Single Star of the West

The Republic of Texas, 1836–1845

Edited by
Kenneth W. Howell
and Charles Swanlund

UNT PRESS

University of North Texas Press
Denton, Texas

Printed in the United States of America.

10 9 8 7 6 5 4 3 2 1

Permissions:
University of North Texas Press
1155 Union Circle #311336
Denton, TX 76203–5017

The paper used in this book meets the minimum requirements
of the American National Standard for Permanence
of Paper for Printed Library Materials, z39.48.1984.
Binding materials have been chosen for durability.

Library of Congress Cataloging-in-Publication Data

Howell, Kenneth Wayne, 1967- editor. | Swanlund, Charles, editor.
Single star of the West : the Republic of Texas, 1836–1845 / edited by
Kenneth W. Howell and Charles Swanlund.
pages cm.
Denton, Texas : University of North Texas Press, [2017]
Includes bibliographical references and index.
ISBN 978-1-57441-671-8 (cloth : alk. paper)
ISBN 978-1-57441-684-8 (ebook)
LCSH: Texas–History–Republic, 1836–1846.
LCC F390 .S57 2017
DDC 976.4/04–dc23
2016049092

The electronic edition of this book was made possible by the support
of the Vick Family Foundation. Typeset by vPrompt eServices.

This book is dedicated to the memory of
Dr. Archie P. McDonald (1935–2012)—
long-time Professor of History at Stephen F. Austin State University, Director of the East Texas Historical Association, scholar, and friend.
—Kenneth W. Howell

To my wife Gail for her unwavering support and belief in me; and to my friend and colleague Ken Howell for guiding me through the sometimes treacherous waters of editing and publishing.
—Charles Swanlund

Contents

List Of Illustrations

Acknowledgments

The publication of this study has taken a herculean effort on the part of all involved. During the past two years, the editors and contributors had to endure unexpected delays as well as the give and take normally associated with edited volumes. Since the genesis of this project, the editors had to replace three of the original contributors, whose time devoted to other endeavors eventually forced them to withdraw from the project. Amazingly, the contributors, whose chapters appear in this volume, stayed with us, providing ardent support through all the highs and lows. Words cannot express our appreciation to them for all their efforts, their patience, and their professionalism. If it had not been for their encouragement and understanding, the publication of this work would not have been possible.

We would like to express a debt of gratitude to our colleagues at Blinn College, especially Brandon Franke, Nathan Giesenschlag, Kirk Bane, Tom Stephens, Steve Kirkpatrick, Harley Haussman, Ron Wright, Pat Johnson, and Diane Lovell. They listened intently as we discussed different topics related to this study, and at times, asked key questions that prompted the development of new ideas. Dr. Steven "Kirk" Bane deserves special recognition. Dr. Bane read many pages of the manuscript and provided valuable suggestions for its improvement. Kirk earned his Ph.D. in History at Texas Christian University, where he studied under Dr. Ben Procter. The experience left at least one lasting impression on his soul—he knows how to write clear and precise prose! Additionally, we would like to thank our students at Blinn College. During different times, we have discussed various topics covered in this book with them in class, asking for their input and feedback. In some cases, our students asked questions about the material that forced us to rethink or clarify our positions regarding the history of the Lone Star nation.

Additionally, we want to recognize the efforts of Ty Cashion. Ken and Ty talked on several occasions regarding the false narrative of the Texas Myth and the elusive nature of defining a singular Texas identity. Ty's insights on the need for a new metanarrative on Texas history and his support for our project are greatly appreciated.

While conducting research on Anson Jones, Charles spent countless hours combing through the shelves of the Star of the Republic Museum's extensive research library. Houston McGaugh and museum staff were gracious enough to give him full access to all their materials on Jones. Their kindness and professionalism are greatly appreciated. A debt of gratitude is also owed to the Texas Parks and Wildlife Department for granting permission to use the previously unpublished photograph of Anson Jones. Catherine Nolte, Complex Superintendent of the Washington-on-the-Brazos State Park, was instrumental in the process. In addition, appreciation is extended to Barb King, Park Interpreter at the Barrington Living History Farm, for her insights and information relating to Jones and his family.

We also would like to extend our gratitude to the staff at the University of North Texas Press, especially Director Ron Chrisman. Ron thank you for staying the course with us and for your willingness to publish such a lengthy manuscript, a task that most press directors would have refused to entertain. Ron's expert guidance through the publication process and positive encouragement kept us moving forward during our most trying days. We would like to also thank Karen DeVinney for her services as copyeditor. She saved us from more than one embarrassing oversight. Finally, we would like to thank reviewers, Patrick Williams and Sam Haynes, who meticulously combed through the originally submitted manuscript. Their expertise and insights served to improve the overall merit of this volume.

While we received many valuable suggestions for improving this work, the editors take full ownership for any mistakes in historical accuracy or presentation. We sincerely hope readers will enjoy this foray into the history of the Republic of Texas, and remain optimistic that this study will in some way inspire future generations of scholars to conduct their own research into this fascinating period of Texas history.

Kenneth W. Howell
Charles Swanlund

INTRODUCTION

The Question of Myth and Identity

Kenneth W. Howell
and Charles Swanlund

One of the earliest authors who considered writing a history of Texas was Mirabeau B. Lamar. Following the Battle of San Jacinto, he began collecting reminiscences of events in Texas that occurred before 1836. Lamar planned to use these documents to chronicle the country's rise from its beginnings as a Spanish frontier to its status as an independent nation. As historian Laura Lyons McLemore suggests, Lamar hoped that such an account would aid Texas's "efforts to obtain diplomatic recognition for the republic."[1] Despite amassing a substantial collection of documents, Lamar never completed his project.[2] Perhaps, the task of writing a comprehensive national history proved too overwhelming, especially given the circumstances of his troubled political career. Regardless, if Lamar had completed his proposed tome, it undoubtedly would have followed the same general patterns found in nineteenth- and early twentieth-century publications, which primarily focused on Anglo history. For more than a hundred years, scholars have concluded that the history of the Republic rested on two basic tenets—Anglo migration west of the Sabine River and white settlers' efforts to secure control of Texas. According to traditional accounts of the Lone Star nation, Texians, who are generally portrayed as courageous, bold, adventurous, and heroic, marched over the land, defeating all who stood in their way. In the wake of their glorious victory over an "oppressive" and "inferior" Mexican government, white Texans established a democratic republic and engaged in a long-standing struggle to eradicate threats posed by savage Indians and Mexican mongrels. For traditionalists, the "real" story of Texas began with the Texians' defeat of Santa Anna at San Jacinto. The problem with the majority of the historical scholarship on Texas, however, is that it presents a false narrative, producing a body of literature commonly labeled by some modern scholars as the "Texas Myth." As with all myths, the traditional narratives contain some elements of truth, but its biased interpretations often denigrate the realities of the past through oversimplification and an unwavering devotion to cultural values that are more aligned to the early decades of the twentieth century than to the modern era.[3]

While correctly identifying that Anglo males eventually dominated the political, social, and economic institutions of Texas, the traditional narrative often ignores, or at least downplays, the impact of Tejanos, American Indians, African Americans, women, and other cultural and ethnic groups.[4] Though most serious scholars have abandoned this position, the Texas Myth endures, perpetuating, in some cases celebrating, the idea of white male superiority. Thus, the legacy of the mythmakers is a body of scholarship based on half-truths and flawed analysis that continues to oversimplify and muddle the past, leaving the general public, as well as students, with an incomplete picture of their Texas heritage.

Perhaps, the limited number of modern studies focusing on the Texas Republic partly explains why the traditionalist interpretation still dominates this historical era. Aside from biographies and topical studies produced in the past three decades, historians have published few comprehensive accounts of the Lone Star nation.[5] In fact, modern scholars have spent more time studying the Texas Revolution than they have examining the Republic.[6] Though the causes of the revolution and its outcome remain important to our understanding of the emergence of the Lone Star nation, it is puzzling that historians have paid scant attention to the Republic, an independent country that survived for almost ten years before its annexation to the United States.

In addition to covering the revolution, modern historians have examined in detail the experiences of Tejanos, Native Americans, African Americans, and women in the years both before and after 1836.[7] These scholars have done much to discredit the Texas Myth and have provided a richer understanding of ethnic and racial diversity within the Republic; yet, at the same time, their efforts have left the story of the Republic fragmented and incomplete. Perhaps, the one exception to this trend is Andrew Torget's *Seeds of Empire: Cotton, Slavery, and the Transformation of the Texas Borderlands, 1800–1850*.[8] Torget provides a sweeping account of how cotton production and slavery shaped events in Mexican Texas, leading eventually to the outbreak of the Texas Revolution and the creation of a new republic, predicated on the idea of becoming the first fully committed slaveholding nation in North America. Torget should be commended for his attempt to break from the traditional narrative and for advancing a thought-provoking analysis that seeks to explain *how* and *why* white males eventually dominated the political, social, and economic institutions of the republic era through early statehood. While there is no doubt that the cotton culture and slavery significantly impacted the development of Texas, one might be concerned that *Seeds of Empire* suggests that a certain homogeneous identity based on a southern model existed in Texas. One is left wondering whether or not this worthwhile contribution to Texas historiography is in some ways a return to the idea of Texas exceptionalism, a retreat back to a pre-1936 identification of Texas as southern.[9] While such an analysis held true for large segments of the Texas population, it ignores regional differences in the Republic that had little or nothing to do with cotton production or slavery. For example, how would the Comanche fit into a narrative based on a southern motif? Are we to believe that they were eager to engage in an economy based on slavery and cotton? Surely, most scholars would agree that the Comanche, as well as other Native American tribes, were just as much a part of the history of the Republic as any other culture group living in Texas at the time.

When the editors first conceived this volume, one of their primary goals was to examine whether or not a unique Texas identity existed in the Republic. They posited that if such an identity ever existed, it surely would be evident in the years between the revolution and annexation, a period when Texas fully functioned as an independent nation. In their efforts to discover something akin to a unique identity, the editors failed. It is evident that a homogenous identity did not exist in the Republic. This discovery will come as no surprise to professional historians, but it will challenge the views of the general public, whose understanding of Texas primarily has been shaped by traditionalist interpretations.[10]

While a single cultural identity remained elusive, the editors did discover that the Republic was a place of cultural confluences. Even though Anglos gained cultural dominance early in the Republic's existence, other groups retained significant influence within society. In fact, one could argue that regional identities within the Republic were more important than any singular homogeneous cultural characteristic. This is not to say that each culture group lived in a vacuum; they certainly did not. They shared common values and beliefs. Excluding slaves, perhaps, the greatest commonality among the various cultural and ethnic groups, both male and female, was their belief that Texas was a land of opportunity. Free blacks, though limited in number, Native Americans, Tejanos, Anglos, and Europeans saw Texas as place of potential prosperity. However, after white Texans gained dominance over the political, social, and economic institutions, the hopes of prosperity diminished for non-whites.

This volume seeks to answer several important questions about the Republic of Texas, including: *Who were the Texans of the Republic era? What were the experiences of Tejanos, African Americans, American Indians, foreign-born immigrants, and women living in the Republic? In what ways did various ethnic and racial groups influence the development of Texas during this era?* While this study does not claim to provide definitive answers to these questions, the chapters that follow discuss the experiences, both positive and negative, of those who resided in Texas between 1836 and 1845. Individually, each contributor provides insights on specific identity groups living in the Republic or particular personalities and events that shaped their future. Collectively, the chapters provide an account of a complex, heterogeneous society that struggled to survive as an independent nation.

The editors have divided the chapters of this volume into four sections, each division relating to a specific aspects of the Republic's development. Section One, "The Birth of a Republic," focuses on events leading to the emergence of the Lone Star Republic. In Chapter 1 "Mexico's Federalist War and the Secession of Texas," Bruce Winders briefly describes key events of the Texas Revolution, providing important context for the remaining chapters by identifying the causes and events leading to the establishment of the Republic. In this chapter, Winders convincingly argues that the struggle between Mexican Centralists and Federalists was part of a larger phenomenon, one in which citizens in various countries were challenging the legitimacy of their own governing bodies. In this regard, Winders places the Texas Revolution within a global context, comparing the Mexican Revolution of 1821 with that of the American, French, and Latin American revolutions of the late eighteenth and early nineteenth centuries. Additionally, Winders reveals how different cultural, ethnic, and social groups in society contributed to Texas independence.

In Chapter 2, "Voices of the Revolution and Republic," Paul Spellman builds upon the ideas introduced in Winders's chapter by examining the leaders of the Texas Revolution, revealing their contributions to the establishment of the Republic. Spellman convincingly illustrates that the emergence of an independent republic resulted from an alliance between Anglo and Tejano leaders, who represented the "voices" of the movement. Furthermore, Spellman notes that many of the "voices" of the revolution were silenced before they could contribute to the founding of their new nation. Many of these individuals either died in battle or succumbed to illness during, or shortly after, the conflict. Spellman leaves the reader contemplating how the development of the Republic might have been different had these individuals survived. Even more importantly, Spellman provides information on leading figures of the era that have been eclipsed in popular memory. Because many of the "second tier" leaders were Tejanos, their absence from scholarly discussions suggests that they were victims of traditional biases.

In the final chapter of this section, "Who were the Texians?: The Creation of a Texas Identity in the Era of the Republic," James Crisp explores the potential development of a unique Texas identity in the Republic era. Crisp is the most successful in arguing that something akin to a Texas identity existed in the Lone Star nation, suggesting that Tejanos' early contributions to the establishment of the Republic reflect ideals which are commonly defined as "Texan." However, Crisp reveals that whatever chance the Republic had to create a unique identity quickly faded away after the failure of the Santa Fe Expedition in 1841 and the subsequent Mexican invasions across the Rio Grande in 1842. Afterwards, Anglos distrusted Tejano loyalty to Texas, resulting in calculated efforts to weaken the civil and legal rights of Mexican Texans.

Section Two, "Defending the Republic," examines the Republic's military forces. In Chapter 4, "Army of the Texas Republic, 1836–1845," Joseph G. Dawson III describes the condition and status of the Texas army. Dawson argues that the army represented a conundrum for the Republic, explaining that while the nation certainly needed a sizeable force to protect its interest, there were inherent dangers to maintaining a large military. In particular, the financial circumstances of the Republic made it difficult for Congress to properly equip and provision its troops, leading to a disgruntled armed force within the nation. Equally problematic, Texas presidents experienced great difficulty in directing the actions of their military commanders. Dawson also provides an informed discussion on the experiences of the common soldiers and officers serving in the army. A remarkable aspect of the Texas army was it was something of a hybrid of cultural confluences. Built on a model established by the United States Army, Texans molded their defensive forces to meet the challenges facing their young nation. In this regard, it should be remembered that the Texas army was initially created to preserve the independent status of the Republic, but evolved into an Anglos-dominated force used to enact control over non-white cultural groups, such as the Cherokees in East Texas.

Chapter 5, "The Republic of Texas Navies," reveals that the Texas navy played an important role in defending the Texas coast. Here, Gary Joiner illustrates the love-hate relationship that developed between the

Republic's political leaders and their naval commanders, especially during the Houston administrations. Despite such tensions, Joiner concludes that the Texas navy during this era was vital in protecting the Republic's coastline from invading Mexican armies; aiding the revolutionary movement on the Yucatan Peninsula, where opposition to the Mexican government blossomed into a full-scaled revolt and distracted Mexican officials' attention away from Texas; and maintaining a working relationship with the United States which in part contributed to the annexation of Texas in 1845.

In Chapter 6, "Crystallization of a Tradition: Texas Rangers and the Republic of Texas," Bruce Glasrud and Harold Weiss, Jr. trace the evolutionary development of this famous regional icon. Glasrud and Weiss effectively recount the trials and tribulations of the Rangers as they confronted border raiders and hostile American Indians on the Texas frontier. The chapter provides a balanced account of Ranger activities, pointing out that Texans often viewed the Rangers from different perspectives; some saw them as "patriot-warriors" while others considered them as "bloody avengers." Interestingly, while the Ranger service emerged as a hybrid of Anglo-European, Native American, and Spanish traditions, Anglo political leaders often used the Rangers to challenge and defeat non-white cultural groups operating on the Texas frontier, especially Native Americans. In this regard, the Rangers ultimately contributed to Anglo dominance in the newly independent nation.

Section Three, "Politics and Economics in the Republic," examines the political environment of the Republic through the eyes of its presidents and diplomats and discusses the economic conditions of the nation. While some might argue that a focus on the presidents of the Republic is a return to the traditionalist views of celebrating prominent white men of the era, such arguments fail to recognize the nuances of these Texas leaders. In Chapter 7, "Sam Houston: The Trials and Tribulations of a President," James L. Haley explores President Houston's successes and failures as he led the nation during his two terms in office. Haley's Houston is a larger than life character, who proved indispensable to the survival of the Republic. However, Haley also suggests that Houston was in many ways trapped between two opposing cultural identities in the nation—Anglos and Cherokees. In part, Houston's devotion to the Cherokee of East Texas almost cost him a promising political career. Houston was one of the few white Texans who understood the cultural dynamics of the Republic and attempted to operate within the gray areas that separated the worlds of Tejanos, Native Americans, and Anglos.

Kenneth W. Howell in Chapter 8, "Mirabeau B. Lamar: Blinded by Delusions of Grandeur," evaluates President Lamar as he prepared to enter office. Howell does not provide a comprehensive examination of Lamar's presidency, but rather gives readers a glimpse into his vision of building the Republic into a vast empire. Perhaps, more important is the revelation that Lamar, as an individual, represented a strange mixture of southern and American cultural identities. Having migrated from Georgia, the president was heavily influenced by southern ideology, including states' rights, a commitment to slavery and a cotton-based economy, and a martial spirit that often prompted him to exercise military action against perceived enemies of the Republic. At the same time, Lamar was influenced by characteristics consistent with American ideology, such as liberty (at least for whites), the spirit of Manifest Destiny, which he used to support his adherence to Texas nationalism, and an inherent belief in white supremacy. It was these characteristics that led to Lamar's meteoric rise in Texas politics, as well as his rapid decline.

In Chapter 9, "Anson Jones: The Forgotten President of Texas," Charles Swanlund provides a comprehensive overview of the Jones presidency, reminding the reader of his importance to the Republic and his controversial role in the annexation of Texas to the United States. Swanlund correctly argues that Jones, who is often remembered for his role in annexation, also served in vital roles in congress and the state department. Perhaps, Jones was the most "Texan" of the three presidents. Unlike Houston, he did not seem to possess the ability to work across cultural lines; yet, he was not a brash cavalier like Lamar. In reality, however, we are primarily left to speculate about a Jones presidency, because his time as president was cut short with the annexation of Texas to the United States.

In Chapter 10, "The Diplomacy of the Lone Star Republic, 1836–1845," Kenneth Stevens explores the rough and tumble activities of Texas diplomats who worked tirelessly to gain foreign recognition of the fledgling republic. Stevens explains that Texas diplomats conducted vigorous negotiations with foreign nations, including the United States, England, France, and Mexico. Though contemporaries often deemed their approach as unsophisticated and inconsistent, the efforts of Texas diplomats resulted in the accomplishment of several important goals, including trade and recognition agreements, and more significantly, annexation to the United States.

In Chapter 11, "Across Many Borders: Persistence and Transformation in the Texas Economy and Culture, 1830–1850," Walter Buenger explores the economic conditions of the Republic from a broad perspective, examining the region's economy from the pre-revolutionary era through early statehood. This longer approach provides valuable insights into the Republic's economy, as well as its background and influence on Texas after annexation. Given that economic factors often shaped political and social developments, this chapter is critical to the understanding of the Republic. Examining the Republic and its economic development from a transnational perspective, Buenger argues that the Texas economy was influenced by the Atlantic world, aligning it in many ways with the Lower South. Nevertheless, he stops short of making a sweeping claim for economic homogeneity. In fact, Buenger convincingly argues that Texas was a confluence of cultures, a place where distinctive and evolving "cultural pockets" or "island communities" persisted and where at least six types of Texans existed: Lower South, Upper South, German, Comanche/Apache, and Tejano. A sixth group resulted from cultural mixing, what Buenger refers to as a "blend." Though Buenger cautions scholars not to overemphasize the diversity of these Texans, he also reminds the reader that we cannot ignore them either.

The final section in the book, "Social and Cultural Vistas," examines a wide range of social and cultural groups living in the Republic, including women, Native Americans, Tejanos, and African Americans. This section also provides an overview of religion during this era. In Chapter 12, "Frontier Bonnets: Women in the Republic of Texas," Mary Scheer explores the lives of Anglo, Hispanic, Native American, and African American women. Scheer explains in detail the varied experiences of women, highlighting the fact that Anglo females benefitted more from living in a white male dominated society than did women of other racial groups.

In Chapter 13, "American Indians in the Republic of Texas: A Case Study for Moving Beyond the Traditional Perspective," Jody Edward Ginn contends that Native Americans were not the homogeneous culture that traditional scholars often describe. Instead, the various tribes functioned independently, seeking to further their own self-interests. In this regard, they were no different from their Anglo counterparts who sought new opportunities in Texas. Ginn examines the complexity of Anglo-Native American relations through the eyes of John Connor, a Delaware chief, who was allegedly the only American Indian to receive an official grant of land for his services to the Republic.

Similarly, Alwyn Barr in Chapter 14, "Freedom and Slavery in the Republic: African American Experiences in the Republic of Texas," explores the lives of black Texans, both free and slave. As readers will surmise, African Americans who lived in the Republic experienced a life of hardship and tragedy, an existence comparable to blacks living in the American South. His detailed analysis of black Texans reveals again how traditional scholarship has ignored the role that non-white culture groups played in the development of the nation.

In Chapter 15, "A Tainted Friendship: The Betrayal of Tejanos in the Republic of Texas," Francis Galan illustrates at length how Tejano rights diminished as the bonds between them and Anglos withered and died. Even some of the most noted Tejano leaders, such as Juan Seguin, eventually witnessed an erosion of their political, economic, and social status in a predominantly Anglo dominated society. Nevertheless, Galan also reminds us of the significant contributions of Tejanos to the creation and development of the Lone Star Republic.

In the final chapter, "God Bless Texas: Religion in the Republic of Texas," John Storey chronicles the growth of the Protestant denominations in the Republic. It is interesting to note that these religious groups developed along similar paths as Protestant churches in the United States. One significant difference, however, was that they had to initially compete with the Roman Catholic Church, an institution with roots that extended back to the Spanish era.

Collectively, these chapters provide an overview of the political, social, cultural, economic, and religious institutions of Texas between 1836 and 1845. As previously mentioned, this era has received limited scholarly attention in the past few decades. The editors hope this volume will inspire new scholarly interest in this fascinating period of Texas history, leading to more in-depth analysis of the people who struggled to survive in the fledgling nation. Additionally, the editors believe that their study will peel back the layers of the Texas Myth, providing a history of the Republic that will prove meaningful and useful to present and future generations of scholar.

Notes

1. Laura Lyons McLemore, *Inventing Texas: Early Historians of the Lone Star State* (College Station: Texas A&M University Press, 2004), 41.

2. Charles Adams Gulick, Jr. and Katherine Elliott, eds., *The Papers of Mirabeau Buonaparte Lamar*, Vols. 1–6 (Austin: Texas State Library, 1920–1927). Lamar's published papers contain numerous documents, sources, and reminiscences of early Texans related to different episodes

in the history of Texas. From the moment that Lamar first entered Texas, he collected these historic accounts with the hopes of writing a history of the Republic (and later state). Lamar never finished his history of Texas even though he wrote notes for such a book periodically through his life.

3. A prime example of the persistence of the Texas Myth is found in T. R. Fehrenbach, *Lone Star: A History of Texas and the Texans* (New York: Macmillan, 1968).

4. In fact, this methodological approach to the Republic era is the genesis of a myth that scholars have systematically applied to subsequent eras, prompting the emergence of modern scholars who question the true nature of the historical identity of the state's past.

5. There are many credible biographies of early Texans who played important roles during the Republic years. For example, James L. Haley, *Sam Houston* (Norman: University of Oklahoma Press, 2002) and Paul Spellman, *Forgotten Texas Leader: Hugh McLeod and the Texan Santa Fe Expedition* (College Station: Texas A&M University Press, 1999). Also, there are numerous studies that examine specific topics and events associated with the Republic, such as Jeffery Stuart Kerr, *Seat of Empire: The Embattled Birth of Austin, Texas* (Lubbock: Texas Tech University Press, 2013); Frederick Wilkins, *The Legend Begins: The Texas Rangers, 1823–1845* (Abilene: State House Press, 1996); Dianna Everett, T*he Texas Cherokees: A People Between Two Fires, 1819–1840* (Norman: University of Oklahoma Press, 1990); Jeffery Robenalt, *Historic Tales from the Texas Republic: A Glimpse of Texas Past* (Charleston: The History Press, 2013); Stephen L. Hardin, *Texian Macabre: The Melancholy Tale of a Hanging in Early Houston* (Abilene: State House Press, 2007); Stephen L. Moore, *Texas Rising: The Epic True Story of the Lone Star Republic and the Rise of the Texas Rangers, 1836–1846* (New York: William Morrow, 2015).

6. The following represent only a small sample of works related to the Texas Revolution; see Gregg J. Dimmick, *Sea of Mud: The Retreat of the Mexican Army After San Jacinto, An Archeological Investigation* (Austin: Texas State Historical Association, 2004); Stephen L. Hardin, *Texian Iliad: A Military History of the Texas Revolution* (Austin: University of Texas Press, 1994); Andreas V. Reichstein, *Rise of the Lone Star: The Making of Texas* (College Station: Texas A&M University Press, 1989); H. W. Brands, *Lone Star Nation: How a Ragged Army of Volunteers Won the Battle for Texas Independence—And Changed America* (New York: Doubleday, 2004); William C. Davis, *Lone Star Rising:*

The Revolutionary Birth of the Texas Republic (College Station: Texas A&M University Press, 2004); Paul D. Lack, *The Texas Revolutionary Experience: A Political and Social History, 1835–1836* (College Station: Texas A&M University Press, 1992); Ron J. Jackson and Lee Spencer White, *Joe: The Slave Who Became an Alamo Legend* (Norman: University of Oklahoma Press, 2015); James Donovan, *The Blood of Heroes: The 13-Day Struggle for the Alamo—and the Sacrifice That Forged a Nation* (New York: Little, Brown and Company, 2012); Phillip Thomas Tucker, *Exodus from the Alamo: The Anatomy of the Last Stand Myth* (Philadelphia: Casemate Publishers, 2010); Richard Bruce Winders, *Sacrificed at the Alamo: Tragedy and Triumph in the Texas Revolution* (Abilene: State House Press, 2004); Randy Roberts and James S. Olson, *A Line in the Sand: The Alamo in Blood and Memory* (New York: The Free Press, 2001); Sam W. Haynes and Gerald D. Saxon, eds., *Contested Empire: Rethinking the Texas Revolution* (College Station: Texas A&M University Press, 2015); Jay A. Stout, *Slaughter at Goliad: The Mexican Massacre of 400 Texas Volunteers* (Annapolis: Naval Institute Press, 2008); Gregg Cantrell, *Stephen F. Austin: Empresario of Texas* (New Haven: Yale University Press, 1999); Edward L. Miller, *New Orleans and the Texas Revolution* (College Station: Texas A&M University Press, 2004); Jonathan W. Jordan, *Lone Star Navy: Texas, the Fight for the Gulf of Mexico, and the Shaping of the American West* (Washington, D.C.: Potomac Books, Inc., 2006); Andrew J. Torget, *Seeds of Empire: Cotton, Slavery, and the Transformation of the Texas Borderlands, 1800–1850* (Chapel Hill: University of North Carolina Press, 2015). Despite the limited number of studies relating to the Republic era, students should be familiar with the following: William Ransom Hogan, *Texas Republic: A Social and Economic History* (1946; reprint, Austin: Texas State Historical Association, 2006); John Edward Weems and Jane Weems, *Dream of Empire: A History of the Republic of Texas, 1836–1846* (1971; reprint, New York: Barnes & Noble Books, 1995); Stanley Siegel, *A Political History of the Texas Republic, 1836–1845* (Austin: University of Texas Press, 1956). Also see Richard B. McCaslin, *Washington on the Brazos: Cradle of the Texas Republic* (Austin: Texas State Historical Association, 2016).

7. In the past three decades, many new studies have been published about the peoples of Texas. An example of such scholarship includes: David J. Weber, *The Spanish Frontier in North America* (New Haven: Yale University Press, 1992); David La Vere, *The Texas Indians* (College Station: Texas A&M University Press, 2004); Juliana Barr, *Peace Came*

in the Form of a Woman: Indians and Spaniards in the Texas Borderlands (Chapel Hill: University of North Carolina Press, 2007); Pekka Hämäläinen, *The Comanche Empire* (New Haven: Yale University Press, 2008); Jean A. Stuntz, *Hers, His, and Theirs: Community Property Law in Spain and Early Texas* (Lubbock: Texas Tech University Press, 2005); Ana Carolina Castilo Crimm, *De León: A Tejano Family History* (Austin: University of Texas Press, 2003); Raúl A. Ramos, *Beyond the Alamo: Forging Mexican Ethnicity in San Antonio, 1821–1861* (Chapel Hill: University of North Carolina Press, 2008); Gary Anderson, *The Conquest of Texas: Ethnic Cleansing in the Promise Land, 1820–1875* (Norman: University of Oklahoma Press, 2005). For an excellent treatment of recent scholarship on Texas prior to 1846, see F. Todd Smith, "Spanish, Mexican, and Republican Texas to 1845," in *Discovering Texas History*, ed. Bruce A. Glasrud, Light Townsend Cummins, and Cary D. Wintz, 169–96 (Norman: University of Oklahoma Press, 2014).

8. Andrew J. Torget, *Seeds of Empire: Cotton, Slavery, and the Transformation of the Texas Borderlands, 1800–1850* (Chapel Hill: The University of North Carolina Press, 2015).

9. During the 1936 Centennial Celebration in Texas, promoters of Texas tourism and economic interest attempted to move the state away from negative identification with the Lost Cause and Confederacy by fostering the notion that Texas was a western state and aligning it with western motifs, such as the cowboy, gunfighters, cattle drives, and etc. For a detailed examination of the 1936 Centennial Celebration, see Kenneth B. Ragsdale's *The Year America Discovered Texas: Centennial '36* (College Station: Texas A&M University Press, 1987).

10. For a more in-depth study of the Texas identity, see Light Townsend Cummins and Mary L. Scheer's *Texan Identities: Moving beyond Myth, Memory, and Fallacy in Texas History* (Denton: University of North Texas Press, 2016).

PART I:
The Birth of a Republic

Chapter 1
Mexico's Federalist War and the Secession of Texas

Richard Bruce Winders

I hope they have sense enough at Monclova to take no part in the civil war that seems to be commencing.

Stephen F. Austin
Mexico City
April 15, 1835[1]

Most Texans upon hearing the phrase "Texas Revolution" immediately recall other words they learned in school: Gonzales, Alamo, and San Jacinto. Students are routinely taught that the Texas Revolution began on October 2, 1835, when colonists drove away Mexican soldiers who had come to retrieve a cannon provided for protection. At the Battle of the Alamo on March 6, 1836, General Antonio López de Santa Anna sent the brutal message that rebels would receive "no quarter" from him. At San Jacinto, on April 21, 1836, the Texans dealt Mexico a stinging rebuke that guaranteed independence for the new Republic of Texas. This grouping of events neatly packages a story with a beginning, a middle, and an end. However, although simple and succinct, it fails to adequately explain one of the most significant events that occurred on the North American continent during the nineteenth century. Unfortunately, what has been presented to the public over the years is more caricature than interpretation.[2]

The missing component in the interpretation of the Texas Revolution has been context. The very name of the event—the Texas Revolution—makes it appear to have been a small regional affair. Texans throughout the ages have taken pride and ownership of the conflict. It is the story of their birth and rise to eminence. Although the subject of American history, many Americans, and almost all Mexicans, have ceded this episode to Texas, glad to separate themselves from Texas and its boastful nationalism. In doing so, however, the true regional and global importance of the event has gone largely unexplained.

So what is the missing context that places the Texas Revolution on a higher historical plateau than it currently occupies? To answer this question, one has to realize that the events occurring in Mexico prior to the Texas Revolution represented a larger struggle between two competing systems of government, one old and the other new. Across the world the institution of monarchy was under attack, an assault made possible by the Enlightenment, the rise of the United States, and the French Revolution.[3] The foes of kings and queens were those who adhered to the new principle of republicanism. This struggle was carried out throughout North and South America as the old colonial powers lost control of their former holdings. Thus, both continents became contested fields as monarchists and centralists vied with republicans to establish new governments during the early nineteenth century.

Serious historians have long tried to establish this struggle between Mexico's competing political factions as the context for the Texas Revolution. Thus, the best evidence-based interpretation of the Texas Revolution is one that views it as an episode within the ongoing war between Mexican centralists and Mexican republicans. This simple statement automatically expands the event to a theater larger than what is traditionally considered Texas.[4] It also involves the issue of states' rights, nullification, and secession—all concepts inherent with a federal system. On the eve of the federalist revolt against centralism, the legislature of *Coahuila y Tejas* lamented, "It is not conceived how a national representation, owing its origin to an existing fundamental pact, can have the power to reform or change it as it may think proper." It asked, "Upon what principal of constitutional right can it be founded?"[5] Austin's response regarding the Decree of October 3, 1835, that officially created a central government was not that different from arguments made by delegates at the Hartford Convention or the Southern fire-eaters of 1861. The famous *empresario* proclaimed, "if carried into effect [the decree] evidently leaves no remedy for Texas but resistance, secession from Mexico and a resort to natural right."[6] What is independence if not secession by another word?

In addition to the lack of context, the Texas Revolution has suffered from the amount of attention focused on its heroes. This is not said to diminish the role or the importance of heroic figures but to contend that many of the individuals most responsible for the course and conduct of the revolt remain largely unknown to the public and students. While Stephen F. Austin, James Bowie, William B. Travis, David Crockett,

James W. Fannin, Sam Houston, Lorenzo de Zavala, and Juan Seguín most certainly will appear in most narratives of the Texas Revolution, the reality is that these men mainly reacted to events instead of shaping them. Ironically, the individuals whose actions and decisions were most influential during the war are fairly obscure to all but the most well-versed scholars of the Texas Revolution. Valentín Gomez Farías, José Antonio Mexía, Agustín Viesca, José Maria Tornel, José Urrea, Carlos de la Garza, Henry Smith, James W. Robinson, Francis W. Johnson, James Grant, and Mosely Baker have rarely, if ever, had even minor roles in the popular culture version of the Texas Revolution.[7] For years the Texas Revolution has been populated by stock characters that can clearly be grouped into specific categories: principal actors, supporting actors, extras, and a villain.

The villain, of course, is Antonio López de Santa Anna, the president of Mexico. Writers and the public have targeted Santa Anna for disdain and blame: Santa Anna, the self-proclaimed dictator, forced his will on both Mexico and Texas.[8] The problem with this interpretation is that "self-proclaimed dictators" usually are institutionalized. Santa Anna had supporters (Santanists) who continually elevated and sustained him in power for nearly thirty years. Casting Santa Anna as a power-hungry politician driven by greed and family honor provides a simple story line but obviates and obfuscates the roles others had in what was truly an important event in Mexican history. Understanding the Texas Revolution depends on not allowing one man to represent an entire nation.

Independence from Spain in 1821 presented Mexicans with new challenges, including questions relating to what type of government would replace the defeated Spanish regime. The struggle to answer this question threw Mexico into a series of civil wars that lasted several decades. Collectively, these civil wars are commonly referred to as Mexico's Federalist Wars. The historic episode known as the Texas Revolution was an event that occurred within this larger Mexico conflict.

Independence failed to bring unity to Mexico. Mexicans were divided into three general political factions following independence. One faction, called monarchists, wanted to preserve the old Spanish system but with a king of their own choosing. A second faction, called centralists, opposed installing another king, wishing instead to establish a strong, centralized national government controlled by Mexico's societal elites. Another group, called federalists, wished to establish a federal republic (like the United States) in which the individual states maintained their sovereignty. Federalists were also known as republicans because of their support for republican principles. Geographically, centralists generally lived in states near Mexico City while federalists often inhabited the areas more distant from the capital. Federalism appealed to the frontier regions because it offered local control.[9]

The form of government that the new Mexican nation would adopt was important because any substantial change threatened the existing social order. Under Spanish rule, several powerful social classes had emerged whose members tended to hold almost all important civil, military, and church offices. The groups controlling Mexico were the military, owners of large estates, and the established church. Monarchists and centralists wished to maintain the status quo they had helped to establish. Federalists, who were composed of Mexico's rising business and professional class, desired sweeping changes that would open offices and create opportunities for more Mexicans. Thus, federalists found opponents in both monarchists and centralists who feared a loss of political power and social status.

Mexico experienced rule under all three factions during its first ten years of existence. Immediately after independence, a Mexican officer named Agustín de Iturbide ruled the nation as emperor from 1822 until 1823. The overthrow of Iturbide created a vacuum in which the federalists ascended to power. Most notable of their achievements was the adoption of the Constitution of 1824, a document that established the federal relationship between the states and the national government in Mexico City. Mexico's first president of the federal republic, Guadalupe Victoria, served out his entire term without any challenge to his authority. Those who followed would not be so fortunate.

In 1829, General Anastasio Bustamante refused to accept his defeat in the race for the Mexican presidency and used his troops to force the legitimate winner into exile. By 1832, federalist revolts broke out across Mexico against Bustamante's centralist administration. Colonists in Texas (objecting to a young rabblerousing lawyer named William B. Travis's imprisonment at Anahuac by its centralist commander, Juan Davis Bradburn) participated in this revolt, explaining their action in a document known as the Turtle Bayou Resolutions. General José Antonio Mexía, a federalist supporter, investigated the incident and vouched for the colonists' actions.[10] The guest list at a ball held at Brazoria on July 22, 1832, to celebrate their vindication included both Austin and Mexía. One Anglo colonist offered a toast that seems ironic given subsequent events: "Genl. Santa Anna—The hero of constitutional liberty, and proscribed patriot under the shackles of tyranny; may the sun of his political glory sit in the ocean of freedom, and the herald to its enemies throughout the habitable globe." Another uttered, "Genl. Santa Anna—May the close of his political existence be similar to that of the great Washington, shroaded [*sic*] in glory." Yet a third proclaimed, "The tree of liberty—Now under the operation of the pruning hook of Gen. Santa Anna; may it hereafter bloom more beautifully, and bear fruit more abundantly."[11]

Antonio López de Santa Anna benefited from the federalist revolt he had orchestrated. Federalists throughout Mexico viewed him as a true defender of the republic, and therefore, a defender of their cause. Elected president of Mexico in 1833, Santa Anna retired to his estate and left governing Mexico to his vice president, Valentín Gómez Farías.[12] With the support of Congress, Farías, an ardent federalist, began implementing policy that threatened to diminish the power and social standing of the military, land owners, and the established church as a way to achieve a society he and more radical republicans envisioned. Leaders of the threatened factions appealed to Santa Anna in the Plan de Cuernavaca (May 25, 1834) to resume his office and reverse Farías' reforms. Granted extra-legal authority to assist him during the crisis, Santa Anna returned to Mexico City. The Plan de Cuernavaca set in motion a chain of events: Vice President Farías was dismissed and his reforms revoked; Mexico's federalist congress was dissolved and replaced with one composed of centralists; Mexican states were stripped of their sovereignty and converted into districts that were to be governed from Mexico City; and the federalist Constitution of 1824 was set aside and a call made for the creation and adoption of a centralist document to replace it. By 1835, a number of Mexican states—including Yucatan, Oaxaca, Coahuila y Tejas, and parts of Tamaulipas—were in revolt against Santa Anna's centralist regime.[13]

Understanding Santa Anna and others like him is vital to deciphering the events unfolding in Mexico. Antonio López de Santa Anna (1794–1876) was born to a Spanish middle class merchant family in Jalapa. His family connections and his association with the port city of Veracruz factored in both his personal and public life. Although his father wanted him to enter business, Santa Anna was "drawn to a glorious career of arms."[14] Accepting a commission as a junior officer, Santa Anna rose steadily, although not meteorically, in a Spanish Army struggling to restore order to New Spain in the wake of Father Hidalgo's 1810 call for revolt. Most notable for his service was a citation for gallantry in the 1813 Battle of Medina outside San Antonio de Béxar in the province of Texas.[15]

With that rebellion crushed, Santa Anna returned to Veracruz where he pursued Indians and rebels as well as held various administrative roles. Santa Anna had risen to the rank of lieutenant colonel by the time Iturbide proposed his Mexican coalition that ultimately resulted in independence in 1821. Iturbide had successfully brought together both Mexican royalists and rebels by presenting the real struggle to be won as one between indigenous Mexicans of all casts against the Spanish. The plan appealed to men like Santa Anna (*criollos* or Mexican-born Spaniards), who readily renounced their Spanish birthright for the elevation in Mexican society that came with the demise of Spanish rule. Subsequent legislation enacted by *criollos* decreed the expulsion of Spaniards, forcing many to return to their homeland.[16]

Santa Anna supported the idea of a Mexican republic and even helped orchestrate the downfall of Iturbide's short-lived empire. He consistently backed federalist administrations throughout the 1820s, winning praise from federalists in places like Texas. His defeat of a Spanish invasion force at Tampico in 1829 made him a national hero and helped propel him to the office of presidency. This well-documented record as an ardent federalist made his alliance with the centralist political faction all the more baffling to former supporters who felt betrayed. The traditional theory has been that Santa Anna was an opportunist who always looked out for his own interests.

However, recent scholarship into the politics of Mexico's early national period offers another explanation for Santa Anna's political behavior.[17] Santa Anna and others of his status were considered *hombres de bien*, men who held a position of stewardship for the nation owing to their upbringing, connections, wealth, history of service, and other honorable virtues. The concept of the *hombre de bien* held that these were responsible men who could be trusted in all matters, even the future of the nation.[18] Frequent barrack revolts and mob actions, especially Mexico City's Parían Riot of 1827, strengthened distrust of the Mexican masses. If the masses were left unchecked, France's Reign of Terror might be replayed in Mexico. Even once ardent republicans like José Moria Tornel, a leading Santa Anna supporter, began to doubt that Mexicans were ready for the type of liberal government enjoyed by citizens of the Unites States. Santa Anna's statement that his countrymen needed a guiding hand was often dismissed by many of his contemporaries and historians, but he and others believed that Mexico and Mexicans had to change before the fruits of federalism would develop.[19] The increasingly popular belief that Mexico's transition into a liberal republic needed more control brought the centralists to power. By 1835, however, the threat of losing Texas temporarily brought a majority of Mexico's centralists and federalists together in an effort to prevent its loss.

Located on the northeastern frontier of New Spain, the Province of Texas had served the Spanish as a buffer by keeping other colonial interests and the barbarous Indians from reaching their more prosperous settled regions. With the establishment of the United States, the role of Texas as a buffer became even more important as U.S. citizens began to spill across the Appalachians and fan out throughout the Mississippi Valley and the Gulf Coast. By 1820, however, the Spanish policy of keeping foreigners at bay changed, a shift brought on by the realization that Texas needed a large, stable population if its traditional role as a buffer was to be maintained.

The Spanish had relied on their standard triad of missions, presidios, and civil towns to extend their presence into Texas. As the nineteenth century dawned, though, Texas could count only three established communities: San Antonio de Béxar, Nacogdoches, and La Bahía (renamed Goliad in 1829). Moreover, the tumultuous years between and 1810 and 1820 actually saw Texas's population plummet. In response, Spanish officials adopted a policy of controlled immigration, a program continued by the newly independent nation of Mexico. Far from an altruistic endeavor, the plan was to allow Americans and Europeans to immigrate to Texas in exchange for their loyalty. The goal of the policy was essentially to bring in grateful immigrants who would defend the frontier, build new communities, and transform Texas from a frontier into an economically prosperous and stable region.[20]

The Constitution of 1824, the document that laid the foundation for the Federal Republic of Mexico, addressed Texas' frontier condition by designating it a department within the twin state of *Coahuila y Tejas*. For Texas, which had been an autonomous province under the Spanish, the new arrangement represented a loss in prestige, political power and economic activity since Saltillo, a town in Coahuila, became the new state capital. Agitation for separate statehood quickly developed within Texas. The loss was particularly galling for Béxar, which was reduced from a provincial to a departmental capital. Elite Béxareños, who were staunch federalists, found allies among the politically active incoming settlers. In fact, the issue of colonization and statehood had been linked by design.[21] By 1833, colonists felt strong enough to petition Congress for statehood, an act that led directly to leading *empresario* Stephen F. Austin's arrest and imprisonment in Mexico City.[22]

Politics within *Coahuila y Tejas* often centered on issues important to its northern citizens. Influential Béxareños formed an alliance with the Monclova faction that contested Saltillo for control of the state. While not always supporting the colonists' attempts to change the state's policies regarding Texas, Béxareños worked to further the colonists' business interests. Beyond their shared federalist ideology, Béxareños saw the prosperity of the incoming immigration linked to their own economic advancement. Thus, on contentious issues such as slavery, Béxareños worked to obtain an exemption for the Department of Texas since economic success depended on reliable work force of slave labor. Interpretations that suggested that slavery was the major cause of the Texas Revolution frequently characterize republican rhetoric as a cover for the desire to extend the institution into Texas. The point overlooked is that early republicans—American and Mexican—desired economic opportunity and saw the republic with its emphasis on individual rights and private property as the form of government best able to promote and protect economic liberty.[23] In San Antonio de Béxar, the most prominent Béxareño family clan included familiar names such as Ruiz, Navarro, Herrera, Veramendi, Flores, and Seguín. The marriage of James Bowie to Ursula Veramendi, the daughter of a wealthy Béxareño merchant and politician, represented much more than a simple love match—it showcased the political and economic alliance between native and immigrant elites.[24]

In reality, Texas had become embroiled in a civil war that pitted the Béxar-Monclova faction against Saltillo even before the outbreak of the revolution in 1835. In 1828, the representatives from the north successfully voted to relocate the capital from Saltillo to Monclova.[25] The act resulted in both sides mobilizing their respective militias and, although no battles were fought, hostilities seemed possible. Santa Anna attempted to settle the dispute but ultimately the Béxar-Movclova faction denounced Santa Anna's centralist shift while Saltillo endorsed it.[26] In a move that angered the central government, legislators in Monclova issued a number of questionable 400 league grants to individuals as a way to raise funds for the state's defense.[27] Although the act initially referenced the Indian frontier, any troops raised could also be used against the centralists. By the summer of 1835, the centralists responded to the threats to their authority, ordering General Martín Perfecto de Cos, the commander of the *Provincias Internas*, to close the legislature at Monclova in an effort to curtail federalist agitation.[28] Before he could arrive, though, a handful of legislators granted Governor Agustín Viecas the authority to relocate the capital temporarily to a point of his choosing. What had been a regional dispute was on the verge of become part of the larger national conflict. According to colonist William H. Jack, "Texas is looked upon by the republicans of Mexico, as the last rallying point of liberty, and to crush its Spirit in the bud, is the end and object of all their military movement."[29]

Positions hardened during the summer of 1835. In May, General Antonio López de Santa Anna had led a column of troops to the city of Zacatecas and crushed a federalist rebellion that had broken out in that state.[30] General Cos intercepted Viesca who was on his way to Texas to establish a temporary government at Béxar. In June, William B. Travis and his supporters captured the Mexican garrison at Anahuac after accusing the forts' commander and local tax officials of tyranny (a buzz word for centralism). Unlike his earlier involvement in the 1832 disturbance at Anahuac, Travis found his actions criticized by many colonists. Both native and immigrant Texans viewed these events as serious developments that appeared to be moving the department toward an inevitable fight with the centralist-controlled government.[31]

Many colonists urged their countrymen to remain calm and do nothing that might worsen the situation. They reminded others that Stephen F. Austin, who earlier had traveled to Mexico City to present a petition detailing the colonists' grievances, still remained a prisoner there. Frustrated with the response he received, the *empresario* had sent a letter telling Texans to proceed with their plan to establish Texas as a separate state within the Mexican Federal Republic. His belligerent stance alarmed authorities, who ordered him arrested and held in prison. Although later released from close confinement, Austin still remained in the Mexican capital awaiting permission to return to Texas.[32] His friends and political allies in the Peace Party wanted no additional incidents that might jeopardize his safety or chance of freedom.

Despite the faction's peaceful wishes, events beyond their control continued. Cos had captured Augustín Viesca, the governor of *Coahuila y Texas*, as that official tried to reach the Department of Texas. The governor and his supporters, who included Benjamin R. Milam, planned to temporarily relocate to San Antonio de Béxar, but Cos' soldiers apprehended them as they rode northward. More disturbing to Texans, though, was word that Cos would soon be on his way with a large number of troops. The rumor was that Texas would receive the same treatment that had been visited upon Zacatecas.[33] As developments unfolded, the warning of the War Party seemed to be coming true. Its supporters even urged an immediate march on Béxar before it could become a centralist stronghold.[34] Colonists throughout the settlements held meetings on possible actions against the centralists. Toward the end of August, Cos ordered the arrest of William B. Travis, Lorenzo de Zavala, Frank W. Johnson, Mosely Baker, and other perceived troublemakers in an effort prevent further anti-government agitation.[35] Austin, who had been absent from Texas for more than two years, returned home in late August to find the region preparing for war with the centralist government of Mexico. John W. Smith, a resident of Béxar, claimed that even the Béxarenos were "hot for a war and think the colonies does wrong in not making war."[36]

The measure that finally provoked the colonists into taking up arms against the centralists was the government order recalling weapons it had loaned to militia and municipalities for their defense.[37] The official explanation that the items were going to be stored in central locations across Mexico where they would be available in the case of regional emergencies appeared to mask the centralists' true intent—they wanted weapons out of the hands of potential rebels. Military contingents visited both Victoria and Gonzales to retrieve small cannons loaned to those communities. Officials at Victoria complied but colonists at Gonzales refused to turn their cannon over to the soldiers and even called on the Mexican troops to surrender. Lieutenant Francisco de Castañada, who led the contingent from Béxar to Gonzales, reported the action to his superior, writing, "I refused to do so [surrender], and I asked them why they had attacked me. To this they replied that it was because I was a Centralist and they were Federalists. I made them see that it was not that way, that up to that date the Government of the Nation had existed under this form, and that their aggression was unjust and would bring down upon them the most dire results, for which they would be responsible."[38] As Castañada predicted, the result of the action at Gonzales was war. Word of the October 2, 1835, skirmish spread quickly and more than four hundred colonists rushed to Gonzales. Quickly organizing themselves into the Federal Army of Texas with Stephen F. Austin at their head, the rebel army moved westward to San Antonio de Béxar.[39]

San Antonio de Béxar was important to the Mexican government both strategically and politically. The town, the population of which in 1835 numbered around 2000, was located on the old *Camino Real* that led from the Rio Grande to the Louisiana border. Béxar was also the traditional seat of political power in Texas, serving as the home of the governor during Spanish rule. Its political role continued after

Mexico won its independence. Occupying the town when the revolution erupted were 650 Mexican soldiers under General Martín Perfecto de Cos. Prominent colonists and even Santa Anna believed that securing Béxar was the key to controlling Texas.[40]

Austin and the Federal Army of Texas arrived outside Béxar in late October to find that Cos had already begun fortifying the town, including the plaza around San Fernando Cathedral and the old mission compound known as the Alamo. Austin sent a 100-man detachment under the command of James Bowie and James W. Fannin to scout out enemy positions on the south side of town. Cos countered by ordering Col. Domingo de Ugartechea to intercept the probe. On the morning of October 28, the two forces fought a brief but fierce battle along the bank of the San Antonio River within sight of Mission Concepción. The outnumbered Texans inflicted heavy casualties on Ugartechea's men, who retreated back to town.[41]

The action then settled down to a siege operation, with the Texans camped on the outskirts of the town and Cos and his men occupying Béxar. On November 8, the Texans scored another victory when William B. Travis and his command located and captured Cos's horse herd grazing near the Medina River. The Texans struck again on November 26 when James Bowie prevented a pack train loaded with forage from entering town. Known as the Grass Fight, the skirmish occurred near Alazán Creek west of the town.[42] Little by little, food, supplies, and time were running out for the Mexican army trapped inside Béxar.

However, despite their successes, the Texans were experiencing their own set of difficulties. Siege life had little appeal for the volunteers and many began to leave as the weather turned colder. Austin, appointed commissioner to the United States by the Provisional Government, left the army to assume his new duties. Although his friends believed he could raise money for Texas, his detractors within the old War Party were glad to have him out of the way. His replacement as commander, Edward Burleson, had trouble controlling the independent minded Texans who remained even though they had elected him. By the beginning of December, strong sentiment emerged, pushed by Houston, for the army to end the siege, withdraw to the east, and establish winter quarters.[43] The men of the New Orleans Greys were dismayed to hear talk of calling off the campaign just as they and other volunteers arrived eager for a fight.[44] On the eve of the army's breakup Benjamin Rush Milam, a respected colonist, spoke out against the withdrawal and asked: "Who will follow Old Ben Milam?" Soon nearly 300 men volunteered to attack the town with him the next morning. The remainder of the Texans agreed to stay and support the attack by protecting the rear of the two assault columns. Entering Béxar on the morning of December 5, Milam and the Texans began a five-day-long engagement that consisted of close range fighting. Battling house-to-house, the Texans gradually seized key Mexican positions around San Fernando Church. Late on the ninth, Cos's men fell back to the Alamo. Soon afterward, Cos asked for terms and surrendered to the Texans on the following day.[45] Many within the rebels' ranks objected to the lenient terms, predicting that they would have to face Cos and his soldiers again.[46]

Other military events had been happening outside of Béxar. The success at Gonzales bolstered supporters of the revolt, who quickly captured the centralist stronghold at Goliad on October 9. Like Béxar, Goliad was a strategic crossroads that needed to be held in order to control the surrounding area and access to the coast. Captain Philip Dimmit and a force of volunteers extended the rebels' reach down to the Nueces River with the centralist garrison at Lipantitlán on November 5. Their success put the Irish immigrant communities of Refugio and San Patricio in the rebel sphere of influence. More importantly, it helped ensure the safety of Copano Bay, which was becoming the revolution's portal to the United States. By the first of the year, one member of the council announced that "a cordon of posts are being established from Bexar by Goliad to San Patrico on the Rio Nueces, and Government agents will be stationed at each post to receive and provide for volunteers, and take charge of all public stores." As for the future, "we hope to extend the line to Matamoros at no very distant time."[47] The goal was to establish a strong frontier line that could repel any centralist counterattack.

One of the most important events in the Texas Revolution did not even happen in Texas. During the late summer of 1835, three exiled Mexican officers met in New Orleans to plan a coordinated federalist response to Santa Anna. These men were Lorenzo de Zavala, former governor of the Federal District of Mexico; Valentín Gómez Farías, Santa Anna's former vice president; and José Antonio Mexía, a former officer of the Mexican Army. Gómez Farías's role was to organize federalist resistance throughout Mexico. He had already passed through Zacatecas and Coahuila on his way to Texas. Zavala's role was to help manage the federalist revolt in Texas, and Mexía's role was to support other Mexican federalists through direct military action. In October 1835, Mexía led an expedition from New Orleans to take the fight to the Mexican state of Tamaulipas. The expedition arrived at Tampico and attempted to capture the important port city, but the expected federalist support faltered and the attack failed. Mexía re-embarked his men and sailed for Texas. While it is easy to discount as a historical tangent, the Tampico Expedition had far reaching ramification for Texas and the rebels.[48]

More than military events occupied the colonists' attention that fall. Delegates had been chosen during the summer for a meeting to be held in October at San Felipe in response to worsening relations with the centralist-controlled government; however, the outbreak of hostilities outpaced their plans. In the excitement of the moment many of the delegates had accompanied the Federal Army of Texas to Béxar, causing the meeting to be rescheduled for early November.[49] Meeting at San Felipe from the fourth through the fourteenth, the members of the Consultation established a framework for a provisional government to see Texas through its current emergency. The absence of Austin and key supporters of the old "peace" coalition allowed more strident delegates a stronger voice, a voice that increasingly called for a total break with Mexico. Moreover, many delegates began to realize that continued aid from the United States depended on independence.[50]

The Consultation dealt with the most pressing issues at hand: establishing a civilian government, organizing a military force, and achieving legitimacy in the eyes of the world. The former was accomplished by a formal proclamation called the *Declaration of Causes*. The delegates explained their actions as a response to the centralist takeover of the Mexican government and the annulment of the federal Constitution of 1824. Contending that the federal pact had been broken, they vowed to govern Texas as a separate entity, declaring a sort of temporary secession in effect until the federation was restored and Texas could rejoin the union as a separate state. To that end, the delegates established a civil government, electing Henry Smith, Political Chief of the Department of the Brazos, to serve as its governor. Austin, the other candidate for the office, received twenty-two to Smith's thirty-one votes. The provisional government also included a general council headed by Lieutenant Governor James W. Robinson, who received the votes of all delegates present. Although the delegates intended for the governor and the council to work together, the two branches quickly embarked on contrary courses. As chief executive, Smith believed himself superior to the council, expecting its support and becoming peeved when he did not receive it. The council believed itself to be Smith's equal and justified in pursuing its own agenda, often disregarding the governor's wishes and advice.[51]

Unfortunately, the delegates created another contentious situation by establishing two distinct military forces for Texas. In reality, Texas already had an army, which consisted of the volunteers who were serving in the field at Béxar and Goliad. These troops had elected their own officers, a standard practice with citizen-soldiers. The delegates recognized the existence of this volunteer corps but also moved to create a regular army, appointing Sam Houston as its commander. In a decision that ultimately created chaos, the delegates announced that Houston had no authority over the volunteers. The result was that Texas was left with a regular, but virtually non-existent army, while the volunteers comprised autonomous and independent commands. Compounding the military blunder, the Béxar garrison sided with the governor while the volunteers around Goliad supported the council. It was a recipe for the disasters that would follow.[52]

Members of the council desired a working relationship with other Mexican federalists, one of the main dictates of the Consultation. Smith early on decided that no Mexican, regardless of ideological leaning, could be trusted and, therefore, no moral or monetary support should be afforded to them. Among the acts that infuriated Smith, the council issued funds to Mexican federalists in order to secure their help, even after the disaster at Tampico.[53] To further exacerbate the developing feud, Viesca—recently freed from captivity—arrived unexpectedly at Gonzales in early November, accompanied by Colonel José María Gonzales and a company of soldiers loyal to the federalist cause. Viesca's supporters expected him to be greeted as the chief officer of the state, especially since he was still the duly elected governor of *Coahuila y Texas*. They were incensed when the post's commander, Philip Dimmit, refused to recognize the authority of the former governor based on the fact that Texas had established its own provisional government while Viesca was imprisoned. Complaints had also been lodged that Dimmit and his men had mistreated local residents, driving these potential allies off into the countryside. Angry letters to Austin and the council resulted in Dimmit's replacement.[54] Texan supporters of the Mexican Federalist party still believed that Viesca, Mexía, and Gonzales with his men could be useful in Texas as well as extending the war beyond its borders.[55] Facing opposition from Smith, however, these Mexican federalists withdrew from the conflict, taking refuge in New Orleans where Mexía later faced legal problems for filibustering.[56] Labeling the council's actions treacherous, Smith demanded it apologize and reverse its actions otherwise he would have no further dealings with it. Equally stubborn, the council declared the governorship vacant and recognized Robinson as Smith's replacement. Their impasse had important ramifications. The conflict, in which alliances had been built on ideological issues regarding federalism and centralism, began to assume a racial tone as Smith maligned and alienated Mexican federalists, bringing secession one step closer. Moreover, civil government ceased to function, leaving Texans waiting for the upcoming constitutional convention to restore order. One observer summed up the situation in a letter to his wife, "The situation of the country in relation to its political condition is anything but settled. The victory at San Antonio & expulsion of the last hostile forces from Texas has left us for the present free from Mexico[.] There is however, as I think much to be found in the ambition of demagogues. There is now issued writs of Election which is to take place next month for members of a convention to meet in March next."[57]

The volunteers at Goliad had already made their intentions clear. On December 20, 1835, the garrison issued its own call for secession, declaring "that the former province and department of Texas is, and of right ought to be, a free sovereign, and independent State." Reflecting on the past controversy surrounding reliance on help from Mexican federalists like Mexía, they proclaimed "It belongs to the North-Americans of Texas to set this bright, this cheering, this all-subduing example." They further explained that "Unless we take this step, no foreign power can either respect or even know us." As for Mexico, "Let us, then, know them hereafter, as other independent States know each other—'enemies in war, in peace, friends.'"[58] Despite their optimistic rhetoric, almost all believed more fighting lay ahead.

The military situation also deteriorated. The problem lay with the Consultation's decision to deny Houston command over the existing volunteer force. With Béxar and Goliad in rebel hands, attention turned towards the Rio Grande and Matamoros. A campaign to capture this inland port would make use of the existing volunteer force, give the provisional government a source of revenue through customhouse receipts, and support Mexican federalists engaged in the larger anti-centralist revolt.[59] In late December, Frank W. Johnson, who replaced Edward Burleson as commander of the volunteers in Béxar, had recruited more than 200 volunteers for the expedition. Both Governor Smith and his council approved the plan but had different ideas as to who should lead it. The governor ordered Houston to oversee the expedition, who in turn assigned the task to James Bowie. The council offered the position to Johnson, who declined because of a dispute over volunteer officer commissions. Next, they selected James W. Fannin. However, in the meantime, Johnson changed his mind, leaving the expedition with three commanders. Bowie abandoned the project but both Fannin and Johnson planned to proceed with the expedition. Smith and Houston quickly soured on the plan. Before leaving for East Texas to ask the Cherokee to stay out the conflict, Houston traveled to Goliad where he convinced many of the volunteers to abandon the expedition. Shortly after the new year, Texas had four distinct and autonomous military forces: (1) the small force of recently recruited regulars, loyal to Smith and Houston; (2) the Béxar garrison under Lieutenant Colonel James C. Neill, loyal to Smith and Houston; (3) the Goliad garrison under Colonel James W. Fannin, loyal to the council; and (4) the remnants of the Matamoros Expedition under Frank W. Johnson, loyal to the council but working for a separate republic that would comprise the watershed of the Rio Grande. Cooperation between the commands could not realistically be expected given the personalities and divided loyalties present.

The ill-fated Tampico Expedition had an additional effect on the military situation. Mexican officials had captured thirty-one of Mexía's volunteers and asked the national government what to do with them. The response they received from Santa Anna was that since Mexico was not currently at war with any nation, the prisoners must be pirates and therefore would be executed. Despite pleas for clemency from diplomats and the men themselves, the prisoners were shot on December 14, 1835.[60] Santa Anna and his Minister of War, José Maria Tornel, sought to apply this principle to the revolt in Texas. Specifically referencing José Antonio Mexía and filibustering expeditions originating from the United States, Tornel—with the approval of Santa Anna and Congress—announced on December 30, 1835, that "Foreigners landing on the coast of the republic or invading its territory by land, armed with the intention of attacking our country, will be deemed pirates and dealt with as such, being citizens of no nation presently at war with the republic, and fighting under no recognized flag."[61] The Tornel Decree, as it came to be called, ensured that executions would become a prominent feature of the centralist campaign to crush the rebels.

By January, the effects of the discord were evident. In Béxar, Neill wrote to the governor and the council lamenting, "It will be appalling to you to learn [of] our alarming weakness" and warning "We have 104 men and two distinct fortifications to garrison." In response, the council and Smith promised aid. The governor asked Houston to take care of the situation before he left to meet the Cherokee. Houston turned to Bowie, asking him to take what men he had to Béxar to help stabilize the situation.[62] Still worried about this frontier post, Smith also ordered Travis, now a lieutenant colonel of cavalry in the regular service of Texas, to take what men he had raised and proceed to Béxar. Travis reluctantly complied after suggesting that a captain command the contingent while he remained behind to recruit more men. By mid-February, when Neill left Béxar on leave, the garrison had risen to approximately 150 men, mainly volunteers with a handful of Texas regulars. A dispute between Travis and Bowie over who should command in Neill's absence left the garrison divided even though the two men ultimately resolved to share joint command for the twenty days Neill was expected to be gone. Frustrated with receiving so little help from the government, Neill had decided to find more men and supplies on his own.

Discord also reigned at Goliad. Houston had succeeded in dissuading all but the most ardent supporters of Johnson and Grant from descending on Matamoros. The expedition's two leaders moved south toward the Nueces River where they planned to gather men, supplies, and horses for their venture. An independent Texas held no appeal for these men. Although a federalist, Grant had a reason to widen the revolt because his property lay in Coahuila and he was in danger of losing it and other concessions if the south remained under centralist control. Houston charged, "Several members of [the council] are aware that the interests and feelings of Dr. Grant are opposed to the independence and true interests of the people of Texas." [63] If there were to be a separation, Grant and his supporters hoped it would yield a new republic centered on the Rio Grande. The volunteers who chose to remain at Goliad were organized into two battalions under Fannin. Although he held a regular commission as colonel that placed him second in rank only to Houston, Fannin supported the council and represented its interests by commanding the volunteers assembled at Goliad. He put the garrison to work strengthening the old Spanish fort which his men christened Fort Defiance.

The Mexican government had not been idle. Authorized by Congress to lead the army back into Texas, Santa Anna organized the upcoming counterattack from his base in San Luis Potosí. The objective of the Texas campaign was to retake Béxar and Goliad, both important political and strategic locations. By reincorporating Cos's Béxar command into a combined force of regular and militia units, he amassed 6,500 troops. At no time in the counterattack, however, would all of these men be concentrated in one place. The plan called for two main columns to reenter Texas. Santa Anna would command a column that targeted

San Antonio de Béxar, while another column, commanded by General José Urrea, would march to Matamoros, suppressing any federalist support he encountered along the Rio Grande before advancing onto Goliad.[64] After securing Béxar and Goliad, the army could fan out eastward and drive the rebels before them, either killing them or driving them out of Texas.

The centralist counterattack had made contact at both Béxar and San Patricio south of Goliad by the end of February. Santa Anna's column entered Béxar on February 23, forcing the rebels to fall back into the Alamo. With Neill still away and Bowie ill, Travis assumed command of the undermanned garrison, immediately sending out couriers carrying written calls for assistance. Texans responded but few could make it because of the time and distance involved in marshalling reinforcements and travelling to the Alamo. The only know contingent to arrive in time was the Gonzales Ranging Company, who lived only seventy miles from Béxar. On March 3, James Butler Bonham brought Travis a letter from Major Robert M. Williamson, reiterating that help was on the way and pleading "For God's sake, hold out until we can assist you."[65] After conducting a two-week-long siege of the Alamo, Santa Anna launched a classic dawn attack on March 6, carrying the fort and putting the garrison to the sword. News of executions following the fort's capture quickly spread, reaching Gonzales on March 11. Santa Anna intended the word of the executions to serve as a warning to the rebels.[66]

After making a show of force along the Rio Grande Valley, Urrea turned and marched northward from Matamoros. On February 25, Fannin, still at Goliad, received an urgent request from Travis. He organized a relief column but called it off the next day when he learned of Urrea's advance.[67] Early on the morning of February 27, Urrea struck, surprising and killing eight and capturing thirteen members of Johnson's command at San Patricio. Johnson and a few others escaped but it marked the beginning of the end of Johnson's and Grant's independent command. On March 2, Urrea ambushed Grant's party at Agua Dulce while the federalists were rounding up horses. Grant and thirteen others were killed and six men taken prisoner. News of the fate of Johnson's and Grant's men, rather than stirring the volunteers gathered at Goliad into action, created confusion. Complicating the situation further, Fannin learned that some colonists who supported the revolt were in danger from Urrea's advance. On March 10, Fannin had sent Amon B. King and a small detachment with wagons to collect these families and escort them back to Goliad. King determined that the enemy force in the area was greater than imagined and asked Fannin to send help while he forted up in the old mission at Refugio. Fannin dispatched William Ward, commander of the Georgia Battalion, to assist King. The arrival of Ward and his men at Refugio initiated a conflict over seniority between the two federalist officers. The squabbling caused the rebels to break into several smaller detachments, each of which was subsequently defeated and its survivors captured and executed by Urrea's troops between March 12 and 15.[68] Urrea's success was greatly aided by the fact that rancher Carlos de la Garza, and other local centralist supporters, provided intelligence and military assistance during the Goliad campaign.

Back at the beginning of March, the long anticipated convention finally convened at the small town of Washington on the Brazos River. The delegates brushed aside the rancorous dispute between the governor and the council, offering neither side the opportunity to revisit old grievances. The delegates reaffirmed Houston as Texas's commanding general but corrected the Consultation's mistake by giving him authority over all troops in the field—regulars and volunteers. They also declared Texas independent from Mexico and set to work creating a governmental framework for the Republic of Texas.[69] Already ideologically separate from centralist Mexico, the public declaration completed the act of secession begun by the Consultation in November. As the delegates worked, several of Travis's pleas for assistance reached them. On the March 6, a letter arrived that made it clear the Alamo's situation was critical. Houston squashed a proposal for the delegates to disband the convention and race to Béxar, proclaiming that he would leave that afternoon for the frontier where he would assume command.[70] Traveling with a small group of military aides, Houston reached Gonzales on March 11 and found Neill with 350 men ready to march to relieve the Alamo. Later that day news of the Alamo's fall arrived. With no reason to risk his newly acquired command in a futile march to Béxar, Houston decided against holding Gonzales and ordered a retreat to the east. The town burned as he marched away. In what became known as the Runaway Scrape, civilians followed Houston, fearing being left behind to face the wrath of the advancing Mexican Army. Another Texan military disaster fuelled the panic sweeping Texas. On March 11, with a clear view of the military situation and using his expanded authority, Houston ordered Fannin to evacuate Fort Defiance and rendezvous with him at Victoria. Fannin procrastinated, hoping the men he had sent south to aid the colonists would return. On March 18, advanced elements of Urrea's command reached Goliad, initiating a skirmish outside the fort. Finally departing the next day, Fannin's 400-man command was caught near Coleto Creek on the open prairie, encircled, and forced to fight. On March 20, Fannin surrendered his command to Urrea, believing he and his men would be treated as prisoners of war. Marched backed to the old presidio, the volunteers were kept for a week before the majority (342) were led out and executed. Urrea, who had already conducted executions on a smaller scale, evidently felt differently about the prisoners at Goliad. It was only after Santa Anna's personal insistence that the Tornel Decree was carried out.[71]

News of the Alamo's fall finally reached the delegates assembled at Washington on March 15, 1835. Even before the unfortunate events at Goliad had occurred, the delegates and the new officials meeting at the small river-crossing settlement felt exposed and in danger. On March 17, one observer to the proceedings, William F. Gray, noted that "the state of the country is becoming every day more gloomy." Later that day the Virginian reported the convention's hasty adjournment, explaining "A general panic seems to have seized them. Their families are exposed and defenseless, and thousands are moving off to the east."[72] The Runaway Scrape had swept up even the new government.

Houston used Texas's geography to his advantage as he retreated. He strategically placed rivers between him and the advancing Mexican Army. With the time he purchased by maneuvering, he collected and incorporated additional bodies of men into his force. He reached San Felipe on March 28, stopping for the night before moving upriver. When two companies refused to retreat any further, Houston ordered their captains, Mosely Baker and Wylie Martin, to guard the crossings at San Felipe and Fort Bend, their home settlements. San Felipe was burned to prevent its use by Santa Anna. From the end of March through mid-April, Houston was able to maintain a training camp at Groce's Plantation on the west bank of the Brazos River near present-day Hempstead. By April 9, Baker and Martin had been forced to give up the river crossings. Santa Anna's approach ultimately forced Houston to abandon his plantation post and resume his withdrawal toward the Louisiana boarder. Critics of his retrograde policy wondered if he ever intended to turn and fight or would he allow himself to be pushed out of Texas.[73]

Both armies were about to converge. Santa Anna had left his main force behind, taking personal command of a 500-man detachment in an attempt to catch President David G. Burnet, Vice President Lorenzo de Zavala, and other officials of the revolutionary government who were reportedly at Harrisburg. He reached the town on April 18 but the government had already fled. Like Gonzales and San Felipe, Harrisburg was burned to the ground. Learning of Santa Anna's venture, Houston moved towards Harrisburg. On April 20, Houston and Santa Anna skirmished inconclusively near the San Jacinto River, after which both sides went into camp along a bayou leading to the San Jacinto River. [74] Outnumbered by Houston, Santa Anna sent a message ordering General Cos to bring reinforcements and join him as quickly as possible.

Houston had finally resolved to give battle to the enemy before him. Santa Anna, reinforced by Cos on the morning of April 21, had roughly 1,300 men within a horseshoe-shaped bend on the river. Houston ordered Vince's Bridge burned, leaving Santa Anna with no escape route. That afternoon, Houston led his 900 men against Santa Anna's camp. Shouting "Remember the Alamo" and "Remember Goliad," the Texans killed 630 Mexican soldiers as they avenged the victims of the Tornel Decree. Another 700 soldiers were finally allowed to surrender once darkness cloaked the battlefield. The Texan losses, by comparison were unbelievably small: nine killed and thirty wounded. The victory was made even more meaningful when Houston's scouts captured Santa Anna the next day.[75]

Following the Battle of San Jacinto, the new Texan government headed by President David G. Burnet undertook diplomatic measures to end the war between Texas and Mexico. On May 14, 1836, captured Mexican president Santa Anna signed a treaty negotiated with Texas officials. In the document, Santa Anna promised to end the war and order all Mexican troops in Texas to retire to the south bank of the Rio Grande. In a secret portion of the treaty, Burnet promised to transport Santa Anna safely to Veracruz so the Mexican president could urge his government to adopt the treaty. The Treaty of Velasco had two important effects on the future. Angry Texans soldiers refused to let Santa Anna go; thus, Santa Anna later declared the treaty voided by the Texans, who had keep him imprisoned for six months before finally allowing him to return home. More importantly, however, was Texas's insistence that the treaty clearly established the Rio Grande as the southern boundary of Texas. This claim later contributed to the outbreak of the Mexican War (1846–48).

The Texas government's insistence that the Mexican Army withdraw from Texas was based on the fact that danger still existed despite the turn of events at San Jacinto. Roughly 4,000 Mexican soldiers remained in the field, ready to continue the campaign. General Vicente Filisola, who took command of the Mexican troops after Santa Anna's capture, had ordered his subordinates to rendezvous east of present-day Houston in the watershed of San Bernardo Creek. As shown by Gregg Dimmick and his associates, it was this gathering of the Mexican Army in this flat, featureless area called the "Sea of Mud" that ultimately forced the Mexican troops to leave Texas. Torrential rains turned the prairie into a bottomless muck that made movement almost impossible. The water and mud disorganized and demoralized the troops to the point where Filisola decided to withdraw to Matamoros where he planned for the army to refit and regroup before resuming its campaign to crush the revolt in Texas.[76]

Mexican forces still occupied Béxar, though. Santa Anna had appointed General Juan José Andrade to take command of the town before leaving on March 31, 1836, to join his troops in their eastward march. Left with "more than 1000 men," Andrade's primary task was to rebuild the fortifications at Béxar, so it could be defended against a Texan attack. His secondary task was to care for the 150 Mexican soldiers who had been wounded during the final assault on the Alamo and another 40 men who had fallen ill. Andrade stated that the troops at Béxar remained loyal and "not demoralized." Ironically, his reports mirrored Neill's earlier complaints of being left with too few men and little funds to carry out his mission. Andrade received medical assistance from an unexpected quarter. Andrade reported, "In La Bahia, two of the foreign doctors [Barnard and Shackleford] who were part of the prisoners left over, were asked by Colonel Ugartechea, to help us." Despite their continued captivity, the two Goliad Massacre survivors, Drs. Joseph Henry Barnard and Jack Shackleford, found their assignment at Béxar relatively pleasant under the circumstances.[77]

The first news of San Jacinto and Santa Anna's capture reached Béxar on May 6, 1836. Confusion reigned as no one seemed to know what would happen next.[78] On May 19, 1836, Andrade received orders from Filisola to evacuate Béxar and reunite with the rest of the Mexican Army which was then withdrawing to Matamoros. It took Andrade several days before he could leave. Andrade's chief of artillery disabled the artillery found at the Alamo.[79] On May 22, Barnard noted, "General Andrade has received orders to destroy the Alamo. They are now busy as bees, soldiers, convicts and all, tearing down the walls &c." At midday on May 24, the doctor wrote, "The Mexican army troops are now leaving town. The last column is this moment crossing the river." He and Shackleford departed Béxar two days later. On June 1, Andrade's command camp near Goliad was in sight of the Texans, who under Rusk had just reoccupied the town the day before. He reached Matamoros on June 18, 1836, where he was reunited with the rest of the Mexican Army, then under the command of Urrea instead of Filisola. One official act still had to be completed at Béxar. Lieutenant Francisco Castañeda, an officer with the local Alamo Company, had remained behind with eighteen soldiers with orders to receive the Texans and turn the town and its public property over to them. On June 4, 1836, Captain Juan Seguín arrived with twenty-two men to reclaim Béxar. After a brief meeting, Castañeda relinquished control of the town to Seguín and departed for Matamoros.[80]

Occupied by soldiers of one side or another since October 1835, Béxar, the town and its residents, had suffered. Two major battles had been fought within its environs. Many of the trees had been cut down either to build fortifications or use as firewood. The town had a desolate, war-torn appearance. Seguín reported that only forty families were left out of Béxar's prewar population of nearly 2000 residents. Many of the inhabitants had fled the town during the fighting to seek safety in the countryside. Others had followed Andrade's column to Matamoros. Within a few weeks, Seguín estimated that besides the soldiers of the Texas Army, only about fifty individuals actually remained.[81]

Reinforcements soon arrived to support Seguín. On June 4, General Rusk, who replaced the wounded Houston as commander of the Texas Army, ordered Colonel James Smith to travel from Victoria to Béxar with his command. His mission was (1) to check the upper route to make sure it was clear of Mexican troops and (2) round up any cattle they encountered. In regards to the residents of Béxar, the general told Smith, "you will be careful on going to San Antonio to prevent any unnecessary interruption to the citizens there. Such conduct as entering their homes and taking their property you will forbid [as] improper [as] those of them who have taken [a] hand against us are gone and those who remain have either been our friends or are no service to either party."[82] On June 8, Smith reported, "Agreeable to your orders I continued to Scour the country on both sides of Antonio river and have found the country to be in a perfect state of quietness, from information recd." Nevertheless, a rumor circulated that Mexicans were planning "to ravage the whole of that part of the country, to murder the inhabitants and rob the country of every thing valuable."[83] This information, true or not, hurried Smith on his journey to Béxar. As Rusk promised, Smith entered the town in mid-June and encamped his men around the Alamo even though many houses in town were vacant. The two Texan officers, Smith and Seguín, set about fulfilling Rusk's orders to both secure the town and acquire information about conditions on the frontier.

Events were about to take a drastic turn that would result in the Texans' unexpected evacuation of Béxar. Rusk had received messages by three Texan officers, Henry W. Karnes, Henry Teal, and William P. Miller, who were being held prisoners in Matamoros. The letters, which had been secreted in the handle of a courier's whip, warned that the Mexican Army was about to reenter Texas to finish the task of crushing the revolt. They stated, "Urea [*sic*] is commander in chief of the Mexican army, and says he will not stop short of the Sabine. … Blow up Goliad and Bexar. You must have a sufficient force in the field at once, and we will whip them again; …"[84] Shaken by the news, Rusk issued a public appeal for action in which he repeated the men's warning.[85] The "Whip Handle Dispatch" seemed to give Texans two options: prepare to fight once again or leave Texas.

Rusk sent an urgent order to Smith at Béxar. "You will with your whole force of Cavalry except thirty men rejoin the Army at Headquarters, with the greatest dispatch possible information has just reached of the rapid advance of the enemy about Six Thousand strong from Matamoros … this information comes in letters from Carnes [*sic*], Teal and major Miller who are arrested and confined in the Mexican Camp. … You will dispatch thirty men and direct them to drive back across the Guadalupe and Colorado all the stock they properly can with as much dispatch as possible keeping a good look out for the advance of the enemy Cavalry. … Great dispatch and promptitude is expected in the executions of this order. There is not one moment to be lost."[86]

Rusk had specific orders for Seguín. In a postscript, he asked Smith to pass the following instructions on: "Col Seguin with his command will also repair forthwith to Head Quarters he will give an order to the citizens to appeal in driving off the cattle."[87] Complying with Rusk's wishes, Seguín issued a public appeal to the residents of Béxar.

TO THE INHABITANTS OF BEXAR

Fellow Citizens:

> Military movements compel me to repair to Head Quarters. I have in consequences to evacuate this town, but previous to doing so, I require your aid to carry off the cattle and place them where the enemy cannot make use of them. I have no doubt that you will assist cheerfully in this measure, thereby furnishing to the supreme government of Texas a proof of your attachment to the just cause, and the beloved liberty we are contending for. If, on the contrary you fail to render the slightest service, your disaffection will be manifest: and although a matter of regret to the supreme government, yet it can then no longer treat you as

> Texians, but, perhaps, as enemies. Be not deceived with the idea we have no forces wherewith to repel force—time will show to the contrary and will convince you that Texas must be free.
>
> Fellow citizens your conduct on this day is going to decide your fate before the general government of Texas. If you maintain your post as mere lookers-on; if you do not abandon the city and retire to the interior of Texas, that its army may protect you, you will, without fail, be treated as real enemies, and will suffer accordingly. My ties of birth and friendship I entertain towards you, cause me to desire your happiness, and I therefore address you in that spirit of truth while in me is characteristic.
>
> Bexians: render every possible aid, and soon shall you enjoy your liberty and your property, which is the wish of your countyman and friend, Juan N. Seguin[88]

Seguín's address made it clear: the residents of Béxar were facing a test of their loyalty to the newly established Republic of Texas. In reality, this test was extended to the entire native-born population in the coming decade that followed Texas's secession from Mexico. Béxareño José Francisco Ruiz cautioned his son-in-law, Blas Herrera, "If for any reason you should remain, then by no means should you take up arms against the Texans. Give the same advice to your friends for only God could possibly return the territory of Texas to the Mexican Government. Texas has the arms and money for her defense and shall remain forever free."[89]

With Smith's and Seguín's departure, Béxar was virtually deserted by the end of June 1836. Throughout the summer, Rusk kept his troops further to the east, positioned to block Urrea if he decided to advance into Texas. Not until late August would he feel safe enough to send any troops back to the frontier and Béxar. Although an uneasy peace settled on the region, years passed before the threat of a Mexican counterattack against the Republic of Texas would finally cease.

Notes

1. John H. Jenkins, ed., *Papers of the Texas Revolution, 1835–1836*, 10 vols. (Austin: Presidial Press, 1973), 1: 69. Hereafter referred to as *PTR*.

2. The goal of this chapter is somewhat grand: present an evidence-based interpretation of what is known as the Texas Revolution. While this interpretation represents the view of this author, it never would have been formulated without the work of other historians who contributed to this

topic, in particular, pioneer Texas historians Euguene C. Barker, Roy W. Smith, William C. Binkley, Ruby Cumby Smith, Carlos E. Castañeda, James Winston, Karle Wilson Baker, Ralph W. Steen, Harbert Davenport, Hobart Huson, Henry W. Barton, Nettie Lee Benson, Kathryn O'Connor, Gerald S. Pierce, and Joseph M. Nance. More recent contributors to the subject include Malcolm D. McLean, Richard G. Santos, David J. Weber, Margaret Swett Henson, Jesús F. de la Teja, Alwyn Barr, Stanley C. Green, Gene Brack, John H. Jenkins, Richard M. Gaines, Thomas Ricks Lindley, Andrés Tejarina, Jaime E. Rodríguez O., James E. Crisp, Stephen L. Hardin, Paul D. Lack, Miguel Soto, Gregg Cantrell, Stephen L. Moore, James L. Haley, Jack Jackson, John Wheat, Ana Carolina Castillo Crimm, Pedro Santoni, Gregg Dimmick, Stuart Reid, Michael P. Costeloe, Timothy Ana, David R. McDonald, Will Fowler, Todd Hansen, Andrew J. Torget, and Michael R. Moore. These and others need to be credited for their efforts in showing the Texas Revolution was an event worthy of serious historical study.

3. Although ignored by many historians during the last half of the twentieth century, the Enlightenment and ideas associated with it are again topics for discussion. For examples of this revival, see, Karen O'Brian, "The Return of the enlightenment," *The American Historical Review* 115, no. 5 (December 2010): 1425–1435; Robert Louden, "A New Enlightenment?" *RSA Journal* 156, no. 5543 (Autumn 2010): 34–39; and John Rajchman, "Enlightenment Today," *Log*, No. 11 (Winter 2008): 131–142.

4. Hobart Huson, *Captain Phillip Dimmitt's Commandancy of Goliad, 1835–1836: An Episode of the Mexican Federalist War in Texas, Usually Referred to as the Texas Revolution* (Austin: Von Boeckmann-Jones Co., 1974), xiii-xiv. Huson was working on a manuscript on the topic of the Federalist Wars when he died in 1983 at age ninety.

5. J. P. Kimball, trans., *Laws and Decrees of the State of Coahuila and Texas, In Spanish and English* (Houston: Telegraph Power Press, 1839; Clark, New Jersey: The Lawbook Exchange, Ltd., 2010), 289.

6. *PTR*, 3: 39.

7. Disney's 2004 movie, *The Alamo*, attempted to introduce James Grant and other lesser know figures into the story but cuts by the studio rendered them unrecognizable.

8. "Mexico and Texas: Part II," *The United States Democratic Review* 3, Issue 12 (December; J. & H. G. Langley, October 1838), 305–20. The author of this early article establishes what will become the common view of Santa Anna.

9. Donald Fithian Stevens, *Origins of Instability in Early Republican Mexico* (Durham: Duke University Press, 1991), 29–45. Must reads for this topic are Stanley C. Green's *The Mexican Republic: The First Decade, 1823–1832* (Pittsburgh: University of Pittsburgh Press, 1987) and Timothy Anna's *Forging Mexico, 1821*–1835 (Lincoln: University of Nebraska Press, 1998).

10. F. H. Turner, "The Mejía Expedition," *Quarterly of the Texas State Historical Association* 7, no. 1 (July 1903): 1–28. Hereafter *QTSHA*.

11. *The Constitutional Advocate* (Brazoria), October 17, 1832; Turner, "The Mejía Expedition," *QTSHA*, 14.

12. The teaming of Santa Anna and Gómez Farías represented a carrot and stick approach to reform with the former the deal maker and latter the enforcer.

13. *PTR*, 2: 23, 39. The decree actually implementing the centralist plan of government was issued by acting president Miguel Barragan on October 3, 1835.

14. Anna Fears Crawford, *The Eagle: The Autobiography of Santa Anna* (Austin: State House Press, 1988), 7.

15. Ibid., 7. "On the sleeve of my left arm I wore a decoration of honor—having distinguished myself in that action."

16. Will Fowler, *Tornel and Santa Anna: The Writer and the Caudillo, Mexico, 1795–1853* (Westport: Greenwood Press, 2000), 66–71, 74–77.

17. Crawford, *The Eagle*, xiv; Will Fowler, *Santa Anna of Mexico* (Lincoln: University of Nebraska Press, 2002), 154–157. The strength of Fowler's work is that writing as a European, he is able to approach his subject without an anti-Santa Anna bias.

18. Michael Costeloe, *The Central Republic in Mexico, 1835–1846: Hombres de Bien in the Age of Santa Anna* (New York: Cambridge University Press, 1993), 16–17.

19. Fowler, *Tornel and Santa Anna*, 143–45; Waddy Thompson, *Recollections of Mexico* (New York: Wiley & Putnam, 1846), 5; Richard B. Winders, *Mr. Polk's Army: The American Military Experience in the Mexican War* (College Station: Texas A & M University Press, 1997), 183–85. Even the U.S. Ambassador to Mexico, Waddy Thompson, claimed of Santa Anna that "He faithfully sustained the government thus established, until it was fairly tried and generally thought, by the most enlightened men, that the experiment had failed." The inability of Mexico to live up to republican standards became a standard theme by the Mexican War.

20. Kimball, trans., *Laws and Decrees of the State of Coahuila and Texas*, 70–74, 75–76, 78–79.

21. Charles A. Bacarisse, "The Union of Coahuila and Texas," *Southwestern Historical Quarterly* 61, no. 3 (January 1958): 341–349.

22. Andrés Tejarina, *Tejanos and Texas Under the Mexican Flag, 1821–1836* (College Station: Texas A&M University Press, 1994), 113–36. The traditional narrative of events in Texas has come from the North American point of view but the work of Andrés Tejarina, Jesús F. de la Tejas, and others have brought attention to another voice. Jack Jackson's and John Wheat's works on the respective trips of Juan N. Almonte and Manuel de Mier y Terán to Texas are invaluable.

23. Kimball, *Laws and Decrees*, 103; *A Visit to Texas* (New York: Goodrich & Wiley, 1834; A Facsimile Reproduction, Austin: The Steck Company, 1952), 10–11, 78–79. Decree No. 18 (September 15, 1827) regulated slavery; Decree No. 56 (May 5, 1828) recognized the link between prosperity and labor and validated contracts made between colonists and servants. In *A Visit to Texas*, a newcomer is told how to evade the prohibition on slavery by obtaining contracts with his slaves. For the most recent work on slavery and the Texas Revolution, see Andrew Torget, *Seeds of Empire: Cotton, Slavery, and the Transformation of the Texas Borderlands, 1800–1850* (Chapel Hill: University of North Carolina Press, 2015).

24. Kimball, 167, 185, 197, 292. Decree No. 159 (October 5, 1830) states "Letter of citizenship is hereby granted to James Bowie, on the supposition that he can accomplish the establishment of cotton and woolen stuffs, which he offers to place in the state." James Grant was granted the right for ten years to establish cotton and woolen factories at Monclova, Saltillo, and Parras. Benjamin R. Milam was granted ten years to establish navigation on the Colorado River as far as Mina. John M. Bangs and Philip Dimmit were exempted from the ban against foreign-born merchants because their families were born in the state.

25. Kimball, *Laws and Decrees*, 107. Decree 64 (September 25, 1828) authorized the relocation of the state's capital to Monclova.

26. Kimball, *Laws and Decrees*, 280, 288–90. On July 23, 1834, the Executive Department of the state announced that it recognized Santa Anna as president of the republic. *The Exposition of April 22, 1835*, issued by federalist legislators clearly indicated Monclova's rejection of the centralist plan of government.

27. Kimball, *Laws and Decrees*, 247–52, 270, 281–82, 283, 287, 301–4, 310–1; Eugene C. Barker, "Land Speculation as a Cause of the

Texas Revolution," *Quarterly of the Texas State Historical Association* 10 (July 1906): 76–95.

28. Joseph E. Chance, *José Maria de Jesus Carvajal: The Life and Times of a Mexican Revolutionary* (San Antonio: Trinity University Press, 2006), 28–31.

29. Kimball, *Laws and Decrees*, 284, 312; *PTR*, 328. Decree 297 (April 7, 1835) warns the public of Cos coming to Monclova. Decree 325 (May 21, 1835) states, "Should the executive think proper, during the recess of congress, to establish his dispatch at any other place in the state than the capital, he is hereby authorized to do so provisionally."

30. *PTR*, 1: 57, 69, 104–6, 139–40, 156, 194–202, 403–2, Josiah Gregg, *Commerce of the Prairies* 2 (1845), 101–2. Gregg, who was in Mexico at the time, reported that "the soldiery amused themselves by sacking the city, and by perpetrating every species of outrage that their mercenary and licentious appetites could devise."

31. Eugene C. Barker, *The Organization of the Texas Revolution*. Reprint from the Publication of Southern Historical Association (November 1901), 1–26. Barker's article gives a cogent account of the activities during the months immediately prior to the outbreak of hostilities.

32. Stephen F. Austin, "The 'Prison Journal' of Stephen F. Austin," *Quarterly of the Texas State Historical Association* 2, no. 3 (January 1899): 183–210.

33. *PTR*, 1: 85, 374, 458, 502; 2: 19–20; 31–2. On April 6, 1835, Cos discusses "dos Batallones de 600 hombres con su tren corresponte. Artilla. Pase a Tejas immediamente." Warned Horatio Alsbury, "I have seen Gentlemen from different parts of the government … who pass troops on every road Marching for Texas;. …"

34. *PTR*, 1: 201, 328. On July 4, 1835, Robert M. Williamson publicly called for capturing Béxar.

35. *PTR*, 1: 291–92; The Alamo, Phil Collins Collection, Accession No. P.399.014, "Arrest Warrant Issued by Wiley Martin, Political Chief, San Felipe, August 10, 1835."

36. *PTR*, 1: 406.

37. William A. DePalo, Jr., *The Mexican National Army, 1822–1852* (College Station: Texas A&M University Press, 1997), 43; Anna, *Forging Mexico*, 233, 259. Kimball, *Laws and* Decrees, 212, 228. On January 25, 1824, the state legislature of Coahuila and Texas suspended executions of the national law of January 31, 1834, that ordered the reduction of the militia.

38. *PTR*, 2: 39–42, 47–49, 95; Malcolm McLean, ed., *Papers Concerning Robertson's Colony in Texas* (Arlington: University of Texas at Arlington, 1980), 11: 562–63; Ana Carolina Castillo Crimm, *De Léon: A Tejano Family History* (Austin: University of Texas Press), 145.

39. Stephen F. Austin, "General Austin's Order Book for the Campaign of 1835," *Quarterly of the Texas State Historical Association* 11, no. 1 (July 1907): 1–55. This document provides a day-to-day account of Austin's attempt to lead the Federal Army of Texas in its effort to capture Béxar.

40. Richard Bruce Winders, *Sacrificed at the Alamo: Tragedy and Triumph in the Texas Revolution* (Abilene: State House Press, 2004), 56–58.

41. *PTR*, 273.

42. *PTR*, 3: 5–8.

43. *PTR*, 3: 64.

44. Herman Von Erhenberg, "A Campaign in Texas," in *Littell's Living Age* 8 (January, February, March, 1846): 415.

45. *PTR*, 3: 160–64.

46. *PTR*, 3: 490–495. William R. Carey, a participant who was soon to die at the Alamo on March 6, 1836, lamented, "we should have made a Treaty and not a childs bargain however it is done now and its too late to alter until we have another fight which we expect shortly."

47. *PTR*, 3: 408–9.

48. *PTR*, 1: 313–15, 416; 3: 134–38, Edward L. Miller, *New Orleans and the Texas Revolution* (College Station: Texas A&M University Press, 2004), 24; Lorenzo de Zavala, *Journey to the United States of North America*, trans. Wallace Woolsey (Austin: Shoal Creek Publishing, 1980), 8–9; Eugene C. Barker, "The Tampico Expedition," *Quarterly of the Texas State Historical Association* 6, no. 3 (January 1903): 169–186; Margaret Swett Henson, *Lorenzo de Zavala: The Pragmatic Idealist* (Fort Worth: Texas Christian University Press, 1996), 70, 89–90.

49. Eugene C. Barker, "Journal of the Permanent Council, (October 11–27, 1835)," *Quarterly of the Texas State Historical Association* 6, no. 4 (April 1904): 249–278.

50. Paul D. Lack, *The Texas Revolutionary Experience: A Political and Social History, 1835–1836* (College Station: Texas A&M University Press, 1992), 38–52. Lack's volume ranks as one of the most important works on the Texas Revolution written to date.

51. John Henry Brown, *The Life and Times of Henry Smith* (Austin: The Steck Company, 1935), 81–82, 96–97. Although biased towards

Smith, Brown give an important account of the troubled workings between the governor and the general council.

52. Roy W. Smith, "The Quarrel Between Governor Smith and the Council of the Provisional Government of the Republic," *Quarterly of the Texas State Historical Association* 5, no. 4 (April 1903): 270–345.

53. *PTR*, 3: 129,144–46, 168–67, 183, 201, 202, 203, 204–5, 234–35, 262–64. Wrote Smith, "I consider it bad policy to fit out or trust Mexicans in any matter connected with our Government, as I am well satisfied that we will in the end find them inimical and treacherous."

54. *PTR*, 2: 385, 408–10, 419–20, 488.

55. *PTR*, 2: 464.

56. Eugene C. Barker, "The United States and Mexico, 1835–1837," *The Mississippi Valley Historical Review* 1, no. 1 (June 1914): 15.

57. *PTR*, 3: 410.

58. *PTR*, 3: 265–70.

59. *PTR*, 2: 321–22. On November 5, 1835, in his advice to the Consultation, Austin recommends the delegates support an expedition against Matamoros to be led by Mexía.

60. *PTR*, 3: 191, 195.

61. *Telegraph and Texas Register*, March 12, 1836. The Alamo Collection; Carlos E. Castañeda, ed., *The Mexican Side of the Texan Revolution By the Chief Mexican Participants* (Washington, D.C.: Documentary Publications, 1971): 53–54. Oddly, The Papers of the Texas Revolution, 3:379, has does not have the full text of this important document but only a one sentence annotation.

62. *PTR*, 1: 339–40. One of the longstanding misconceptions about the Battle of the Alamo is that the garrison's commanders (Neill, Bowie, and Travis) disobeyed his orders to "blow up the Alamo" and leave Béxar. Thus, according to Houston and his supporters, the garrison bore responsibility for its own death. While he did suggest to Smith the fortification in town be destroyed, the Alamo blown up, and the cannon, men, and supplies brought back east because the post could be held with volunteers, his request for this course of action clearly stated "if you should think well of it." The governor, however, did not like the plan and ordered Travis to reinforce Béxar's small garrison.

63. Kimball, *Laws and Decrees*, 158, 162, 247; *PTR*, 4: 190–91. In Decree 145 (April 30, 1830), the legislature accepted Grant's offer to build a road between Saltillo and Parras that he would pay for with his own funds. On September 25, 1830, Decree No. 152 bestowed citizenship on Grant. In Decree No. 272 (March 25, 1834), Grant was given

permission to produce cotton and woolen goods in the departments of Monclova, Saltillo, and Parras for a period of ten years. Houston expressed his opinion of Grant to Smith, writing, "Then, who is Dr. Grant? is he not a Scotchman, who has resided in Mexico for the last ten years? does he not own large possessions in the interior? has he ever taken the oath to support the organic law? is he not deeply interested in the hundred-league claims of land which hang like a murky cloud over the people of Texas? is he not the man who impressed the property of the people of Bexar? is he not the man who took from Bexar, without authority, or knowledge of the government, cannon and other munitions of war, together with supplies necessary for the troops at that station, leaving the wounded and the sick destitute of needful comforts? Yet this is the man whose outrages and oppressions upon the rights of the people of Texas are sustained and justified by the acts and conduct of the general council!"

64. Patricia Roche Herring, *General José Cosme Urrea: His Life and Times, 1797–1844* (Spokane: The Arthur H. Clark Company, 1995), 45–65, 90–91. Herring's volume details the life of Urrea, a federalist who would participate in an anti-centralist revolt in 1838. Ironically, a coconspirator in the endeavor was José Antonio Mexía.

65. Todd Hansen, ed., *The Alamo Reader: A Study in History* (Mechanicsburg: Stackpole Books, 2003), 601. Williamson's letter, found in Travis' coat pocket, undermines the need to "draw the line in the sand," one of the main highlights of the traditional story of the battle. Williamson's letter was written before it was learned that Fannin had turned back and abandoned an attempt to march to relieve the Alamo.

66. For a current narrative of the siege and battle of the Alamo, see Winders, *Sacrificed at the Alamo*, 111–129.

67. *PTR*, 4: 443–444. Historians and the public have always been critical of his decision not to carry through with his plan to march to help Travis but given the situation he faced, his action, if not gallant, is reasonable. Explained Fannin to Robinson, "The Council of War consisted of all the commissioned officers of the command and it was by them unanimously determined, that, inasmuch as a proper supply of provisions and means of transportation could not be had; and, as it was impossible, with our present means, to carry the artillery with us, and as by leaving Fort Defiance without a proper garrison, it might fall into the hands of the enemy, with the provisions, etc., now at Matagorda, Dimmit's Landing and Cox's Point and on the way to meet us; and, as by reports of our spies (sent out by Col. Bowers) we may expect an attack upon this place, it was deemed expedient to return to this post and

complete the fortifications, etc., etc. ..." Subsequent events prove that Urrea's column was a serious threat to the Texans.

68. Hobart Huson, *Refugio: A Comprehensive History of Refugio County from Aboriginal Times to 1953*, 2 vols. (Woodsboro: The Rook Foundation, Inc., 1953), 1: 258–314. Huson's chapter entitled "War Comes to Refugio" sheds important information on Urrea's activities in the area.

69. *PTR*, 159, 263–65. The traditional Alamo story is that Travis and his men died without knowing independence had been declared. In truth, it was the outcome they desired, even sending two delegates of the town to vote for independence. Writing on March 3, 1836, Travis claimed he would lay down his sword and leave the Alamo if the convention did not declare independence.

70. William Fairfax Gray, *The Diary of Col. William Fairfax Gray* (Houston: Fletcher Young Publishing Co., 1965), 119–125. The convention received Travis's February 23 letter on February 26; his famous February 24 letter on February 26; his February 25 letter on March 2; and his March 3 letter on March 6. The convention received word of the Alamo's fall from Houston on March 15.

71. "Mexico and Texas," in *The United States Democratic Review* 3, Issue 10 (October; J. & H. G. Langley, October 1838), 137–38; *PTR*, 5: 175–176; Castañeda, *The Mexican Side*, 221–22. While Urrea attempted to elude blame for the execution of Fannin's command, he had previously noted on March 16, 1836, "Prior to leaving Refugio: I authorized the execution, after my departure from camp, of thirty adventurers taken prisoner during the previous engagements [San Patricio & Refugio], and setting free those who were colonists or Mexicans."

72. Gray, *Diary of Col. William Fairfax Gray*, 131, 133–34.

73. Stephen L. Hardin, *Texian Iliad: A Military History of the Texas Revolution* (Austin: University of Texas Press, 1994), 179–93.

74. Stephen L. Moore, *Eighteen Minutes: The Battle of San Jacinto and the Texas Independence Campaign* (Dallas: Republic of Texas Press, 2004), 278–80. One of the most important results of the skirmish for Houston would be Mirabeau B. Lamar's attention-grabbing heroics, which thrust him into the limelight. Lamar would become Houston's harshest critic and serious political rival in the Republic of Texas.

75. Moore, *Eighteen Minutes*, 242–386.

76. Gregg G. Dimmick, *Sea of Mud: The Retreat of the Mexican Army After San Jacinto, An Archeological Investigation* (Austin: Texas State Historical Association, 2004), 193–224.

77. Richard G. Santos, *Santa Anna's Campaign Against Texas, 1835–1836* (Waco, TX: Texian Press, 1968), 92; Juan José Andrade, *After the Battle of the Alamo: Documents Published by General Juan José Andrade on the Evacuation of San Antonio de Béjar, Texas, May, 1836*, edited by Roger Borroel (East Chicago, IN: La Villita Publications, 1997), 10, 11, 12, 13, 15, 17–183; J. H. Barnard, *Dr. J. H. Barnard's Journal* (1912; repr. Aransas Pass, TX: Biography Press, 1983), 29–30.

78. Barnard, *Journal*, 31–32.

79. Andrade. *The Evacuation of San Antonio de Béjar*, 14.

80. Andrade. *The Evacuation of San Antonio de Béjar*, 17–18; Barnard, *Journal*, 33; Gerald S. Pierce, *Texas Under Arms: the Camps, Posts, Forts, & Military Towns of the Republic of Texas, 1836–1846* (Austin: Encino Press, 1969), 125–26; Andrade. *The Evacuation of San Antonio de Béjar*, 17.

81. Pierce, *Texas Under Arms*, 125–26.

82. Pierce, *Texas Under Arms*, 125–26.

83. *PTR*, 7: 75–76.

84. *PTR*, 7: 90–91; R. M. Potter, "Escape of Karnes and Teal from Matamoros," *Quarterly of the Texas State Historical Association* 4, no. 2 (October 1900): 71–84.

85. *PTR*, 7: 186.

86. *PTR*, 7: 187.

87. *PTR*, 7: 187.

88. *PTR*, 7: 244.

89. The Daughters of the Republic of Texas Library, José Francisco Ruiz (at Columbia) to Blas Herrera (at Béxar), December 27, 1836. For an overview of the continuing conflict between Texas and Mexico, see Richard B. Winders, *Crisis in the Southwest: The United States, Mexico, and the Struggle over Texas* (Willington: Scholarly Resources, 2002), 31–69.

Chapter 2
Voices of the Revolution and Republic

Paul N. Spellman

During the transitional period from the pre-revolutionary agitation in the early 1830s through the latter days of the Republic in 1845, disparate voices rose and fell across the increasingly volatile Mexican state of Texas. The earliest agitators decried the restrictive Law of April 6, 1830, while mistakenly, as it turned out, supporting the presumably federalist leadership of Antonio Lopez de Santa Anna. When Santa Anna laid aside the Mexican Constitution of 1824, new voices arose in anger and frustration followed by yet another wave of potential leaders in Texas beginning to ponder a more militant response. The objectives of the several conventions and interim governing bodies swung from one cause to another, leading first to revolution, then to independence, and ultimately to annexation and statehood.

The leading voices most often associated with the Texas Revolution and Republic—Sam Houston, David Burnet, Stephen F. Austin, Mirabeau Lamar, Thomas J. Rusk—either came late to the debate on Texas independence or tended to support the "wait and see" attitude following the dictatorial takeover by Santa Anna in Mexico City in 1834. Of the more recognizable personalities, perhaps only Lorenzo de Zavala, briefly the interim vice-president of the Republic, held a prominent position in the "revolutionist" cause prior to 1836.

Importantly, a "second tier" of voices raised the clarion alarm against Santa Anna's centralist shift, some as agitators, some involved with either Texas separation from Coahuila or the Monclova Federalist movement, and still others as participants in the "400 Leagues" debate over the infamous land speculation laws of 1834 and 1835. Also among the second tier, the far from unanimous voice of the *Bexareños* represented some of the confusion and detachment by Mexicans living in the San Antonio area, and poorly defined "War" and "Peace" parties dotted the Texas political landscape. A significant number of Texas colonists fell into the category of loyalists to the Mexican government—even during the early months of Santa Anna's dictatorship, with what some called "the Tory sentiment."[1] Finally, even as late as the summer of 1835, the largest majority of Texians called for peace and patience, what Stephen F. Austin called repeatedly "a dead calm."[2]

However, by late August 1835, new voices began a more urgent call for independence from Mexico and, when Colonel Austin shifted his stance away from conciliation and towards freedom, the revolution swept across Texas like a prairie fire. A provisional government stumbled along through the opening weeks of the revolt, and a March convention of delegates ratified a declaration of independence and a constitution, establishing an interim government that would carry through to the end of the conflict. After the April 21, 1836, victory at San Jacinto, several factors led to the emergence of yet another group of leaders who became the voices of the fledgling Republic. Despite the fact that many of these leaders had gained prominence during the struggle to win independence from Mexico, they now represented competing visions for the future of Texas. As witnessed during the revolution, a lack of a unified voice among the Texans presented new challenges to the establishment of the Republic. One of the most controversial and divisive issues confronting the newly established government was the issue of annexation to the United States. The list of the founders of the revolution and a Republic turns out to be larger, and more fluid, than history has since taught. The purpose of this chapter is to identify the earliest voices aligned to Mexico's centralist regime under Santa Anna followed by an examination of the transitions in leadership between 1834 and 1837.

The roundly decried Law of April 6, 1830, brought a growing sense of frustration among Anglo Texans who had heretofore enjoyed nearly a decade of economic freedoms and, for many, the very prosperity that had been their siren call to Texas. Despite the entreaties of first *Empresario* Stephen Fuller Austin to government officials in San Antonio and Saltillo, the constricting new law, which included a threat to the future of slavery in Texas as well as an end to duty-free trade and the closing of the borders to American immigration, held its ground into the spring of 1832. Growing sentiment by those Texans involved in trade to the United States turned momentarily violent that June with the first of the so-called "Anahuac Disturbances."

One of the first "agitators," as Mexican authorities would call them, during this prelude to the revolution was John Austin, born in Connecticut in 1801, a distant kin to the *empresario*. John Austin, who briefly had been imprisoned in Mexico following Long's 1819 filibustering expedition, and his brother James E. B. Austin allied with

Stephen F. Austin in the early organization of the colony. Despite his opposition to the April 6 restrictions, John became the port officer and *alcalde* of the Brazoria Municipality in 1831 and 1832. When the confrontation with the customs officials in Anahuac became imminent, John Austin led a small group of Texans to the Brazos River to procure a cannon, an action that precipitated the battle of Velasco on June 26, 1832, the first armed conflict between Texans and Mexican officials that would foreshadow the coming insurrection. An almost certain, potentially larger uprising was then abruptly postponed by a savage outbreak of cholera across Coahuila y Texas, and John Austin's voice silenced prematurely when he, along with his two daughters, succumbed to the disease in August 1833.[3]

Also involved at Anahuac in 1832 was South Carolinian William Barret Travis, who came to Texas in 1831 from Alabama under suspicious personal circumstances, received a then-illegal land grant (because of the April 6 law), and opened a law practice in Anahuac. His open conflict with the customs duties officials at the port earned him a reputation as a defiant voice of the still-unorganized "War Party" politicos, and his subsequent arrest in 1832 led to the first disturbances there and, for at least a short period, the abandoning of the customs office by the Mexican government. Travis moved his law practice to San Felipe, but three years later almost to the day, a second "disturbance" at the recently reestablished customs offices on the Texas coast witnessed his leading a company of twenty-five men and capturing the Mexican officials and garrison at Anahuac. This aggressive action earned mostly heated criticism of Travis as an agitator and caused the ostentatious young lawyer to defend his actions well into the first months of the revolution. With that said, William Barret Travis's historic legacy to the Revolution is his famous defense of and death at the Alamo on March 6, 1836.

The Menefee brothers agitated as early as the spring of 1832 against the April 6 law and the situation involving the customs duty officials along the coast. Thomas Menefee, born in Virginia and raised for a time in Tennessee and later Alabama, came to Texas with his brother William and their families to settle in Jackson County, part of Austin's colony. Thomas's son John Menefee wrote years later: "From the time, 1832, till the latter part of 1832, we lived in peace and quiet, no taxes or duties to pay, no law but a law unto ourselves, all friendly, sociable, sober, honest and moral; good crops and prosperous times." After the trouble at Velasco and Anahuac, it all changed. "These were hardy days, the like of which we never expect to see again."[4]

William Menefee organized what later became known as "the Menefee meeting" in June 1832, that led to rising anger among the colonists and carried over to the Conventions of 1832 and 1833. John wrote in his 1880 memoirs, "The object [of our meeting] was to determine whether or not we would permit the [Mexican] soldiers from the west side of the Lavaca to pass, in case they attempted to go to the relief of the fort at Velasco. We met again with our arms a mile or two above the road," but let the soldiers pass.[5] William Menefee represented the Jackson County citizens at the conventions—the November 1835 Consultation and the ensuing General Council—and was a signer of the Declaration of Independence at that time representing Colorado County as judge.

Other early agitators in Texas included the three Jack brothers—William, Patrick, and Spencer—and James Bowie. The Jacks of Georgia arrived together with their families at San Felipe in 1830. Roundly critical of the 1830 law, Patrick was arrested in 1832 at the same time as Travis, while his brother Spencer became entangled in a shooting incident on a Brazos River blockade runner one year earlier. All three were engaged in the early stages of the revolution, but Spencer died unexpectedly at age twenty-eight while his two brothers died of yellow fever only sixteen days apart in 1844. Bowie, born in Kentucky and brother of Rezin whose long-bladed knife became famous on the American frontier but is more associated with James, may have been in Texas as early as 1819, accompanying the filibustering expedition of Dr. James Long. More certain, however, the historical record places James in Nacogdoches in 1830, before he traveled across Coahuila y Texas, settled in San Antonio and wed Governor Veramendi's daughter Ursula in 1831. In 1833 while away on a business venture, Bowie learned of the deaths of his wife and two daughters to the cholera epidemic. The disconsolate and ill widower chased Indians and his nightmares across Texas. Following the Monclova land speculation fiasco, Bowie wandered back in 1835 to San Antonio, where he died with Travis and the other defenders of the Alamo.

Irishman John Joseph Linn arrived in Texas in 1829 as a colonist in Martin De Leon's town of Victoria. The multilingual "Juan Linn" as he was known operated a successful mercantile business out of Victoria and on Lavaca Bay, established the town of Linnville in 1831, and was one of the first to oppose openly President Santa Anna. He and Placido Benavides served on Victoria's Committee of Safety in 1835. Linn was present at Gonzales in October 1835, served as quartermaster of the nascent Texian forces, represented Victoria at the Consultation, and was elected to the March Convention but did not arrive in time to sign the Declaration of Independence, opting instead to assist James Fannin at Goliad and reinforcing defenses around Victoria. Linn also missed the battle at San Jacinto aiding the *ad interim* government's escape to Galveston Island, but assisted Sam Houston in the subsequent interviews with the prisoner Santa Anna. Suspicions that Linn was a Mexican spy prevented his further involvement in the Republic's upper echelon of leadership, serving instead as the last *alcalde* and first mayor of Victoria. Later, Linn was elected to the Republic Congress as a pro-Houston supporter. These "second tier" voices made substantive contributions to the early stages of discontent and pre-revolution, but most of them took a back seat to the leaders who emerged in 1836.

On March 26, 1834, Coahuila y Texas Governor Augustin Viesca signed into law a resolution to sell vast amounts of land across the Mexican state purportedly to raise funds for a militia to defend the settlers against marauding Indians along the frontier. The largely federalist leadership in Monclova, the capital of Coahuila y Texas, may have been thinking more about funding its own resistance to the now-Centralist shift of Santa Anna in Mexico City. Less than a month later, on April 19, Viesca accepted the petitions of four Texians intent on purchasing the leagues of land, then subdividing and selling them as speculators. Some four hundred leagues of land were available for purchase from the government; an astounding amount of land (over 1.7 million acres) was now obtainable in the very kind of land grab that Stephen F. Austin and other colonial leaders had warned against for more than a decade. Ironically, one of the speculators was none other than Samuel May Williams, Austin's friend and colony secretary since 1822. In addition to Williams, Robert Peebles, Francis W. Johnson, and John Durst were involved in this hotly debated controversy.[6]

On March 14, 1835, a sizable portion of those original 400 leagues was granted to the petitioners, but by then the situation in Monclova had become dangerous to the federalists, and when Dr. James Grant attempted to procure an additional three hundred leagues under the 1835 law, the Centralist forces annulled the petitions and sent a Mexican army marching towards Monclova as Viesca and others fled for their lives. The debate surrounding the land speculation events of 1834 and 1835 did not precipitate the Texas Revolution, but the controversy accentuated the deterioration of the Coahuila y Texas government's authority and became a major distraction for the settlers well into the summer of 1835.[7]

Samuel May Williams had fled to Texas more than a decade earlier from a perilous financial situation in Louisiana, arriving at San Felipe under the name E. Eccleston and earning the trust of Austin, who assigned him the task of recording the first colonial land grants. His involvement in the Monclova intrigue—the "400 Leagues" as many in Texas called it—met with a disheartening sense of betrayal and not a little anger by Austin. While under arrest in Mexico City, Austin wrote on several occasions about his disappointment in Williams's involvement in the scheme. In 1833, Williams collaborated with Thomas McKinney in a successful commercial venture out of Galveston. Their partnership allowed them to assist in raising money and supplies for the revolution. During the Republic years, Williams invested in the banking business, actively supported the Houston administrations, served briefly in the Texas congress, and contributed to the early growth of Galveston.

Robert Peebles, a licensed physician in partnership with Dr. James B. Miller, after the failure of the land grab in 1835, helped with the revolutionary government's record-keeping into early 1836, and fled with the records for safekeeping into Louisiana during the April "Runaway Scrape." He served in several capacities during the Republic years. Francis W. Johnson, popularly condemned as a land speculator, attempted to redeem himself during the Revolution, but became disgusted with the leadership—particularly Governor Henry Smith who reciprocated in kind—and left Texas. He returned briefly but left again for good in 1839.

John Marie Durst, whose brother Jacob was also a longtime Texas resident, had come to Nacogdoches as a child with his family in 1806, and so was one of the oldest residents involved in these events. Durst, like Peebles, actually took up temporary residence in Monclova in preparation for petitioning the government for the leagues and served in the state government, but fled with the others back to Texas before the coming army in April 1835. During the revolution, he joined a company of Texians stationed along the Angelina River, but saw no action and eventually retired from the public eye in the Nacogdoches area.

In the correspondence and records of the events leading up to the Revolution, these were the more prominent names on the minds of the vast majority of settlers. Another contingent found in Monclova in early 1835 was a group of men who had designs not only on the land that the government was offering, but also in the authority that might come to them as *empresarios* of large settlements on those lands.

Impressed with the successes of the colonies settled during the 1820s by Stephen F. Austin (San Felipe), Green DeWitt (Gonzales), and Martin De Leon (Victoria), a remarkable delegation of suitors for such a role arrived in Monclova over the winter of 1834–1835 with the intention of obtaining still-available tracts of land mostly across the northern and northwestern part of the state, and bringing settlers into those areas under their supervision and authority. For their part they intended to agree to the terms of the sales of the leagues by establishing and paying for a regional militia to protect the settlers from Comanche and Tawakoni Indian raids. In response, Governor Viesca appointed "commissioners" from the delegation to supervise the sale of the tracts, the recruitment of the several militias, and so on. Among these appointments were George A. Nixon, George W. Smyth, and Charles S. Taylor for "Eastern Texas," Talbot Chambers for the colony of Benjamin F. Milam, Dr. Peebles for Austin's colony, and Francis Johnson for the region around Gonzales. James Bowie was also present at that time and appointed to supervise the purchase belonging to speculator General John T. Mason from the United States. Mason had unsuccessfully applied a year earlier for nearly twenty *million* acres of Texas frontier, a controversial prelude to the Monclova intrigue that followed.[8]

Others gathered at the state seat of government in early 1835 were: Thomas J. Chambers, W. H. Steele, James Carter, James Grant, Ben Milam, John Cameron, David J. Toler, and a resilient Haden Edwards attempting a return eight years after the Fredonian debacle. These collectively would be referred to over the next several months as "the foreigners" by Santa Anna and General Martin Perfecto de Cos, whose army now directed its attention to ridding Coahuila y Texas of these intruding speculators and agitators. At the same time, in May of 1835, the now-dictator General Santa Anna personally led another army to Zacatecas, a seat of increasing unrest and defiance, and on May 10 and 11 savagely destroyed the Zacatecan defenses and ruthlessly pillaged the city. In Monclova, the "foreigners" fled in company with Viesca and most of the legislature before Cos's assault: However, Spanish troops captured Viesca outside the city, sending him to prison.[9]

Again, these events may not have directly led to the coming revolution except by stirring the settlers to either defy Santa Anna's centralist turn and the military movements, or for the vast majority, sending families fleeing to Louisiana or at least closing their doors to the agitation. But the turmoil in Coahuila y Texas was seen from Santa Anna and Cos's perspective, largely incorrectly, as a gathering storm not unlike Zacatecas and with a similar consequence planned for the near future. Cos's assembling of forces for a march to San Antonio, instead of dispelling the agitators and quelling the resistance, would engender the very opposite reaction across Texas.

"Calm, a dead calm, is all that Texas needs," wrote Stephen F. Austin on February 6, 1835, from his position under house arrest in Mexico following the well-known account of his arrest for treason on January 3, 1834. One month later, he wrote again that Texas "must have calm, no party divisions, no excitements," and on April 1 and again on April 15 he wrote his erstwhile compatriot Samuel May Williams, "we must keep clear of civil wars."[10]

In the midst of the growing chaos and confusion across Texas, the power of Austin's pen would be the one—and often only—source of restraint and patience. If that attitude were to be altered, which of course would occur five months later, Texas agitation would most likely dissolve into a "revolutionary movement."

The phrase "revolutionary movement" emanated from one of the true revolutionaries to emerge during the turmoil of 1835, Lorenzo de Zavala, who spoke about the merits of revolution on May 8, 1835, prior to his controversial and inflammatory arrival in Texas in July alongside another Mexican revolutionary, General José Antonio Mexia.[11] Contemporaries recognized Zavala from the beginning as a radical opponent of Santa Anna and his supporters' shift toward a stronger centralized government. Born in Yucatan and deeply involved in Mexico's politics for decades, Zavala supported democratic ideals for his native country, founded and wrote fervently in several newspapers, suffered imprisonment on more than one occasion, but never wavered from his federalist views. He served in various congresses representing Yucatan, held the position of secretary of the treasury under the federalist presidency of Vicente Guerrero, and was summarily ousted, and exiled, when the centralist Bustamante administration took over late in 1829.

For the next two years, Zavala sharpened his democratic ideology in New York City and in England. He returned to Mexico to serve in Santa Anna's initially federalist government, but resigned his post when Santa Anna assumed dictatorial status in 1834. Following his resignation, Zavala traveled back to New York where he continued to agitate against Santa Anna's government. Thus, his arrival in Texas in the summer of 1835 caused an alarm across Mexico, some seeking his arrest while others feared that his presence would further inflame the already chaotic atmosphere. Warrants for his arrest appeared in late July, but Zavala eluded the authorities, took up with the nascent Texas revolutionaries, served on the Permanent Council, and then represented Harrisburg at the Convention of 1836. He and his family hid on Galveston Island from Santa Anna's approaching army until after San Jacinto, at which time,

Texas authorities appointed him as the peace commissioner to Mexico City under the terms of the Treaty of Velasco, a mission that never took place because of Zavala's sudden death.[12]

José Antonio Mexia arrived in Texas with Zavala and with a bounty on his head as well. Having spent a number of years living in the United States, Mexia embraced the democratic ideals as did Zavala, but served in Mexico's army during the Guerrero administration. He returned to the United States as secretary of the Mexican legation and then as a lobbyist for the Galveston Bay and Texas Land Company; Mexia backed Santa Anna initially but joined the federalists in protest in 1834. Exiled to New Orleans by Santa Anna, Mexia attempted but failed to enlist supporters to fight for the Texian cause. Ultimately, the Mexican army captured Mexia during an abortive military campaign to oust the revived Centralists in 1839. Shortly after his capture, Santa Anna ordered the troublesome rebel executed.

Taking the brunt of the assaults on Texas during the revolution—and again in 1842—the city of San Antonio withstood those attacks and managed to continue be the rather singular voice of the *Tejanos* from the period of colonialism to American statehood. Deeply involved in the affairs of Coahuila y Texas during the days of discontent with the Centralist regime in Mexico City, the voices of distinction from Bexar included: José Antonio Navarro, his brother José Angel Navarro, and their uncle José Francisco Ruiz; the elder Don Erasmo Seguin, his son Juan Nepomuceno Seguin and his son-in-law Manuel Flores; José Maria Jesus Carbajal; and José Antonio Menchaca. In addition, Ramon Musquiz served as Political Chief of the Texas District from 1828 until 1834, was committed to federalism during his political tenure, generally supported Anglo-American colonization, and mediated attempts to assuage the growing sentiments in favor of independence on the one side and military suppression on the other.

Like Musquiz, Placido Benavides stood against Santa Anna's dictatorship without advocating Texas independence. He grew up in De Leon's colony in Victoria. In September 1835, Benavides gained notoriety by warning Texans of Cos's approaching army, earning him the sobriquet as "the Paul Revere of Texas." Later the young Tejano fought at Goliad and at the siege of Bexar, but fled in 1836 to Louisiana, where he died the following year.

José Antonio Navarro led a long and glorious life in service to his birthplace of San Antonio, to Texas independence, and to early Texas statehood. Navarro marched with Gutierrez in 1813, befriended Stephen F. Austin early on, supported the revolutionists and signed the Texas

Declaration of Independence alongside his uncle. During the Republic years, Navarro supported President Mirabeau Lamar and marched with the ill-fated Texan Santa Fe Expedition as special commissioner right into Mexican imprisonment for nearly two years, but survived the ordeal and escaped to Texas. Navarro was the only Hispanic to attend the 1845 statehood convention, and continued in Texas politics as an ardent anti-Houston voice even as late as the 1860s.

Navarro's older brother Angel, also an in-law by marriage to James Bowie and the Veramendis, served as Political Chief of Bexar in the 1830s, resisted the call to arms during the Monclova intrigue despite his pro-federalist views, and as late as August of 1835 remaincd insistent that the people of San Antonio supported Santa Anna's new government against revolution. Because of that stance, revolutionaries condemned Navarro during the last year of his life. The Navarros' uncle, José Francisco Ruiz, lived his entire life in San Antonio and participated in the Gutierrez-Magee Expedition in 1813 but did not participate in the Texas Revolution after signing the Texas Declaration of Independence on March 2, 1836. He represented the Bexar District in the Republic Congress for its first year, and successfully negotiated treaties with Texas Indians until his death.

The Seguin family experienced a wide spectrum of responses to their legacy in Texas. The elder Juan José Maria Erasmo Seguin, a native *Bexareno*, served as postmaster of his native town on several different occasions, as well as *alcalde* and other posts. Although as a friend and associate of Stephen F. Austin he supported Anglo colonialism in Texas and an increased independence for Texas from Coahuila and although General Cos forced him into exile on the family's ranch near Floresville during the Revolution, in his later years Seguin came under attack from Anglo Texans who accused him of being a collaborator against Texas independence. Under such suspicions, Sequin again retired to his ranch, where he lived out his last years.

Seguin's son, Juan Nepomuceno, on the other hand, was deeply involved in the Texas Revolution, served in various positions in the Republic government and as mayor of San Antonio, and outlived all of his contemporaries. Juan Seguin was *alcalde* of his hometown in 1833 and Political Chief in 1834. In the spring of 1835, he led a small detachment of soldiers to Monclova, where he and his men narrowly escaped the clutches of Cos's approaching army. Seguin commanded a small scouting company of Tejanos during the Revolution that was the only Hispanic unit to fight at San Jacinto. He accepted the Mexican surrender of San Antonio two months later, and served in the Republic's Senate for four years. In 1840 Seguin participated in the failed attempt to reassert federalism in Mexico City, was castigated in Texas for land speculation investments, lived in Mexico until Texas became a state of the United States, and returned to San Antonio, where he lived for many years until his retirement in Nuevo Laredo and death in 1890. The Texas city of Seguin was named in his honor.

Juan Seguin's brother-in-law Manuel Flores, not to be confused with the agitator and spy of the same name, was a lifelong *Bexareño* who fought with Seguin at San Jacinto, aided in the defense of San Antonio during the Vazquez Raid in 1842, and retired to Atascosa County after 1842.

José Maria Jesus Carbajal, brother-in-law of Placido Benavides and a *Bexareño*, lived for a time in the United States where he was educated, returned to Texas as surveyor for Martin De Leon's colony where he laid out the town of Victoria, and was serving in the Coahuila y Texas legislature in 1835. Texas Commandant Domingo Ugartechea ordered Carbajal's arrest on August 8, 1835, one month after James Kerr named him as an agitator and land speculator, along with Samuel May Williams, Francis Johnson, and Jim Bowie. Carbajal eluded the warrant, fled briefly to Louisiana where he acquired a sailing vessel and aided the revolution by shipping supplies to Texas until his ship was captured and Carbajal imprisoned. Escaping from a Matamoros jail, Carbajal kept a low profile for the next four years. Scholars have well documented his activities over the next four decades, including involvement in expeditions and the Mexican War, until his death in Hidalgo County, Texas, at age sixty-five.

José Antonio Menchaca, like Carbajal and Juan Seguin, was a native of San Antonio. Not to be confused with a Mexican loyalist of the same name, Menchaca became actively involved in the revolution as a soldier in Seguin's company at San Jacinto. During the Republic years, he served as mayor of San Antonio and commanded a frontier defense force that failed to defend the city against Woll's invasion in 1842. For the remainder of his long life he remained active in Texas and San Antonio politics, and was a Mason of the Holland Lodge, first lodge of Texas. The Travis County town of Manchaca [*sic*] was named after him.

The *Bexareños* represented the largest community of Hispanics in Texas between 1835 and 1845. In many ways, they made significant contributions to the Texas Revolution and the founding of the Lone Star Republic—they were the some of the most significant voices of Mexican Texas.

The term "revolutionist" became the identification of those Texans calling for more than simply a Texas independent of Coahuila, but the term itself was not commonly used until the middle of 1835. As early as the Conventions of 1832 and 1833 such voices were referred to as the "war party," and included brothers William and John Wharton, R. M. Williamson, Branch T. Archer, and Philip Sublett, along with the previously identified Patrick Jack, Jim Bowie, and William Barret Travis; another still-subdued voice among this faction in 1833 was Nacogdoches resident Sam Houston of Tennessee. During Stephen F. Austin's incarceration in Mexico in 1834 and 1835, the "war faction" continued to agitate for independence. However, the majority of Texans were awaiting Austin's return before taking action against the Mexican government.[13]

William Harris Wharton and John Austin Wharton were raised in Nashville by an uncle following the deaths of their parents, and both came to Texas as well-educated lawyers between 1829 and 1833. Of the two, William was the more gregarious and an accomplished orator, and thus the center of attention in 1833 during the rising agitation that pitted his voice (the war party) against the moderate Stephen F. Austin (the peace party). At the 1833 convention, delegates selected Wharton over Austin to preside over the proceedings. Both Whartons favored the separation of Texas from Coahuila and supported the Mexican Constitution of 1824, which Santa Anna soon abrogated, making himself a virtual dictator. The Whartons set aside their differences with Austin as the revolution unfolded in late 1835. William Wharton, Stephen F. Austin, and Branch T. Archer served as special commissioners to the United States, seeking financial and military support for the Texas rebels. In the early days of the Republic, William Wharton served briefly as secretary of state charged with sealing recognition by the United States. Unable to secure such a promise, Wharton retired from public service, was briefly captured and imprisoned in Mexico, and died tragically from the discharge of his own rifle.

John Wharton served in the Texian army during the revolution, received awards of valor for his participation at San Jacinto, served as secretary of war for President Houston, and then retired to Brazoria to a law practice with Elisha Pease and John Woods Harris. Wharton died after a brief illness only a few months before his brother. Later, Texans named the town and county of Wharton in honor of the brothers.

Robert McAlpin "Three Legged Willie" Williamson, a native of Georgia, suffered from an illness when he was fifteen years old that caused his right leg to draw back at the knee. In order to walk, Williamson wore a wooden leg fitted from his knee to the ground, earning the moniker "Three Legged Willie." Williamson, who arrived in Texas perhaps as early as 1829, entered a partnership with Godwin Cotton to publish the newspaper the *Cotton Plant*. He also was involved with the publication of two other Texas papers. Williamson represented Mina at the 1835 Consultation and fought at San Jacinto. He was associated with the "war party" from the earliest debates, and was so supportive of Texas becoming part of the United States that he named his son Annexus. Williamson appears on an arrest warrant in August 1835, along with Zavala, Johnson, and the others. During and after the Republic years, Williamson served Texas as congressional representative, and later as a judge until his death in 1859. Texas legislators named Williamson County in his memory.

Branch Tanner Archer arrived in Texas in 1831 following a successful political career in Virginia, with a diploma from William & Mary College and a medical degree in hand. He supported the war faction at the Convention of 1833, and as a result, Mexican authorities named him as an "agitator" along with the Whartons and the Jacks in a circular issued on June 24, 1835.[14] Even though he favored independence, Archer continued to support the Mexican Constitution of 1824 until the tide had turned to revolution. He joined William Wharton and Stephen F. Austin as special commissioners to the United States, returned at the end of the revolution to support Austin in the Republic's first presidential election, and then served in the Lamar administration as secretary of war. Archer remained active in Texas politics out of his home near Brazoria until his death. Later, Texans named Archer County after him.

Kentucky native Philip Allen Sublett was living in Durango, Mexico, in 1824. Sometime either at the end of the decade or in the early 1830s he moved to San Augustine on Ayish Bayou in the Nacogdoches District of Texas, where the citizens elected him to represent them at the 1832 and 1833 conventions as part of the "war party." Sublett served in the revolutionary army at Concepcion and the siege of Bexar, and remained active in San Augustine and Sabine Pass during the Republic years.

Wylie Martin and Moseley Baker were among that "second tier" of voices generally associated with their fierce defiance of General Houston's orders to retreat from Gonzales in March of 1836, the infamous "Runaway Scrape." Both served valiantly in holding off Santa Anna's approaching army. Prior to the revolution, both men were advocates for a separate Texas state. After authorities listed them as agitators in the spring of 1835, they became staunch voices for war against Santa Anna's dictatorial regime.

Martin served briefly as Political Chief of the Brazos District in 1835. At about the same time, Ugartechea issued a warrant for Baker's arrest in July 1835.[15] Baker fought in most of the major conflicts of the Revolution, but scholars generally remember him for his role in defending the Brazos River crossing with a small contingent of sharpshooters against a larger Mexican force, thus allowing Houston more time to gather and train the Texian army at Groce's Retreat.

The term "revolution" as the independent clarion to separate altogether from Mexico did not fully appear until the spring of 1835, as the agitation and frustration across Texas continued to be aimed until that time at the April 6 law, the Monclova land deal, and the customs officers along the Gulf Coast. For example, as late as April 3, 1835, Colonel Ugartechea wrote General Cos that "there is anarchy in Coahuila," but his reference was to the federalist resistance by Viesca and the Monclova legislature. Eight days later, William Barret Travis proposed "kindling a flame in Texas," but still the objective seemed to be a Texas independent of Coahuila not from Mexico. Moreover, on April 15 Francis W. Johnson wrote from Monclova of "wars and rumours of war" as the Mexican army approached.[16]

On May 8, 1835, in a letter addressed from New York City to friends and colonists in Texas, Lorenzo de Zavala declared perhaps melodramatically, "there's a Revolutionary Movement in Texas." For perhaps the first time in a popular circular, the term had now been unveiled for what it would soon become, a call for an independent Texas free from Mexican authority and Santa Anna's dictatorship.[17] General Cos, who understood the implications of an Anglo Texas agitated to the point of separation, sent stern warnings across the Rio Grande on May 12 and 28, and again on June 1 and July 5, prophesying "a certain revolution" would result if Mexican authorities allowed the Monclova federalists to reach San Felipe and join with the war faction there. On July 7, Cos wrote, "The object of these perverse men is to cause a revolution." Conversely, at about the same time, Ben Milam wrote to Francis Johnson that "revolution was the sure result" of the agitation. Moreover, Austin, who was still being detained by Mexican authorities, expressed his belief that "some [here in Mexico] wish [Santa Anna's] army to Texas so they can revolt here."[18]

The response in Texas to this new and dramatic turn toward total independence was mixed with a significant number of Texans preferring to avoid open rebellion against Santa Anna, while others began to warm to the "kindled flame" of freedom. On July 13, Ugartechea wrote Cos that "those malcontents in San Felipe" should be dealt with promptly. However, the following day a self-styled "Commission for Peace" in San Felipe organized itself to press for moderation and patience. Numbered among this peace faction were Sterling McNeel and his three brothers, James Knight, James Perry, Josiah Bell, Alexander Somervell, and John A. Wharton—all of them calling for compromise, not war.[19]

Voices responding to the "revolutionist cause" now rose. Ugartechea sent a plea for peace across Texas on July 15, and still considered Zavala to be the real culprit behind this perilous new turn. James H. C. Miller called for moderation ten days later and claimed that agitator Wylie Martin had come to his senses. Peter Ellis Bean promised that the Mexican army would "quell any move by the revolutionists," and Thomas M. Thompson, commissioned in the Mexican Navy and altogether disliked by most Texians, warned the agitators to calm down and "let there be no Revolution."[20]

By mid-summer of 1835, the agitation for resistance to the approaching Mexican army had reached enough of a crescendo to cause several individuals and communities to call for conciliation. A group of "moderates" in Columbia had already signed off on a petition for peace on June 28, and J. B. Miller, Thomas Chambers, and John A. Williams had echoed similar sentiments in letters to General Cos. James H. C. Miller joined the moderates in a July 25 letter, and Colonel Ugartechea himself pled for peace in a circular to the Texians on July 15.[21] A trio of agents even offered and then tried, unsuccessfully, to mediate the conflict.

One of those hoping for a peaceful solution was Whitfield Hamlet Sledge, who arrived in Texas from Troup County, Georgia, in 1834. Shortly after his arrival, he attempted to organize a meeting with both sides in an effort to negotiate a plan of reconciliation. On July 19, 1835, Sledge wrote that he was suspicious of the inflammatory speeches of Lorenzo de Zavala, and feared that his intentions for Texas would only lead to increased violence. A second voice of compromise came from Edward Gritten, a British subject and secretary to Col. Juan Almonte during his visit to Texas, who now offered to work as an agent for peace in Mexico City. Rumored to be a close acquaintance of Santa Anna, Gritten made an exhaustive effort to prevent bloodshed by writing both General Cos and the citizens in Texas early in July that a peaceful resolution was still possible. On July 7, Gritten spoke passionately to the citizens of Gonzales, assuring them that Mexican troops would not come into Texas, briefly assuaging the growing panic. Now seen as an agent of the Mexican government, his proposals for mediation on August 8 went largely unheard. Vermont native Don Carlos Barrett, who was raised in New York and arrived in Texas by April 1835, seconded the offers by

Sledge and Gritten, but by November the three were objects of derision and accused of being spies for Mexico by Gov. Henry Smith. Their fading voices signaled the final attempt to prevent wholesale violence and war.[22]

Mary Austin Holley wrote of September 1835:

> By this time Gen. Stephen F. Austin, who had been so long confined to the dungeons of Mexico, re-appeared in Texas, when he immediately became the rallying point of the colonists. Prudent as he always had been, he was never a cringing slave, and now that he saw the dearest rights of his fellow-citizens jeopardized by the despotism of Santa Anna, he who had once been his friend like the noble Zavala, became his foe, conscious that the triumph of the despot would be the fall of his own country.[23]

On September 1, Austin arrived aboard the schooner *San Felipe* at the mouth of the Brazos River, where his nephew William Joel Bryan warmly greeted him and friend Thomas McKinney, who landed nearby on the ship *Laura.* Austin biographer Gregg Cantrell describes what may have been the empresario's mood: "Later that evening Austin excused himself and walked the beach until late in the night [where] he had ample time to ponder the course he would pursue in the coming days and weeks." Cantrell continues, "That course was still not clear in all its details, it depended on what he found in the interior and what moves the Mexicans made next. But in his own mind he had already reached the most critical conclusion: Texas must be free of Mexico."[24]

One week later, Austin attended a joyous reception in his honor at Brazoria, where he made an impassioned speech clarifying the options for Texans at that moment: active support for the 1824 Constitution and defiance against Santa Anna's dictatorship; peace and conciliation with Mexican authorities; or, a general forum to debate the possibility of a declaration of independence for Texas. "The constitutional rights and the security and peace of Texas," he concluded, "they ought to be maintained; and jeopardized as they now are, they demand a general consultation of the people."[25]

Nevertheless, on September 19, Austin's personal stance on the more perilous alternatives for Texas crystallized. In a letter penned to the Committee on Safety in Columbia, he wrote this famous utterance, the penultimate turning point for Texas: "Conciliatory measures with Gen. Cos and the military at Bexar are hopeless. *War is our only recourse.*"[26]

It is not an exaggeration to note that Austin's clarion call in mid-September finally changed the course of the debate in the minds of a vast majority of Texas settlers, as well as the several voices of calm and compromise still holding desperately to a hope for peaceful resolution. The estimable Austin had in one stroke of his pen turned Texas towards the fight for independence.

Thirteen days after Austin's statement, a single cannon shot near the small community of Gonzales signaled the beginning of the Texas Revolution.

There is little hyperbole in any statement assessing Texas's revolutionary governance as confused, polarized, and of little value to furthering the cause of independence. The General Consultation called for October 15 did not actually convene until November 1, and during those three weeks Stephen F. Austin attempted unsuccessfully to establish a "Permanent Council" representing the districts across Texas. Fewer than a dozen delegates arrived at San Felipe, although they managed to elect Richard Royall as Council president and Charles B. Stewart secretary. With no consensus or broad support and as other delegates began to head for the Consultation, the Council disappeared without a trace. Richard Royster Royall, born in Virginia and a longtime associate of Austin who settled his family in Matagorda after moving from Alabama, managed to accomplish very little during the sixteen days of his tenure. He served briefly with the Provisional Government but roundly decried Governor Henry Smith, returned to Matagorda, and served briefly as captain of a Ranger company charged with rounding up stray cattle.

Charles Bellinger Stewart was active during the period of agitation in 1832, fought at the Battle of Velasco, kept brief records for the Council, and served in a similar position in the Provisional Government, and took on the largely implausible role as "secretary of state." Though he signed the Texas Declaration of Independence on March 2, 1836, Stewart bowed out of the public eye after the Revolution except for stints in the Republic Congress and later the Texas legislature. After the revolution, Stewart lived out the remainder of his life in Montgomery County.

The sordid story of the Provisional Government is one of heated debate, personal antagonism and, finally, failure. For three months, Henry Smith served as governor and James W. Robinson as lieutenant governor. Also part of this less than august congress were revolutionists Francis W. Johnson, Richard Ellis, Samuel Carson, Robert Potter, and others, several of whom also served as delegates at the March Convention. When the administration could not organize itself properly, it lost the confidence of the people and disintegrated by the end of January 1836, as Governor Smith skulked home. The more accomplished leaders in Texas at that time were nowhere to be found: Austin, Wharton, and Archer were in the United States, Lamar and McLeod hadn't arrived yet in Texas, and Sam Houston, a general in command of a nonexistent army, spent several weeks with his Cherokee brethren in East Texas before heading for San Felipe and then towards San Antonio to meet Santa Anna's army.

Henry Smith managed to antagonize nearly everyone in his administration and at the Consultation, despite outpolling Austin 30-22 for the governorship. In September following the end of the Revolution, he was defeated by Houston in his attempt to win the Republic presidency. He served briefly in the Republic congress, but in 1849, he headed for the California gold fields, where he died two years later. Convention president Richard Ellis served briefly in the Republic congress, but retired from public service in 1840. Delegate Samuel Price Carson distinguished himself at the Convention with his broad educational background and common sense approach to the tasks, but lost the election for ad interim president to David Burnet. At the behest of Burnet, Carson headed to Washington, D. C., as a special envoy, but when Texas leaders sent other commissioners to the United States, the confusion exasperated Carson who resigned and, in ill health, died shortly after.

George C. Childress came to Texas very late in the proceedings, accompanying his uncle Sterling Robertson in the establishment of Robertson's Colony, and taking up permanent residence in Texas in late 1835. He and his uncle attended the Convention, and it was Childress who first presided over the meeting, established a committee to write a declaration of independence, and penned most of the document himself. Childress was another of the confusing array of commissioners to the United States in 1836, and upon his return to Texas he tried unsuccessfully to practice law in Houston and then Galveston. Tragically, he committed suicide on October 6, 1841.

Leaving North Carolina under suspicious circumstances, Robert Potter arrived in Nacogdoches on July 1, 1835. He was a delegate from that district at the Convention, signed the Texas Declaration of Independence and helped write a Constitution for the new Republic. His previous experience in the U. S. Navy earned him the appointment as secretary of the Texas Navy. He fought at San Jacinto before retiring to his home on Caddo Lake, where he became embroiled in the Regulator-Moderator War in 1842 and was killed in a shootout.

These and other "voices" of the Revolutionary Government(s) made several important contributions during the short time that there was any governance between Gonzales and San Jacinto, but few of them distinguished themselves and a remarkable number of them died before the Republic era ended.

Two weeks after the Declaration of Independence was signed on March 2, 1836, the *ad interim* government of the Revolution began its work, a complex and confusing process that would last in some form or another until October 22 when the new Republic was formed. During the course of this administration's business, Santa Anna's approaching army resulted in the ignominious but necessary retreat later known as "the Runaway Scrape." Included among the settlers and Houston's still-forming army was the government itself, on the run from San Felipe to Harrisburg and then a desperate race ahead of the enemy to sanctuary on Galveston Island. The four months following San Jacinto were filled with the business of ending the war through the Treaties of Velasco, and the transition from a selected slate of officials to those democratically elected in "national" elections for offices created under the newly created constitution of the Republic of Texas.

As the March 2 Convention prepared to adjourn, its delegates elected the slate of officers who would serve Texas for the next seven months in the *ad interim* government of Texas. David Burnet was elected president, Lorenzo de Zavala was named vice-president, Samuel P. Carson was selected secretary of state, Bailey Hardeman was chosen secretary of the treasury, David Thomas became attorney general, Thomas J. Rusk was appointed secretary of war, and Robert Potter became secretary of the navy.

David Burnet arrived in Texas briefly in 1827 to establish a colony under the laws issuing *empresario* grants, but the venture failed. After his efforts to secure a land grant, Burnet left Texas only to return in 1831 to operate a marginally prosperous mill on the San Jacinto River for the next four years. Initially, he seemed to oppose Texas independence, but as he increasingly became frustrated with Santa Anna's dictatorial regime, Burnet warmed to the idea of secession from Mexico. As a result, he attended the 1833 Convention representing the residents of Liberty and later served as an observer at the 1836 Convention. Burnet's intellect and personality impressed enough delegates to elect him president of the *ad interim* government over the more well-known Stephen F. Austin.

Burnet's presidency seemed to generally irritate everyone around him, especially Sam Houston, commander of the Texian Army: The two swapped vituperative messages during the Runaway Scrape, and even after the San Jacinto victory they remained at odds for the remainder of their days in Texas. Burnet sided with the Lamar administration against annexation, making him the target of pro-annexation groups. Burnet's later years paled in significance to the one position of authority he enjoyed as *ad interim* president.

Born near Nashville, Tennessee, Bailey Hardeman fought in the War of 1812, crisscrossed the American West as a trader out of Santa Fe, and moved with his family to Texas late in 1835. After arriving in Matagorda, Hardeman quickly involved himself in revolutionary actives, gaining the attention of his superiors during the siege at Bexar. Hardeman represented Matagorda at the March Convention, was elected secretary of the treasury and later served as secretary of state, replacing Carson. He served on the committee drafting the Texas Constitution, carried out his duties through the summer, but died of a fever in September 1836. Counties in Tennessee and Texas are named for him and his family.

David Thomas, attorney general for the ad interim government, came to Texas from Tennessee in 1835 and was in Nacogdoches when the revolution began. Thomas was commissioned lieutenant for the Matamoros Expedition, and returned to San Felipe in time to attend the Convention and sign the Declaration of Independence. He served simultaneously as secretary of war in April 1836, but died when a gun was accidentally discharged while he stood aboard the steamship *Cayuga* five days before the battle at San Jacinto.

It is important to recognize that one of the factors in the transition of voices from the initial agitation through the Revolution and into the middle years of the Republic was the remarkable number of deaths among those earlier leading figures, thus creating a void of leadership that was quickly filled with the likes of Lamar, Rusk, McLeod, and other latecomers to Texas. It is impossible to know how the earlier voices might have fared in the complex new roles of leading an independent nation, but there is no question that the transition in leadership largely played out in tragedy: the respective ages of revolutionary leaders at the time of their deaths indicate premature ends to what might have been.

One of the first "agitators," John Austin, died in the cholera epidemic in 1833 (31 years old). Three years later an astonishing number of Texian voices were silenced. James Bowie (39) and William Barret Travis (27) died at the Alamo on March 6, 1836. James Fannin (32), a native of

Georgia, who supported standing against Mexican authorities in August 1835, died in the Goliad Massacre on March 27, 1836. Ad interim attorney general David Thomas (35) was gone in April, and Angel Navarro (52) died in June. Placido Benavides (36) and Spencer Jack (28) were gone in 1837, Samuel Carson (39), D. Carlos Barrett (49), and William Wharton (37) passed away in 1838, and Texas lost John A. Wharton (31) in early 1839. Federalist champion and *Bexareño* Gen. José Antonio Mexia (38) was executed by Santa Anna in 1839, moderator W. H. Sledge died in 1840 (47) as did *Bexareño* and signer of the Declaration of Independence José Francisco Ruiz (56), and the influential George Childress (37) and Robert Potter (42) were buried in 1842.

Without question, however, the two most significant deaths of all the early voices occurred six weeks apart in late 1836, literally and ironically as the era of Revolution folded into the era of the Republic. On November 15, forty-eight-year-old Lorenzo de Zavala, vice-president of the *ad interim* government, the leading Hispanic voice of revolution, died of pneumonia after an accidental plunge into an icy river. And on December 27, Stephen F. Austin, first of the *empresarios*, voice of wisdom and conciliation, one of the most respected men of Texas's early epoch of colonization, and secretary of state for the nascent Republic, died from exhaustion and pneumonia at the age of forty-three.

The elections held across Texas on September 5, 1836, marked the transition from Revolution to Republic, but did not settle the protracted debate over whether Texas should remain an independent republic or seek annexation to the United States. The distinguishable political factions for the next decade stood on two sets of arguments: Republic versus statehood; and for or against the policies and leadership of the most polarizing figure of them all, Texian General and the first elected president of the Republic, Sam Houston. While some of the "second tier" voices continued to serve their districts and counties during political debates, the distinctive and recognizable voices now belonged to men such as Thomas Jefferson Rusk, Hugh McLeod, Anson Jones, Mirabeau Lamar, and, of course, Sam Houston. And, not coincidentally, these rising figures of the early Republic—and later statehood—emerged as the heroes of the pivotal Battle of San Jacinto, which was fought less than five months prior to the elections.

Thomas Jefferson Rusk, born of Irish stock in South Carolina in 1803, came to Texas late in 1834 chasing—literally—company managers from Clarksville, Georgia, who had absconded with investment funds and fled to the frontier. On the trail of the culprits, Rusk arrived in Nacogdoches, but he failed to apprehend the thieves or recover his money. Sometime after his arrival in East Texas, Rusk apparently grew tired of the pursuit, but rather than return to Georgia he decided to remain in the northern province of Mexico. The amiable Rusk soon became involved in the independence movement, signing a resolution on August 15, 1835, calling for a general convention later that fall (a clarion matched by similar petitions already spreading from Gonzales, Mina, San Felipe, Matagorda, and Columbia). "War is a fearful scourge," declared the Nacogdoches resolution that also included the signature of Sam Houston, but "we must live free or die."[27]

Rusk led a contingent of citizen-soldiers to Gonzales in early October, and then pressed on to San Antonio. By December he had been named inspector general of the army for the provisional government, and later accepted the appointment as secretary of war under the *ad interim* government. He aided Burnet's staff in their retreat to Harrisburg and towards Galveston as Santa Anna's army gave chase, and then arrived at San Jacinto in time to distinguish himself in the ensuing battle on April 21, 1836. For the six months following San Jacinto, Rusk served as commander in chief of the Army of the Republic, but relinquished that position when the new government of the Republic was seated.

In the years that followed, Rusk continued to be a significant voice in the affairs of Texas, most importantly as Chief Justice of the Texas Supreme Court from 1838 to 1840, and as one of the first United States senators to represent the twenty-eighth state of the Union. A successful lawyer in partnership with James Pinckney Henderson and, for a time, Kenneth Anderson, Rusk once acknowledged that a law practice on the frontier "barely supports a man, owing to the poverty of our people caused by our disturbances with Mexico and the overstock of young men in the profession."[28] He refused to run for president of the Republic in 1838, deferring to Mirabeau Lamar, and eighteen years later saw his name being considered by the Democratic Party as a potential U. S. presidential candidate. Despondent over his own ailments and the death of his wife on April 23, 1857, Rusk committed suicide ninety-seven days later.

Hugh McLeod was born in New York City, raised in central Georgia, graduated from West Point—though last in his class—and was at his post at Ft. Jesup, Louisiana, in 1836 when he crossed into Texas to join the revolution. Instantly respected for organizing the defenses at Nacogdoches, McLeod served as the Republic's first adjutant general under both Presidents Houston and Lamar, and clearly established himself as a Lamar supporter and fierce anti-Houston man. Colonel McLeod fought bravely at the Battle of the Neches and was one of the officials present at the 1840 Council House Fight in San Antonio.

Recognized during his lifetime and career as one of the leading orators and political figures in Texas, McLeod continued to take the losing side of most issues and elections, and was the poorly prepared commander of the Santa Fe Expedition in 1841 whose abject failure was partly responsible for moving Texas closer to another military conflict with Mexico. McLeod stood beside Lamar opposing annexation and supporting the expansion of the Republic westward. During the early years of statehood, McLeod managed a decent law career in Galveston, avidly supported the cause of secession in the 1850s, and died of pneumonia in Virginia awaiting command of a Texas regiment during the Civil War.[29]

Mirabeau Buonaparte Lamar, born and raised in Georgia, arrived in Texas in late 1835, seeking a fresh start on life. Lamar brought within him a cultured personality, the curiosity of a successful newspaper editor, and a keen insight and perspective that would serve him well throughout his estimable Texas career. His heroic acts during the initial conflict at San Jacinto on April 20 earned him a battlefield promotion to colonel and the respect of the Texian army; Lamar led a cavalry unit the next day into the Mexican camp. He was appointed commander of the army by Burnet but did not serve, and in the 1836 elections became the Republic's first vice-president.

In the 1838 elections, Lamar won a remarkably easy victory to the presidency, succeeding his political enemy Sam Houston and essentially reversing most of Houston's policies during the three years of his administration. Ever opposed to annexation, President Lamar envisioned a Texan nation spreading from the Gulf of Mexico to the Pacific Ocean, a vision cut short by the failed Santa Fe Expedition in 1841. Often referred to as Texas's "Father of Education," Lamar proposed to Congress a plan to establish public schools and universities across the Republic. Additionally, he unraveled Houston's Indian policies, sending armies to vanquish and remove the Kickapoos, Cherokees, and Comanches. With his exorbitant spending unchecked, Lamar led Texas to the brink of bankruptcy by the end of his term, and left the office to his old political foe, Houston, whom many trusted to right the economic woes of the Republic as well as confront the escalating and seemingly imminent confrontation with Mexico.

Mirabeau Lamar left to Texas a vigorous but often impulsive energy that helped create a more civilized, educated environment and encouraged the establishment of the Philosophical Society of Texas and a new capital on the upper Colorado River named Austin. However, he also led Texas down a precarious path of economic distress, military conflict, and an implausible vision of a permanent Republic struggling against the overwhelming tide moving toward annexation to the United States, a *fait accompli* during his lifetime. Lamar died at his plantation home in Richmond, Texas, in 1859, and was buried with full Masonic ceremony in Richmond's Morton Cemetery.

Anson Jones, like McLeod, Rusk, and Lamar, came late to the revolution. However, unlike these men whose respective contributions during the period of the Republic and early statehood afforded them a certain familiarity to future generations of Texans, Anson Jones has become an enigmatic character almost forgotten to history, except for the role he played in the annexation of Texas to the United States.

A native of Massachusetts, Jones earned a license to practice medicine in New York at age twenty-two. He later spent two years in New Orleans as a merchant prior to coming to Texas late in 1833. Once in Texas, Jones returned to his medical practice in Brazoria, participated in the 1835 Consultation, and finally supported the side calling for an independent Texas. He fought at San Jacinto, then was briefly appointed apothecary general of the Texian army.

Dr. Jones served in the First Congress of the Republic of Texas, urging the withdrawal of any annexation proposals and taking sides with the Lamar faction. President Houston sent him to Washington, D. C., as Texas's minister, but President Lamar recalled him. Back in Texas, he finished the senatorial term of the late William H. Wharton. By 1840 Jones opposed Lamar's plan to expand Texas to the West Coast and argued against funding the Texan Santa Fe Expedition. During Houston's second term, Jones served Texas as secretary of state, working with Houston to develop a foreign policy while struggling still with the issue of Texas statehood. Recognition of Texas's independence by Mexico became for Jones a paramount factor in the decision whether to pursue annexation with the United States, and colored his choices during his term as the last president of the Republic between 1844 and 1846. President Jones remained ominously silent in 1845 while awaiting word from Mexico and holding off rising sentiment for annexation across Texas. Jones's delay prompted public outrage which nearly cost him his office.

During the early years of statehood, Jones lived out his life on his Barrington plantation near Washington-on-the-Brazos, bitter that he was not elected to the U. S. Senate, a despondency that, along with a variety of physical ailments, led him to commit suicide in 1858. His name is generally, but not entirely correctly, associated with the annexation movement of 1844 spurred by U. S. President James Knox Polk and the majority of Texans, and his memorial still retains the banner statement he declared on February 19, 1846, introducing the twenty-eighth state of the Union: "The Republic of Texas is no more."[30]

"Elias, remember my words. I will yet be the President of a great Republic. I will bring that nation to the United States, and if they don't watch me closely I will be the President of the White House yet." With that likely apocryphal declaration to Arkansas Marshal Elias Rector as he stepped across the border into Texas for the first time late in 1832, the legend of Sam Houston in Texas was born.[31]

There is no more polarizing figure during the Revolution-Republic-Statehood Era in Texas, nor one with more significance throughout, than "the General" himself, Sam Houston. Born auspiciously on March 2, 1793—the future day of Texas independence—the Tennessee native rose to political prominence as state attorney, twice-elected Democratic congressman from his home state's Ninth District, and governor. His resignation from the governor's office in 1832 due to complications from personal issues more so than any political defeat, in conjunction with continuing interest in land opportunities in Texas since 1822, combined to put him on the westward trail in search of a new start. "I will practice law [in Texas], and with excellent prospects of success," he wrote on July 31, 1833, during a brief stay in Arkansas, "and I have purchased about 140,000 acres of choice land [in Texas's Leftwich Grant] in which I am equally interested." Nothing would come of the land purchase, however, but the growing drama in Texas would soon envelop him.[32]

Sam Houston represented the U. S. War Department over the winter of 1832–33 negotiating with the Texas Cherokees, attended the San Felipe convention in April 1833, as a somewhat subdued supporter of Wharton's "war faction," and was practicing law in Nacogdoches and San Augustine by the late summer. Following him, however, were swirling rumors of his being an agent of President Andrew Jackson, "spying" on the situation of a possibly-soon independent and annexation-minded Texas. Houston's biographer Llerena B. Friend addressed the persistent question on the minds of many: "What the devil was Sam Houston doing in Texas? He was there to make a living and a name for himself. His separation from his wife had shattered his personal life and his political future... Texas was adjacent [to Arkansas] and offered a chance, political and financial. A political change was inevitable there, and he had political experience which he might use to advantage, but in what direction he was not sure."[33]

Disappearing from Texas in 1834, his whereabouts and reasons still unsettled today, Houston was back in Nacogdoches and signing on to a Nacogdoches Resolution for a Convention on August 15, 1835, and from that moment on situated himself at the forefront of the Revolution. On August 29 he circulated a call to arms in his area, and by the fall was already being referred to as "General Houston" and "commander-in-chief."[34] Officially appointed to that position in March 1836, his leadership of the Texian army at San Jacinto became the stuff of legend, but he was equally known for his penchant to stir controversy, including the harsh orders that became "the Runaway Scrape" to the infighting with his own officers, soldiers, and President David Burnet, who accused him of cowardice in his ordered retreat from Santa Anna's approaching army. Additionally, Houston was heavily criticized by his detractors regarding the ultimately correct but unpopular decision to spare Santa Anna's life after the Mexican president's surrender at San Jacinto.

While in rehabilitation in New Orleans after surgery on his shattered ankle, a battle wound from San Jacinto, Houston accepted his friends' urging to put his name on the ballot for the presidency of the new Lone Star Republic and, despite the animosity by many of his former soldiers and families who had lost everything in the Runaway Scrape, he won an easy and resounding victory. Houston served as the first and third President of the Republic of Texas, sparring throughout those formative years with his political opponents, especially Mirabeau Lamar and his supporters and was elected to the United States Senate along with his colleague Thomas J. Rusk in the 1845 statehood elections, and re-elected in 1852. As Governor of Texas, Houston struggled with secession and the war effort to his last breath in 1863.

Houston's support for annexation throughout the Republic years proved to have a powerful impact and was ultimately a successful objective. "I am in favor of annexation," he wrote A. J. Donelson, "if it can take place on terms mutually beneficial to both countries. I have, on all occasions, evinced the most anxious solicitude touching the matter, and have withheld no means in my power, towards its completion." A dying President Andrew Jackson declared in 1845: "Texas comes into the Union with a united voice, and Genl. Houston, as I knew, puts his shoulder to the wheel to roll it in speedily."[35]

Although the period of transition from the Texas Revolution into the years of the Lone Star Republic is often associated with the familiar voices of Sam Houston, Mirabeau Lamar, Lorenzo de Zavala, David Burnet, Anson Jones, and Thomas J. Rusk, a "second tier" of leadership directed the movement of frustration and agitation towards revolution and even into the controversy of Republic vs. Statehood. Too often ignored or lost to history, the myriad voices of both Anglos and Tejanos between 1832 and 1846 represent a broader—and earlier—call to action across Texas than that of a handful of notables at the helm by the end of the period.

Notes

1. Margaret Swett Henson, "Tory Sentiment in Anglo-Texas Public Opinion," *Southwestern Historical Quarterly* 90, no. 1 (July 1986): 32–34. Henson provides a lengthy and important list of those earliest agitators and loyalists in Texas.

2. Stephen F. Austin, February 6, 1835, in *Papers of the Texas Revolution*, vol. 1, ed. John H. Jenkins (Austin: Presidial Press, 1973).

3. *Handbook of Texas Online*, "Austin, John," accessed March 06, 2016, http://www.tshaonline.org/handbook/online/articles/fau09.

4. Interview with John S. Menefee, "Texas Clarion" (Jackson County), June 1880.

5. Menefee's interview continued, "Texas Clarion," July 1880.

6. Michael P. Costeloe, *The Central Republic of Mexico, 1835–1846: Hombres de bien in the Age of Santa Anna* (Cambridge: Cambridge University Press, 1993), 50–52; Stanley Siegel, *Political History of the Texas Republic* (Austin: University of Texas Press, 1956), 19–20.

7. Eugene C. Barker, "Public Opinion in Texas Preceding the Revolution," *Annual Report of the American Historical Association for the Year 1911*, vol. 1 (Washington, D.C., 1913), 219–228.

8. Monclova Controversy through various correspondence, cf. Francis W. Johnson, April 15, 1835; Ugartechea to Cos, May 24, 1835; Travis letter, June 9, 1835, in *Papers of the Texas Revolution*.

9. Barker, "Public Opinion in Texas Preceding the Revolution," 5–8.

10. Stephen F. Austin to Samuel May Williams, April 1 and April 10, 1835, in *Papers of the Texas Revolution*.

11. Lorenzo de Zavala, May 8, 1835, in *Papers of the Texas Revolution*.

12. Margaret Swett Henson, "Understanding Lorenzo de Zavala," *Southwestern Historical Quarterly* 102, no. 1 (July 1998): 2–16.

13. Llerena B. Friend, *Sam Houston, The Great Designer* (Austin: University of Texas Press, 1954), 57.

14. Siegel, *Political History of the Texas Republic*, 18ff.

15. Circular from Martin Perfecto de Cos, July 5, 1835, *Papers of the Texas Revolution.*

16. Frank W. Johnson, April 15, 1835, in *Papers of the Texas Revolution.*

17. De Zavala, May 8, 1835, in *Papers of the Texas Revolution.*

18. Ben Milam to F. W. Johnson, July 5, 1835; Cos, July 7, 1835, in *Papers of the Texas Revolution.*

19. Domingo de Ugartechea to Cos, July 13, 1835, in *Papers of the Texas Revolution.*

20. Ugartechea, July 15, 1835; Peter Ellis Bean, July 30, 1835, in *Papers of the Texas Revolution.*

21. James H. C. Miller, July 25, 1835, in *Papers of the Texas Revolution.*

22. *Handbook of Texas Online*, Julia L. Vivian, "Gritten, Edward," accessed March 06, 2016, http://www.tshaonline.org/handbook/online/articles/fgr69; *Handbook of Texas Online*, Thomas W. Cutrer, "Barrett, Don Carlos," accessed March 06, 2016, http://www.tshaonline.org/handbook/online/articles/fba81; *Handbook of Texas Online*, Ralph W. Steen, "Smith, Henry," accessed March 06, 2016, http://www.tshaonline.org/handbook/online/articles/fsm23.

23. Mary Austin Holley, *Texas* (Austin: Texas State Historical Association, 1985), 334–335.

24. Gregg Cantrell, *Stephen F. Austin: Empresario of Texas* (New Haven: Yale University Press, 2001), 309.

25. Cantrell, *Stephen F. Austin: Empresario of Texas*, 311

26. Cantrell, *Stephen F. Austin*, 312. Cantrell quotes Austin as using the word "resource" rather than "recourse."

27. "Nacogdoches District Resolution," August 15, 1835, in *Papers of the Texas Revolution.*

28. Rusk to Edward Harden, September 16, 1845, as quoted in William Ransom Hogan, *The Texas Republic: A Social and Economic History* (Norman: University of Oklahoma Press, 1946; reprint, Austin: Texas State Historical Association, 2006), 247.

29. For more on Hugh McLeod see Paul N. Spellman, *Forgotten Texas Leader: Hugh McLeod and the Texan Santa Fe Expedition* (College Station: Texas A&M University Press, 1999).

30. Anson Jones, *Memoranda and Official Correspondence Relating to the Republic of Texas, Its History and Annexation* (New York: D. Appleton and Company, 1859), 604.

31. Houston to Elias Rector, as quoted in Friend, *Sam Houston*, 36.

32. Sam Houston to John Houston, July 31, 1833, as quoted in Friend, *Sam Houston*, 59.

33. Sam Houston, as quoted in Friend, *Sam Houston*, 55.

34. Sam Houston, August 15 and August 29, 1835, in *Papers of the Texas Revolution*.

35. Friend, *Sam Houston*, 153–155.

Chapter 3
Who Were the Texians? The Creation of a Texas Identity in the Era of the Republic

James E. Crisp

When Moses Austin, the founder of formal Anglo-American settlement in Texas, returned in 1821 to his Missouri home from San Antonio, where he had negotiated a contract with the Spanish government to bring to the under-populated province three hundred families from the United States, he wrote to his seventeen-year-old son to recommend a college transfer. James Elijah Brown Austin was following in the footsteps of his older brother Stephen by studying at Transylvania University in Lexington, Kentucky.[1] His father informed Brown of his Texas plans, and promised him that "I can get you introduced at the College at *Monterey* a large City about *500* miles south of *St Antonio* … and you will learn there the Spanish language which will be of more Consiquence [*sic*] to you than you can now conceive of … [T]he college … has now *400 students* from every part of the Spanish provinces, by which means you will have an opportunity to visit the City of Mexico and become acquainted with the Country generally and make friends with the young men of the first families in that Country."[2]

Barely two months after writing this letter Moses Austin was dead, and it was Stephen F. Austin rather than his little brother who made the trip to the "City of Mexico" in order to secure from the newly independent country the permission to proceed with the contract his father had made with the now-defunct government of New Spain. The goal of assimilating the Austin family into Mexican life and society, however, was still alive. Upon departing Texas for the Mexican capital in March 1822, Stephen left brother Brown behind in San Antonio to learn Spanish at the home of Erasmo Seguín, a leading citizen of the town and the guide who had crossed the Sabine River with the future *empresario* as he began his great adventure and his life's work.[3]

Brown Austin broke his brother's heart when he died of yellow fever on a trip to New Orleans in 1829, but Stephen pressed on with his perceived duty to become a full-fledged and loyal Mexican citizen in the decade after his first, and very successful, visit to the capital. After a year spent in Mexico City, he was fluent in Spanish, and more importantly, in the political culture of Mexico, not only understanding and obeying the laws, but helping to write them both as an intimate of native-born politicians and eventually as a member serving in the legislature of the joint state of *Coahuila y Tejas*. Most of the thousands of English-speaking colonists that Austin brought into Texas, however, never made such profound adjustments to life in Mexico.

All of the settlers in Austin's colonies, both under his first contract and four subsequent colonizing arrangements, lived between the San Jacinto and Lavaca rivers, with the majority located in and between the valleys of the Brazos and the Colorado, far from the existing Mexican municipalities of San Antonio, Goliad (previously La Bahía), and Nacogdoches.[4] Few saw the need or benefit of learning Spanish, but Austin, according to Mexican General Manuel de Mier y Terán, made sure that his colonists at least tried to understand and obey the laws of Mexico. Terán contrasted this with what he saw on his 1828 inspection tour amid the factious and fractious settlements in East Texas, where even the local Mexican government officials were in his view incapable of administering justice without oversight from the central government.[5]

Writing from Nacogdoches to the president of Mexico, Terán described dangerous developments in the region of his country nearest to the United States. Scattered among what he considered the ill-educated Mexicans and the untrustworthy immigrant tribes of semi-civilized Indians, Terán found

> colonists who have come from another, more advanced, society, better educated but also more malicious and mistrustful than are the Mexicans. Among the foreigners there are all kinds: fugitive criminals, honorable farmers, vagabonds and ne'er-do-wells, laborers, etc. They all go about with their constitution in their pocket, demanding their rights and the authorities and functionaries that [their constitution] provides.[6]

Even among his quieter colonists in central Texas, Austin was having his own problems. He wrote to his cousin Thomas Leaming in Philadelphia in June 1830 that his colony was firmly established, but that he was finding his own settlers even more difficult to "manage" than the Mexican government. This was an extraordinary statement, in light of the fact that Austin had just learned of the Mexican government's recent decision (with the passage of the Law of April 6, 1830, which had been inspired by Terán's warnings) to ban the further emigration of people from the United States. Yet Austin could declare to Leaming: "I do say that the North Americans are the most obstinate and difficult people to manage that live on earth, [al]tho[ugh] I have had many 'backwoods men' and 'rough fellows' to do with."[7]

Historian Stephen L. Hardin has argued that Texans characteristically "bristle under restraint." "Their tendency to strike an independent course, to observe their own customs," notes Hardin, "annoys foreigners."[8] This tendency towards the obstinacy and fierce independence that Austin and Terán witnessed among the Anglo-Texans became even more pronounced during the era of the Texas Republic, but the foreigners could be impressed as well as annoyed. Arthur G. Wavell, a British soldier of fortune who knew the Texans well, opined to Her Majesty's Foreign Office in 1844 that in addition to their great talents, energy, and practical knowledge, "they add a reckless hardihood, a restless Spirit of Adventure, resources and confidence in themselves, keen perception, coolness, contempt of other men, usages, and Laws, and of Death, equal to the Wild Indian."[9]

"Rampant individualism," was the central theme of William Ransom Hogan's classic 1946 account of the lives of the ordinary citizens of the Texas Republic, and historian Gregg Cantrell notes that this spirit "accounted for both the remarkable strengths and the deplorable flaws of the young frontier nation."[10] Living among such rampant individualists was not always pleasant. Although Hogan believed that the Anglo-Texan settlement of San Augustine "must provide a notable exception to any attempt to characterize the Republic of Texas as devoid of the best in the civilization of the period," those who saw it first-hand did not necessarily agree.[11] Writing from San Augustine in the summer of 1842, Bird Holland declared that he

> must say something about these Red-Landers—this is the dambest [*sic*] community I ever saw. I have not seen half a dozen respectable people since I have been here—and this Red land is the dambest, meanest area that any White man ever lived in, though it corroborates with the people—they are fighting, stealing, scrigling [*sic*], and every other kind of thing that is mean.[12]

The summer of '42 was a rough time for the Texas Republic—there had been a Mexican invasion that captured San Antonio in the spring, and an even more serious incursion in the fall would capture not only San Antonio but many of its prominent citizens. Holland had mentioned earlier in his letter that he soon might have to serve in a military unit, but he found that obstinance and independence in East Texas reached an extreme that could be dangerous for the nation:

> The Red-Landers say the Mexicans never did them any harm—and swear they never will shoulder a gun to invade Mexico or any other co[untry]. I have not seen a solitary individual in this city who says he is willing to go—Drafts have been held—[but] they laugh at the idea of being forced to do anything.[13]

It was not only draft-dodgers in Texas who laughed at the idea of following orders. The volunteer soldiers who made up the bulk of the Texas revolutionary army in 1835–36 were notorious for literally marching to their own drummers, and their officers were often no better disciplined than they were. The same could be said for the civilian leadership during the conflict. In 1991 historiographer Paul D. Lack summed up the conclusions of William C. Binkley's path-breaking 1950 lectures on the Texas Revolution thusly:

> A malcontented and poorly provisioned army, respecting no outside authority and thus divided into hopelessly independent units, lurched from one strategic vision to another with the result that no concerted policy prevailed. Political disunity contributed to the overall malaise, as Texas leaders established and destroyed no fewer than five governments during the year after hostilities commenced.[14]

"Political disunity," Texas-style, could be brutal. Imagine yourself sitting on the General Council of the provisional revolutionary government of Texas on January 9, 1836, as Governor Henry Smith tells you that "your services are now no longer needed." (The council responded by impeaching and attempting to remove Smith.) Here is how Smith described the council to itself:

> Look around upon your flock, your discernment will easily detect the scoundrels. The complaint; contraction of the eyes; the gape of the mouth; the vacant stare; the hung head; the restless fidgety disposition; the sneaking sycophantic look;

> a natural meanness of countenance; an unguarded shrug of the shoulders; a sympathetic tickling and contraction of the muscles of the neck anticipating the rope; a restless uneasiness to adjourn, dreading to face the storm themselves have raised.[15]

What could be the source of such contumelious orneriness? Noah Smithwick had a theory: "The Redlands had a hard name, and there is no denying the fact that there were many hard characters there, its geographical position making it a convenient retreat for renegades, who infested the border along the Sabine, just as they do now [1899] along the Rio Grande."[16] There is no doubt that the Texas border had provided a haven for rogues ever since the creation of the "Neutral Ground" between Texas and Louisiana by Spanish and American military authorities in 1806, and under both Mexico and the Republic, the Texas border represented a very specific kind of freedom to those headed west to escape debts, arrest, bad marriages, and perhaps that hangman's noose.[17]

Smithwick, dictating his memoirs at the end of the nineteenth century, was quick to assure his readers that he did not intend to smear the entire Anglo-Texan population with one broad brush:

> … I want it distinctly understood that the disclosures I make are not to be construed as reflecting on the whole population of the Redlands, who were no more responsible for the evil emanating therefrom than it is that of any other section tyrannized over by a band of ruffians.[18]

Yet even in Stephen F. Austin's bucolic capital of San Felipe de Austin, the following lyrics were penned:

> *The United States, as we understand,*
> *Took sick and did vomit the dregs of the land.*
> *Her murderers, bankrupts, and rogues you may see,*
> *All congregated in San Felipe.*

There was, said Smithwick, "more truth than poetry" in this "doggerel rhyme" (which, he noted, had a number of ribald verses that named names of prominent San Felipians). An inventive local musician fitted the words to a tune, "which tempted the disinterested to sing it, [and this] was several times productive of blood-shed."

"Many hard things," noted Smithwick in his twilight years, "have been said and written about the early settlers of Texas," and the old man had to admit that much of it was "unfortunately true." But he claimed that historians had failed to discriminate between the "true colonists" who came to Texas to improve it, and the "outlaws and adventurers who flocked into the towns." [19] The coming of independence and the Republic exacerbated, if anything, the lure of Texas towns for scamps and shysters of all varieties, and the many unemployed veterans of the Texas Army who ended up hanging around the new national capital of Houston produced, as Stephen L. Hardin has so brilliantly displayed in his *Texian Macabre*, a dangerous population of "rowdy loafers."[20]

The British observer Francis Sheridan, who spent much of his time in Texas in 1840 in Houston (even as the national capital had been moved northwest to Austin), estimated that based on his observations, "the comparative ratio of honest men to rogues in Texas, is tantamount to the number given by Hamlet, for one in the world[.]" Sheridan's twentieth-century editor helpfully notes that in Act II, scene 2, Hamlet exclaims: "To be honest, as this world goes, is to be one man picked out of ten thousand." [21]

Mary Austin Holley, whose writings about her cousin Stephen's colony in 1833 and the Revolution in 1836 were some of the most widely read (and very favorable) contemporary descriptions of Texas, visited Houston during its early heyday, in the years immediately following the death of the former *empresario* in December 1836. She was undoubtedly shrewder than Sheridan when she surmised that this great "scene of vice" was hardly representative of the Republic as a whole. The swampy capital city "concentrates the rascals," she told her daughter in March 1838, "& leaves the rest of the people in peace."[22]

Sheridan's exaggeration of the percentage of rogues and rascals in the Texas population, and his observation that "The use of the Bowie Knife [was] in general practice among high & low," however, contained a kernel of truth that William Ransom Hogan explicated as he gave the Texas Republic a "final inspection" a century after its demise.[23] His conclusions are worth quoting at length. The experience of warfare during the Revolution and the embattled state of the Republic, argued Hogan, bred a "fighting spirit" which "arose not alone from national compulsion but from individual necessity."

> In the years immediately following the Texas Revolution, law enforcement agencies were still in the process of organization precisely at the time that the country was in a state of postwar

> unrest and in the grip of a paroxysm of speculation. Disputes between persons of upper-class backgrounds were settled by resort to the Code Duello, and men of all classes engaged in other forms of personal conflict. Indians, Mexicans, desperadoes, drunken ruffians, gamblers, trigger-quick duelists who sought to have their honor offended—any of these might assail normally peaceable citizens. Hence they learned to defend themselves, and, if necessary, take the offensive. Their confidence in their ability to look any man in the eye gave them a feeling of strength in their own opinions.[24]

Hogan's generalities about national and international strife becoming personal find vivid and specific confirmation in a letter sent in September 1839 to the Secretary of War by Lieutenant John Browne from the Texan Army post at San Antonio concerning dangerous conditions on the southern frontier of the Republic. When Browne visited Victoria, he found the town:

> filled with a set of men who have given themselves the title of *a band of Brothers*[.] I soon found [wrote Browne] that what they said was Law[;] they are all in the cow stealing business and are scattered all over this frontier[.] [T]hey pretend to say that they only steal from the enemy but I am convinced to the contrary that they steal from the Texians as well as Mexicans[.]

So far, so good—but a closer look at Lieutenant Browne's extensive report to the government reveals a critical aspect of the Texan identity that Hogan left largely unexplored. At the heart of the matter is a deceptively simple question: Who were the Texians?

Browne had "been told that [the band of Brothers] drove off from Carlos Rancho a Caballarda [*caballada,* or horse herd] belonging to Alderetta [*sic*] and Seguin[,] that the owners know well where their property is but dare not to proceed to recover it."[25] These owners were José Miguel Aldrete and Juan Nepomuceno Seguín. The former had married into Victoria's founding De León family, and was one of the largest ranchers and landholders in South Texas. An ardent supporter of the Texas Revolution, he was one of the few native Mexicans to sign the Goliad Declaration of Independence in December 1835, supporting separation from Mexico even before the majority of Anglo-Texans were ready to endorse such a bold move.[26] Juan Seguín was the son of Stephen Austin's friend Erasmo Seguín, and one of the first Texan officials to take up arms against the Centralist regime of Santa Anna, in the spring of 1835. At the time of Lieutenant Browne's report, Seguín was not only serving in the Texan Congress, but was also Chairman of the Senate Committee on Military Affairs (despite his lack of fluency in English).[27] These men were clearly *not* "the enemy"!

Lieutenant Browne reported that while he was in Goliad, "one of the Gang … [declared] that he was one of the *band of Brothers* and wished me to understand that they could defend themselves against any force the Government could send to oppose them. …" Browne was not a government commissioner sent to investigate conditions on the border, but rather he had been "requested by a number of citizens of Carlo's [*sic*] Rancho[,] Goliad[,] and San Antonio to make a report of their condition to the Government[.]" Now he told the Secretary of War that "The Government can have no idea of the deplorable conditions on the San Antonio River[.] [T]he constant dre[a]d of being murdered obliges them to receive the Rob[b]er as a friend[.]" The gang had recently robbed and killed a party of Mexican traders at the Nueces River, but it was "the Mexican citizens her[e] [who] say it will not do for them to take up arms against the Americans no matter how agrivated [*sic*] the circumstances may be[,] but that they will leave it to the Government to redress their wrongs. …"[28]

Who were the Texians, indeed? Were they only the "Americans" in Texas, or did their number include the "Mexican citizens" of the San Antonio valley who had asked Browne to bring *their* government to their aid? In the preface to *The Texas Republic*, William Ransom Hogan announced that:

> This volume contains no extended treatment of the Mexicans, Germans, and Indians. The explanations are simple: There was more culture conflict than assimilation between the Anglo-American immigrants and the resident Mexicans, whose influence and numerical strength were comparatively insignificant. Spanish and German influences began to make themselves felt while Texas was independent, but they produced no sharp modifications of Anglo-American culture.[29]

Hogan has his point, but the *identity* of the Texians during the period of the Republic would be incomprehensible without reference to Mexico, and to the "Mexicans" on both sides of the border, whether that line was drawn at the Nueces or the Rio Grande. Gregg Cantrell surmised in 2006 that if Hogan were writing his book in the twenty-first century, he "would undoubtedly pay more attention to African-Americans, Tejanos, and women."[30] Today the same should be said for the inclusion of the Native Americans who inhabited a major proportion of the vast territory claimed by the Republic of Texas.

One of best of the new, more inclusive, generation of Texas historians suggested by Cantrell has been Paul D. Lack, whose prize-winning monograph, *The Texas Revolutionary Experience,* is one of the most innovative and thorough works on the subject in recent years. Lack's provocative conclusion with regard to the place of "minorities" in this story is that:

> For Texans of Hispanic and African descent the outcome of the Texas Revolution was a sudden reversal of fortunes. Powerful racial and ethnic antagonisms—expressed not only institutionally in slavery but also by custom in the form of endemic Tejano-Anglo hatred, suspicion, and conflict—*became fixed in the Texas identity during its brief experience of nationhood.*[31]

This statement contains a great deal of truth, but Lack failed to realize that the Tejano experience in the Texas Republic was profoundly different from that of blacks, as well as that of Indians.

Lack's dubious claims that "[b]y 1836 the [revolutionary] conflict had become a race war" and that "it became virtually inevitable that [Texan] military authorities would treat all Tejanos as enemies" were partially the result of his having relied far too heavily on a blatantly racist speech, long mistakenly attributed to Sam Houston.[32] We now know that the oft-published and oft-quoted speech, cited as proof of Sam Houston's "anti-Mexican attitudes," was in fact a garbled version of an address put into Houston's mouth by Hermann Ehrenberg, a young Prussian veteran of the Texas volunteer army who first wrote the speech, in German, in a memoir published in Leipzig in 1843. The attitudes, as well as the words, belong to Ehrenberg, not Houston.[33]

Houston, in fact, as the first elected president of the Texas Republic, was largely responsible for limiting and to an extent reversing the anti-Mexican sentiments, sometimes expressed in purely ideological terms, sometimes in clearly ethnic and racial terms, that flourished and grew during and immediately after the Revolution. For instance, provisional Governor Henry Smith vetoed legislation of the General Council calling for cooperation with Mexican Federalists, as well as legislation allowing "the Mexican population within our limits" to vote for delegates to the convention that would declare Texas independence, in each case on the grounds that Mexicans simply could not be trusted.[34] In both instances, however, Smith was overruled by the Council.[35] And while it is true that the Texas Declaration of Independence voiced "the melancholy conclusion, that the Mexican people ... are unfit to be free, and incapable of self-government," the same body that approved this document also wrote a Constitution that ostensibly granted the Hispanic citizens of the Texas Republic full citizenship and guaranteed to them (as Sam Houston put it) "the same rights as ... Anglo-Saxons."[36]

In the earliest and most desperate days of the Republic, when its public officials as well as its common citizens were fleeing eastward from General Santa Anna and the Mexican army, interim President David G. Burnet and even Stephen F. Austin used blatantly racial language to appeal directly to United States senators for American aid for their cause. Both claimed that the Mexicans were a "mongrel" race of mixed blood, depraved and barbaric.[37] Moreover, even after Sam Houston's victory over Santa Anna at San Jacinto, actions against the "Mexicans" living in the Texas Republic spoke louder than words.

After Houston left for New Orleans to have his battle-wounds from San Jacinto treated, a Texan army made up mostly of "new-comers" under General Thomas J. Rusk, while stationed at Victoria, "required the utmost exertion of their general to control them." According to the city's Irish-Texan mayor, John J. Linn, these troops' "creed was the total extermination of the Mexican race and the appropriation of their property to the individual use of their exterminators."[38] Almost all of the extended De León family, many of whom had greatly aided the Texas cause during the conflict, were forced into exile by the vicious assaults of the insubordinate and under-provisioned troops.[39]

Things were significantly different in San Antonio, however, where unlike Victoria and Goliad, local Tejanos remained the majority not only in the city's population but on the City Council.[40] Civil government there was restored under the watchful eye of Texas Lieutenant Colonel Juan N. Seguín. This Tejano officer, who incidentally as army commandant at San Antonio gave the eulogy (in Spanish) at the ceremonial burial of ashes of the Alamo defenders with whom he had served, was himself distrusted by such "new-comers" as Felix Huston, a Mississippi lawyer and planter "of volatile temper and decidedly aggressive intentions toward Mexico" who had brought hundreds of troops from the United States to Texas, but arrived too late to participate in the Revolution. Huston found himself in command of the Texas Army in December 1836 when Rusk became the Secretary of War in President Houston's new cabinet.[41]

Huston complained to the president that Seguín was "unfit for command" because he could not speak English.[42] Moreover, Huston trusted no "Mexican" (including those from San Antonio) living in Texas, and wanted to leave not a single one of them remaining between his army and the Mexican border.[43] He accordingly ordered Seguín to evacuate and effectively destroy San Antonio early in 1837.[44] The Tejano commandant appealed this drastic course of action to President Houston, who rescinded Huston's order, assuring Seguín that his honor was not being questioned, and enjoining the Tejano officer to use his post at San Antonio to exercise "sleepless vigilance" against "the enemy you have to guard against"—the armed forces of Mexico.[45]

Sam Houston's biggest problem upon taking office—and incidentally the greatest threat to the Tejanos—was not Mexico. It was an out-of-control Texas Army. He solved it with a master-stroke. About the same time that Huston issued his infamous order to Seguín, the President asked the would-be Supreme Commander to come to the capital to discuss strategy. Since there was only one bed in the executive mansion, the Chief Executive, always the generous host, slept on the floor. In the meantime he dispatched his Secretary of War on a midnight mission to furlough General Huston's army out from under him.[46] To use an old Texas expression that not only reflects the Hispanic ranching tradition, but also nicely skewers inflated pretensions to status, we can say that by the time Felix Huston realized what had happened, he was "all hat and no cattle."

Three or four months into his presidency, Sam Houston had largely reversed a vicious circle of ethnic polarization that had begun during the Revolution and was being exacerbated by the flood of belligerent volunteers streaming into Texas after San Jacinto, looking for Mexicans—any Mexicans—to attack. Victoria's Mayor John Linn believed that Houston had literally "save[d] the people of San Antonio," the historic center of Hispanic life and culture in Texas. Moreover, by confirming Juan Seguín in command of the San Antonio garrison in 1837, and by using his presidential prerogative to nominate Juan's father, Erasmo Seguín, as Chief Justice of the Bexar County Court in the same year, Houston had placed the highest local civilian and military authority in Tejano hands, and given tangible reality to a "Texian" identity that extended across ethnic bounds.[47]

During the first half of the Texas Republic's existence—until the series of crises that followed in the wake of the Mexican army's invasions of 1842, "Texians" of Mexican heritage found places not only in the Vice-Presidency briefly held by the prominent Mexican statesman Lorenzo de Zavala, but also in the Congress, the Army, the ranger companies, the judiciary, municipal governments, and on the juries in Bexar County that passed judgment on Anglos and Tejanos alike. Significantly, in May of 1838, the Houston *Telegraph and Texas Register* was welcoming back into Texas the many "Mexicans who fled the country at the time of [Santa Anna's] invasion." The editor exclaimed:

> We are glad to learn that our government is pursuing a mild and forbearing policy towards these fugitives, many of whom fled to the settlements on the Rio Grande, not so much on account of hostility to us, as to withdraw their wives and children from the scene of war.[48]

Even after the so-called Córdova Rebellion in Nacogdoches of August 1838, when dozens of armed and mounted Tejanos, allied with some old Anglo settlers, dissatisfied Indians, and even a few free blacks, challenged the authority and legitimacy of the local and national governments, there was no backlash against Texas Mexicans generally.[49] The Houston *Telegraph* continued to welcome new immigrants from Mexico who were flocking to Bexar County in the spring of 1839, and "opening new farms in every direction around the city" of San Antonio.[50]

Sam Houston, of course, was known far and wide not so much for his efforts to assure ethnic harmony and national tranquility as for leading the Texans (including a Tejano company commanded by Captain Juan N. Seguín) to an improbable, almost miraculous, lopsided victory over Santa Anna at San Jacinto. According to the official report of the battle, 630 Mexicans were killed and 730 taken prisoner, and of the 910 Texans who saw action that day, only 9 were killed or mortally wounded, with another 30 wounded less seriously.[51] No other event was more important in securing for the citizens of the Texas Republic a reputation for self-reliance, for martial prowess—and perhaps for a tendency toward exaggeration.

All of these characteristics existed in embryo among the Texans even before the Revolution. The Tejanos themselves, usually far from the minds of the politicians of Mexico City and either ignored or damaged by their policies, had a long history of self-reliance. Under Spain as well as Mexico, writes Stephen L. Hardin, the Hispanic "colonists of Tejas learned to fend for themselves. … Tejanos developed their own customs, clothing, music, tactics, food, even a variant of the Spanish language."[52] Contrary to William Hogan's assessment, aspects of this self-reliance and the Tejanos' adaptation to the Texas environment had rubbed off on the Anglo-American settlers even before the Revolution. Tejano historian Andrés Tijerina has described the development of the *"compañía volante,"* or "flying company" of mounted rangers that became the Tejanos' standard method of policing and defending the vast and under-populated areas of Texas; he also traces the adoption of such tactics by the Anglo-Texans in both the Austin colonies and the Republic.[53]

Herman Ehrenberg, the Prussian teenager who came to Texas with the New Orleans Grays in 1835 to win the "liberty and sovereignty" of the settlers of the "prairie country" from Mexico, not only fought at Béxar and Coleto, but also served the Republic in a frontier ranging company in the spring and summer of 1840 before returning to Europe to sing the praises of

> the exhilarating life that the prairie, teeming with game, offers those who roam and hunt there … The ranger … has no worries about a house, food, or even clothes. … He is happy just to roam across the magnificent western territory. He visits the settlements only infrequently. But when election day comes, when the highest ranking government official is elected, then the ranger is right there among the other citizens of the nation to cast his vote for the good of the country.[54]

Ehrenberg was by no means alone when, writing as a "Citizen of the [Texas] Republic" in 1842, he linked the virtues of individual self-reliance to the importance of collective self-government.[55] The Anglo-Texans, as the contest over their status in Mexico intensified in 1835–1836, increasingly referred to themselves as "sons of '76," and clearly desired to be brought into the fold of the American Union in the immediate aftermath of San Jacinto.[56] But after Texas was denied annexation in 1836 and again in 1838, its citizens began to forget just how extensive the massive aid from citizens of the United States had been in sustaining their revolution, and began to craft a national narrative that emphasized their self-liberation and their inordinate pride in having created a country of their own.[57] But again the question arises: if they were not "Americans," then who were the "Texians"?

Self-reliance did not come only with the Republic. Even in the colonial period, when they were ostensibly under the Mexican flag, the Anglo-Texans, like the Tejanos, were largely on their own—for good or ill. For the first decade of their settlement in Mexican Texas, the colonists were exempted from paying tariffs on the many goods they imported from abroad. It was the rather heavy-handed imposition of these new tariffs, and the presence of a Mexican soldiery to enforce the nation's laws, that sparked the violent disturbances in Texas in 1832. For the next three years—until the arrival of new troops sent by Santa Anna in 1835—few in Texas felt the hand of the distant national government at all. Victoria's Irish colonist John J. Linn recalled that during this halcyon period of *de facto* independence, "[a] live mastodon would not have been a greater curiosity than a tax-collector."[58]

In 1835, as in 1832, the Texans (Tejanos and Anglos alike) were successful in forcing the total evacuation of the Mexican soldiers whose presence they so resented. The following year did not go so well. Until the remarkable victory at San Jacinto, the Texans lost—badly—virtually every military engagement with the Mexican army (though they were more successful against the Mexican navy). But one big victory was enough to give the Texans bragging rights and a reputation as fierce and effective fighters, despite the fact that their forces had been utterly vanquished by General José Urrea as he drove up the Texas coast in 1836 from Matamoros to the Brazos River. The Day of San Jacinto meant that it would be the Alamo's sacrifice and Santa Anna's ultimate humiliation that would be remembered, and not General Urrea's triumphs.[59]

The end of the Revolution did not mean the end of danger for the Republic, of course, and the fighting spirit was kept alive in Texas by the threats from the Rio Grande to the Southwest, the Comanche country to the northwest, and the "disconnected Bands [of Indians] from the U. States dispersed throughout" the (eastern) border. Self-reliance had a military corollary, and the Texans were self-consciously a besieged people. We are, the Secretary of State reminded the infant Republic's representative in Washington, "a small nation of people spread over an extensive territory, at the same time battling against vast odds" with potential enemies in every direction.[60]

The enemies of Texas in the United States, most notably the abolitionists who opposed the annexation of Texas, were capable of giving a kind of backhanded compliment to the prowess and exaggerated ambitions of the Texans and those Americans who had helped them separate this vast land from Mexico. The Unitarian preacher William Ellery Channing wrote that

> Some crimes, by their magnitude, have a touch of the sublime; and to this dignity the seizure of Texas by our citizens is entitled. Modern times furnish no example of individual rapine on so grand a scale. It is nothing less than the robbery of a realm. The pirate seizes a ship. The colonists and their coadjutors can satisfy themselves with nothing less short of an empire.[61]

More friendly observers, who still saw much room for improvement in the Texas Republic, were quick to acknowledge their admiration of this soldierly society on the frontier. A group of Christians sent Bibles and religious tracts in 1837 to the "chivalrous, but morally destitute" people of Texas.[62] An 1839 Second of March speaker on Texas Independence Day in Houston, who voiced his hope that "the rude points of our national character [would] gradually and forever disappear," began his oration by telling his audience that "together we have come up to the common altar of our country, to render our united homage to the God of battles."[63] When Sam Houston and Mirabeau B. Lamar, despite their political differences, got together with twenty-four other men of intellect to form the Philosophical Society of Texas in Houston on December 5, 1837, they proclaimed: "Texas has her captains, let her have her wise men."[64]

The Society, unfortunately, was moribund within a year, done in to a great extent by the political tension between Houston and Lamar. These were men of very different temperaments and beliefs, and the latter, who served as president between Houston's two terms, did much to narrow the definition of "Texian" during his time in office, both purposefully and inadvertently.

Lamar's first major move was to expel (and threaten to exterminate) the Cherokee, with whom Houston had negotiated a treaty during the dark days of the Revolution. The Texan Congress had refused to ratify the document, which guaranteed to the Indians their extensive lands in East Texas in exchange for their friendly neutrality during the war. Houston, who had lived with a Cherokee band as a youth in Tennessee and fluently spoke their language, bitterly resented Lamar's stated determination to rid Texas of every single red man.[65]

Lamar pursued a similar course with regard to the few hundred free African-Americans in the Republic, supporting a law passed in February 1840 that required "all free persons of color" to remove themselves from the Republic within two years. Exactly two years later, as president, Houston issued a proclamation forestalling the operation of that law, noting that there were "a number of honest and industrious persons of that description, who have been *citizens of this country* for a number of years."[66]

Sam Houston loved the grand gesture, and his mode of dress was sometimes exotic, but he was a prudent and cautious man, as shown both by his masterful San Jacinto campaign (many retreats, but only one true battle) and his conciliatory Indian policy. Mirabeau Lamar was nothing of the kind. It was Lamar's imperial overreach toward New Mexico, ironically, that doomed his presidency and indirectly brought devastation to Juan Seguín and the Tejanos whom Houston had tried so hard to include in the definition of "Texian."

Superficially, Lamar's gambit to extend the actual rule of Texas to its claimed boundaries on the far reaches of the upper Rio Grande was the high-water mark of Anglo/Tejano cooperation in the Republic. When Lamar visited San Antonio in 1841 to promote his grand "Santa Fe Expedition," which was intended to bring the people of New Mexico (along with their trade routes and their silver) under the control of Texas, the festivities began with a waltz led by President Lamar and the mayor's wife: "Mrs. Juan N. Seguin."[67] Moreover, Lamar had named to accompany the expedition the sole surviving Tejano signer of the Texas Declaration of Independence, José Antonio Navarro, as one of the four Texian "civil commissioners" to serve in New Mexico (all completely unauthorized by the Congress, as was the expedition itself).[68]

Lamar's proclaimed motives for expanding into Santa Fe were as dubious as the expedition's legality. He wrote to the people of Santa Fe that

> not from any desire to promote our own interest … but for the exalted purpose of diffusing the blesings of our institutions, and of giving to all who reside within our teritory [*sic*] the freedom we enjoy.—Activated by this spirit of Philanthropy alone, we now throw wide the doors of the Temple which we have erected to Liberty, and ask you to enter as members of the same family.[69]

He also had a speech written for Navarro, to be delivered to the people of Santa Fe, announcing that the Republic of Texas "with the innate vigor of Hercules, had risen from its very birth, invincible, …" and would soon become "the richest, most powerful nation in America."[70]

Both the public and private statements of Lamar and his officers in Texas, however, show that they were hoping that the expedition to Santa Fe would "revive the drooping finances" of the Republic, which Lamar's policies (including a drastically inflated currency) were driving into bankruptcy, as well as save them from their own personal debts.[71] It is also clear that the Lamar Administration was prepared to *compel* New Mexico to submit to Texas, if possible, and that the New Mexicans would not have rights equal to those of other Texas citizens.[72]

The result of all this bluster was, of course, a fiasco. The Santa Fe Expedition became lost, stumbled into New Mexico only to be captured without a shot, and its members sent to prison in Mexico. José Antonio Navarro came in for special punishment, and remained in irons for years before his escape to Texas was accomplished in 1845.[73] No one exemplifies the downside of Texan braggadocio more perfectly than Mirabeau Buonaparte Lamar—he left office in disgrace, barely avoiding impeachment, and (according to his nemesis, Sam Houston, who succeeded him) left, "not a dollar" in the nation's Treasury.[74] Anson Jones, who in turn succeeded Houston in office in 1844, claimed to have warned Lamar and his cabinet in 1839 the government's

> *scale* of operations was too large; and that this was a great fault, thinking and acting as a great nation, when we were but a first rate *county*; and that there were counties in the United States ahead of us in wealth and population, and that we were about to realize the fable of the frog and the ox—and burst.[75]

What burst upon Texas in 1842 as a result of the Santa Fe Expedition were two retaliatory raids by which the Mexican Army set in motion events that eventually destroyed civil government in San Antonio, the career of Juan Seguín, and the tentative place of Tejanos within the Texian identity.[76] General Rafael Vásquez, who descended upon the town in March, spread rumors of his collusion with Seguín, though Juan had actually warned both the city council and the national government of the impending attack.

Now accused of treason despite being declared innocent by Edward Burleson, the Republic's Vice-President, Seguín's life was threatened and his Tejano neighbors attacked. In April he submitted his resignation as mayor, and by the summer he was in exile in Mexico, where he was offered the choice of prison or joining the second raid, which was led by General Adrián Woll in September. After appearing in San Antonio with the Mexican Army, Seguín was branded an arch-traitor, though his actions that fall were mostly centered on accompanying to the Rio Grande two hundred Tejano families who were fearful (with good reason) of abuse by the unruly Texan soldiers who were streaming toward the unfortunate city.[77]

Seguín's personal tragedy was reflected on a larger scale all over the Republic, where, as historian Jack Jackson put it, "at last the ugly line [had] been drawn for Texas."[78] It was this moment of alleged "Mexican treachery" that crystallized what David Montejano has called the legitimizing myth of Texas history, a myth that justified so much violence and shame along the border.[79] The repercussions certainly reached the city of Houston, where twelve former prisoners of war—Mexican soldiers from Santa Anna's army who had elected to claim Texas citizenship rather than return to Mexico—published a statement in the *Morning Star* that although they, after recent events, were "looked upon with suspicion and distrust," they were "willing ready at any moment to defend this soil. … Our motto is: 'where Liberty dwells—there is our country.'"[80] Unfortunately, after this season of distrust in the last years of the Republic was multiplied in its effects by the bloodshed and terror of the war between the United States and Mexico which followed the annexation of Texas, the popular understanding of the "Texan identity" would not include its Hispanic component for more than a century to follow.[81]

Why was 1842 so different from 1838, when the Republic shrugged off the threat of rebellion by Vicente Córdova in Nacogdoches? Bertram Wyatt-Brown, in his analysis of the response to rumors of slave revolts in the Antebellum South, concludes that a massive response is often more indicative of external sources of anxiety among the dominant group than on a calculated effort to make the retribution match the presumed offense.[82] Mexico, and after Seguín's fall from grace Mexicans generally, received much of the blame for the dire straits in which the Republic of Texas found itself in the early 1840s. The border was unsafe, the treasury was empty, immigration had slowed to a trickle, the currency was virtually worthless, and the postal system had come close to collapse. By mid-1843, three expeditions aimed at punishing Mexico for its impertinence ended badly, with the Texans defeated and embarrassed.[83] Texas was experiencing, concluded William R. Hogan, a "psychological depression" which exacerbated the financial one.[84]

The editor of the *Telegraph and Texas Register* "tremble[d] for the stability" of the Republic, and mourned that "the Lone Star pales before the foul mists of dishonor that are gathering …"[85] Some in Texas worried that the tropical climate or proximity to Mexicans might cause the Anglo-Texans to become lazy and untrustworthy.[86] Texans had ceased to be "Americans" in nationality—could they also cease to be "Americans" in character and principles? The answer was given in starkly racial terms: white men—Anglo-Americans—go where they might, would "*never* retrograde"![87] Never, said the new President Anson Jones in 1844, have they "degenerated," even "in the islands of Australia and the Pacific, nor the wilds and prairies of the west."[88] If Texas was in trouble, it was because "worthless and incompetent men" had been entrusted with the government.[89] Yet the nation's leading editor could still believe that "a high and brilliant destiny awaits our beloved Republic." Why? Because

> [t]he banner of the Single Star is but the advanced standard of the all-conquering race, that is sweeping onward with a slow but irresistible current from the shores of the Atlantic. Our republic is but the left wing of the mighty army of Anglo-Americans that is marching to the Pacific, and is destined to establish the true principles of freedom throughout the dark regions of the "West."[90]

This is essentially a racial formula of the Texan identity, and one that had no room for the likes of Juan Seguín.

With all of the Texas Republic's problems and deficiencies, what, asked William R. Hogan at the conclusion of his study, held it together long enough to be annexed by the United States? Optimism for a better tomorrow was an inherent component in the mindset of virtually all who ventured into this frontier nation, and Hogan saw the basic bounty of the vast territory as the key the people's survival under duress:

> Shelter, food, and clothing could always be obtained. Life could be sustained regardless of the price of cotton, and hopes that the future would bring increased security and added value to landholdings were never abandoned.[91]

Not everyone could measure up to the struggle. A young man who came to Tyler County as late as 1845 exclaimed to those who were waiting for better times:

> I don't see how a man can live as you folks do ... the Ticks, the black Mud, the sand flies, and the musketoes [*sic*]—dry beef, black coffee, sweet potatoes ... would ruin me. ...It is the most perfect purgatory of any place on the Earth.[92]

According to Catholic theology, all of those in purgatory can look forward to going to heaven, if they can only endure. This is essentially what Benjamin B. Peck told his mother in Rhode Island that he was going to do when he wrote her from Gonzales in November 1841 that "times are very hard." Texas was, he said, "the hardest country in the world for a young man to [get] along in," but if only a man had "a family and a little money," he could buy a piece of land cheaper than any he had ever seen, as low as twenty-five cents an acre if one risked moving "out of the settlements." With a family and a little capital, the new settler could do very well in Texas, "for if a man would be industrious here he can raise anything he wants to live on." This Rhode Island Yankee, however, was not as impressed by the Texans of the present as he was hopeful about the Texas of the future. "The people in general here are very indolent," he complained, "If they can get plenty of corn bread and beef they are well contented to lay down and sleep the biggest part of the time."[93] It seems that in the Republic of Texas, one man's purgatory could be another man's paradise.

As the political winds in the United States finally blew in the direction of the annexation of Texas in 1844–45, helping to revive the economy and brighten the future, it seemed as if the only Tejano who remained welcome in the Republic was the one who could not be there. Although all other Texian prisoners from the Santa Fe Expedition had been released from Mexican prisons by June 1842, José Antonio Navarro remained incarcerated under harsh conditions until his escape by boat from the island fortress of San Juan de Úlloa in December 1844. After a circuitous return to Texas by way of Havana and New Orleans, he was welcomed by crowds at Galveston, Houston, and other cities as he made his way back to his rancho above San Antonio.

It is possible that for some Anglo-Texans, Navarro's loyalty under duress and renewed presence in the Republic's fading days might mitigate the negative image of all "Mexicans" in Texas that had predominated since the difficult days of 1842. That sanguine hope is challenged, however, by the unrepentant reaction, echoed elsewhere in the Republic, of one Galveston editor to Navarro's return:

> Although born and reared in the deserts surrounded [*sic*] city of San Antonio … Col. Navarro is not of the abject race of Mexicans. His father was a Corsican of good birth, and, what is worthy of remark, was born under the same roof with that [prodigy] of the human race, Napoleon Bonaparte.[94]

Notes

1. David B. Gracy, *Moses Austin: His Life* (San Antonio: Trinity University Press, 1987), 213.

2. Moses Austin to James E. B. Austin, April 8, 1821, in Eugene C. Barker, ed., *The Austin Papers*, Annual Report of the American Historical Association for the Year 1919, 2 vols. (Washington, DC: Government Printing Office, 1924), vol. 2, pt. 1, 386.

3. Gregg Cantrell, *Stephen F. Austin: Empresario of Texas* (New Haven, CT: Yale University Press, 1999), 88–91, 110.

4. Cantrell, *Stephen F. Austin*, 163–64.

5. Terán to the Governor of Coahuila y Tejas, June 24, 1828, in *Texas by Terán: The Diary Kept by General Manuel de Mier y Terán on His 1828 Inspection of Texas*, Jack Jackson, ed., John Wheat, trans. (Austin: University of Texas Press, 2000), 96.

6. Terán to the President of Mexico, June 30, 1828, in *Texas by Terán*, 100–01.

7. Stephen F. Austin to Thomas F. Leaming, June 14, 1830, in Eugene C. Barker, ed., *The Austin Papers*, Annual Report of the American Historical Association for the Year 1922, 2 vols. (Washington, DC: Government Printing Office, 1928), vol. 2, 415. See also Cantrell, *Stephen F. Austin*, 250.

8. Stephen L. Hardin, "Texas: The Word That Explains It All," *Texas Heritage* 1 (2014): 22–23.

9. Wavell, quoted in Justin H. Smith, *The Annexation of Texas* (New York: Macmillan, 1919), 34.

10. Gregg Cantrell, "Foreword," in William Ransom Hogan, *The Texas Republic: A Social and Economic History* (1946; reprint: Austin: Texas State Historical Association, 2007), vii–viii.

11. Hogan, *Texas Republic*, 153.

12. Bird Holland to "Dear Woodhouse," June 19, 1842, in *Letters of Hard Times in Texas, 1840–1890*, David Holman, comp. (Austin: Roger Beacham, 1974), 12–13. The name "Redlands" came, of course, from the color of the soil in the area. It was not an epithet, but was embraced by the residents. The *Red-Lander* was an important newspaper published in San Augustine during the Republic. Randolph Lewis, "SAN AUGUSTINE RED-LANDER," *Handbook of Texas Online* (http://www.tshaonline.org/handbook/online/articles/ees24), accessed January 09, 2015. Uploaded on June 15, 2010. Published by the Texas State Historical Association. The old Texas settler Noah Smithwick testified that "the Redlands" is what "the country between the Sabine [River] and Ayish Bayou was called." Noah Smithwick, *The Evolution of a State, or Recollections of Old Texas Days* (1900; reprint, Austin: University of Texas Press, 1983), 60. Smithwick had more to say about the Redlands, as we shall see below.

13. Holland to Woodhouse, June 19, 1842, in *Letters of Hard Times in Texas*, 12–13.

14. Paul D. Lack, "In the Long Shadow of Eugene C. Barker: The Revolution and the Republic," in *Texas Through Time: Evolving Interpretations*, Walter L. Buenger and Robert A. Calvert, eds. (College Station: Texas A&M University Press, 1991), 147. See William C. Binkley, *The Texas Revolution* (Baton Rouge: Louisiana State University Press, 1952), vi. Binkley's work has enjoyed multiple reprints by the Texas State Historical Association.

15. Smith to Council, January 9, 1836, in John H. Jenkins, ed., *The Papers of the Texas Revolution, 1835–1836*, 10 vols. (Austin: Presidial Press, 1973), 3: 459–60.

16. Smithwick, *Evolution of a State*, 60.

17. John V. Haggard, "NEUTRAL GROUND," *Handbook of Texas Online* (http://www.tshaonline.org/handbook/online/articles/nbn02), accessed January 09, 2015. Uploaded on June 15, 2010. Published by the Texas State Historical Association.

18. Smithwick, *Evolution of a State*, 60.

19. Smithwick, *Evolution of a State*, 55.

20. Stephen L. Hardin, *Texian Macabre: The Melancholy Tale of a Hanging in Houston* (Abilene, TX: State House Press, 2007), xvii.

21. *Galveston Island, Or, A Few Months off the Coast of Texas: The Journal of Francis C. Sheridan, 1839–1840*, Willis W. Pratt, ed. (Austin: University of Texas Press, 1954), 88, n. 99.

22. Mary Austin Holley to her daughter, March 21, 1838, quoted in Hogan, *Texas Republic*, 270.

23. Sheridan, *Galveston Island*, 100.

24. Hogan, *Texas Republic*, 297.

25. Lt. Jno. Browne to A[lbert] S[idney] Johnston, Sept. 13, 1839, in *The Papers of Mirabeau Buonaparte Lamar*, Adam Gulick, Jr. et al., eds., 6 vols. (1921–1927; reprint, New York: AMS Press, 1973), III: 106.

26. Ana Carolina Castillo Crimm, *De León: A Tejano Family History* (Austin: University of Texas Press, 2003), 67; Hobart Huson, "ALDRETE, JOSE MIGUEL," *Handbook of Texas Online* (http://www.tshaonline.org/handbook/online/articles/fal04), accessed January 16, 2015. Uploaded on June 9, 2010. Published by the Texas State Historical Association.

27. *A Revolution Remembered: The Memoirs and Selected Correspondence of Juan N. Seguín*, Jesús F. de la Teja, ed. (2nd ed.; Austin: Texas State Historical Association, 2002), 23, 33. It is possible that the horse herd to which Browne referred belonged to Erasmo Seguín, but the point remains valid. Erasmo in 1838 had become the Chief Justice of the District Court of the Texas Republic's Bexar County.

28. J. Browne to A. S. Johnston, Sept. 13, 1839, *Lamar Papers*, III: 106–07.

29. Hogan, *Texas Republic*, ix–x.

30. Cantrell, "Foreword," in Hogan, *Texas Republic*, viii. "Tejano" is a term used at least since the mid-twentieth century to designate Texans of Mexican descent and ethnicity. In the mid-nineteenth century, the first and usually the only language of virtually all Tejanos was Spanish.

31. Paul D. Lack, *The Texas Revolutionary Experience: A Political and Social History, 1835–1836* (College Station: Texas A&M University Press, 1992), 265. (Emphasis added.)

32. Lack, *Texas Revolutionary Experience*, 86, 160.

33. Lack, *Texas Revolutionary Experience*, 327. For the full story of the Ehrenberg memoir and its effects on Texan historiography, see James E. Crisp, "Sam Houston's Speechwriters: The Grad Student, the Teenager, the Editors, and the Historians," *Southwestern Historical Quarterly* 92, no. 2 (October 1993): 202–37; see also James E. Crisp, "In Pursuit of Herman Ehrenberg: A Research Adventure," *Southwestern Historical Quarterly* 102, no. 4 (April 1999): 422–39.

34. Smith to Council, Dec. 9, 1835, *Papers of the Texas Revolution*, 3: 129; Smith to Council, December 12, 1835, ibid., 3: 174 (quotation); see Lack, *Texas Revolutionary Experience*, 77, 160.

35. H. P. N. Gammel, comp., *The Laws of Texas, 1821–1897 ...*, 10 vols. (Austin: Gammel Book Company, 1898), 1: 644, 660.

36. "Texas Declaration of Independence," March 2, 1836, in Gammel, comp., *Laws of Texas*, 1: 1066; Sam Houston to George W. Hockley and Samuel M. Williams, February 3, 1844, in Amelia W. Williams and Eugene C. Barker, eds., *The Writings of Sam Houston, 1813–1863*, 8 vols. (1938–1943; reprint, Austin and New York: Pemberton Press, 1970), 4: 241.

37. Burnet to Henry Clay, March 30, 1836, *Papers of the Texas Revolution*, 5: 238–39; Austin to Sen. L[ewis] F. Linn, May 4, 1836, in Eugene C. Barker, ed., *The Austin Papers, October, 1834-January 1837* (Vol. III; Austin: University of Texas Press, 1927), 345. Burnet was writing from Harrisburg, as he and his cabinet fled from Washington-on-the-Brazos toward refuge on Galveston Island. Austin was writing from New York City, where he was desperate to find monetary support for what appeared to be a failing revolution. His biographer, Gregg Cantrell, believes that Austin's "racist diatribe" was totally out of character, and most probably not in keeping with his actual beliefs. See Cantrell, *Stephen F. Austin*, 344. Less than two weeks later, while in Washington, DC, Austin heard the "glorious news in relation to the capture of Santana." Austin and W. H. Wharton to [James] Treat, May 16, 1836, *Papers of the Texas Revolution*, 6: 308. After passions had cooled, and the Republic was relatively safe, Austin wrote in August that Mexico's "state of chaos, [was] produced by the sudden transition from extreme [S]panish slavery and ignorance, to extreme republican liberty." Austin to W. S. Archer, August 15, 1836, *Austin Papers*, 3: 416.

38. John J. Linn, *Reminiscences of Fifty Years in Texas* (1883; reprint, Austin: State House Press, 1986), 200.

39. Crimm, *De León*, 165–67.

40. Minutes of the City Council, Volume One: 1839–[1844], Office of the City Secretary, Victoria, Texas; Minute Book of the [Goliad] Common Council, Volume I: 1841–1852, Photostat, Briscoe Center for American History, University of Texas, Austin; Minutes of the City Council of the City of San Antonio from 1837 to 1849, Journal "A," typescript with English translations, Briscoe Center for American History, University of Texas, Austin, 1–32.

41. Thomas W. Cutrer, "HUSTON, FELIX," *Handbook of Texas Online* (http://www.tshaonline.org/handbook/online/articles/fhu46),

accessed January 21, 2015. Uploaded on June 15, 2010. Published by the Texas State Historical Association.

42. De la Teja, ed., *Revolution Remembered*, 31.

43. Huston to Houston, December 16, 1836, Houston Correspondence, Catholic Archives of Texas, Austin.

44. De la Teja, ed., *Revolution Remembered*, 31.

45. Houston to Seguín, January 16, 1837, in De la Teja, ed., *Revolution Remembered*, 152–153.

46. Marshall De Bruhl, *Sword of San Jacinto: A Life of Sam Houston* (New York: Random House, 1993), 239–41.

47. Houston to the Senate, November 7, 1837, in Williams and Barker, eds., *Writings of Sam Houston*, 2: 148–49.

48. (Houston) *Telegraph and Texas Register*, May 19, 1836.

49. On the complexities of the Córdova Rebellion, see James E. Crisp, "*¡Mucho Cuidado!* Silencing, Selectivity, and Sensibility in the Utilization of Tejano Voices by Texas Historians," in Monica Perales and Raúl Ramos, eds., *Recovering the Hispanic History of Texas* (Houston: Arte Público Press, 2010), 111–135, and the many sources cited therein.

50. (Houston) *Telegraph and Texas Register*, March 13, 1839. See also ibid., April 10, 1839.

51. L. W. Kemp, "SAN JACINTO, BATTLE OF," *Handbook of Texas Online* (http://www.tshaonline.org/handbook/online/articles/qes04), accessed January 22, 2015. Uploaded on June 15, 2010. Modified on February 5, 2014. Published by the Texas State Historical Association.

52. Hardin, "Texas," 21–22.

53. Andrés Tijerina, *Tejanos and Texas under the Mexican Flag, 1821–1836* (College Station: Texas A&M University Press, 1994), 80–92.

54. Hermann Ehrenberg, *Texas und seine Revolution* (Leipzig: Otto Wigand, 1843), [6], 129. Translation by Louis E. Brister. Ehrenberg's name appears on the payroll and muster roll of the militia company of Captain Constantius Pierce, Militia Rolls, Texas State Library and Archives, Austin. This company, also known as the Pitkin Guards, was organized in Houston in March, 1840. See the (Houston) *Morning Star*, March 7 and March 14, 1840.

55. Ehrenberg, in *Texas und seine Revolution*, identified himself on the title page as "Bürger der Republik."

56. Sam W. Haynes, "'Imitating the Example of Our Forefathers': The Texas Revolution as Historical Reenactment," in *Contested Empire: Rethinking the Texas Revolution*, Sam W. Haynes and Gerald D. Saxon, eds. (College Station: Texas A&M University Press, 2015), 47.

57. For an important account of just how crucial the aid from the United States was for the Texas rebels, see Edward L. Miller, *New Orleans and the Texas Revolution* (College Station: Texas A&M University Press, 2004); see also James E. Crisp, "Beyond the Battleground: The Competing Legacies of San Jacinto," *Houston History* 4, no. 2 (Spring 2007): 12–19.

58. Linn, *Reminiscences*, 23. Significantly, Linn reported in July 1835 that "the well disposed Mexicans" of San Antonio were mightily upset that their city was now being occupied by Mexican troops, and that they wanted the "Americans" in Texas to help resist, and not to "let the country be poluted [*sic*] with a worse than Savage set with impunity." Linn to James Kerr, July 30, 1835, *Papers of the Texas Revolution*, 1: 288–89.

59. Stephen L. Hardin, *Texian Iliad: A Military History of the Texas Revolution* (Austin: University of Texas Press, 1994), 250.

60. [Robert A.] Irion to [Memucan] Hunt, Sept. 20, 1837, in George P. Garrison, ed., *Diplomatic Correspondence of the Republic of Texas*, 3 vols. (Vol. 1 published as Vol. II of the *Report of the American Historical Association for the Year 1907* [Washington, DC: Government Printing Office, 1907]; Vols. 2 and 3 published as Vol. II (in two parts) of the *Report of the American Historical Association for the Year 1908* [Washington, DC: Government Printing Office, 1908]), 2: 261.

61. William Ellery Channing, *A Letter to the Hon. Henry Clay, on the Annexation of Texas to the United States* (Boston: James Munroe and Company, 1837), 20–21.

62. Hogan, *Texas Republic*, 218.

63. Henry Thompson, *Oration Delivered on 2nd March, 1839, on the Anniversary of the Independence of the Republic of Texas* (Houston: National Intelligencer Office, 1839), 5 (second quotation), 8 (first quotation).

64. Dorman Hayward Winfrey, comp., *A History of the Philosophical Society of Texas, 1837–1987* (Austin: The Philosophical Society of Texas, 1987), 73–74.

65. Gary Clayton Anderson, *The Conquest of Texas: Ethnic Cleansing in the Promised Land* (Norman: University of Oklahoma Press, 2005), 171–74. See also Mirabeau B. Lamar, "Second Annual Message to Congress," November 12, 1839, *Lamar Papers*, 3: 166. The strength, endurance, and singularity of Houston's pro-Indian views and policies are shown by Carol A. Lipscomb, "Sam Houston: Indian Agent," in Richard B. McCaslin, Donald E. Chipman, and

Andrew J. Torget, eds., *This Corner of Canaan: Essays on Texas in Honor of Randolph B. Campbell* (Denton: University of North Texas Press, 2013), 82–105.

66. PROCLAMATON BY THE PRESIDENT OF THE REPUBLIC OF TEXAS, February 5, 1842, in Williams and Barker, eds., *Writings of Sam Houston*, 2: 476–77. Italics added for emphasis.

67. Rena Maverick Green, ed., *Memoirs of Mary A. Maverick* (San Antonio: Alamo Printing Co., 1921), 55. Juan N. Seguín was elected mayor of San Antonio in 1841 and re-elected in 1842. See De la Teja, *Revolution Remembered*, 40–43.

68. H. Bailey Carroll, "TEXAN SANTA FE EXPEDITION," *Handbook of Texas Online* (http://www.tshaonline.org/handbook/online/articles/qyt03), accessed January 26, 2015. Uploaded on June 15, 2010. Published by the Texas State Historical Association. Of the other two signers, Lorenzo de Zavala (originally from Yucatán) died in 1836, and José Francisco Ruiz in 1840.

69. Lamar to the People of Santa Fe, June 5, 1841, *Lamar Papers*, 3: 490.

70. The speech, written at Lamar's behest by Reuben M. Potter, is quoted in Crisp, "*¡Mucho Cuidado!*" 127.

71. Lamar, "Message to Congress," November 3, 1841, quoted in William C. Binkley, *The Expansionist Movement in Texas, 1836–1850* (Berkeley: University of California Press, 1925), 60. See also Hogan, *Texas Republic*, 100; and the letters of Branch T. Archer to Thomas Jefferson Green, May 1, May 15, and August 31, 1840, T. J. Green Papers, Southern Historical Collection, University of North Carolina at Chapel Hill.

72. Lamar, "Address to Citizens," June 5, 1841, quoted in Mark E. Nackman, *A Nation within a Nation: The Rise of Texas Nationalism* (Port Washington, NY: Kennikat Press, 1975), 98–99; Samuel A. Roberts to William G. Cooke, J[osé] Antonio Navarro, Richard F. Brenham, and William G. Dryden, June 15, 1841, *Diplomatic Correspondence of the Republic of Texas*, 2: 738.

73. For Navarro's imprisonment and escape, see George Wilkins Kendall, *Narrative of the Texan Santa Fé Expedition*, Gerald D. Saxon and William B. Taylor, eds., 2 vols. (Dallas, TX: DeGolyer Library and William P. Clements Center for Southwest Studies, 2004), 2: 237–38.

74. Sam Houston, "First Message to Congress, Second Administration," *Writings of Sam Houston*, 2: 402.

75. Anson Jones, *Memoranda and Official Correspondence Relating to the Republic of Texas, its History and Annexation* (1859; reprint, New York: Arno Press, 1973), 36.

76. Joseph Milton Nance, *Attack and Counterattack: The Texas-Mexican Frontier, 1842* (1964; digital edition, TSHA Online: A Digital Gateway to Texas History), 7.

77. De la Teja, *Revolution Remembered*, 42–50. Though he remained in the Mexican service throughout the rest of the Texas Republic's existence, and fought against the United States in that country's war with Mexico, Seguín kept in contact with friends in Texas (such as Sam Houston), and returned to San Antonio in 1848 to regain his Texas citizenship.

78. Jack Jackson, *Los Tejanos* (Stamford, CT: Fantagraphics Books, Inc., 1982), 90.

79. David Montejano, *Anglos and Mexicans in the Making of Texas, 1836–1986* (Austin: University of Texas Press, 1987), 82, 165, 223–25.

80. Statement of Bernardo Arze et al., (Houston) *Morning Star*, October 10, 1843.

81. See Don Graham, "Remembering the Alamo: The Story of the Texas Revolution in Popular Culture," *Southwestern Historical Quarterly* 89, no. 1 (July 1985): 35–66.

82. Bertram Wyatt-Brown, *Southern Honor: Ethics and Behavior in the Old South* (New York: Oxford University Press, 1982). See in particular Chapter 15, "Policing Slave Society: Insurrectionary Scares," 402–434.

83. Nackman, *Nation within a Nation*, 102–103.

84. Hogan, *Texas Republic*, 82. See also ibid., 65, 94–95, 100.

85. (Houston) *Telegraph and Texas Register*, July 27, 1842.

86. See the observations by the British observer William Bollaert for May 27, 1844 in Eugene W. Hollon and Ruth Lapham Butler, eds., *William Bollaert's Texas* (Norman: University of Oklahoma Press, 1956), 350; and those of Thomas Jefferson Green, *Journal of the Texian Expedition Against Mier*, Sam W. Haynes, ed. (Austin: W. Thomas Taylor, 1993), 64.

87. (Houston) *Morning Star*, Sept. 14, 1843.

88. Anson Jones, "State of the Republic Address," December 16, 1844, *Journals of the House of Representatives of the Ninth Congress of the Republic of Texas* (Washington[-on-the-Brazos]: Miller & Cushney, 1845), 66.

89. (Houston) *Morning Star*, Jan. 6, 1842.

90. (Houston) *Telegraph and Texas Register*, March 8, 1843.

91. Hogan, *Texas Republic*, 293.

92. Quoted in Wayne Gard, "Life in the Land of Beginning Again," in Stephen B. Oates, ed., *The Republic of Texas* (Palo Alto, CA: American West Publishing Company, 1968), 44–45.

93. Benjamin B. Peck to Mrs. Nikolas Peck, November 10, 1841, in David Holman, comp., *Letters of Hard Times in Texas, 1840–1890* (Austin: Roger Beacham, Publisher, 1974), 7–8.

94. From the (Galveston) *Civ[ilian]*, quoted in the (Clarksville) *Northern Standard*, March 6, 1845.

PART II:
Defending the Republic

Chapter 4
Army of the Texas Republic, 1836–1845

Joseph G. Dawson III

Moses Austin Bryan, nephew of Stephen F. Austin, recalled that the "Father of Texas" had once stated, "the salvation of Texas depends on the army being sustained. …" Concerned about the Army's preparedness, President Sam Houston asserted that the Republic's Army "is the salvation of the country." Rumors swirled around the threat of a Mexican campaign in Texas, as Mexican offensives were possible after the Battle of San Jacinto in April 1836 until the United States annexed Texas in 1845. For the Republic to survive, Texans believed that it needed its own army.[1] Respectable armies demand soldiers, of course, but also require financing, logistics, and citizen support. Operating without adequate funds, the Texas Congress routinely limited the Army's finances. Such limitations rendered the Republic's continued existence uncertain when its enemies attacked and also, ironically, when Texans assumed the offensive. An inadequate army raised doubts about the Republic's ability to effective engage its two primary enemies—Mexico and Native Americans. The Texas Army's meager strength never dissuaded either Mexicans or the Comanche from taking aggressive actions but it never had to fight a European army.

Uniting in their views about the importance of an army to the Republic, famous Texas leaders gave the fledging nation an element of exceptionalism. And long after the Texas Republic faded into a glorious memory, Texans, especially Anglo Texans, were still proud that Texas had stood independent. Across the years, Anglo Texans proclaimed that many factors, encrusted by myth and legend, made their state distinctive.[2] For instance, Texans asserted that their region afforded extraordinary opportunities exemplified by plentiful land and widespread property ownership, at least for Anglos, putting aside the matter that Native Americans as well as Mexico contested the claim of Texans for that land. Throughout a spacious territory, an energetic image (or marvelous mirage) formed of thriving ranches employing hundreds of cowboys driving big herds of cattle to distant markets. Texans appeared to demonstrate remarkable readiness for military service, using firearms, and defending liberty, as represented by the renowned battles of the Alamo and San Jacinto.[3] Other Texans, including the Texas Rangers, also declared they had a belligerent prowess in fighting Indians.[4] Larger-than-life adventures hid controversies surrounding the Texas Rangers. Nevertheless, the Rangers created a reputation about arresting bandits and suppressing riots supposedly unmatched by any other law enforcement agency. Swaggering with a take-on-all-comers attitude, Texans recounted their stories with braggadocio and projected an independent, irrepressible outlook.[5]

While none of these factors has been exclusive to Texas, surviving as an independent Republic in a highly contested region for over a decade was a *substantive factor* that Texans could contend made their state "exceptional."[6] Naturally, Texans dismissed assertions of other states that claim to have been a republic on par with the Republic of Texas during their early history, especially California but also other regions within the *initial* forty-eight states of the United States.[7] Texans asserted that each of these so-called republics, unlike the Lone Star Republic, functioned independently under its own government for only a brief period of time and that the only republic recognized by European nations was Texas. Having their own army seemed to strengthen the Texans' assertions.[8]

Although Anglo Texans marked their state as "exceptional," depending on how historians define this term, it may attach to others. For example, historian Pekka Hämäläinen applies the term "exceptional" to describe the extensive and long-lasting "Comanche Empire," one of the Republic's major enemies. Hämäläinen argues that for more than a century the Comanche dominated numerous Native American tribes and held at arm's length such powers as Spain, Mexico, France, Britain, and the United States. In his analysis, the "Comanche Empire" lasted longer, covered a bigger area, and exercised greater influence on international and intertribal relationships than Texas. Therefore, Hämäläinen concludes, "exceptional" appropriately pertains to the Comanche Empire but should *not* apply to Texas.[9] No doubt, the debate over Texas "exceptionalism" will continue.

The army of the Republic attracted citizen support, including when temporary troops also served. These troops contributed to a military mystique; some even said a military tradition.[10] Texans, especially Anglo Texans, recounted how sincere settlers started a risky revolution and American adventurers rushed to help. They overcame defeats at Goliad and the Alamo. Although outnumbered, Texans won independence at San Jacinto, defeating the bigger and better organized Mexican Army led by the self-proclaimed "Napoleon of the West," General Antonio Lopez de Santa Anna. Subsequently, enrolling hundreds of undisciplined volunteers from the United States and supplemented by controversial units of Rangers, the Republic's Army struggled to protect Texas and respond to its enemies.[11]

After San Jacinto, General Sam Houston demanded that Santa Anna concede an independent Texas that included a vast area, spilling beyond the traditional borders of the former Mexican province of Coahuila y Tejas. From east to west, the new Republic stretched from the Sabine River (along the U.S.A.'s Louisiana boundary) westward to the Rio Grande, supposedly including Santa Fe, the capital of Mexico's province of Nuevo Mexico. From north to south, Texas reached from the Red River and the Staked Plains down to the Rio Grande. Expansive and demanding, Texas swallowed the small numbers of troops that the Republic kept under arms.[12]

Seeking the trappings of a sovereign government, unrealistic Texas leaders envisioned formal army units commanded by capable commissioned officers and comprised of reliable sergeants and enlisted soldiers. Modeling its army partly on the U.S. Army, the Republic called for its regular soldiers to enlist for three years, though the U.S. Army required five-year enlistments. Texas issued commissions, specified army ranks and units, printed regulations, and designed uniforms. The descriptions of its uniforms revealed the Texas Army's high expectations for itself, though its War Department often ran short of supplies.[13]

The Texas Congress passed laws to establish its conventional army and revised statutes over the years. If fully funded by the Congress and directed by the president, the Army's Infantry Regiment, Cavalry Regiment, and Artillery Batteries could have totaled between 2,500 and 3,500 officers, sergeants, corporals, and privates. Several factors reduced the army's strength, however. Financial shortfalls and political squabbles led presidents to muster out some soldiers, making it rare for them to serve full enlistments. Units never recruited up to full strength, and routine attrition resulted from death by disease and accidents, desertions, and discharges due to illness, injury, and courts martial.[14]

According to an 1840 plan, the Army wanted to scatter posts along a defensive perimeter guarding the western settlements. Maintaining patrols presented challenges, as few of the conventional units were mounted. Cavalry was the most expensive form of military organization.[15] Without a steady national income, Texas continually operated at a deficit. Consequently, like other governmental departments, the War

Department had difficulty paying either its soldiers or its creditors. Instead, the government often issued promissory notes or script. Somehow finding businesses willing to sell products on credit, the War Department purchased some weapons and supplies, but often was unable to outfit all its troops.[16]

In contrast to the United States, where the federal government stipulated how to commission its army officers, enlisted men in the Texas Army voted to elect many of their officers, a procedure only approved among American volunteers and militia. Texas soldiers elected those closest to them, company officers such as lieutenants and captains, but also more senior officers, majors through colonels, creating rivalries within the ranks. The president and the secretary of war assigned the Army's three generals, as well as designating other officers. Though the U.S. Army prohibited such public expressions by its soldiers, Texas privates and sergeants were able to state their dissatisfaction with their officers. When a majority of their troops did not support them, Texas officers sometimes resigned. A notable example occurred in 1836, when General Mirabeau B. Lamar resigned suddenly after outspoken troops opposed him.[17]

Despite the bedrock democracy of the Texas Army, considerable authority still rested with the Republic's president, as commander in chief, to raise, discipline, direct, and discharge military personnel. In a significant example of presidential action, deciding to undermine General Felix Huston's wild plan to attack Mexico in 1837, President Houston "furloughed" the army's soldiers, effectively discharging most of the army.[18]

In emergencies, Texas supplemented the Army by gathering men of uneven quality in undisciplined outfits: volunteers, Rangers, and militia. None belonged to the regular Army establishment, and circumstances influenced their service. County militia sometimes did not rendezvous unless imminent danger menaced their homes. Temporary volunteers sometimes enlisted reluctantly, as they knew that the Republic usually could not pay them. Ranger companies favored operating on their own.[19] Paid or not, men in these outfits signed on for short terms, usually for a particular campaign. Even with these necessary supplements, a conventional army often enrolling only one thousand men or fewer, was inadequate to defend the large Republic, proved incapable of conducting offensives into Mexico, and had limited success against the strongest Indians.

Abiding by the precepts of many Americans, Texans established a small conventional army that posed no danger to civilian governance, knowing it needed assistance from temporary troops, but the Army was not a reflection of Texas society. In 1836, the Texas population was estimated at about 30,000 Anglos, 3,500 Tejanos, and 5,000 African Americans, most of whom were slaves. In addition, perhaps 14,000 Native Americans lived across Texas. The population grew in the next decade.[20] The U.S. Army set the example, limiting who could serve for a specified term. The Texas Army accepted unmarried recruits "of good character," enlisting on their own choice, who were "free white male persons ... who speak and understand the English language." Therefore, much in contrast to the U.S. Army of the late twentieth and twenty-first centuries, the Texas Army enlisted no women, no African Americans (free or slaves), and no Indians. Unofficially, slave owners brought slaves into Army camps and took them in the field. Officers arranged for Indian scouts, but none officially enlisted as soldiers. On the other hand, dozens of Hispanics served as soldiers, including several high-profile Tejanos such as José Antonio Navarro and Juan N. Seguín, leaders who influenced other Tejanos to join.[21]

Responsibility for administering the Army went to a civilian, the member of the president's cabinet serving as secretary of war.[22] Texans followed the U.S. cabinet system, where presidents sought capable administrators but chose all appointees for political reasons. To serve as Texas secretary of war, appointees were not required to be veterans but most had military experience. Most of them had arrived in Texas from the slave states during the 1830s. Having few resources, most war secretaries still fulfilled the job satisfactorily. In the hectic year of 1836, finishing the Revolution and getting the Republic's government underway, several men served as secretary of war, leading to a high turnover rate.[23]

Among the most logical choices, Kentuckian Albert Sidney Johnston held the war portfolio from December 1838 to March 1840. Excellent credentials hid the fact that he disliked dealing with soldiers who served for only a few months. Naturally, Johnston's education and years in the U.S. Army shaped his outlook. Graduating in 1826 from the U.S. Military Academy at West Point, New York, eighth in his class of forty-one cadets, Johnston was the rare professional officer among Texas Army officers and war secretaries. He served in the U.S. Army at the lowest commissioned ranks of first lieutenant and second lieutenant before resigning in 1834 and moving to Texas in 1836. Catapulting to the rank of general, he learned that Texans bridled at the regimentation expected of U.S. Army soldiers, and he and President Houston often disagreed on policy matters. Of greater concern to Johnston and everyone who decried Texans' lack of discipline, subordinate officers sometimes were unwilling to respond to Johnston's orders. Although dueling violated Texas Army regulations (as it violated U.S. Army regulations), Johnston yielded to his emotions in January 1837 and used pistols to fight a duel with a disputatious subordinate general, Felix Huston. Johnston outranked Huston, but Huston's questioning of Johnston's authority to command was a matter of honor. Huston's pistol bullet seriously wounded Johnston, who took months to heal. According to Anglo Texans, Johnston, after recovering from his wound, earned notoreity in the campaign against the Cherokee in 1839.[24]

Turning to cabinet appointees, Presidents Houston and Lamar naturally selected cabinet members they favored. A Tennessee friend of President Houston, George W. Hockley, moved to Texas in 1835. In the rank of colonel with the Revolutionary Army, Hockley was adjutant (supervising records and assisting General Houston) during the San Jacinto campaign. He later directed the War Department's Ordnance section (dealing with weapons and ammunition). He accepted the post of secretary of war under Houston in 1841–1842. Originally from Virginia, Branch T. Archer was one of the best-educated Texas officials but his military résumé was thin. He earned a medical degree from the University Pennsylvania in 1808, practiced medicine back home, and was elected to the Virginia legislature. He arrived in Texas in 1831. During the Revolution, Archer engaged Mexicans at the Battle of Gonzales in 1835, accompanied Stephen Austin to represent Texas as a special delegate to the United States, and then voters elected him to the First Texas Congress. Picked by President Lamar, Archer held the War Office from March 1840 through July 1841.[25]

Compiling his military record, William G. Cooke, also a Virginian, joined the "New Orleans Greys," a company raised in Louisiana during the Texas Revolution. Soldiers elected Cooke lieutenant and later a captain and he fought at San Antonio in 1835 and served as an aide to Sam Houston. Houston made Cooke acting secretary of war in November 1836, but switched him to be the Army's Inspector General (inspecting unit capabilities) and Quartermaster General (dealing with housing soldiers). As a colonel, Cooke established garrisons on the frontier and commanded the First Texas Infantry Regiment, one of the Army's largest units, briefly enrolling hundreds of soldiers.[26] Accompanying the Texan Santa Fe Expedition in 1841, Cooke was taken prisoner and detained in Mexico until 1842. To obtain his release, he had to swear never again to engage in military action against Mexico. Instead, upon returning to Texas, he promptly rejoined the Texas Army to oppose General Adrián Woll's Mexican offensive in 1842. President Houston designated Cooke to be

Quartermaster General and he went with the Somervell Expedition to the Rio Grande. In December 1844, President Anson Jones again appointed Cooke secretary of war.[27]

Leading the soldiers, Texas officers typically lacked a formal education, military training, or prior service in a professional army. This was not out of the ordinary in the nineteenth century, when many Americans and Texans believed in the concept of "natural soldiers"—men with little or no military experience springing to the battle line in wartime. They recalled glorious heroes from the American Revolution, such as George Washington, Nathanael Greene, and Daniel Morgan and, more recently from the War of 1812, Andrew Jackson. All of them won reputations as excellent officers who became generals without benefit of attending a military academy or even graduating from college.

Despite duplicating features of the U.S. Army, Texas politicians demonstrated practicality by deciding *not* to establish a military college. In the era of the Texas Republic, one-third of U.S. Army officers received appointments directly from civilian life without having enrolled in college. The U.S. Military Academy admitted fifty or more cadets per year, but gradually cadets dropped out and numbers of graduates varied annually. Through the class of 1838, West Pointers even had the option to resign from the Army immediately following graduation. It was only after 1838 when the U.S. Government required West Point graduates to serve in the Army for four years.[28] Thus, Americans and Texans knew that many officers gained commissions without attending an academy or college.

Therefore, unlike Albert Sidney Johnston, most Texas officers had little interest in establishing a professional ethos. Among Texans, such attitudes about "natural soldiers" being appointed from civilian life produced an ambiguous attitude about serious points of military protocol and behavior. As with Felix Huston, Texans felt no compulsion about standing on rank or ceremony, and frequently did not acknowledge a superior officer's authority as something that came with their rank.

Empresarios sang the praises of the Republic but it attracted few men from the U.S. Military Academy. Those who came to Texas exerted little positive influence. For instance, William S. Stillwell graduated from the Academy in 1827. Stillwell resigned in 1833 and joined the Texas Revolution, fought at San Jacinto, but died in 1837. John T. Collinsworth earned his diploma in 1830 and resigned in 1836. For a time, Collinsworth held the post of Texas Inspector General, but he also died in 1837.

George B. Crittenden finished at West Point in 1832. He soon resigned. Moving to Texas, Crittenden accepted a lieutenancy in the Army and marched with the Somervell-Mier Expedition. Taken prisoner, Crittenden's health suffered badly, limiting his contribution to the Texas Army.[29]

Two exceptions stood out among West Pointers. Albert Sidney Johnston was notable as a general and secretary of war. The other was Hugh McLeod. Nearly denied graduation for academic deficiency, he finished fifty-sixth of fifty-six cadets in 1835 and resigned a few months later. Although youthful, McLeod was dynamic and served in Texas as Adjutant General, Inspector General, and a field commander (to be discussed below).[30]

Others also attended West Point. James W. Fannin enrolled at the Academy in 1819 but left in 1821, before he was eligible to graduate. During the Texas Revolution, Fannin wrangled a major command at Goliad, some 650 men, one of the largest contingents of Texans. Indecision haunted Fannin, however. Plummeting to ignominy, he surrendered his troops to the Mexicans in 1836 and they executed him. Fannin's slipshod leadership tarnished West Point's reputation among Texans.

Thomas Jefferson Green entered West Point in July 1822 but resigned only four months later. Leaving the Academy did not stop Green from serving the Republic militarily. However, his actions on the Somervell-Mier Expedition were questionable at best. Joseph Bonnell was a unique case. Graduating with the Academy class of 1825, Bonnell was still serving in the U.S. Army at the same time he was a special aide to Sam Houston in the Texas Army in 1835. Bonnell briefly represented Texas (not the United States) in official negotiations with the Caddo Indians.[31]

In contrast to heroic stereotypes, the Republic's army officers featured a hodge-podge of literacy, skills, and accomplishments. Personal impressions, meritorious actions, and rhetorical ability might converge, resulting in an officer getting a major command. Those attaining high rank seldom held it throughout the Republic years and the officer corps usually was in flux, however. Texas officers at all ranks, from lieutenant to general, came and went, resigning their commissions when they wished and returning to the Army later. Upon resigning, some joined the volunteers, Rangers, or the militia. If a man ran for political office, he cited this checklist of military credits. Among the many officers who were not West Pointers, Edward Burleson, William Fisher, Felix Huston, Thomas Rusk, Alexander Somervell, and Juan Seguín ranked among the most important, though not always for winning victories as combat leaders.

Edward Burleson. Army Officer and Vice President, Republic of Texas. 1850 Daguerreotype. Courtesy of the Texas State Library and Archives Commission.

Edward Burleson made his mark as a combat officer. A North Carolinian, Burleson had served in the War of 1812 as well in the militias of Missouri and Tennessee before moving to Texas at age thirty-two. In 1835, Burleson's personality and capability persuaded Stephen Austin, then a Texas general, to make Burleson a lieutenant colonel. Temporarily promoted to the rank of general in command of the Revolutionary Army, Burleson fought at San Antonio before the army temporarily disbanded in 1835 and took the field again at San Jacinto. With independence seemingly secured, Burleson joined the militia but accepted President Lamar's commission to command the Army's Frontier Regiment, fighting against the Cherokee in 1839 and the Comanche in 1840. Following Burleson's exploits, Texans elected him vice president in 1841. Having been in and out of the Army, he returned to oppose two major Mexican Army invasions in 1842.[32]

Like other Texans, William Fisher entertained a high opinion of his own military abilities. To his credit, he raised a company of soldiers and led them at San Jacinto. His leadership impressed Sam Houston, who appointed Fisher secretary of war for several months (1836–1837). Later, President Lamar assigned Fisher as an Army colonel. Fisher opened fire on Comanche treaty negotiators at San Antonio's Council House in 1840. Demonstrating his lack of military acuity in 1842, Fisher failed to understand the desperate plight of Somervell's Expedition to the Rio Grande. Continuing the expedition after Somervell wisely advocated retreat, Fisher led a rump portion of Texas troops to disaster at Mier. He languished in Perote Prison for months and, after his release, died in 1845. Fisher's importance is not due to his success in battle or praiseworthy leadership. Despite holding high rank and responsibility, he was an official who failed to grasp tactical realities and underestimated the Mexican Army.[33]

Although promoted to high ranks, Felix Huston rivaled Fisher for demonstrating bad leadership. A Mississippian, Huston was an example of a headstrong southerner who found it impossible to serve as a capable subordinate until promotion came his way, perform assignments, and lead under pressure. Intrigued by Huston's personality, President Houston designated him as junior brigadier general of the Texas Army, but then posted Albert Sidney Johnston to take command. As described above, Huston reacted by challenging Johnston to a duel instead of either resigning his commission or staying on as a brigadier general in a subordinate capacity. Huston lacked a realistic understanding of the fiscal and military circumstances in Texas, recommending to Houston that the

Republic raise an army of five thousand to enforce the Rio Grande as the Republic's boundary. Houston rejected the plan as impossible. Huston's highlight came in 1840 when he commanded Texas forces in a victory over the Comanche at Plum Creek. Seeing no further military prospects, Huston abandoned Texas to practice law in New Orleans before returning to Mississippi, where he died in 1857.[34]

Thomas J. Rusk joined the list of high-ranking officers with more faults than accomplishments. In Rusk's case, he flew from one office to another as though he collected titles for his résumé. Rusk closed a law practice in Georgia and pledged himself to Texas independence. Enlisting, he left the army before fighting at San Antonio in 1835. Nevertheless, he latched on to the post of inspector general for three months. Present at the creation, Rusk signed the Texas Declaration of Independence. He added the office of ad interim secretary of war to his list before fighting bravely at the Battle of San Jacinto, impressing Sam Houston. In a questionable move, Houston designated Rusk commander in chief and brigadier general in the Army from May to October 1836, when Rusk again took the post of secretary of war. He soon resigned from the cabinet. As a militia officer (not in the Army), Rusk suppressed a suspected Tejano plot in the Cordova Rebellion, helped defeat the Kickapoo in 1838, and fought the Cherokee in 1839. He rose to a seat on the Texas Supreme Court but soon resigned to open a law practice. As a high-ranking officer, Rusk never focused on developing an effective military for Texas.[35]

Alexander Somervell became controversial by showing more caution and willingness to analyze enemy forces than most senior officers. Born in Maryland in 1796, Somervell resided in Louisiana and Missouri and then pursued ventures in Texas in 1833. Supporting the Texas Revolution, he fought at San Jacinto, served as secretary of war, and was twice elected to the Texas Congress. Soldiers were skeptical of Somervell's cautious approach when Sam Houston appointed him to the rank of brigadier general to lead an expedition in response to the Mexican Army's incursions of 1842. In command of one of the largest combined forces of Texans (perhaps eight hundred men, including militia, volunteers, Rangers, and Army soldiers), Somervell marched to Laredo. After capturing Laredo and the town of Guerrero, Somervell grew concerned that continuing the expedition was too risky. Reports indicated that Mexican troops moved toward them, the Texans' supplies were running out, and hundreds deserted the expedition. Somervell called for retreat, ending his military service, but William Fisher decided to forge ahead. The Mexicans defeated Fisher at Mier.[36]

Juan Nepomuceno Seguín was distinctive in several ways. Winning political offices in San Antonio before 1835, Seguín joined the Revolution and became the most important Tejano in the Army. Stephen Austin made Seguín an Army captain. An effective cavalry leader, Seguín was popular with Revolutionary leaders and Tejano troopers elected him to higher ranks. He fought at San Antonio and San Jacinto. Seguín's army record resulted in his return to politics. Voters elected him to Congress three times, and as mayor of San Antonio. Then he turned away from the Republic. Colluding with Mexican General Rafael Vásquez during 1842 stained Seguín's reputation. Further accusations of treason dogged him due to being involved in General Adrián Woll's incursion. Seguín thus rose and fell in the eyes of Anglo Texans, leading many to question the loyalty of other Tejanos. Significant to winning Texas independence, Seguín might have enhanced Anglo acceptance of Tejanos in the future if he had remained devoted to the Texas Republic.[37]

Three men were president of the independent Republic: Sam Houston, Mirabeau Lamar, and Anson Jones. They possessed varied military experiences but were untutored in military studies (as were most U.S. presidents). Victorious due to aggressive leadership at San Jacinto, Houston had acted cautiously before then, correctly understanding the fragility of the Revolutionary Army. Lamar had held the ranks of colonel and general in the Republic's Army, though he was a general for only a short time before resigning from the military. Jones, a medical practitioner and pharmacist, had been a surgeon for the Army during the San Jacinto campaign. While guiding Texas toward annexation to the United States, one of Jones's greatest fears was renewed hostilities with Mexico, a situation that might prompt Americans to reconsider adding Texas to the Union.

Strategy is complex, but Houston and Lamar's options boiled down to either offense or defense. In both of his presidential terms, Houston stressed defense. Financial and political realities reinforced Houston's choice. Rather than military actions, Houston expected diplomacy with Indian tribes to yield results. Houston acknowledged that Mexico remained a threat but he explained that until Mexican troops crossed the Rio Grande, logic dictated forgoing offensives and keeping a small army. To deal with temporary emergencies, Houston persuaded Texans to rely on county militias, Rangers, and short-term volunteers. Succeeding Houston into office, Lamar chose a contrasting strategy. Believing in Texas exceptionalism and knowing Texans' belligerence, skill with firearms, and reputed enthusiasm for combat, Lamar took risks by approving poorly calculated offensives.[38]

Texas presidents never wished to antagonize the United States, the friendly power bordering the Republic on the east and north. America sent immigrants rather than invaders to Texas, but elsewhere, Texas confronted serious enemies. Native Americans inside Texas competed for use of the land. Some Texans concluded that only completely removing the Indians, including some tribes that were either weak or not belligerent, would cancel any threat they posed. More directly, Mexico possessed military forces capable of attacking Texas. Additionally, some Texans worried that Tejanos might plot with either Mexico or Indians inside the Republic, fomenting an internal war. It was possible that Texas might fight internal and external enemies simultaneously.

To the south and west, Mexico was the Republic's primary external enemy, and Mexico intended to reassert its sovereignty over Texas, as Mexico's leaders trumpeted the likelihood of attacks. The Mexican army numbered upwards of 20,000 soldiers, a substantial force with considerable potential.[39] Several factors hindered Mexico's chances to regain control of Texas, however. Since winning independence from Spain in 1821, Mexican nationalism had struggled. Multiple provinces tried to secede, including Texas, Yucatán, Tabasco, and Zacatecas. Therefore, the government stationed its best regiments in Central Mexico to protect the capital, Mexico City. Garrisons in Mexico's "Far North," such as California and Coahuila y Tejas, hosted the least proficient troops.[40] Most soldiers were poor, unenthusiastic draftees anxious to go home. Furthermore, Mexicans mismanaged their national budgets, producing financial insolvency and rising debts. The army suffered from uncertain pay, uneven training, and unreliable muster rolls.[41] Therefore, the Mexican army operated short of funds, quality firearms, and other necessities that expeditions needed to advance across hundreds of miles. Mexico did maintain a small military college attended by cadets training to become junior officers, but setting bad examples, senior officers often interfered in politics, making it impossible to foster military professionalism—the expectation that military officers trained seriously, respected election results, took orders from elected civilian officials, and served conscientiously for twenty years or more. Mexico's Army was top-heavy with officers obtaining commissions for pay and prestige but absent from their posts. Despite these drawbacks, some extraordinary army units, including most cavalry squadrons and select infantry regiments, demonstrated good training, capable officers, and adequate supplies.[42]

An international dispute with a major power revealed the overall inadequacy of Mexico's Army. To collect loans owed to French bankers,

France's military intervened in Mexico from March 1838 to February 1839. France's intervention insulted Mexican nationalism but helped Texas by shifting the Mexican Army's attention away from the Republic to activities closer to Mexico City. In addition to dealing with French intruders, Mexican garrisons repeatedly failed to provide an adequate defense against Comanche raiders, who ventured far south of the Rio Grande. Nevertheless, despite such deficiencies, Mexico's Army still posed a serious danger to Texas, one that peaked in 1842.[43]

Some of General Santa Anna's subordinates were of good quality. Six Mexican generals active during the years of the Texas Republic had compiled fifteen to twenty years of military service, including Pedro de Ampudia, Mariano Arista, Valentin Canalizo, Vicente Filisola, Rafael Vásquez, and Adrián Woll. They developed knowledge of soldiering, logistics, expeditionary planning, and battlefield tactics. Such officers should have had demonstrated advantages over novice Texan commanders.[44]

While Mexicans struggled to pacify secessionists and deal with the French, numerous Native American tribes inhabited Texas and Mexico. These included Comanches, Kiowas, Lipan Apaches, Cherokees, Shawnees, Choctaws, Caddos, Karankawas, Kickapoos, Tonkawas, and Wichitas. The United States had pushed some of them into Texas from east of the Mississippi River. Each tribe wanted to maintain a place in the region, but they existed separately, seldom cooperated, and did not unite in a confederation.[45]

The Comanche distinguished themselves as more belligerent and mobile than the rest. Along with their ally the Kiowa, the Comanche presented substantial dangers to all Texas residents and the Republic's assertion of sovereignty. The Comanche perceived only a cosmetic change in the transition from Mexican political administration to Texan governance. The tribe remained implacable foes of Anglos, Tejanos, and Mexicans.[46]

In a meeting with Sam Houston in 1844, Chief Old Owl plainly stated the Comanche outlook: Texas was "Comanche land and ever has been."[47] Texas formed a part of the Comanche "empire" encompassing lands stretching from modern Kansas into Chihuahua and Durango south of the Rio Grande. From 1750 to 1850, Spaniards, Mexicans, Anglos, Tejanos, and other Indians resided in "Comancheria" at the sufferance of the Comanche, who had displaced rival tribes and put their empire and everyone living within it to their own use. Never intimidated by the Spanish colonial army or the Mexican Army, the Comanche had proved their military advantage over Mexico's settlers and small garrisons as they hunted bison, their main sustenance. Participating in their own method of warfare, hundreds of mounted Comanche successfully conducted economic raids for weeks at a time, moving at will across Texas and other provinces, seizing animals, property, and especially captives. Captives were incorporated into the tribe, ransomed, or sold as slaves. The Comanche usually avoided towns, which were typically populated by well armed residents who could inflict casualties and make a raid costly. Looking ahead to the next raid to take more animals, supplies, and captives, the Comanche often left surviving settlers with enough to rebuild. In addition to seizing what they wanted, the Comanche bargained with adventurous traders for all sorts of goods and employed diplomacy to their advantage, demanding tribute or negotiating, as the situation warranted. They effectively manipulated these combinations, and the region appeared to belong to them—"nuanced, orderly, and reassuring," according to historian Pekka Hämäläinen's interpretation.[48]

A key element in the Comanche empire meant that they were "expecting others to conform to their cultural order," as Hämäläinen concludes. In that arrangement, Comanche society reveled in hunting, raiding, and imposing their will, including on other Indians. Their empire would last until some other competitor brought considerable power to bear against them.[49]

Texans wished to gradually tighten their grip on lands the Republic claimed, placing them on a collision course with the Comanche. Texans further upset the Comanche cultural order by defeating or driving out smaller tribes, such as the Cherokee, Choctaw, Shawnee, Caddo, Kickapoo, and Wichita. The Texas capital at Austin, a small town of fewer than one thousand residents, was vulnerable to attack.[50] Some recognized that their conventional Army and defenses were inadequate but reacted to the Comanche mostly with mobile forces of Rangers, militia, and temporary volunteers. Even if it took many years, Texans vowed to eventually defeat the Comanche.[51]

Battles of the Republic involved small numbers of combatants, but they loomed large to Texans. The size of battles in Texas contrasted with the War of 1812, the U.S.-Mexican War, the Civil War, or the post-Civil War Indian campaigns. However, they occurred at a time when many still recalled notable small battles from the American Revolution and the War of 1812. For instance, in the American Revolution, at Bunker Hill only around one thousand Americans fought two thousand British troops. Washington crossed the Delaware River with 2,400 Americans to engage 1,400 Hessians at Trenton, New Jersey. At King's Mountain,

South Carolina, one thousand British encountered about nine hundred Americans. In Daniel Morgan's amazing victory at Cowpens, South Carolina, each side fielded about one thousand soldiers. In the War of 1812, General Winfield Scott raised U.S. morale by winning at Chippewa, Canada, where 1,300 Americans defeated 1,700 British. Andrew Jackson led two thousand Americans against nine hundred Creek warriors at Horseshoe Bend, Alabama.[52]

During 1837 and 1838, Texans fought no major battles with either Native Americans or Mexico. This relative peace resulted from Sam Houston's stress on not antagonizing any enemy, giving the Republic of Texas time to establish itself. Houston especially sought peace with the Cherokee, even as the Comanche conducted their accustomed raids.[53]

In December 1838 the new president, Mirabeau Lamar, discarded Houston's approach and changed strategy to offense. At Brushy Creek in February 1839, Texans skirmished with the Comanche outside of Austin. On July 15–16 on the Neches River, Texans won a major battle over the Cherokee, Delaware, Shawnee, and Kickapoo. Leading volunteers and other Texas troops, General Thomas Rusk and Colonel Edward Burleson attacked a Cherokee camp. Casualties totaled at least six Texans killed and forty wounded, and Cherokee losses amounted to one hundred wounded and twenty dead, including Chief Bowl, a leader distinguished for his efforts at peace. Lamar's aggressive approach led many members of several tribes to abandon Texas and relocate across the U.S. border into the "Indian Territory" (modern Oklahoma). This outcome opened Indian lands to Anglo settlement and reduced the number of tribes that the Comanche plundered, altering the social conditions in Texas.[54]

The next year the Comanche opened negotiations with Texans. A temporary truce or a treaty lasting several months could have allowed the Comanche to focus on other vulnerable prey without expecting hostilities with Texans. Texans might have benefited from a truce if it allowed them to turn their attention "to cope with Mexico."[55] Preceding substantive negotiations, President Lamar demanded that one band of Comanche, the Penateka, return several Anglo captives Texans accused them of taking. They agreed to confer in San Antonio in March 1840.

Bringing their families, a large delegation of Penateka leaders arrived at a meeting place called the Council House. But they brought only one captive, thus violating how Texans interpreted the preliminary arrangement. Anticipating trouble, Lamar's Special Commissioners, including Hugh McLeod and William Cooke, had come armed to the meeting. Inside the Council House, Texans killed several Comanche negotiators.

Outside, Texans killed some sixty Comanche, including women and children. Surviving the fusillade of bullets, other Comanche escaped, bent on revenge.[56]

The Comanche considered the Council House meeting a massacre and in August they retaliated, campaigning through Central Texas, down to the Gulf Coast. Led by Chief Buffalo Hump, warriors attacked the towns of Victoria and Linnville, taking revenge on Anglo and Tejano civilians, but not seeking battle with Rangers or the Army. However, on August 11–12 battle was joined along Plum Creek, in Caldwell County, east of San Antonio. General Felix Huston led a Texan combined force, perhaps one hundred strong, but he was apprehensive about engaging the Comanche, who were burdened with plunder from the raid. Huston trusted Colonel Edward Burleson, plus Rangers under Benjamin McCulloch, to carry the fight. The Comanche suffered casualties of around forty killed and wounded. The Comanche balanced those losses against their success of obtaining hundreds of horses and mules and other plunder. Texans claimed to have low casualties, only one killed and seven wounded, but their undefended towns had made easy targets.[57]

Having struck back at the Comanche, in 1841 Lamar lashed out at Mexico. The president planned an expedition to seize Santa Fe, New Mexico. Texans reckoned it was part of the Republic. Mexicans dismissed the claim as ridiculous, as Santa Fe had never been part of Texas before. Lamar offered the expedition to an experienced campaigner, Edward Burleson, who declined due to an unnamed illness. Instead, Lamar turned to his young friend, General Hugh McLeod, who accepted command. Though Lamar persuaded a prestigious Tejano, José Antonio Navarro, to join the venture, no other Tejanos enlisted.[58]

Ostensibly intending to open access to the lucrative Santa Fe trade, McLeod's "Pioneers" included 270 soldiers and 50 merchants. Setting out from Austin on June 18, 1841, they had to cross more than seven hundred miles of inhospitable terrain. McLeod revealed his serious shortcomings. He failed to conduct adequate reconnaissance along alternate routes and disregarded the need to know about water availability. He and fellow officers packed insufficient supplies for such a trek. They had neither interviewed merchants familiar with Santa Fe to gain information, nor sent spies to ascertain Santa Fe's highly negative attitudes toward Texans. McLeod fell victim to the false outlook that those he expected to conquer would welcome him.

Mexican authorities learned of the expedition's small size and prepared to meet it. Without adequate rations and water, McLeod and his desperate troops arrived exhausted. On October 5, 1841, they surrendered to Mexican authorities, who locked them in prison.[59]

McLeod's Santa Fe Expedition exposed several points to everyone. Instead of easily seizing a defenseless city, the catastrophe showed Texans and others that campaigning in Mexico proved more difficult than they anticipated. Attackers needed to plan for a well-supplied force three or four times the size of McLeod's. In turn, the expedition gave Mexicans no reason to increase their respect for the Texas Army. Although Texans had struggled across terrain that some thought was nearly impassable for an expeditionary force, they failed to take Santa Fe but had revealed its vulnerability. Santa Fe craved reinforcements, but Mexico's government provided none, leaving it vulnerable to attack by the United States five years later.[60]

In partial response to the Texan Santa Fe Expedition, in 1842 President Santa Anna acted to reassert Mexican sovereignty over Texas. A Mexican army of 1,400 soldiers assembled near the Rio Grande and in February, some five hundred under General Rafael Vásquez advanced on San Antonio. Although its population had dwindled to fewer than one thousand residents, both Texans and Mexicans recognized that the city still represented a strategic location as a trade and financial center. Controlling it was symbolically important to both sides.[61]

On March 5 the city fell easily to Vásquez, demonstrating conclusively that the Texas Army was incapable of defending its frontier. Vásquez's organized force, more cohesive than any that Texans had mustered, could have occupied the city. Instead, after gathering some loot, on March 6, the Mexicans retreated. An army capable of conquering was instead conducting a temporary incursion.[62]

The Mexicans' offensive looked genuine and galvanized Texans to respond. Quickly reacting, Vice President Edward Burleson recruited three companies of short-term volunteers, and hundreds more, including militia and Rangers, flocked to join them, creating the combination that Texas substituted for a conventional army. Placing his own officer in charge, President Houston sent his cautious general, Andrew Somervell, to command, resulting in a standoff between Burleson and Somervell. Expressing themselves, the troops endorsed Burleson. While many Texans clamored for a counterattack, Houston planned to raise troops for *defense*. Opposing the president, Congress called for war against Mexico. Houston knew that an offensive was likely to fail, just as McLeod's had failed. As a politician, however, the president sensed the public attitude. He heard that "Burleson was at San Antonio with 1500 men" most of them supposedly "snorting" like bulls to attack Mexico. Switching his rhetoric, Houston publicly promoted an offensive, in contrast to his defensive intent, but he warned Somervell that "Texas at this time is not in a situation to invade Mexico" in the next four months.[63]

Although hundreds of Texans had mustered in response to Vásquez's "imposing" raid, Houston declined to dispatch an expedition. South of the Rio Grande, Mexican General Mariano Arista arranged a defense and requested reinforcements but only one hundred effective troops reached him. During June, undisciplined Texans idled, drank alcohol, and gambled in assembly camps. No combat seemed imminent and it appeared to Houston that recruits showed "a spirit of utter insubordination and mutiny openly prevailed." The war scare subsided and many Texas volunteers went home. However, in early July the Mexicans conducted a reconnaissance in force. The ensuing skirmish on July 7 at Lipantitlan, along the Nueces River northwest of Corpus Christi, resulted in light casualties on both sides.[64]

In an action unprecedented until the U.S.-Mexican War in 1846, during August a much bigger Mexican expedition of 1,500 under General Adrián Woll crossed the Rio Grande. Accompanying him were dozens of Cherokee and Vincente Córdova, leader of a Tejano plot against the Republic in 1838, reminding Texans of their internal enemies. On September 11, 1842, Woll occupied San Antonio. He captured the town as easily as Vásquez had six months earlier, confirming again the inadequate Texas defenses. This time Woll and his forces remained in the city a week. Making an ad hoc response, by September 17, about six miles northeast of San Antonio, illustrious Ranger officers John Coffee Hays, John H. Moore, and Mathew Caldwell had assembled outfits of volunteers, militia, and Rangers from several counties. Around three hundred men prepared a hasty defense. Meanwhile, Hays spurred scouts to San Antonio.[65]

Woll ordered hundreds of troops to pursue Hays's scouts. Near Salado Creek, the Mexicans began skirmishing with Caldwell and the others. With unlimbered cannon, Woll's artillerists fired salvos into the Texans' positions, shielded by groves of trees. Multiple Mexican attacks, resulting in numerous casualties, failed to dislodge the Texans. Because of the high casualty rate, Woll withdrew.[66]

Meanwhile, riding toward San Antonio from Fayette County, Captain Nicholas Dawson led fifty-three men to join Hays. Following behind them was a larger company of some eighty riders. Combined, their units would have been formidable. Scouts told Dawson about the battle at Salado Creek. He decided against waiting for the trailing troops and pressed ahead.

Five miles from the Salado Creek battle, Dawson encountered Lieutenant Colonel Cayetano Montero commanding four hundred Mexicans. The Texans found refuge in a grove of mesquite. Dismounting, they jolted the Mexicans with well-aimed musket fire. The Mexicans wisely responded by blasting the Texans with several artillery shots, forcing Dawson to offer to surrender. The Texans were trapped and, in no mood to be generous, Montero ordered the cannon to resume firing, wounding Dawson and several others. Dawson then urged Montero to accept their surrender, but again he refused.[67]

Mexican troops entered the mesquite grove and began killing the wounded Texans. Casualties of the Dawson fight totaled thirty Texans killed, including a black slave traveling with the detachment, along with thirty Mexicans killed and sixty wounded. Two Texans escaped but the Mexicans took fifteen prisoners. They were imprisoned in Mexico. The Mexicans' refusal to allow Dawson's surviving men to surrender added to the Texans' residual bitterness.[68]

Sympathizers told Woll that hundreds of Texans rushed to oppose him. During the night of September 18, leaving his campfires burning to feign his continued presence, Woll began his retreat from San Antonio.[69]

Only a few weeks after the battles near Salado Creek, Texans launched a major campaign reacting to the Vásquez and Woll incursions. Ironically, this big offensive came under Houston, who had stressed defense. Houston again assigned General Somervell, whose caution and modest demeanor contrasted with the obstreperous Edward Burleson, to command the expedition of more than eight hundred men who were enlisted into a motley group of regulars, militia, Rangers, and volunteers. While many of the men wanted to truly defend their nation, others enlisted as part of the invasion force, hoping to gain personal wealth from plunder acquired in Mexico. Their first objective was Laredo, north of the river. Finding Laredo undefended on December 8, the expedition seized and pillaged the town. Discipline began to collapse and several dozen men deserted. Somervell's campaign had started with many enlistees, reached the Rio Grande, and posed an ostensible threat to Mexico. For Somervell, he had achieved enough.[70]

On December 19 Somervell decided against crossing the river. He intended to end the campaign and urged retreat. Several men deserted. Not satisfied with Somervell's leadership or retreating without more plunder, others nominated Captain William Fisher (the former secretary of war) to take command at the rank of colonel. Somervell withdrew with 189 men, including Hays and most of the Rangers, leaving Fisher with three hundred men.[71]

Fisher's weakened contingent, slightly more than McLeod's Santa Fe Expedition, should have given the colonel pause. Another disaster loomed. General Pedro de Ampudia assembled nearly one thousand Mexicans (about six hundred soldiers along with militia) to defend Mier, a town eighty miles south of Laredo on the Mexican side of the Rio Grande. Texas scouts notified Fisher of the Mexican defenses. Unimpressed, Fisher led his men into Mier on Christmas Day. The resulting two-day battle trapped Fisher with no hope of escape. The battle was the Texans' second sequential failed offensive campaign. More than thirty Texans were killed and wounded, while Mexican casualties amounted to one hundred or more. Somervell had been right to end the campaign. Ampudia forced Fisher to surrender and marched the Texans to Perote Prison. Fisher's foolishness came to an ignominious end, demonstrating more Texan deficiencies in leadership, discipline, logistics, and reconnaissance.[72]

Nevertheless, the Mexican Army was unable to regain control of Texas after seven years of promising to conduct offensives, crowned by two major attacks in 1842. General Vicente Filisola had been overheard to say in 1839: " … Texas is lost to Mexico. We will never be able to retake it." Filisola had made the right assessment.[73]

There are several conclusions to draw about the Republic's Army. First, though it was always quite small, the Army contributed to the independence of Texas from 1836 to the eve of annexation by the United States. During the Republic era, Mexico tried and failed to reclaim Texas. In 1844, a wave of "Manifest Destiny" washed across the United States. The existence of the Republic, plus the intention of U.S. leaders to obtain California from Mexico, combined with America's annexation of Texas, led to the U.S.-Mexican War in 1846.[74]

For a decade, Mexico and Texas conducted bilateral negotiations, dramatized their mutual mistrust, and disputed their boundaries. Both sent armed forces into territory each had claimed. This confrontation was analogous to a "cold war." Leaders in both nations understood that combat during the military campaigns of 1841–1842 had occurred *without* a declaration of war. Trying to gain advantage, Mexico and Texas involved other nations in their disputes, especially Britain and America. After 1844, Mexicans and Texans were mired in an intensifying crisis, with neither willing to compromise: Mexico rejected the idea of Texas independence and Texas refused to change its boundary. War started not only over the Rio Grande boundary but over the question of whether all of Texas was a Mexican or an American state.[75] The war resulted in important consequences. It confirmed Texas annexation, resolved the Rio Grande boundary, and subdued Mexico, which never tried again to use military force to regain sovereignty over its former province.

Next, existing under tense conditions, the Texas Army, often only a few hundred soldiers, started small and remained small. It was not a deterrent to Mexico. The Texas Army contrasted with the Mexican Army of 20,000 and the U.S. Army of 8,000 or more. Sometimes, given the Republic's financial woes, its Army was barely more than an army on paper. The Texas military never matched in size what the Republic needed to defend its boundaries. Armed Texans failed to seize Santa Fe in 1841 or Mier in 1842. Mexican troops twice attacked San Antonio in 1842. Those belligerent actions did not prompt Texas or Mexican leaders to raise all capable men to the colors and conduct a major war. When those campaigns concluded, no diplomacy produced a formal treaty to officially end a war. Both sides backed off but antagonisms remained unrelieved.

Therefore, crises led each Texas president to request temporary volunteers, county militia, and Rangers to assist the Army, and often those unofficial supplements formed a greater percentage of the forces available than official Army units, as in campaigns against Indians. To the regret of the Cherokee, and sometimes the regret of the Mexican Army and the Comanche, those labels for armed Texans meant distinctions without differences, however. Once in motion toward an enemy, employing mobility and firepower, Texas troops were formidable combatants, no matter what their official label or designation.

The existence of the Texas Republic's Army outweighed its size and overcame its lack of uniforms and equipment and haphazard procedures for selecting officers. Unsurprisingly, Texas Army officers ran the gamut from ruthless to cautious and capable to incompetent, and they yielded mixed results. Nevertheless, the Army contributed leaders while providing a nucleus for temporary outfits to cluster around for expeditions and defense.

Many Texans took remarkable pride in their Republic. In Europe and North America, to be a nation-state in the 1830s and 1840s meant establishing a functioning government and raising an army. The United States and Mexico furnished nearby examples, and both produced constitutions, congresses, presidents, and armies. Texans mirrored all of those. Although they generated a military mystique, Texans learned that it was much more difficult to create and maintain an army than it was to write a constitution, convene congresses, and inaugurate presidents.

Notes

1. Moses Austin Bryan described a speech by his uncle in Moses Austin Bryan to James F. Perry, October 26, 1835, in John H. Jenkins, ed., *The Papers of the Texas Revolution, 1835–1836*, 10 vols. (Austin: Presidial Press, 1973), 2: 223; Sam Houston to Albert Sidney Johnston, February 11, 1837, in Marilyn McAdams Sibley, ed., "Letters from Sam Houston to Albert Sidney Johnston, 1836–1837," *Southwestern Historical Quarterly* 61 (October 1962): 256. Regarding the perpetual threat of Mexican offensives, see Joseph Milton Nance, *After San Jacinto: The Texas-Mexican Frontier, 1836–1841* (Austin: University of Texas Press, 1963), 11, 27, 33, 68–77, 420–30. An excellent brief introduction is Thomas W. Cutrer, "Army of the Texas Republic," *Handbook of Texas Online* (http://www.tshaonline.org/handbook/online/articles/qja03), accessed July 1, 2015.

2. Representing what may be termed traditional Anglo-Texan approaches to what makes Texas distinctive or "exceptional" are Stephen Hardin, "Texas: The Word that Explains it All," *Texas Heritage* magazine 1 (2011): 20–23, and, succinctly, T. R. Fehrenbach, "Texas Mythology: Now and Forever," in Robert F. O'Connor, ed., *Texas Myths* (College Station: Texas A&M University Press, 1986), 204–26, and more fully in T. R. Fehrenbach, *Lone Star: A History of Texas and Texans* (New York: Macmillan, 1968).

3. To many Texans, it was no matter that the Alamo was a defeat. In Texas lore, the Alamo showed determination against tyranny, even in the face of long odds. To overcome that defeat led to another battle against the odds, producing the decisive and grand victory at San Jacinto over the same enemy leader and part of the same army that fought at the Alamo. A contemporary assessment by Joseph Eve, an American, helped establish the stereotype. In Eve's opinion, "the Texans bould [*sic*] and fearless to a fault, chivalrous, intelligent enterprising and patriotic, who fight in defence [*sic*] of their all, their wives and children, their homes and property, and their civil and religious liberty. …" Joseph Eve to U.S. President John Tyler, October 11, 1842, in Joseph M. Nance, ed., "A Letter Book of Joseph Eve, United States Chargé d'Affaires to Texas," *Southwestern Historical Quarterly* 43 (January 1940): 98.

4. Many books recount the Rangers' history. An excellent place to start is Robert M. Utley, *Lone Star Justice: The First Century of the Texas Rangers* (New York: Oxford University Press, 2002).

5. Representing what may have been a prevailing attitude among his fellows, a Republic soldier wrote: "we … feel as if we could whip our weight in Wild Cats And five times our weight in Mexicans." Joshua H. Davis to My Dear, May 31, 1837, "A Letter from the Army of the Early Republic," *Quarterly of the Texas State Historical Association* 10 (April 1907), 347–48, quote on 347.

6. Of course, "exceptionalism" is a term with multiple meanings, and Texans recognized that claiming "exceptionalism" for Texas always provoked debate. They responded by relishing the debate and enhancing their claims. On the debate, see Mark E. Nackman, *Nation within a Nation: Rise of Texas Nationalism* (Port Washington, NY: Kennikat Press, 1975). Contrasting approaches include Walter L. Buenger and Robert W. Calvert, "Introduction," in Buenger and Calvert, eds., *Texas Through Time: Evolving Interpretations* (College Station: Texas A&M University Press, 1991), ix-xxxv; Walter L. Buenger, "Three Truths in Texas," in Walter L. Buenger and Arnoldo DeLeon, eds., *Beyond Texas Through Time: Breaking Away from Past Interpretations* (College Station: Texas A&M University Press, 2011), 1–49; Walter L. Buenger, "Texas Identity: Alternatives to the Terrible Triplets," in Richard B. McCaslin, et al., eds., *This Corner of Canaan* (Denton: University of North Texas Press, 2013), 3–36; Glen Ely, *Where the West Begins* (Lubbock: Texas Tech University Press, 2014), especially 3–17; Ty Cashion, "The Great Enigma of the Lone Star State in the American West," *Montana: The Magazine of Western History* 55 (Winter 2005): 2–15; Ty Cashion, "The End of Texceptionalism: A Postmodern Metanarrative for the New Century," *International Journal of the Humanities* 10, no. 3 (2013). Ty Cashion, *The Lone Star Mind: An American Intellectual History* (Austin: University of Texas Press, forthcoming) will be an important study. I thank Professor Cashion for providing me an early look into parts of his provocative book.

7. California's short-lived "Bear Flag Republic" popped up at the time of war between the United States and Mexico. On June 14, 1846, some American settlers announced that they had taken control of the Mexican province of California. A few days later, having been dispatched weeks earlier by U.S. President James K. Polk, American military and naval forces invaded Mexico at several points on the Pacific Coast and occupied key locations. In July those troops claimed the province

for the United States, bringing the "Bear Flag Republic" to an end after it existed for only a few days. During the next four years, regular officers of the U.S. Army and U.S. Navy administered California. The U.S. Congress approved California for statehood in 1850. See Neal Harlow, *California Conquered: The Annexation of a Mexican Province, 1846–1850* (Berkeley: University of California Press, 1989). In September 1810, American settlers rebelled against Spain in an area known as "West Florida." Those rebels proclaimed the West Florida Republic containing Spanish lands from Baton Rouge to Mobile, thus including parts of present-day states of Louisiana, Mississippi, and Alabama. The rebels immediately sought annexation into the United States. Only a few weeks later, in October, President James Madison added "West Florida" to United States territory. When Louisiana was admitted to the Union in 1812, the "Florida parishes" formed the eastern section of the new state between the Mississippi River and the Perdido River. The U.S. government divided the remaining stretch of "West Florida" between the territories of Mississippi and Alabama, but incorporating that area required U.S. military units to occupy Mobile during the War of 1812. See William C. Davis, *The Rogue Republic: How Would-be Patriots Waged the Shortest Revolution in American History* (Boston: Houghton Mifflin Harcourt, 2011). West Florida and the Bear Flag Republic each existed for a matter of days, held no gubernatorial elections, and recruited no armies. No other nations extended diplomatic recognition to either one, all in contrast to Texas.

8. Prior to the American Revolution, in a narrow zone between Great Britain's colonies of New Hampshire and New York, contentious settlers asserted themselves by carving out a separate place they called "Vermont." While some Vermonters proposed becoming part of British Canada, many others supported breaking with Britain in 1775 and fought on the American side in the Revolution, helping produce independence for the United States in 1783. After thirteen states ratified the U.S. Constitution between 1787 and 1790, Congress approved Vermont as the fourteenth state admitted to the Union in 1791. Vermont did not raise its own army or entertain ambassadors from other nations, making its status as an independent republic questionable. See Charles T. Morrissey, *Vermont: A Bicentennial History* (New York: Norton, 1981). Hawaii was an independent monarchy in the Pacific Ocean located 2,300 miles from California. Sometimes the islands had fragmented into four governing entities before European contact. Between 1820 and the 1870s, American merchants and investors gradually increased their influence as more traders and missionaries arrived. In 1893, American settlers overthrew the monarchy, but maintained no

military forces. They arranged for the United States to annex the islands four years later, making them an American territory. (Separately in 1898, U.S. military forces defeated Spanish imperial forces in the Pacific and the Caribbean. In the Pacific, America took the former Spanish colonies of the Philippines, Guam, and Wake, as well as Puerto Rico and Cuba in the Caribbean.) From 1898 to 1941 many doubted the need for Hawaiian statehood, but during World War II the islands and the naval base at Pearl Harbor assumed strategic importance. Congress admitted Hawaii as a state in the Union in 1959. See Ruth Tabrah, *Hawaii: A Bicentennial History* (New York: Norton, 1980).

9. Pekka Hämäläinen, *The Comanche Empire* (New Haven: Yale University Press, 2008), 345.

10. Joseph G. Dawson III, ed., *The Texas Military Tradition: From the Texas Revolution to World War II* (College Station: Texas A&M University Press, 1995); Alexander Mendoza and Charles David Grear, eds., *Texans and War: New Interpretations of the State's Military History* (College Station: Texas A&M University Press, 2012).

11. An excellent treatment is Stephen L. Hardin, *Texian Iliad: A Military History of the Texas Revolution, 1835–1836* (Austin: University of Texas Press, 1994).

12. Actually, however, neither Texas nor Mexico controlled an ungoverned dangerous zone between the Rio Grande and the Nueces River called the "Nueces Strip." On the size of the Army, Texas counted variable number of troops on duty. See Gerald S. Pierce, "The Army of the Texas Republic, 1836–1845" (Ph.D. dissertation, University of Mississippi, 1963), 10–12, and Nance, *After San Jacinto*, 18–19, 94–95, 243, 329, 384, 402–403.

13. *General Regulations for the Government of the Army of the Republic of Texas* (Houston: Intelligencer Office, 1839), is a detailed two-hundred-page document reflecting debts to the U.S. Army. See also Bruce Marshall, *Uniforms of the Republic of Texas and the Men Who Wore Them, 1836–1846* (Atglen, PA: Schiffer Military History, 1999). Marshall bases his illustrations on careful research into sources of the 1830s and 1840s, including the Texas Adjutant General's General Order No. 5, dated May 23, 1839, which Marshall quotes, 59–73. For other illustrations, see Stuart Reid, *The Texan Army, 1835–1846* (Oxford, UK: Osprey Publishing, 2003).

14. Regarding unit strengths, regiments varied from five hundred to one thousand men, companies varied from fifty to one hundred, and batteries varied from fifty to one hundred, depending on numbers of

cannon. Pierce, "Army of the Texas Republic, 1836–1845," 10, 29–37, 45–46. Rather than Texans displaying discipline, desertion was endemic and debilitating. See Nance, *After San Jacinto*, 231, 259, 302–303, and Joseph Milton Nance, *Attack and Counterattack: The Texas-Mexican Frontier, 1842* (Austin: University of Texas Press, 1964), 191, 203, 245, 253, 461–62, 472, 477, 501.

15. Confirming the high cost of cavalry, see Sam Houston to the Texas Congress, December 27, 1842, Amelia W. Williams and Eugene C. Barker, eds., *Writings of Sam Houston*, 8 vols. (Austin: University of Texas Press, 1938–1943), 3: 251–52, quote on 251.

16. Charles P. Roland, *Albert Sidney Johnston, Soldier of Three Republics* (Austin: University of Texas Press, 1964), 67. Nance details examples of successful purchases of weapons. See Nance, *After San Jacinto*, 92–95.

17. See Henry W. Barton, "The Problem of Command in the Army of the Republic of Texas," *Southwestern Historical Quarterly* 62 (January 1959): 299–311, and Pierce, "Army of the Texas Republic," 22.

18. Houston's mass furlough: Stanley Siegel, *A Political History of the Texas Republic, 1836–1845* (Austin: University of Texas Press, 1956), 67, and James L. Haley, *Sam Houston* (Norman: University of Oklahoma Press, 2002), 193–94. For examples of Texas laws, see H. P. N. Gammel, ed. and comp., *The Laws of Texas*, 10 vols. (Austin: Gammel Book Co., 1898), 2: 381–386, outlined the structure Congress intended for the army in 1840. During the Republic years, the army varied in size and numbers of units, but usually hovered around 1,000 officers, noncommissioned officers, and enlisted men, with most units not up to full strength. Adjusted by later laws, presidential authority is described as of 1839 in ibid., 2: 84–85.

19. The county militia dated back to England and the English settlement of North America, expecting every able man, from age seventeen to fifty, to bring his own weapons to defend his locality. In America, militia included only free men, property owners and their sons, typically excluding Indians, slaves, prisoners, vagrants, and indentured servants. By the 1830s, militia units continued in the South and West but declined elsewhere in the United States, as foreign and Indian threats receded. In most but not all counties, Texas formed militia units. They varied drastically in strength and quality and occasionally deployed outside their county. "Volunteers" was a flexible term, often applied to undisciplined men recruited in the United States who had no weapons. Texas would supply them. Recruiters lured recruits promising land in Texas when they

completed their term. Volunteers were temporary soldiers who served for six months or one year or for a single expedition. "Rangers" were Texas men mounted on their own horse and carrying their own weapons, officially authorized by the government to "range" or patrol in a region or county for a specific term of duty. Once the government organized a Ranger company (around fifty men), it might be dispatched elsewhere. See John K. Mahon, *The Militia and the National Guard* (New York: Free Press, 1983), 6–77, and Nance, *After San Jacinto*, 11, 21, 28, 40–42, 46, 77, 88–89, 91–92, 242–44, and Nance, *Attack and Counterattack*, 3–4, 26, 32, 44, 59–60, 72–73, 98, 100–101, 114, 116, 149–51, 192–93, 226, 271, 273–74, 281, 473–76, and passim.

20. "Census and Census Records," *Handbook of Texas Online* (http://www.tshaonline.org/handbook/online/articles/ulc01), accessed July 14, 2015. A lower estimate of Native Americans, perhaps only around 7,000, is in Gary Clayton Anderson, *The Conquest of Texas: Ethnic Cleansing in the Promised Land* (Norman: University of Oklahoma Press, 2000), 120. American worries over the central government's misuse of a conventional standing army derived from the era of the American Revolution and early U.S. republic. See Russell F. Weigley, *History of the United States Army* (1967; enl. ed., Bloomington: Indiana University Press, 1984), 75, 77, and Richard H. Kohn, *Eagle and Sword: The Beginnings of the Military Establishment in America* (New York: Free Press, 1975), 2–6, 87–88, 282–83.

21. For types of enlistees, see *General Regulations for the Government of the Army*, 97–107, quotations on 98–99. After their first enlistment, soldiers and sergeants were permitted to marry. Regarding *Tejanos*, see Stephen L. Hardin, "Efficient in the Cause," 52–61, in Gerald E. Poyo, ed., *Tejano Journey, 1770–1850* (Austin: University of Texas Press, 1996); David McDonald, *José Antonio Navarro: In Search of the American Dream in Nineteenth Century Texas* (Denton: Texas State Historical Association, 2010), 166–80; Jesús F. de la Teja, ed., *A Revolution Remembered: The Memoirs and Selected Correspondence of Juan N. Seguín* (Austin: State House Press, 1991). See also a listing of *Tejanos* by Ruben R. Luzano, *Viva Tejas; The Story of the Mexican-born Patriots of the Republic of Texas* (San Antonio: Southern Literary Institute, 1936), esp. 41–46.

22. It may have seemed pretentious for Texas to have a "secretary of war" along with uniformed officers assigned for responsibilities as Adjutant General, Inspector General, Quartermaster General, and Chief of Ordnance for an army of only around 3,000 soldiers. One general and three staff colonels should have been able to fulfill

those administrative duties. From 1836 to 1845 in a nation covering a larger geographical area, the U.S. Army had the same types of administrative departments and fluctuated between 8,500 and 12,400 officers and enlisted men. During several of those years, 1836–1842, the U.S. government assigned thousands of soldiers to Florida in a stubborn, ongoing war against the Seminole Indians. See Weigley, *History of the United States Army*, 597, listing U.S. Army strength, and 161–63 on the Seminole War.

23. During the Republic, secretaries of war and their former states included Thomas Jefferson Rusk (South Carolina and Georgia), William S. Fisher (Virginia), Barnard Bee, Sr. (South Carolina), Albert Sidney Johnston (Kentucky), Branch T. Archer (Virginia), George W. Hockley (born in Pennsylvania but he had established residency in Tennessee before moving to Texas), George W. Hill (Tennessee), Morgan C. Hamilton (Alabama), and William G. Cooke (Virginia). Alexander Somervell (Maryland) and Mirabeau B. Lamar (Georgia) also served briefly as war secretary during 1836. Of these, George Hill held one of the lengthiest appointments, January 1843 to December 1844, in the second Houston administration. For each of these officials, consult essays in the *Handbook of Texas Online*, passim.

24. Roland, *Albert Sidney Johnston*, 67–71, 83–99, 115. Regarding the role of honor in southern men's lives, see Bertram Wyatt-Brown, *Southern Honor: Ethics and Behavior in the Old South* (New York: Oxford University Press, 1982). Dueling among Texans occurred often. See Thomas W. Cutrer, "Dueling in the Republic of Texas," *Handbook of Texas Online* (http://www.tshaonline.org/handbook/online/articles/jgd01), accessed August 25, 2015.

25. Carolyn Hyman, "Hockley, George Washington," and David Minor, "Archer, Branch Tanner," *Handbook of Texas Online* (http://www.tshaonline.org/handbook/online/articles/fho08), accessed July 10, 2015.

26. Fluctuations of numbers of soldiers are described by Nance, *After San Jacinto*, 18–19, 94–95, 243, 329, 384, 402–403.

27. Steven A. Brownrigg, "Cooke, William Gordon," *Handbook of Texas Online* (http://www.tshaonline.org/handbook/online/articles/fcobv), accessed July 15, 2015.

28. William B. Skelton, *An American Profession of Arms: The Army Officer Corps, 1784–1861* (Lawrence: University Press of Kansas, 1992), 138, and Samuel J. Watson, *Peacekeepers and Conquerors: The Army Officer Corps on the American Frontier, 1821–1846* (Lawrence: University Press of Kansas, 2013), esp. 547note24.

29. Although Collinsworth and Crittenden had graduated commendably in the middle of their classes, twenty-fourth of forty-two and twenty-sixth of forty-five cadets, respectively, Stillwell finished thirty-six of thirty-eight. All of them went into the infantry, meaning none entered the more prestigious branches of the engineers, artillery, or cavalry. When the United States annexed Texas, Crittenden returned to the U.S. Army in 1846. Basic information for Stillwell, Collinsworth, and Crittenden is found in George W. Cullum, *Biographical Register of the Officers and Graduates of the United States Military Academy at West Point*, available on-line by entering the search phrase "West Point Class of [year] in Cullum Register" then clicking on the graduate's name.

30. Basic information for McLeod is in Cullum, *Biographical Register*, available on-line by entering the search phrase "West Point Class of [year] in Cullum Register" then clicking on the graduate's name. A biography is Paul N. Spellman, *Forgotten Texas Leader: Hugh McLeod and the Texan Santa Fe Expedition* (College Station: Texas A&M University Press, 1999).

31. On Fannin, see the analysis in Hardin, *Texian Iliad*, 134–35, 160–61, 165. See also Clinton P. Hartmann, "Fannin, James Walker, Jr.," Robert Bruce Blake, "Green, Thomas Jefferson," and Seldon B. Graham, Jr., "Bonnell, Joseph," in *Handbook of Texas Online* (http://www.tshaonline.org/handbook/online/articles/ffa02), accessed July 15, 2015. Haynes, *Soldiers of Misfortune*, negatively assesses Green and his misadventures, 28–29, 31, 72–77. Bonnell continued to serve in the U.S. Army until he died in 1840. Perhaps Bonnell might be categorized with the modern term of a "liaison officer" on special assignment. Bonnell is briefly described in Cullum, *Biographical Register of the Officers and Graduates*, available on-line by entering the search phrase "West Point Class of [year] in Cullum Register" then clicking on the graduate's name.

32. Voters disappointed Burleson when they elected Anson Jones president instead of him in 1844. John H. Jenkins and Kenneth Kesselus, *Edward Burleson: Texas Frontier Leader* (Austin: Jenkins Publishing Company, 1990), 13, 16–17, 50, 57, 66–86, 93, 107–19, 136, 150, 178, 196–206, 251–58, 259, 267–68, 297–302, 316–17, 350–51.

33. Sam W. Haynes, *Soldiers of Misfortune: The Somervell and Mier Expeditions* (Austin: University of Texas Press, 1990), 61–62, 66–71, 74. See also Nance, *After San Jacinto*, 30–31, 36–37, 89, 208–209, and David M. Vigness, "Fisher, William S.," *Handbook of Texas Online* (http://www.tshaonline.org/handbook/online/articles/ffi24), accessed July 10, 2015.

34. Thomas W. Cutrer, "Huston, Felix," *Handbook of Texas Online* (http://www.tshaonline.org/handbook/online/articles/fhu46), accessed July 11, 2015.

35. Priscilla Myers Benham, "Rusk, Thomas Jefferson," *Handbook of Texas Online* (http://www.tshaonline.org/handbook/online/articles/fru16), accessed July 10, 2015. See also Mary W. Clarke, *Thomas J. Rusk: Soldier, Statesman, Jurist* (Austin: Jenkins Publishing, 1971), 79–95, 111–18, 123–36.

36. Haynes, *Soldiers of Misfortune*, 12–13, 52–65.

37. Hardin, "Efficient in the Cause," 52–61, in Poyo, ed., *Tejano Journey*; Jesús F. de la Teja, "Juan N. Seguín: Federalist, Rebel, Exile," 212–30, in Jesús F. de la Teja, ed., *Tejano Leadership in Mexican and Revolutionary Texas* (College Station: Texas A&M University Press, 2010).

38. Haley, *Sam Houston*, 180–83, 203–206, 242–50, 257–58; Randolph B. Campbell, *Sam Houston and the American Southwest*, 2nd ed. (New York: Longman, 2002), 100–102, 116–20, 123–24. Herbert P. Gambrell, *Mirabeau Buonaparte Lamar, Troubadour and Crusader* (Dallas: Southwest Press, 1934), 238–39, 241–43, 254–56, 263. Spellman, *Forgotten Texas Leader*, 38, 54–58.

39. A contemporary observer estimated the Mexican Army at 20,000. See Charles Folsom, *Mexico in 1842* (New York: C. J. Folsom, 1842), 148.

40. David J. Weber, *The Mexican-American Frontier, 1821–1846: The American Southwest Under Mexico* (Albuquerque: University of New Mexico Press, 1982), 108–109.

41. Regimental strengths were never consistent. Ideally, each regiment enrolled as many as one thousand soldiers but often fielded half that. Troop numbers were unreliable because the government asked Mexican generals to report the number of soldiers under their command, then sent soldiers' pay to the generals to disburse. Thus, adjutants still listed soldiers on muster rolls who had died, deserted, or been discharged. See William A. DePalo, Jr., *The Mexican National Army, 1822–1852* (College Station: Texas A&M University Press, 1997), 70–89.

42. Ibid.

43. Ibid., 67–70; Hämäläinen, *Comanche Empire*, 219–32, 314.

44. Canalizo was senior with twenty-five years in uniform. David M. Vigness, "Arista, Mariano," David M. Vigness, "Ampudia, Pedro de"; "Vasquez, Rafael," *Handbook of Texas Online* (http://www.tshaonline.org/handbook/online/articles/far04), accessed July 16, 2015, Joseph Milton Nance, "Adrian Woll: Frenchman in the Mexican Military Service,"

New Mexico Historical Review 33 (July 1958): 177–186, and DePalo, *Mexican National Army*, 49, 66, 81–84, 99.

45. David La Vere, *The Texas Indians* (College Station: Texas A&M University Press, 2004).

46. An introduction to Native Americans in Texas is Pekka Hämäläinen, "The Emergence of a New Texas Indian History," in Walter Buenger and Arnoldo De León, eds. *Beyond Texas Through Time* (College Station: Texas A&M University Press, 2001), 50–84. Supplementing that essay are Matthew M. Babcock, "Native Americans," and F. Todd Smith, "Spanish, Mexican, and Republican Texas to 1845," in Bruce Glasrud, et al., eds., *Discovering Texas History* (Norman: University of Oklahoma Press, 2014), 20–25 and 169–96.

47. Chief Old Owl quoted in Dorman H. Winfrey and James M. Day, eds., *The Indian Papers of Texas and the Southwest*, 5 vols. (Austin, 1965; reprinted, Austin: Texas State Historical Association, 1995), 2: 8.

48. Hämäläinen, *Comanche Empire*, 12. See also the descriptions and analysis of how extensive and damaging the Comanche raids were to Mexico before 1846, in Brian DeLay, *War of a Thousand Deserts: Indian Raids and the U.S.-Mexican War* (New Haven: Yale University Press, 2008), 41–222.

49. Hämäläinen, *Comanche Empire*, 16.

50. Houston stated: "Austin is no defense to the frontier, as the last three years have demonstrated." Houston to Sec. of War George Hockley, March 22, 1842, in Williams and Barker, eds., *Writings of Sam Houston*, 3: 509–30, quote on 530.

51. Anderson, *The Conquest of Texas*, 134 and passim. A resolution to the struggle finally came more than thirty years after Texas was annexed into the United States. From 1845 to 1865, the Comanche empire reaped benefits from the U.S.-Mexican War (1846–1848) and the American Civil War (1861–1865)—major wars that interrupted Anglo encroachment and appeared to give the Comanche and Kiowa nearly a free hand until 1865. When their state officially returned to the Union, Texans relentlessly prosecuted their war against the Comanche with the aid of the U.S. Army from 1865 to 1875. Along with the slaughter of the bison, U.S. forces and the Texans gained a superior advantage by 1878 that they never relinquished. Driven from Texas and pushed into reservations, the Comanche yielded their empire—one major step in what historian Peter Maskowski calls "the 300-year war." Peter Maslowski, "The 300 Year War," 129–54, in Matthew Moten, ed., *Between Peace and War: How America Ends Its Wars* (New York: Free Press, 2000).

52. At one of American's most illustrious victories, only three thousand Americans stood in Jackson's battle lines at New Orleans in January 1815. During the U.S.-Mexican War, 1,200 Americans captured Santa Fe, New Mexico, and around one thousand American soldiers, sailors, Marines, and volunteers seized all of California.

53. Haley, *Sam Houston*, 108–109, 119, 191, 204–205; Campbell, *Houston and the Southwest*, 100–102.

54. Anderson, *Conquest of Texas*, 178–79; Haley, *Sam Houston*, 215; Jenkins and Kesselus, *Edward Burleson*, 200–206; Mary W. Clarke, *Chief Bowles and the Texas Cherokees* (Norman: University of Oklahoma Press, 1971), 57–58, 106–111.

55. Capt. Clark L. Owen to Col. Joseph Rogers, March 2, 1838, in L. W. Kemp, ed., "The Joseph H. D. Rogers Letters," *Southwestern Historical Quarterly* 55 (July 1951): 107.

56. Anderson, *Conquest of Texas*, 181–83; Spellman, *Forgotten Texas Leader*, 41–50.

57. Jenkins and Kesselus, *Edward Burleson*, 257; Anderson, *Conquest of Texas*, 187–89; Thomas W. Cutrer, *Ben McCulloch and the Frontier Military Tradition* (Chapel Hill: University of North Carolina Press, 1993), 41–44.

58. Jenkins and Kesselus, *Edward Burleson*, 267–68; Burleson to Lamar, June 4, 1841, in Charles A. Gulick, Jr., and Katherine Elliott, eds., *The Papers of Mirabeau Buonaparte Lamar*, 6 vols. (1922; reprint, New York: AMS Press, 1973), 3: 531–32. On Navarro's role, see Andrés Resédez, trans., *A Texas Patriot on Trial in Mexico: José Antonio Navarro and the Texan Santa Fe Expedition* (Dallas: DeGolyer Library and Southern Methodist University, 2005), 28–29, 55–56, 59–60, 69–71, and McDonald, *José Antonio Navarro*, 166–67, 172–74, 180–99.

59. An excellent account of McLeod's part in the expedition is Spellman, *Forgotten Texas Leader*, 63–93.

60. Joseph G. Dawson III, *Doniphan's Epic March: The 1st Missouri Volunteers in the Mexican War* (Lawrence: University Press of Kansas, 1999), 28–79.

61. Jenkins and Kesselus, *Edward Burleson*, 295. It appeared to Santa Anna that Vásquez and his troops should have conducted a serious campaign, but the result was less than Santa Anna had wished. See Will Fowler, *Santa Anna of Mexico* (Lincoln: University of Nebraska Press, 2007), 225–26, and DePalo, *Mexican National Army*, 83.

62. DePalo, *Mexican National Army*, 82–83; Nance, *Attack and Counterattack*, 39, 47–51.

63. Volunteers rushing to enlist were described by Joseph Eve to John J. Crittenden, April 3, 1842, in Nance, ed., "A Letter Book of Joseph Eve," 372. Houston's warning to Somervell: Houston to Somervell, March 18, 1842, in Williams and Barker, eds., *Writings of Sam Houston*, 2: 509–510 (Houston's emphasis). Houston's comment about Burleson, Houston to William H. Daingerfield, April 1, 1842, ibid., 3: 14–16, quote on 15. See also Jenkins and Kesselus, *Edward Burleson*, 300; Nance, *Attack and Counterattack*, 55–116.

64. Houston labeled the Vásquez raid "imposing" and described volunteers going home: Houston to Texas Congress, June 27, 1842, Williams and Barker, eds., *Writings of Sam Houston*, 3: 74–83, esp. 74–75; "Insubordination": Houston to Texas Senate, July 18, 1842, ibid., 3: 105. Nance, *Attack and Counterattack*, 229–30, 236, 245–50.

65. Nance, *Attack and Counterattack*, 311–19; George R. Nielsen, "Mathew Caldwell," *Southwestern Historical Quarterly* 64 (April 1961: 478–502, especially 496–500.

66. Utley, *Lone Star Justice*, 44–46.

67. Nance, *Attack and Counterattack*, 364–73.

68. Nance, *Attack and Counterattack*, 374–76, and Utley, *Lone Star Justice*, 46–49. The Mexicans had executed Texans prisoners at Goliad and granted no quarter at the Alamo. The bitter results of the Dawson fight added to Texan hostility, which continued into the U.S.-Mexican War. Texas volunteers and Rangers often showed no quarter to Mexicans during that war. See James M. McCaffrey, *Army of Manifest Destiny: The American Soldier in the Mexican War, 1846–1848* (New York: New York University Press, 1992), 125–28.

69. Woll inflated Texan losses and downplayed Mexican losses in the campaign. See Joseph Milton Nance, trans. and ed., "Brigadier General Adrian Woll's Report on his Expedition to Texas in 1842," *Southwestern Historical Quarterly* 58 (April 1955): 523–52, esp. 545. See also Nance, *Attack and Counterattack*, 382–408.

70. Haynes, *Soldiers of Misfortune*, 48–61.

71. Ibid., 61–64.

72. An excellent analysis is ibid., 66–79. The Mier prisoners managed to escape but were recaptured. In response, Mexicans proposed executing all of them, but settled on literally decimating them. In March of 1843, 177 Texan veterans of Mier picked colored beans from a container. Mexican firing squads shot the seventeen who drew black beans, further intensifying hostility between Texans and Mexicans. Ibid., 104–27. For additional details on the events of this campaign, see Joseph Milton Nance, *Dare-Devils All:*

The Texan Mier Expedition, 1842–1844, Archie P. McDonald, ed. (Austin: Eakin Press, 1998).

73. Filisola quoted in Nance, *After San Jacinto*, 7.

74. Weber, *Mexican-American Frontier*, 267–68. An introduction to Manifest Destiny is Thomas R. Hietala, *Manifest Design: American Exceptionalism and Empire* (1985; rev. ed. Ithaca, NY: Cornell University Press, 2003).

75. Although the United States before and after 1846 annexed other territories, provinces, or islands, adding Texas to the Union was the only time such a step had led directly to war with a European or Latin American nation.

Chapter 5
The Republic of Texas Navies

Gary D. Joiner

No nation on Earth possessing a seacoast can protect itself without commanding the seas adjacent to and near it. So it was for the newly declared Republic of Texas. Early Anglo-Texans largely came to Texas by sea from the eastern and central Gulf of Mexico ports of Pensacola, Mobile, and New Orleans. The broad coastal Gulf plain was a natural destination: flat, well-drained, easily farmed and ready to accept cattle ranching. North of this lay more inhospitable lands, which were drier and inhabited by often hostile Indians. From 1810 to 1821, Mexico broke away from Spanish control and begin its long, often turbulent path to nationhood. Mexico originally not only accepted the Anglos, particularly Stephen F. Austin and his colony, but, they did not anticipate the flood of immigrants. Among the principal causes for consternation by the Mexican authorities was that most of these new people were Protestants. If the flood was not stemmed, Mexico might face not only a sizeable minority of non-Catholics, but a potential rival on its northern border, wherever that might be. Clumsy overreaction by the government in Mexico City set events in motion. Mexican authorities decided to exact customs duties on all goods entering Texas ports. This became an early source of animosity on the part of the Texans and, if not the spark, certainly set the fuse for the Texas Revolution.[1]

Texas, rife with individualism and harboring a deep sense of Manifest Destiny, broke away from Mexico in the fall of 1835. Most of the immigrants were Southerners, who held strong views that the Mexican government consisted of foreigners who tried to dominate them.[2] The fact that these settlers had come to the northernmost province of an independent nation did not matter. They still believed, behaved, and acted as if they were United States citizens moving west. Texans first, but Americans also.

Geography played an enormous role in the potential survival of the fledgling republic. To understand the events that followed, one must examine the western Gulf of Mexico. Shaped like an enormous letter "C," the Gulf stretches west from the mouth of the Mississippi River across Louisiana, Texas, and the eastern shore of modern day Mexico to the Yucatan Peninsula. From the Tropic of Cancer to Corpus Christi lay an inhospitable desert, which was equally harsh to both the Mexicans and Texas.[3] During the first half of the nineteenth century, only a few ports provided facilities to provision armies and to carry on trade, the most important being Matamoros at the mouth of the Rio Grande. Texans found that establishing ports was a difficult process. Natural harbors were limited, with Galveston Bay and Matagorda Bay offering the best potential locations. South of the Rio Grande, the ports of Tampico, Tuxpan, and Vera Cruz were the principal sites. Among these, Vera Cruz was undoubtedly the most important, providing direct access, via road, to Mexico City.[4] South of these ports, the Mexican coast turned swampy. Communications over land were difficult at best and often nonexistent. The Yucatan Peninsula was an important part of Mexico. Rich in population, containing the bulk of boat- and shipbuilding, the Yucatan was far removed from Mexico City and its Indian population was not impressed by the national government. It was often in rebellion.[5] Off the northern shore of the Yucatan lay two groups of islands, the Alacaranes and the Arcas. The two largest islands were Mujeres and Cozumel. The Mexican navy was not large enough to patrol this entire huge coastline from the Sabine Pass, the western edge of the United States, to the Yucatan. The Texans would use this to their advantage. It became obvious very quickly that control of the coast would play a pivotal role in whether Texas gained independence or Mexico retained its northernmost province of *Tejas*.

If independence and war came, strategy was straightforward for both sides. The Texans must protect their coast, keep the vital supply lines open to New Orleans, and deny any amphibious attack from the sea, while simultaneously disrupting Mexican commerce and naval activity on her eastern coast. The Mexican government must be able to sustain what is today called force projection. They must transport or march a large army into Texas and keep it supplied so that the land forces can hold their positions and intimidate any Texans who wish to cause trouble. They also had to monitor events in the Yucatan. Despite the seemingly inpenetrable advantage of the Mexicans, the Texans could expect to hold their own, if they had a navy.

The Mexican government dispatched its northern army sector commander, General Manuel de Mier y Terán, to Texas to enforce Mexico City's will. The Mexican army held garrisons at Bexar (San Antonio), Fort Velasco (at the mouth of the Brazos River), Anahuac (at the northern end of Galveston Bay), and Nacogdoches. The Texans bristled at this and a group of them decided to drive out the garrison at Anahuac in June 1832. They realized that they could not succeed without naval support.

They asked private merchant vessel captains for help and three vessels, *Stephen F. Austin, Water Witch,* and *Red River* aided the insurgents. With small crews and few armed men, these vessels halted supplies coming into the loyalist Fort Davis and captured three Mexican boats loaded with supplies.[6] The tiny blockade worked and the garrison at Fort Davis was forced to vacate. About the same time as the Anahuac siege, the loyalist fort at Velasco, built in early 1832 to "protect" the mouth of the Brazos, intimidated the Austin colony headquartered at San Felipe. Texans sailed the schooner *Brazoria* down the Brazos with two small cannon and thirty infantry to the fort. Initially turned back, the *Brazoria* returned with additional sharpshooters on land. They caused several casualties along the fort's walls and the garrison commander surrendered on June 27.[7] Mexican control over the northeastern coast of Texas disintegrated. The Mexican garrison at Nacogdoches left their compound. The Texans, led by Austin, convinced the Mexican government that they were actually helping the government by driving out over-zealous malcontents in the Mexican garrisons. It bought them three years of peace.

The Gulf of Mexico was by no means a "Mexican lake." The United States, Great Britain and Mexico all kept naval vessels in the region. The U.S. Navy kept the powerful frigate USS *Constellation* at New Orleans, along with smaller armed vessels. This was primarily an anti-piracy role for the sister of "Old Ironsides," the USS *Constitution.* Another, less overt mission was to protect American interests with regards to Texas. The British had a Caribbean squadron that was responsible for interdicting slave traders and keeping the Americans from grabbing former Spanish lands as they declared independence. During the 1820s the Mexicans contracted with foreigners to lead and man their navy. The most notable was Commodore David Porter. He brought several senior officers with him. Porter was under suspension from the U.S. Navy for insulting the mayor of a town in Puerto Rico. He held the post as the Mexican naval commander until 1829.[8]

Internal financial and political problems within the Mexican government between 1830 and 1835 saw a dramatic decrease in funding for the Mexican navy. The east coast fleet, based in Vera Cruz, was reduced to the schooners *Moctezuma, Vera Cruzana, Campecheano,* and *Papaloapan.* The government could not maintain and man these vessels to the point that only *Moctezuma* could regularly sail. By June 1835 only *Vera Cruzana* and *Moctezuma* were seaworthy and manned.[9] Although records are incomplete regarding the size of the Mexican navy, this reduction in force would cost the Mexicans dearly.

Smaller armed vessels appear on the list sporadically, often when they became embroiled in incidents.

Political turmoil in Mexico increased during 1834. The Federalists, led by General and President Antonio Lopez de Santa Anna, strengthened their hold, expunged their Centralist rivals, and Santa Anna dissolved the Mexican Congress. The Federalists were not willing to cooperate with the Texans, whom they viewed as a direct threat to Catholic Mexico. The Texans viewed the new government as openly hostile to them and a naval incident heightened tensions. Texans still bridled at the fact that the Mexican government imposed tariffs on them. On September 1, 1835, two merchant ships, the *San Felipe* and the *Laura,* intercepted and engaged the Mexican revenue schooner *Correo Mejicano*, while it was escorting two smaller supply vessels, the *Ana Maria* and *Josepha*, near Velasco.[10] The Texans accused the *Correo*, her captain, and crew of piracy. The vessel was sailed to New Orleans where it was held for three months until the Mexican government secured the officers and crew and the vessel's release.[11] The Texas coast lay unguarded for those three months and supplies and men poured into Texas. Open revolt was simply a question of time. Public opinion in Mexico rose in anger at the incident. The Mexican outcry was one of the factors that led Santa Anna to launch a punitive attack on Texas the following year.

Two months after the *Correo* incident, on November 1, 1835, Texas revolted against Mexican authority. The revolutionary government was led by Stephen F. Austin and Sam Houston with the capital at Washington-on-the-Brazos. Three weeks later, on November 24, the new Texas General Council created an official navy, authorizing four schooners. These purchased vessels became the *Invincible, Independence, Brutus*, and *Liberty*.[12] The 60-ton *Liberty* was the smallest. The other three were each 125-ton vessels.[13] The Navy was under the command of Commodore Charles Edward Hawkins.[14] The Council also commissioned privateers through six letters of marque and reprisal.[15] (These were commissions authorizing an individual, known as a privateer, to attack and seize enemy vessels and return them to a friendly port where an admiralty court would condemn the vessel and then sell them. It was a form of legitimate piracy.) By mid-December these independent contractors were in action. The Mexican navy had captured an American mercantile schooner *Hannah Elizabeth*. It was carrying cannons and supplies to Texas. One of the Texan privateers, *William Robbins*, intercepted the prize and recaptured it on December 19.[16] The loss of *Correo Mejicano* and *Hannah Elizabeth* forced a change in tactics by the Mexican navy. The privateers were considered to be the most dangerous threat. The convoys system would now be used to supply future Mexican units moving into Texas.

Santa Anna considered the northern Mexican state of Coahuila and coastal Texas to be a single political unit. The Mexican Constitution of 1824 created this entity. This was to keep the concept of rebellion from spreading. The two entities shared similar geography and hardships on whoever controlled them. Santa Anna dispatched a six-thousand-man army to deal with the Texans. He quickly discovered that the army was unsustainable solely by land. His senior commander called the region "extensive and frightful deserted lands."[17] This harsh environment made control of the coast by both sides vital. The small Texan fleet augmented by the privateers denied the Mexicans ease of access. During the winter of 1835–1836, Santa Anna gathered his six thousand hungry troops at Coahuila and in the early spring he moved into Texas. The privateers captured several small prizes.

As the Mexican army moved across the Rio Grande, Texas declared itself independent and became a republic on March 2, 1836. Four days later the Alamo fell to Santa Anna's army. Goliad fell the next week. Sam Houston's tiny army of about one thousand men fled on a route near the sea. The Mexican navy could not get near them. With Santa Anna in pursuit, it appeared the little republic might become extinct. However, Houston played the Mexicans into a place and time of his own choosing and penned them beside Buffalo Bayou. The Battle of San Jacinto lasted just eighteen minutes. The Mexican army was destroyed and Santa Anna was captured.

The Texas navy still guarded the coast and took Sam Houston to New Orleans for medical attention. *Liberty* operated in the waters around Yucatan in early March and captured the Mexican schooner *Pelicano* off Sisal on March 3 before escorting Houston to New Orleans.[18] *Invincible*, patrolling the coast, captured the American brig *Pocket*, attempting to supply the fleeing Mexican army on April 3.[19] These were the halcyon days for the Revolutionary Texas Navy. Hard sailing, no time to refit, and crew exhaustion all played roles in what followed.

Liberty went into refit in New Orleans. The Texas government could not pay the bills and the ship was eventually sold by the shipyard to recover the cost of the job.[20] *Invincible, Brutus*, and *Pocket* were dispatched to blockade Matamoros in an attempt to prevent the resupply of the retreating Mexican army. They were kept at that station until all three needed repairs. Since Texas did not possess any repair facilities, *Brutus* and *Invincible* sailed to New York and *Pocket* sailed to New Orleans.

Both *Brutus* and *Invincible* were held for nonpayment and might have been sold if it had not been for Samuel Swartwout, the customs collector for New York City.[21]

As 1836 ended and 1837 began, new challenges faced the Texas Navy. The new cutter *Independence* was purchased as surplus from the U.S. Revenue Service in New Orleans.[22] Captained by Commodore Hawkins, the vessel began a three-month cruise covering the Mexican coast. It was ordered to patrol outside Galveston Bay to ward off a possible landing by the Mexican Navy and then to New Orleans for repairs.[23] While overseeing the work, Commodore Hawkins contracted and died from smallpox and the cutter was turned over to Captain George W. Wheelwright.[24] Wheelwright sailed the *Independence* back to Texas waters where it was overtaken by two Mexican naval vessels attempting to enforce the blockade. The cutter fought a running duel, but was forced to surrender within sight of Galveston.[25]

The Mexican navy, through capture and purchase, had amassed seven warships in the Gulf of Mexico. The *Independence,* now renamed *Independencia*, brought the total to eight. The most powerful were three brigs and two schooners tasked with blockading Galveston and other ports as needed. The Mexican captains began capturing American-flagged vessels and the U.S. Navy sent the sloop-of-war *Natchez* captained by William Mervine, to sort things out.[26] Mervine entered the Rio Grande, freed an American-flagged merchantman and captured one of the Mexican brigs. It was later returned and the U.S. apologized.[27]

Brutus and *Invincible* raided the Caribbean and captured five Mexican vessels before returning to Galveston. On August 26, 1837, *Brutus* entered the bay but *Invincible's* draft was too deep for the tide. Mexican warships enforcing the blockade caught the waiting *Invincible* and attacked. *Brutus* came to her sister's aid, but grounded. *Invincible* was burned at night and *Brutus* sank in a storm in October.[28] This left Texas without any combatant vessels. Texas made an attempt at rebuilding the navy through the purchase of an antiquated merchant brig, *Potomac*, from L. M. Hitchcock in Galveston for $8,000.[29] Purchased as a harbor boat, the vessel never sailed and was of little value.

Texas was largely saved at this time by a combination of factors. The Mexican government could have strangled the sea trade and supply lines to the new republic, but world events took center stage. The great Panic of 1837 wreaked havoc with world economies and no international parties had excess funds. In 1838 Mexico was forced to almost abandon her blockade stations off the Texas coast and redeploy her warships to home waters. The French and Mexicans became involved in what has been termed the "Pastry War." The French fleet bombarded Fort San Juan de Ulua, which guarded Vera Cruz. They also captured the Mexican naval fleet. The French seized Vera Cruz and held it until 1839 when peace was restored. They kept the Mexican ships.[30] Neither the Mexicans or Texans could take naval action against its opponent.

Sam Houston was not allowed by law to run for another term as president. He was succeeded by Mirabeau Buonaparte Lamar, a Texas nationalist and strong proponent for the Texas army and navy.[31] Lamar commissioned Frederick Dawson of Baltimore to build six vessels for the Texas Navy. The vessels were the *San Jacinto*, *San Antonio*, *San Bernard*, *Louisville*, *Wharton*, *Austin*, and *Archer*. They were delivered as completed between March 1839 and April 1840.[32]

These ships became the core of the Second Texas Navy. Edwin Ward Moore, at the time only twenty-nine years old, was named Commodore of the Texas Squadron. He picked *Austin* as his flagship. Moore recruited crews and then sailed the squadron to Mexican waters to show the flag and attempted to influence stalled peace negotiations. He made an alliance with the rebel faction in Yucatan before returning to map the Texas coast.[33] The squadron lost the schooner *San Jacinto* in a storm off Arcas Island.[34] Weather and illness did much more damage to the Texan vessels than did the enemy on that cruise. Bad luck continued with the weather as the primary antagonist. The steamer *Zavala* was heavily damaged on October 3 in a storm off Frontera as she was wooding. Her rudder shipped and her steering was heavily damaged. The crew made emergency repairs and, during her return, they broke up furniture and fixtures for fuel.[35] She was so damaged that, upon return to Galveston, repairs were not made and the vessel rotted in place. She grounded in Galveston Bay in the summer of 1842 and was scrapped in 1843.[36]

President Lamar continued to wage war on Mexico by launching offensives on land and sea in 1841. His major overland expedition was against Santa Fe and failed. The naval portion was designed to defend Yucatan against a strengthening threat from Mexico. The Yucatan rebels assisted in paying for the naval assistance and this financial boost lasted until April 1842. Lamar's term ended on December 13, 1841, and Sam Houston again assumed the presidency. On Lamar's last day in office, the Texas Squadron set sail again for the waters off Vera Cruz. The fleet consisted of *Austin*, *San Bernard*, and *San Antonio*, followed by *Wharton*. With periods of inactivity during peace negotiations, the vessels operated on this mission until April 26, 1842. They captured four Mexican merchantmen.[37]

Commodore Moore encountered constant problems with manning the vessels and, worse, paying the crews. Part of the problem was with President Houston, who was never a proponent of the navy. The *San Antonio* suffered a mutiny while it was in port at New Orleans. One man, an officer, was killed by the mutineers before the ringleaders were jailed and the ship was placed on lockdown.[38] Punishment was severe. Three men received one hundred lashes and four were hanged.[39]

Commodore Moore and President Houston were both strong-willed men. Houston advocated annexation to the United States and did not want to expend funds on the Navy, which he viewed as a tremendously expensive luxury. Moore was a nationalist who wanted to project the power of the Navy to Mexico and beyond. Houston ordered the *Austin*, *San Antonio*, and *San Bernard* to be refitted in New Orleans.[40] He provided no funds for the extensive repairs, hiring of new crews, or resupply of the vessels. Commodore Moore garnered support from New Orleans businessmen while Houston refused to expend any money on the navy for a full year. Houston believed he had solved his problem with Moore and the Navy by bottling them up in New Orleans. He sent his last remaining ship, *Wharton*, to New Orleans for much needed refitting.[41] He also refused to allow the ships' officers and crews to share in bounty prizes for the capture of enemy vessels. He threatened to veto any legislation that would reverse his position. Robert Potter attempted such legislation, which failed through Houston's intimidation. He reintroduced a joint resolution in January 1842 authorizing the Secretary of War to issue certificates of bounty land to all officers, seamen, and marines for their service.[42] Houston refused to follow the lead and the measure failed and was not brought up again.[43] Commodore Moore made a desperate gamble in September 1842 to bypass the president. He dispatched the *San Antonio* to Yucatan to make contact with the rebels again and attempt to reinstate the agreement to help pay for the Texas Navy's activities. That fall witnessed an extremely powerful hurricane in the Gulf that month. The *San Antonio* disappeared and the *San Bernard* was wrecked in Galveston.[44]

Mexico decided to reinvest in its navy and 1842 saw a resurgence. It purchased two new schooners from Brown and Bell Shipyard in New York City. One was lost on a reef near Florida. The other, *Aquila*, was armed with new French Paixhan 42-pounders.[45] The Mexican navy also acquired a seagoing tug, which it named *Regenerador*.[46] During July and August 1842 the Mexican navy carried out missions against the rebel navy in Yucatan, adding to their fleet five small vessels. They besieged the ports of Yucatan.[47] The Mexican navy also purchased two new large sidewheel steamers, *Guadalupe* and *Moctezuma*. Both were armed with Paixhan pivot guns of 68-pounders and 42-pounders respectively.[48] Both large vessels could outrun and outgun any ship in the Texas Navy. Most of the vessels' crews were British. The Texans were forced to retool their cannons as Paixhan 18-pounders while their ships were being refitted in New Orleans.[49] By autumn 1842, the Texas Squadron consisted of only two sea-worthy ships, *Austin* and *Wharton*. They floated at piers in New Orleans with too few men to man them and a president who wanted to abandon them.[50]

Mexico began a re-conquest of the Yucatan and it appeared to European and American observers that Texas would be next.[51] President Houston played an artful diplomacy, seemingly warlike while complaining that the Navy was a drain on resources and that the treasury could not afford to keep it. As he continued this tactic, he negotiated with the United States and Great Britain to help end the war.

Commodore Moore received the help he so desperately needed from Yucatan and, without Sam Houston's approval, secretly sailed the *Austin* and *Wharton* from New Orleans on the night of April 19, 1843.[52] The officers and crew of the sloop-of-war USS *Ontario* gave three cheers for the Texans as they left the Mississippi River.[53]

At the time, it seemed as if the two vessels were sailing on a suicide mission. *Austin* and *Wharton* sailed into familiar waters off Yucatan but against an enemy of unknown number with much more powerful guns. Some of the vessels would be their own former sisters. Others were vessels that they had previously defended. *Austin*'s armament consisted of sixteen 24-pounders and two 18-pounders. *Wharton* carried fifteen 18-pounders.[54] The Mexican fleet, which could sail faster and shoot farther, consisted of *Moctezuma* with six 42-pounder Paixhans, *Guadalupe,* with two 68-pounder Paixhans and two 32-pounders, *Mexicano*, rated at sixteen guns, *Aquila* with seven Paixhans, *Iman* with nine guns, and *Campecheano* with three guns. They were escorted by several smaller vessels, including the steam tug *Regenerador*.[55] The three larger combatants were steamers. The Texans fleet was comprised only of sailing ships.

Ten days of sailing across the Gulf of Mexico brought Commodore Moore and his Texans to the waters off Campeche. The next morning, April 30, five Mexican warships appeared to the south just above the horizon. They were the *Moctezuma*, *Aquila*, *Mexicano*, *Iman*, and *Campecheano.*[56] Moore did not and could not know that the flagship *Guadalupe* was ten miles away at Lerma. Her skipper, Captain Cleveland, had contracted yellow fever and had died the previous night. At least forty of his crew were sickened by the deadly disease.[57]

Both groups of ships maneuvered from first light until 7:35 as the Texans attempted to draw close to the Mexican sloops. The Mexicans kept four to five miles ahead of their pursuers. The larger Mexican warships began firing, but very inaccurately, with most of the shells falling short or passing harmlessly overhead.[58] At 9 a.m. the sea becalmed and the *Austin* and *Wharton*, finding themselves in a dire predicament, ceased firing. The Mexicans, remarkably, did not fire or attempt to close on the hapless Texans.[59] Two hours later the Mexican warships began firing. A gentle breeze wafted from the north and the *Austin* and *Wharton* were able to get underway. A single 68-pound shell crashed into the Commodore's cabin and exited through the stern. It did not explode. This was the only round that hit the flagship.[60] The Texans fled to the port of Campeche. Although little damage was done to either side, the battle broke the Mexican siege and encouraged the Yucatan rebels to remain defiant.[61] Campeche was spared the wrath of the Mexican vessels by the presence of the Texan ships. The Mexicans were forced to land troops fifteen miles away.[62] Some of the British officers, led by the *Guadalupe*'s Commander Charlewood, resigned and most went back to England.[63]

The Mexican government was mortified by the action. Commodore Francisco Lopez, commander of the Mexican fleet, was removed from command and arrested for incompetence.[64] He was replaced by Commodore Tomas Marin. He immediately began complaining about the state of his vessels and crews, particularly that the vessels were infested with yellow fever and the healthy crewmen were too few to operate the ships.[65] The government ordered the army to complete the crews. The fact that they had no experience aboard ships did not seem to matter in the least.[66] Marin was in the unusual position of possessing too many armed vessels and not enough men. He sent the smaller vessels away and retained *Moctezuma*, *Guadalupe*, and *Aquila*.[67]

At the same time Moore received two long-range 18-pounder cannon for *Austin* and one long barreled 12-pounder for *Wharton* given by the authorities of Campeche and taken from their fortified walls. All during this time, the sea was a glassy calm except for the brief, tantalizing fickle breeze. Finally on May 16, an easterly breeze arrived and the *Austin* and *Wharton* moved out to do battle.

The Texans sailed about three miles and the winds died. The Mexicans, in steamers, saw their opportunity and bored in, firing their heavy 68-pounder and 42-pounder cannon while still far from the range of the

Texans' smaller guns.[68] The Mexican warships pounded the Texans for two hours, shredding some of the sails and spraying shell fragments from their Paixhans down on the decks and among the crewmen.[69] A small breeze arose and Moore took advantage of it, maneuvering directly into the midst of the enemy ships. This startled the Mexican commanders. For the next three hours *Austin* (*Wharton* could not maneuver in close enough to matter) herded *Moctezuma* and *Guadalupe* close in to the coast. Their commanders were more interested in escaping than waging a hard fight. The larger guns on the Mexican ships were of less use in close quarters. *Austin* was hit fourteen times and suffered casualties of three dead and twenty-two wounded.[70] Just as the *Austin* almost completely exhausted her ammunition, firing 530 rounds, *Moctezuma* and *Guadalupe* managed to extricate themselves and steamed ahead to safety.[71] American, British, and French observers all noted the difference the guns made. Although technically applauded, beyond the world of the ordnance men, few people appreciated what had occurred. These two naval engagements were the first time in history that exploding shells, fragmentation rounds, had been used a sea. They were also the only time in history that sailing ships soundly defeated steamships.[72] *Austin* was heavily damaged. Her rigging was in shreds as were her sails. She also had a large hole below the waterline that flooded her magazine.[73] Hasty repairs were made and no further action occurred due to both sides having a severe lack of ammunition. The Mexican navy failed in its objective of securing the harbor of Campeche and the companion army siege failed due the lack of heavy gunfire from the navy.

President Houston believed that the actions of Moore and his crews were not only counter to his efforts to negotiate a peace, but were illegal and he branded the Commodore and his men pirates. The May 6 declaration was almost universally condemned in Texas and across the South.[74] Perhaps the harshest sentiment, and widely copied, was that of the *New Orleans Picayune*:

> We hear but one opinion expressed in relation to Sam Houston's recent proclamation and that is deep indignation and merited rebuke. The opinion obtains alike, in this city as well as in Texas, and the President is universally pronounced either as a black-hearted traitor to his country or a mad man.[75]

The only contact Moore had with Texas in the coming days was a resupply of powder on June 16.[76] The rebel government in Campeche paid for the repairs to *Austin* and *Wharton* and resupplied the ships with gunpowder and ammunition. As they sailed from the safe haven, crowds cheered them from the battlements.[77]

In what seemed to be a world turned upside down, Moore and his valiant crews returned to Galveston on July 15, where people thronged to see and cheer them and militia members fired 21-gun salutes.[78] Sam Houston promptly dismissed the commodore from the Navy.[79] In Mexico City, to put a brave face on a bad situation, Commodore Marin was praised for his efforts and awarded a special medal, the *Cruz de Honor*. Located in the National Museum of History, Chapultepec Castle, in Mexico City, the medal reads (translated) "Through Courage he Defeated the Texas Navy—obverse—In Campeche on 16 May, 1843."[80] Sam Houston got most of his wishes. The United States became a de facto guarantor of Texan sovereignty for another three years. The U.S. Navy protected the Texas coast as if it were part of the "mother country." Texas entered the Union on December 29, 1845, after much wrangling over the slavery issue and balance of power in the U.S. Senate. The four remaining Texas Navy combat vessels *Austin*, *Wharton*, *Archer*, and *San Bernard* were transferred to the U.S. Navy upon statehood. They were scrapped in 1848 due to their poor condition.[81] Commodore Moore and John Lothrop, captain of the *Wharton*, urged the Texas authorities to overturn Houston's declaration regarding piracy through a court martial. Moore was exonerated, but Lothrop died before the verdict was announced.[82]

The Texas Navy created a proud tradition which still exists today. In guarding the "Sacred Soil of Texas" it prevented multiple invasions, denied the Mexicans open access to its own coast, assisted in keeping two revolutions on opposite ends of Mexico thriving, and in spite of the actions of the president of its own country, kept the door open for assistance from the United States and entry into the Union.

Notes

1. Fleet Admiral Chester W. Nimitz in *The Texas Roundup* at Moana Park, Honolulu, Hawaii, January 16, 1944.

2. Jonathan W. Jordan, *Lone Star Navy: Texas, the Fight for the Gulf of Mexico, and the Shaping of the American West* (Washington, D.C.: Potomac Books, 2006), xii.

3. E. M. Eller, et al., *The Texas Navy* (Washington, D.C.: Naval History Division, Navy Department, 1968), 2.

4. Ibid.

5. Ibid.

6. Margaret Swett Henson, *Juan Davis Blackburn: A Reappraisal of the Mexican Commander at Anáhuac* (College Station: Texas A&M University Press, 1982), 97–98, 120–145.

7. Jordan, *Lone Star Navy*, 4–5.

8. Richard S. West, Jr., *The Second Admiral: A Life of David Dixon Porter 1813–1891* (New York: Coward-McCann, 1937), 18–27.

9. Jordan, *Lone Star Navy*, 7.

10. Austin *Texas Republican*, September 19, 1835; *Telegraph*, October 10, 1835.

11. *New Orleans Commercial Bulletin*, January 18, 1836.

12. James M. Daniel, "TEXAS NAVY," *Handbook of Texas Online.* http://www.tshaonline.org/handbook/online/articles/qjt02. Published by the Texas State Historical Association.

13. Eller, *The Texas Navy*, Table, 26.

14. www.tshaonline.org/handbook/online/articles/fhaax

15. Eller, *The Texas Navy*, 5.

16. Ibid.

17. Vicente Filosa, *Evacuation of Texas: translation of the Representation Addressed to the Supreme Government by Gen. Vicente Filosa in Defence of His Honor, etc.* (Waco, TX: Texian Press, 1965), 60.

18. Eller, *The Texas Navy*, 28.

19. *New Orleans Bee*, May 21, 22, and 24, 1836.

20. Daniel, *Texas Navy.*

21. B. R. Brunson, "SWARTWOUT, SAMUEL," *Handbook of Texas Online* www.tshaonline.org/handbook/online/articles/fsw03. Published by the Texas State Historical Association.

22. Eller, *The Texas Navy*, Table, 26.

23. Jordan, *Lone Star Navy*, 69–70.

24. Ibid., 79–80.

25. San Felipe de Austin. *Telegraph and Texas Register*, June 8, 1837.

26. Eller, *The Texas Navy*, 8.

27. Ibid.

28. Daniel, *Texas Navy.*

29. Jordan, *Lone Star Navy*, 110.

30. Eller, *The Texas Navy*, 11.

31. Herbert Gambrell, "LAMAR, MIRABEAU BUONAPARTE," *Handbook of Texas Online* (http://www.tshaonline.org/handbook/online/articles/fla15) Published by the Texas State Historical Association.

32. Eller, *The Texas Navy*, 29.

33. Marie Giles, "MOORE, EDWIN WARD," *Handbook of Texas Online* (http://www.tshaonline.org/handbook/online/articles/fmo24. Published by the Texas State Historical Association.

34. Douglas V. Meed, *The Fighting Texas Navy 1832–1843* (Plano, TX: Republic of Texas Press, 2001), 137.

35. Jordan, *Lone Star Navy*, 162–165.

36. Eller, *The Texas Navy*, 12.

37. Jordan, *Lone Star Navy*, 195–200.

38. *New Orleans Commercial Bulletin*, February 11, 12, 14 and 17, 1842.

39. Eller, *The Texas Navy*, 14.

40. Roy F. Sullivan, *The Texas Navies* (Bloomington, IN: Author-House, 2010), 79.

41. Eller, *The Texas Navy*, 14.

42. Harriet Smither, ed., *Journals of the Sixth Congress of the Republic of Texas, 1841–1842,* 1 (January 7, 1842): 210.

43. Ernest C. Fischer, *Robert Potter: Founder of the Texas Navy* (Gretna, LA: Pelican Publishing, 1976), passim.

44. Jordan, *Lone Star Navy,* 222–226.

45. Eller, *The Texas Navy*, 16.

46. Sullivan, *The Texas Navies*, 80.

47. Ibid.

48. Eller, *The Texas Navy*, 16–17.

49. Ibid., 17.

50. M.T. Roberts, ed., *The Personal Correspondence of Sam Houston,* vol. 1 (Denton: University of North Texas Press, 1996), 106.

51. Jordan, *Lone Star Navy*, 231–232.

52. E.W. Moore, *To the People of Texas* (N.P.: Galveston, TX, 1843), 80.

53. Commodore Moore quoted in Eller, *The Texas Navy*, 18.

54. Eller, *The Texas Navy*, Table, 26.

55. Ibid., 18.

56. Moore, *To the People of Texas*, 151–153.

57. Eller, *The Texas Navy*, 18.

58. Moore, *To the People of Texas*, 152–153.

59. Ibid.

60. Eller, *The Texas Navy*, 18–19.

61. Ibid., 19.

62. Sullivan, *The Texas Navies*, 104–106.

63. Ibid., 106.

64. Jordan, *Lone Star Navy*, 259.

65. *Houston Morning Star*, May 23, 1843 reported on information filtered by Commodore Moore.

66. Ibid.

67. Jordan, *Lone Star Navy*, 263–264.

68. Meed, *The Fighting Texas Navy*, 205.

69. Ibid.

70. Eller, *The Texas Navy*, 22.

71. Sullivan, *The Texas Navies*, 117.

72. Eller, *The Texas Navy*, 22.

73. Jordan, *Lone Star Navy*, 269.

74. See *Houston Morning Star* May 17–31, 1843, ff.; *New Orleans Commercial Bulletin,* May 26, 1843, and *New Orleans Picayune*, May 26, 1843, among others.

75. *New Orleans Picayune*, May 25, 1843.

76. Eller, *The Texas Navy*, 22.

77. Meed, *The Fighting Texas Navy*, 215.

78. Ibid., 219.

79. Eller, *The Texas Navy*, 25.

80. Ibid., 22, 25.

81. Ibid. 25.

82. Ibid.

Chapter 6
Crystallization of a Tradition: Texas Rangers and the Republic of Texas

Bruce A. Glasrud and Harold J. Weiss, Jr.

> *The Rangers have both a black side and a white side but mostly, like all institutions composed of people, a range of grays separating the two. Sound history records the range as well as the poles.*[1]
>
> — Robert M. Utley

The years before, during, and after the Republic of Texas (1836–1846) witnessed the transformation of troops of temporary mounted volunteers doing ranging service as needed for defense into the Texas Rangers who have since been both idolized and condemned in the annals of the state and of the nation. The metamorphosis from part-time and untrained volunteers to the more formally administered companies of citizen-soldiers that protected the frontiers during the years of the Republic of Texas required three elements in this changing scene: a forceful leader, a unique weapon, and a defining moment.

These three elements found fruition in January 1844 when John C. Hays raised a company of men for the western frontier. "The model for all subsequent captains, John Coffee (Jack) Hays," one historian noted, "pioneered mounted combat by adopting the first revolving pistol, the five-shot Paterson Colt."[2] At Walker's Creek in 1844, Rangers, Colts, Comanche, and other Indians all came together in a defining battle that reshaped warfare in the Lone Star State and the American Southwest.[3] These elements and traditions are present in the latter nineteenth as well as the twentieth and twenty-first centuries. In the strict sense, tradition denotes the passage of beliefs and modes of activity, often in oral formats, from one generation to another. In popular usage, though, the term can refer to some of the cultural traits in this generational shift. When this occurs, long-standing cultural norms, as happened with the empire-building Texas Rangers, become a source of legitimacy,

John Coffee "Jack" Hays (1817–1883): He had a boyish look and mild manners, which surprised those looking for a rugged Ranger leader. Hays and his men used revolvers, carried out horse charges, gave the Texas Yell, and built a Ranger tradition that captured the public's imagination. Jack Hays became the prototype for future Ranger officers. Courtesy Texas State Library and Archives Commission.

i.e., the authority to act gained from the accumulation of pragmatic experiences. As did United States' citizens, Texans committed themselves to a set of ideals, values, and processes in the body politic as well as legal precepts laid down by governmental institutions.[4]

The early Texas Rangers evolved into a formidable peacekeeping force. No single dramatic event like the Alamo or San Jacinto marked their transition, yet in the first half of the nineteenth century, a Ranger tradition was established. The pioneers who moved from the Old South and elsewhere into the Texan lands in the 1820s and 1830s relied upon an era that lionized volunteer companies of citizen-soldiers. In the frontier lands (with their low man–land ratio) and in the more settled regions in Texas, an informal ad-hoc system arose. Settlers sporadically came together to protect families and settlements from Indian attacks and threats from Mexican nationals. These ingrained beliefs and actions to maintain their livelihood made citizen soldiers take the battlefield, often without authorization from those in authority, during the colonial and early statehood periods. These volunteer men at arms had a disdain for the chain of command and the discipline of soldiers in the regular army. Rangers became irregulars and, in the words of one historian, they "fought under no flag, wore no uniforms, and in practice observed no prescribed length of service."[5]

Two factors stand out in the crystallization of a Ranger tradition. By the beginning of the 1840s, the Rangers had become more organized. Under the leadership of officers like Robert McAlpin "Three-Legged-Willie" Williamson, Jack Hays, and John H. Moore, the Rangers added more experienced members and began to build an esprit de corps. In the forging of this tradition, a significant element was the adaptability of the Rangers to the changing culture in Texas. During the years of the Republic, for example, Presidents Samuel "Sam" Houston and Mirabeau B. Lamar differed in their policies for handling Indian tribes. The former stressed peaceful coexistence and the latter advocated aggression and expulsion. To carry out the aims of the state, the Rangers adjusted their mindset, their strategy, and their tactics.[6]

To uphold time-honored values, symbols, and shibboleths, those engaged in the ranging service had to be brave and honorable in everyday affairs, self-reliant in carrying out their duties, and heroic in the face of the enemy. An additional feature is essential to understanding the role of captains of a Ranger company in the field. In the realm of philosophy, scholars define the hero in history either as an "event-making man" or as an "eventful man" (who happened to be in the right place at the right time).[7]

William Alexander Anderson "Bigfoot" Wallace (1817–1899): Standing six feet two inches and weighing about 240 pounds, Wallace approached the physical appearance of the legendary citizen-soldier Ranger in the public's mind. Yet his impact on the formative years of the Rangers never equaled that of the more prominent Texans in his day. But the picturesque Wallace surpassed his fellow Rangers as a storyteller and folk hero. Courtesy Texas State Library and Archives Commission.

Through either careful thought or sheer luck, Jack Hays, for example, had a foot in each camp.

The earliest ranging citizen-soldiers in the Texas countryside took the field in fits and starts. The genesis of the Rangers began with one man—the driven and enigmatic Stephen F. Austin. The famous empresario first used the word "ranger" in an address to his colonists in 1823. However, when the term was applied to an armed force in Texas has been debated by Ranger enthusiasts and scholars ever since. Some scholars argue that the designation began with a militia company formed in that year (1823) in the field under the command of Moses Morrison. He and his nine men, armed with rifles and one musket, had orders to build blockhouses and small boats for protection against the Indian tribes, especially the Karankawa, along the coast. To others, the word "ranger" has more meaning when applied to the actions of the Kuykendalls who organized a small ranging party in 1827 to detect inroads in the colony by northern Indians like the Waco. One must remember that these faint beginnings of the Texas Rangers took place in Mexican Texas. That means, then, that the Ranger service in the Lone Star State has been a cultural mix: a hybrid of Anglo-European, Native-American, and Mexican and Spanish traditions.[8] These generational beliefs and practices especially included the use of horses and their accoutrements, from the southern rangers on horseback in the American colonies to the Spanish flying companies of horsemen and the Comanche fusion of horse and rider into a formidable fighter.

In the 1830s, two events put the Texas Rangers on a more systematic leadership basis. During the summer of 1835, the brave but impulsive Robert M. Coleman and his company of mounted riflemen fought a bloody battle with Tawakonis and other Indians (who dug rifle pits) in present-day Limestone County. The captain and those who survived fell back until reinforcements arrived from other companies. The combined force then took the field under the command of John H. Moore, an organizing process supported by Captain Coleman. The state later paid Coleman and others for engaging in the "ranging service." To some, this action was a step in putting together a Ranger command system.[9]

The second significant event of 1835 affecting Ranger development derived from legislative action taken by the provisional government in establishing defensive forces. On November 24, 1835, statutes addressing a militia and setting up all military units under the general in charge of the regular army became law. At the same time the government established a "corps of Rangers," the first statutory mention of the force.

The swashbuckling "Three-Legged Willie" Williamson was selected the Ranger commander with the rank of major. At least one captain, John J. Tumlinson, Jr., and his company took the field against Indian tribes and aided settlers in the Runaway Scrape during the Texas Revolution.[10]

The following year, a little more than a month after the Texas victory at San Jacinto, twenty Texas Rangers, commanded by Isaac Burton, became henceforth known as "Marine Rangers" when they captured a Mexican schooner in Copano Bay; and within a couple of weeks they captured two more vessels with considerable supplies that now became forage for the Texans rather than for the Mexican army. As historian Mike Cox put it, the supplies "fed and armed Texas troops."[11]

Texian officials who gained independence from Mexico called for elections in September 1836 to accomplish three purposes: ratify a constitution, elect officers of the new government, and ascertain public opinion on annexation to the United States. In that month, voters overwhelmingly approved the constitution and expressed a desire to join the American Union. They also elected Sam Houston as president and Mirabeau Lamar as vice president. The newly formed Republic of Texas, which was supposed to have an ephemeral existence, lasted for nearly a decade. Governing bodies in an independent republic were no longer figments of the imagination.[12]

The Republic's political establishment and its popular base were born in wartime and had its difficulties for years to come. "The Republic of Texas had a difficult birth," Randolph B. Campbell, a leading historian of Texas wrote, "and rarely enjoyed a calm moment during its ten years of life. Plagued by factional politics and chaotic finances, unable to win annexation to the United States or recognition of its independence by Mexico, the Republic never developed a national identity and struggled constantly just to survive. Yet Texas attracted more immigrants than ever before. No amount of political turmoil or diplomatic uncertainty could discourage those who saw opportunity in the cheap lands of the new republic."[13] Of necessity, this influx of settlers precipitated conflict with Native land occupiers and the Texas Rangers' import and traditions emerged.

The Constitution of the Republic of Texas reflected the Anglo-American preference for the legal system and branches of government of the United States. The founders established a bicameral legislature, giving it the powers to declare war and maintain an army, navy, and militia. The lack of financial resources coupled with the needs of frontier defense meant a pressing demand for men at arms within a shrinking military establishment. In emergencies in combating ancient foes, Texians could always fall back upon their mobile hit-and-run forces: the Rangers.[14]

In the political arena during the Republic era, the leading lights were Houston and Lamar. Colorful, demanding, and not always tactful, Houston served two terms as president (1836–1838 and 1841–1844). In between, his archrival, Lamar, a gifted writer and orator, presided over a presidential administration (1838–1841). Houston's goals while in office were to handle the nation's debt, dampen the conflict with Mexico, coexist with the Indian tribes, and join the American federation of states as soon as possible. Lamar, on the other hand, did not worry about finances and dreamed about building an empire to the Pacific Ocean. To do so Texians needed to be resolute and forceful in their dealings with Indian tribes and Mexico.[15] Both of these leaders utilized ranger companies to implement their policies. One of Lamar's schemes was to expand the geographical area of Texas by seizing control of what became the New Mexico territory, then under control of Mexico. Texas authors frequently refer to the episode as the "Santa Fe Expedition," while New Mexico historians call it the "Invasion of New Mexico." The effort turned into a fiasco for Lamar and Texas. Although Texas Rangers were not officially involved, numerous men either had served in ranging companies, such as Mathew Campbell, or later would become involved with the organization.[16]

During the initial years of Houston's presidency, Congress passed laws to augment the armed forces by raising large numbers of mounted riflemen or gunmen to enter into the ranging service but Houston tried to keep the military establishment to the minimum. Preparing for warfare, however, President Lamar pushed to use the regular army and the militia with laws passed accordingly. At the same time, Congress enacted legislation authorizing ranging companies to protect individual counties. Lamar's aggressive posture appealed to frontier settlements. In his second term as president in the 1840s, Houston approved several laws that raised companies of mounted men in arms to act as Rangers. By now, the Republic not only needed the Ranger service, but the mounted force became more economical and effective as an arm of the state. The actions of Hays and his cohorts would confirm such a view in the years to come.[17]

The Ranger service in the era of the Republic can be approached from several vantage points: first, more organized Ranger companies in the field with more experienced manpower; second, the adaptability of the Rangers to the shifting goals of Texan political leaders in the age of Manifest Destiny; third, the rise of the Ranger mystique of the patriot-warrior and its counterpart, the bloody avenger; and fourth, the images of the Rangers as seen by artists, folklorists, newspaper reporters, novelists, and the public at large.

Dressed in wide-brimmed hats of some sort (even straw hats in the summers), with shirts, jackets, and pantaloons of the frontiersmen, armed with Kentucky-Pennsylvania-Tennessee rifles, single-shot pistols (carried in belts or in holsters on either side of the saddle horns), and Bowie knives or even tomahawks, the early Texas Rangers on horseback were more recognizable than uniform. In popular literature, writers often depicted the Rangers operating in the middle of the 1800s as wild-eyed individuals, huge, bearded, and carrying fearsome weapons. The pop culture image, though, resembled too much the way people envisioned mountain men in the wilds of the American West.[18]

In the formative years of the Ranger service during the Republic and its aftermath, four men rose through the ranks and showed an ability to lead. First, and foremost, stood the mild-mannered Jack Hays. Three others joined Hays, sometimes together, sometimes separately, as rough-and-ready fighters: Benjamin "Ben" McCulloch, Samuel H. "Sam" Walker, and John S. "Rip" Ford. All four laid the foundations for the distinctive role played by the Rangers in military affairs.[19]

During the second half of the 1830s the Ranger service, formed and reformed, faced numerous threats from Indian tribes and Mexican nationals. In the year that the Republic came into being, a violent act occurred that had regional and national overtones. Members of the Parker clan and other inhabitants with similar religious beliefs built a settlement in North Texas. The settlers erected a fortified community, consisting of cabins, a stockade, and blockhouses guarding the gates. Contemporaries often referred to the frontier fortification simply as Fort Parker. In May 1836, while most of the men were working in the fields, Comanche and other Indians attacked those inside the fort. Several were killed, including Silas Parker, leader of a Ranger district, and a number of settlers were taken captive, the most prominent being Cynthia Ann Parker. Her life thereafter became part of Texan folklore, from giving birth to Quanah Parker, famed Comanche chief, to her recapture decades later, part of the enduring story of the political career of Lawrence Sullivan "Sul" Ross.[20]

During the days of the Republic, central Texas became a meeting ground between Texians and the various Indian tribes. They met, they talked, they traded, and they fought. More often than not, each side lost combatants but those who survived would fight another day. For a time, battles could be seen as set-piece maneuvers. However, the usual guerilla fighting called for surprise attacks, with both sides killing men, women, and children in bloodthirsty ways.

This happened in November 1837 at the "Stone Houses," a rock formation in present-day Archer County. Here an eighteen-member Ranger party under the command of Lieutenant A. B. Vanbenthuysen, looking for stolen horses, encountered a mixed group of Indians, about 150 strong, some of whom were armed with rifles. In the ensuing battle, the Texans made a defensive stand in a ravine. Heated firing took place for an extended period, continuing even after the Texans had downed their attackers' chief. Finally, after suffering numerous casualties, the Indians temporarily withdrew. By then the Rangers had lost four and had a number of horses killed. When the hostile Indians returned, they set fire to the dry grass and brush. The remaining Rangers made a foot charge against their rifle-armed foe. In the attack, the Indians shot and killed six more Texans and wounded three more. The Ranger officer in charge reported that his men had killed approximately fifty of their attackers during the course of the battle. The few remaining Rangers, with the help of some friendly Indians, returned to white settlements. In this back-and-forth warfare, the Ranger service could not carry out an effective campaign without the support of the regular army or the militia.[21]

When Lamar assumed the presidential office of the Republic in 1838, a more aggressive policy towards Indian tribes and Mexican nationals became the law of the land. In his initial speech the new president called for hostile actions against the Indians "that will admit of no compromise and have no termination except in their total extinction or total expulsion."[22] However, as one historian noted: "Even with a fledgling regular army and a large corps of ranging companies (although many on paper only), he could not even defend the frontier settlements, much less exterminate the tribes. The one clear success of his policy was expulsion—expulsion of the Cherokees from eastern Texas."[23]

Tensions between the Cherokee and Anglo settlers in Northeast Texas resulted in the Cherokee War of 1839. Negotiations to find a peaceful settlement broke down although tribal leaders found common ground with Houston but not with Lamar. When this happened the military—regulars, militia, Rangers, and Indian allies, over a thousand strong—moved into East Texas to remove the Cherokee. Chief John Bowles led the Cherokee, while Kelsey H. Douglass, who was a compromise selection in the contest for command of the military, led the Texans.

The initial contact between the two forces went through several stages: talk, maneuver, and fight. In the end, two bloody engagements took place in present-day Henderson and Van Zandt counties. The first occurred on Battle Creek in July 1839, while the second more decisive engagement, known as the Battle of the Neches, happened a day later. In the latter struggle, the Cherokee and their Indian allies, numbering in the hundreds armed with rifles and bows and arrows, took a defensive position in a ravine and thicket. The Texans, down to about 500 men in arms, charged and drove their foe from the ravine toward the river. In the process the aging Chief Bowles, decked out in a vest and hat with a sword and sash given to him by Houston, tried to rally his tribesmen before being shot and killed. Most of the remaining Cherokees fled across the Red River into Indian Territory. In the fighting, the number of Indians killed was greater than the number of Texans, who suffered more wounded than their enemy. In time, the Shawnees also agreed to leave Texas for the Indian country—in a peaceful way.[24]

By the end of the 1830s, a clear and coherent policy by officials of the Republic to handle the issues posed by Indian tribes and Mexican nationals remained elusive. Diplomatic and military actions by Texan leaders seemed to be an indecisive hit-or-miss process. Three factors became important in this scenario: local concerns about everyday life in Texas settlements; infighting among Anglos, Indians, and Mexicans, which handicapped their ability to make decisions; and the intransigence shown by individuals, both Indian and white, that prevented compromised agreements from being made and carried out.

One official report in the early days of the Republic listed twenty-seven bands of Indians living in Texas. They were scattered from East Texas to the western lands. The Texan approach to relations with these tribes looked haphazard in response to local concerns about safety and welfare. Events that fit into this picture included Rangers versus Indians in the Elm Creek fight in 1837; in the Kickapoo War in 1838; in the Battle of Brushy Creek and its aftermath in 1839; and in the continuing struggle with the Comanche at the end of the decade.

At times Anglos, Indians, and Hispanics rode and fought together in the wars of the Republic. A notable example occurred with the campaign of John H. Moore against the Comanche in 1839, with Lipan Apache and Tonkawa volunteers with the Rangers in the engagements. Even more striking was the movement of Indian Rangers at the Red River against the Cherokee in 1839. This Texan force featured Captain James H. Durst's mixed company of whites and Indians, including

Captain Panther, a Shawnee leader, and his mounted company as well as Captain Lewis (Luis) Sánchez and his ranging company with numerous Tejanos. Anglos alone did not insure the survival of the Texas Republic.[25]

Two issues in the relations between Texas and Mexico seemed intractable: the placement of the southern border of Texas and Mexico's refusal to recognize the independence of Texas after the revolution. Events at the end of the 1830s between the two states were preliminary to the momentous clash of arms in the following decade. Also, one should make note of other incidents occurring during this preparatory stage, including the encounter of Captain Erastus "Deaf" Smith's Rangers (including Jack Hays) with Mexican forces near Laredo in 1837; the rebellion by Vicente Córdova, Tejanos, and Indians in 1838; and the Córdova fight at Mill Creek and the struggle with Manuel Flores in 1839. Texas, Mexico, and eventually the United States could not find the resolve to settle their differences in a peaceful and orderly way.[26]

The violent interplay among the Texans, the Indian tribes, especially the Comanche, and Mexican nationals in the early 1840s was a striking and confusingly complex state of affairs. Several events stood out in the headlines of the day: the Great Comanche Raid, the battle of Walker's Creek, the invasions by Mexican forces under the command of Generals Rafael Vásquez and Adrián Woll, and the subsequent Somervell and Mier expeditions. From all these endeavors, a folklore narrative of the intrepid Texas Rangers as well as the last days of the Republic took shape.[27]

With suddenness and overwhelming numbers, the Comanche (and Kiowa) struck Texas settlements. The Comanche raid of 1840 resulted from two important motivations: the thirst by the Indians for revenge after the deaths of their chiefs at the Council House fight in San Antonio and the encouragement to take such action given by Mexican officials and citizens. The Comanche, numbering in the hundreds, moved from their bastion in the Hill Country through the unsettled portions of central Texas, mostly undetected.

Two Texas towns bore the brunt of the Comanche onslaught. In late summer, the Indians first struck Victoria. They encircled the settlement, killed and wounded several inhabitants, and seized a large number of cattle and horses. Then, unexpectedly, the Comanche traveled the distance to the Gulf of Mexico and burned the seaport of Linnville. Townspeople fled into the water for safety. Comanche warriors plundered the town's stores and warehouses. On the return trip the Comanche wore tall hats and coats and their horses had bright ribbons and calicos tied to their manes and tails. Such an Indian war party might never again appear in the annals of history.

As word about the raid spread through Anglo Texas, armed parties began to gather at Plum Creek in present-day Caldwell County. Even Edward Burleson and his fighting force with their Indian auxiliary, Chief Placido and his Tonkawa, arrived to do battle. Numbering about 200, the Texans, following usual procedure, dismounted to form a line (here a hollow square) to meet a charge by the enemy. Although the Texan commander, Felix Huston, had no ranging experience, others on the field of battle, such as Mathew Caldwell, did. They led a mounted charge and a running fight took place for several miles over the countryside. In the end, more Comanche were killed than Texans. The result was a severe blow to this formidable Comanche-Kiowa offensive thrust into Anglo Texas.

The leaders of the Republic believed that an additional show of force was needed against the warlike tribes. Near the end of 1840 a ranging party of about ninety volunteers under John H. Moore, accompanied by Chief Castro and his Lipan scouts, moved into Indian Territory. They scouted, attacked, and destroyed a Comanche village on the upper Colorado River, killing over a hundred men, women, and children, leaving Texans with the belief that they had avenged the brutal raids on Victoria and Linnville.[28] That effort also enhanced the Texas Ranger tradition.

Tall talk and explosive actions between the Texas Republic and Mexico resulted in several serious armed clashes in the 1840s. Early in 1842, General Rafael Vásquez crossed the Rio Grande with a large Mexican force of regulars and militiamen, including Caddo Indians, and made a quick raid on San Antonio. After looting the town, the Mexican military withdrew. A small party of Texan volunteers, led by Jack Hays who was rising in Ranger ranks, watched the coming and going of Vásquez's armed body, even following them to the border with Mexico. By design, the incursion tested the Texan defenses and showed that Mexico still claimed the lands of the Lone Star State.[29]

Then the invasion came. In the fall of 1842, a Mexican army, commanded by General Adrián Woll, crossed the Rio Grande and once more occupied San Antonio. This force consisted of nearly 1,000 regulars, infantry, cavalry, and artillery, together with another 200 or 300 irregulars and militia, and accompanied by a contingent of Cherokee Indians under Vicente Córdova. Around 200 Texans, with Mathew Caldwell and Jack Hays in charge, faced the invaders. They established strong defensive lines in different directions along Salado Creek. Then Hays and a mounted Ranger company acted as decoys, riding close to San Antonio and taunting the Mexicans to come out and fight. Woll took the bait and his entire command soon reached the positions of the Texans. After skirmishing indecisively, the Mexican soldiers made a mass attack, with cannon, drums, and music. The Texans, firing their rifles from their cover, killed or wounded dozens of Mexican fighting-men with little loss of life themselves. Woll and his force moved back to San Antonio, and in time, they evacuated the town and retreated across the border to the safety of Mexico. The Battle of Salado Creek was over.[30]

President Houston knew that the Republic did not have the manpower and arms to mount an invasion of Mexico. Nevertheless, to quiet public opinion he appointed a militia general, Alexander Somervell, to take charge of the troops at San Antonio and move south towards the Mexican-Texas border. Inept and indecisive, Somervell took his time, his undisciplined force weakened by defections and lack of provisions. At the border, this motley military force disbanded at the end of 1842. Several hundred Texans, though, decided to cross the boundary line and seize and plunder the Mexican community of Mier, where they fought and lost to a large body of Mexican troops. At one point, the Texas militiamen captured at Mier tried to escape. After their recapture, a Mexican firing squad executed seventeen Texans, who selected black beans from an earthen jar of white beans. The "black-bean" episode enraged Anglo Texans. Mexican authorities imprisoned the rest of the Mier prisoners at Perote Castle near Vera Cruz. Some of the captives escaped, while other succumbed to the harsh conditions of their confinement. In 1844, Mexico released the last of the Mier prisoners, returning him to Texas.[31]

The year 1844 was a key moment in Ranger history. By then Jack Hays and the Ranger service had obtained revolvers manufactured by Samuel Colt. While on a scouting mission in the Hill Country, Hays and a small detachment of Rangers, with famed Sam Walker and Robert Addison Gillespie as members, encountered a large Comanche war party led by Yellow Wolf. At the Battle of Walker's Creek, June 8, 1844, both sides maneuvered, attacked, and stood off counterattacks. At one point, Hays and his Rangers charged, fired, and dropped their rifles, and used their five-shot Paterson Colts in close combat. In the end, the Comanche suffered greater losses—slain or wounded—than the Rangers. The coming of the Colt revolver revolutionized warfare in the American Southwest.[32]

To some inside and outside Texas, Jack Hays and those who followed him were the best fighters in the last days of the Republic. He and his Rangers engaged Indians or Mexicans in a number of important conflicts: at Laredo, at Uvalde Canyon, and at the Llano River in 1841, in the Vásquez Raid and the Woll invasion in 1842, near the Medina River in 1843, and at Walker's Creek and near the Nueces River in 1844. At the same time two of the more famous Republic fights fought by Hays and his Rangers—Enchanted Rock in 1841 and Bandera Pass in 1842—have become controversial. They mix history and folklore because of disputes about location, time (day, month, year), and the use of conflicting records, if any exist. Yet Hays has become the quintessential Ranger.[33]

For several U.S. presidential administrations from Andrew Jackson to James Polk, settlement, revolution, independence, and statehood for Texas was an important topic in national politics. The federal government had to decide whether to admit Texas to the Union, and if so whether to admit Texas by treaty or joint resolution of Congress. The latter procedure resulted in a favorable passage of an annexation resolution in both houses of the United States Congress in early 1845. President Anson Jones delayed a Texas vote of acceptance in order to pursue diplomatic aims with European countries as well as with Mexico. In October of that year, however, Texans approved annexation by an overwhelming vote. Elections for a new state government took place and the final ceremony marking completion of joining the United States was held on February 19, 1846, with the Lone Star flag being lowered and the Stars and Stripes being raised to the top of the flagpole. Outgoing Texas President Jones concluded: "The final act in this great drama is now performed. The Republic of Texas is no more."[34]

Texans had not forgotten the efforts of the Ranger service. The newly elected Texas legislature passed a resolution praising the courageous actions of Jack Hays, Ben McCulloch, and Robert Gillespie. In a decade of sporadic military engagements probably several hundred Texans, called Rangers, spies, volunteers, were killed or wounded on the battlefields. The most serious loss of life, thirty-six, resulted from the actions of Captain Nicholas Dawson and his company of Texan volunteers who tried to reach the Texas lines during the Woll invasion but were cut down by irregular Mexican cavalry.

In addition, several Ranger companies were formed, one headed by Captain Gillespie, with Major Hays commanding the new battalion. A key duty of these mounted troops would be to scout and report to General Zachary Taylor and the United States Army as they moved into Texas.[35] The subsequent war with Mexico offered Anglo Texans one more opportunity to fight Mexicans south of the border as United States military leaders recruited several Ranging companies during the U.S.-Mexican War (1846–1848).

In the time of the Republic, the Rangers evolved into a more organized body of irregulars with an esprit de corps. They became regional icons who gained a reputation either as patriot-warriors or as bloody avengers in their struggles with Indian tribes and Mexican nationals. The Rangers carried this dual identity into the U.S.-Mexican War, which gave them a national reputation. As prominent Ranger historian Robert Utley put it: "Until 1846, hardly anyone outside Texas had heard of the Texas Rangers. The Mexican War nationalized the Ranger tradition and earned it an enduring place in the imagination of Americans."[36]

By the middle of the nineteenth century, the Texas Rangers had come of age. From ad hoc parties of citizen-soldiers they assumed a more definite shape during the Republic and thereafter. The Rangers became an organized body of experienced horse soldiers with an esprit de corps ready to carry out a nationalistic tradition. This common spirit inspired enthusiasm, devotion, and a regard for the masculine attributes (strong, brave, and honorable) of being Rangers. The fighting columns of early Texans—Rangers, militiamen, and army regulars—carried out what one recent historian has called the "Texas Way of War."[37]

Notes

1. Robert M. Utley, "Images of the Texas Rangers," in *The Way West: True Stories of the American Frontier*, ed. James A. Crutchfield (New York: Tom Doherty Associates, 2005), 263.

2. Ibid., 258.

3. The general histories of the Rangers in Texas will give you a bird's-eye view of these luminaries and events. See, for example, Mike Cox, *The Texas Rangers: Wearing the Cinco Paso, 1821–1900* (New York: Forge, 2008); Charles M. Robinson, III, *The Men Who Wore the Star: The Story of the Texas Rangers* (New York: Random House, 2000); Robert M. Utley, *Lone Star Justice: The First Century of Texas Rangers* (New York: Oxford University Press, 2002); and Walter Prescott Webb, *The Texas Rangers: A Century of Frontier Defense* (Boston: Houghton Mifflin, 1935); Bruce A. Glasrud and Harold J. Weiss, Jr., eds., *Tracking the Texas Rangers: The Nineteenth Century* (Denton: University of North Texas Press, 2012).

4. For the use of traditionalism and other interpretive schemes in historical writings about Texas, see Walter L. Buenger and Arnoldo De León, eds., *Beyond Texas Through Time: Breaking Away from Past Interpretations* (College Station: Texas A&M University Press, 2011).

5. Steven L. Hardin, *The Texas Rangers* (London: Osprey Publishing Ltd, 1991), 4. See also Mark E. Nackman, "The Making of the Texan Citizen Soldier, 1835–1860," *Southwestern Historical Quarterly* 78 (Jan. 1975): 231–53.

6. For a vivid look at the nature of the Rangers, see Stephen L. Hardin, "'Valor, Wisdom, and Experience': Early Texas Rangers and the Nature of Frontier Leadership," in *Tracking the Texas Rangers: The Nineteenth Century*, eds., Bruce A. Glasrud and Harold J. Weiss, Jr. (Denton: University of North Texas Press, 2012), 50–61.

7. Sidney Hook, *The Hero in History* (1943; repr. Boston: Beacon Press, 1943, reprint 1955), 151–83.

8. For a look at the origins of the earliest Rangers, see the differing viewpoints in Allen G. Hatley, *The Indian Wars in Stephen F. Austin's Texas Colony, 1822–1835* (Austin: Eakin Press, 2001); and D. E. Kilgore, *A Ranger Legacy: 150 Years of Service to Texas* (Austin: Madrona Press, 1973).

9. Stephen L. Moore, *Savage Frontier: Rangers, Riflemen, and Indian Wars in Texas, 1835–1837* (Plano, TX: Republic of Texas Press, 2002), Vol. 1, pp. 21–29. Malcolm D. McLean, compiler of the papers of the Robertson Colony, recognized the role played by Coleman in organizing the Rangers. See Utley, *Lone Star Justice*, 306–07, n. 8.

10. Frederick Wilkins, *The Legend Begins: The Texas Rangers, 1823–1845* (Austin: State House Press, 1996), 13–24. For a succinct look at the early Rangers, see Darren L. Ivey, *The Texas Rangers: A Registry and History* (Jefferson, NC: McFarland & Co., 2010).

11. Mike Cox, "Isaac Burton and His Horse Marines," in *Texas Ranger Tales II* (Plano, TX: Republic of Texas Press, 1999), 1–12, quote on 5.

12. Numerous works have been published on the revolutionary era and the beginnings of the Republic. See, for example, Stephen L. Hardin, *Texian Iliad: A Military History of the Texas Revolution* (Austin: University of Texas Press, 1994); and Paul D. Lack, *The Texas Revolutionary Experience: A Political and Social History, 1835–1836* (College Station : Texas A&M University Press, 1991).

13. Randolph B. Campbell, *Gone to Texas: A History of the Lone Star State* (New York: Oxford University Press, 2003), 159. For a short history of the state with an extensive chapter on the Republic, see Archie P. McDonald, *Texas: All Hail the Mighty State* (Austin: Eakin Press, 1983).

14. For a starting point about the ins and outs of the Republic, see Seymour V. Connor, *Adventure in Glory, 1836–1849* (Austin: Steck-Vaughn, 1965); and William R. Hogan, *The Texas Republic: A Social and Economic History* (Norman: University of Oklahoma Press, 1946).

15. Wilkins, *The Legend Begins*, 102–103.

16. Of the many biographical studies, see James Haley, *Sam Houston* (Norman: University of Oklahoma Press, 2002); and Stanley E. Siegel, *The Poet President of Texas: The Life of Mirabeau B. Lamar, President of the Republic of Texas* (Austin: Jenkins, 1977).

17. For a brief summary of the military laws, see Webb, *Texas Rangers*, 29–34. Stephen Moore in an appendix entitled "Texas Ranger Companies of the Republic of Texas, 1835–1845" has listed over two hundred units. See *Savage Frontier: Rangers, Riflemen, and Indian Wars in Texas, 1842–1845* (Denton: University of North Texas Press, 2010), Vol. 4, Appendix, pp. 207–19. Moore's four-volume chronicle is encyclopedic in nature.

18. For images and analyses of attire and accoutrements, see John L. Davis, *The Texas Rangers: Images and Incidents* (San Antonio: University of Texas Institute of Texan Cultures, 1991); and Wilkins, *Legend Begins*, 59–70.

19. Thomas W. Cutrer, *Ben McCulloch and the Frontier Military Tradition* (Chapel Hill: University of North Carolina Press, 1993); James K. Greer, *Colonel Jack Hays: Texas Frontier Leader and California Builder* (New York: E. P. Dutton & Co., 1952); Richard B. McCaslin, *Fighting Stock: John S. "Rip" Ford of Texas* (Fort Worth: Texas Christian University Press, 2011).

20. Paul H. Carlson and Tom Crum, *Myth, Memory and Massacre: The Pease River Capture of Cynthia Ann Parker* (Lubbock: Texas Tech University Press, 2010); Jo Ella Powell Exley, *Frontier Blood: The Story of the Parker Family* (College Station: Texas A&M University Press, 2001); S. C. Gwynne, *Empire of the Summer Moon: Quanah Parker and the Rise and Fall of the Comanches, the Most Powerful Indian Tribe in American History* (New York: Scribner, 2010).

21. Moore, *Savage Frontier*, Vol. 1, pp. 267–78.

22. Utley, *Lone Star Justice*, 24.

23. Ibid.

24. Stephen L. Moore, *Savage Frontier: Rangers, Rifleman, and Indian Wars in Texas, 1838–1839* (Denton: University of North Texas Press, 2006), Vol. 2, pp. 235–304. For a look at the Cherokee Tribe, see Dianna Everett, *The Texas Cherokees: A People Between Two Fires, 1819–1840* (Norman: University of Oklahoma Press, 1990).

25. Moore, *Savage Frontier*, Vols. 1 and 2.

26. Ibid.

27. Detailed coverage of these events will be found in two works by Stephen Moore: *Savage Frontier: Rangers, Riflemen, and Indian Wars in*

Texas, 1840–1841 (Denton: University of North Texas Press, 2007); and *Savage Frontier: Rangers, Riflemen, and Indian Wars in Texas, 1842–1845* (Denton: University of North Texas Press, 2010).

28. For a study of these events, see Donaly E. Brice, *The Great Comanche Raid: Boldest Indian Attack of the Texas Republic* (Austin: Eakin Press, 1987). For an up-to-date revision, see Donaly E. Brice, "The Great Comanche Raid of 1840," in *Tracking the Texas Rangers: The Nineteenth Century*, edited by Bruce A. Glasrud and Harold J. Weiss, Jr. (Denton: University of North Texas Press, 2012), 62–86.

29. The Vásquez raid is retold in detail in Joseph Milton Nance, *The Texas-Mexican Frontier, 1842* (Austin: University of Texas Press, 1964).

30. For the particulars and sources for the Woll invasion, see Utley, *Lone Star Justice*, 43–52.

31. Sam W. Haynes, *Soldiers of Misfortune: The Somervell and Mier Expeditions* (Austin: University of Texas Press, 1990); Joseph M. Nance and Archie P. McDonald, *Dare-Devils All: The Texan Mier Expedition, 1842–1844* (Austin: Eakin Press, 1998). See also Sterling B. Hendricks, "The Somervell Expedition to the Rio Grande, 1842," *Southwestern Historical Quarterly* 23 (October 1919).

32. Moore, *Savage Frontier*, Vol. 4, pp. 139–154; Utley, *Lone Star Justice*, 3–12.

33. Most of these Ranger-Indian-Mexican events are covered in volumes 3 and 4 of Moore, *Savage Frontier*.

34. Campbell, *Gone to Texas*, 182–186, quote on 186.

35. Moore, *Savage Frontier*, Vol. 4, pp. 75–84, 187–200.

36. Utley, *Lone Star Justice*, 58. The iconic view of the Texas Rangers at the end of the Republic was not of a singular mindset. The images varied in number and kind: heroes like Jack Hays; rogues in the mold of Mabry "Mustang" Gray; folkloric figures, such as William A. A. "Big Foot" Wallace; and incompetent captains in the field, as, for example, John Bird.

37. Nathan Jennings, *Riding for the Lone Star: Frontier Cavalry and the Texas Way of War, 1822–1865* (Denton: University of North Texas Press, 2016).

PART III:

Politics and Economics in the Republic

Chapter 7
Sam Houston: Trials and Tribulations of a President

James L. Haley

On October 22, 1836, Sam Houston took the oath of office as the first elected president of the Republic of Texas.[1] He was not prepared, he had no speech, and he hurriedly wrote out a succession of platitudes.[2] Provisional President ad-Interim David Burnet had resigned unexpectedly, two months early, in the face of near-mutiny in the Texas Army. Though elected with nearly 90 percent of the vote, Houston could look at the political landscape and know that just as many Texas leaders loathed him as idolized him.

At the time Houston arrived in Texas, on December 2, 1832, he was already one of the most famous men in America: a former governor of Tennessee and presidential prospect, but a man who had suffered political and social ruin. Also, many knew of his ferocious reputation that people either admired or despised in proportion to their feelings about his scandalous failed marriage, about his friendly relations with Native Indians, and most of all about his mentor, Andrew Jackson, the immensely polarizing president of the United States.

Houston was born in Virginia, but not the polite, English-descended Tidewater region that produced Washington and Madison. He was from Rockbridge County, near the Shenandoah Valley, a wild country settled by Scotch-Irish immigrants who journeyed down the Great Philadelphia Wagon Road. When Houston was thirteen his widowed mother moved the family to a raw new farmstead near Maryville, in the foothills of the Great Smoky Mountains of eastern Tennessee. Loathing work at the family farm or general store, he ran away at sixteen and lived for three years with a band of Cherokee Indians who lived on Hiwassee Island in the Tennessee River. There he learned to roam, drink, and love free life in a way more direct than other Americans' rhetoric about "liberty." He also acquired a respect and love for Indians that made polite people profoundly uncomfortable.

Sam Houston. President of the Republic of Texas. Courtesy of the Library of Congress.

Paradoxically, he also loved classical literature. When he left home, he took with him Pope's translation of *The Iliad*, a book that became a lifelong touchstone, and he began amassing a knowledge of Roman history that dwarfed that of his contemporaries. He returned home at nineteen and taught for a term at the Maryville school—a cheeky occupation for a youth who himself had withstood less than a year of formal education. He made a success of it, however, and paid off debts he had run up supplying gifts to his Cherokee friends. At twenty, with his mother's permission, he enlisted in the army. The War of 1812 was in full roar, and Jackson as a Tennessee militia general was raising a force to punish hostile (and British-influenced) Creek Indians guilty of the Fort Mims Massacre. In the climactic Battle of Horseshoe Bend, Houston received three grievous wounds, and battlefield surgeons believed he would not survive the night. Despite the medical prognosis, Houston recovered, slowly, but his wounds never completely healed.

His pluck and gallantry were rewarded by a succession of mentors. Congressman John Rhea of Houston's district helped him to win a permanent commission in the army; Jackson placed him on his staff, and then made him the government's sub-agent to the Hiwassee Cherokees, with the goal of removing them from Tennessee to new lands in the West. They did not want to go and Houston hated doing it, but Governor Joseph McMinn counseled him through the removal, which Houston carried out so humanely that the Cherokee never blamed him for it. (The infamous "Trail of Tears" lay many years in the future.) He imposed on family friend Judge James Trimble to sponsor him in reading for the law; merchant Isaac Golladay extended him credit to enter practice, and after less than a year, voters elected him solicitor general for Nashville. He rose to become the most prominent of Jackson's political aides, and he served four years in Congress. In 1827, Tennessee voters elected Houston governor. After serving a successful term in office, many believed President Jackson's young protégé was on the path to his own presidential bid. During his campaign for reelection, what had seemed like a brilliant marriage to Eliza Allen of Gallatin ended disastrously when she left him after ten weeks and returned to her parents. She had been pressured into the marriage by her ambitious family, who forced her to jilt a suitor whom she did love and wed Houston, whom she did not—which Houston discovered only after they exchanged vows. Contrary to the calumnies circulated by her family and his enemies, he did not leave her; she left him—an injustice he bore with a gentleman's silence, though it sent him into a free fall of drink and depression.

A broken Houston resigned his office and undertook a three-year exile to the Indian Territory, living again with the former Hiwassee Cherokees, taking an Indian wife (without Christian ceremony) in Diana Rogers, and for a time giving himself up to despair. Jealous competitors for Jackson's attention lost no time in capitalizing upon his fall, energetically discrediting him to their stunned principal.[3] Not until 1832 did Houston, once again in Washington on Cherokee business, vindicate himself into Jackson's confidence. The president had been attempting to purchase the Mexican province of Texas, but authorities in Mexico City summarily had rebuffed his efforts. American colonists in Texas, however, were growing increasingly dissatisfied with the Mexican government. As such, Jackson began to ponder an alternative route to securing Texas for the United States.

With ringing oratory, Houston restored his celebrity by defending himself on the floor of the House against an assault charge, for his beating an Ohio Congressman for calumnies uttered against Houston in that chamber.[4] Ginning up a pretext about meeting with Comanche Indians, Jackson sprung Houston into Texas, where he obtained land, entered politics, consulted with his many Tennessee associates who had located there, and began riding events as they careened toward revolution. The 1836 Convention that declared Texas independence also named Houston Commander-in-Chief of the Texas forces. He departed the gathering even as the Alamo fell, and from Gonzales he led a gaggle of volunteers on a retreat across the breadth of Texas that his "army" found humiliating almost to the point of mutiny.

For many years, to historians who have favored Houston, the purpose of the "Run-away Scrape" was to lure the Mexican dictator, Antonio López de Santa Anna, to chase the retreating Texas army, stretching his supply line until any mistake he made would be fatal. More recently, revisionist scholars have depicted Houston as a drunken poseur, dragged along by his own troops and forced to fight at San Jacinto.[5] Now, however, it has become increasingly clear that neither narrative hits the mark. The reason for Houston's silence was that he was prosecuting a plan to which absolute secrecy was essential. Indeed, he was luring Santa Anna eastward, even as General Edmund Pendleton Gaines was assembling an American force in the piney woods of western Louisiana. If Houston could bait Santa Anna into crossing the Neches River—the stream that Jackson claimed as the international boundary—Gaines would pounce across the Sabine and end the conflict with one stroke. As Anson Jones later realized, the Mexican-American War of 1846 would have been fought in 1836.[6]

It was a plot that required deep intrigue, including Houston's placement of a minion in the very cabinet of Ad-Interim President David Burnet, who hated Houston to the depth of his being and who had placed his own spies on Houston's staff in the attempt to discredit his command. They failed, but Houston's spy, Burnet's Secretary of State Samuel Price Carson, under the guise of a mission to the United States to raise money and volunteers, went instead to western Louisiana and served as liaison between Houston and Gaines. "You should fall back, if necessary, to the Sabine," Carson wrote Houston from Gaines's camp, "Volunteer troops will come on in numbers from the United States. You must fall back, and let nothing goad or provoke you to a battle, unless you can, without doubt, whip them."[7]

As events developed, Santa Anna did not take the bait. As the Texas government broke and stampeded for the coast, the President-General turned and pursued them, thinking to scotch the whole rebellion at once and then get on with his main business, which was enforcement of the Sabine River that he claimed as the international boundary. When Santa Anna turned, Houston turned also, forced his men fifty-five miles through sucking mud in two and a half days, and in the gory vengeance of San Jacinto, without doubt whipped them.

Houston's campaign and victory are the most instructive imaginable introduction to his subsequent presidency: pursuing an object that required profound planning and forecast, while fighting rear-guard political actions against other Texans motivated by personal animus. Having failed to get Houston replaced as commander, Ad-interim President David G. Burnet refused Houston's request to seek medical treatment in New Orleans for his ankle shattered by a musket ball during the Battle of San Jacinto. Burnet gave in only after the captain of the steamboat *Yellow Stone* defied him and refused to sail without Houston. However, the president took some satisfaction when his newly minted secretary of war, Mirabeau Lamar (whom the army repudiated) cashiered surgeon Alexander Ewing for desertion when he left with Houston, continuing to treat the general's wounds while en route to the Crescent City.

During his months of convalescence, Houston allowed supporters to enter his name in the first official election for President of the Republic of Texas. Stephen F. Austin, founder of the original colony, should have been the obvious choice, but his too-long-held loyalty to Mexico (principally among various other things) cost him popularity, and he received only 586 votes to Houston's 5,119.

Realizing that his defiantly insubordinate army might mutiny and topple the fragile civilian government, Burnet performed the one statesmanlike act of his tenure: he resigned early and turned affairs over to his archenemy, who was the one man who could control the troops. Caught by surprise and without a prepared inaugural speech, Houston assumed the presidency on October 22, 1836. The same election that swept Houston into the presidency included a referendum on annexation, and in all of Texas, only ninety-four men voted against joining the United States. Thus, it was widely assumed that Houston's tenure would last only long enough to formalize Texas's admission to the Union.

Indeed, Andrew Jackson ached to acquire the Lone Star Republic, but the political difficulties proved insuperable. Power in the Senate had been evenly balanced between slave states and free since the Missouri Compromise of 1820. Northern states refused to hand the South the advantage of admitting Texas as a slave state, plus annexing Texas potentially would lead to a war with Mexico, which repudiated the Treaties of Velasco as soon as Santa Anna was safely home. The chagrin in Texas was nearly universal when the final act of Jackson's administration was to recognize the independence of the Republic of Texas, and Houston had to confront the myriad tasks of launching a new country.

Though Stephen F. Austin was angry and bitter over his crushing defeat in the contest for the presidency, he accepted the portfolio of secretary of state to formalize the cessation of hostilities (not quite peace) with Mexico and open the campaign for annexation. From getting an office open (sending to New Orleans for sealing wax and blank log and account books) to starting a national currency (beginning with promissory notes that Houston ordered be floated only gradually so as not to deflate their value), the presidential office was a hive of activity. Houston was the one personage known throughout the United States, and his letterbox overflowed with correspondence—letters of introduction, inquiries into the fate of relatives who disappeared during the revolution, and queries regarding the republic's terms for land grants for settlement.[8]

The nation's capital was located in Columbia, mostly because it was one of the few towns not burned during the revolution. It was inadequate to the purpose, and during the spring of 1837, Congress relocated the seat of government fifty-five miles to the northeast to a purpose-built capital city named for the president. Houston was on Buffalo Bayou, upstream from Texas's principal port of Galveston. It was the entrepreneurial project of two brothers named Allen, who threw in construction of a spacious frame Capitol if the government would relocate to their city.

There the trials Houston endured as head of government were partly compensated by the distinction of being head of state: he received distinguished visitors such as the naturalist John James Audubon, presided over the first meeting of the Philosophical Society of Texas, attended the first professional theatre performance given in the new country (his entrance accompanied by "Hail to the Chief") and on April 21 he opened the first San Jacinto Ball in shoes specially fashioned to support his shattered ankle. Still, the personal demons that earlier drove him to drink still spurred him, causing him to frequently make a spectacle of himself. While he became the favorite and champion of the rougher class of frontiersmen, those who meant to establish polite society in Texas found him as odious as ever.

Increasingly the latter coalesced into a faction around Mirabeau Lamar, one of whose partisans wrote that Houston "dresses himself gaudily in self peculiar taste viz. black silk velvet gold lace crimson vest and silver spurs." Inebriated, "he makes himself again *Hector* upon his feet and no longe [*sic*] the wounded Achilise of San Jacinto … and with a tread of dominion in his aroganic [*sic*] step strides … across his own nominated metropolis … to the barkeeper."[9]

Feelers arrived by post from Tennessee that his estranged wife was ready to forgive all and come be first lady of the new nation, to which the president apparently did not respond.[10] He found some solace in opening a courtship with Anna Raguet of Nacogdoches—beautiful, cultured, and seventeen—but she kept a polite distance until she married his secretary of state, Robert Irion.[11] He also found a congenial roommate in a new surgeon general, Ashbel Smith, who arrived with a library full of classics of Greece and Rome and the Renaissance, and who became his friend for life.

Letters from the countryside, however, let him know that all was not well in the infant country, particularly concerning the overbearing military. Soldiers of the Texas Army had killed an ox belonging to one Daniel Elam of China Grove, as Elam wrote indignantly to the president, "without giving me any notice of the same—or giving me any thing to show for the damages they had done." He brought this to Houston's attention, "believing as I do that you for one will not suffer such depredation" to be committed upon private citizens.[12]

Indeed, Houston undertook an inspection tour and determined that the army was emerging as a serious threat to Texas's democracy itself. The revolution had ended so suddenly that it caught huge numbers of volunteers still on road or ship from the United States: included among their numbers were companies of hotspurs ambitious for personal glory in Texas and would-be martinets and latter-day filibusters who had trouble accepting that they missed the fight. The most unruly was Felix Huston of Mississippi. His belligerence had been a large factor in President Burnet's resignation, and now his particular hobbyhorse was an intended invasion (which would have been a pillaging raid) of Matamoros. For months Houston answered his too many and too familiar letters with friendly stalling, until he appointed Albert Sidney Johnston as senior brigadier and commander-in-chief of the forces. Huston was scalded; he resigned what he thought was his intimacy with the president, wounded Johnston in a duel, and retained command for himself. Unwilling to take him head-on, Houston summoned the would-be generalissimo to the capital for a conference, and in dead of night dispatched his secretary of war, S. Rhoads Fisher, with orders furloughing the excess troops and offering them free transport back to the United States. When Huston returned to camp, he discovered he had almost no army left. Local merchant (and later governor) Francis Lubbock called this the greatest act of Indian cunning he ever witnessed,[13] and it may well have preserved civilian rule in the new republic.

Mexico remained a threat, and Houston procured four small ships to form a Texas Navy. He also pursued friendship with Great Britain—a thorny goal because Texas depended on cotton, a cash crop cultivated by slaves, and the English increasingly disapproved of slavery. He went as far as he could without alienating his own people. With the British consul to Tampico, Joseph Tucker Crawford, with him on the podium, Houston denounced the slave trade to the Texas Congress as he backed legislation outlawing the African slave trade in Texas, which he was able to argue went no farther than U.S. law had done for a generation. After dispatching J. Pinckney Henderson as envoy to Britain, Houston instructed him (via Irion) that when he was pinned down about slavery, "you can speak with candor and truth, admitting that its institution was cruel and impolitic," but that Texas's economy was, for the time being, beholden to it.[14]

Crawford and many in England were favorably impressed, but recognition was not to come during Houston's brief term of office. The Republic's Constitution barred presidents from serving consecutive terms, and by an additional quirk, the first president's tenure in office was limited to two years with subsequent presidential terms set at three years. Houston's many enemies coalesced behind Mirabeau Lamar. His campaign was scurrilous, and neither of Houston's approved candidates survived the campaign for the office. Calumnies uttered against Peter Grayson had so undone the candidate that he blew his brains out, and James Collinsworth, drunk or despondent or both, either fell or threw himself from a boat into Galveston Bay.

Lamar, whom Houston had elevated from corporal to colonel of cavalry during the Battle of San Jacinto, had gone over to Burnet bag and baggage, and Houston, never one to go quietly, materialized at the inauguration dressed as George Washington, and according to one observer, "he really looked more like the [Gilbert Stuart] portrait than ever did Washington himself."[15] Houston also held the podium, and spoke, for three or four hours, leaving Lamar so apoplectic that his secretary had to read his speech for him.

Winning the election virtually by default, Lamar's vastly different vision of Texas and its place in the world seemed dedicated to erasing Houston's imprint from the country: The new president launched a war to the knife against the Texas Cherokee whom Houston had patiently courted and aggression toward Mexico which Houston had avoided antagonizing. Both presidential positions required Congress to create a monetary policy that sent the Republic's economy into a tailspin. More importantly, Lamar proposed a continental vision for Texas, which froze annexation in its tracks.

Houston intended a long respite through the United States, cashing in some of his San Jacinto laurels, and ultimately sojourning with Jackson at the Hermitage. Unhappy with the first draft at a passport, he had the word "citizen" struck out and replaced with "late president" of the Republic of Texas.[16] By the time of his return to Texas, Houston was energized, first by having become engaged to the young woman of his dreams in Margaret Lea of Marion, Alabama, and second by fury at how the country was being governed in his absence. Lamar had removed the capital from Houston City to the raw new village of Austin, eighty miles northeast of San Antonio, where lurking Comanche warriors picked off citizens who ventured beyond the edge of town. Houston took a seat in Congress as Representative from San Augustine, where he rebuilt his power base and gathered allies to regain the presidency.

Differences in policy mingled with personal insults, as one of Lamar's first acts was to banish Houston's beloved Lone Star flag of a golden star on an azure background and replace it with a red, white, and blue tricolor. He also returned to Houston furniture in the executive residence, the use of which Houston had allowed him until Lamar could make his own arrangements. The furniture, however, was so ruined that Houston filed a lawsuit for damages, which Lamar ultimately had to pay after delaying disposition of the suit for nearly a decade. Houston had always been a political lightning rod. One either loved him or hated him, and during the campaign in the autumn of 1841, Texans commonly framed political issues in terms of one's stance with Houston, or against Houston.

His campaign for restoration to the presidency was waged against Lamar's preferred successor, former Ad-interim President Burnet whose hatred of Houston if anything exceeded Lamar's. The canvass was epic in its ugliness, from both sides. The result was Burnet's crushing defeat that led to his disappearance from public life. Houston meant to exult in his triumph, and had the French chargé, Alphonse du Bois, Comte de Saligny, order from Paris a costume in moss-green velvet, "a la Henry V," in which to be sworn in. He thought better of it, fortunately, and dressed as a frontiersman in "linsey-woolsey hunting shirt" to assume office for the second time.[17] Eschewing the "President's House" that Lamar had ensconced himself in—which in his haste to live in suitable grandeur had been built of green lumber and was now pulling apart at the seams—Houston took up residence at Angelina Eberly's boarding house.

Lamar's administration was not without accomplishment, most importantly achieving recognition by France and Great Britain, which gave Houston the tools he needed to make another run at annexation by the United States. More urgent, however, was to mitigate the worst damage from Lamar's term. The Comanche were openly hostile and the Brazos Valley tribes—the Waco, Keechi, Anadarko, Tawakoni, and others—barely less so, and Houston undertook carefully staged councils with the latter, whom he employed to attest his sincerity to the former, which brought a measure of quiet to the frontier. Lamar's provocations toward Mexico, which had included renting the Texas Navy to rebels in Yucatan and trying to annex New Mexico under the fig leaf of the Santa Fé "trading" expedition, resulted in two Mexican invasions during 1842. This prompted Houston to move the capital from the exposed village of Austin about a hundred miles east to the site of Texas's independence, Washington (only later called Washington on the Brazos).

Most urgent of all, Houston had to pursue his objectives while slashing public spending almost to nothing, as what became known as the "Retrenchment Congress" passed a budget of shocking austerity. Lamar's imperial ambitions, while his government engraved ever-prettier issues of paper currency, had deflated that money to as low as three cents against the American dollar. Real commerce was reduced virtually to barter; a blood feud had broken out in East Texas, from where Houston's attorney general Robert W. Terrell wrote him that, "It really appears to me as if society were about to dissolve itself into its original elements."[18]

When Houston removed government operations as far east as Washington on the Brazos, he left his land commissioner, Thomas William Ward, at his station in Austin, unfunded and dependent for kindness and credit upon an increasingly hostile population. Moreover, Houston twice sent Rangers to Austin to coordinate with Ward in removing the government papers from the city, thus kindling the "Archives War." Austin citizens sent the first party back to Washington with their horses' manes and tails shaved. When they discovered the second party loading documents into wagons in the dead of night, Mrs. Eberly alerted the town by firing the cannon that was kept loaded on Congress Avenue as an Indian alarm. (Some recent historians have doubted that the incident occurred as traditionally related, if at all, but Ward's own report states that the cannon was fired on them, not once but eight times). The Rangers attempted a get-away with as much of the archives as they had loaded, but an Austin mob overtook them on Brushy Creek. After a brief gunfight in which no one was hurt, the Austinites recovered the documents and placed them for safekeeping with Mrs. Eberly. The conflict left land commissioner Ward in a more precarious predicament than ever, but his entreaties to Houston for payment netted only a friendly gift of tobacco. "For your present of tobacco I am much obliged," Ward wrote him, "I would be more obliged if I could obtain the amount due me by the Republic."[19]

Similarly, James Reily, a lawyer and Ohio native who had been T. J. Rusk's aide-de-camp and then law partner, went to Washington, D.C., in high hopes as Texas's chargé d'affaires there, but soon found himself stranded without funds. For months, he maintained a witty banter on the subject of being paid, at one point remarking that he had met a lady to whom, as a young woman, Houston had given a ring when she defended him from her seat in the gallery during his assault trial before the House of Representatives. "My terms just now are one thousand dollars" for his salary and expenses. "I tell you what it is General both you and your Secretary of State had better keep me here & *pay me well* & promptly for staying, for if I come home in a bad humor … I shall be armed with facts enough to ruin your peace with your families."[20]

Eventually Reily gave up and resigned, and he appears to have borne home no romantic tales of Houston's earlier life. The new Secretary of State that Reily mentioned was Dr. Anson Jones, a legislator of some ability whom Houston had sent on a diplomatic mission to Washington during his first term. He was also, however, emotionally unstable, a dyspeptic misanthrope who was convinced to the depth of his being that he was the true leader of Texas, that only his influence prevented Houston from careening down a path of extremism and ruin, and that Houston was meanly appropriating all the laurels for himself. A disproportionate amount of Houston's correspondence to him was intended to cheer him up, but if the president had seen Jones's diary he likely would not have bothered. Houston, Jones wrote, "is not so strong in what he does himself, as in what his enemies do: it is not *his* strength, but *their* weakness—not his *wisdom* but their *folly*. Cunning, Indian cunning, is the secret of his business."[21]

Jones also threatened to quit when Houston allegedly broke his promise to pay the Secretary for his services in par money. What seemed to elude both Reily and Jones was that *nobody* in government service was being paid. The president could not even present his own five-thousand-dollar salary voucher to the treasury for payment, and instead wrote to his friend Tom Bagby back in Houston, "Pray do help me by renting my house … to some good man for $15 or $20 per month, and by the month. … It will help me some."[22]

If these penurious circumstances made anything clear, it was Texas's need to join herself to the United States, but as Houston turned his attention toward annexation, it was clear that previous appeals had not worked. He realized that the United States, whose schizophrenic record of alternately courting and spurning Texas now had a long public record, might never approve annexation unless adding Texas was an economic or military necessity. Slowly, Houston formulated a plan to achieve his purpose.

On one hand, he could tout Texas's increasingly warm relations with the British government, whose chargé d'affaires, Captain Charles Elliot, Houston had turned into a warm friend. Part of the wreckage of Lamar's administration was that several hundred Texans were now held in the dungeons of Mexico's Perote Castle—survivors of the Santa Fé "Trading" Expedition, along with hostages taken during the Mexican invasions of 1842, and the remnants of the mutineers from the Somervell Expedition, who disobeyed orders, invaded Mexico, and were defeated in the Battle of Mier. On January 24, 1843, he wrote Elliot to ask British help in obtaining their release; almost lost in the letter was his glancing mention of how Britain's growing profile in Texas was helping them keep a grip on Oregon in the face of expansionist pressure from the United States.[23] Elliot forwarded Houston's request to the British minister in Mexico, Sir Richard Packenham, who consulted with the American minister Waddy Thompson. Concerned that a growing British-Texan friendship could be potentially troubling for the United States, Thompson quickly alerted Washington—just as Houston hoped.

At the same time, Santa Anna returned one of his prisoners, James W. Robinson, who had convinced the dictator that he could effectively use his influence (he was former acting governor of Texas early in the revolution) to bring about a peaceful reunion of Texas with Mexico. From Washington-on-the-Brazos, Robinson reported to Santa Anna that Houston was open to the proposition, and that "if your Excellency had thought proper to have released all the Texian prisoners ... it would have had a good effect on the people."[24] It is highly likely that Houston dictated the contents. Incredibly, Santa Anna bought it, and between Robinson's assurances and foreign encouragement, Mexican authorities began to free the Texan prisoners.

On another tack, Houston provoked an international incident with the United States. American trade with Mexico passed over the Santa Fé Trail, which under the terms of the Treaty of Velasco, crossed through Texas's sovereign territory. Houston dispatched one of his trusted operatives, Jacob Snively, with two hundred "privateers" to interdict that trade, which they did until they were captured and disarmed by American soldiers. In opening the Eighth Texas Congress on December 13, 1843, Houston's only mention of the United States was this "infraction of our revenue laws by citizens of the United States attended with circumstances of a very unpleasant character."[25] In the same speech, his praise of Great Britain was little short of extravagant. At the same time, Houston began penning editorials, published anonymously through the connivance of friendly newspaper editors such as Thomas "Ramrod" Johnson of the *National Vindicator*, extolling the economic benefits of friendship with Britain and minimizing the benefits of union with the United States.[26]

Eventually, such relentless skullduggery had its effect. The United States did not want to annex Texas, but the only thing that scared them more than admitting Texas as a southern slave state, was the prospect of Texas as a British protectorate. Houston cast so much chaff into the air that even Jackson doubted his intentions. Jackson wrote Houston an alarmed letter on the same point. If Texas aligned with the British, England "would form an iron hoop around the United States, with her West India Islands that would cost oceans of blood, and millions of money to Burst asunder."[27]

Houston's diplomatic shell game was dazzling. He had commissioners in Mexico, signing an armistice that, to Santa Anna's satisfaction, referred to Texas as a Mexican Department—a document to keep the dictator off balance and guarantee the Texas commissioners time to get out of the country safely.[28] Ashbel Smith, now in Paris, was exchanging pleasantries with the French king on the subject of peace and Texas's reliance on French friendship.[29] With Jackson's backstage support and in deep secrecy, and with nothing more secret than the American pledge to defend Texas from Mexico during the negotiations, Texas and the United States signed an annexation treaty on April 12, 1844. Truly, Houston was earning his sobriquet as the "Talleyrand of the Brazos."

With Senate debate, and again rejection in June, the cat was out of the bag, however. Santa Anna's wrath was Jovian; he declared war on Texas, which Houston answered with suitable insults of his own on July 29, and extracted a promise of protection from the U.S. consul, General William Sumter Murphy—which he had no authority to give and was recalled. U.S. dithering over annexation was settled in the presidential election of 1844 by the narrow victory of Tennessean (and Jackson minion and Houston friend) James Knox Polk.

The outgoing president, John Tyler, decided to cooperate on the issue. While the treaty had been defeated, the annexation faction realized that nothing in the constitution forbade taking in new territory by joint resolution of the Congress, which only required a one-vote majority, where a treaty required two thirds. Fearing Houston's friendship with the British, they offered Texas a measurably sweeter deal than the terms of the rejected treaty: Texas could enter the Union directly as a state, although its population fell short of that requirement. Once part of the United States, Texans could later split their state into as many as five states if they wished. Congress also agreed to allow Texans to keep their public domain to defray their national debt. The resolution passed the House comfortably; in the Senate, sectionalism broke down, and it passed 27–25 on an individual conscience vote. A. J. Donelson was packed off to Texas with the terms, which would be open until the end of the year. Texas must draft a state constitution, and hold a referendum to ratify the decision.

Annexation was now all but accomplished. After three years of arduous puppeteering, Houston's term ended and voters elected the querulous Dr. Jones to be the Republic of Texas's last president to oversee the formalities. Texas officially joined the Union on December 29, 1845, and the exchange of executive authority, with the lowering of the Texas flag and raising of the Stars and Stripes, taking place in Austin six weeks later.

Houston intended a triumphal progress through the United States that would end at the Hermitage and a reunion with Jackson. In New Orleans, a jostling crowd at the Arcade insisted that at last, after years of keeping the United States off balance and guessing, Houston commit himself on whether or not he favored annexation, exclaiming there was no danger in revealing his position. In a speech punctuated by the audience's roars of laughter, Houston vivisected the newspaper editors who had accused him of selling out to the European powers. "My friends," he wagged, "I have been accused of lending myself to England and France; but, I assure you, I have only been *coquetting* with them."

It was an analogy that deserved some amplification. "Supposing a charming lady has two suitors," he explained. "One of them she is inclined to believe would make the better husband, but is a little slow to make interesting propositions. Do you think if she was a skillful practitioner in Cupid's court she would pretend that she loved the other 'feller' the best and be sure that her favorite would know it?" He was interrupted by laughter and applause. Well, "if ladies are justified in making use of coquetry in securing their annexation to good and agreeable husbands, you must excuse me for making use of the same means to annex Texas to Uncle Sam."[30]

A letter from Jackson's one-time ward and Houston's friend from his days in Congress, E. G. M. Butler, that the Old Chief could not last much longer, sent the Houston family on the road to Nashville at a redoubled pace. It was to no avail, for they received word outside the city that Jackson had died, denying Houston the one accolade that would perhaps have meant the most to him.

Notes

1. Of the scores of Houston biographies now on the shelf, Marquis James's *The Raven: A Biography of Sam Houston* (New York and Indianapolis: Bobbs-Merrill, 1929) was long considered the gold standard. However, several of its incidents did not actually happen, and were included to emphasize points of Houston's character, as was the style of biography in the 1920s. Although deeply researched, it is now considered a portrait, not a photograph. Llerena Friend's *Sam Houston: The Great Designer* (Austin: University of Texas Press, 1954) remains the best study of his politics, and Marion K. Wisehart's *Sam Houston: American Giant* (Washington, D.C.: Robert B. Luce, 1962) is the most detailed and most intuitive. James L. Haley's *Sam Houston* (Norman: University of Oklahoma Press, 2002) is the most recent and most personal.

2. Houston, Inaugural Speech, 22 October 1836, Texas State Library and Archives, later included in Eugene C. Barker and Amelia W. Williams, *The Writings of Sam Houston*, 1: 448–52 (hereinafter cited as *Writings*).

3. These years are summarized in Jack Gregory and Rennard Strickland, *Sam Houston with the Cherokees, 1829–1833* (Austin: University of Texas Press, 1967).

4. *Congressional Debates*, vol. 8, pt. 2 (1831–32), 1810–21, reprinted in *Writings*, 1: 207–24.

5. Espousing the latter contention see, e.g., Houston's treatment in Stephen Hardin, *Texian Iliad* (Austin: University of Texas Press, 1994), and the more vociferous William C. Davis, *Lone Star Rising* (New York: Free Press, 2004); compare with the more traditional approach of Haley, *Sam Houston* (Norman: University of Oklahoma Press, 2002), and H. W. Brands, *Lone Star Nation* (New York: Doubleday, 2004).

6. Jones, *Memoranda and Official Correspondence*, 83–84.

7. Carson to Houston, 14 April 1836, in Jenkins, *Papers of the Texas Revolution*, 5: 470. Jenkins notes that the original letter was lost, and cited to Yoakum, *History of Texas*, 2: 169. Houston lent his personal papers to Yoakum to prepare his book. Many papers were lost in two subsequent fires, one when the widowed Margaret Houston began burning them in anger at being unable to interest a publisher in a Houston biography, and the second many years later in a house used for storage by Andrew Jackson Houston, which he was using to store his vast collection of Houston papers.

8. A representative selection of early correspondence is offered in James L. Haley, ed., *Most Excellent Sir: Letters Received by Sam Houston, President of the Republic of Texas, Columbia, 1836–1837* (Austin: Duncan & Gladstone, 1987).

9. William D. Red to Lamar, 23 May 1837, in C. A. Gulick, Jr., et al., eds., *The Papers of Mirabeau Buonaparte Lamar*, 6 vols., 1: 552.

10. J. P. Clark to Houston, 5 October 1836, Sam Houston Papers, Catholic Archives of Texas; Robert McEwen to Houston, 13 December 1836, Sam Houston Hearne Collection, Dolph Briscoe Center for American History, University of Texas. Clark was Eliza Allen's cousin; when that avenue proved unproductive, the second attempt came through McEwen, who was Houston's cousin.

11. Houston's missives to Anna are reproduced by descendent Sam Irion, *Ever Thine Truly: Love Letters from Sam Houston to Anna Raguet* (Austin: Jenkins Garret Press, 1975). Far from being a jealous suitor, Houston bowed out with such grace that the couple named their first child Sam Houston Irion.

12. Elam to Houston, 2 January 1937, A. J. Houston Collection, Texas State Library and Archives.

13. Lubbock, *Six Decades in Texas*, 74–75; Haley, *Sam Houston*, 195 and notes thereto.

14. Irion to Henderson, 25 June 1837, in George P. Garrison, ed., *Diplomatic Correspondence of the Republic of Texas*, in Annual Reports of the American Historical Association for the Years 1907 and 1908 (Washington, D.C.: U.S. Government Printing Office, 1907–11), pt. 3, 809.

15. Red, "Allen's Reminiscences of Texas," 295. The incident was also recounted in Guild, *Old Times in Tennessee*, 289, although he ascribed it to the first inaugural.

16. Sam Houston, Passport, Domestic Records of the Secretaries of State, Texas State Archives.

17. Bateman, "Waterloo Scrapbook," *Austin American-Statesman*, 12 December 1986; Gregg, *Diary and Letters of Josiah Gregg*, 109. The "Henry V" cap is preserved in the Sam Houston Memorial Museum in Huntsville.

18. Terrell to Houston, 25 July 1841, Sam Houston Papers, Catholic Archives of Texas.

19. Ward to Houston, 28 September 1842, Nancy Burch Collection, Sam Houston Regional Library and Research Center, Liberty.

20. Reily to Houston, 13 April 1842, Sam Houston Papers, Catholic Archives of Texas.

21. Jones, *Memoranda and Official Correspondence*, 34–36.

22. Houston to Bagby, 18 December 1842, in *Writings*, 3: 236.

23. Houston to Elliot, 24 January 1843, in *Writings*, 3: 299–302.

24. "Robinson" to Santa Anna, 10 April 1843, in *Writings*, 3: 351–53.

25. Houston to the Texas Congress, Annual Message, 13 December 1843, in *Writings* 3: 459, 464.

26. See, e.g., "Annexation Again" by "A Texian," *National Vindicator*, 2 December 1843, whose language, logic and stock phrases could only have come from Houston.

27. Jackson to Houston, 15 March 1844, in Remini, *Andrew Jackson and the Course of American Democracy*, 492–95.

28. Houston to Isaac Van Zandt and J. Pinckney Henderson, 29 April 1844, in Garrison, *Diplomatic Correspondence*, pt. 2, 274–76.

29. Smith to Houston [undated?], Nancy Burch Collection.

30. Address in Houston, in Barker and Williams, *Writings of Sam Houston* 6: 5–13. While the editors of Houston's correspondence place the speech in Houston City before his departure, it is virtually certain that he repeated the subject in his New Orleans appearances. See Haley, *Sam Houston*, 469 n.64.

Chapter 8
Mirabeau B. Lamar: Blinded by Delusions of Grandeur

Kenneth W. Howell

On December 10, 1838, President-elect Mirabeau B. Lamar sat patiently as President Sam Houston stood to deliver his "Farewell Address" in front of the crowd that had gathered to watch the inauguration of the new chief executive. Unfortunately for Lamar, the outgoing president had a score to settle with the critics of his administration, and the Hero of San Jacinto was ready to confront his political enemies before handing over the reins of government by offering an uncompromising defense of his decisions while in office. Lamar and the others present at the ceremonies should have guessed Houston's strategy even before he rose to speak, especially given that the former president was adorned in attire reminiscent of the style worn by George Washington, a symbolic overture clear to all. Houston believed that he was the true "Father of the Republic" and wanted the people of Texas to know that the president-elect could do little more than stand in the shadow of his greatness. For three hours, President Houston painstakingly defended his administration. Houston's theatrics served its purpose: Lamar became so frustrated that when it came time for him to deliver his inaugural address, he simply handed his speech to his private secretary, Algernon P. Thompson, instructing him to read it to the few individuals who had not already abandoned the ceremony. To his credit, Thompson did his best to relay Lamar's visions for the fledgling Republic of Texas, but his effort to give life to another man's speech paled in comparison to Houston's earlier performance. For Lamar, this fiasco proved to be only the first of many disappointing episodes that plagued his presidency.[1]

If the inaugural ceremonies had proceeded differently, Lamar might well have inspired a new sense of hope among those gathered at the steps of the capitol, then located in the city of Houston. Having spent several days preparing his remarks, Lamar planned to share his vision of a new Texas, a country that he believed would become the envy of the world. Disappointingly, Lamar's dream of a new Texas never fully

Mirabeau B. Lamar. Second President of the Republic of Texas. This image originally appeared as *"Mirabeau B. Lamar*—Genl. Lamar, Ex-President of Texas." It was a portrait engraving by J. Sartain, Philadelphia, designed as a frontispiece illustration opposite the title page to *Verse Memorials* by Mirabeau B. Lamar, published by W. P. Fetridge & Co.: New York, 1857. Courtesy of the Texas State Library and Archives Commission.

materialized, leaving his political enemies, especially Sam Houston and his supporters, to characterize his administration as a complete disaster, an assessment that modern scholars continue to embrace just as much as their admiration for the Hero of San Jacinto.[2] Such criticism, however, reveals little about Lamar as he stood on the threshold of his presidency, leaving many questions about the Republic's second president unanswered. Were his proposed policies doomed from the beginning? Did his contemporaries view his policies as outrageous and out of step with their own beliefs? What was the foundation of Lamar's political views as he accepted the challenges of leading the fledgling republic? Was Lamar's vision for the future of Texas based on delusions of grandeur, or were his ideas the product of serious reflection and sound principles? The answers to these questions are important to any objective understanding of Lamar's successes and failures. In order to answer these questions, as well as others, it is necessary to examine Lamar's earliest plans for establishing a vibrant and successful nation. The two best expressions of Lamar's early views were his inaugural address and his first official message to the Texas Congress. These two documents make it possible to ascertain, at least in part, the presidential mindset of this tarnished Texas leader, providing scholars an objective basis for judging the merits of his leadership.

In the beginning of his inaugural speech, Lamar showed humility by stating, "when I reflect upon the g[re]at unanimity of the popular voice by which I am called t[o thi]s station, I cannot repress the painful apprehension that I [may] not be able to fulfill the high expectations which such gen[erous] confidence implies."[3] Despite this reservation, Lamar made a solemn promised to his fellow countrymen, declaring "every effort in my power [wi]ll be made to strengthen and retain the confidence reposed in [my dis]position to advance the happiness of the people and to [widen] and confirm the foundations of our national institutions."[4] Whether or not the incoming president truly doubted his abilities to serve as president is highly questionable. More likely, Lamar chose his words for political effect. At the time of his election, the people of Texas, disillusioned with the Houston administration, viewed Lamar as the possible answer to the major challenges confronting the Republic.[5] Typically when voters place all their hopes in a newly elected official, they often are disappointed when their perceived "savior" only achieves moderate improvements or gains. It seems reasonable to assume Lamar would have been aware of this political reality. Thus, by downplaying his own abilities, Lamar could effectively temper the people's enthusiasm for his presidency, rendering any future accomplishments even more significant in their minds. Given Lamar's life-long interest in history, it was natural for him to contemplate his own legacy even at this early stage of his political career.[6]

Influenced by the same spirit that characterized Americans' belief in Manifest Destiny, Lamar wanted Texas to expand westward toward the Pacific Ocean. In this regard, his strong adherence to Texas nationalism was another unique feature of his address. Using language commonly associated with American expansionists during the Jacksonian era, the incoming president commented:

> I place a high trust, my fellow citizens, in the protection of the Great Ruler of nations who has never yet deserted a people whose virtues may have entitled them to the blessings of freedom. Driven into the assertion of our rights and the defense of our lives by the tyranny and oppression of those with whom it was our misfortune to be associated in government, Providential interference in our behalf, from the beginning of the revolution up to the present period,—guiding us in the paths of victory, an[d] sustaining us in the hour of difficulty when our own wisdom had failed us, has been so manifest and signal, that I cannot but indulge the cheering belief that the Great Dispenser of all blessings will not continue to prosper us in our future career; will be with us in all our trials and struggles, and in the end enable us to rear such a political superstructure for the preservation of freedom as tyranny cannot shake and time shall continually strengthen.[7]

Furthering his argument that God had ordained the success of the new republic, Lamar called on his fellow Texans to give reverence to "that Divine Being who hath thus far conducted us to glory and prosperity" by demeaning "ourselves individually and nationally in such a manner as not to forfeit all claim to the munificence solicited by the selfishness of our motives, or the [f]olly of our measures."[8] In Lamar's mind, the past and the future success of Texas rested in a belief that Providence had played a hand in laying "the corner stone of a young Republic" which might "excel those nations which have arr[i]ved at maturity, in the purity of her institutions and the stability [of her] freedom."[9]

Having established the context for his remaining remarks, Lamar addressed some of the most pressing issues then troubling the country.

While serving as President Houston's vice president between 1836 and 1838, Lamar spent much of his time traveling outside of the country, especially in his native home of Georgia. Even though he neglected his Constitutional duty of presiding over the Texas Senate, Lamar kept pace with developments in the Republic. During his sojourn through the southern region of the United States, friends kept him informed of troubles confronting the Texas government and complained of President Houston's ineffective leadership. Houston's harshest critics made numerous and open references to the president's frequent episodes of drunkenness. More than likely, it was during his travels that Lamar began to think about solutions to the problems that troubled his adopted country. The most significant concerns confronting Texas resulted from the government's failure to negotiate a peace treaty with Mexico, potentially leaving Texas vulnerable to invading Mexican armies, and its inability to stabilize the Republic's finances. Regarding these problems, Lamar generalized, "We have peace to procure; the public credit [to] establish and the resources of our country to develop."[10] However, before discussing his solutions to these problems in detail, Lamar warned against the formation of political factions and expressed the necessity of developing trust between the people and their government, both necessary ingredients for the future success of the Republic. He contended that solutions

> are not to be attained … without union amongst the people; and without reciprocal confidence between the public depositories of power. If distrust and jealousy be allowed to take root in the different departments of government, and factious dissensions spring up in the bosom of our present peaceful and united [po] pulation, all the efforts of the patriot to advance the public weal will prove unavailing and abortive, and the nation, instead of moving onward to that proud elevation that awaits her, must necessarily recede into a debased condition, and possibly sink into irretrievable ruin.[11]

Lamar undoubtedly knew that the Republic was ripe for political factions. While competing political parties had not yet emerged, there was a clear division among those who supported the incoming president and those who remained faithful to Houston. Even though he had not claimed to be the leader of an anti-Houston faction, Lamar was clearly perceived as such by the political elite and the general public. Despite his call for unity, however, Lamar's actions as president would eventually serve to solidify further political divisions.[12]

The remainder of the president-elect's inaugural address focused on specific issues. He began by briefly defining his approach to domestic and foreign policy. While not going into detail, Lamar believed that "agriculture, commerce, and the useful arts" were the true "basis of all national strength and glory." He pledged that his administration would follow policies designed "to awaken into vigorous activity, the wealth, talent and enterprise of the country; and at the same time, to lay the foundation of those higher institutions for moral and mental culture, without which no government, on democratic principles, can prosper, nor [th]e people long preserve their liberties."[13] However, the new president did not offer any additional insights regarding his economic policies. It seems likely that Lamar had given the matter some thought, because less than a month later during his first address to the Texas Congress, he presented a comprehensive economic plan to the members of that legislative body.

Regarding foreign intercourse, Lamar was more introspect. He called on his fellow Texans to "deal justly with all nations, aggressively to none; preserve friendly and amicable relations with such as may be supposed to reciprocate the policy, and avoiding all protracted and perplexing negociations [*sic*], [and] court free and unrestricted commerce wherever it may be the interest of our people to carry the national flag."[14] Lamar's position on foreign trade was hardly a departure from that of the Houston administration, and in many ways reflected the inevitable course of expedient action. At the time of his address, Lamar knew that the country was in no position to dictate terms to developed nations of the world. Still, he felt compelled to give credence to the idea of free trade with friendly foreign powers. Perhaps more surprising was the incoming president's statements regarding the possibility of going to war should it be necessary. Lamar boasted, "Preferring peace, but not averse to war, I shall be ever ready to adjust all differences with our enemies by friendly discussion and arrangement, at the same time be equally prompt to adopt either offensive or defensive operations, as their disposition and our own safety may render necessary."[15]

Given the economic conditions of Texas, Lamar knew that his assertion on waging war was virtually meaningless. So, why did he make such a bold statement? The answer was simple: he had no other choice. Relations with Mexico, which still had not recognized Texas independence, were tenuous at best, and rumors of an invading Mexican army circulated throughout every corner of the Republic. Furthermore, Lamar had to compete with Sam Houston's reputation as a war hero. While Houston may not have been politically popular in 1838, Texans still revered him as the "Hero of San Jacinto," and many citizens credited him with winning Texas independence. Lamar's own military reputation remained questionable. Even though he had served bravely at the Battle of San Jacinto, the Texas army later rejected Lamar's appointment as its commander.[16] Thus, the new president would have deemed it politically expedient to declare his intentions of using military force to defend the Republic in times of crisis, avoiding any signs of weakness toward the nation's enemies.

Next, Lamar outlined his domestic policies. He began by confirming his willingness to work with all those "who have the good of the country, and not their own aggrandizement in view" for the betterment of the nation, protecting the "equal and impartial balance between the rights, claims and interests of every class of our fellow citizens. ..."[17] In this regard, Lamar promised to

> sustain the freedom of the press, the purity of elections, the right of opinion, and the freedom and sanctity of religion; maintain the integrity and independence of the judiciary as the great dispensary of justice, and the correction of civil, criminal and constitutional abuses; economize the public resources; protect the frontiers; recommend equality of taxation, burthening none of the branches of industry for the benefit of others; discourage multiplicity of legislation; patronize talents, integrity and sobriety; support wi[th] becoming liberality all laudable and patriotic institutions founded i[n] reason and tested by experience.[18]

Finally, the president pledged to uphold the laws of the nation, guarding against public fraud and holding "every individual in official station to strict accountability."[19]

Exactly what thoughts permeated Lamar's mind when he labored to outline his domestic policy during the days before the inaugural ceremony may never be completely known. Largely, Lamar's policies were simply an extension of rights coveted by Americans and protected by the United States Constitution. However, the chief executive might also have intended to refute ideals associated with Andrew Jackson and his supporters, especially the remarks pertaining to taxation, patronage, and patriotic institutions. In order to understand the subtlety in Lamar's politics, it is necessary to examine briefly the evolution of his career prior to arriving in Texas.

Lamar formed the basis of his political beliefs in the heat of Georgia politics during the 1820s and early 1830s. His earliest introduction to politics came when he served as Governor George M. Troup's private secretary between 1823 and 1826. After marrying Tabitha Jordan, who suffered from tuberculosis, Lamar resigned as Troup's secretary in order to take care of his ailing bride. Despite Tabitha's ill health, she gave birth to a daughter, Rebecca. Shortly after his daughter's birth, Lamar moved his family Columbus, Georgia, and established a local newspaper—the *Columbus Enquirer.* In 1829, Lamar successfully ran for the Georgia Senate, but resigned his seat in 1830, when his wife died from complications related to her illness. Following Tabitha's death, Lamar suffered bouts of depression and temporarily abandoned politics, taking solace in traveling and writing poetry, one of his favorite pastimes. Two years after his wife's death, Lamar attempted to reignite his political career, running unsuccessfully for Congress in 1832 and again in 1834. Unfortunately, whatever political future he had in Georgia seemingly had met the same faith as his young bride. Between these two defeats, however, Lamar went through something of a political transformation. As Governor Troup's private secretary and during his time in the Georgia legislature, Lamar was a staunch supporter of Andrew Jackson, primarily because the president sided with Georgia on the issue of Indian removal. Nonetheless, Lamar changed his opinion about Jackson following the Nullification Crisis in 1832. In Lamar's mind, the president had become a tyrant, forcing South Carolina to yield to the collection of federal taxes (in the form of tariffs). Many citizens in the American South agreed with Lamar's position, believing that their states received no practical benefits from the revenue generated from tariffs. As a result, the young Georgian initiated efforts to organize a political party that supported nullification and states' rights as defined by South Carolinian John C. Calhoun. From this moment, Lamar held a deep-seated hatred for Jackson and his policies.[20]

In 1835, while on his way to Texas, Lamar revealed his contempt for Jackson in a speech delivered in Montgomery County, Alabama, where local citizens asked him to make a public address on states' rights. Though he discussed at length the virtues of states' rights and the destructive nature of protective tariffs, his closing comments regarding the character of Jackson succinctly summarized his views on the issues. Lamar stated:

> Who is Andrew Jackson? Let me not attempt to describe his character—to draw him in his proper colors, the foulest

> language is too fair. Who can do justice to Calligula [*sic*] & Nero? and who can properly portray the man who combines all that is revolting in the one with the disgusting ferocity of the other? As an individual, a rebrobate [*sic*]; as a military man, a murderer; and as a public functionary, the alternate flatterer & base betrayer of all principles and all parties. To him let the foes of my State, pour their mean apostate worship; my devotions are given to a smilig [*sic*] deity that dwells upon the mountain tops & frolics in vallies [*sic*]; who presence cheers the poor man's cottage & animates the revels of the rich-man's pallace [*sic*]. I mean the Goddess of freedom ....[21]

Given that Lamar's hatred of Jackson solidified before he first entered Texas in 1835, it is not surprising that his inaugural address contained subtle hints of his anti-Jackson views. His call for "equality of taxation, burthening none of the branches of industry for the benefit of others" was certainly intended to prevent the passage of a protective tariff that would benefit only a select group in the nation. His statement on patronage characterized how his own appointments to public office would be based on merit, not political expediency, such as Jackson had done during his terms in office. Finally, Lamar's reference to support of "patriotic institutions founded in reason and tested by experience" was an indirect reference to Jackson's Bank War that ended with the destruction of the Second Bank of the United States and the endangerment of the American economy. Later, this connection was even more evident when Lamar recommended that the Texas Congress create its own national bank. Viewing each of these circumstances as evidence of Jackson's failures, Lamar affirmed that he would avoid making the same mistakes in Texas. Perhaps, Lamar's scorn for Jackson explained in part his similar feelings toward Houston, especially given that the "Hero of San Jacinto" was a protégé of the "Hero of New Orleans."

Lamar intended his inaugural address to be nothing more than a cursory introduction of his vision for the country. He acknowledged this fact by declaring, "As this is not the occasion for the Executive to offer his recommendatory councils for the action of congress; I must pass by for the present, the development of those measures by which I hope to carry out the cardinal principles of my administration." Lamar did promise, however, to present as soon as practical his "views of general policy, and to suggest such a course for legislative conduct, as may seem … the most essential to an energetic and successful direction of public affairs."[22] While he remained evasive about his administration's policies for future development and growth, Lamar discussed at length one issue he deemed detrimental to the future of the Republic—the annexation of Texas to the United States.

Steadfast in his opposition to annexation, Lamar stated, "I have never been able myself to perceive the policy of the desired connexion [*sic*], or discover in it any advantage either c[i]vil, political or commercial, which could possibly result to Texas." He continued, "But on the contrary a long train of consequences of the most appalling character and magnitude, have never failed to present themselves whenever I have entertained the subject … that the step once taken would produce a lasting regret, and ultimately prove disastrous to our liberty and hopes, as the triumphant sword of the enemy."[23] Lamar devoted the remainder of the speech, more than half of his total prepared remarks, to explaining his hostility toward annexation.

First, after clarifying that he felt no animosity toward the character and institutions of the United States, Lamar stressed that his position on annexation was based on an "allegiance and affection" to the Republic, claiming that "her glory and happiness must be my paramount consideration, and I cannot allow myself to speak in any other than the language of freedom and frankness on all matters involving her safety, dignity and honor."[24] In other words, Lamar considered himself the guardian of the Republic and believed annexation would produce dire results regarding the future of Texas—none more appalling than the "surrender of her Independence."[25] President Lamar defined the rights that the Republic would yield if annexation became a reality:

> the right of making either war or peace; the right of controlling the Indian tribes within her borders; the right of appropriating her public domain to purposes of education and internal improvements; of levying her own taxes; regulating her own commerce and forming her own alliances and treaties—when I view her divested of the most essential attributes of free government; reduced to the level of an unfelt fraction of a giant power; or peradventure divided into Territorial districts, with Governors and judges and excise men appointed from abroad to administer laws which she had no adequate voice in enacting, and gather imposts for the benefit of those who

> levy them—when I look upon her, as she soon will be, the cornucopia of the world, pouring her abundant treasurers into the lap of another people than her own; a tributary vassal to remote and uncongenial communities; communities as widely separated from her in pursuits as in distance, who are known to be opposed to her peculiar and essential interests, and who are daily sending forth their denunciations against her from the fire-side, the pulpit and the council chamber; and when I bear in mind that all this sacrifice of rights and dignity and character is to be made, for what![26]

Lamar could have ended his diatribe against annexation at this point but chose instead to buttress his argument. To those listening, it was obvious that Lamar's position was influenced in part by his earlier pronouncements in favor of states' right, a position espoused in his 1835 Alabama speech. Lamar had no desire to become part of the United States, a nation that he believed did not respect the rights of citizens of individual states. In essence, his prior devotion to the states' rights doctrine had made him into a demagogue, who was committed to building an empire rather than becoming a part of one that already existed. Lamar made this point abundantly clear as he continued to quell the call for annexation by arguing that the Republic could not afford to hand over its sovereignty:

> for the privilege of going into a union in which she carries wealth without proportional influence—for the glory of identifying her fortunes with a government in which a large portion of the inhabitants are alarmed for the safety of the very institutions upon which her own hopes of happiness are based; a government embracing conflicting interests and irreconcilable prejudices with lasting causes of domestic quarrel, where Texas can hope for nothing but a participation in the strifes [*sic*] that distract the public councils, and [after] passing through many throes and convulsions be the means perhaps of producing or accelerating an awful catastrophe which none could be more ready to avert or sincerely deplore than herself ...[27]

Lamar's perception of the Republic as it then existed and his views for its future would not allow him to contemplate annexation. One should also note that Lamar's comments related to "peculiar and essential interest" and the "safety of the very institutions upon which her own hopes and happiness are based" were direct references to Texans' desire to build a slave-based cotton economy, which many believed had fallen under attack in the United States.[28] In his mind, Texas was on the threshold of greatness, destined to build an empire that might one day be revered worldwide. Lamar described this new empire in detail, asking his fellow Texans to contemplate the "high destiny that awaits our country: the great prosperity which lies within her attainment if sh[e] will but appreciate her … incalculable resources." Lost in the dream of Texas greatness, he reflected:

> when I view her vast extent of territory, stretching from the Sabine to the Pacific and away to the South West as far as the obstinacy of the enemy may render it necessary for the sword to make the boundary; embracing the most delightful climate and the richest soil in the world, and behold it all in the state of high cultivation and improvements—her mountain of minerals yielding their vast treasures to the touch of industry; her luxuriant pastures alive with flocks and herds, and her wide fields whitening with a staple commodity, in the production of which she can have no rival; with the whole world for her market; and then consider the noble purposes to which this immense and exhaustless wealth may be applied, in adoring and beautifying the country, providing for its safety and defense, endowing institutions for the spread of virtue, knowledge and the arts, and carrying to the door of every citizen of the Republic, peace, plenty, and protection—and when in addition to these glorious and grand results, I look still farther to the important improvements which she will be able to devise in government, and to the entire revolution which her example in free trade will effect in the commerce of other nations, emancipating it from the thralldom of tariff restrictions and placing it upon the high ground of equitable reciprocity, all of which will certainly flow from the maintainence [*sic*] of her present independent position as the sun courses the heavens.[29]

If this was not enough, Lamar completed his portrait with warnings of pending despair, declaring that he could not regard annexation "in any other light than as the grave of all her hopes of happiness and greatness … and [if annexation occurred] that a young Republic just rising into high distinction among the nations of the earth" would be "swallowed up and lost like a proud bark [ship] in a devouring vortex."[30]

To bolster his argument, Lamar had to dismiss the Texans' overwhelming vote for annexation in the 1836 election. He carefully stated that when voters cast ballots in favor of joining the United States, they had acted in their own self-interest, especially considering the unstable condition of Texas following the Battle of San Jacinto. He reminded his audience that the Republic was "without means and without credit; her settlements broken up; her villages desolated by ruthless invasion; and amidst all still threatened in her defenceless [*sic*] situation with a return of the foe and a renewal of the sad calamaties [*sic*] of war." The president continued, "under such a state of things, no wonder that the people, harassed and almost ruined … should be willing to purchase momentary security by surrender of their national Independence."[31] Though annexation may have been desirable in 1836, Lamar argued that circumstances in Texas had changed and that the reasons for joining the Union no longer existed. Reflecting on the two years that had followed the favorable vote for annexation, Lamar asserted, "We [now] behold a powerful and prosperous people, daily increasing in wealth and numbers happy in their present possessions and looking forward to still higher and more glorious results. Invasion too, has lost its terrors. Conscious of our own strength, we know very well that the enemy has greater reason to apprehend danger from us, than we from him." Lamar then asked the rhetorical question, "And shall we now, in the midst of glory[ous] hopes and increasing vigor, persevere in a suicidal policy, origi[nal]ly founded in necessity rather in choice?"[32] Of course, his answer was unequivocal—NO!

Furthering his argument, Lamar suggested that Texans had an opportunity to improve the American system of government. He contended that the United States Constitution "is certainly the highest effort of political wisdom, and approaches more nearly to perfection than any other social compact for government of man; yet a fair trial of fifty years ha[s] detected in that sacred chart many se[r]ious and alarming errors." Lamar believed, however, that if Texans adopted the finest features of the American government, while correcting its flaws, they could "devise and perfect a system of our own which shall surpass its model."[33]

Defining the principles of this new government, Lamar claimed that "virtue and justice" were essential and that a "government reared upon the one and administered upon the other, cannot fail to be an eternal bulwark to the rights of man."[34] The president acknowledged that a written compact between the people and their rulers was wise, because it established the boundaries of governmental power and limited the opportunity for misrule. However, Lamar believed that written compacts were equally important in protecting the rights of every individual. Those cherished rights were ensured "by virtue of a high instrument, the standard of all rule and law, adopted by the special servants of the people and clearly defined, approved and ratified by a whole community."[35]

Lamar concluded his speech with a warning, claiming that the Texans' new government could not survive if "the people or the public functionaries, unmindful of their obligations to its authority … shall suffer themselves to be hurried by the violence of baleful passions, or be seduced by the selfish suggestions of its solemn injunctions." If they succumb to such selfish interest, Lamar feared that "the inevitable consequence will be, the loss of public credit, the destruction of private confidence, and the subversion of all order, morality and safety."[36] Lamar suggested that the people's adherence to patriotism was the only way to avoid a failed government, stating:

> As individuals, we are restr[ain]ed from the violation of *laws*, by the fear of punishment; but as communities, we have nothing to withhold us from an infringement of the *constitution*, except that high morality and honest pride w[h]ich make the virtuous and enlightened bosom feel that its country's [hon] or is its own. Hence I esteem it the first duty of a patriot, and the [h]ighest evidence of his patriotism, to cherish and respect the constitution of his country. Nor can I conceive of a more dangerous enemy to liberty than the popular chief who shall discard its authority under the hollow pretext that he is acting for the good of the people. No reason of state policy, nor pretended exigencies, can justify its violation. Under any and all circumstances its infraction is more dangerous than treason, and its dethronement is the death of liberty. Let me invoke the people of Texas to stand by their constitution. Let us offer no violence to its precepts and restrictions. Let us bow to the supremacy of its authority. Let it be our cloud by day and our pillar of fire by night.[37]

His comment about the dangers of a rogue "popular chief" was another veiled reference to President Jackson's actions during the

Nullification Crisis, an event that moved Lamar toward an adherence to states' rights. Alternatively, Lamar's target may have been Houston, whom many Texans believed had exceeded his constitutional authority as president.[38] In reality, Lamar believed that both Jackson and Houston were tyrants who had violated the rights of their constituents. Furthermore, realizing that Texans were dividing into pro- and anti-Houston factions, the president was attempting to unite the people behind his administration. Overall, Lamar conceived his address with one purpose in mind: Texas was destined to become a great empire that would someday be the envy of the world. As such, it would be foolish for the Republic to relinquish prematurely its sovereignty to the United States, a nation whose government, according to Lamar, was eroding the rights of states in order to secure stronger federal control. Given that Texas had recently fought a revolution to win independence from Santa Anna's dictatorial government, it was apparent that Lamar was unwilling to replace one master for another.

Lamar's inaugural address provides scholars with a glimpse into the mind of its creator, but it does not yield a comprehensive understanding of his vision for Texas. To understand further Lamar's ambitions, it is also necessary to examine his first official message to Congress. Less than a month after his inaugural speech, the president detailed the course of action that Congress should follow in order to address the obstacles confronting Texas, including foreign affairs, education, frontier defense, and deteriorating economic conditions.

President Lamar began his message by addressing foreign affairs. Acknowledging that the United States had recognized the independence of Texas, he was convinced that other nations would follow suit, especially Great Britain and France. Lamar understood that slavery was an obstacle to British recognition of Texas independence. However, like many Texans, he was confident that the potential for commercial benefits would outweigh England's aversion to slavery. Additionally, Lamar predicted that France would be forced to extend diplomatic recognition to Texas, because of fears that the British government's relationship with the Republic would allow England to monopolize European trade with the new nation. Despite desires to forge relations with Europe, Texans' immediate concern was the threat posed by Mexico, which still claimed Texas. However, Texas political leaders realized that recognition from Mexico would not be forthcoming. Lamar reiterated his earlier sentiments, stating that Texas desired a peaceful solution to the continued problems with their southern neighbor, but if "peace can be obtained only by the sword, let the sword do its work."[39]

This was the extent of Lamar's observations regarding foreign nations. Despite its importance, he remained cautious, taking a wait-and-see attitude toward relations with Europe. Perhaps, the president realized that future negotiations were in the hands of diplomats sent overseas with the purpose of securing the recognition of Texas independence, formalizing trade agreements, and if possible, securing loans, both public and private. Given the nature of the ongoing deliberations, Lamar understood that he could do little to influence the decisions abroad—a clear reminder that the future of the Republic was linked to events and circumstances beyond his immediate control.[40]

Lamar next addressed public education, which surely puzzled his audience, considering the more pressing issues facing the nation. However, from the president's perspective, an educated citizenry was vital to the longevity of a republic. He eloquently stated, "education is a subject in which every citizen, and especially every parent, feels a deep and lively concern … [and all agree that a] cultivated mind is the guardian genius of Democracy … the noblest attribute of man. … It is the only dictator that freemen acknowledge, and the only security which freemen desire."[41] Lamar's plan for establishing public education was straightforward—Congress should fund the system through a suitable appropriation of land. According to the president, the immediate designation of public land for educational purposes would not be an "inconvenience, to the government, or the people, but defer it until the public domain shall have passed from our hands, and the uneducated youths of Texas will constitute the living monument of our neglect and remissness."[42] Lamar furthered explained that by waiting to address this issue, Congress would be forced to levy new taxes to fund the proposed educational system. Given the dire state of the economy, the president surmised that Texans would view tax increases as detrimental to their financial security. As such, any delayed attempt to educate the Republic's youth would prove difficult. In a final attempt to convince Congress of the need for immediate action, Lamar proclaimed, "A liberal endowment which will be adequate to the general diffusion of a good rudimentary education in every district of the Republic, and to the establishment of a university where the highest branches of science may be taught, can now be effected without the expenditure of a single dollar—postpone it a few years, and millions will be necessary to accomplish the great design."[43]

Lamar, echoing the philosophy of Thomas Jefferson, believed that an educated citizenry was vital to a republic. He also maintained a special interest in education that stretched back to his childhood. As a youth in Georgia, he received an elementary education, but never attended college. Despite his own circumstances, Lamar understood that even rudimentary instruction would benefit Texas children and believed in the necessity of establishing a system of higher education to prepare the nation's future leaders. Lamar's devotion to founding schools in the Republic has prompted biographers to applaud him as the "Father of Texas Education."[44]

Next, after briefly mentioning the necessity of correcting flaws in the legal code, Lamar moved to a topic that captured the attention of every Texan: frontier dense. At this point, the president discussed in detail threats confronting the nation, especially the distressing issues associated with Mexico, border raiders along the Rio Grande, and American Indians spread throughout Texas. Given that his predecessor had reduced drastically the army and the navy had fallen into disrepair, Lamar proposed that Congress pass legislation to strengthen the Republic's armed forces, and if necessary, use the newly organized military against its enemies.[45] To bolster his argument, the chief executive provided further details on what he considered the most immediate risks to national security.

Even though Mexico had not posed a major challenge since the Battle of San Jacinto, Lamar believed that the Mexican government's internal problems might be temporary, arguing, "We ought by no means to permit them to beguile us into negligence."[46] However, a more pressing issue was raids along the southern border. Lamar advised Congress to pass legislation that would "visit a just and severe retribution upon such Mexican citizens, not in the actual service of their government, as shall be formed in arms, or convicted of any hostile practices within our territory." He further explained, "An honorable warfare we will reciprocate. But the predatory aggression of unauthorized banditti, have always received, as they justly merit, the severest chastisements that an indignant community can inflict."[47]

Lamar was also concerned about the presence of American Indians in Texas. His perspective was clear and undoubtedly reflected his earlier experiences with tribes in Georgia. The president reminded his audience, "It is a cardinal principle in all political associations, that protection is commensurate with allegiance, and the poorest citizen whose sequestered cabin is reared on our remotest frontier, holds as sacred a claim upon the government for safety and security as does the man who lives in ease and wealth in the heart of our most populous city."[48] Believing that government's first responsibility was to protect its citizens, Lamar called on Congress to deal with "Severity with the enemy," claiming that "as long as we continue to exhibit our mercy without shewing [*sic*] our strength ... the Indian [will] continue to bloody the edge of the tomahawk, and move onward in the work of rapacity and slaughter."[49] President Lamar revealed his visceral hatred of American Indians when he boldly asserted:

> If the wild cannibals of the woods will not desist from their massacres; if they will continue to war upon us with the ferocity of Tigers and Hyenas, it is time we should retaliate their warfare, not in the murder of their women and children, but in prosecution of an exterminating war upon their warriors, which will admit of no compromise and have no termination except in their total extinction or total expulsion.[50]

In particular, President Lamar commented on the tensions developing between Anglos and the Cherokees in East Texas. The key question was whether the Cherokees owned official title to their lands. Lamar left no room for doubt concerning his answer to this question, arguing that the "Emigrant Tribes" had no legal or equitable claim to any lands in Texas. He pointed out that the Cherokees were intruders, who came to Texas "against the public wish, and at the sacrifice of the public tranquility."[51] Mexican authorities had viewed the Indians as "objects of disquietude and terror; and if any instance a promise of lands was made to their Chiefs or Head-men, they were either induced by fear, or proceeded from a design to array the tomahawk and scalping-knife against American settlers of Texas."[52] For Lamar, "Such promises (if ever made) under such circumstances can impose no moral obligation on us."[53] Regarding any promises that Texas officials made to the Cherokees during the revolution, Lamar dismissed any such agreements outright, claiming that any treaty between the tribe and the Consultation government in 1835 was never "ratified by any competent authority, and therefore can in nowise be legally considered as binding or obligatory upon us."[54] Then, he stated that even if such treaty had been ratified by all the solemnities of the constitution, "this government is now wholly absolved from the performance of its conditions, by the notorious and habitual violation of its principal stipulations by the Indians."[55] Finally, Lamar revealed his true feelings regarding the

Cherokees, "To admit their claim to any extent on any other conditions would entail interminable vexation on our posterity. It would be parceling out our territory to strangers and intruders, and introducing in the very viscera of body politic, an alien, independent and innately hostile people, who know no restrains of law and are subordinate to no authority."[56]

Lamar's position regarding the Cherokee undoubtedly stirred the ire of Sam Houston, who had a longstanding relationship with the Cherokees. Prior to coming to Texas in 1832, Houston had lived with the Cherokees on two different occasions. During his initial four-year stay with the tribe in Tennessee, the elders had adopted Houston, giving him the name "the Raven." During his second stay, the tribe renamed him "Big Drunk," because Houston attempted to drown his sorrows of a failed marriage and the end of his career in Tennessee politics in whiskey. At the start of the Texas Revolution, General Houston and others successfully negotiated a treaty that stipulated the Texas government would give the Cherokees permanent title to their lands once the revolution ended and the Texans gained their independence from Mexico, providing that the tribe remained neutral during the conflict. Unfortunately for the Cherokees, the First Texas Congress refused to ratify the treaty, leaving the tribe's lands legally open to white settlers. Houston, who was then serving as president, protested the actions of Congress and refused to support the congressional representatives' call to remove the Cherokees from their East Texas lands. President Houston's opposition to Congress led western settlements of the Republic to turn against him. In turn, Houston refused to carry out the laws of December 1836 that provided for an increase in the number of military personnel stationed on the frontier, claiming that he was concerned about the financial cost of housing, equipping, and maintaining troops along the western frontier. Given his close connection with the Cherokees, no one was surprised to see Houston vehemently oppose President Lamar's Indian policies. Furthermore, even fewer were shocked when Houston, while serving in the Texas Congress between 1839 and 1841, sought political retribution against Lamar by opposing legislation that his administration favored, especially his nemesis's plans to strengthen the western region's position within the national government.[57]

President Lamar's plan to protect the frontier was multifaceted: He called on Congress to establish a line of military posts on the frontier; argued that all interactions between American Indians and Texans should be strictly controlled by the government; proposed that

Congress create reservations, where Indians would be forced to live and abide by all Texas laws; suggested that Indian agents should be appointed to preside over the activities of the tribes living on the reservations; and requested that Congress form a commission charged with the task of making treaties with the various American Indian groups in Texas. He further stipulated that Texas authorities would treat all tribes that entered into treaties with the Republic as friends of the state, while they would consider those who refused to enter into peace treaties as enemies.[58]

In order to defend the frontier effectively, Lamar strongly believed that it was imperative that Texas strengthen its military forces, especially since the Houston administration had reduced the size of the army.[59] Thus, the president called for the immediate organization of a regular, permanent standing army, arguing that a strong show of force would "deter the Indians from his depredations—inspire a confidence which would lead to a rapid settlement of our present frontier, and at the same time form a nucleus around which the chivalric yeomanry of the land would rally in the event of another invasion from our national foe [Mexico]."[60] Anticipating that some Texans might perceive a standing army as a potential threat to their form of government and individual civil liberties, Lamar suggested that local militias should be established and be ready to answer the call of duty if necessary. The chief executive was also concerned with defending the "maritime frontier." Knowing that foreign commerce was vital to the future economic success of the Republic, he called on Congress to improve the deplorable conditions of the existing Texas Navy and to expand the number of ships in its fleet, charging it with the duty of protecting commercial trade on the high seas.[61]

Many of Lamar's contemporaries agreed with his plan to increase the military presence in the western regions and along the southern border, but they were uncertain how the Republic would pay for military expenditures. In an attempt to answer this question, President Lamar suggested specific ways to fund increases in military spending as well as other government programs deemed vital to national growth and prosperity. He commented that the future of the Republic was tied to nature, believing:

> In a few years, when agricultural exports shall exceed in value all that the most sumptuous extravagance can desire from abroad, and our unexplored minerals shall be in process of extraction, the people of Texas will find no difficulty in rendering

> ample means of support to their government, and protection to themselves.[62]

However, that was the future. How would the government, and the Texas economy, survive until that time when the Republic's natural resources could be exploited? Lamar was clear that the government could not levy burdensome taxes on the farmers who were still struggling to rebuild their farms following the devastation of the Texas Revolution. Instead, the president believed that it was necessary to secure foreign loans, which would allow the Republic enough time to develop its economic resources. In order to generate revenue, Lamar requested that Congress continue to collect import tariffs. Despite a belief that the production of raw materials in Texas was more conducive to duty-free trade policies, the president argued that "the ultimate adoption of free trade … would in the present situation of our country, exhibit an apparent recklessness and imprudence, which could not fail to affect our credit abroad; for it should never be forgotten, that fickleness and instability in a young government like ours, is as destructive to its character, as a vitiated currency is to its wealth, or oppression to its peace."[63] Furthermore, Lamar stated that "the credit of our public issues, which must most certainly sink into a disastrous and degrading depreciation with the repeal of the impost," would leave the government treasury destitute.[64] A depleted treasury would leave the country, especially the frontier, vulnerable to its enemies.

The remainder of Lamar's message related to his views on the Republic's money supply and the need to create a government-owned national bank. First, he believed that Congress should create a practical mode of meeting the general demand for currency, claiming "precious metals are the only uniform standard of value; and no paper representative can acquire general confidence, and answer the legitimate purposes of trade, unless it be convertible at the pleasure of the holder into gold or silver; for there are occasions … when nothing else than specie … will satisfy the demands … of creditors."[65] In order to manage the monetary circumstances of the nation, Lamar suggested that Congress create a nation bank—the Bank of Texas. The president spent a great deal of time outlining the basic operational and managerial structure of the proposed institution. Critical to the success of the bank were two principles: First, the government would own and control the bank, believing that private involvement with the institution would lead to eventual corruption. Second, the bank would be supported with what Lamar called a "triple security," which included real estate, specie, and public faith.[66] The public's faith in the bank would be secured by assuring the management of the institution would be placed in the hands of "honest and efficient business men of the country, without reference to their particular callings, or political opinions."[67] To ensure that the officers of the bank were able men, the president suggested that Congress establish specific policies for appointing individuals to these positions.[68]

At the end of his message, Lamar appealed to the emotions of the congressmen present, hoping that he could convince them of the validity of his views for the future of Texas. In doing so, he invoked all the key terms commonly associated with Manifest Destiny, including God, patriotism, glory, greatness, and power. Confidently, Lamar stated:

> Providence has placed her [Texas] before you a perfect blank, ready to receive the finest, or the worst impressions. You may shape her to the noblest purposes, or work her to the most debasing and pernicious ends. … Let us then, gentlemen, duly appreciate the privileges of our peculiar position—let us not lose the opportunity which God has given us of doing good—but let us love our country, and looking with a single eye to her glory and greatness—do whatever wisdom and experience may suggest for the spread of knowledge, virtue, and the useful arts; and for the development of those vast resources which are slumbering in her mountains, and lying dormant in the germinating power of her soil. … In a word, let us sacrifice all narrow-minded selfishness upon the hallowed alter of patriotism, and by an energetic and enlightened discharge of the trusts confided to us, elevate our young Republic in that proud rank which her unrivaled beauty and unbounded wealth entitle her to take among the nations of the earth.[69]

Thus, early in his presidency, Lamar laid before the people his vision for the future of Texas. The majority of the Republic's political leadership seemingly welcomed with open arms his dream of a new empire. However, as is often the case with such grandiose schemes, Lamar's Texas never materialized, and posterity has remembered his administration as one of the most disastrous in the annals of Texas history. Even though scholars have detailed Lamar's failures at length, few have adequately identified the reasons *why* his policies failed. As a result, they leave us with an incomplete picture of his presidency. Additionally, historians often dismiss completely Lamar's successes during his first year in office. While there is no doubt that Lamar had many shortcomings, his failures, in large part, were the result of circumstances beyond his control and poor counsel from trusted advisers.

In the first months of his presidency, Lamar experienced some success, at least in the eyes of Texans who supported the administration's policies. With the support of Congress, Lamar moved the capital from Houston to its present location in Austin and waged a successful, and popular, war against the Cherokee from East Texas. Additionally, the president secured congressional support for the development of an educational system in the republic. Furthermore, the administration experienced minimal success in foreign affairs. When Lamar took office, the United States was the only foreign country that had officially recognized Texas independence. By the end of his term, France had acknowledged the republic's existence, and Texas diplomats had successfully negotiated trade agreements with Belgium, the Netherlands, and England; however, they failed in their attempts to earn the most important country's endorsement—that of Mexico. As long as Mexico refused to recognize the independence of Texas, European nations remained reluctant to invest in the future of the fledgling republic, depriving the Texas government of a vital resource: money.

Without financial assistance from European countries, Lamar's vision of building a great Texas empire became an impossibility. The president's subsequent actions only contributed to the economic woes of the Republic, especially his continued war against the Plains Indians on the western frontier, his attempt to revitalize the Texas navy, and his disastrous Santa Fe Expedition.[70] To stem the tide of growing financial collapse, the administration followed the only possible solution at their disposal: They printed more paper money, hoping to buy enough time to secure foreign loans. Their hopes for such funding went unrealized, and their economic gamble only compounded the nation's financial problems as the increased amount of paper in circulation steadily fell in value. As economic conditions grew worse, the pro-Houston faction increasingly gained momentum. No longer lurking in the shadows, Houston supporters were now engaged in a full-fledged political war with the administration. Ultimately, the pro-Houston faction would triumph over the president by restoring Sam Houston to the presidency in the 1841 election and destroying the reputation of Lamar in the process.[71]

At the end of his term, Lamar's failures proved greater than his successes. Even though the president "transformed the republic into a racially homogeneous democratic republic for slaveholding, fostered growing diplomatic clout within the international community, gained command of the seas," and created the foundation for an educational system, his policies also "bankrupted the republic."[72] Lamar and his supporters realized that their chance to mold Texas into a great empire had passed, providing momentum once again to the annexation movement. As Lamar's vision of building a great empire faded, so did the Texans' opportunity to create a unique and enduring identity. Beginning in 1841, the fate of Texas was entwined with the United States, replacing delusions of grandeur with a solidified American identity.

Notes

1. Stanley Siegel, *The Poet President of Texas* (Austin: Jenkins Publishing Company, 1977), 51; Kenneth E. Hendrickson, Jr., *The Chief Executives of Texas: From Stephen F. Austin to John B. Connally, Jr.* (College Station: Texas A&M University Press, 1995), 35; John Edward Weems with Jane Weems, *Dream of Empire: A History of the Republic of Texas, 1836–1846* (1971; reprint, New York: Barnes & Noble Books, 1995), 138; Philip Graham, *The Life and Poems of Mirabeau B. Lamar* (Chapel Hill: The University of North Carolina Press, 1938), 50; Llerena B. Friend, *Sam Houston: The Great Designer* (Austin: University of Texas Press, 1954, reprints 1969, 1979), 92–93; Stanley Siegel, *A Political History of the Texas Republic, 1836–1845* (Austin: University of Texas Press, 1956), 103–04; George Lankevich, ed., *The Presidents of the Republic of Texas* (Dobbs Ferry, NY: Oceana Publications, Inc., 1979), 31; James Haley, *Sam Houston* (Norman: University of Oklahoma Press, 2002), 208; and Jeffrey Stuart Kerr, *Seat of Empire: The Embattled Birth of Austin, Texas* (Lubbock: Texas Tech University Press, 2013), 48–50.

2. Archie P. McDonald, *Texas: All Hail the Mighty State* (Austin: Eakin Press, 1983), 93. Archie McDonald makes an interesting observation that Lamar in attitude was the exact opposite of Sam Houston. According to McDonald, Lamar's view of finance was to spend; his policy toward Mexico was to force recognition; and his policies toward Native Americans in Texas was removal or extermination. Also, unlike Houston, Lamar had bold dreams of building an empire. McDonald makes an even more interesting observation about the differences in

the two men, writing that "Ironically, the brash, bold Texan image so prevalent throughout the world is owed more to Lamar than to Houston, although most would imagine it to be just the opposite. The irony is the more noticeable because of the physical and intellectual differences between them. Despite numerous wounds and an apparent disregard for his health as witnessed by his well-known appetite for alcohol, Houston remained robust throughout his life, while Lamar suffered numerous physical ailments and such poor health that his absence from his capital was required on several occasions. Yet Lamar was the dreamer of bold action for Texas. He always wanted the Republic to do more than it was doing, perhaps more than it could do, to establish its independence, to gain recognition from foreign governments, and to put the economy and the educational system on a sound footing." While I believe McDonald's assessment of Lamar is accurate, most scholars would disagree, choosing instead to embrace Houston and excoriate Lamar. In their eyes, Houston is the great hero of the Republic and Lamar is the villain. With Houston erected as the centerpiece of an intellectual pantheon devoted to Texas politicians, Lamar's reputation has suffered greatly. Understandably, Lamar is deserving of criticism: There is no doubt that he made many mistakes during his term as president—the same as those who served as president before and after him. However, he was also the victim of poor counsel and uncontrollable circumstances, which few historians take into account when examining his presidency.

3. The Inaugural Address of Mirabeau B. Lamar, President of the Republic of Texas, To Both Houses of Congress, December 10, 1838, in *The Papers of Mirabeau Buonaparte Lamar*, eds. Charles Adams Gulick, Jr. and Katherine Elliott, vol. 2 (Austin: Texas State Library, 1922), 316. The quotes taken from *The Papers of Mirabeau Buonaparte Lamar* are copied exactly as each appear in the papers, including the editors' corrections and insertions.

4. The Inaugural Address of Mirabeau B. Lamar, December 10, 1838, 316–17.

5. Stanley Siegel, *A Political History of the Texas Republic, 1836–1845*, 99.

6. Charles Adams Gulick, Jr. and Katherine Elliott, eds., *The Papers of Mirabeau Buonaparte Lamar*, Vols. 1–6 (Austin: Texas State Library, 1920–1927). Lamar's published papers contain numerous documents, sources, and reminiscences of early Texans related to different episodes in the history of Texas. From the moment that Lamar first entered Texas, he collected these historic accounts with the hopes of writing a history of the

Republic (and later state). Lamar never finished his history of Texas even though he wrote notes for such a book periodically through his life.

7. The Inaugural Address of Mirabeau B. Lamar, December 10, 1838, 317.

8. Ibid.

9. Ibid. It should not be surprising that Lamar embraced Manifest Destiny, especially given his political experience in Georgia, where he supported Indian removal and the continued Anglicization of southern territories in the United States and the northern province of Mexico (Texas).

10. Ibid.

11. Ibid., 317–318.

12. James Morgan to Samuel Swartwout, February 5, 1838, in *Fragile Empires: The Texas Correspondence of Samuel Swartwout and James Morgan, 1836–1856*, eds. Feris A. Bass and B. R. Brunson (Austin: Shoal Creek Publishers, 1978), 66; Haley, *Sam Houston*, 213–214; Friend, *Sam Houston: The Great Designer*, 94–95; Archie P. McDonald, Comp., *The Texas Experience* (College Station: Texas A&M University, 1986), 42–44; Siegel, *A Political History of the Texas Republic*, 137–172; Andreas V. Reichstein, *Rise of the Lone Star: The Making of Texas* (College Station: Texas A&M University Press, 1989), 162; Kerr, *Seat of Empire* , 43–47; Margaret Swett Henson, comp., and Donald E. Willett, ed., *The Texas That Might Have Been: Sam Houston's Foes Write to Albert Sidney Johnston* (College Station: Texas A&M University Press, 2009), 19–22.

13. The Inaugural Address of Mirabeau B. Lamar, December 10, 1838, 318.

14. Ibid.

15. Ibid.

16. Siegel, *A Political History of the Texas Republic*, 42–42; A. K. Christian, "Mirabeau B. Lamar," *Southwestern Historical Quarterly* 23, no. 3 (January 1920): 163–165; Siegel, *The Poet President of Texas*, 23–28.

17. The Inaugural Address of Mirabeau B. Lamar, December 10, 1838, 318.

18. Ibid.

19. Ibid.

20. Kerr, *Seat of Empire*, 40–42.

21. M. B. Lamar, Montgomery County, Alabama, Speech at a Public Dinner; State Rights; The Killing of Owens; Against War with

France; Jackson's Character, January 1835, in *The Papers of Mirabeau Buonaparte Lamar*, eds. Charles Adams Gulick, Jr. and Katherine Elliott, vol. 1 (Austin: Texas State Library, 1920), 197; Kerr, *Seat of Empire*, 43.

22. The Inaugural Address of Mirabeau B. Lamar, December 10, 1838, 319.

23. Ibid.

24. Ibid.

25. Ibid., 320.

26. Ibid.

27. Ibid.

28. For more on Texas commitment to creating a slave-based cotton economy, see Andrew Torget's *Seeds of Empire: Cotton, Slavery, and the Transformation of the Texas Borderlands, 1800–1850* (Chapel Hill: The University of North Carolina Press, 2015).

29. The Inaugural Address of Mirabeau B. Lamar, December 10, 1838, 320–21.

30. Ibid., 321.

31. Ibid.

32. Ibid., 321–22.

33. Ibid., 322.

34. Ibid.

35. Ibid.

36. Ibid.

37. Ibid.

38. For specific details on Houston's troubled first term as president, see Siegel, *A Political History of the Texas Republic*, 56–92. On page 92, Siegel summarizes Houston's first term, "With a mediocre score of accomplishments in the problems of land, finance, and Indian relations, coupled with the failure to attain annexation in the sphere of foreign affairs, the Houston party could boast of no major political triumphs in its first term of office. The President had disregarded the will of Congress in refusing to open the land offices, in sanctioning treaties with Indians that he knew Congress would not honor, and in instructing Anson Jones, as minister to the United States, to withdraw the petition for annexation. Added to this, the Old Hero was as controversial a figure as ever as ever before, and those who hated him still did so with a passion. Tales of his drinking made the rounds again, and his past life was held up to public ridicule." Also see Weems, *Dream of Empire*, 135–36.

39. Message of the President, Submitted to Both Houses, December 21, 1838, in *The Papers of Mirabeau Buonaparte Lamar*, eds. Charles Adams Gulick, Jr. and Katherine Elliott, vol. 2 (Austin: Texas State Library, 1922), 347–48.

40. Jack C. Ramsay, Jr., *Thunder on the Brazos: A Biography of Mirabeau B. Lamar* (Austin: Eakin Press, 1985), 90–110; A. K. Christian, "Mirabeau Buonaparte Lamar," *Southwestern Historical Quarterly* 24, no. 3 (January 1921): 195–234; Siegel, *The Poet President of Texas*, 63–86; Siegel, *A Political History of the Texas Republic*, 113–36 and 147–65; Weems, *Dream of Empire*, 145–151 and 179–183; Reichstein, *Rise of the Lone Star*, 166–70; Dorman H. Winfrey, "Mirabeau B. Lamar and Texas Nationalism," *Southwestern Historical Quarterly* 59 (October 1955): 184–205; Herbert Pickens Gambrell, *Mirabeau Buonaparte Lamar: Troubadour and Crusader* (Dallas: Southwest Press, 1934), 241–42.

41. Message of the President, Submitted to Both Houses, December 21, 1838, 348.

42. Ibid., 349.

43. Ibid.

44. Ramsay, *Thunder on the Brazos*, 138–39; Gambrell, *Mirabeau Buonaparte Lamar*, 218–37; A. K. Christian, "Mirabeau Buonaparte Lamar," *Southwestern Historical Quarterly* 23, no. 4 (April 1920): 233–36; Graham, *The Life and Poems of Mirabeau B. Lamar*, 53; Mary Scheer, "Mirabeau B. Lamar: Poet, President, and Namesake for a University," *East Texas Historical Journal* 52, no. 1, (Spring 2014): 52; Archie P. McDonald, "Lone Star on the Rise," in *Texas: A Sesquicentennial Celebration*, ed. Donald W. Whisenhunt (Austin: Eakin Press, 1984), 87.

45. Siegel, *A Political History of the Texas Republic*, 65–67 and 78–79; Jonathan W. Jordan, *Lone Star Navy: Texas, The Fight for the Gulf of Mexico, and the Shaping of the American West* (Washington, D.C.: Potomac Books, Inc., 2006), 74–123.

46. Message of the President, Submitted to Both Houses, December 21, 1838, 350–51.

47. Ibid., 351–52. Interestingly, Lamar's position on Mexican raiders echoed Santa Anna's declaration that Texas rebels were nothing more than pirates.

48. Ibid., 352.

49. Ibid.

50. Ibid., 352–53.

51. Ibid., 353.

52. Ibid.

53. Ibid.

54. Ibid.

55. Ibid.

56. Ibid., 354.

57. Siegel, *A Political History of the Texas Republic*, 140; Haley, *Sam Houston*, 216.

58. Message of the President, Submitted to Both Houses, December 21, 1838, 354.

59. McDonald, "Lone Star on the Rise," 85–86; Haley, *Sam Houston*, 193–95.

60. Message of the President, Submitted to Both Houses, December 21, 1838, 354.

61. Ibid., 354–56.

62. Ibid., 356.

63. Ibid., 359.

64. Ibid.

65. Ibid., 360–61.

66. Ibid., 361–65.

67. Ibid., 365.

68. Ibid., 365–66. Lamar suggested that Congress would elect the members of the board of directors, and the president of the Republic would nominate the bank's president and cashier, who would have to be approved by the Senate before assuming office. Congress would have complete oversight of the bank's board of directors.

69. Ibid., 368.

70. As the country continued its economic plunge, Lamar sought ways to save the Republic from financial ruin. Knowing that there was a rich trade between Santa Fe and Missouri, the president hoped to redirect the network of goods passing between these two points through Texas to Galveston, thereby increasing the amount of trade goods coming into and out of the port city. If Galveston's reputation as a trading center could be strengthened in the eyes of foreign merchants, perhaps they would put added pressure on their government to provide financial assistance to Texas. In other words, if Texas could become economically significant to the economies of foreign countries, perhaps the governments of those nations would be more willing not only to recognize Texas as an independent country, but also to provide needed loans to economically sustain the Republic.

71. Ramsay, *Thunder on the Brazos*, 151–56; McDonald, "Lone Star on the Rise," 87–89. While it was easy for Houston supporters to criticize the actions of Lamar for political expediency, modern scholars seem to have lost sight that the president did not act alone—Lamar was not a dictator. The president often sought the counsel of leading government officials during this era and developed his policies based on their advice. For more on Houston's election to his second term, see Siegel, *A Political History of the Texas Republic*, 172–184.

72. Henson and Willett, *The Texas That Might Have Been*, 22.

Chapter 9

Anson Jones: The Forgotten President of Texas

Charles Swanlund

Anson Jones, the last president of the Republic of Texas, was a participant in most of the major events of the Texas Revolution, and was a key contributor to the survival of the resultant republic for most of its brief and colorful history. Jones was reputed to have offered the first public resolution calling for the convening of an assembly to discuss independence from Mexico in 1835, participated as a combatant in the penultimate battle of the Texas Revolution, served as the Apothecary General of the Texas army in the immediate aftermath of that conflict, served in the Second Texas Congress in the House of Representatives, was appointed as Texas's Minister to the United States in Sam Houston's first presidential administration, served in the Texas Senate in the Fourth and Fifth Texas Congresses, occupied the office of secretary of state during Sam Houston's second term, and served as the last president of the Republic of Texas. In view of all of these accomplishments, scholars still question: Why does Jones remain a little known figure in Texas history? The answer to this question is somewhat complex, and in many respects, Jones's legacy was tarnished not only by the political turmoil that surrounded the issue of annexation to the United States, but also by his own efforts to reclaim credit for his contributions to the Republic, a seemingly self-serving attempt to secure his legacy for posterity.

To develop a greater understanding of Anson Jones, one must first examine his background and experiences prior to arriving in Texas in 1833, which in reality were not very different from many other individuals who came to Texas during the same period. Jones's first ancestor in America was William Jones, who served as Deputy Governor of New Haven and Connecticut from 1683 to 1698. William was the son of Colonel Sir John Jones and Catherine Cromwell, the second sister of the Lord Protector of England.[1] The Joneses were among the elites of New England, but when Anson's father, Solomon, was seven years old, the family's fortunes were reversed when both his parents died, leaving him and his brothers orphans. Solomon Jones would come of age during the tumultuous period of the

Portrait of Anson Jones. Third and Last President of the Republic of Texas. This image is located at the Washington on the Brazos State Park. Courtesy of Texas Parks & Wildlife.

American Revolution, and Solomon and his brothers served in the Continental Army. Solomon served for five years and saw action at Bunker Hill and Saratoga. British soldiers captured two of Anson's uncles, keeping them prisoners aboard the "Jersey prison-ship" until an exchange was arranged. Another uncle, Phineas Jones, lost a leg during the war.[2] After the Revolution, Solomon married Sarah Strong and eked out a living as an itinerant tanner and tenant farmer. Anson, born in 1798 in Great Barrington, Massachusetts, was the thirteenth of fourteen children, four of whom died in "extreme infancy."[3] The family would move ten times during his first eighteen years, and struggled just to get by. Despite their extreme poverty, the Jones family apparently appreciated the value of education, and from an early age, Anson received what rudimentary education was available to him. "I was very fond of reading and study" he would write in his memoirs, "and employed every means in my power in purchasing books, and all the time which could possibly be spared in reading them, or in the prosecution of my academic studies."[4] During his formative years, Anson was an introvert, preferring the company of books to that of most people. Imbued with the family penchant for patriotic service, he tried to enlist in the army at the age of fourteen during the War of 1812, but his father forbade him to serve, preferring that his son further his education instead. Solomon enrolled young Anson in the Lenox Academy.[5] Anson's mother died when he was seventeen, creating additional hardships on his family and forcing him to undertake a career. His older brothers preferred that he learn a trade, but his father and older sisters had greater things in mind for him, urging him to become a physician. Though Anson had dreams of becoming a printer, he acquiesced to his father's wishes and agreed to study medicine. Jones would later comment that his decision "entailed years of unhappiness upon me."[6]

The study of medicine in the nineteenth century was less regulated and structured than today. As with the study of law, medicine still offered opportunities through apprenticeship rather than a formal education. Jones was probably not an ideal candidate for this type of education. He apparently had little self-confidence, and would later recall that "I had no knowledge of the world—was shy and timid to a fault—had no wealthy or efficient friends—and my brothers, from whom alone I had a right to expect counsel or assistance, were opposed to the occupation I had determined upon, and consequently withheld either."[7] In 1817, he moved to Litchfield, Connecticut, where his sister had arranged for him to study under Dr. Daniel Sheldon. He made little progress in his studies, and after a year, faced with mounting debt, became a schoolteacher in

Goshen, "occupying my intervals of leisure in reading such medical or other books as I could *borrow*, for I was not able to *buy* any."[8] In 1818, he moved to Utica, New York, where he lived with his brother and earned his keep clerking in his brother's store while studying under Dr. Amos G. Hull. He once again found himself with mounting financial obligations, so he returned to teaching to make ends meet. His brother's business floundered, forcing Anson to take up residence in the home of a man named Hinman. During this time, he continued his apprenticeship with Dr. Hull. This decision to board at the home of Hinman would later have profound ramifications for Jones.

In 1820, Jones earned his certification to practice medicine through the Oneida Medical Society. He then relocated to Bainbridge where he opened a practice, which would fail after slightly more than a year. He was then persuaded to open a drugstore in Norwich, Connecticut, and armed with references from Dr. Hull and others, purchased a supply of medicines and drugs on credit, and went into business. Not long after opening the store, Hinman, whom Jones thought to be a friend, sued him for his board in Utica, and obtained a judgment against him. In order to satisfy the judgement, Anson had to liquidate the stock of the store, putting him out of business once again. Ruined, Jones arranged to relocate in Harpers Ferry, Virginia, where he opened another medical practice. On his way to his destination however, he was arrested by one of his creditors in New York, where he was forced to give up his watch "and every dollar I had in the world but twenty" to settle the debt.[9] Now without means to travel, he decided to open a practice in Philadelphia, but again his practice failed. As he had in the past, the distraught doctor resorted to teaching, an occupation that offered him little joy but did provide a source of income. Six months later, Jones despaired of being able to make a living in Philadelphia and chanced to meet a Mr. Lowry, the American Consul to Venezuela. Lowry persuaded the young doctor that he could make it as a physician in the Latin American country. In 1824, Jones sailed for South America, where he would split his time between Laguayra and Caracas until 1826.[10]

On his return to the United States, Jones again opened a medical office in Philadelphia. Again having little success, he decided that maybe his problem was the lack of a formal medical degree, so in the winter of 1826–27, he enrolled for a "full course of lectures in Jefferson Medical College" from which he was awarded a diploma in 1827. [11] Still failing to achieve great success, he decided to expand his circle of personal acquaintances in an effort to stimulate business; he joined the Society of Odd Fellows. This was the beginning of Jones's lifelong involvement with fraternal organizations. He would also become involved with the Masons and International Order of Foresters. By October of 1832, despite achieving great success in the Odd Fellows, rising to the post of the Grand Master of all Pennsylvania lodges, he still had not achieved solvency. [12] During another chance meeting, a man named Thomas J. Spear offered Jones the opportunity to become a partner in a mercantile house in New Orleans. Spears convinced Jones to once again relocate and forsake medicine. Jones arrived in New Orleans in the fall of 1832, only to learn that he had cast his lot with a man "devoid of principle, and reckless of character, and everything else."[13] Apparently, Dr. Jones believed that his new partner was a man with no redeeming qualities. He immediately disassociated himself from Spear, and in the spring of 1833, he opened yet another medical office, which subsequently failed. He took stock of his life and reached the conclusion that he could not make a living in New Orleans. He also realized that his time in residence there was leading to several bad habits, "I found the pernicious habit of gambling, to which I had always had an inclination, was growing upon me there."[14] He further noted, "Whilst in this place, also, partly from having frequently little else to do, and partly to overcome the feelings of disappointments I had so often endured, and more particularly about this time, I also found myself learning to imitate the practice of taking a 'julep' much oftener than was at all necessary."[15]

Another chance encounter on the streets of New Orleans was to alter the destiny of Anson Jones, and perhaps Texas as well. He happened to meet Captain Jeremiah Brown, the skipper of the *Sabine*, a ship that regularly engaged in the Texas trade.[16] Captain Brown told Jones that there was a need for physicians in Texas, particularly at Brazoria with which Captain Brown was well acquainted. Jones later remembered this pivotal moment in his life: "My impressions of Texas were extremely unfavorable. I had only known it as a harbor for pirates and banditti, and at first I was wholly opposed to going there to reside. Upon further inquiry and conversation, however, I concluded it was not so bad as it had been represented; that whatever its former character had been, it now had assumed an entirely different one. ..."[17] He decided to make the journey, and as a result, the destinies of Anson Jones and Texas become inextricably combined.

Jones, aboard the *Sabine*, arrived at Velasco in October of 1833. He then made his way to Brazoria where he immediately concluded that his initial misgivings had been correct, and he quickly booked passage back to New Orleans (leaving him with the princely sum of $2.00 in cash) aboard the *Sabine*, which would not sail for two weeks.

Before she sailed, Jones became acquainted with John A. Wharton, who was able to convince him that he should give Texas a chance, and assured him that he could make it in Brazoria, because the other two physicians in the area had just died of cholera. Given that Jones was still $2,000 in debt and had little or no prospects of success in the United States, he decided to stay on. As he would recall in 1849, "The consequences to myself is, that I am in Texas still—the consequences to the country will be, to be judged of hereafter, when history shall have given her truthful and impartial award."[18]

Jones established his practice, and enjoyed immediate success. Before the year was out, he had a practice that encompassed a circuit of about forty miles, and was able to take on his own apprentice, John N. Berryman.[19] His newfound success almost ended in 1834 when he contracted "bilious remittent fever" while treating a patient, and was confined to his bed for two months before making a recovery. In 1835, he brought his sister Mary to Texas to keep house for him, and added his cousin, Dr. Ira Jones as an apprentice. During this period, Jones also applied for and received a charter to form a Masonic Lodge, which became Holland Lodge No. 36. This lodge would eventually become the Grand Lodge of Texas when it transferred to Houston in 1838. Jones would serve as the Grand Master of the lodge for many years, and would be active as a Mason for the rest of his life.[20]

As the pace of the political unrest in Texas quickened in 1835, Jones tried to remain detached as he felt befitted his status as a doctor. As it became more and more obvious that a change needed to occur, he started to become involved, but maintained a moderate tone, he would later recount:

> I was one of those, however, who counselled forbearance, and the maintenance of peace as long as the one was proper or the other possible. I consequently did not join in the war-cry early, and was not one of those who early this year secured the appellation of "war dogs," most of whom afterwards, when the struggle actually came on, showed themselves true disciples of Falstaff, and that they believed "discretion the better part of valor," by leaving the country.[21]

He concentrated his efforts on his practice, and for the first time in his life, seemed to reap the rewards of his profession. He soon realized, however, that events were moving too fast to avoid taking a stance on

Texas's situation. Jones signed the petition crafted by John A. Wharton calling for a convention to discuss matters, and his cousin Ira went to join the Texian forces besieging Bexar. Anson decided to travel to San Felipe in the fall of 1835 to observe the proceedings of the General Consultation. While traveling through Columbia, Jones made the acquaintance of the Reverend Jose Maria Alpache e Infante. Padre Alpache had served the Church in Tabasco, had been a senator in the Mexican Congress, was an outspoken critic of the Centralist regime in Mexico City, and claimed to be a friend of Lorenzo de Zavala.[22] The two men decided to travel together, a long and arduous journey given the weather. After spending several days in the company of the good father, Jones concluded that his companion "was in the first place a *coward*, and in the second place, *untrustworthy* in other respects. …"[23] In what would become a pattern for Jones from this point forward when later recalling incidents from his life, he would give greater significance to the actual events than perhaps were warranted by them. Jones wrote in his memoirs, "This was doubtless a great service, for afterwards it became known to me that it would have been unfortunate for Texas if his [Padre Alpache] advice had been followed [at the General Consultation]; and in that it was not followed, was probably owing to me, in a great measure."[24]

After arriving in San Felipe, Jones then turned his attention to the proceedings and to the participants. "There appeared to me to be plenty of recklessness and selfishness, but little dignity or patriotism."[25] In his journal, he described his disgust with many of the figures who would become central to the revolutionary and republic periods. He describes his initial impressions of Jim Bowie and Sam Houston, noting that Bowie was "dead drunk" and commenting that Sam Houston's "appearance was anything but decent and respectable, and very much like that of a broken-down sot and debauchee."[26] When he expressed his displeasure with what he described as a drunken "orgie" in which Bowie, Houston, Branch T. Archer, and others made base and callous references about Stephen F. Austin, John Wharton warned Jones that "his life might be at some risk unless he closed his mouth."[27] Nothing happened, but Jones was disgusted with the entire Consultation, and later recorded his belief that "History will not be able to say much in favor of that 'Consultation,' nor of the Provisional Government they established."[28]

By the time he returned to Brazoria, Jones had decided that the only solution to the problems of Texas was a complete break from Mexico. He stated his belief that it was "not only useless, but *false*, to talk about sustaining the 'principles of the Constitution of 1824.'"[29] He became an advocate of immediate separation from Mexico, and noted that he "refused to have anything to do with any other policy, or the advocates of any other."[30] In December of 1835, Dr. Jones, who had been so reluctant to dabble in politics, was one of the leading voices in calling for a declaration of outright independence from Mexico at a meeting in Brazoria. As he would recollect later, "I believe, therefore, that I took the first efficient step for the *independence* of Texas, and advocated the first resolutions for that purpose."[31]

In February of 1836, Jones presided over elections to the convention at Washington-on-the-Brazos, and would later reminisce that voters would have elected him as one of the Brazoria delegates but that he "declined all requests to become a candidate."[32] He then went about preparing for the "storm" that was about to occur. He sent his sister Mary back to New York, and in March, he enlisted as a private in Captain Calder's Company of the 2nd Infantry Regiment. As the army was camped in the Brazos River bottom in April, there was a virulent outbreak of measles and dysentery. At the "very urgent solicitation of Col. Sherman" Jones agreed to serve as the regimental surgeon with the proviso that the colonel would allow him to rejoin the ranks as a private as soon as the necessity for his medical services had ceased.[33]

Jones also performed another function in the Texian army, serving as Judge Advocate in the court martial of two Texas soldiers, privates John Garner and an A. Scales who were charged with mutiny and desertion. The court found both men guilty and sentenced them to death, but the court also recommended clemency for both.[34] By this time, Jones had apparently become intimate friends with Sam Houston. At Groce's Landing on April 15, General Houston invited Jones to dine with him. Jones reported that he found Houston to be "thoughtful and irresolute. …" He added that Houston hoped to "get a bloodless victory" and that the conversation ended with "an expression of earnest hope" on his part, "that the next move would be *towards* the enemy."[35]

As the army crossed Buffalo Bayou to move to San Jacinto, Jones left his medical duties and met the army at Lynchburg. He makes no mention of his involvement in the fighting at San Jacinto, only that he "participated in the battle" and worked through the night tending to the wounded. He then accompanied the wounded Sam Houston to Galveston, where he was appointed as Assistant Surgeon-General and Medical Purveyor to the army and dispatched to New Orleans for the purpose of procuring medical supplies.[36]

After a month in New Orleans, Jones returned to Texas. Upon his return to Brazoria, he was stricken with a severe bout of dysentery and confined to bed at William Wharton's house for two months. After he recuperated, he returned to Brazoria to find that looters had broken into his office, and "everything taken from it that was valuable and portable."[37] He also found two attorneys occupying and working from his office. When Jones finally succeeded in evicting the two men, James Collinsworth, who was evidently a friend of the two men, challenged him to a duel. Jones accepted the challenge to "fight with pistols at ten paces," but Thomas F. McKinney intervened and the duel never occurred. Jones would later record that Collinsworth, "ever after, however, hated me, and being in the habit of drinking to excess, threw himself away, and was finally lost in Galveston Bay the following year."[38]

At the end of 1836, Jones severed his ties with the army and prepared to revive his medical practice. After a few months, political leaders persuaded him to once again delay the practice of medicine and stand as a candidate for the Texas House in 1837. By this time, Jones had become a keen observer of Republic politics, and had become convinced that the First Congress "had committed the most woeful blunders, and there had been much reckless and interested legislation."[39] Particularly odious, as far as Jones was concerned, was the charter for the Texas Rail Road, Navigation, and Banking Company, which he cites as one of the main reasons why he decided to run for Congress, and which he described as being "one of the most corrupt schemes of iniquity ever sanctioned by a Legislature and a President. …" He also evinces great dissatisfaction with the selection of the nascent city of Houston as the capital, and the "sale of Galveston Island" as reasons to run.[40] Jones thus entered a crowded field of candidates for Brazoria's two seats, which included Matthew C. Patton, a merchant, William J. Russell, and Patrick Jack. Jones won decidedly, and Jack would win the other seat after a contentious process that went to the House Rules and Privileges Committee, which was presided over by none other than Anson Jones.[41]

Anson Jones would become what his biographer Herbert Gambrell called the "indispensable man" of the Second Texas Congress. In addition to chairing the House Rules and Privileges Committee, he also was the chair of the Ways and Means and Foreign Relations committees. In addition to these leadership positions, he served on the Committee of the State of the Republic and the Finance Committee. Because of his experiences in Venezuela, he served as the un-appointed job of "master" of protocol in the House, a position that required him to assume the task of scrutinizing enrolled bills and reporting any new business to the chamber. Additionally, he participated in a number of select committees, such as the one that was to consider the repeal of the Texas Rail Road, Navigation, and Banking

Company charter (which was natural considering that his opposition to this bill was what induced him to run for office in the first place). Other committees that Jones served on included those formed to explore ways to reward veterans of Bexar and San Jacinto; to revise the land system of the Republic; to fund the national debt; to select a permanent site for the national capital; to "digest" the report of the secretary of state; to articulate an education policy; to revise the tariffs of the Republic; to undertake amendments to the judicial system; to consider claims; and another committee formed to charter railroads.[42] Jones's personality and background made him, perhaps more than any other member of Congress at the time, exquisitely suited to legislative work. He was analytical and methodical, and he seemed to have not yet developed a number of the personality traits that others would find so irritating in later years.

Among his crowning legislative achievements were that he proposed bills to regulate the practice of medicine in Texas, to come up with a coherent national education policy, and of perhaps greatest importance, he introduced legislation designed to withdraw Texas's proposal for immediate annexation to the United States.[43] The latter was the one of his proposed bills that would become the most important to his future. Not only did it bring him to the attention of Sam Houston as being knowledgeable about foreign affairs and lead to his increasing rise within Houston's diplomatic service, but it also furthered future speculation on his attitudes regarding the ultimate annexation of Texas.

The logic of Jones and others regarding annexation seems on the surface to be unassailable. Given the current political climate in the United States, annexation at the time was simply not going to be possible. In order for the Republic to survive economically, it was crucial to begin establishing trade relations with the major powers, particularly, Great Britain and France. As long as the issue of annexation was undecided in the United States Congress, there could be no formal recognition forthcoming from Europe. In addition to the economic considerations, there was also the constant specter of a continued conflict with Mexico. If Texas could intertwine her economic interests with England and France, that could most certainly provide Texas with even more protection against further Mexican aggression. Many of the accusations against Jones during the final stages of annexation seemed to begin with his proposal of this bill without really considering the realities involved at the time.[44]

While in Houston attending to his duties in Congress, Jones also found time to involve himself in other matters close to his heart. In November of 1837, Jones presided over the foundation of the

Holland Lodge of the Masonic order, where members elected him as that lodge's first Worshipful Grand Master. Other august members of Texas's first Masonic lodge were David G. Burnet, Sam Houston, Mirabeau Lamar, Thomas Rusk, Thomas J. Green, Francis Lubbock, and "some sixty Texans who had stormed San Antonio."[45] Furthermore, he was instrumental in the creation of the Philosophical Society of Texas, which included a veritable "Who's Who" list of important Texans from the period. Lamar served as the society's president, and Jones as the Vice President.[46]

At the conclusion of the session of Congress, Jones made preparations to return home to Brazoria, but before departing the capital, Jones managed to become engaged to Mrs. Mary McCrory, a widow whom he had met while boarding at the home of her stepfather, John Woodruff. The couple's nuptials were set to take place the following June, but events would dictate that the union would ultimately not take place for some time after. Jones returned to Brazoria at the end of his term, believing that he was through with government service; however, Sam Houston summoned him to discuss an appointment to another government post. Jones surmised that the president was going to ask him to serve as an agent to procure a navy for Texas, a position that the Brazoria doctor was resolved to refuse. When he arrived at the capital, however, he soon learned that Houston had other plans for him. Memucan Hunt had resigned as Texas's Minister Plenipotentiary to the United States, and Houston's first choice to replace him, Peter Grayson, had turned down the job believing that he would be the next president of Texas. When Houston offered the job, Jones initially replied in the negative, remembering later that Houston "had then urged and insisted on my taking the office as Minister," largely because he "did not know of anyone else he could get whom he could trust. …" Jones later recalled that when he appeared to be less than excited about accepting the "honorable exile," Houston "appealed to my patriotism to induce me to consent."[47] Dr. Jones left the meeting without accepting the job, but the president knew he had his man. Even before Jones agreed to accept the post, Houston had prepared his credentials, giving the paperwork to Secretary of State Dr. R.A. Irion for delivery. Irion delivered the credentials to Jones, and after securing an agreement that he could withdraw Texas's proposal for annexation, Jones reluctantly agreed to go. This would prove to be a fateful decision, as the job would carry him away from Brazoria, and cause him to delay his wedding. Not only would the mission affect his personal life, but also it would ultimately send him on a new trajectory, which would contribute mightily to the anguish he experienced at the end of his life.

While traveling to Washington, D.C. to take up his duties, Jones received the news that both Peter Grayson and his old nemesis James Collinsworth had committed suicide.[48] Jones, who had begun keeping his *Memoranda* journals on the journey, prophetically wrote as one of his initial entries on July 29:

> I shall be surprised at no one's committing suicide after hearing of Col. Grayson's doing so. It is the first time in my life that anyone in the circle of my acquaintance has done such an act; and it has shocked me more than the death of a dozen others would have done in the usual course. I believe party abuse has been the cause, acting upon some predisposition to morbid melancholy. Col. Collinsworth's drowning himself was a thing in course. I had expected it, as I knew him to be deranged, and when excited by liquor, almost *mad*. In all the annals of suicide, perhaps no parallel to these two cases can be found.[49]

Jones arrived in Washington on August 23, only to discover that the other members of the Texas Legation were strangely absent. Jones then wrote Secretary of State Irion to report his arrival, and spent the next ten days acquainting himself with the Legation's files. In the files, Jones was somewhat taken aback to learn that President Houston had, on May 19, 1838, already issued instructions to withdraw the annexation proposal. He noted that this was why he had thought it odd that Irion had so readily agreed to this stipulation to take the job, without tipping Sam's hand on the matter. Hunt had left Washington prior to the president's transmission of the order, and so it would fall to the new minister to carry it out. He further understood what few else did, that there was no realistic hope of annexation in the current political climate, and that the entire exercise was aimed primarily at Great Britain and France in order to effect recognition and trade agreements. To his surprise, the United States did not officially recognize Jones as Texas's official representative until he was properly presented to President Van Buren upon his return to Washington in October. He spent the intervening month busying himself with the negotiation of the boundary agreement between Texas and the United States, drafting the official withdrawal of the annexation proposal, and perhaps most importantly, reading Elliot's *Diplomatic Code*, and familiarizing himself with the intricacies and niceties of international diplomacy.

On October 12, 1837, Jones proceeded to the U.S. State Department and delivered the formal communication officially withdrawing Texas's request for annexation to the Union. After delivering the letter, Jones also received a certified copy of the boundary agreement between Texas and the United States, which Memucan Hunt had negotiated before his departure. This document was extremely important, because it was vital to the second phase of the Texas diplomatic plan: diplomatic recognition from the European powers. Sovereign nations insisted on clearly defined boundaries of Texas, before they would consider formal recognition of the new republic. Jones then composed a letter to Texas's representative to the courts of England and France, J. Pinckney Henderson, notifying him of the boundary agreement and the formal withdrawal of the request for annexation. Hopes were high of quickly gaining recognition from France, who was on the threshold of the "Pastry War" with Mexico. Recognition from the mighty British Empire was to prove more problematic. The British had invested large amounts of capital in Mexico, and to complicate matters further, anti-slavery sentiment was at its high-water mark in Britain. Even armed with the boundary agreement and the official notification of the withdrawal of the annexation request, Henderson achieved little in England other than securing a limited trade agreement between the two countries.

After performing his task, Jones had little else to do as the representative of his country. He made the requisite social calls as befit his position, and attended state dinners, which were so much a part of diplomatic relations, but had relatively little else to do. To occupy his time, Jones often visited the Library of Congress, where he read up on a variety of subjects, the most important of which was economics. Through self-study, Jones grasped the significance of Texas cotton. England had an insatiable desire for raw cotton, and Texas's undefined tariff policy could very well make sure that Texas cotton would provide the in-road for a mutual self-interest with Britain that could ultimately lead to diplomatic recognition, "If England does not take the 'blind Staggers,'" he wrote, "she cannot much longer remain indifferent. ..."[50] The major difficulty for the state department was gently nudging England toward the same conclusions.

Even though Jones diligently made the diplomatic rounds, Britain's emissary to the United States was a peculiar individual named H. S. Fox, an individual whom contemporaries often referred to as the "spectre minister" owing to his unusual ways and even more irregular personal appearance.[51] Try as he might, Jones was unable to establish a dialog with Fox. He was, however, able to cultivate an important contact in the form of Christopher Hughes, America's *Charge d'Affaires* to Sweden.

The two men formed a fast friendship, and Hughes enthusiastically agreed to use his contacts to bring the topic of Texas up with his old friend, Lord Palmerston, the British Foreign Minister. Palmerston forwarded the communication provided by Jones to Hughes to the Prime Minister, and provided Hughes with letters of introduction to other British emissaries in Europe. Hughes then travelled to Paris, where he met with J. Pinckney Henderson, and together they called on M. Patois, the French Minister to the United States. They won over Patois, and soon thereafter, France recognized Texas and acknowledged Henderson as Texas's official representative in Europe. Even though Jones was not directly involved in the process, he certainly paved the way for Henderson's diplomatic successes, and set the tone for official recognition of Texas by the major European powers. While this process was ongoing, Jones received little news from officials in either Texas or Europe; therefore, he continued the mundane work of cultivating European and American officials.

Jones finally received word from Texas in January 1839, when the new secretary of state, Barnard E. Bee, informed him that the voters had elected Mirabeau B. Lamar as president of Texas. Jones realized that Lamar's election to office would lead to his recall, but he continued working as he had before. Finally, in February 1839, the state department notified Jones that Richard G. Dunlap would soon replace him as Texas's minister to the United States. While he waited for his replacement to arrive, Jones avowed that he would never again serve in public office. In May, he departed for Texas aboard the Texas warship *Viper*, determined to re-enter the practice of medicine, leaving public service to others. His time in Washington though, had apparently transformed Jones. Moses Austin Bryan, who served as Jones's secretary in Washington noticed; in a letter home, he expressed his opinion that "Doct. Jones … is a different man here, from what he was in Texas."[52]

When the *Viper* arrived in Galveston on June 21, 1839, Dr. Jones's newfound aversion to public service evaporated quickly. As soon as he landed, he learned that the citizens of Brazoria had elected him to finish out the Senate term of his friend John A. Wharton, who had died the previous December. Jones's initial reaction was to decline the office, but when supporters informed him that Lamar had fought his election, Jones accepted the job, noting that he was desirous of placing himself "in constant contact with an administration which was gradually sucking the life-blood of the country away."[53] It is also apparent that as early as this, Jones had become convinced that Texas's future survival was almost solely dependent on establishing relations with England. He further understood that the key to establishing this relationship would be cotton. Upon his arrival in Galveston, Jones learned that a sailing vessel named the *Ambassador* was being sent to Great Britain by Samuel May Williams loaded with Texas cotton. Jones remarked to an assembled crowd that "You have sent the best possible negotiator for the Government to England, a ship loaded with cotton, the staple production of the country."[54] After travelling to Houston to report to the administration that had dismissed him, Jones returned to Galveston where he basked in the approbation of the locals at a series of dinners. In mid-July, he returned to Brazoria where celebrations in his honor continued. Before he took up the reins of his new office in November, Jones found time to note in his journal that:

> The folly of Lamar is in nothing more apparent than his threats of *offensive* war against Mexico—and whenever a campaign is set on foot it will be disastrous. Texas is overwhelmed with army and navy officers—there are enough for Russia—and Texas is without the means to support them many weeks longer. Borrowing may serve to protract the crisis awhile, but come it must with a tremendous crash ere long. Gen. Lamar may mean well—I am not disposed to impugn his motives—he has fine belles-lettres talents, and is an elegant writer. But his mind is altogether of a dreamy, poetic order, a sort of political Troubadour and Crusader, and wholly unfit by habit or education for the active duties, and the everyday realities of his present station. Texas is too small for a man of such wild, visionary "vaulting ambition."[55]

Jones arrived in Austin to take his seat on November 1. Even though he opposed Austin as the new seat of government, he quietly began buying up some of the choicest town lots for himself. He also sought to renew his acquaintance with his fiancé Mary McCrory, who had moved to Austin while he was in Washington. He also served as master of ceremonies at a dinner in honor of Sam Houston, who had been elected to the House of Representatives from St. Augustine. Despite his outward support for Houston, Jones found time to note in his journal on November 19, "Gen. H. is not so strong in what he does himself, as what his enemies do: it is not *his* strength, but *their* weakness—not *his* wisdom, but their *folly*. Cunning, Indian cunning is the secret of his success. Old Bowles, the Cherokee Indian chief, learned him all he knows—though he has native tact, was an apt scholar, and learned *Indian* well."[56] Five days later, Jones recorded that "No man is more completely master of the art of appropriating to himself the merit of others' good acts, and shifting on to others the odium of his bad ones, than Gen. Houston."[57] This pattern would continue with Jones for the next decade. Publicly he would ally himself with Houston, while privately excoriating him.

Jones inserted himself into the affairs of the government with great gusto. He assumed the chairmanship of the Senate Foreign Relations Committee, the chairmanship of the Judiciary Committee, and served as a member of the Education, Finance, Post Office, and Roads Committees, as well as appointments to a number of special committees. Although a staunch supporter of the anti-Lamar faction, Jones rarely expressed his dislike in his political discourse. One exception came when a senator from Nacogdoches complained that a Senate resolution demanding information from the president was "indecorous and disrespectful." Jones rose and inquired, "if the honorable gentleman from Nacogdoches would do the senate the favor, to submit some code of refinement and etiquette, by which they can address His Excellency the President of the Republic of Texas:—sir, shall we do it in grand oriental style? In French, Italian, Hebrew, or Spanish?" Jones continued, "Or will he invent some new and courtly language in which we will salute his royal ears? Sir, if His Excellency is too dignified to listen to common language, he had better not preside over the destiny of this nation!"[58] But he was also quick to defend what he considered to be the prerogatives of the presidency. He opposed his cousin Oliver Jones when he demanded that the Senate have a say in the office hours kept by Lamar's staff.

Despite his keen involvement in the affairs of state, Anson Jones once again found himself growing more and more disenchanted with the process. When the Fourth Texas Congress adjourned on February 5, 1840, Jones recorded in his journal, "Senate adjourned—freedom and liberty was once again restored, *aucon j'respire*."[59] With no further legislative duties until the next congress convened the following November, Jones once again hung out his shingle to practice his trade. He also continued to engage in land speculation and to rekindle his relationship with the widow McCrory. On May 6, 1840, Dr. Jones headed to the courthouse and purchased the second wedding license issued in the capital. The next morning, he and Mary entered into holy matrimony. Jones's journal entry for this auspicious day simply says, "Sunday Morng May 17th Married."[60] After the nuptials, Jones concentrated on the completion of his house on

Pecan Street and on developing his private business. That September, he returned to Brazoria to visit his constituents, but it was becoming increasingly clear that politics, which had once excited him, were now becoming a burden. He wrote a letter to Mary on October 14 in which he declared, "I am much disposed to fix myself here in future and to leave the noise and clamor of politics entirely. I regret, indeed, that I ever entered their arena at all."[61] However, recalcitrant as he may have been, when the Fifth Congress convened on the first Monday in November, Dr. Jones took his seat in the Senate. In December, his colleagues elected him President *pro tem* of the Senate. From that point forward, he would be involved with great events, despite his growing disdain for politics.

When President Lamar secured a leave of absence, Vice President David G. Burnet vacated his position of presiding over the Senate to assume the duties of Acting President, leaving Jones to fill his vacancy in the Senate. Jones seemed to enjoy his new responsibilities. He wrote, "Deciding questions of order suited me, gave me employment, and filled time which otherwise would have hung very unpleasantly on my hands; for in the proceedings of a Congress, when the government was rushing downward with hourly increasing velocity, I, of course, could feel neither interest nor pleasure. It was at best only, locking the stable door after the horse was stolen."[62] Jones confined himself to presiding over the Senate, voting sometimes to accept the administration's nominations for cabinet positions, and other times rejecting them. He voted to confirm Thomas W. "Peg Leg" Ward as commissioner of the General Land Office and voted with the majority to confirm George W. Terrell as secretary of state. However, he voted against Branch T. Archer's appointment to the post of secretary of war, primarily because of the nominee's affiliation with the Texas Rail Road, Navigation and Banking Company. Regardless, Archer received enough ballots in his favor to win confirmation.

Shortly after the Senate vote, General Felix Huston visited Dr. Jones to deliver a challenge to a duel on Archer's behalf. Jones was no more willing to duel Archer than he had been to engage Collinsworth in 1836. On December 9, Jones responded to Archer, "You complain of no *personal wrong* or *injury* which I have done you nor ask of me any redress. I can therefore only regard your note as intended to make a gratuitous, wanton, unprovoked attack upon me, and more in the character of a malignant assassin seeking life than that of an honorable gentleman demanding satisfaction for any grievance." Jones continued, "The charge in your note that I am a plunderer of public property is as false as it is contemptible—facts well known to yourself. You may perhaps be the defender of public property, but you will recollect that it was not by my vote, and I sincerely regret that the defense of my country's interest has not fallen into better and abler hands. …"[63] Archer decided to drop the matter.

As the session of the Fifth Congress began to wind down, Jones again focused on his personal affairs. He arranged to trade his house and property in Austin for land in Brazoria, and began to pack up his household. On February 26, 1841, the Jones family welcomed the arrival of their first child, a boy named Sam Houston Jones, and a month later departed the capital. [64] Anson Jones again believed that his time in politics had passed. He planned to return to Brazoria and resume the practice of medicine as a private citizen. Jones most certainly cared deeply for what would come next for his adopted country. Prior to his return from Washington, Jones firmly believed that Sam Houston would right the ship of state; but after serving with him in Congress the two years, Jones saw another side of the Hero of San Jacinto. On New Year's Day 1840, he wrote that Houston was "only intent upon making Lamar's administration as odious as possible. … He is willing the government should be a failure in order that he may have it to say there is no one but 'Old Sam' that the people can depend upon, & that he is the only man that can successfully administer the Govt. of Texas." Jones commented further: "Lamar is certainly no statesman, & he and his friends are ruining the country and going to the Devil as fast as Gen. Houston can possibly wish—This he sees and chuckles at. … He is skillful to destroy his enemy, but will do nothing to stay the impending ruin."[65] If not Sam Houston then, who would it be? There was David G. Burnet, whose association with Lamar politically damaged him as a candidate; there was Thomas J. Rusk, who declined to be nominated; or Henry Smith, the former Revolutionary governor in whom Jones placed little faith in achieving success. That left only Sam Houston as a viable candidate. There was even talk of a Houston-Jones ticket in 1841.

Jones would not hear of it. Though supporters placed his name in nomination, he declined to accept. He instead devoted himself singularly to the practice of medicine. Reflecting on the situation later in life, he recorded, "By fall I had succeeded in establishing a business about as extensive as I could attend to. But my office-holding had impoverished me, and embarrasses my affairs just at a time when the wants and expenses of a family were beginning to be felt."[66] This sentiment would not last overly long. Houston would win the election with an almost two-thirds majority. While Jones was in Austin taking care of some personal business at the Land Office, a letter from "Old Sam" caught up with him. Houston was offering him the post of secretary of state in his cabinet. Jones was certainly intrigued, and promised the General he would consider his offer. By the time of Houston's inauguration in Austin, Jones had determined to take the job, primarily at the urging of the Speaker of the House, Kenneth Anderson. Politics was once again at the center of Jones's life.

Before agreeing to take the post, Jones apparently had several discussions with the new president concerning his role in the administration. President Houston had apparently selected Jones for the cabinet position because of his knowledge of diplomatic relations. Seemingly, Houston held Jones in such high regards that he built the remainder of his cabinet around him. In addition to his duties as secretary of state, Jones would also serve as *de facto* secretary of the treasury, a position he held until Houston identified a suitable candidate for that position. Houston was certainly aware of Jones's fascination and knowledge of economics. In the beginning, the two men seemed to be of like mind regarding the challenges facing the Republic. Upon his confirmation by the Senate, Jones took up the reins of his new job and noted that he would fulfill his duties "with a determination to snatch the country from the verge of destruction upon which she was tottering, and to save her if possible, notwithstanding the almost insurmountable difficulties. …"[67]

As he moved on to this next phase of his political career, Anson Jones seemed to have been in a positive frame of mind and was confident that he was the best man for the job. He knew the challenges ahead of him were daunting but appeared to have been equally sure that he was up to meeting them. Assessing the state of the post-Lamar Republic, Jones commented, "The country was brought to the extremest point of depression—Her means exhausted—Her credit utterly prostrated—The loan, sought all over the U.S. and Europe, refused on any terms—Pressed and oppressed with debts—Her currency at a discount rate of 97 1/2 % —The Navy gone to Yucatan—The Army to Santa Fe and captivity—The frontiers of a thousand miles assailed by hostile Indians—Mexico, exasperated by the executive menace."[68]

Jones was certainly qualified for the new position that he held: He knew Sam Houston, with all of the warts that came along with him; he had a good working knowledge of the mechanics of international diplomacy; he apparently had the ability to form a positive first impression; and he possessed a first-rate mind. Dr. Ashbel Smith, a friend of Jones's for twenty years would later recall that the secretary of state "took no one-sided views, he was never misled by seeing only the benefits or only the disadvantages of any measure … [he] struck a just balance between them. This is what made him a statesman; and it was this quality that caused his contemporaries to misunderstand him during the annexation crisis." Smith continued, "Texans wanted action at once; their president wanted to lay before them all the facets and alternatives—and he expected them to contemplate the present effects and future consequences of their choice as calmly as he had."[69]

Charles Elliot, Great Britain's representative to Texas during the annexation negotiations and well-respected player in the international affairs of his time, described Jones as being "worthy, friendly, plain in speech, simple in manner, sound in judgment, 'remarkably cautious and reserved', and endowed with a moderate degree of the skill and finesse of his predecessor."[70] Alphonse DuBois, Compte de Saligny, France's representative to Texas during the Republic years, noted to his superiors after meeting Jones for the first time that he "appeared to me to be a well-intentioned man of good faith. …"[71] Saligny, however, would have a vastly different opinion of Dr. Jones as the events of annexation played out.

As Anson Jones embarked on his tenure as secretary of state, he was confronted by a host of problems that he knew about, as well as some of which he was as yet unaware. He had to deal with the aftermath of Lamar's failed Santa Fe Expedition. He had to smooth over relations with France, which had soured because of the so-called "Pig War." Additionally, he needed to conclude a new and more equitable trade agreement with Great Britain. In his role as *de facto* secretary of the treasury, he had to find a way to repair the Republic's financial woes.

One of the problems that came to his attention after he took office was the ever-expanding rift between him and the chief of state. Jones believed that he had the authority to act autonomously, but in fact, Houston's view on the subject would turn out to be diametrically opposed to Jones's understanding. Another problem that surprised him came when the past president challenged him to a duel. In January 1842, an item had appeared in a local newspaper, the *Weekly Texian*, proposing that the perfect solution to recovering the prisoners from the Santa Fe Expedition would simply be to swap them for Mirabeau Lamar. The piece in the paper, which was very much indicative of the public grumbling about the way the entire fiasco had transpired, was simply signed by "A." Upon reading the piece, Lamar decided the "A" was Anson Jones, and immediately dispatched an emissary, James Webb, to confront Jones about the article and to "Accept no equivocation or explanation … require of him a categorical reply. …" Webb was also to inform Jones, "Had the production emanated from the Editor of the *Texian* or from any irresponsible scoundrel like him, it might be suffered to pass unnoticed … but coming from one of the highest of our public functionaries & bearing the aspect of a govmt. Measure, the people at large are as interested of myself. … The malignant spirit which pervades the piece, as well as the flagicious & diabolical proposition which it contains, calls aloud for redress at my hands …"[72] Webb apparently never had the opportunity to deliver this message, but several months later, Lamar's former secretary of war, Gen. Albert Sidney Johnston, confronted Jones in his office, handing the secretary of state a note signed M. B. Lamar. The note inquired "whether you are the author of a certain communication signed A., which appeared in the *Weekly Texian* on the 26th ult., or whether you had any agency in advising, or any connection whatever with said publication … I must demand a prompt reply, and an unequivocal answer." Jones simply dismissed Johnston, and scrawled a response directing Lamar to his former secretary of the Navy, Memucan Hunt who would provide him with "any or all information you require."[73] The matter went no further. Once again, Jones escaped the consequences of a duel.

Secretary of State Jones attacked the more pressing problems one by one. His first order of business was to immediately recall all of Lamar's appointed officials under his purview. He wanted to make sure that the men who held these positions would implicitly carry out his policies. He sacked Texas's ambassador to the United States, Barnard Bee, and replaced him with Major James Reily, a former member of the Texas House of Representatives who possessed the Irish "gift of gab" and perhaps more importantly, a wife who happened to be the niece of the extremely influential member of the American Whig party, Henry Clay. He instructed Reily to conclude the trade agreement between Texas and the United States, which had been languishing for two years. Also, the ambassador was to inform the United States in no uncertain terms that their Indians were not welcome in Texas, and he was to quietly and informally renew discussions concerning the annexation of Texas to the United States.

Jones had one other task he desired Reily to perform on his way to Washington, D.C. Texas needed to heal the rift with France caused by the "Pig War" as quickly as possible. Jones, who genuinely liked the French legate, Saligny, knew that repairing the relationship between

Texas and France would have to be done through official channels.[74] Jones wrote an official apology to the French government, which his European representative delivered, but directed Reily to show it to Saligny, who was then residing in New Orleans, before it was officially sent forward to France. The portion of the correspondence he most wanted Saligny to see stated, "Though accidental circumstances may have placed individuals in public stations who have been mistaken in giving proper expression to national feelings and sentiments … the present administration would not be doing justice to these sentiments if it failed to disclaim … the abusive language of which in moments of unfortunate excitement M. De Saligny was the object."[75] The note struck the right tone, and this and other communications apparently mollified the French legate. The French diplomat ultimately return to Texas.

Jones's next order of business was to shore up his diplomatic team in Europe. At the time, Gen. James Hamilton, a Lamar appointee, represented Texas in Europe. Hamilton was a bellicose and bombastic South Carolinian who was reputed to have participated in fourteen duels, and to have wounded all fourteen of his opponents.[76] Hamilton had been appointed by Lamar as a sort of commissioner at large, and was associated with several somewhat questionable loan schemes, one of which involved a seven-million-dollar loan from Belgium.[77] Hamilton had managed to conclude a more palatable trade agreement with Great Britain and convinced British officials to enter negotiations with Mexico concerning the independence of the Republic of Texas. Unfortunately, from the administration's position, in order to get Britain to consent to the first two agreements, Hamilton had to sign an anti-slave trade agreement. Even though he was opposed to the anti-slave trade agreement, Jones realized its necessity. The secretary of state successfully shepherded the treaty through the Sixth Texas Congress, thus opening the door to his larger plans for the diplomatic affairs of the Republic. After setting the table for his upcoming initiatives, Jones replaced Hamilton with his long-time colleague, Dr. Ashbel Smith. Not only was Smith of like mind, he offered the added advantage of also being a close friend of Sam Houston, which Jones certainly must have viewed as an asset for ensuring that the chief executive would support his foreign policy initiatives.

Among his immediate priorities, Jones included a comprehensive program to intertwine Texas's affairs with the economic interests of Europe. If successful, Secretary Jones envisioned that European powers would intercede with Mexico on Texas's behalf. Part of this plan was to encourage as much immigration from Europe as possible. He would do as much as he could to attract *empresarios* from France, England, Belgium, and Germany so that they might "bring population and Money from the Storehouses of Europe."[78] Towards this end, Jones appointed Henri Castro as Texas's Consul General to Paris, and William Kennedy as Texas's Consul to London. Kennedy was an Englishman who had published a two-volume work on Texas in England, which stimulated public interest in the Republic. Additionally, Kennedy had close ties to Lord Aberdeen, the British Minister of Foreign Affairs. Jones also offered assistance and assurances to Prince Solms Braunfels who was establishing a German colonization company.

While Jones proved extremely adept at dealing with the more sedate, mundane matters of state, he proved less successful in dealing with the two Mexican raids into Texas in 1842, which brought the Republic to the brink of war with Mexico. Up to this point, Jones's policy toward Mexico appeared to have been one of strict avoidance. Jones believed that the best way to deal with the Mexican threat was for Texas to completely ignore Mexico, and rely instead on Great Britain and France to use their influence with Mexico to preserve the sovereignty of Texas. As the crisis unfolded, Jones seemed to have slipped into a frame of mind in which he had great difficulty in deciding upon a course of action. While it is easy to speculate, there is no way to know if this period of indecision was a harbinger of the mental instability that finally came to dominate Dr. Jones at the end of his life.

In response to Lamar's "invasion" of New Mexico, Santa Anna, who had once again risen to power in Mexico, ordered Mexican troops into Texas twice in the spring of 1842. In both instances, the Mexicans occupied San Antonio briefly before returning to Mexico. On the second occasion, the invasion force captured approximately sixty Texans and carried them back to Mexico as prisoners. The public demanded that the government answer this violation of Texas sovereignty, forcing the hand of Sam Houston. He knew that Texas was broke and did not have the resources necessary to conduct almost any sort of meaningful military response to the incursions. He decided to make a symbolic military gesture by dispatching 750 men under General Alexander Somervell to patrol the Rio Grande border. Houston intended that Somervell's force would be a show of force along the border and might prevent further Mexican raids into Texas. This small force, known as the Somervell Expedition, encountered absolutely no Mexican presence, and the president ordered Somervell to abandon the search.[79] Houston then dispatched Secretary Jones to New Orleans to see if he could secure loans to aid the dire financial condition of the Republic. By the end of June, Jones was back in Texas, having successfully secured the loan of a million dollars from Alexandre Bourgeois d' Orvane.[80]

After returning home from New Orleans, Jones went on an unusual extended leave of absence for three months as the crisis with Mexico intensified. Dr. Jones apparently was concerned about his own personal finances, sending out bills for medical services, and trying to collect whatever debts were due him. Seemingly, he was preparing for the future just in case things went badly for Texas. He also apparently decided during his absence that he would leave the service of the government. When summoned by the president to explain his absence, Jones reluctantly started out for Houston, only to fall ill as he made his way. He would languish for eighteen days at the home of Col. William Austin before resuming his journey.

This sojourn from his office most likely resulted not only from Jones feeling that he had let his own personal affairs slide, but also seems to mark the end of Jones's patience with Sam Houston. One of the conditions of Jones's accepting the post had supposedly been a promise from Houston that Jones would have absolute autonomy to conduct state business. At the end of 1843, Jones ranted against Houston in his personal memoranda, stating "I have also strenuously opposed his system of petty and vindictive warfare upon individuals and the 'Honorable Congress', which are gotten up by him to make political capital for himself, but are injurious to the interests and character of the country. Genl. H. and myself are drifting away from each other hourly."[81] He vented against Houston's appointments to the government, claiming that they violated the "implied understanding" between the two men, which had induced Jones to take the job in the first place. He explained his decision to return to the government by noting:

> I have a vitally important object to accomplish in completing the salvation and safety of the country,—the complete restoration of its finances, and its ultimate annexation to the United States, or ultimate peace and independence; and from this purpose I have resolved not to be diverted by minor considerations, and more especially by private griefs. I may have to play the part of "Curtius", and if so, I am prepared to make a Sacrifice like his, if the gulf of destruction which has so long

> yawned for Texas can happily be closed. I am also content to let Gen. H. be the "Caesar", for it is only by yielding to his vanity and ambition that we can get on together; and the whole safety of the country, and the successful issue of the important measures now pending, require that we should co-operate; for, however powerless he might be to do good, his *position* as President puts it in his power to do great harm; and the condition of public affairs is becoming too critical to sustain any violent jar or shock. It therefore becomes my duty to yield to much private wrong, which I am resolved cheerfully to do.[82]

Once the Mexican crisis abated, and Jones returned to office, relations between the two men to some degree returned to the status quo. Jones would spend the rest of his tenure as secretary of state courting the Europeans, while at the same time pursuing annexation to the United States.

The next phase of Anson Jones's life was about to begin; as Houston's term wound down, the great speculative pastime in Texas was to try to handicap who would become the next president of the Republic. Many Texans were concerned that Lamar would run again, but Lamar quickly allayed those fears by averring that he had no interest in a second term. Lamar's choice was James Webb, but Webb refused to entertain the notion. Many wanted to see Houston's second-term vice president, Edward Burleson, run but were also not sure whether Burleson would represent the Houston or Lamar faction. Most voters waited to see what Thomas J. Rusk would do. Most Houston supporters, as well as many of his detractors, seemed to favor Anson Jones. Houston himself was silent on the matter, although several of his intimate friends hinted to Jones that he was Sam's choice to succeed him. Jones remained uncharacteristically quiet about this period in his reminisces, but one can almost see him waiting to see who would run, and weighing his chances of success against various prospective opponents. He most assuredly by this point in his life had gained enough self-confidence to believe he could do the job, but he also most certainly would not be prepared to run unless he was reasonably sure he would win. It seems as if he was most satisfied to finish out his term as secretary of state, and to return to his private affairs. His wife was again pregnant, and home life and his business affairs seemed to preoccupy his thoughts at this juncture.

As the end of Houston's second term approached, Jones began to receive more and more feedback that he was indeed the candidate of choice for many in Texas. At the end of October, Jones received word that a convention in Washington County had nominated him as a presidential candidate. When Jones received word of the nomination, he wrote that he was pleased to note that it "was the spontaneous act of the *people of Texas*, and without agency on my own part. Party had nothing to do with it. …"[83]

Despite the fact that the election was looming, the affairs of state had to continue. Jones continued his diplomatic efforts with England, France, and the United States. U.S. President James Tyler was an advocate of expansion, and wanted the annexation of Texas to form his presidential legacy. Tyler appointed Secretary of State Abel Upshur to negotiate an annexation deal with Texas. Upshur died in a naval mishap, however, and the president sent in his place the South Carolina firebrand John C. Calhoun. Negotiations proved fruitful, resulting in a treaty of annexation. The treaty, which needed a two-thirds majority in the U. S. Senate for approval, failed to get the required number of votes. The Senate's vote was not surprising, especially to Houston and Jones.

Once the U.S. Senate rejected the treaty of annexation, the British Foreign Office under Lord Aberdeen called on Parliament to pass a "Diplomatic Act" to ensure that Texas and Mexico remain at peace. Lord Aberdeen informed Ashbel Smith, the Texas representative in Europe, that should Mexico refuse to acknowledge Texas's sovereignty, then Mexico would find itself without the "friendship of England and France."[84] Smith enthusiastically forwarded Aberdeen's plan to Sam Houston, who was anxious to see the proposal accepted.

In the meantime, the election for Texas president neared. Jones ran against Edward Burleson, and neither candidate garnered widespread support. Burleson was pilloried by Jones supporters as being uneducated; they also charged that a vote for Burleson would be a vote for the continuation of the disastrous policies of Lamar. Burleson supporters countered with the argument that Jones was little more than a marionette of Sam Houston. Support for the two candidates tended to break down along sectional lines. Burleson's electoral base was in the west, while Jones's political strength came from the much more heavily populated east. With neither candidate garnering a great deal of enthusiastic support, it was up to the extremely divisive but also immensely popular "Hero of San Jacinto" to shift the election toward one candidate or the other. On August 5, 1844, Sam Houston, who up to that point had remained silent on the election, offered a lukewarm endorsement of his secretary of state:

> I am not opposed to his [Jones] election. If I have not been a noisy advocate for his success, it has not been because I did not confide in him. … He has conducted the foreign relations of the govt. and I have confidence that if the choice of the people should devolve the duties of president upon him, he would consult the true interests of the country, and that he would endeavor to carry out a policy which he might conceive would but promote its honor and prosperity. I have arrived at this conclusion from the fact that I know him to be intimately acquainted with the true and abiding interests of the people.[85]

This was hardly a ringing endorsement, but it pushed Jones over the top. Jones won the election, garnering 7,037 votes to Burleson's 5,568.[86] Anson Jones was poised to be the next president of the Republic.

Even though the question of annexation was the burning issue of the day, Jones had won the election without publicly announcing his own views on the subject. After the election, Jones then returned to his duties as secretary of state for the last several months of Houston's term. Houston instructed Jones to accept Britain's offer of approaching Mexico with the "Diplomatic Act," and Jones, as president-elect, chose to ignore these instructions, writing later that he had done so because "it would either defeat annexation altogether, or lead to a war between Europe and America. Besides, it would directly complicate our relations and entangle us with France and England, produce disturbances and revolutions at home, and probably render it very difficult, if not impossible for me to administer the government of Texas successfully." Jones continued, "Gen H. has furnished no explanation of his motives for this course of policy. If they be to defeat annexation, produce a war, or break down my administration [about to commence] I cannot favor any of these objects, and can conceive of no other."[87]

On December 9, 1844, the last president of the Republic took the oath of office. Anson Jones took to the lectern in front of Independence Hall at Washington-on-the-Brazos and delivered his inaugural address. In this speech, Jones outlined his priorities as president, and those assembled anxiously awaited to see what the new chief executive would have to say about annexation, which most Texans overwhelmingly supported.

Jones opened his remarks by announcing that the present occasion was not the suitable one for a discussion of policy, and then proceeded to outline his priorities. He discussed financial policy, education, Indian relations, and a host of other topics. Noticeably absent from his inaugural address however, was any sort of statement regarding the president's views on annexation. When pressed on the issue later, all Jones would say was that "I had a right to be silent, and the grave keeps not its counsels more safely than I did mine."[88]

As Jones accepted the reins of power in Texas, events elsewhere were occurring that really took the whole process of annexation out of the newly elected president's hands. John Tyler, the lame-duck president of the United States, had interpreted the results of the nation's 1844 presidential election, which James K. Polk had won, as a mandate for westward expansion, including the annexation of Texas to the Union. Tyler determined that the admission of Texas to the Union would be his presidential legacy, and he re-opened the issue with Congress. Remembering the recent vote in the Senate, President Tyler presented annexation to Congress as a joint resolution. Even though both houses of Congress had to approve a joint resolution, the measure only needed a simple majority to pass. In accordance with Tyler's plan, the resolution for annexation made its way through the House by a comfortable margin and narrowly passed in the Senate.

Congress's annexation bill was substantially different from the one that had been defeated before. The conditions of the bill were less favorable to Texas. The new bill specified that the United States would admit Texas to the Union under a republican form of government no later than July 1, 1846, requiring three basic conditions: First, any questions of boundaries were to be settled by the U. S. House of Representatives. Second, the state of Texas would retain all of the debts of the Republic. However, Congress allowed Texas to retain all of its public lands, reinforcing the idea that the state could use any income derived from these lands to retire its public debt. Finally, Texas retained the authority to divide its vast territory into four additional states, providing that any new states to the north of the Missouri Compromise boundary prohibited slavery.

Once the resolution passed, European powers mounted an intense effort to obviate Texas's acceptance of annexation, while the United States tried to exert as much pressure as it could for immediate acceptance.[89] Jones remained quiet on the subject, but continued to meet with all interested parties. It was at this point that most of the later controversy surrounding the president's views on annexation emerged. After meeting with the envoys of Great Britain and France, Jones agreed to wait ninety days before acting on annexation. In essence, the delay gave the European powers a last chance to make a counter-offer to annexation. Charles Elliot,[90] the representative from Britain, and the Compte de Saligny, France's envoy, wanted the time to see if they could coerce Mexico to recognize Texas independence, hoping that this would convince the Texans to remain out of the Union, thereby thwarting Polk's plans for westward expansion. Texans viewed the delay as a sign that Jones secretly opposed annexation.

Jones remained steadfast to the end of his days that his purpose in granting the delay was to provide Texans with options. He had spent the last seven years working tirelessly with the Europeans to achieve this goal, and he most certainly had a desire to complete the process. Also, by granting this "cooling-off" period, Jones probably hoped to re-open negotiations with the United States, securing more favorable terms for Texas. However, Jones apparently misjudged the depth of feeling in Texas regarding the issue. At this point, most of his countrymen were tired of independence and desired the security and prosperity that they believed would result from joining the Union. Jones's silence on the matter allowed rampant speculation about his motives and certainly cost him whatever political support he may have enjoyed to this point. Jones soon became the target of many Texans, especially newspaper editors, who launched a vitriolic smear campaign against him. The political environment grew increasingly tense. Secretary of State Dr. Ashbel Smith revealed to his politically berated friend that long-time associate Memucan Hunt had relayed to him that he would do nothing to stop the people from "tarring and feathering President Jones or his cabinet members."[91] Jones remained stoic through it all, and stayed the course despite accusations that he had taken bribes from the British to sabotage the process.[92]

As planned, Jones convened Congress at the end of May, and called for a Constitutional Convention to convene in Austin on July 4. On May 30, Elliot returned from Mexico with an agreement in hand. The Europeans had successfully negotiated with Mexico an agreement that recognized the independence and sovereignty of Texas, as long as Texas rejected annexation. Jones now had achieved his goal. He was able to present the Mexican offer to the Texas Congress, allowing that body to make the choice. At the capitol, he shared with congressional members that he was able to offer the people of Texas "peace with the world and independence, or annexation and its contingencies."[93] While Jones had most assuredly achieved his goal of presenting Texas with options, he completely misjudged the public sentiment. Texans were calling for immediate annexation to the Union. The Texas Congress, called into special session, immediately and unanimously accepted the annexation deal and overwhelmingly rejected the Mexican offer. After their vote, Congress passed a resolution thanking Andrew Jackson for the part he played in annexation but made no mention of Jones. Instead of recognizing his diplomatic efforts, the Texas senators introduced a resolution to censure the president. While members tabled the resolution, it remained part of the official record. Congress then stripped Jones of all but ceremonial powers. The Constitutional Convention convened on July 4, and by the end of August, delegates had completed their task. In the middle of October, the voters approved annexation by a wide margin and ratified the new state constitution. The United States Congress voted to accept Texas as a state, and by the middle of December, Texas held statewide elections in which Democratic candidates won a majority of the offices. In the gubernatorial election, voters elected James Pinckney Henderson as governor. Interestingly, despite all his service during the era of the Republic, the political career of Anson Jones was almost at an end.

Following Texans' approval of annexation, Jones spent the remaining months of his presidency as a figurehead, especially since Congress had stripped away his presidential powers. On February 19, 1846, Jones performed his last official duty on behalf of Texas when he gave a valedictory speech at the formal ceremonies marking the entrance of Texas into the Union. Clearly, Jones understood the unpopularity of his course of action regarding annexation:

> I lay down the honors and the cares of the Presidency with infinitely more gratification than when I assumed them … Whatever injustice may have been done me in moments of excitement … the public mind will settle down into proper conclusions … my fellow-citizens will then judge me rightly. At least I have the approbation of my own conscience—a reward in itself above all price, and repose upon the assured belief that history and posterity will do me no wrong.[94]

After the ceremonies, Jones returned to his family home at Barrington Farm, near Washington-on-the-Brazos. He expected the new Texas Senate to appoint him as one of Texas's two United States Senators, but the call never came. Instead, the seats went to Sam Houston and Thomas Rusk. Jones would spend the remainder of his life becoming increasingly embittered at what he considered the denial of his rightful place in the pantheon of Texas heroes. He primarily placed the blame on Sam Houston, whom he accused of lying about his role in the proceedings of annexation, and spent the balance of his time on earth trying to balance the scales of justice. After injuring his arm in a fall from a horse, Jones found himself in constant pain, and heavily medicated himself with increasingly larger doses of laudanum. In 1858, Jones sold his beloved plantation and planned to move his family to Galveston. He visited the city of Houston in January 1858 and checked into the Capitol Hotel (the former Capitol building of the Republic). He spent an evening drinking heavily with friends, one of whom later reported that Jones had told him, "My public career … began in this house, and I have been thinking it might close here."[95] The next morning, hotel staff found Anson Jones dead in his room, his death seemingly from an obviously self-inflicted gunshot wound to the head.

Any discussion of the mental state of Anson Jones at the time of his death would be speculative at best. Once he had been ostracized from public life after annexation, he obviously became more and more despondent about the lack of recognition and respect he was afforded by Texas. And he most assuredly became increasingly bitter, particularly with Sam Houston, whom he blamed (with some justification perhaps), for appropriating the lion's share of the credit for annexation. His increasing animosity towards Houston becomes readily apparent through Jones's journals, as he went back and added rants against Houston and others while preparing his memoirs for publication. This bitterness extended beyond Houston to almost everyone who supported him. After the injury to his arm, Jones apparently began to take increasingly large doses of laudanum for the pain, which certainly exacerbated his feelings of paranoia and despondency. His actions immediately prior to his death, the selling of his beloved Barrington Farm, and his decision to move to Galveston without even consulting his wife, can certainly be construed as the actions of a less than rational man. In addition to these contributing factors, there may also have been organic forces at work. Without having access to the man himself, it is perhaps reckless to attempt some sort of pop psychology diagnosis of his condition, but certainly it is possible to assume that Jones was perhaps what today would be classified as Bi-Polar, and quite probably suffered from severe depression, which the large doses of laudanum he took for his arm intensified.

Regarding Anson Jones, students of Texas history are left with an important question: What is the significance of the last president of Texas? He certainly participated in most of the great events during the formative years of Texas, although perhaps in some instances, not to the degree he would have liked us to believe. According to the historical record, he was indeed the "Architect of Annexation," seeing the process brought to a successful conclusion. He was responsible for initiating diplomatic contact with Europe, leading to the recognition of Texas by important foreign countries. Finally, he had aided the economic survival of the tenuous Republic through trade agreements with France and Great Britain. During his tenure in the Texas Congress, Jones had been instrumental in keeping a modicum of restraint upon not only that body, but the policies of the executive branch as well. As secretary of state, Jones played a valuable role in not only the duties entailed by that office, but also as a moderating influence on Sam Houston. His expertise in the areas of diplomacy and finance served Texas well.

Jones himself is partially responsible for his tarnished legacy. By all accounts, he was possessed with a somewhat abrasive personality and was never afraid to extol the virtues of his intellect. He poisoned the well of posterity to some degree when he went public with his disagreements with Sam Houston and others after his presidency. His memoirs and personal correspondence are replete with vitriolic attacks on Houston (and others), many in scrawled notes in the margins. While certainly responsible for much of his own misfortune, Jones was also a victim of the legacy of Sam Houston. Houston was much more politically adept than Jones and was indeed a master of taking credit for the good acts of others. In the controversy over annexation, for example, Houston let Jones do most of the work and then swooped in at the last moment and appropriated most of the credit.

In the final analysis, Jones simply did not possess the personal qualities necessary to become one of the larger than life figures lionized in Texas history. His role in the events of the time are at least worthy of additional study, and there can be no doubt that his many contributions to Texas deserve more credit than usually apportioned to him. Dr. Anson Jones himself may have best summed up his career in a response to a letter Hamilton Stuart wrote to him in 1845. Stuart wrote to Jones, "Public opinion will yet do you justice." Jones seemingly agreed. He responded, "Not until I am dead. Contemporary malice, jealousy, injustice and selfishness will prevent its being done sooner! Yet though 'I am stricken, and my heart is like a bruised reed, waiting to be broken,' I have the highest consciousness of having faithfully performed my great trust, of having 'acted well my part'—a consciousness I would not exchange for all the world can give or take away."[96]

Notes

1. Herbert Gambrell, *Anson Jones: The Last President of the Republic of Texas* (Austin: University of Texas Press, 1964), 3.

2. Anson Jones, *Memoranda and Official Correspondence Relating to the Republic of Texas, Its History and Annexation. Including a Brief Autobiography of the Author*, Classic Reprint Series (El Paso: Forgotten Books, 2012), 2–3.

3. Ibid., 3.

4. Ibid., 3.

5. Ibid., 3.

6. Ibid., 4.

7. Ibid., 4.

8. Ibid., 5.

9. Ibid., 6.

10. Ibid., 6.

11. Ibid., 7.

12. Gambrell, *Anson Jones*, 17.

13. Jones, *Memoranda and Official Correspondence*, 7.

14. Ibid., 8.

15. Ibid., 8.

16. Jonathan W. Jordan, *Lone Star Navy: Texas, the Fight for the Gulf of Mexico, and the Shaping of the American West* (Washington, D.C.: Potomac Books, 2007), 47. The *Sabine* was a merchant schooner that smuggled some of the first cotton out of Texas. Brown would later captain the *Liberty* and *Invincible* in the Texas navy.

17. Jones, *Memoranda and Official Correspondence*, 8.

18. Ibid., 9.

19. Ibid., 10. Berryman would not stay with Jones long. He was killed in a duel with R.A Stevenson in 1835.

20. Gambrell, *Anson Jones*, 66. In fact, Jones had the charter for the lodge in his saddlebags when he participated in the Battle of San Jacinto.

21. Jones, *Memoranda and Official Correspondence*, 11.

22. Gambrell, *Anson Jones*, 52.

23. Jones, *Memoranda and Official Correspondence*,12.

24. Gambrell, *Anson Jones*, 52. Alpache was also an active Mason, and this is what most likely drew the two men together in the first place.

25. Jones, *Memoranda and Official Correspondence*, 12.

26. Ibid., 12.

27. William C. Davis, *Lone Star Rising: The Revolutionary Birth of the Texas Republic* (College Station: Texas A&M University Press, 2004), 172.

28. Jones, *Memoranda and Official Correspondence*, 13. As James Haley points out in *Sam Houston*, this story would serve as the "fusebox" for a number of anti-Houston stories throughout the years. For more depth, see James L. Haley, *Sam Houston* (Norman: University of Oklahoma Press, 2002), 17.

29. Jones, *Memoranda and Official Correspondence*, 13.

30. Ibid., 13.

31. Ibid., 14.

32. Ibid., 15.

33. Ibid., 15.

34. Haley, *Sam Houston*, 135. While the two were found guilty and sentenced to death, Houston granted clemency, but used the sentence as a warning to the rest of the army.

35. Jones, *Memoranda and Official Correspondence*, 16.

36. Ibid., 17.

37. Ibid., 17.

38. Ibid., 17.

39. Ibid., 18.

40. Ibid., 18. The Texas Railroad, Banking and Navigation Company had been issued a charter by the First Congress, which was approved by Sam Houston. The charter would allow the formation of a company controlled by speculators that would have had sweeping powers such as eminent domain, and the permission to issue its own currency. Jones describes it as the "great feudal landlord of the whole" and compares it with the British East India Company. The company never got off the ground.

41. Gambrell, *Anson Jones*, 93, 101.

42. Ibid., 101–104.

43. Ibid., 104.

44. Ibid., 128. The revocation of the annexation proposal was first introduced in the Senate by a Dr. Everitt in the same year. Jones introduced the House version. Both measures failed.

45. David C. Humphrey, *Peg Leg: The Improbable Life of a Texas Hero, Thomas William Ward, 1807–1872* (Austin: Texas State Historical Association, 2009), 48.

46. Gambrell, *Anson Jones*, 113.

47. Ibid., 131.

48. Ellen M. Murray, *Notes on the Republic* (Washington-on-the-Brazos: Star of the Republic Museum, 1991). Collinsworth was not the only signer of the Texas Declaration of Independence to take his own life. George Childress, Thomas J. Rusk, and James Woods would also do so.

49. Jones, *Memoranda and Official Correspondence*, 28.

50. Gambrell, *Anson Jones*, 151.

51. Ibid., 151.

52. Ibid., 166.

53. Stanley Siegal, *A Political History of the Texas Republic: 1836–1845* (Austin: University of Texas Press, 1956), 141; Gambrell, *Anson Jones*, 168–169. In fact, Lamar apparently had the opportunity to turn Jones into a staunch ally at this point. Samuel A. Roberts, the secretary to the Texas legation to the United States in Washington, D.C (commonly referred to during the Republic era as Washington City), wrote to Lamar urging him to curry favor with Jones upon his return. Lamar chose to ignore this advice, and Jones would gradually succumb to the vortex surrounding Sam Houston.

54. Andrew J. Torget, *Seeds of Empire: Cotton, Slavery, and the Transformation of the Texas Borderlands, 1800–1850* (Chapel Hill: University of North Carolina Press, 2015), 202.

55. Jones, *Memoranda and Official Correspondence*, 34.

56. Ibid., 35.

57. Ibid., 35.

58. Gambrell, *Anson Jones*, 188.

59. Jones, *Memoranda and Official Correspondence*, 38. Literally translated, *aucon j'respire* means: I can breathe!

60. Gambrell, *Anson Jones*, 195.

61. Gambrell, 197.

62. Jones, *Memoranda and Official Correspondence*, 35; Gambrell, *Anson Jones*, 198. Jones was not an admirer of Burnet. On November 25, 1839, Jones had written of Burnet that "D.G. Burnet is a good, honest man enough, has patriotism, and means well enough, and has decided talent; but he lacks tact and judgment, and is always too much under the influence of his prejudices, which are very powerful. He has every kind of sense but common sense, and consequently will never do for a statesman."

63. Jones, *Memoranda and Official Correspondence*, 200.

64. Ibid., 425. In a note scrawled in his original memorandum book, Jones wrote, "In 1848, Sam Houston having turned Traitor, I changed the name to Samuel Edward."

65. Jones, *Memoranda and Official Correspondence*, 37.

66. Gambrell, *Anson Jones*, 211.

67. Ibid., 226.

68. George Lankevich, *The Presidents of the Republic of Texas* (Dobbs Ferry, NY: Oceana Publishing Company, 1979). This passage is representative of the vitriol that Jones quite often used when referring to Lamar's legacy.

69. Texas State Historical Association, *Southwestern Historical Quarterly* 60; "Notes and Documents: Anson Jones, Master of Barrington" (An Address at the Dedication of the Anson Jones House, March 2, 1958, by Herbert Gambrell), 526.

70. Justin H. Smith, *The Annexation of Texas* (New York: Barnes and Noble, 1941) , 374.

71. Nancy Nichols Barker, ed., *The French Legation in Texas: Vol. I, Recognition, Rupture, and Reconciliation* (Austin: Texas State Historical Association, 1971), 433.

72. Gambrell, *Anson Jones*, 230.

73. Ibid., 238.

74. Ibid., 187. In fact, Jones had sold his Austin home to Saligny when he liquidated his holdings in Austin.

75. Ibid., 233.

76. Ibid., 234.

77. Ibid., 234–235. According to the terms of the Belgian agreement, the King of Belgium agreed that he would back a seven-million-dollar loan to the Republic, at 6 percent interest over twenty years, provided that Texas secure the loan with a combination of customs excises, taxes, and public lands. Texas would also be required to make a deposit in the Belgian treasury of three and a half million dollars in advance as a guarantee. Belgium in return would receive trade concessions and immigration rights, essentially bringing the Republic almost exclusively into Belgian orbit. Jones passed the treaty on to the Texas Senate without comment, and the treaty died there when the Senate refused to consider it. Hamilton resigned in a snit, returned to South Carolina, and whiled away his days complaining that Texas had refused to reimburse him for $200,000 in personal expenses.

78. Ibid., 240.

79. In December of 1842, approximately 350 of Somervell's men decided that they would ignore his orders and occupy the Mexican town of Mier, which they would use as a base to launch a search and rescue mission to recover their fellow Texans taken earlier in the year from

San Antonio. They met little resistance and took Mier, but they were quickly confronted with a much larger Mexican force. Once they ran low on ammunition, they were left with no alternative but to surrender. While being marched down to Mexico City, the prisoners staged a mass escape attempt. In retaliation, Santa Anna ordered that the ranks of the Texans be decimated. After a lottery involving the use of black and white beans (black meant death), seventeen Texans were executed and the rest sent to imprisonment in Perote castle. This became known as the "Black Bean Incident."

80. Lankevich, *Presidents of the Republic of Texas*, 44. According to Jones's biographer, Herbert Gambrell, Jones also had a personal motive for securing the loan. Gambrell avers that Jones received a $10,000 commission for securing the loan (Gambrell, *Anson Jones*, 251).

81. Jones, *Memoranda and Official Correspondence*, 39.

82. Ibid., 40.

83. Gambrell, *Anson Jones*, 295.

84. Siegal, *A Political History of the Texas Republic*, 233–234.

85. John H. Jenkins and Kenneth Kesselus, *Edward Burleson: Frontier Leader* (Austin: Jenkins Publishing, 1990), 349.

86. Ibid., 350.

87. Siegal, *A Political History of the Texas Republic*, 234.

88. Gambrell, *Anson Jones*, 372.

89. Lankevich, *The Presidents of the Republic of Texas*, 54. And what pressure it was! At the end of December 1844, the American Consul to Texas, Duff Green, tried to bribe Jones with stocks and bonds to immediately accept annexation. Outraged, Jones had Green's diplomatic credentials revoked, and he had Green escorted out of Texas rather than to have him shot.

90. Various sources either spell Elliot with one "L" or two. I have used the more common spelling throughout.

91. Elizabeth Silverthorne; *Ashbel Smith of Texas: Pioneer, Patriot, Statesman, 1805–1886* (College Station: Texas A&M University Press, 1982), 98.

92. There was also a major intrigue involving Sam Houston's old nemesis, Sidney Sherman, in concert with Commodore Edwin Stockton which could have resulted in war between Mexico and the United States. For more information on this, see Robert W. Merry's fine study, *A Country of Vast Designs: James K. Polk, the Mexican War and the Conquest of the American Continent* (New York: Simon and Schuster, 2009).

93. Lankevich, *The Presidents of the Republic of Texas*, 56–57.

94. Gambrell, *Anson Jones*, 419. Jones concludes his remarks with the famous line, "The final act in this great drama is now performed. The Republic of Texas is no more." Jones's biographer, Herbert Gambrell, offers the rather apocryphal story that as Jones lowered the flag of the Republic, the flagpole broke in half. While a great story, no supporting documentation was found.

95. Ibid., 439.

96. Ibid., 502.

Chapter 10
The Diplomacy of the Lone Star Republic, 1836–1845

Kenneth R. Stevens

In the nine years, from 1836 to 1845, that Texas was an independent nation, it pursued a vigorous course in its foreign relations, initiating diplomatic efforts with several nations, including the United States, European countries, and Mexico. While Texan diplomacy was generally unsophisticated and inconsistent, it managed to accomplish some important goals, including trade and recognition agreements, and most significantly, annexation to the United States.

Texas diplomacy began even before the declaration of independence from Mexico on March 2, 1836. Texans held a Consultation at San Felipe in November 1835, which established a provisional government and appointed Henry Smith as governor. Because outside financial support was critical, on December 7, 1835, the Consultation appointed Stephen F. Austin, Dr. Branch T. Archer, and William H. Wharton as commissioners to the United States. They were ordered to negotiate a million-dollar loan and, in separate instructions, given broad power to procure and fit out armed vessels; arrange for provisions, weapons, and munitions; seek donations; enlist the sympathies of Americans; and determine whether the Texas could obtain the intervention of United States government in its cause. They were to ascertain whether Texas could "by any fair and honorable means" become part of the United States and, if not, whether the U.S. would recognize Texas independence.[1] The commissioners were an incongruous lot. Austin had been a member of the "peace party" of mainly established settlers who had tried to maintain a working relationship with Mexican authorities as long as possible. They had opposed the more impetuous "war party," including Wharton, whose members embraced conflict with Mexico and independence.[2] The two were implacable enemies. Austin complained that the true interests of Texas had been jeopardized "by inflamatory men, by political fanatics, political adventurers, would-be-great-men[,] vain talkers, and visionary fools."[3] Wharton issued a public card rejecting Austin's "false and ridiculous charges" which he said displayed a "bloated mass of disgusting self conceit—of arrogant dictation, and of inconsistent stupidity."[4]

As they prepared to depart, both men expressed doubts about their mission. Austin agreed to the assignment "from a sense of duty" but doubted much could be accomplished. Wharton, he told a friend, lacked "political honesty," and his efforts were "more devoted to injure me than serve the country." Archer, he continued, had "pure intentions," but was "wild" in his politics. "Associated with such men," he complained, "what have I to expect? Or what has the country to hope?"[5] Wharton had so little confidence in the undertaking that he at first declined the appointment. But at least the two agreed on one thing: unless Texas declared independence, it would not receive effective financial support or other aid from the United States.[6] Austin still spoke of developing a working relationship with Mexican federalists, but if that was not achieved, he considered the only alternative to be a "direct declaration of independence." [7] So things stood on December 26 when the commissioners sailed from Velasco for New Orleans on board the schooner *Liberty*.

The time spent together on the voyage from Texas to New Orleans allowed them to repair their differences. They all agreed about the "main principles" of their mission, "and especially as to independence."[8] In a letter to his brother-in-law James F. Perry, Austin was even more effusive. The "most perfect harmony" existed between the commissioners. Archer, he said, was "a noble fellow," and "Wharton and myself are on the best of terms." Their past disagreements were only because they had not "known each other personally as we might and ought to have."[9]

The commissioners arrived in New Orleans on January 1 and attracted much attention. On January 6, they spoke before what the New Orleans *Bee* said was one of the "largest and most respectable meetings" ever held in the city. The meeting passed resolutions in favor of Texans' fight for "truth, light and liberty, against tyranny, priestcraft and military domination."[10] William Fairfax Gray, a Virginia land agent and speculator then in the city, noted that the vote in favor was loud and unanimous and when the nays were called for "not a *no* was heard, but a person in the crowd sang out *yes*, which caused the remark that the vote was unanimous *and one over*." Gray, however, observed that the commissioners "seem not to know very well how to go about their business. They wish to raise funds to support their army and government on a pledge of the public domain, but have declared no plans, have offered no terms."[11]

Offering land scrip valued at fifty cents an acre, the commissioners secured loans from multiple subscribers, one for $200,000 and a second for $50,000 (but with only 20 percent of the funds advanced).[12] Subsequently they negotiated another loan for $100,000, but the lenders advanced only $10,000 until the Texas government approved an agreement giving the option of taking land at twenty-five cents an acre.[13]

Wharton left for Tennessee in mid-January, leaving Austin and Archer in New Orleans to conclude loan details.[14] From Nashville Wharton wrote to President Andrew Jackson and friends in Congress about Texas, but the administration was preoccupied in a diplomatic dispute with France over unpaid spoliation claims.[15] Nonetheless, Austin believed that Texas would get all the aid it needed and did not think it would be difficult to obtain the recognition of the United States.[16]

Austin and Archer joined Wharton in Nashville in February. A Texas meeting on the eleventh was attended by "ladies and gentlemen of the first rank in point of intelligence and wealth," including members of the state legislature, Governor Newton Cannon, and former governor William Carroll. At the end of the month, Austin and Archer left for Louisville, leaving Wharton, who was ill with the flu, in Nashville.[17]

Though they were met with public enthusiasm, raising money and other practical support remained difficult. They repeatedly urged their government to declare independence because while many Americans supported the cause, Texas would "sink in their estimation" if independence was not declared.[18] From Nashville, Austin wrote on February 18, 1836, "enthusiasm in favor of Texas is very great and universal all over this country, and we can get aid to sustain our independence I have no doubt of it and I think there will not be much difficulty in procuring the recognition of the U.S. Govt. Nothing is wanting but union, and harmony, and concert of action and of purpose, at home; and an unquallified [*sic*] declaration of independence."[19] At Louisville, Austin and Archer wrote their government that it would be "almost useless" for them to seek recognition for Texas in Washington until Texas declared independence. Without a formal declaration of independence, the Texas delegation would not be "received in any public capacity whatever."[20]

While the commissioners traveled toward Washington, events had continued apace back home. Texas declared independence on March 2, 1836. The Alamo fell on March 6 and the Goliad Massacre took place on March 27. Then, at San Jacinto, on April 21, Sam Houston defeated Santa Anna. The Mexican leader signed two treaties, one public and one secret, at Velasco on May 14, 1836. In the public treaty, Santa Anna agreed to withdraw Mexican forces beyond the Rio Grande and not to take up arms against Texas again. In the secret treaty, he promised to "so prepare matters" in Mexico that Texas independence would be recognized. In exchange, the Mexican leader would be freed and returned to Mexico.[21] Santa Anna boarded the Texas schooner *Invincible*, but before the vessel got underway for Vera Cruz, an unruly crowd demanded that he be taken off. The general and his chief aide Col. Juan Almonte were confined at James A.E. Phelps' Orozimbo Plantation in Brazoria. Soon after, word arrived from Mexico that the Mexican Congress had disavowed the Treaty of Velasco.[22] Many wanted Santa Anna executed for war crimes, but Houston maintained that "faithless" as Santa Anna was "if he were to renew his pledges to Texas through the Government of the United States, he would not dare to violate them" or, if he did, American indignation would ensure "their zealous aid in our behalf, should it ever be required."[23]

The commissioners were unaware of the political drama that had unfolded in Texas since their departure. Governor Henry Smith was increasingly at odds with the Provisional Council. After a number of quarrels with the members, he adjourned the body, calling them "scoundrels" and accusing them of "low intrigues." They in turn charged Smith with "official perjury" and "slanders and libels," and removed him from office.[24] On January 23, 1836, Acting Governor James Robinson wrote the commissioners with the "painful and humiliating" news that Smith had been impeached and removed.[25]

Without informing Austin, Archer, and Wharton, the provisional government, now headed by David G. Burnet, appointed a host of additional Texas agents. George C. Childress and Robert Hamilton were sent to Washington to seek recognition of Texas independence.[26] On the way, Childress learned from newspapers that Austin, Wharton, and Archer were "acting as Commissioners under the authority" of "*the late* provisional Government," which he informed Burnet, "would place both us and them in a very awkward situation."[27] To add even more confusion, on April 1, Burnet directed Samuel P. Carson, a former North Carolina congressman who briefly served as Texas secretary of state, to Washington to join the other commissioners in seeking recognition and to "take in charge a general Supervision of all the interests and concerns of Texas in that Country."[28] In addition, John T. Lamar and Thomas J. Green were commissioned to raise men, money, and supplies.[29] Then, on May 26, 1836, the government appointed James Collinsworth and Peter W. Grayson to replace the other commissioners.[30] The welter of diplomatic appointments seems to confirm Gray's impression that the Texans did not know "how to go about their business."

In Louisville Austin and Archer attended a Texas meeting on March 7, 1836, at the Second Presbyterian Church. Austin stirred the audience when he said that the cause of Texas was "the cause of light and liberty;—the same holy cause for which our forefathers fought and bled." An independent Texas, he said, would "extend the principles of self government over a rich and neighboring country, and open a vast field there for enterprise, wealth, and happiness." He went on to identify independence with the slavery question, saying that Texas independence would help protect the United States from "wild fanatics" who might interfere with Southern slavery.[31] That sentiment, while reassuring to his Southern audience, surely reinforced Northerners fears of an aggressive slave-driving South.

Archer, Austin, and Wharton arrived in Washington at the end of March 1836. They complained to their government that they had learned of the Texas declaration of independence through newspaper accounts but still had not received official word, and the United States would not recognize Texas "until it is presented to them by some one with ministerial powers from the same Convention that made the declaration." If the commissioners had had such powers, "Texas would have been, by this time, recognized, if not admitted into this Union." Wharton sent a separate confidential letter stressing the importance of accrediting a minister before the Congress adjourned. The current session was favorable to Texas, but the next might "have a preponderance of Northern and Eastern jealousy."[32] As if to verify the problem, when Wharton had dinner with Jackson, on May 31, 1836, the president asked him, "Where are your letters from your Government?" Texas needed to make public the "true situation of your country and every thing that goes to shew you are a *de facto government*."[33]

Since little could be accomplished at Washington, the three split up. In Philadelphia Austin approached Bank of the United States president Nicholas Biddle about a $500,000 loan for Texas, but nothing came of the effort.[34] From New York Austin wrote President Jackson and "any member of the Cabinet or Congress" complaining that Santa Anna was waging war in Texas "under the *bloody* flag of a Pirate." It was a "war of barbarism against civilization, of despotism against liberty, of Mexicans against Americans." He asked the administration and Congress to give Texas part of the surplus in the national treasury and to make the struggle in Texas "a *National war*" that reflected "the noble feelings of the American people."[35]

Austin wrote to Missouri Senator Lewis F. Linn that he had labored for years "to *Americanize* Texas—to form a nucleus around which my native countrymen could collect and grow into a solid body that would forever be a barrier of safety to the southwestern frontier, and especially to the outlet of the western world—the mouth of the Mississippi." The Americanization of Texas would do more to protect Louisiana, Arkansas, and Missouri than spending thirty million dollars on forts or more than an army of 10,000. An expression of support from Congress or the president would end the war, cost nothing, and "violate no treaty or other obligation," but it would "inspire confidence" and encourage moneylenders so Texas could secure the funds it needed. Austin also told Linn that Mexico's war against Texas was "waged by the mongrel Spanish-Indian and Negro race, against civilization and the Anglo-American race."[36] Such virulent bigotry, says Austin biographer Gregg Cantrell, was not normally part of Austin's personality. He knew that support for Texas would come from Southerners, and he spoke and wrote accordingly.[37]

Austin quit the mission in May and arrived back in Texas on June 27. He had concluded that his efforts in the United States had been a mistake. The wealthy did not see Texas as a sound investment and were unwilling to risk their capital. "Had I known as much of those kind of people last winter as I do now, I should not have spent any time upon them," he confided to his cousin Mary Austin Holley.[38]

Archer and Wharton followed Austin back to Texas. The three met at Velasco and prepared a report for President Burnet describing the "insuperable difficulties" they had encountered during their mission. They had only obtained loans on "disadvantageous terms" primarily because of events in Texas, including the dispute between Governor Smith and the Council, the failure to declare independence in a timely way, the losses at the Alamo and Goliad, Houston's retreat as far as San Jacinto, the supposed threat of an Indian uprising, the government's refusal to ratify the first loan they negotiated, and as they pointedly remarked, the failure of the government "to correspond with us and ratify our powers and appointment."[39] The commissioners' lack of success highlighted the serious problems that would plague the nascent republic.

The victory at San Jacinto sparked discussion about Texas in the United States. Congress received memorials from several states urging recognition of Texas independence. The House and Senate foreign relations committees considered the issue and recommended that the government recognize Texas whenever it received sufficient evidence that Texas had "in successful operation a civil Government, capable of performing the duties and fulfilling the obligations of an independent power." The joint resolution passed unanimously in the Senate and by a vote of 128 to 20 in the House in June 1836.[40]

Based on the committees' recommendations, Jackson sent Henry M. Morfit, a State Department clerk, on a special mission to investigate whether Texas could sustain itself as an independent nation. Morfit's reports, submitted in a series of letters between July and September 1836, did not support recognition. Mexico was preparing another assault headed by General José Urrea and Texan forces were not adequate to the challenge. Morfit heard that Urrea had proposed alliances with Indian tribes in which they would receive land in exchange for waging war against the Texans. Texas, he concluded, might continue in an "embryo state for many years."[41]

In fear of an alliance between Mexico and hostile Indian tribes, President Burnet wrote U.S. General Edmund P. Gaines suggesting that if placing troops at Nacogdoches would "secure peace" it "would be perfectly satisfactory" to Texas.[42] In July 1836, Gaines ordered troops to Nacogdoches where they remained through November.[43] Under the guise of protecting the United States frontier from Indian attacks, it seemed clear to many, ordering troops beyond the Sabine was motivated by support for the Texans against Mexico. The Mexican minister to the United States, Manuel E. de Gorostiza, demanded his passports over the affair, charging that "the partiality of General Gaines in favor of the Texans, is a matter of notoriety."[44]

While the United States Congress debated recognition, Santa Anna was on his way to Washington, undertaking a journey to convince Jackson to mediate between Texas and Mexico. The plan originated with Austin, who had met with Santa Anna when he returned from the United States. Austin proposed that the general write to Andrew Jackson asking for United States intervention. In the letter, suggestively dated July 4, Santa Anna informed Jackson that a Mexican army was preparing to invade Texas and "war and its disasters" were "inevitable, unless a powerful hand interpose." Jackson would make a "great a service to humanity" if he used his influence to bring peace by mediation. Austin also wrote Andrew Jackson urging him to accept the proposal.[45] Jackson politely declined Santa Anna's offer because the Mexican government had informed the United States that it would not consider any agreement made by Santa Anna binding as long as he was a prisoner.[46] Nonetheless, by year's end, Santa Anna was on his way to Washington.

In September 1836, Texas voters elected Sam Houston as the first president of the republic. At the same time, Texans overwhelmingly voted in favor of annexation to the United States by a vote of 3,277 to 91.[47] Establishing the foreign policy of the republic was, of course, an immediate concern. Houston appointed Stephen F. Austin secretary of state and William H. Wharton as minister to the United States.[48] Among his first acts, Houston approved sending Santa Anna to the United States to meet with Andrew Jackson. Accompanied by his aide Juan N. Almonte, and escorted by Colonel George W. Hockley, Barnard E. Bee, Sr., and Major William H. Patton, Santa Anna departed in November for Washington.[49]

Houston's major foreign policy goal was to gain recognition of Texas independence, followed by annexation to the United States. By pursuing recognition as an independent nation first, Texas would escape the territorial stage of government and enter the union on an equal footing with other states. As minister, Wharton had clear instructions: he should explain that Texas claimed the Rio Bravo del Norte as a boundary; the issue of future divisions of Texas into additional states "should be left entirely to the option and decision of the people of Texas"; the location of Indian tribes south of the Red River should be "guarded against" and Indians now in that area should be removed with "just terms of indemnity"; laws and land claims enacted by Texas should be valid and there should be no restrictions on slavery different from those applied to other states in the union; and if Texas was to pay its existing debts, it should retain "the absolute disposal of all the Public lands."[50]

Wharton also received "private and special instructions" that he should not agree to anything that might cause rejection of an annexation treaty by Texans. Despite the overwhelming vote in favor of annexation, Austin felt that "very many people of influence who voted for that measure, merely yielded to the peculiar circumstances of the times, and incline strongly to the opinion, that Texas ought to remain a separate and independent Republic." In Austin's view Texas was making "a great sacrifice by agreeing to the annexation at all," and if the United States did not wish to annex Texas or failed to offer "not only liberal, but even munificent terms," Wharton engage in "full and free conversations with the British, French and other foreign Ministers." If the United States acknowledged Texas independence but declined annexation, then he should seek a treaty of amity, limits, and commerce, and if possible, a treaty of alliance.[51]

Despite the official position, Houston was frank when he wrote privately to Andrew Jackson informing him that both Wharton and Santa Anna were on their way to Washington. "My great desire," he said, "is that our country Texas shall be annexed to the U. States. … It is policy to hold out the idea (and few there are who know to the contrary) that we are very able to sustain ourselves, against any power, who are not impotent, yet I am free to say *to you* that we cannot do it. … I look to you, as the friend and patron of my youth and the benefactor of mankind to interpose in our behalf and save us."[52] Subsequent events would show that Houston's fears were well founded.

Wharton reached Washington in December 1836, after an exhausting trip from Texas to New Orleans, up the Mississippi to the Ohio, to Wheeling, and then to Washington. He arrived the day after President Jackson sent Congress a special message on Texas.[53] Jackson's message, of December 21, Wharton reported, surprised everyone and pleased no one "except perhaps the abolitionists."[54] The president said that it was too early to recognize Texas independence. Acknowledging a new state was "an act of great delicacy," especially because a premature recognition while Mexico still claimed dominion over it would be a "justifiable cause of war." Because Texans were so connected to the United States by language, political principles, and other bonds, and had indicated the wish to become part of the United States, prudence suggested that the United States should "stand aloof" until Mexico or another major power recognized their independence.[55]

Just as important but left unstated in the message was domestic politics. Recognition or annexation of Texas would create political turmoil in the United States. Jackson did not want to saddle his chosen successor, New Yorker Martin Van Buren, with the burden of dealing with the impact of Texas on the slavery question or another difficult issue with Mexico.

Santa Anna arrived in the capital on January 17 and saw Jackson on the nineteenth. The president hosted a dinner for him that evening, and the next day the two generals discussed Texas. Santa Anna later recalled that Jackson offered Mexico six million pesos if it recognized Texas independence, to which he had replied that only the Mexican Congress could agree to such an arrangement. In Jackson's account, Santa Anna himself proposed ceding Texas in exchange for a "fair consideration," but the president rebuffed him. Whatever was said, the leaders parted amicably. Jackson ordered an American vessel to convey Santa Anna to Vera Cruz. Wharton talked with both Santa Anna and Jackson about their meetings and told them that recognition of Texas independence was an "indispensable prerequisite" for any agreement. Texas insisted "the question of Independence should be acted on immediately, unconnected and unembarrassed with any other, and that it be decided on the broad and naked grounds of our being an organized de facto Government, with ample physical ability to maintain our national existence."[56]

Wharton was frustrated. Throughout his time as minister, he complained that his government did not keep him informed of events or even send instructions. On December 31, 1836, Wharton grumbled in a letter to Austin, "Up to this moment I have not received a single line from Texas. … I implore you again and again to write to me more frequently—at least once a week. You know how embarrassing it is to be asked fifty times a day what news from Texas and to be compelled to reply I have had no despatches."[57]

At least part of the reason for the lack of communication was Secretary of State Austin's health, which had been weakened by his imprisonment in Mexico for most of 1834 and the rigors of travel during his 1836 mission in the United States. In Columbia, Texas, then the capital, Austin lodged and held office in a shed that lacked a fireplace or a stove. In December 1836, when a norther blew in, Austin contracted pneumonia. Friends and doctors tended him, but he continued to fail. On the morning of December 27, he woke from a fitful sleep and deliriously declared, "The independence of Texas is recognized! Don't you see it in the papers? Doctor Archer told me so!" Those were his last words. He died within a half hour.[58] It was a sad end for the "father of Texas" at the age of forty-three.

The pace of diplomatic relations with the United States quickened when James Pinckney Henderson, who had emigrated to Texas from Mississippi after San Jacinto, replaced Austin as secretary of state. His first act was to order Memucan Hunt, another post-San Jacinto Texan from Mississippi, to join Wharton in Washington. The two were to work together to win recognition followed by annexation to the United States.[59]

In February, Wharton and Hunt sent an impassioned note to Jackson objecting to the American government's delay in recognizing Texas. Because of this, they said, public confidence in the government was destroyed, immigration had fallen, financial resources could not be developed, and credit was damaged even though Texas' claim to recognition was a hundred times greater than Mexico or South American states had given in the past. Such coldness was bound to alienate the people of Texas and compel them to seek friends overseas. Once diplomatic and trade relations were established with England or France, Texas would be "forever lost to the United States as far as annexation is concerned."[60]

Actually, recognition was at hand. On February 28, 1837, the House of Representatives passed a resolution providing for the outfit and salary of a minister to Texas whenever the president believed there was "satisfactory evidence that Texas is an independent power." A resolution proposed by Mississippi Senator Robert J. Walker for recognition passed the Senate on March 1, 1837. On his last full day in office, March 3, President Jackson signed the measures and appointed Alcée La Branche, a Louisiana sugar planter, as chargé d'affaires to Texas. Jackson invited Wharton and Hunt to the executive mansion that evening for a glass of wine to celebrate the occasion. The Texas representatives wrote their government that "Jackson has closed his political career by admitting our country to the great family of nations."[61]

Achieving recognition had not been easy. Though Jackson had almost eagerly embraced testy diplomatic relations with France over American spoliation claims, he was reluctant to offend Mexico. The politics of slavery in the United States also made him more cautious. Jackson did not wish to encumber his successor Martin Van Buren with political opposition at the outset of his administration.[62]

The effort to gain recognition by the United States was Wharton's final diplomatic effort. He left Washington for home as soon as the U.S. Congress adjourned.[63] On the voyage from New Orleans his vessel, the Texas schooner *Independence,* was captured by the Mexican navy—within sight of Velasco—and Wharton along with other passengers and crew were taken as prisoners to Matamoros. He eventually escaped and made his way back to Texas.[64]

Admission to the union as a state remained the primary goal of Texas foreign policy. The republic was, in fact, desperate. "On the success of this measure," declared Robert A. Irion, who had replaced Henderson as secretary of state, "our permanent prosperity, and perhaps, existence as an organized Government, mainly depends."[65] Texas leaders hoped that political conditions were more favorable now that the 1836 election was over and Van Buren was president. In June 1837, Irion instructed Hunt to make a formal request for annexation. In a long note to Secretary of State John Forsyth, on August 4, 1837, Hunt reviewed the history of Anglo settlement in Texas, the events that led to rebellion and the political and familial connections between Texans and Americans. He suggested that annexation would protect the western frontier of the United States and give the United States control of the Gulf of Mexico. If Texas did not become part of the union, he warned, it could become a rival.[66] Hunt told Irion that he had believed Forsyth favored bringing Texas into the union, but then he was shocked to learn that Forsyth was "violently opposed to annexation!!" He was, Hunt declared, a "traitor" to the interests of the South.[67]

Forsyth officially replied to Hunt later that month, and it was as discouraging for Texas as Hunt had feared. Though the struggles of Texans had won the sympathies of the American people, the annexation of an independent foreign nation had never been an issue before, and whether it would even be constitutional was not known. Furthermore, since Texas was at war with Mexico, annexation would involve the United States in hostilities with a country with which the United States had a treaty of friendship and commerce. As "powerful and weighty" as Hunt's arguments were, they could not override "treaty obligations and respect for that integrity of character by which the United States have sought to distinguish themselves."[68]

Though Hunt's efforts fell short of annexation, Texas and the United States settled by treaty two diplomatic disputes. The first involved the American merchant ships *Durango* and *Pocket*, which had been prized by the Texas navy in 1836. The *Durango* had been captured in Matagorda Bay in March, taken to Galveston and its cargo of badly needed supplies appropriated for the Texas army. The vessel was never returned to its owner. The *Pocket* was prized in April as it transported provisions and war materiel to Mexico for Santa Anna. Both seizures were unjustified, and in a treaty signed in April 1838, Texas agreed to pay $11,750 in damages.[69]

The same month Texas and the United States signed an agreement marking the boundary between Louisiana and Texas. In the Transcontinental Treaty of 1819 the United States and Spain had agreed on a boundary at the Sabine River, but before the Texas revolution the Jackson administration claimed that the border was the Neches, which was farther west. In fact, the claim that the boundary extended as far as the Neches was unconvincing, and the United States agreed to the Sabine River as the proper limit.[70]

The Van Buren administration's rejection of annexation exasperated Texans. In April 1838, the Texas Congress narrowly defeated a resolution that the annexation proposal should be "unconditionally withdrawn," but despite the congressional vote, President Houston ordered Anson Jones, who was named to replace Memucan Hunt in Washington, to withdraw the annexation offer.[71] On October 12, 1838, Jones informed Secretary of State Forsyth of "the formal and absolute withdrawal of the proposition for the annexation of Texas to the United States."[72]

The election of Mirabeau B. Lamar to the presidency in 1838 seemed to close the issue for good. In his inaugural address of December 10, 1838, Lamar disparaged annexation, saying that he had never seen the desirability of annexation and in fact felt it would have proven as "disastrous to our liberty and hopes" as "the sword of the enemy." In the notes for the address, he wrote even more vehemently. Because the United States had so decisively rejected annexation, Texas could not with any sense of "national pride or dignity of character renew the negotiation."[73] On January 23, 1839, the Texas Congress passed a joint resolution approving withdrawal of the annexation proposal.[74]

Even before withdrawing the annexation offer, Texas sought recognition and trade agreements in Europe. In 1837, Texas sent James Pinckney Henderson, at the time secretary of state, as an agent to Britain and France. Henderson met with Foreign Secretary Lord Palmerston but was unable to convince him to extend formal recognition because, Palmerston told him, the government was not convinced that Texas could sustain its independence. Equally important in shaping British policy, as Henderson understood, was the existence of slavery in Texas, the interests of British trade in Mexico and creditors who held substantial Mexican debts, and the possibility that recognition by Britain might encourage the United States to annex Texas.[75] Britain did agree to a trade arrangement by which Texas vessels were allowed access to English ports without formal recognition.[76]

Frustrated in London, Henderson went to Paris in April 1838.[77] His timing was fortunate, because hostility between Mexico and France worked to the advantage of Texas. French citizens had claims of 600,000 pesos against Mexico for damages resulting from civil disorder, including one dispute that involved a large claim from a French pastry chef, and in April 1838 the French minister in Mexico City suspended diplomatic relations. The French navy blockaded the coast of Mexico from Yucatan to the Rio Grande and, on November 27, 1838, bombarded the Mexican fortress of San Juan de Ulúa, and Vera Cruz.[78]

France's trouble with Mexico made it more receptive toward overtures from Texas. In September 1838, the French government ordered Alphonse Dubois de Saligny, a secretary at the French legation in Washington, to visit the republic and report on conditions there.[79] Saligny arrived in Texas in February 1839 and remained until May. He completed a favorable report assuring his government that Mexico could never reconquer Texas, the decision against annexation to the United States was "irrevocably resolved," and hostile Indian tribes were "more annoying than dangerous." There was no reason to doubt the ability of Texas to "maintain its existence as an independent state." Recognition of Texas independence, he concluded, would bring "great advantages to France for many years to come."[80] Based on Saligny's report, the French Foreign Office opened treaty talks with Texas. Henderson pressed for a separate treaty of recognition before negotiating a trade agreement, which would allow Texas to negotiate a commercial agreement as an equal power, but conceded the point when France insisted on a single agreement.[81]

Once more, however, Texas diplomacy fell apart from the government's lack of focus and failure to coordinate its actions. During Henderson's negotiations, James Hamilton, the South Carolina nullifier and speculator in Texas land, and Albert T. Burnley, a New Orleans commission merchant, were appointed agents to seek a five-million-dollar loan for Texas in Europe. The agents had no success in London so Hamilton left Burnley in England while he went to France.[82] In Paris Hamilton and Henderson were soon working at cross purposes. Henderson wanted to reach the best terms possible for Texas, but Hamilton urged him to make more concessions in order to increase his chances of obtaining a loan. In private talks with French Foreign Minister Marechal Soult, Hamilton promised to obtain better terms from the Texas Congress than Henderson had offered. His position weakened by Hamilton's back-stairs dealing, Henderson gave in to demands for lower duties on French exports to Texas and was unable to secure a favorable agreement on the importation of Texas cotton into France.[83] The Franco-Texan treaty of September 25, 1839, recognized the republic but otherwise conferred few benefits.[84] After concluding their treaty negotiations, Henderson and Hamilton returned to Texas separately. Henderson established a law practice in St. Augustine; Hamilton prepared to return to Europe in his quest for a five-million-dollar loan.[85]

The beginning of Lamar's administration seemed a good time to try to end hostilities with Mexico. Peace would increase Texas's international standing and might make it easier to obtain the large loan that the republic needed to repair its finances. Perhaps Mexico, just emerging from its difficulties with France, would be amenable to an agreement.

Barnard Bee, who had served as Santa Anna's escort to Washington in 1836, was appointed a special agent to Mexico in February 1839. He was given full powers with two caveats: unconditional recognition of Texas independence and the Rio Grande boundary for which he was authorized to compensate Mexico up to $5 million.[86] Secretary of State Forsyth instructed Powhatan Ellis, the U.S. minister in Mexico, to offer assistance to any negotiations that took place.[87] On his way to Mexico, Bee stopped in New Orleans, where he met with James Hamilton and representatives of the international banking house Lizardi and Company. They proposed that, working through the British, Mexico could discharge $5 million of debt in exchange for recognizing Texas independence and accepting the Rio Grande boundary.[88] Bee arrived in Vera Cruz in early May, but the government refused to receive him if his object was Texas independence. Bee personally was treated with courtesy, but the Vera Cruz *Censor* quoted an official who said he was "not aware of the existence of a nation called the republic of Texas, but only a horde of adventurers in rebellion against the laws of the government of the republic." The mission, Bee concluded, had been a mistake.[89] Samuel A. Roberts, secretary of the Texas legation in Washington, wrote Lamar that Joel R. Poinsett, the U.S. secretary of war and a person of much experience in Mexico, said sending Bee as a public minister rather than a secret agent doomed the mission. In that capacity, Mexico would have to recognize Texas in order to meet with him.[90] It seems doubtful, however, that Mexico would have recognized Texas independence in any case.

Another effort to reach an agreement with Mexico involved James Treat, a New York merchant who had long experience in Mexico. He was fluent in Spanish, known to Santa Anna, and was a friend of Juan Vitalba, an Italian living in Mexico who was reputed to be a secret agent of Santa Anna. Vitalba spoke with Bee before the Texas emissary left Vera Cruz and convinced him that another mission, properly conducted, could be successful. Hamilton met Treat in New York and recommended him to Lamar. Acting through Vitalba, Hamilton said, Mexico might agree to a mediation by the United States, which could take place in the "better atmosphere" of Washington. The "way would have to be paved with gold," Treat said, but the money could be taken from the $5 million he was authorized to expend.[91]

Treat's instructions as a "Private and Confidential Agent," dated August 9, 1839, included "the absolute independence of Texas" and the Rio Grande boundary for which he was authorized to compensate Mexico up to $5 million. If those goals were accomplished, he could negotiate a treaty of amity and commerce. Powhatan Ellis, the U.S. Minister in Mexico, was authorized to provide his good offices if called upon. The British Minister in Mexico, Richard Pakenham, also offered his assistance.[92]

Treat arrived in Mexico City in December 1839, but found the government unwilling to negotiate because of Texan support for the Republic of the Rio Grande, a Federalist effort to separate the northern states of Mexico from the Centralist government of Santa Anna. Lamar declared neutrality, but Texan filibusters joined the Republican army and, following combat with Mexican forces at Saltillo, they retreated to safety north of the Rio Grande. Meanwhile, Mexico suffered more instability when separatists in Yucatan declared independence in June 1840.[93] Foreign Minister Juan de Dios Cañedo told Treat that Mexico would discuss an armistice with Texas, yet the government took no steps to accomplish that goal. Mexico, it seemed, simply wished to talk while it worked to end the Federalist rebellions in the Republic of the Rio Grande and Yucatan.[94]

In the end, the Mexican government agreed to nothing. In October 1840, Mexico informed British Minister Pakenham that it would not consider an armistice or agree to a boundary south of the San Antonio River. Pakenham told the Texan agent that "under present circumstances, nothing would be gained by further overtures to the Mexican Government upon this subject."[95] Treat sailed that month on the Texan warship *San Antonio* for Galveston. He died of consumption on the voyage, on November 30, 1840.[96] In a message to Congress reporting Treat's death, David G. Burnet, acting as president while Lamar visited the United States, urged Congress to prepare for war.[97] A mission that began with great optimism had come to a distressing conclusion.

Despite the lack of success with Mexico, diplomatic endeavors continued in Europe. James Hamilton had returned to Europe in May 1840 to continue his efforts on behalf of recognition, commercial treaties, and much-desired loans.[98] In September, he signed a trade agreement with the Netherlands and renewed trade discussions begun by Henderson with Belgium.[99] Talks with Belgium resulted in a scheme that would provide a seven-million-dollar loan in exchange for Belgian commercial privileges and the right to settle colonists in Texas.[100]

Hamilton's great effort was to reach an accord with Britain. He met with Foreign Secretary Palmerston in October 1840 and gave him a memorandum outlining the reasons Britain ought to recognize Texas and agree to a commercial treaty. It included the benefits of trade and peace between Mexico and Texas that would accrue for Britain and the disadvantages that would result if no agreement was reached.[101] Hamilton signed three treaties with Britain in November 1840: a treaty of commerce conferring most-favored-nation status to both nations, a treaty in which Britain offered mediation between Mexico and Texas according to which, if successful, Texas would assume one million pounds sterling of Mexico's foreign debt contracted before 1835, and a third for suppression of the African slave trade that provided for a limited mutual right of search.[102] The search issue had a tempestuous history in Anglo-American relations, and no doubt, the South Carolina slave owner disliked it, but Palmerston had insisted.[103] The Texas Senate ratified the first two treaties in January 1841 and the slave trade convention in September 1842. Britain appointed Charles Elliot, a colonial service officer, as chargé d'affaires to Texas and Ashbel Smith was appointed Texas chargé to Britain and France.[104]

Hamilton's loan efforts, however, ended in frustration. He had always been as invested in the search for large loans (on which he would enjoy substantial commissions) as for diplomacy. He returned to Texas in February 1842 eager to present his agreement with Belgium. Instead, Congress terminated Hamilton's appointment as commissioner. Sam Houston, who had regained the presidency in December 1841, had little use for European loans.[105]

Lamar made another attempt for peace with Mexico, based on the offer of British mediation, when he sent Secretary of State James Webb to Mexico in March 1841. If the Mexican government rejected his overture, Webb was to go to Yucatan and determine if the rebels there were willing to join Texas in a war against Mexico.[106] Webb arrived at Vera Cruz in May and immediately contacted British minister Richard Pakenham, who approached the Mexican government.[107] Mexico flatly rejected the overture, informing Pakenham that "honor and justice" would not allow Mexico to accept the "dismemberment" of its territory.[108] Webb was unable to travel to Yucatan, but he informed Lamar that Mexico had made clear that it would never "discuss, or ever receive propositions, *from any source whatever*, which have for their object, the separation of Texas from Mexico." The question for Texas was simply "whether it is better for us to let things remain as they are, or to take such steps without farther delay, as will coerce an acknowledgement of our rights?" Webb urged Lamar to recognize Yucatan and Tabasco and join them in a war against Mexico.[109]

Lamar retaliated against Mexico by opening Texas ports to Yucatan and signing a treaty of friendship, on August 17, 1841, with its agent. According to the agreement, the Texas navy would patrol Yucatan's coast and Texas would receive compensation of $8,000 a month. The navy captured several prizes off Yucatan, but Sam Houston, re-elected president in September 1841, repudiated that policy and ordered the return of the fleet. In any case, the alliance proved pointless because Mexico and Yucatan reached an agreement that settled their differences.[110]

Imperial ambition and the deplorable state of Texas finances led to the greatest foreign relations humiliation of the Lamar administration. Trade over the Santa Fe Trail between New Mexico and Missouri was highly profitable, and its allure appealed to the free-spending Lamar, who had increased the national debt by millions. He had twice proposed diplomatic and trade missions to Santa Fe, but the Texas Congress had rejected the idea. In 1841, Lamar acted on his own. He authorized an expedition, partly commercial and partly military, to Santa Fe and issued a proclamation announcing that Texas desired trade and inviting the people to become part of Texas.[111]

On June 18, 1841, the expedition comprised of about 320 men and twenty-three wagons of trade goods and supplies departed Brushy Creek, just north of Austin. Among the merchants and military troops went civilian commissioners to establish political relations with Santa Fe. George Wilkins Kendall, the publisher of the New Orleans *Picayune*, also made the journey and later wrote an account of the expedition. The men made their way northwest, but the country proved too much for them. On October 5, the exhausted adventurers were captured by the Mexican army shortly after entering New Mexico. The prisoners suffered brutal treatment on a march from Santa Fe to Mexico City. The survivors were released in 1842 through the intervention of the United States.[112] Texans, who often boasted of their military prowess over Mexicans, had suffered an embarrassing military defeat, took heavy financial losses, and required assistance from the United States to free the prisoners.

Sam Houston, inaugurated for his second term as president on December 13, 1841, headed a country with many problems. The republic's finances had gone to ruin as the government spent recklessly and issued "Redback" currency that steadily devalued. Mexico still refused to acknowledge Texas's independence, and the precise diplomatic relations of Texas with the United States, Britain, and France remained uncertain.[113]

The Texas Congress's approaches to foreign relations remained impetuous and amateurish. In response to news about mistreatment of the Santa Fe prisoners, the legislature passed a law claiming that large portions of northern Mexico, New Mexico, and California were part of Texas. Houston vetoed the measure in February 1842, pointing out that "It would appear curious to nations in amity with us, that a people destitute of means to meet their own pressing wants" would presume to declare authority over two thirds of Mexico. It would also, he said, prove an impassable barrier to British mediation. Despite the correctness of his views, Congress passed the measure over his veto.[114] After Mexican troops briefly occupied San Antonio, Goliad, and Refugio in 1842, Houston proclaimed a blockade of Mexican ports, but vetoed a declaration of war by Congress, pointing out that, among other issues the republic did not have the resources for an invasion of Mexico.[115]

In September 1842, Mexican forces under Gen. Adrian Woll occupied San Antonio and took about sixty prisoners, including three congressmen who were in town for court business. After a skirmish between Texans and Mexican soldiers at Salado Creek, about six miles from town, General Woll retreated. But Captain Nicholas M. Dawson and thirty-five of his men were killed; fifteen more were taken to Mexico and imprisoned in Perote Castle.[116]

In November, Houston ordered military action against Mexico in retaliation for the Mexican incursions. Texan forces under the command of Alexander Somervell took Laredo and Guerrero in December, but when Somervell ordered a withdrawal, many of the poorly disciplined troops refused. Two hundred men returned to Texas with Somervell. The others fought Mexican troops at the town of Mier on the Rio Grande on December 25. The outnumbered Texans surrendered on December 26 and were marched to Matamoros and then south. On February 10, 1843, about two hundred of the prisoners escaped but nearly all were recaptured. In the notorious "black bean episode," 159 white and 17 black beans were placed in a container, and every man that drew a black bean was executed by firing squad. The survivors joined other Texan prisoners at the Perote Castle in Vera Cruz.[117]

As had been the case with the Santa Fe prisoners, Texans quickly remembered their American roots once they were in trouble. In the United States, friends and relatives of the prisoners appealed to the American government to intervene in the matter. The Tyler administration, particularly Secretary of State Daniel Webster and the United States Minister to Mexico Waddy Thompson, expended considerable effort on their behalf.[118]

Houston pursued an armistice with Mexico with greater success than Lamar. The opening arose through James Robinson, one of the men taken captive in Woll's raid on San Antonio. Santa Anna released Robinson so he could deliver a proposal that Texas return to Mexico with a large measure of self-rule. Robinson met with Houston and the president dictated a response—ostensibly written by Robinson—in which he proposed an armistice. Through the good offices of Charles Elliot, the British chargé to Texas, and Percy Doyle, Britain's chargé in Mexico City, the two sides agreed to cease hostilities in June 1843. In February 1844, commissioners from Mexico and Texas met at Salinas to draft terms for the armistice.[119] The armistice made sense for both Mexico and Texas. By 1843, several failed attempts must have convinced Santa Anna that Mexico would not reconquer Texas. For Houston even a temporary official peace with Mexico would limit defense expenditures and might help curtail adventurers and hotspurs intent on making war. Moreover, the stability that would accompany peace with Mexico would improve the standing of the republic in the eyes of Europe and especially England. If differences with Mexico were resolved, the United States also might be more interested in annexation in the event Texas chose that path.

In 1843, annexation to the United States again began to seem a realistic possibility. John Tyler, a Virginia slave owner who became president upon the death of William Henry Harrison in April 1841, was an exemplar of Manifest Destiny, the idea that the United States was an exceptional nation meant to serve as a model of republican institutions to the rest of the world. He believed that the future of America depended on "extending the sphere" and annexation of Texas was a critical component of his national vision, a goal he had in mind from his first day as president. Like many other Americans, Tyler failed to see how slavery contradicted that vision.[120]

His own secretary of state, Daniel Webster, was an obstacle to Tyler's plans. In 1841, Tyler had proposed a Texas annexation treaty to him and asked, "Would any thing throw so bright a lustre around us?"[121] The president held little hope for a positive response, because he knew that Webster, a New Englander, would never consent to bringing Texas into the union, so he eased him out of the cabinet in May 1843.[122] As Webster's replacement, Tyler chose Abel P. Upshur, a fellow Virginian and expansionist.

Tyler and Upshur were concerned about British influence in Texas. The British were leaders in a world antislavery crusade, and many Americans believed their mediation between Mexico and Texas was part of a plot to spread abolition. Tyler's agent in England, Duff Green, reported that Foreign Minister Lord Aberdeen had promised to guarantee a Texas loan if the Republic would abolish slavery.[123] Upshur warned the United States chargé d'affaires to Texas, William S. Murphy, that this was part of a plan "to abolish domestic slavery throughout the entire continent and islands of America."[124]

To block British plans, Upshur initiated annexation talks in October 1843 with Texan chargé d'affaires Isaac Van Zandt. Recent events in Europe, he said, had "engaged the serious attention of this government."

The administration would be prepared to conclude an annexation treaty.[125] Texas, which the United States had turned away twice, was wary. Houston wrote Andrew Jackson that another refusal "would forever terminate expectation on her part and it would then not only be left for the United States to expect that she would seek some other friend."[126]

Another important issue for Texas was concern that Mexico might reopen hostilities between the time an annexation treaty was signed and its ratification, when it could depend on the protection of the United States. Van Zandt posed that question to Upshur on January 17, 1844, and received verbal assurance that "the moment" a treaty was signed a naval force would protect the Texas coast and troops would be stationed on the Texas border.[127] Convinced that the United States annexation proposal was serious, Texas dispatched James Pinckney Henderson to join Van Zandt in Washington to help complete the negotiations.[128] On February 27, the treaty draft was completed. Upshur informed William S. Murphy, the chargé d'affaires in Texas that "*a clear constitutional majority of two thirds, are in favor of the measure*" in the Senate.[129]

The next day Van Zandt joined President Tyler, Upshur, and other gentlemen and ladies for an excursion on board the Navy's newest vessel, the *Princeton*, a steam frigate of advanced design. On the Potomac, the guests were treated to repeated firing of the *Princeton's* massive iron cannon, the "Peacemaker." As the vessel passed George Washington's Mount Vernon estate, a crowd gathered around the cannon for a final salute. In that moment the gun exploded, sending shrapnel through the air and killing eight. The dead included Secretary of State Upshur and another key supporter of annexation, Secretary of the Navy Thomas Gilmer. President Tyler had gone below deck or he probably would have been among the casualties.[130]

The *Princeton* tragedy was a severe blow to the treaty process. A week after the gun exploded, Tyler chose Senator John C. Calhoun of South Carolina as his new secretary of state. Confirmed unanimously by the Senate, Calhoun resumed discussion of the treaty's final details with the Texas representatives. Upshur and Gilmer, Van Zandt wrote, had been "ardent and devoted friends" of annexation and Upshur's political skills were finely tuned.[131] Calhoun was as committed to slavery as Tyler and Upshur, but his political skills were less adept.

In their talks with Calhoun, Van Zandt and Henderson introduced a new expectation. In January, Upshur had verbally affirmed that United States military forces would protect Texas from the moment an annexation treaty was signed. The Texas representatives now wanted a written commitment and Calhoun promised that President Tyler "would deem it his duty to use all the means placed within his power by the Constitution to protect Texas from all foreign invasions."[132]

The annexation treaty was signed on April 12, 1844. According to the agreement, Texas would cede its public lands to the United States and enter the union as a territory. In exchange, the United States would assume the public debts of Texas. The word slavery did not appear in the treaty, but said that the citizens of Texas "would be maintained and protected in the free enjoyment of their liberty and property … consistent with the principles of the federal Constitution."[133] Van Zandt and Henderson assured their government that the right of property included "our right to slaves, as the constitution of the United States recognizes that species of property." If the treaty failed to win the required two-thirds majority vote in the Senate, the president said he would submit a joint resolution to Congress annexing Texas to the union "under that provision of the constitution of this Government, which authorizes Congress to admit new states into the union." Texas supporters in Congress had no doubt that, if necessary, such a law would pass.[134]

Tyler submitted the treaty and accompanying papers to the Senate on April 22. Treaties were generally discussed in executive session with an injunction of secrecy until they were ratified, but a few days after the Texas treaty was submitted, Ohio Senator Benjamin Tappan, the brother of the well-known abolitionists Lewis and Arthur Tappan, disclosed the contents to the New York *Evening Post* with explosive results. Among the documents was a letter from Secretary of State Calhoun to British minister Pakenham, in which the secretary of state defended slavery as beneficial to blacks, criticized British antislavery efforts, and announced that maintaining slavery was "essential to the peace, safety, and prosperity" of the southern states. The treaty came to a vote in the Senate on June 8, 1844, and was defeated, 36–16.[135]

Two days after the Texas annexation treaty was defeated, President Tyler sent a message to the House. Though the treaty had failed to obtain a two-thirds majority in the Senate, he believed that the "power of Congress" was "fully competent in some other form of proceeding to accomplish everything that a formal ratification of the treaty could have accomplished."[136] He had in mind, of course, admitting Texas by joint resolution based on Article IV, section 3 of the Constitution, which gave Congress the power to admit new states. That provision, however, had only been used to admit existing national territory to statehood. What Tyler proposed was a novel approach to congressional power.

Territorial expansion was the primary issue in the 1844 presidential contest. The Democrats nominated James K. Polk of Tennessee, who stood for American acquisition of the whole of the Oregon territory and Texas; his Whig opponent, Henry Clay, initially opposed Texas annexation but shifted his position during the campaign, stating that he had "no personal objection" to the prospect if it could be accomplished with the "common consent of the Union, and upon just and fair terms." After an unsuccessful effort as an independent candidate, Tyler withdrew and endorsed Polk, who won in a close election. It was all the evidence Tyler needed to press forward for annexation by resolution.[137]

When Congress gathered in December 1844, Tyler recommended annexation by joint resolution. The election had shown, he said, that "a controlling majority of the people and a large majority of the States have declared in favor of immediate annexation."[138] The resolution passed the House on January 25, 1845, and the Senate on February 28.[139] The United States government would take charge of boundary questions while the state would retain its public lands and would apply income derived from the lands to the republic's debts. With the consent of Texas, up to four additional states could be formed from its territory, but slavery would not be allowed in land north of the Missouri Compromise line.[140] President Tyler signed the bill on March 1, and on March 3, the day before he would surrender office to James K. Polk, he sent the resolution to Texas for its approval.[141] The Mexican minister at Washington, Juan Almonte, immediately broke diplomatic relations with the United States.[142]

Actually, Texas had another offer under consideration. When it became clear that annexation was in the works, British Foreign Secretary Lord Aberdeen and French Foreign Secretary François Guizot ordered their representatives in Texas, Elliot and Saligny, to offer mediation between Mexico and Texas.[143] They met with Anson Jones, Houston's successor as president, to propose a settlement in which Mexico would recognize Texas independence if Texas pledged not to become part of the United States.[144] In Mexico City, the government agreed to the arrangement, which Elliot delivered to Jones on June 3, 1845. The next day Jones announced an end to hostilities with Mexico and said he would submit Mexico's proposal to the people.[145]

United States agents were also at work. Andrew Jackson Donelson, the American chargé to Texas, had meetings with Houston and Anson Jones.[146] In addition, President Polk sent special agents, including former Kentucky governor and Postmaster General Charles A. Wickliffe, Congressman Archibald Yell of Arkansas, Navy Captain Robert Stockton, and the ubiquitous meddler Duff Green. All these men, according to Ashbel Smith, were visiting the settlements of Texas and touting the benefits of annexation to the United States. According to Texas Attorney General Ebenezer Allen, they organized public meetings in favor of annexation and lured ambitious politicians with the possibility of federal offices.[147] Sam Houston himself had objected to provisions of the annexation proposal, which he felt was disrespectful and "not to have been expected by any one who regarded annexation as a compact between two nations, where each had substantive and acknowledged sovereignty and Independence."[148] Even so, Houston, who had political aspirations for the U.S. Senate or even the American presidency, favored annexation.[149]

The Texas Congress convened on June 16 to consider the proposals from Mexico and the United States. It was clear that the public favored annexation over reunion with Mexico. Congress unanimously voted for annexation and President Jones called a convention, which met at Austin on July 4, 1845. With one dissent, the delegates voted in favor of annexation to the United States. The convention drafted a state constitution and, on October 13, 1845, the constitution and the proposal for annexation were sent to the people for ratification. The United States Congress certified the state constitution and, on December 29, 1845, James K. Polk signed the law admitting Texas to statehood.[150] The Lone Star Republic had come to an end.

Notes

1. Commission of Austin, Archer, and Wharton, December 7, 1835, in George P. Garrison, ed., *Diplomatic History of the Republic of Texas* (Washington, D.C.: Government Printing Office, 1908–1911), 1: 51–52 (hereafter *DCRT*); Henry Smith to Austin, Archer, and Wharton, December 8, 1835, *DCRT*, 1: 52–54.

2. Jodella D. Kite, "The War and Peace Parties of Pre-Revolutionary Texas, 1832–1835," *East Texas Historical Journal* 29 (Spring 1991): 11–24.

3. Stephen F. Austin to James F. Perry, August 25, 1834, in Eugene C. Barker, ed., *The Austin Papers* (3 vols. in 4. Washington, D.C.: Government Printing Office, 1928 and Austin: University of Texas, 1927): 2 (Part 2): 1075–85.

4. Wharton to the Public, November 9, 1834, in Barker, *Austin Papers* 3: 25–26.

5. Austin to Richard R. Royall, December 25, 1835, in Barker, *Austin Papers*, 3: 292–294.

6. Wharton to Branch T. Archer, November 26, 1835, in Barker, *Austin Papers*, 3: 266–267.

7. Austin to Provisional Government, December 2, 1835, in Barker, *Austin Papers*, 3: 273–274.

8. Austin to Richard R. Royal, December 25, 1835, in Barker, *Austin Papers*, 3: 293.

9. Austin to James F. Perry, March 4, 1836, in Barker, *Austin Papers*, 3: 317–318.

10. New Orleans *Bee*, January 7, 1836, quoted in Gregg Cantrell, *Stephen F. Austin: Empresario of Texas* (New Haven: Yale University Press, 1999), 334.

11. Paul Lack, ed., *The Diary of William Fairfax Gray: From Virginia to Texas, 1835* (Dallas: De Golyer Library and William P. Clements Center for Southwestern Studies—Southern Methodist University, 1997), January 4 and January 6, 1836, pp. 55, 58.

12. Austin, Archer, and Wharton to Henry Smith, January 10, 1836; Austin and Archer to Henry Smith, January 20, 1836, *DCRT*, 1: 55–57, 57–59. See also Eugene C. Barker, "The Finances of the Texas Revolution, *Political Science Quarterly* 19 (December 1904): 629–632.

13. Austin to [David G. Burnet?], April 3, 1836, with enclosure, Garrison, *Austin Papers*, 3: 341–344.

14. Austin and Archer to Smith, January 20, 1836, *DCRT* 1: 57–59.

15. Wharton to Smith, Nashville, February 7, 1836, *DCRT* 1: 65–66.

16. Austin to Henry Austin, February 14, 1836, in Garrison, *Austin Papers*, 3: 314.

17. Austin, Archer, and Wharton to Henry Smith, February 16, 1836, and Austin and Archer to the Governor of Texas, March 3, 1836, *DCRT*, 1: 66–69, 72–73; Austin to James F. Perry, March 4, 1836, Garrison, *Austin Papers*, 3: 317–318.

18. Austin to Don Carlos Barrett, January 17, 1836, and Austin to McKinney, January 21, 1836, Garrison, *Austin Papers* 3: 305–306, 308–309; Austin, Archer, and Wharton to Henry Smith, February 16, 1836, *DCRT* 1: 66–69.

19. Austin to [Smith (?)], February 18, 1836, *DCRT* 1: 70–71.

20. Austin and Archer to Governor of Texas, March 3, 1836, *DCRT* 1: 72–73.

21. "Public and Secret Treaties of Velasco, May 14, 1836," enclosed in Austin to William H. Wharton, November 25, 1836, in Kenneth R. Stevens, et al., *The Texas Legation Papers, 1836–1845* (Fort Worth: Texas Christian University Press, 2012), 39–44.

22. Will Fowler, *Santa Anna of Mexico* (Lincoln: University of Nebraska Press, 2007), 179–180; Stanley Siegel, *A Political History of the Texas Republic, 1836–1845* (Austin: University of Texas Press, 1959), 40–41.

23. Houston to the Texas Senate, November [1]6, 1836, in Amelia W. Williams and Eugene C. Barker, *The Writings of Sam Houston, 1813–1863* (8 vols.: Austin: University of Texas Press, 1938–1943), 1: 469–474.

24. Henry Smith to Council, January 9, 1836, quoted in W. Roy Smith, "The Quarrel between Governor Smith and the Council of the Provisional Government of the Republic," *Quarterly of the Texas State Historical Association* 5 (April 1902): 324 (hereafter *QTSHA*); Paul D. Lack, *The Texas Revolutionary Experience: A Political and Social History, 1835–1836* (College Station: Texas A&M University Press, 1992), 58–60.

25. James Robinson to Austin, Wharton, and Archer, January 23, 1836. *DCRT* 1: 64–65.

26. Commission of George C. Childress, March 19, 1836, *DCRT* 1: 73–74; Ethel Z. Rather, "Recognition of the Republic of Texas by the United States," *QTSHA* 13 (1910): 193–195.

27. Childress to David G. Burnet, Natchitoches, March 28, 1836, *DCRT* 1: 74.

28. David G. Burnet to Samuel P. Carson, April 1, 1836, *DCRT* 1: 75–76.

29. Joseph W. Schmitz, *Texan Statecraft, 1836–1845* (San Antonio: Naylor Co., 1941), 7.

30. Burnet to Collinsworth and Grayson, May 26, 1836, *DCRT*, 1: 89–91; Schmitz, *Statecraft*, 26.

31. Cantrell, *Austin*, 339–341.

32. Wharton to Governor of Texas, April 9, 1836, *DCRT* 1: 81–82.

33. Wharton to Austin, June 2, 1836, Barker, *Austin Papers*, 3: 363–364.

34. Archer, Austin, and Wharton to Government of Texas, April 6, 1836, *DCRT* 1: 79–80; Austin to Biddle, April 9, 1836, in Barker, *Austin Papers*, 3: 328–330.

35. Austin to Andrew Jackson, et al., April 15, 1836, in Barker, *Austin Papers*, 3: 332–333.

36. Austin to L.F. Linn, May 4, 1836, in Barker, *Austin Papers*, 3: 345–348.

37. Cantrell, *Austin*, 344–345.

38. Austin to Mary Austin Holley, May 29, 1836, quoted in Cantrell, *Austin*, 346–347.

39. Austin, Archer, and Wharton to Burnet, July 21, 1836, *DCRT* 1: 111–112.

40. Samuel F. Bemis, *John Quincy Adams and the Union* (New York: Knopf, 1956), 357–358; Robert V. Remini, *Henry Clay: Statesman for the Union* (New York: W.W. Norton, 1991), 485–486; Schmitz, *Texas Statecraft*, 27–29.

41. Morfit to Forsyth, August 27, 1837 and Morfit to Forsyth, September 14, 1836, in "Message of the President of the United States, Relative to the 'Political, Military, and Civil Conditions of Texas,'" *Senate Document* 20, 24th Cong., 2d sess. (Serial 297), pp. 12–15, 29–36.

42. Burnet to Collinsworth and Grayson, July 8, 1836, *DCRT* 1: 104–105.

43. James W. Silver, *Edmund Pendleton Gaines, Frontier General* (Baton Rouge: Louisiana State University Press, 1949), 206–213.

44. Gorostiza to Asbury Dickins, October 15, 1836, *Sen. Doc.* 1, 24th Cong., 2d sess., pp. 100–105.

45. Santa Anna to Jackson, July 4, 1836, *DCRT* 1: 106–107; Austin to Jackson, July 4, 1836, Williams, Austin *Papers*, 3: 380–383; Cantrell, *Austin*, 348–349.

46. Andrew Jackson to Antonio Lopez de Santa Anna, September 4, 1836, in Stevens, *Texas Legation Papers*, 11–15.

47. George P. Garrison, "The First Stage of the Movement for the Annexation of Texas," *American Historical Review* 10 (1904): 74.

48. Cantrell, *Austin*, 360–361; Siegel, *Texas Republic*, 54.

49. Fowler, *Santa Anna*, 182–183.

50. Austin to Wharton, November 18, 1836, Stevens, *Texas Legation Papers*, 19–29.

51. Austin to Wharton, "Private and Special Instructions," November 18, 1836, Stevens, *Texas Legation Papers*, 30–36.

52. Houston to Jackson, "Private," November 20, 1836, Barker, *Austin Papers* 3: 457–458.

53. Wharton to Austin, November 28, 1836 and December 22, 1836, *DCRT* 1: 144, 157–158.

54. Wharton to Austin, No. 2, December 28, 1836, *DCRT* 1: 158–160.

55. Andrew Jackson to the Senate and House of Representatives, December 21, 1836, in James D. Richardson, ed., *A Compilation of the Messages and Papers of the Presidents* (20 vols. New York: Bureau of National Literature, 1897), 4: 1484–1488.

56. Wharton to Rusk, No. 9, [February 16, 1837], *DCRT* 1: 187–192; Robert V. Remini, *Andrew Jackson and the Course of American Democracy, 1833–1845* (New York: Harper and Row, 1984), 364–366; Will Fowler, *Santa Anna of Mexico* (Lincoln: University of Nebraska Press, 2007), 182–183.

57. Wharton to Austin, December 31, 1836, No. 3, *DCRT* 1: 166–168. See also Wharton to Austin, No. 2, December 28, 1836 and Wharton to Austin, No. 4, January 6, 1837, *DCRT* 1: 158–160, 168–172.

58. Cantrell, *Austin*, 363–364.

59. James P. Henderson to William H. Wharton, December 31, 1836, in Stevens, *Texas Legation Papers*, 87–89; James P. Henderson to Memucan Hunt, December 31, 1836, in Stevens, *Texas Legation Papers*, 89–95.

60. James P. Henderson to William H. Wharton, December 31, 1836, in Stevens, *Texas Legation Papers*, 87–89; James P. Henderson to Memucan Hunt, December 31, 1836, in Stevens, *Texas Legation Papers*, 89–95.

61. Wharton and Hunt to Henderson, No. 11, March 5, 1837, *DCRT* 1: 201; Remini, *Jackson and Democracy*, 367–368.

62. For more on Andrew Jackson's foreign policy see John M. Belohlavek, *"Let the Eagle Soar!" The Foreign Policy of Andrew Jackson* (Lincoln: University of Nebraska Press, 1985).

63. Wharton to Rusk, No. 8, February 8, 1837 and James Pinckey Henderson to Wharton, February 28, 1837, *DCRT* 1: 184–186, 200.

64. Jonathan W. Jordan, *Lone Star Navy: Texas, the Fight for the Gulf of Mexico, and the Shaping of the American West* (Washington, D.C.: Potomac Books, 2006), 83–87.

65. Robert A. Irion to Memucan Hunt, June 26, 1837, Stevens, *Texas Legation Papers*, 247–251.

66. Hunt to Forsyth, August 4, 1837, William R. Manning, *Diplomatic Correspondence of the United States: Inter–American Affairs, 1831–1860* (12 vols., Washington: Carnegie Endowment for International Peace, 1932–1939), 12: 129–140.

67. Hunt to Irion, August 10–11, 1837, No. 25, *DCRT* 1: 252–256.

68. Forsyth to Hunt, August 25, 1837, in Stevens, *Texas Legation Papers*, 262–266.

69. Hunter Miller, *Treaties and other International Acts of the United States* (8 vols. Washington, D.C.: Government Printing Office, 1931–1948), 4: 125–131; Jordan, *Lone Star Navy*, 53–55, 64–66.

70. Hunt to Irion, No. 35, April 28, 1838, *DCRT* 1: 325–326; Hunter Miller, *Treaties and other International Acts of the United States*

(8 vols. Washington, D.C.: Government Printing Office, 1931–1948), 4: 133–143.

71. Irion to Jones, July 12, 1838, Stevens, *Texas Legation Papers*, 294–296; Schmitz, *Texan Statecraft*, 61–62.

72. Jones to Aaron Vail, October 12, 1838, Manning, *IAA* 12: 173–174.

73. Mirabeau B. Lamar, "Inaugural Address of Mirabeau B. Lamar," December 10, 1838, and Lamar, "[Notes for the Inaugural Address] on the Annexation of Texas," in Charles A. Gulick, ed., *The Papers of Mirabeau Buonaparte Lamar* (6 vols., Austin: Texas State Library, 1920–1927), 2: 316–323, 324–327.

74. H.P.N. Gammel, comp., *Laws of Texas, 1822–1897* (Austin: Gammel Book Company, 1898), 2: 75.

75. Henderson to Irion, October 14, 1837, December 22, 1837, January 5, 1838, *DCRT* 3: 812–820, 831–836, 839–842; J.L. Worley, "The Diplomatic Relations of England and the Republic of Texas," *QTSHA* 9 (1905): 4–5.

76. Henderson to Irion, No. 7, April 12, 1838, *DCRT* 3: 853–860; Schmitz, *Texan Statecraft*, 64–66.

77. Henderson to Irion, No. 1, June 2, 1838, *DCRT* 3: 1206–1217.

78. Fowler, *Santa Anna*, 186–192; Herbert R. Edwards, "Diplomatic Relations between France and the Republic of Texas," *Southwestern Historical Quarterly* 20 (1917): 209–211.

79. Department of Political Affairs Memorandum for the Minister, September 5, 1838, in Nancy N. Barker, ed. and trans., *The French Legation in Texas* (2 vols., Austin: Texas Historical Association, 1971), 1: 47–48.

80. Saligny to Mole, Feb 20, 1839; Saligny to Jean de Dieu, Duke of Dalmatia, June 24, 1839, in Barker, *French Legation*, 1: 52–55, 95–103.

81. Henderson to Secretary of State, July 26, 1839, *DCRT* 3: 1264–1265.

82. Robert Tinkler, *James Hamilton of South Carolina* (Baton Rouge: Louisiana State University Press, 2004), 178; Siegel, *Texas Republic, 113–115*; Schmitz, *Texan Statecraft*, 49, 82, 142.

83. Tinkler, *Hamilton*, 184–185; Siegel, *Texas Republic*, 118–119; Edwards, "France and the Republic of Texas, *Southwestern Historical Quarterly* 20 (1917): 223.

84. Gammel, *Laws of Texas*, 2: Appendix, 655–662.

85. Tinkler, *Hamilton*, 185–188.

86. James Webb to B. Bee, February 20, 1839; Webb to Bee, March 7, 1839, *DCRT* 2: 432–437, 437–438.

87. Dunlap to Lamar, "Private," May 16, 1839, *DCRT* 1: 383–385.

88. Ephraim D. Adams, *British Interests and Activities in Texas, 1838–1846* (Baltimore: Johns Hopkins University Press, 1910), 26–27; Siegel, *Texas Republic*, 123–124; Schmitz, *Texan Statecraft*, 92.

89. Bee to Webb, May 24, 1839, *DCRT* 2: 447–449; Siegel, *Texas Republic*, 124–125.

90. Roberts to Lamar, July 9, 1839, *Lamar Papers* 3: 35–38; Siegel, *Texas Republic*, 125–126.

91. Hamilton to Lamar, June 22, 1839; Hamilton to Lamar, "Private and Confidential," June 28, 1839; Bee to Webb, July 6, 1839; Bee to Webb, July 9, 1839, *DCRT* 2: 450–452, 453–454, 456–457, 460–462; Joseph M. Nance, *After San Jacinto: The Texas-Mexican Frontier, 1836–1841* (Austin: University of Texas Press, 1963), 181–182; Siegel, *Texas Republic*, 126–127.

92. Burnet to Treat, August 9, 1839; Treat to Lamar, "Confidential," January 31, 1840, *DCRT* 2: 470–472, 538–542; Schmitz, *Texan Statecraft*, 111–115.

93. Nance, *After San Jacinto*, 355–360.

94. Treat to Lamar, "Private," December 12, 1839; Treat to Lamar, "Private," December 31, 1839; Treat to Lamar, "Private," February 7, 1840, with enclosures, *DCRT* 2: 506–507, 523–527, 548–558; Siegel, *Texas Republic*, 129–132; Schmitz, *Texan Statecraft*, 109–123.

95. Pakenham to Treat, October 15, 1840, *DCRT* 2: 726–727.

96. Vitalba to Lamar, December 8, 1840, *DCRT* 2: 720–721.

97. Nance, *After San Jacinto*, 386.

98. Tinkler, *Hamilton*, 188.

99. Gammel, *Laws of Texas*, 2: 905–912.

100. Hamilton to Lipscomb, October 3, 1840; Hamilton to Lipscomb, January 4, 1841, *DCRT* 3: 1532–1533, 1525–1527; Tinkler, *Hamilton*, 189–190, 199–201; Herbert Gambrell, *Anson Jones: The Last President of Texas* (2nd ed., Austin: University of Texas Press, 1964), 234–235.

101. Adams, *British Interests and Activities*, 53–54; Tinkler, *Hamilton*, 192–193.

102. Hamilton to Lipscomb, January 4, 1841, *DCRT* 3: 921–925; Worley, "Diplomatic Relations of England and Texas," *Southwestern Historical Quarterly* 9 (1905): 11–16.

103. Adams, *British and Activities*, 58–59; Tinkler, *Hamilton*, 194–195.

104. Gammel, *Laws of Texas*, 2: 880–885, 886–888, 889–904; Tinkler, *Hamilton*, 195–196.

105. Anson Jones to James Hamilton, Austin, January 26, 1842, *DCRT* 3: 943–944; Tinkler, *Hamilton*, 199–202.

106. James S. Mayfield to Webb, March 22, 1841, *DCRT* 2: 732–736.

107. Webb to Richard Pakenham, June 1, 1841, *DCRT* 2: 752–755.

108. Sebastian Camacho to Pakenham, Mexico City, June 8, 1841, *DCRT* 2: 757–758.

109. Webb to Lamar, June 29, 1841, *DCRT* 2: 760–766.

110. Nance, *After San Jacinto*, 455–456; Jordan, *Lone Star Navy*, 188–200; Siegel, *Texas Republic*, 155–156.

111. Address to the Citizens of Santa Fe, June 5, 1841, *Lamar Papers*, 3: 488–496.

112. Kenneth E. Shewmaker, et al., *The Papers of Daniel Webster: Diplomatic Papers, 1841–1843* (2 vols., Hanover: University Press of New England, 1983), 1: 375–463; George W. Kendall, *Narrative of the Texan Santa Fe Expedition* (2 vols. New York, 1844); Siegel, *Texas Republic*, 164–17; Noel Loomis, *The Texan-Santa Fe Pioneers* (Norman: University of Oklahoma Press, 1958) is a thorough account.

113. Siegel, *Texas Republic*, 184.

114. "Veto of an Act to Define the Boundaries of the Republic," February 1, 1842, in Williams and Barker, eds., *Writings of Sam Houston*, 2: 462–465. Siegel, *Texas Republic*, 191–192; Schmitz, *Texan Statecraft*, 171–172.

115. "Message to the House of Representatives, July 22, 1842, Williams and Barker, *Writings of Sam Houston*, 3: 116–124; Siegel, *Texas Republic*, 192–193, 197–201; James L. Haley, *Houston* (Norman: University of Oklahoma Press, 2002), 242–243.

116. Nance, *Attack and Counterattack*, 322–323, 364–381, 404; Siegel, *Texas Republic*, 203–204.

117. Nance, *Attack and Counterattack*, 483–577; Siegel, *Texas Republic*, 206–209; Sam W. Haynes, *Soldiers of Misfortune: The Somervell and Mier Expeditions* (Austin: University of Texas Press, 1990) is a complete account.

118. Shewmaker, *Webster Diplomatic Papers*, 1: 463–481.

119. Houston to Santa Anna, April 10, 1843, in Williams and Barker, *Writings of Houston*, 3: 351–353; Charles Elliot to Anson Jones, June 10, 1843, and Anson Jones to Charles Elliot, June 15, 1843, *DCRT* 3: 1090–1091, 1092–1093; Adams, *British Interests and Activities*, 128–137; Siegel, *Texas Republic*, 222–224; Schmitz, *Texan Statecraft*, 195–197.

120. Edward P. Crapol, *John Tyler: The Accidental President* (Chapel Hill: University of North Carolina Press, 2006), 26, 176.

121. Tyler to Webster, October 11, 1841, C.H. Van Tyne, *Letters of Daniel Webster* (New York: McClure, Phillips, 1902), 239–240.

122. Lyon G. Tyler, *Letters and Times of the Tylers* (2 vols., Richmond: Whittet and Shepperson, 1884–1885), 2: 263–264; Robert V. Remini, *Webster: The Man and His Time* (New York: W.W. Norton, 1997), 582–583.

123. Duff Green to John Tyler, July 3, 1843, cited in Oliver P. Chitwood, *John Tyler: Champion of the Old South* (Newtown, CT: American Political Biography Press, 1990; reprint 1939), 347; Crapol, *Tyler*, 194–195.

124. Abel P. Upshur to William S. Murphy, August 8, 1843, in Manning, *IAA* 12: 44–49.

125. Upshur to Van Zandt, October 16, 1843, Manning, *IAA* 12: 53–54; Siegel, *Texas Republic*, 227.

126. Houston to Andrew Jackson, February 16, 1844, in William C. Crane, *Life and Select Literary Remains of Sam Houston of Texas* (Dallas: William G. Scarff, 1884), 370–373.

127. Van Zandt to Upshur, January 17, 1844, in *House Executive Document* No. 271, 28th Congress, 1st sess., Serial 444, pp. 88–89; Van Zandt to Anson Jones, January 20, 1844, *DCRT* 2: 239–243.

128. Jones to Henderson, February 15, 1844, *DCRT* 2: 252–253.

129. Abel P. Upshur to William S. Murphy, No. 14, January 16, 1844, in Manning, *IAA* 12: 59–65.

130. Crapol, *Tyler*, 207–209.

131. Van Zandt to Jones, March 5, 1844, *DCRT* 2: 261–262.

132. Calhoun to Van Zandt and Henderson, April 11, 1844, Robert L. Meriwether, et al., eds., *The Papers of John C. Calhoun* (28 vols., Columbia: University of South Carolina Press, 1959–2003), 18: 208–209; Crapol, *Tyler,* 212.

133. "Annexation of Texas," Miller, *Treaties*, 4: 689–696.

134. Van Zandt and Henderson to Jones, April 12, 1844, *DCRT* 2: 269–273.

135. Calhoun to Pakenham, April 18, 1844, in Wilson, *Calhoun Papers*, 18: 273–278; "Proceedings of the Senate and Documents Relative to Texas, from which the Injunction of Secrecy has been Removed," May 16, 1844, *Senate Document* No. 341, 28th Cong., 1st sess., pp. 1–119); *Congressional Globe*, 28th Cong., 1st sess., p. 652.

136. "To the House of Representatives," June 10, 1844, in Richardson, *Messages and Papers*, 5: 2176.

137. Frederick Merk, *Slavery and the Annexation of Texas* (New York: Knopf, 1972), 94–96; Crapol, *Tyler*, 218–219.

138. Tyler, "Fourth Annual Message," December 3, 1844, in Richardson, *Messages and Papers*, 5: 2197–2198.

139. *Cong. Globe*, 28th Cong., 2d sess., 362–363, 371–372.

140. Merk, *Annexation of Texas*, 158.

141. Lyon Tyler, *Letters and Times of the Tylers*, 2: 363; Crapol, *Tyler*, 220. The text of the annexation resolution is in *Senate Document* 2, 29th Cong., 1st sess., pp. 37–38, serial 480.

142. Almonte to Calhoun, March 6, 1845, *Senate Document* 2, 29th Cong. 1st sess. pp. 130–132.

143. Adams, *British Interests and Activities*, 198–200.

144. Adams, *British Interests and Activities*, 210–211.

145. Schmitz, *Texan Statecraft*, 233; Siegel, *Texas Republic*, 252.

146. Pletcher, *Diplomacy of Annexation*, 176.

147. Merk, *Texas Annexation*, 172–173.

148. Houston to Donelson, April 9, 1845, in Williams and Barker, *Writings of Sam Houston*, 4: 417.

149. Merk, *Texas Annexation*, 173.

150. Schmitz, *Texas Statecraft*, 233–235; Siegel, *Texas Republic*, 251–253.

Chapter 11

Across Many Borders: Persistence and Transformation in the Texas Economy and Culture, 1830–1850

Walter L. Buenger

Less than a decade after the unmourned demise of the Republic of Texas, Frederick Law Olmsted toured the state and vividly described a young stock raiser whose father and mother brought him to Texas while it was still a part of Mexico. This stock raiser lived just west of the Brazos River near the Central Texas community of Caldwell. According to Olmsted: "For about a month in the year he had to work hard, driving his cattle into the pen, and roping and marking the calves; this was always done in a kind of frolic in the spring—the neighboring herdsmen assisting each other." The young stock raiser and his family grew a little corn to grind into meal and tended a few hogs, but acquired what else they needed by selling or trading their cattle. The fellow claimed he was a "regular Texan" as if that were a unique or exceptional breed isolated unto itself.[1]

A close reading of what Olmsted wrote of this stock raiser, however, qualifies any insistence on the exceptionalism or isolation of those who grew up in the Republic era. The free range techniques described by Olmsted were common from South Carolina westward and the use of the rope and the horse may indicate a Spanish or Mexican cultural influence picked up either in Louisiana or Texas. As to isolation, if Texas cattle had not eventually reached a market, probably in New Orleans, there would have been far fewer opportunities for their sale or barter. Coffee, skillets, metal tools, and cloth, all of which Olmsted mentioned as commonly owned by stock raising families, came in from the outside, again probably through New Orleans. Thus as part of both a larger circle of trade and as a product of a blending of cultures from across distant borders, this regular Texan was more than he appeared at first glance. A second glance, as well as the broader history of Texas from 1830 to 1850, demonstrated that economic and cultural traits carried to Texas by migrants persisted and that the economic and cultural transformation of those migrants sprang from connections with numerous other groups and other places.[2]

That first glance suggesting exceptionalism and isolation, however, has long dominated our consciousness. In 1946 William Ransom Hogan published *The Texas Republic: A Social and Economic History*, and it has remained the standard if not the only work on the social and economic history of the era.[3] Perhaps this unusual longevity derived from the quality of Hogan's lively prose, but it also likely sprung from the general decline in historians' interest in economic history, the difficulty in finding useful sources on the economy, and the often insular nature of Texas studies before 1980. Hogan's approach also fit nicely into the parameters of traditional Texas history, virtually ignoring women, children, Indian Texans, Mexican Texans, German Texans, and African American Texans. He closed his book by claiming: "So there arose a Texan way of life that still exists, even in the face of all the mass promotion and standardization of machine civilization. Stamina, individualism, 'go-ahead' initiative, pride in everything Texan—those were and still are, in varying degrees, among the ingredients of the Texas spirit." Such sentiments and approaches to the Texas past still have intense appeal in some quarters.[4]

This essay argues for a different approach. Understanding Texas history, especially the economic history of the region, requires conceiving of the boundaries around Olmsted's stock raiser and all other Texans as fluid and connected. People, ideas, habits, crops, capital, goods, and services in varied degrees went back and forth across those boundaries. Atlantic World connections in particular united all Texans and pulled them into the orbit of the Lower South. By 1850, however, these border crossings also created distinctive and evolving cultural pockets or island communities in the diverse regions of Texas. Instead of a "regular Texan" at least six types existed: Lower South, Upper South, German, Comanche/Apache, Tejano, and blended of which Olmsted's stock raiser was an excellent example. Overdrawing the differences between these communities would be a mistake, but so would ignoring their particular cultures. Texas, however, was part of an evolving and growing capitalist economy, and even the barter and livestock-based world of stock raisers felt the specific influences of markets, money, and credit, and the governmental policies and laws intended to promote and undergird slave-based capitalism.[5]

Thus in examining the borders around and between Texans this essay concentrates on three areas: connections to the Atlantic World including migration, commerce, urbanization, crop selection, and labor systems; the evolving household economies in the six cultural regions of Texas; and the flow of money, credit, law, and capitalist culture across and within the borders of Texas. Each of these three focal points revealed both persistence and transformation, and in that sense, this essay responds to absolutists such as Hogan who insisted on Texas exceptionalism or his more modern equivalents who tout the southerness or westerness of Texas. Absolutism obscures change over time and the intermingling of persistence with transformation. Atlantic connections made Texas increasingly like the Lower South by stimulating the spread of cotton and slavery, but in the midst of that, Tejano cattle raising practices and German free labor customs remained. Distinct household economies and cultures, moreover, splintered Texas into islands often widely divergent from a Lower South model. Money, credit, and law, in comparison, thrust Texas and Texans emphatically toward a Lower South model. Yet even here older connections across borders, most distinctively with Spanish community property law, persisted. By 1850 Texas and Texans had moved toward a Lower South model and perhaps had passed a tipping point in that transformation, but significant anomalies remained.[6]

Such anomalies could also be found in the Lower South and the Upper South, but both those regions had a dominant form and structure not present in Texas before 1850. There were, for example, pockets of the Lower South such as northern Georgia and Alabama where slave holding was less common and on a smaller scale. Like much of the Upper South, stock raising or smaller scale cultivation of crops other than cotton, rice, or sugar predominated. There were also pockets of the Upper South, such as western Tennessee and eastern Arkansas, with larger scale cotton plantations dependent on slave labor. Taken as a whole, however, the states of the Lower South stretching from South Carolina and Georgia westward to Louisiana were dominated by slave-plantation agriculture and an export economy. Slaves made up a much higher percentage of the total population in these states than in the Upper South. On the other hand, the Upper South states that stretched from Virginia and Maryland west to Missouri had more mixed agriculture, more intensive stock raising, and fewer slaves as a percentage of the total population. Unlike either the Upper or Lower South, through the 1840s no one pattern predominated, but Atlantic connections were pulling Texans toward the Lower South.[7]

Trade, people, habits, and patterns of behavior that crossed a variety of borders into and within Texas made the region a subset, not an exact replica, of the rest of the Atlantic World. This emerging world grew all

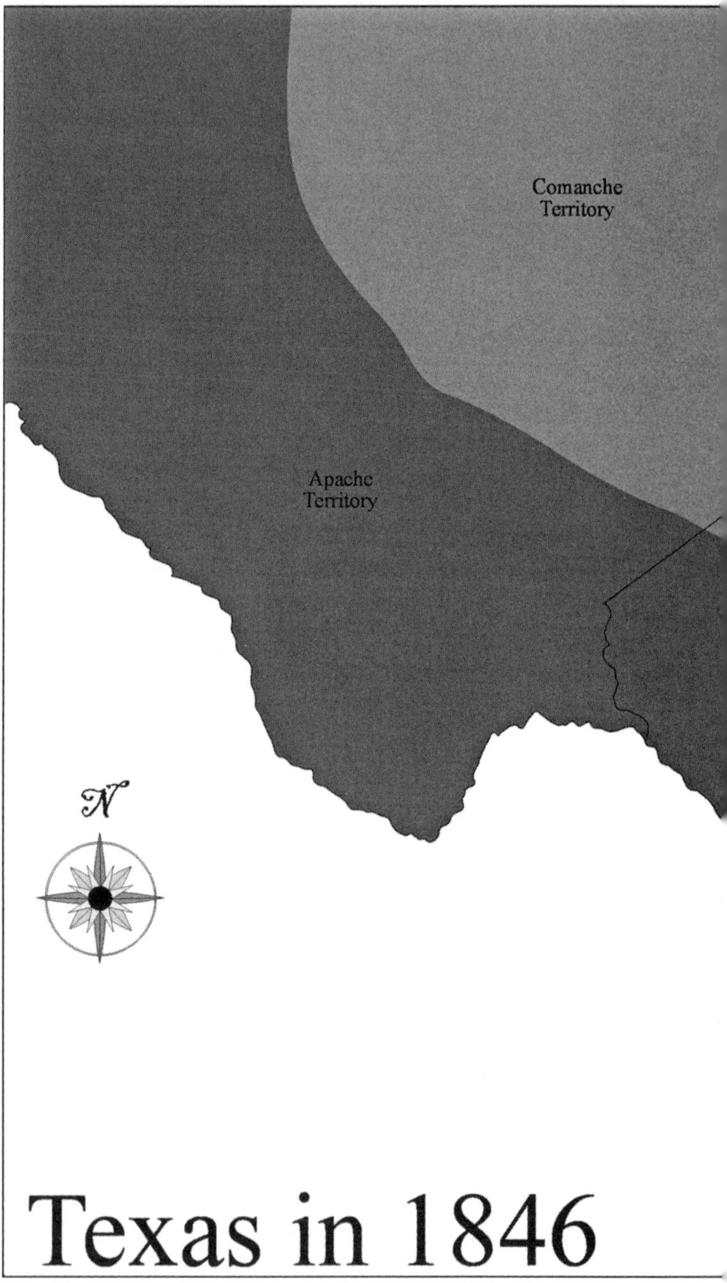

Texas in 1846

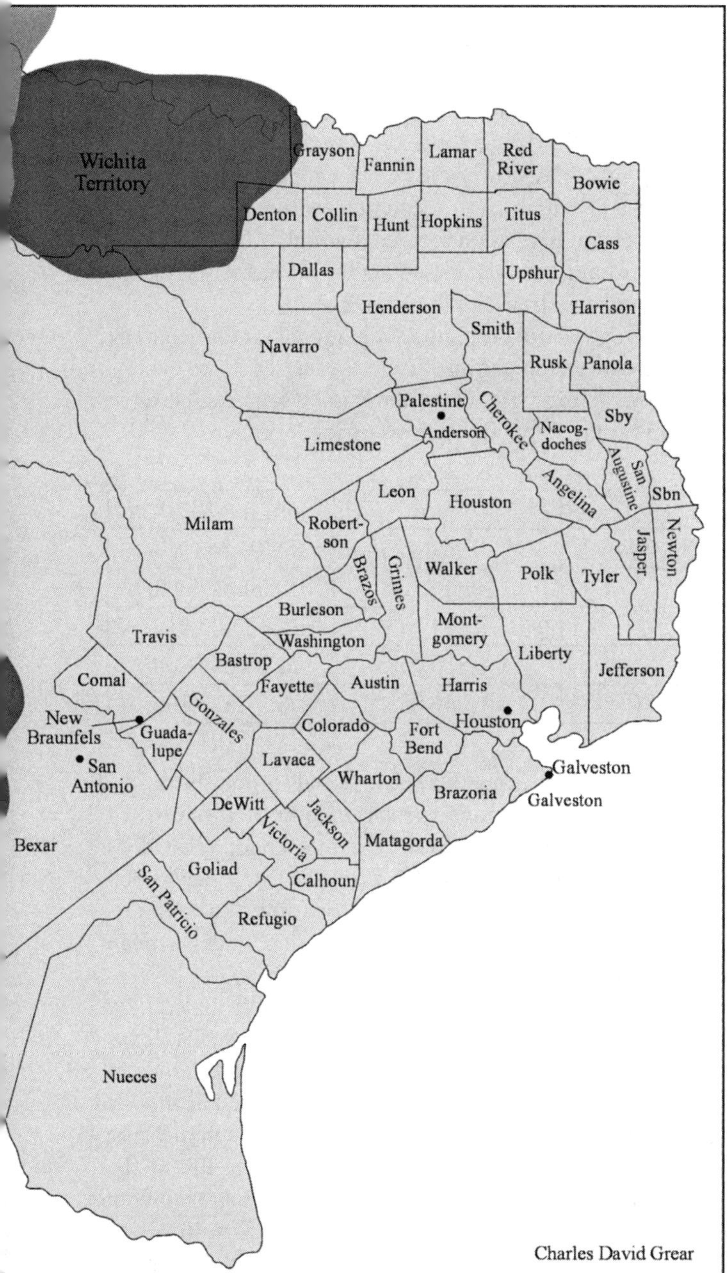
Wichita Territory
Grayson
Fannin
Lamar
Red River
Bowie
Denton
Collin
Hunt
Hopkins
Titus
Cass
Dallas
Upshur
Henderson
Harrison
Smith
Navarro
Rusk
Panola
Palestine
Anderson
Cherokee
Sby
Nacog-doches
Limestone
San Augustine
Angelina
Sbn
Leon
Houston
Milam
Robert-son
Jasper
Newton
Brazos
Grimes
Walker
Polk
Tyler
Burleson
Travis
Washington
Mont-gomery
Liberty
Bastrop
Jefferson
Comal
Fayette
Austin
Harris
Gonzales
New Braunfels
Guada-lupe
Colorado
Houston
Fort Bend
San Antonio
Lavaca
Wharton
Galveston
Galveston
Brazoria
DeWitt
Jackson
Victoria
Matagorda
Bexar
Goliad
Calhoun
San Patricio
Refugio
Nueces
Charles David Grear

the more connected to New Orleans, more like Mississippi in some areas, but in others the culture and economy gradually took on some aspects of the Caribbean, Central Europe, Mid-continent North America, and Northern Mexico. Texas grew more connected to the broader world, not more insular and exceptional. Yet as those far-flung streams of people, concepts, habits, and practices slowly interacted with each other, some distinctive economic and cultural traits emerged within Texas. While certainly containing several plantation regions, through the 1840s Texas as a whole grew closer but remained distinctive from Mississippi just as Virginia remained distinctive from South Carolina.[8]

Statistical sources suggest not only substantial growth in the economy but how this Atlantic conversion unfolded from the late 1820s to the late 1840s. The table below, for example, shows the leading sources of taxable wealth in 1846, the year the Republic of Texas officially ended.[9]

Taxable property of Texas	*1846*	*Constant $ (2013)*
Land	$ 27,520,223	$ 703,881,824
Slaves	$ 10,488,548	$ 268,264,480
Horses	$ 1,504,288	$ 38,475,015
Cattle	$ 1,510,950	$ 38,645,408
Misc. Property	$ 1,089,855	$ 27,875,106

Several observations jump from this table. Land, primarily farms, ranches, and land held for speculative purposes, dominated the list of major types of taxable wealth, but slaves came in second. What does that imply? The number of slaves increased from approximately 5,000 in 1837 to almost 40,000 shortly after annexation, a sure sign of movement toward a cotton-based Lower South model. In this model African Americans were human property and as such were taxed by the government of Texas, rented out, bought and sold, and used as collateral for loans as well as a source of labor. As was true of the United States, Texas Anglos turned other human beings into fungible commodities. In a bizarre and barbarous sense, an increase in slavery indicated economic growth. Using the increase in the number of slaves as a rough measure of economic growth, the economy grew eightfold over the life of the Republic. Economic growth also far outstripped population growth with the total population excluding Indians increasing from about 40,000 to 142,000 during the time of the Republic. Thus, the non-Indian population grew less than fourfold, meaning that average per capita wealth for free people increased although most Texans remained relatively poor by modern standards. Still, instead of struggling in the grip of some grim economic malaise, as often represented, the free population enjoyed improving conditions by 1847.[10]

Statistics can obscure as much as they reveal, however, and several important qualifications need to be made to this picture of economic growth and increasing prosperity. Population growth did not occur at an even pace each year or at the same rate in every county. The place and date of birth of children listed in the 1850 and 1860 censuses for Texas indicated that the non-Indian population grew relatively quickly from about 1833 to 1837 as prices for agricultural commodities increased. Even in the face of a sharp economic downturn, that momentum continued through 1839 as the economic collapse of 1837 pushed some Americans to try their chances in Texas. But population grew slowly from 1839 into 1844 as cotton prices slumped and Texans fought the headwinds of an unstable military and political future. Since part of the local economy depended upon population growth and the demand for livestock, corn, food crops, and labor that came with new arrivals, the years from 1839 to 1844 were tough times for both the export and the local economy. Once general economic conditions bottomed out and the chances of annexation to the United States brightened in 1844, overall non-Indian population and the slave population surged, especially in those counties with the best transportation links and best soil for the cultivation of cotton and other plantation crops. Obviously, as the Atlantic World went so went Texas. Moreover, as this surge occurred and prices for cotton, sugar, slaves, and land improved, wealth (especially as measured by slaveholding) increasingly concentrated in the top 20 percent or so of wealth holders and especially concentrated in the hands of the top 1 percent. By 1850, elites held as great a share of wealth and the political and social power that went with wealth as in any other part of the United States. So much for exceptionalism.[11]

For the other some 80 percent of the free, non-Indian population who lay outside the elite or near elite, rapid gains in wealth proved elusive, but they too probably benefitted from the upturn of the overall Atlantic economy after 1844 and if they owned land, the increased value of that land. While the gap between the rich and the less rich widened, almost every free person was a bit better off by the late 1840s, just as was true of much of the rest of the Atlantic World.[12]

For this other 80 percent of the population, livestock, not wheat, cotton, or sugar cane, typically provided a way to move beyond occasionally owning one or two slaves and growing corn, a bit of cotton or wheat, and food crops like sweet potatoes. Livestock brought entry to a larger market, and unlike cotton it could be consumed and used locally and regionally, insulating it a bit from the price shocks characteristic of cotton. Urbanization in Texas and the arrival of newcomers provided increased demand for all types of livestock within Texas. Outside of Texas, the sale of livestock and hides grew with urbanization and industrialization in the Atlantic World. As the demand for meat or leather in more urban and industrialized places increased, or as demand for horses and mules in the fast-growing agricultural regions of the Mississippi Valley increased, the economy of Texas rode up. When demand slackened, the Texas economy slowed. Indeed demand for livestock outside of Texas probably set a floor and a ceiling for livestock prices at the local level. Thus, even small-scale producers operating in a barter-based economy were in some respects connected to the Atlantic World market.

Livestock may have been a relatively small part of the recorded exports from Texas in some years, but either as part of trade that paid tariffs and taxes or as part of the often large illicit trade that avoided such duties, it offered a revealing look at the intricacies of the Texas economy. As the flow of stock (not to mention cotton and sugar) out of Texas and goods back into the region increased in scale and scope, larger-scale producers and dealers drew on the ever more interconnected financial markets of the United States and Western Europe. Moving increasing numbers of animals over greater distances often brought greater return per animal, but required a larger initial expenditure of capital. Such capital often came via New Orleans, the long-time destination point for Texas livestock and the central connecting node to the Atlantic World.[13]

By 1830, Tejanos and Indians as well as Anglos were closely linked to New Orleans and to Louisiana more broadly. As early as 1779 Tejanos drove herds of Texas cattle to the New Orleans area to help feed the troops of Bernardo de Galvez who led Spanish forces in their successful efforts to assist the Americans in their revolt against Britain. Texas horses and mules were probably marketed in the Crescent City even earlier than that. After Mexican independence, instead of trading with Central Mexico or even northern Mexico, Tejanos increasingly crossed the border to the United States to trade, even if Mexican authorities suppressed such trade. Martín de León and other Tejano ranchers and entrepreneurs also built ties to New Orleans. Long before 1830, many Indian groups in Texas also habitually sent hides, horses, and captives to Louisiana in exchange for firearms, metal implements, and other trade goods.[14]

Into the 1830s, cattle, horses, and hides joined cotton and other agricultural products taken to New Orleans and coffee, tobacco, cloth, metal implements, firearms, and other trade goods came back and were sold by merchants such as José Antonio Navarro in the San Antonio area and Samuel May Williams in the Anglo portions of Texas. After the Texas Revolution this connection with New Orleans increased dramatically as merchants who dealt in cattle, such as Francis Richard Lubbock, began business in Houston and Galveston. Navarro, Williams, and Lubbock all lived and did business in New Orleans before the Texas Revolution. Indeed cultural geographer Terry G. Jordan has argued that stockmen from the Carolinas, like Lubbock, learned more about Hispanic ranching techniques and culture in Louisiana than they did in Texas.[15]

Lubbock and Navarro grew increasingly involved in ranching and the cattle industry from 1830 to 1850 as cattle, hides, and horses moved to local markets and from Texas to New Orleans in greater numbers. As Lubbock put it, "At that time Texas furnished many cattle to New Orleans." Indeed, New Orleans served as the major trailhead and destination point for Texas cattle long before the more famous post-Civil War trailheads. In many ways, this was a carryover from the pre-1830 period and a good example of the blending of Anglo and Tejano customs and practices.[16]

As late as 1848, still taking advantage of the well-established New Orleans market, new emerging markets, and expanding local demand sparked by rapid population growth, the total value of horses and mules and the total value of cattle produced in Texas surpassed the value of cotton. In fact, in 1848 cattle alone were more valuable than any other agricultural or manufactured product. For most years from 1830 to 1850, cotton led all other exports from Texas, but the value of cattle indicated the economy was never simply export driven. The total dominance of cotton both in terms of value and percentage of Texans involved in its cultivation and marketing may have been right around the corner, but it had not yet arrived.[17]

Still for most of the years from 1830 to 1850, dreams of fortunes to be made growing and dealing in cotton captivated a large number of Texans. Cotton booms with glittering prospects of a rapid increase in wealth rolled through the South from the 1810s forward and certainly hit Texas by the 1820s. Even before the Revolution in those parts of Texas where cotton could be transported to market, those glittering opportunities encouraged southerners to move to Texas and take their chances on uncertain protection for slaves. After the Revolution, cotton moved in even larger amounts through Galveston and to New Orleans and the outside world. Cotton had no local manufacturing market and the use of by-products lay far in the future. Cotton's value depended entirely on transportation and export out of Texas. In that sense, it amplified existing economic ties to New Orleans and the Atlantic World, and merchants like Samuel May Williams used their connections to the broader economy to profit from the cotton trade. Moreover, to the extent that local demand for something like cattle depended upon the income from the export of cotton, swings in the price of cotton took the entire Texas economy up or down. What happened in New Orleans and the Atlantic World mattered even in a barter economy.[18]

Culture as well as economics tied Texas to New Orleans. After control of Louisiana passed from Spain back to France in 1800 and then to the United States in 1803, long-established patterns of trade continued and connections between the economy and culture of Texas and New Orleans grew stronger. Commenting on San Antonio in 1828, Jean Louis Berlandier argued: "In their gatherings, the women prefer to dress in the fashion of Louisiana, and by so doing, they participate both in the customs of the neighboring nation and of their own." A new border culture and economy emerged in parts of Texas over the years between the 1820s and 1840s, a culture and economy that blended the habits and culture found in Louisiana with those already in place in Texas. When Lubbock married his French-speaking wife, Adele, and then brought her from Louisiana to Texas in the mid-1830s, he provided a visible symbol of this ongoing connection and amalgamation. His wife and her family provided capital for some of Lubbock's business ventures and she inspired him to learn French. Lacking major cities or centers of finance and industry, through 1850 Texas remained closely tied to Louisiana.[19]

Glimmers of change appeared in the 1840s as the surge of Anglo and African American southerners made much of Texas more like Mississippi than Louisiana, and as rapidly increasing immigration from the Upper South and Central Europe created unique cultural and demographic pockets. Victory in the Mexican War also extended the effective control of Texas and the United States from the Nueces River south to the Rio Grande. This brought Texans north of the Nueces into closer contact with Spanish-speaking people who had long been more closely tied to Mexico than those who lived to their north and east. That transition, however, came immediately after the life of the Republic of Texas, and even after this transition, New Orleans remained the central market, major source of financing, and the key connecting point to the outside world.[20]

This last point requires elaboration. The capital and trade goods that came to Texas from New Orleans did not all originate there and the cotton, sugar, livestock, and hides that went to New Orleans did not all stop there. By 1850 New Orleans was the fifth largest and one of the fastest growing cities in the United States and the only city in the South with a population of over 100,000. The Mississippi River connected the city to the broad interior of the United States and stimulated commercial development and migration to the city. Moreover, the Atlantic linked New Orleans to New York, London, Havana, and the other major centers of trade, commerce, and finance in the Caribbean, American Northeast, and Western Europe. In the first decade of the nineteenth century, thousands of French-speaking migrants (whites, free persons of color, and slaves) displaced by the Haitian Revolution came to New Orleans either directly or after a stopover in Cuba. By 1810 New Orleans was among the most cosmopolitan and diverse cities in the United States. The pattern continued in the decades that followed and the city became a destination point for both German and Irish immigrants in the 1830s and 1840s. By 1850 foreign-born residents were a higher percentage of the total population of the city than native born whites or African Americans. New Orleans was a German and Irish city by 1850, but it also retained a large percentage of native-born whites and blacks who spoke French. Not only did a plurality of the people have non-Anglo roots, so did the bankers, financiers, and factors of New Orleans who connected much of the South to external markets and the laborers who built the transportation links that made New Orleans such a vibrant place.[21]

Galveston, initially developed in the mid-1830s and incorporated in 1839, soon emerged as a close copy and connecting link to New Orleans. Merchants with established ties to New Orleans, such as Lubbock and Williams, quickly relocated there. Trade and capital went back and forth between New Orleans and Galveston, and slowly either through New Orleans or eventually more directly the economic ties radiating out of Galveston reached New York, Havana, and Great Britain. Galveston's population grew increasingly diverse, and by 1850, Germans and a scattering of others born outside of the United States and Texas made up close to 50 percent of the free population. By that year the total Galveston population reached 4,117, passing San Antonio to become the largest city in Texas. Besides its diversity and status as one of only five Texas cities with a population over one thousand, Galveston differed from the rest of Texas in one other fundamental way. Slaves made up about 16 percent of its people as compared to 28 percent for the state as a whole.[22]

Galveston's status as a culturally diverse port fronting on the Atlantic World, a major distribution center, and the site of limited manufacturing also altered the nature of slavery in the Island City from the norm in other parts of Texas. Instead of closely supervised labor on relatively isolated plantations, slaves in Galveston had access to a constant stream of foreign ships, some with free blacks and opponents of slavery among the crews. The possibility of flight or insurrection seemed higher in Galveston to many local whites, but the profits of slavery probably dictated that, nonetheless, owners rented out slaves to work at the docks, in various small metalworking or manufacturing enterprises, as domestic help for the growing mercantile class, or as some other type of semi-skilled labor. Such slaves often came into daily contact with working-class Germans and Anglos, and perhaps class bound these groups together even if race drew them apart. Conflict between foreign-born and native-born free labor may also have given Galveston's slaves some opportunities lacking elsewhere. Such limited degrees of freedom from the strictest and harshest forms of slavery and white supremacy probably also existed in New Orleans and other major southern ports, but at any rate the status of Galveston's slaves provided another significant example of ties to New Orleans and to the Atlantic World.[23]

Just across Galveston Bay, however, lay among the largest concentrations of plantation slaves and the center of sugar cane cultivation in Texas. Here again Galveston resembled New Orleans in being a diverse and pluralistic center of population that profited from the commerce generated by nearby major slaveholding regions and serving as the connecting point to the outside world for an even more distant hinterland.[24]

Indeed, Galveston, again like New Orleans, developed close ties with the Caribbean and served as the center of the domestic and for a time the African slave trade in Texas. While surveying the reasons for immigrating to Texas in 1836, David B. Edward sang the praises and potential of Galveston, a city then very much still in the planning and promotion stage. He considered Galveston's harbor superior to that of New Orleans and even better suited for foreign commerce. As he put it, "The situation of Galveston for foreign commerce is very felicitous. The Gulf of Mexico is spread out before it; Cuba is near at hand; and all the islands of the West Indies are within a few days sail; as also the entire coast of Central America, of Venezuela, and of Columbia."[25]

Of the non-U.S. places listed by Edward, Cuba proved the most important to Galveston and to the nearby sugar producing region at the mouth of the Brazos River. As early as 1833, slaves captured in Africa and brought to Havana were sold to planters along the lower Brazos, and that trade continued through the close of the decade. Some small numbers of transported Africans may have been brought as slaves to scattered parts of Texas as late as the 1850s, but they lived in the most concentrated numbers near the lower Brazos. One historian estimated that a thousand or more enslaved Africans reached Brazoria County. That is half of a common estimate of the total number of slaves imported from Africa to Texas, and it offered another example of the connection of the greater Galveston area to Cuba, Africa, and the broader Atlantic basin. A more general trade with Havana, either directly or through New Orleans, also benefitted Galveston and the surrounding area. Hides, cattle, and foodstuffs went to Cuba. Slaves and trade goods came back. Havana also served as a routine stopping point on voyages to and from England.[26]

Over the course of the Republic, as Galveston emerged as a significant connecting point between Texas, New Orleans, and the Atlantic World, tentacles of trade and culture reached deeply into the Texas interior. Through Houston and more directly through traffic along the Gulf coast and up the lower Brazos and Colorado rivers Galveston's role as a central market grew larger. As the discussion of slaves from Africa indicated, a chief feature of this market was the buying and selling of human beings in and through Galveston. John S. Sydnor, often regarded as the largest slave dealer in Texas, called Galveston home and served as the city's mayor. Most close students of slavery in Texas insist that the majority of slaves were brought to the region with their masters, but as the Texas economy expanded, the market for additional slaves grew and most of these slaves came from the domestic slave trade. Many of these slaves came into Texas from New Orleans and through Galveston where they were auctioned to the highest bidder or sent on to the interior of Texas for sale by slave merchants. In 1854, Olmsted came upon a group of slaves near Victoria and described them as "consigned to some planter in the interior, probably by his factor in New Orleans, as part of the proceeds of his crop." Cotton and other commodities flowed out through Galveston and New Orleans. Slaves flowed in. Slave prices reflected the fluctuations of commodity prices and the availability of credit, and the price of slaves in Texas went up and down with the health of the larger economy and fluctuations in access to credit. Still slave prices trended up through the mid-1840s as commodity prices improved and Texans gained political stability through annexation. Higher prices for agricultural commodities and slaves, like higher numbers of slaves, heralded the return of general prosperity.[27]

Slave owners willingly paid this higher price for labor because land was cheap in comparison with other regions of the South and the price of cotton was rising. Inexpensive and fertile land, readily available slaves, and soaring cotton prices drove the Texas economy to new heights by 1850, setting the stage for an even more dynamic decade to follow and pushing Texas into the Lower South. Cotton's rise to dominance, however, required moving production away from the coast where torrential rains and numerous insects often limited crop yields. Moving too far from the coast or past the end of navigation on the often narrow and difficult to traverse Texas rivers, however, meant that you could not easily and cheaply get Texas cotton to market. Thus the highest production of cotton and the largest number of slaves were found in four regions of the Republic of Texas: an area in Northeast Texas that enjoyed access to New Orleans via the Red River, an area close to the Sabine River with access to New Orleans via the Gulf of Mexico, an area along the Trinity River north of Houston, and a larger area along the lower Colorado and Brazos rivers to the west and southwest of Galveston. In all four cases water transportation proved essential, but so did the existence of market centers that could store, finance, and transship the cotton and provide necessary supplies and equipment. As many observers recorded, primitive roads and the famed Texas mud could bog down the best of teamsters. Cotton production depended not just on good soil, slave labor, and knowledgeable growers, but also on the ability to connect to the outside world. This was true not only of planters who owned twenty or more slaves, but of smaller producers who often sold or bartered their cotton to larger producers. These larger producers then took the cotton on to market, usually dealing with merchants and cotton factors in Houston, Galveston, and New Orleans.[28]

This pattern of moving cotton to market was part of the customs and knowledge cotton growers brought with them from the Lower South. Those knowledgeable growers from the Lower South, moreover, brought experience with the cultivation of cotton with them, and they taught it as well as marketing patterns to others they encountered in Texas. Much of that knowledge concerned when to plant, what varieties of cotton to plant, how to cultivate or thin the cotton, when and how to harvest it, how to combat insects and bad weather, and perhaps of most importance how to brutally coerce or in a few cases creatively encourage the most efficient labor from slaves. Yet when to sell, how to secure capital, and how and when to invest in more land were also cultural traits as much as they were economic calculations. When farmers from Germany, the Upper South, or the Midwest took up cotton farming in Texas, a process occurred very similar to the acquisition of Mexican cattle ranching techniques by Anglos. One clear indicator of this process was the use of mules instead of horses or oxen in farming. Before the 1880s, most of the weeding and cultivation of cotton was done by hand with hoes, but early in the growing stage, some cultivation could be done with primitive implements drawn by either horses or mules. Preparation of the soil before planting was usually done during the Republic years with wooden plows tipped with iron or cast iron plows, and these could be pulled by oxen, horses, or mules. Farmers from the Lower South often favored the mule because they were smaller, stronger pound per pound, and more nimble around emerging cotton plants and in tight corners. They also typically lived longer and withstood more abuse than oxen or horses. Some claimed mules were smarter than horses or oxen, but whether that was true or not the use of the mule by Germans, those from the Upper South, and those from the Midwest to cultivate cotton was a sign of cultural transmission, just as was the use of the horse and rope by Anglo herdsmen. The transition from traditional draft animals to mules probably began in the 1840s in cotton producing counties with a growing number of migrants from the Gulf South.[29]

As the gradual use of the mule indicated, cotton growers of all cultural groups brought certain practices with them from their point of origin, but they pragmatically adapted to what their new locations demanded or what they observed worked best. In one important area, however, other Texans did not adopt the habits and practices of the Lower South before 1850. Germans, Mexicans, and those from the Upper South or Midwest never used slave labor with as much enthusiasm as Texans from South Carolina, Mississippi, and Alabama. Of course there were exceptions, but in the main these folk practiced a type of agriculture such as the cultivation of wheat or small scale cotton production that did not require large gangs of slaves, and they seldom owned more than two or three slaves. These slaves often lived with them or adjacent to them instead of in their own quarters, and the owners worked side by side with them. Germans and to some extent those from the northern border of the South also gained labor by hiring newcomers to the area. Germans commonly used relatives or newly arrived family friends as farm labor. These individuals often lived with the family and worked side by side for wages. After accumulating enough capital, they purchased land and farmed on their own.[30]

In essence, before 1850 crop selection, marketing, and agricultural practices changed more quickly than labor systems. Some of this reluctance to change may have derived from the lack of capital to purchase slaves, but in other cases, the culture of non-Lower South Texans overrode the pragmatic attraction of slavery and the examples of its extensive use. Undoubtedly, however, the influence of Mexico from the mid-1820s into the 1830s also allowed competing labor systems to flourish enough to resist the pull of slavery. The Mexican government took an increasingly hard line against slavery through the 1820s, but active intervention on slavery's behalf by prominent Tejanos and Anglos allowed the institution to persist in some form or fashion. Still, the Mexican government's lack of sympathy for slavery and its active recruitment of Germans and others from outside the Lower South created islands of limited use of slave labor combined with extensive use of wage labor. Obviously Galveston was one such center of mixed free and slave labor, but other free-labor islands established before 1850 made parts of Texas more like Appalachia, the Upper South, or German dominated areas of the Midwest than like Mississippi. To take the German example as the most distinctive case, settlement began in the early 1830s and continued through the Civil War and beyond. News of a welcoming culture and economic opportunity in Texas spread through German-speaking regions at a time when wages and landholdings were shrinking in many parts of Central Europe. Because particular locations in Texas were increasingly familiar, a place where other German speakers had found success and limited competition from slave labor, Germans crossed the Atlantic to Texas by the thousands. Midwesterners and those from some parts of the Upper South followed a like pattern.[31]

These extensive pockets of free labor, especially in rural areas, and the early official encouragement of free labor by the Mexican government, marked Texas through 1850 as distinctive among the slave holding regions of the South. Even in a region like Austin or Colorado counties where German immigrants lived nearby to slaveholders, residents of the large German settlements established in the 1830s preferred a more traditional German form of labor and did not rush toward slavery. This provided opportunities for enterprising Germans such as the Leyendecker extended family to immigrate to Texas, and it provided a very pragmatic reason why Germans clustered together. They worked as hands and skilled labor for each other.[32]

In urban areas and in the major sugar and molasses producing counties, slavery's growth and profitability may have actually created opportunity for skilled free labor. Sugar and molasses production required expensive and relatively complicated machinery and that in turn meant that producers with the largest acreage and most numerous slaves made greater profit per acre because they kept their equipment in steady use. Operating, repairing, and maintaining the mills, boilers, and other equipment in Brazoria, Matagorda, and Ft. Bend counties often fell to free labor, sometimes provided by German immigrants or former residents of the Upper South. In Galveston and Houston free labor built, operated, and maintained cotton presses and other equipment needed to move agricultural commodities to distant markets. Free labor, often skilled German labor, built the houses, office building, warehouses, and wharves springing up as the economy grew. In San Antonio and elsewhere free labor built and ran the grain mills, breweries, and other manufacturing enterprises. As in the case of German farmers who hired German hands, German mill and brewery owners hired other Germans. Demographic patterns fixed before 1850 created a welcoming atmosphere for free labor in parts of Texas, but so too did the realities of slavery in the region. High demand for slaves in the cotton and sugar cane fields and climbing prices for slaves created labor niches for free labor in an urban and sugar-based economy. Essentially, pockets of the Texas economy offered higher wages than available in Central Europe or the Upper South, and labor flowed to Texas as part of a classic process in which across the Atlantic World high-wage areas drew labor from low-wage areas until wages equalized. This was true even in sugar producing areas highly dependent upon slavery.[33]

Except for a few place names such as Sugarland, Texas, memory of the role of sugar production and sugar processing has largely vanished from Texas. Yet around 1840, many large planters along the lower Brazos and Colorado rivers began to shift from the production of cotton to sugar cane. Cotton prices had plunged down in 1837, again in 1839, and again in the early 1840s sending the most entrepreneurial planters looking for alternatives. Torrential rains near the coast also made cotton cultivation unreliable. Prices were more stable and growing conditions more favorable in the low-lying areas for sugar cane than for cotton. By 1848, the combined value of sugar and molasses, the two products made from sugar cane on Texas plantations, surpassed the value of cotton or corn. Only cattle had a higher value that year.[34]

Nothing more clearly demonstrated the connection of Texas to the Atlantic World than the production and processing of sugar cane.

The methods used to grow cane and manufacture sugar and molasses came from the Caribbean either via the greater New Orleans area or directly from Cuba and other sugar-producing centers. The machines used to manufacture sugar came from New York. While Texans consumed some of the locally produced sugar and molasses, most of it went through Galveston to New Orleans or other distribution points in the United States or the Caribbean. Intriguingly, since many of the slaves used in the cultivation of sugar cane came from Africa they may have learned cultivation techniques during their stopover in the Havana area. Almost none of the major planters along the lower Brazos or Colorado had previous experience with sugar cane, but they clearly understood the opportunities the new crop presented, and they knew to look to Louisiana and the Caribbean for the information they needed. Local soil type, rainfall patterns, and available transportation combined with market conditions in the Atlantic World to lead them to new endeavors.[35]

Especially in the case of sugar cane, but to some extent in every phase of the economy from 1830 to 1850, old world habits met new world opportunities and challenges. Those opportunities usually came because of increased connections to the Atlantic World, and the challenges were often met by extensive borrowing by one cultural group from another group. Out of that came a world shaped by place, time, and interaction between groups. By 1850 slavery, cotton, and sugar increasingly united Texas with Mississippi and other Lower South states, but to argue that it was identical by that point would grossly oversimplify the economy and culture of the state. It would overlook not only many distinctive characteristics on the macro level, but also the details of life in each household and in each section of Texas.

Potatoes offered a telling example of fluidity, integration, continuity, and transformation on the household level, and a counterpoint to the rapid adaptation, transformation, and innovation demanded by sugar cane. Potato consumption and production varied across the southern United States, the source of the majority of new Texans from 1830 to 1850. Most southerners grew far more sweet potatoes than white potatoes, however, and this was particularly true in the states that bordered the Gulf of Mexico where the sweet potato was an important food source. In contrast, sweet potatoes were virtually unknown in Central Europe and in Northern Mexico, the other main sources of the Texas population between 1830 and 1850. Instead, especially in Germany, white potatoes were a major crop both for home consumption and for sale and barter. By 1850, however, Germans in the eastern part of Texas, with a climate much like other Gulf South states, grew about five pounds of sweet potatoes for every pound of white potatoes. This compared with Texans from the South who grew about ten pounds of sweet potatoes for every pound of white potatoes. Significantly, Germans in the eastern counties of Texas lived surrounded by both white and black southerners and frequently observed the cultivation of sweet potatoes. Cultural transformation in Texas from 1830 to 1850 resulted as much from German and southern families living in close proximity as it did from soil type, climate, and a pragmatic assessment of yields per acre.

Still, German Texans never shifted completely to the sweet potato and always grew a higher percentage of white potatoes than Texans from the South. Moreover, such groups as the Cat Spring Horticultural Society continually experimented with ways to grow more and better white potatoes in eastern Texas. As German Texan farmers experimented successfully with white potatoes and as a growing number of German immigrants settled around them, the cultivation of white potatoes increased. By 1880, German Texans in the eastern counties grew as many white potatoes as they grew sweet potatoes.[36]

On the micro level as well as the macro level then, culture, demography, and movement across borders mattered. More specifically, proximity to other cultural and demographic groups and the pace of migration across those borders determined household economies and localized cultural practices. In a time when most Texans were born elsewhere they brought with them more than favored crops, methods of production, sources of labor, ways of making a living, and patterns of buying, selling, and financing. They brought more than an ability to adapt to new market opportunities and the challenges of a new environment. They brought dietary preferences and basic ways of constructing their household economies that often persisted for decades and separated them from other Texans. If challenged by soil, climate, and market forces and exposed to people of other cultures, however, economic practices could shift rapidly, but as the case of white potatoes demonstrated, they seldom shifted completely. If over time demographic and cultural realities altered and if experimentation or changes in the market opened up new possibilities, Texans could shift again. In the process, their culture as well as their economy changed, but long after 1850, especially on the household and community level, Texas remained a place of cultural islands not a unified and homogeneous world. Moving down to the household and regional level then demonstrated persistence of traits brought to Texas as well as change.[37]

From 1830 to 1850, six types of cultural islands with distinct economic practices and household economies existed in Texas. Five of these were relatively homogenous: Lower South, Upper South, German, Comanche/Apache, and Tejano. A sixth type, a collection of two or more of those cultural types living in close proximity also existed, and not surprisingly change occurred most rapidly in these more heterogeneous zones. The conflict and cooperation between groups, their borrowing back and forth, and the relative size and immigration flow of each group created differences in the various heterogeneous islands. By 1850, however, they were becoming much more the norm for Texas, especially urban Texas and in areas with recent and rapid migration from the Lower South. A more in-depth look at representative samples of the homogenous and heterogeneous islands suggests how this process unfolded.[38]

Near the border with Louisiana and Arkansas a string of counties from Harrison, Marion, and Cass south and west to Cherokee and Rusk, increasingly resembled the Lower South. By 1850, more slaves lived in Harrison than any other county in Texas and plantation agriculture and cotton cultivation set the tone of everyday life. While Harrison County, with good transportation routes available down the Red and Mississippi rivers to New Orleans, enjoyed the fastest establishment of a Lower South model, almost all the other neighboring counties experienced growth in slavery and cotton cultivation after 1830. Very few Anglos from the Upper South or other parts of the United States lived in this region, and not surprisingly, it came the closest to resembling Mississippi or the other Gulf states in its culture and economy. Before 1850, the transformation to a slave dominated place also benefitted from greater distance from the Mexican border. Unlike regions to the south and west, Harrison County-area slaves could not easily reach freedom across the Mexican border and slavery was considered a safe and remunerative investment. While containing some large plantations with holdings of fifty or more slaves, the Harrison County area also contained plantations with ten to fifty slaves, farms with a few slaves or no slaves, and various types of stock raising enterprises that often utilized public land.[39]

Some 60 percent or more of the region's slaves lived on plantations with more than ten slaves. As was true of slaveholding regions throughout the South, plantation masters mouthed notions of paternalism or patriarchy claiming that whites and blacks lived as one extended family headed by the male landowner. In reality, masters often practiced an extreme form of capitalism that grotesquely exploited labor. Conditions varied, of course, from master to master. Some masters fed and clothed their slaves relatively well, because of either religious beliefs, a sense of empathy, or a managerial choice that healthy and relatively happy slaves had more children and worked harder. In pursuit of profit, other masters routinely beat and tortured slaves to ensure maximum productivity. In this, they copied methods perfected in the 1820s and 1830s in Mississippi and Alabama where productivity per slave on cotton plantations increased dramatically. Cotton growers worked their slaves in gangs doing repetitive tasks with one of the hardest working slaves as the pacesetter. Those who failed to keep up were warned by the white overseer and then whipped if they still lagged behind. Again, in pursuit of profit, some slave owners provided only the barest of essentials in terms of diet and clothing, and they forced women into the fields until the moment they delivered children and soon after their birth. In any case, assertions that slavery existed in some pre-capitalist universe not driven in large part by profit maximization and a frenetic struggle for ever more efficient production were and are self-serving and delusional. For even the most benign masters, coerced and unpaid labor equaled profit. Former slave Jacob Branch of Chambers County summed up slavery succinctly and accurately as "pretty rough," and argued that "every plantation have to answer for itself."[40]

Economic activity on cotton plantations varied from the norm found among stock raisers and on smaller scale farms. The plantation master and mistress were more often managers instead of workers with men managing the fields and various other enterprises. Women managed the home and the production of food and clothing in the home. Women, however, often managed activities outside the home in the absence of their husbands. This included giving orders to white male overseers. Children might work in the fields or the home, especially on smaller plantations, but they also were trained in managerial responsibilities and were reasonably well educated. Slaves enjoyed a small measure of freedom from direct supervision by owners and managers and sometimes were allowed to have their own gardens, but this was typically less common than in sugar producing areas. Slave women and children worked in the fields, but they also might have specialized tasks. Indeed some level of specialization was common among the slaves of larger plantations. Women and girls might provide household help. Boys might help with the stock. Men might work as mechanics or blacksmiths. As this specialization suggested many planters sought a large measure of economic self-sufficiency with their own gins and foodstuff production, but seldom met this goal. Food, clothing, and supplies also came from their neighbors or more distant sources.[41]

Some Anglo neighbors operated smaller farms where slaves often worked side by side with their masters growing cotton and corn. These slaves were under close supervision most of the time. Families, slave and free, were the basic unit of production. Women often had specialized tasks such as cooking, cleaning, and the making of clothing, but they went into the fields in peak seasons. White women usually did less fieldwork than black women, but the labor of women proved essential for the profitable operation of farms. Children also went to the fields early with boys helping their fathers and girls their mothers. Again, fieldwork fell more heavily on African American children, but all children worked at a fairly early age, and the need for farm labor typically encouraged large families.[42]

For slave and free, rich and poor the normal diet revolved around flour, coffee, and other basics brought in from New Orleans or from the wheat producing regions of Texas. Corn produced locally and ground into meal was consumed in some form or fashion at almost every meal. In some cases and in some times of the year cornmeal was almost the sole source of nourishment. Pork produced by the stock raisers or on the farms and plantations, locally raised beef, wild game, and sweet potatoes or other produce grown on area farms or plantations added to the food supply. Relatively little attention was given to the production of dairy products, probably because of the hot climate and difficulty in storing and preserving milk. Chicken and egg production supplemented the diet, but was not as common as in other regions of Texas.[43]

Stock raisers also typically grew corn for human and animal consumption and they sometimes had gardens. They used free range methods most associated with South Carolina, and did not use the horse and lariat that Olmsted found common in other parts of Texas. Instead, they often used dogs to help them herd cattle and hogs. As in the case of small-scale farmers, women and children had specialized tasks but when demands for labor were high they worked alongside men. In some ways, however, stock raisers existed in a type of semi-subsistence economy where women and children played a vital role. They made the clothing, preserved the food, tended the garden, and thus minimized buying, selling, and bartering in the marketplace.[44]

Even stock raising families, however, were closely connected to farmers and planters in the local economy. Planters depended on stock raisers and farmers to provide the foodstuffs they did not produce on their own plantations or import. Farmers often depended on larger planters to gin and market their cotton in New Orleans. Plantations provided a market for surplus livestock. Before 1850, a few mules, horses, and especially barrels of flour moved from the Upper South region to the Harrison County area, but that cross regional trade was limited by transportation difficulties. Instead, New Orleans and local neighborhoods were the main hubs of economic activity in the Lower South communities.

Into the 1830s, these Lower South counties had been the home of numerous Indian groups including the Caddo and the Cherokee. Starting in about 1810, the Cherokee drifted into East Texas from Arkansas and the Southeast, and even those who came to Texas or Arkansas to preserve a remnant of their traditional ways had been steadily assimilated into the Anglo/African culture of the Carolinas, Georgia, and Alabama. They often owned slaves, had intermarried with whites, sometimes grew cotton and had begun to abandon some traditional forms of behavior. In that sense, they were among the earliest of nineteenth century migrants to Texas from the Lower South. They generally sought peace with Anglos, but when forced to fight to protect what they viewed as their land were a well-armed threat to Anglo expansion. In the late 1830s, following the orders of Mirabeau B. Lamar, the president of the Republic of Texas, the Cherokee along with most other Indian people were violently driven out of East Texas. Some 100 Cherokees were killed in a battle near Tyler, Texas, in the summer of 1839 and almost all remaining native people east of the Trinity River were forced north across the Red River into what is now Oklahoma. Most historians argue that the opportunity to profit from growing cotton on the fertile land occupied by the Cherokee motivated their deadly removal by Anglos. Thus instead of living alongside and trading with Indians as had been common earlier in the Lower South, the expansion of the Atlantic World cotton economy motivated something akin to ethnic cleansing in the Lower South areas of Texas. Lamar, a native of Georgia, avid defender of slavery, and later a keen exponent of secession, personified this trend. By 1839, for Lamar and others influenced by a Lower South culture and dreams of the expansion of slavery and cotton, Indian expulsion was the only possible course of action for a good white southerner.[45]

Meanwhile to the northwest of former Cherokee territory and of Harrison County and other Lower South counties an economic and cultural island that resembled the Upper South or even the lower Midwest grew steadily from the 1820s on. From Lamar County over to

Dallas County wheat and to some extent oat cultivation and stock raising on a more intensive scale set the area apart from the Lower South. Limited transportation, not soil or climate, prevented the cultivation of cotton. This held true through the mid-1850s when Daniel Strickland writing of Denton County pointed out: "The soil appears well adapted to the raising of cotton, but on account of the distance to market it is not cultivated." The climate and soil, however, also favored the cultivation of wheat, and that remained the dominant crop until the arrival of railroads in the post-bellum period. Still migrants came to the region in part for those very reasons. They were used to growing wheat and it was part of their culture.[46]

These migrants established a way of life different from Lower South Texans. Slaves were relatively uncommon with only 207 in Dallas County in 1850. Instead, often following an Ohio Valley or Missouri model, locals mixed wheat cultivation with raising cattle, horses, and hogs sometimes with the use of pens and fenced pastures. They also occasionally raised mules for sale or barter. As was typical of the Upper South, however, horses were generally used for plowing and fieldwork instead of the oxen and mules favored in other regions of Texas, and in almost all these counties, the value and number of horses far outstripped the value and number of mules or in most cases cattle. This more intensive form of stock raising occasionally entailed feeding corn, oats, or hay to the stock. Settlers drove some cattle to the Indian reservations north of the Red River and by 1850 also sold their surplus flour there.[47]

Wheat and oat cultivation led to a far different home life than cotton. Typically, wheat and oat producers utilized more machines and required less hand labor, although most machines may not have been brought into the region until the late 1840s. Thus, as Dallas County demonstrated, small-grain growers required fewer slaves and like the Germans may have used newly arrived relatives for labor. If farmers owned slaves, they usually owned fewer than five and slaves worked on specific tasks instead of in gangs. Farms also tended to be more balanced with corn and wheat grown in different seasons in the same fields. Newly sprouted wheat, typically grown over the winter, could also be used to graze horses, mules, and cattle at least in the early stages of its growing cycle. Farm families also strove to feed themselves with what they produced in their fields, gardens, and orchards. Like many Texas farm folk, wheat growers also butchered their own hogs and cattle. Here once again women and children provided essential labor. They maintained the gardens, herded stock, pitched in at butchering time, and preserved the food. Families were often large with six, seven, eight or more children common. Houses were often crude and crowded, but as one old settler remembered, without the work of women homes would have been "fit habitations" only for "owls, bats, and all kinds of vermin."[48]

Limited transportation made self-sufficiency necessary and improving houses difficult. While not totally removed from the market, they were more removed than the Harrison County cotton producers who enjoyed easy access to water routes to New Orleans. In contrast, as J. T. Allen remembered, residents of the Honey Grove area on the border between Fannin and Lamar counties used Jefferson, a town more than 125 miles to the east, as their market center. Jefferson in those days enjoyed water connections to New Orleans, but according to Allen for decades everything was "hauled from this point by an ox team attached to ox wagons, and those trains could be seen for miles hauling supplies from Jefferson and returning with loads of skins and products of the land." While many of these Upper South counties lay just to the south of the Red River, snags, sand bars, and various other obstacles made that river virtually impassable above Shreveport. Thus, ox carts to Jefferson and water transportation from there to Shreveport and on to New Orleans were the only viable route to the Gulf of Mexico.[49]

That distance and degree of difficulty in transporting agricultural products made wheat and the milling of flour ideal economic activities, and wheat and flour shaped the culture and economy of the region in far different ways than cotton. Wheat, once milled into flour, commanded a higher price per pound and was less bulky than cotton. Those characteristics eased the burden of difficult and costly transportation, but also eventually led to higher levels of urbanization and industrialization in the region. Dallas first emerged as a milling center, and when the mills were not producing flour, their machinery could be harnessed for other purposes. Sawmills also were frequently found adjacent to grist and flour mills in the region. Fabricating and repairing mill equipment, threshers, and harvesters helped develop a capable workforce and machine tool capacity. In this sense before the introduction of cottonseed-oil mills in the 1890s the spin offs from wheat production outstripped those from cotton, and that made for a more diversified local economy. It bears repeating, however, that before 1850 limited transportation, usually by ox cart over dirt trails, slowed the marketing of flour and added an extra expense. Much of the flour and all of the oats were consumed in or near where they were grown and milled. The rest went either north to the Indian reservations or to Jefferson.[50]

Allen's mention of skins hauled to Jefferson suggested that hunting and the tanning of cattle and buffalo hides added to the local economy. Early settlers found plentiful game in the river bottoms and more forested areas of the Upper South region, and buffalo could be found on the plains in the 1830s and 1840s. They also routinely butchered cattle for their own consumption and tanned the hides. The game and beef added to their food supply. The hides and furs not used locally went to Jefferson and on to New Orleans. Again only items relatively compact and high in value made the cost of transportation worthwhile.[51]

Thus before 1850, the Upper South portion of Texas lay distantly connected to New Orleans and the cattle, cotton, or sugar centered world of so much of the rest of Texas. Yet hides, flour, machines, and basic supplies still moved back and forth between New Orleans, Jefferson, and the Lamar and Fannin County region. Cotton, however, did not travel that long and costly route, meaning fewer slaves lived in the region and the basic culture brought from the Upper South only slowly changed. Full integration into an Atlantic economy and the spread of cotton awaited the post-bellum arrival of railroads. As that happened, like so much of the rest of Texas the Lamar and Fannin County region evolved into a Lower South cultural world, but that lay ahead in 1850.[52]

To the southwest of the Upper South counties in the 1840s, a band of counties from Comal to Mason increasingly filled up with German immigrants. In many ways, family activities in these counties resembled those in other Texas counties. Similar to the situation in Upper South counties families here did not grow much cotton, but instead grew wheat or corn and raised stock. Each family supplied much of its own labor, and women, men, girls, and boys worked in the fields. Distance and reliance on ox carts to reach major trade centers and the coast limited economic activity. While they did not commonly use horses or mules for plowing in the pre-Civil War era, they did use oxen, a draft animal common in Lower South and Tejano areas. Germans also seem to have picked up very early and perhaps on their way from the coast to their new homes, the habits and practices of Lower South/Tejano ranching. They soon had herds of Longhorns, used ropes, and herded from horseback. As in other Texas ranching areas cattle offered Germans their surest and steadiest connection to the economy of the Atlantic World. Indeed, after 1850 ranching emerged as the primary economic activity in many German areas in western Texas. In significant ways, however, German Texans in the west differed from Upper South and Lower South Texans, especially in the density of their settlements, the specifics of their labor systems, their experimentation with different horticultural endeavors, and their integration into the Comanche economy.[53]

In 1844 on the eve of annexation, a group of German nobles organized as the Verein zum Schutze deutscher Einwander in Texas began transporting German speakers to Texas. By 1847 when the Verein went bankrupt, almost 8,000 Germans had arrived in Texas, and Comal and Gillespie counties had emerged as centers for their settlement. Other organized efforts and immigrants coming on their own filled the surrounding areas with German speakers by 1850. Most came from parts of Central Europe where farm families clustered in villages and walked out to their fields, and they continued this practice in New Braunfels, Castroville, and Fredericksburg. Indeed, New Braunfels in 1850 was one of the few cities in Texas with a population of over a thousand. This pattern did not hold beyond the mid-1850s in part because land holdings grew larger, increasing the distance to their fields and pastures for most families. Still the early clustering created economic and cultural opportunities. Grist and sawmills flourished. Newspapers and schools grew in importance. Closer proximity encouraged hiring free labor and trade and bartering in fruit, vegetables, wine, and beer. Specialization in blacksmithing, carpentry, wagon making, barrel making, and other such skilled trades also increased. In this microclimate, a relatively sophisticated economy grew that created a local market for farmers, tradesmen, and laborers. While they still depended on oxcart trains to San Antonio and the coast for many of their supplies, trade, goods, and money circulated more rapidly and in greater volume in these local areas than in most parts of Texas.[54]

As in the Upper South counties, slaves were scarce in these western German counties, but it may have been as much by choice as because of barriers to plantation agriculture. Writing in the mid-1850s, D. A. Rees of Kerr County declared: "Our German inhabitants are mostly opposed to slavery." Germans in Boerne, Sisterdale, and Comfort, at the time in Kerr County, had fled Central Europe to escape political chaos in the 1840s and they probably brought with them a more fully developed opposition to slavery on political and ideological grounds. This fit nicely with the German tendency to hire their nieces and nephews and to house them in their own homes when they arrived from Europe. As was true farther east, free labor filled the labor requirements of most German families and German-owned businesses. These laborers were often in transition, saving their money until they could start their own farms and businesses.[55]

Olmsted, always glad to see examples of free labor competing successfully with slave labor, lavished praise on the Germans in West Texas for shunning slavery, but he praised their food even more effusively. To hear him tell it, the poor man went without a decent meal from the time he crossed the border into Texas from Louisiana until he hit the German areas in western Texas. In Medina County, he came upon a German family with "a large kitchen garden, in which was growing a greater quantity and variety of vegetables than I have seen in any planter's garden, with two exceptions, at the South." While Olmsted had a special fondness for Texas Germans, other contemporaries supported his observation that they customarily had large gardens where they grew vegetables unseen in other parts of Texas. Germans typically planted two gardens, one in the early spring and another in the late summer or early fall. Women and girls usually worked the gardens and preserved what they produced. Of course, they grew sweet potatoes, something they picked up quickly, but cabbage, kohlrabi, turnips, peas, onions, leeks, garlic, parsley, spinach, and other greens could often be found. White potatoes, however, often proved even more difficult to grow in the western German counties then to the east and until the 1870s were usually imported. Germans also experimented with numerous fruit trees before settling on peaches as the most reliable fruit crop. They also gathered wild pecans. In New Braunfels and nearby areas, however, vegetables, fruit, and nuts not only were consumed at home they were sold in San Antonio, perhaps to other Germans. Dietary preferences translated into profit, and the price commanded by fresh vegetables, fruit, and nuts justified the cost and difficulty of transportation. Thus even if they did not grow large amounts of cotton, vegetables, fruit, and nuts offered German farm families another avenue for entering a wider economy.[56]

That wider economy also entailed trade with the Comanche who still controlled much of Texas just to the west, south, and north of the German settlements. Germans pursued peace with the Comanche very early on, and the Indians evidently needed or benefitted from their business. Germans purchased or bartered for horses, mules, venison, and other game. Once their farms were operating they sold or traded corn and other foodstuffs to the Comanche who depended on trade to supply them the carbohydrates required for a balanced diet. They also soon entered into the well-established Comanche hide trade and became a conduit for Comanche deer and buffalo hides. Germans benefitted from this trade because they pursued peace, and the Comanche conceived of them as being a different people from Anglo Americans or Tejanos. In the 1850s,

Theodore Sprecht and other early settlers complained openly about the Texas government and the U.S. army ruining the trade and close relationship between Germans and the Comanche, indicating the past importance of their close connection.[57]

These more homogenous German counties to the west of San Antonio and Austin offered a telling insight into the process of crossing borders in Texas. Germans picked up some Anglo and Tejano practices very quickly, especially cattle ranching, the growing of sweet potatoes, and some limited experimentation with cotton. Yet the greater density of their settlements, their resistance to the use of slave labor, their marketing of garden crops, and their trade with the Comanche varied from the Anglo and Tejano norms. Because of their relative isolation and the homogeneity of their settlements, these German traits persisted long after 1850.[58]

To the north, south, and west of the German counties lay a large swath of territory controlled by either the Comanche or the Apache. Like the Cherokee, after 1830 the Comanche and their Apache rivals faced increased pressure from the advance of Anglo settlements in Texas. Yet unlike the Cherokee, they maintained a presence in Texas and existed as a distinct cultural island until about 1880. Comanches in the 1830s and 1840s participated in a lively and vibrant economy in which they raided in Northern Mexico and some parts of Texas, hunted buffalo and deer in their home region, and then traded for or purchased weapons, tools, and food supplies from those they trusted in Texas, New Mexico, and the area north of the Red River. The Comanche very seldom grew crops of any type, but women did occasionally gather edible plants and nuts. That, along with the foodstuffs gained by trade, tribute, and raiding, gave them a balanced diet that allowed for mobility, good health, and a relatively high birth rate. Indeed despite repeated cholera epidemics, thanks in part to integrating others into their group, the Comanche still numbered about 25,000 in 1830.[59]

Mobility allowed the various branches of the Comanche to maintain gigantic horse herds, herds so large that they could not long remain in one place without depleting the grass that fed the horses. Mobility also allowed them to follow buffalo herds and preserve their meat while processing their hides. Mobility, at least as long as their numbers remained at 1830 levels, also made their raids and military actions difficult to counter by their often less mobile enemies. This military effectiveness, in turn, kept their access to buffalo herds and grasslands open.

By 1830 buffalo hide processing consumed more and more labor and encouraged the Comanche to turn captives into slaves. Before the spread of African American slaves into Louisiana and Texas, the Comanche took captives on their raids and sold or traded those captives through intermediaries to New Orleans or smaller mercantile centers. Many of those captives were Apache but others were New Mexicans or Tejanos. Traditionally, however, some women and children taken as captives often became part of the band. By 1830, the Comanche had modified this tradition. Some captives could still eventually become fully Comanche as was famously true of Cynthia Ann Parker, the Anglo mother of Comanche chief Quanah Parker. Yet more and more women and children taken as captives were simply slaves who processed buffalo hides or tended the large horse herds. In all likelihood, here was another case in which the expansion of the Atlantic World market economy fostered the growth and spread of an ever harsher and more coercive form of slavery.[60]

Unlike some East Texas Indians, Comanche women, such as Cynthia Ann Parker, did not enjoy an elevated status, but they were essential to the decision-making process of each band and to the group's economy. As in the case of the move to something more akin to Anglo/African slavery, the status of women may have declined as the importance of raiding, war, and hide production increased. Wealthier males often had multiple wives by 1830, and the line between wife number four or five and slaves may have been thin. Still in the 1830s and 1840s, women provided much of the labor to turn buffalo into trade goods, and they maintained the food supply. Since the Comanche frequently moved their camps, women spent much time packing and setting up camps, and when adult males were away hunting or on raids, they along with older men, boys, and girls tended the horse herds and stood watch against possible raids by their rivals. Clearly all Comanche were influenced by both Tejano and Anglo cultures, adapting the use of the horse and European-developed weapons, tools, and clothing to their own uses and responding to changes in Atlantic World trade patterns. Yet if anything, they grew more nomadic and moved away from even limited production of crops and manufacturing of weapons. They traded or raided for grains and other sources of carbohydrates as well as firearms. They herded horses but not cattle, depending instead on buffalo. Their culture changed because of the presence of other groups in Texas and their connections to the Atlantic World, but as in the case of the Germans, they retained significant cultural traits through 1850. They certainly fit into broader trade patterns and helped other groups turn a profit in the Atlantic World economy. Still, except for the Germans, most other Texans regarded the Comanche as enemies to be killed or expelled.[61]

Certainly the Apache regarded the Comanche as enemies, and by 1830 the two groups had a very long history of raiding and attacking each other. Interdependent in many ways, each defined themselves as not the other and each needed to raid the other. Yet they also had distinct cultural characteristics. Most Apache in Texas were Lipan and largely set apart from other Apache groups. They generally lived to the south and east of the Comanche and sometimes migrated into Northern Mexico. Like the Comanche, the Lipan absorbed other groups into their bands including the shattered remnants of various Texas Indian peoples. Yet unlike the Comanche, Lipan women often either cultivated small amounts of corn and other crops or they gathered food from the wild. While the Lipan hunted buffalo, by 1830 they were not as intensively involved in the buffalo trade as the Comanche who drove them from the best hunting spots. They also had a long association with the Spanish settlements of Texas, Mexico, and New Mexico where they took captives and were taken as captives. In both cases, captives over time became part of the Tejano and Lipan population. Lipan leaders often spoke Spanish and during the revolution against Spain that began in 1810 served with one side or the other. After Mexican independence in 1821, they entered a long period of alternating among raiding, trading, and working for the people of Mexico's far northern frontier. While it is difficult to gage the exact Lipan population, in 1840 the group probably numbered between 600 and 900. Despite being a far smaller group than the Comanche, they remained a people to be reckoned with through the Civil War, and after the war they probably slowly merged with the Tejano and Mexican population on both sides of the Rio Grande. In this way, their influence continued after the end of a Comanche presence in Texas.[62]

Despite the antipathy of most other Texas groups for the Lipan and the Comanche and despite the tendency to ignore their contributions to the economy and culture of antebellum Texas, like the other residents of the cultural islands they were part of the Atlantic World, part of their own worlds, and contributors to change among other groups. Some historians have argued, for example, that the level of violence directed at African Americans by Anglos after the Civil War originated in part in Anglos' constant struggle with the Comanche and Lipan. Other Texas groups probably adopted methods of war and hunting from the Comanche and Lipan, and the Lipan in particular were often part of Spanish, Mexican, Tejano, and later Anglo military campaigns. Indeed it appears increasingly likely that the Comanche and Lipan influenced the outcome of military campaigns, and the constant raiding by these two groups in

Northern Mexico made U.S. victory in the Mexican War all the simpler. Obviously we cannot understand the economic and cultural development of Texas west of Austin and south of San Antonio after 1830 without understanding the Comanche and Lipan[63].

Nowhere was the influence of the Comanche and Lipan more apparent than in the most clearly Tejano region—a cluster of counties between the Nueces River and the Rio Grande. While Tejano ranching operations, trade, and commerce probably expanded overall through 1850, Tejano communities hardest hit by Indian raids declined. As mentioned, however, Lipan often lived, worked, and merged into the Tejano population. Other than this close association with the Lipan, Tejanos south of the Nueces lived in relative isolation from other Texans through 1850, and until the conclusion of the Mexican War probably considered themselves more a part of Mexico than of Texas. Not surprisingly, through the close of the nineteenth century this would be the most distinctively and thoroughly Tejano area in Texas. While they shared some common Texas connections to New Orleans, Tejanos in this region also traded with citizens of Northern Mexico, and cattle ranching, more completely than in any other region of Texas, powered their economy.[64]

Conflict between the Texas and the Mexican governments and persistent Indian raids led to considerable churn in the local economy—enough churn for some students of the area to suggest that the economy declined precipitously from 1830 to 1850. More likely, however, ranchers moved their herds and their families back and forth across the Rio Grande often enough to escape the record books, compounding the difficulty of accurately assessing economic activity. In fact, a more realistic outline of the Tejano territory and economic activity would include the south side of the Rio Grande as well as the north side.[65]

Before 1800, settlers from the interior of Mexico stocked and established ranches in the area between the Lower Rio Grande and the Nueces. Through the end of the Spanish colonial era, these stock raisers supplied beef and leather to the silver mines of Northern Mexico and like Tejanos in other sections of Texas slowly established ties with New Orleans. Expansion of the ranching economy continued through the Texas Revolution in 1836, but silver mining declined, robbing Tejanos along the Rio Grande of an outlet for the products of their ranches. Fortunately, Matamoros at the mouth of the Rio Grande expanded as a trade and export center and linked the region to the Atlantic World. By the 1830s cattle, hides, and wool went out of Matamoros, often to New Orleans or Cuba. Flour, tools, and fabric came in. Profits from mule trains and ox carts traveling from the interior to Matamoros bolstered the economy. As Matamoros grew, agriculture expanded slightly in the Lower Rio Grande, but cattle and to some extent sheep remained the primary driver of the economy. In that sense the region resembled the hinterland around Galveston. Cattle, hides, and wool moved out and foodstuffs, cloth, tools, and supplies moved in through a growing metropolis near the coast.

In important ways, however, the region clearly differed from the Galveston area, especially in the lack of a vibrant slave/plantation economy, the development of a salt trade, and habits and practices of ranching reflecting either the influence of coastal Mexico or the high plains of the northern interior instead of Anglo influences. Tejanos grew corn, beans, peppers, and other crops, but on a fairly small scale probably because of the lack of adequate rainfall and the availability of wheat from Northern Mexico. Slavery played almost no role in the economy. Salt as well as cattle were exchanged for the wheat and other commodities needed in the region, and salt deposits were taxed by first the Spanish and then the Mexican government through the mid-1840s. Cattle tended to be rounded up monthly instead of twice a year as was more common in Anglo areas, and sheep raising and cattle raising often complimented each other with weather patterns, the availability of grass, and market conditions dictating the shift in emphasis from one to the other. This move back and forth between cattle and sheep distinguished the region from all other stock-raising regions in Texas prior to 1850, and it probably was a result of diffusion from the plateau region of Northern Mexico. Not surprisingly further up the Rio Grande around Laredo sheep became even more common. Nearer the coast, ranching techniques more clearly resembled those found on the Gulf Coast of Mexico and it was here that the well-known Longhorn cattle developed. This hardy breed could travel long distances, resisted the insects found near the coast, and multiplied quickly. Along with the Longhorns, a host of ranching terms, techniques, and practices would gradually pass into common use in other regions of Texas, but until after 1850, as mentioned before, the diffusion point may have been western Louisiana or the Texas Coastal Bend and not the Trans-Nueces, a region still set apart from much of the rest of Texas.[66]

Social and demographic characteristics further set the region apart from not only the rest of Texas but from the interior of Mexico. Social and economic classes certainly existed including relatively wealthy folk of mainly European heritage, those in the middle economically often of mixed Spanish and Indian heritage, and Indians and servants at the bottom. Yet the region had more class fluidity and relative equality than other parts of Mexico. Women and children were expected to work and society was often patriarchal, but again border conditions opened up some opportunities for women to move into land-owning and more independent roles. Children may have worked hard and early in their lives, but they also may have escaped some of the social structures and class rigidity of more settled regions. A border region in almost every way imaginable existed from the Nueces to south of the Rio Grande before 1850.[67]

For Tejanos in the Trans-Nueces an upsurge in attacks by groups of Comanche and Lipan clearly told them they inhabited a border area. After more than thirty years of relative peace, raids by these groups on Tejano settlements picked up in the late 1820s and grew even more intense through the 1830s and into the 1840s. In the Laredo area, Indian raids pushed settlement and economic activity southward, and in most of the Trans-Nueces, raids slowed economic growth. Living in a type of no-man's-land between Mexican and Texan control, and unable to effectively maintain peace with the Lipan and Comanche, Tejanos suffered sharp losses of life and livestock. Still nearer to Matamoros and in some other isolated cases Lipan and Comanche attacks proved less disastrous. When annexation and the Treaty of Guadalupe Hidalgo secured the region for the United States in the late 1840s, however, settlement was less widespread than two decades earlier. Total population seems to have increased with one reliable estimate placing the Spanish-surnamed population in Texas in 1836 at about 8,000 as compared to 14,000 in 1850. Given the concentration of Spanish-surnamed people south of the Nueces, the economy must have grown at least marginally. Population and economic growth concentrated near Matamoros, while pockets of abandoned land dotted the western Trans-Nueces by 1850.[68]

North of the Nueces and in between the other largely homogenous islands were numerous areas that shared multiple characteristics of at least two of these distinctive types. Nowhere was this truer than in a band of counties from Harris and Galveston on the coast to Bexar and Travis in the west. Here were found the three largest cities of Texas: Galveston, Houston, and San Antonio. All those cities had a significant Central European population, and San Antonio also had a strong Tejano presence. All also had some residents from the Lower South, Upper South, and other portions of the United States. Here the sharing of traits and movement from one form of household economy to another proved common, but within all of these counties smaller distinctive rural neighborhoods and communities preserved many traits brought from their point of origin. Place mattered in the creation, evolution, and maintenance of household economies.[69]

When those Upper South origin planters switched to sugar cultivation in response to bad weather and plunging cotton prices and used German immigrants to operate and maintain the extensive machinery required for sugar production, they demonstrated the importance of place. Place mattered not only because those long established planters had access to examples of a sugar culture and sources of free labor, but also because of climate, soil, transportation, and connections to market centers like Galveston and New Orleans. Through those market centers, elite families in particular also enjoyed connections to much of the Atlantic World. New knowledge and information and close association with those from a different culture fostered more rapid change, such as moving in and out of the cultivation of cotton, expanding stockraising as the New Orleans market grew larger, adopting steam-powered sugar-refining machines, or changing roles for women in the family.[70]

Women's roles, and gender roles in general, offered a particularly important and revealing example of change and the limits of change. As with the cultivation and consumption of potatoes by German immigrants, the conditions on the ground, particularly economic conditions, forced change in traditional cultural norms, but the pull to return to those norms proved powerful. With time, families tended to behave in ways similar to where they came from, but certainly by 1850 that return to customary ways remained in the future. Indeed Texas gender roles, especially in heterogeneous zones, may have never completely returned to those traditionally associated with Lower South, Upper South, German, Comanche, or Tejano communities.[71]

Economic reasons partially explained this slow bounce back to old ways. Community property laws continued over from the Spanish and Mexican era in the Republic offered the most obvious example of deviation from a more patriarchal system. Such laws limited the ability of profligate sons-in-law to throw a daughter and her family into poverty, but they also allowed for a smooth managerial transition when a husband died and reflected the reality that free women often managed land, slaves, and other assets in the absence of their husbands. Beginning in 1835 Spanish community property law and other laws concerning the property of spouses were combined with the English common law familiar to many Anglo Texans and the Louisiana civil code to form a type of hybrid system that governed the property rights of married women. By 1840, however, the Republic had moved back to community property and separate property laws similar to the Spanish system. In a sense, this move from a hybrid system to something similar to the Spanish system reflected legal changes in the Lower South that limited husbands' control over their wives' property. In the 1830s common law traditions slowly shifted in the Lower South, as fathers feared that profligate sons-in-law would squander their daughters' and grandchildren's property. Others sought to protect at least some of the family's property, especially slaves, from creditors by moving toward separate property laws that defined some property as the husband's and some as the wife's. Such sentiment grew especially strong after the sharp downturn in the economy in the late 1830s and the resulting calling in of loans secured by slaves. No doubt the desire to protect a wife's inherited property and a desire to protect family property from creditors influenced thinking in Texas, but Texans went even further than their cousins in Mississippi. Many male Anglo Texans, having observed Mexican-era laws in operation, supported moving back to something akin to Spanish community property law, and in 1845, the creators of the first state constitution included community property laws and other provisions along the Spanish legal model that protected the rights and property of married women. Thus while the entire Lower South moved toward the protection of the property of married women, Texans moved further and faster because of their heterogeneous culture and close-up experience with a Spanish-based legal system.[72]

Similarly, Germans brought with them a culture in which men and women more nearly equally provided the livelihood for the family and they shared in an obligation to keep the family afloat financially and economically. This example may also have influenced some change in the economic patterns of Anglo women. Men provided the bulk of the farm labor, but women might manage the mill, sell vegetables, or in other ways contribute to the family's prosperity. Community property made even more sense in such cases. Conditions on the ground such as a fairly high mortality rates, less-formal marriages outside the bounds of a church, war, and violence all influenced gender roles and the patterns of behavior of men and women, but so did the availability of other models that perhaps better suited the economic and social realities of the time and place.[73]

With the always useful caveat to avoid over-simplification, a type of rough framework emerged that explained economic behavior in the heterogeneous regions and to some extent in all of Texas. Behavior sprang from the various interactions between cultural groups; the growth rate, settlement patterns, and relative size of those groups; the challenges and realities of a place; and the economic opportunities presented by the times. Two examples help tease out how this worked: Germans and slavery, and Tejano cartsmen based in San Antonio.

In the counties between the cities of San Antonio and Houston, German immigrants increasingly lived near slave owners from the Lower South. Yet only a few owned slaves. They had other sources of labor and slavery had never been part of their culture. They preferred making other investments and perhaps lacked the access to credit available to some Anglos. Still as slavery became more common and as profits from cotton increased, some Germans tried slave ownership, moving them into a Lower South cultural orbit that encouraged them to support secession. Reflecting on his boyhood in Austin County, William A. Trenckmann observed, "With the exception of a few who had been in the country for a long time and to whom slavery was less repulsive because they had become accustomed to it, most of the Germans were opposed to slavery and voted against secession." The high rate of return from cotton growing and slave ownership never overcame the cultural disdain for slavery, but time and exposure to a Lower South culture weakened it.[74]

In the San Antonio area, Tejanos using solid-wheeled ox carts had long dominated the transportation industry. As San Antonio grew after 1836, the cart drivers normally traveled a route from San Antonio to Indianola or some other small port on the Gulf of Mexico south of Galveston. Starting in the early 1840s, however, the demography of the region began to change rapidly as Germans, Anglos, and African Americans entered the area. By the mid-1850s, Germans and Anglos outnumbered Tejanos in the region. As this process unfolded Tejano cart drivers held their own because their carts and oxen were well equipped to move through the Texas mud and they charged less. Anglos in Karnes County and elsewhere along their route reacted by ambushing and shooting Tejano cart drivers. Anglo defenders and apologists for this violence charged that Tejanos were not white and that they harbored runaway slaves. While Tejanos and Germans resisted the splitting of society into a typical black/white Lower South binary, leading Tejanos such as Jose Antonio Navarro moved to make Tejanos more American in behavior, but they also encouraged Tejanos and Anglos to accept differences with each other. Continued economic prosperity demanded some level of cultural change and accommodation by Tejanos and Anglos, but not total conformity. As was true of secession and slavery among the Germans, those with the longest association with Anglos and a higher level of wealth and status, such as Navarro, moved more quickly toward a Lower South model, and he eventually owned African American slaves. Navarro and other Tejano elites, however, also resisted efforts to depict Tejanos as the equivalents of African Americans and they loudly and effectively protested actions that threatened the Tejano community's ability to prosper economically.[75]

In this heterogeneous middle region of Texas the strongest impulse may have been to move toward a Lower South model based on slavery and where skin color determined economic activity. Yet the presence of Germans and Tejanos modified this impulse and it gave the economy greater variety. Solid wheeled carts and the marketing of vegetables and other specialized crops persisted. This variety of economic activity and the presence of the largest cities in Texas opened this region to more rapid change than the rest of Texas, making it the most receptive to market forces, new business methods, and new technology.[76]

Moving down to the household level then offers a useful counterpoint to an Atlantic World perspective. As the 1840s closed, Texas remained divided into distinct cultural and economic zones, and those zones were more distinctive than in 1861 when most Texans followed the Lower South in secession. Large-scale migration from the Lower South in the 1840s moved Texas in that direction, but it was not there yet. A similar climate and range of economic opportunities also moved much of Texas toward the Lower South. Yet because of transportation difficulties that kept some areas on the margins of the Atlantic World economy and the stubborn allegiance of many Texans to the cultural norms of their point of origin, several regions had not moved much toward a Lower South model by 1850. Cotton and slavery did not yet dominate the local economy. Even in the heterogeneous zones, cattle raising and other blended economic practices did not follow a typical southern pattern.

By 1850, however, a shared system of money, credit, and law joined the profits of an Atlantic World economy and the increasing migration from the Lower South in pushing Texans toward a Lower South economy and culture. Money, credit, law, and their underpinning culture, more clearly and more decisively than Atlantic connections and household economies, pulled Texans together and into a black/white, slave/free, binary.

Money and credit provided the lubricant that allowed commodities, including slaves, to move back and forth across the borders of Texas. Laws passed during the Republic and enforced by its legal system gave every area of Texas that fell under the control of the government a measure of uniformity. Increasingly from 1830 to 1850, money, credit, laws, and regulations followed a Lower South pattern, extending the reach of that culture into new areas. Yet as community property laws demonstrated and banking laws confirmed, Texas on the eve of annexation differed sharply from Mississippi. Texans had a distinct government, different connections to the credit markets of Europe, and an almost absolute ban on the creation of banks. Their complete failure to adequately build a tax, banking, debt repayment, and credit structure regulated by the state, however, encouraged Texans to look for financial salvation through alignment with the United States.

On the eve of the Texas Revolution, most Texans depended upon specie, barter, or various promissory notes, bonds, and bills from the United States or Europe to speed the buying and selling of goods and services, and they were part of the rapid expansion in lending of that era. Keeping large amounts of silver or gold on hand proved both dangerous and bulky to transport, and barter best suited local and small-scale transactions. Thus, larger-scale and longer-distance transactions depended upon U.S. or European notes, bonds, and bills or lines of credit with merchants in New Orleans. Antonio Menchaca, who served in the victorious Texas army at the Battle of San Jacinto in 1836, was asked after the battle to find food for the captured General Antonio Lopez de Santa Anna. After recording that he purchased coffee, sugar, and flour from a trader, Menchaca commented that he paid the trader "in bills of a bank in New Orleans of which I had $7,000 in my belt; and they were on par with gold and silver with us, and even at a premium with the latter, as they were so much easier to carry in large quantities without danger of losing them." In another example of the centrality of New Orleans in the economic and cultural life of Texans, even before the creation of the Republic notes issued by that city's banks were the commonly accepted and agreed upon medium of exchange.[77]

Large-scale planters, stock raisers, and merchants and traders like Menchaca enjoyed direct access to New Orleans merchants and bankers, but smaller-scale operators either worked through neighboring planters, stock raisers, and merchants or through emerging Texas firms such as McKinney and Williams or later R. & D. G. Mills. The principals in these firms typically had close relationships and were often partners in larger-scale firms in New Orleans, New York, and Philadelphia. McKinney and Williams, for example, enjoyed a very close connection to the Bank of the United States in Philadelphia. That firm also received a bank charter from the state of Coahuila and Texas before the Texas Revolution and put the bank into limited operation during the Republic period. No other chartered bank operated during the period 1830 to 1850, but an increasing number of mercantile firms provided banking services as part of their larger business. Thus, Texans were without a regulated or state-backed banking system, but they did have access to various financial instruments that served as money and large-scale credit. They were part of the rapid inflation in the effective supply of money and credit in the Atlantic World in the 1830s and part of the bursting of that inflation and credit bubble in 1837 and again in 1839.[78]

Success in dealing with financial instruments and in lending depended on accurate information and mastery of arbitrage, the simultaneous buying and selling of notes, bonds, and other financial instruments in different markets. Accurate information and skillful arbitrage lessened risk to firms like McKinney and Williams or to planter/merchants like David G. Mills whose extensive connections let them deal in financial instruments that were reasonably secure and discount them according to their level of security. They could also profit by the spread between the purchasing and selling price of financial instruments. This required the extensive and trustworthy connections (often through family members or close friends) to the outside world of such firms and individuals, and it also required training not available to most Texans. Ability to use the financial system of the day to their advantage was another reason that wealth gravitated to the top during the 1830s and 1840s. It also meant the financial elite grew more tightly bound to the United States with each passing year of the Republic period.[79]

Men like David Mills plowed their profits from banking and mercantile activity into slaves and land, and those were also the security for most loans in Texas. To suggest some measure of the profits available to those skilled and blessed with good connections to the financial markets, by 1860 David Mills and his brother Robert owned 800 slaves and 200,000 acres of land. Slaves were in many ways the key to the entire financial system, not only of the Mills brothers, but of the Republic of Texas. Land was relatively cheap and did not appreciate much in value, but slaves did. As financial panic spread through the American Southeast in the late 1830s planters escaped foreclosure on their slaves by moving them to Texas. Thus to some extent the Texas economy grew because of the Panic, not in spite of it. Planters with holdings in both the United States and Texas also purchased slaves on credit in the New Orleans market and moved them to Texas. They were hurt by the collapse of cotton prices, but like the Mills brothers, they could shift to sugar or they could simply continue to evade foreclosure back in the United States by moving their operations increasingly to Texas. Abandon then any lingering happy notions that slaves were part of the planter family and that "Gone to Texas," the famous saying used to explain the quick departure of so many in the Southeast, was for the little man escaping debt back east. For planters and slave traders, slaves were a commodity that increased in value through the birth of a new generation and by moving slaves from place to place. Slaves shielded owners from debt collectors and allowed for extensive access to credit.[80]

A trail of credit relationships stretched from Texas slaveholders, to Texas merchant/bankers, to merchant /bankers in New Orleans, to various state-chartered and state-secured banks in the South, to banks in New York and Philadelphia, and across the Atlantic to such wealthy investment firms as Baring Brothers. The weak link in the chain turned out to be those southern state-chartered and state-backed banks often created in such a way that the entire population of a state stood behind a bank in case of failure. When cotton prices dipped in the late 1830s the upward spiral of lending and transfer of bills of exchange and bank notes through the economy reversed into a downward spiral. Northeastern and European investors began to ask for payment. Those state banks in turn asked for repayment from planters who used their slaves as collateral. In response slave owners in the Southeast who put their faith in and bet their future on steady growth in slavery and cotton prices moved to Texas with their slaves to avoid losing them to the banks. The banks failed, and the various forms of bills, notes, and the equivalent of paper money associated with them shrank in value or in many cases became worthless. As so often happens after a period of rapid economic expansion built on an insecure financial platform, their failure pulled the economy of the region and of the interconnected Atlantic World downward.[81]

Masters of arbitrage in Texas like Samuel May Williams survived the downturn, but it became increasingly difficult for him to get the legislature of the Republic of Texas to back his effort to set up a bank. Indeed anti-bank sentiment grew in Texas in the wake of the collapse of the state banks of the South, and eventually when Texans entered thc Union they banned all banks in their first state constitution.[82]

Ironically, in some ways the Republic itself became one of those so-called "wildcat" banks. It printed the equivalent of money to supply a medium of exchange and it printed more money to help pay its substantial debt from financing the Texas Revolution and from subsequent military schemes. Such a strategy might have worked if the Republic had held specie or bullion in reserve or had developed a coherent long-term strategy to repay its debt. Instead the government of the Republic's poverty prevented the accumulation of specie or bullion, and Texas leaders completely failed to either monetarize their debts in a way that would turn them into mediums of exchange or establish any level of faith that those debts could be repaid. The poverty and failure persisted when despite trying one tax scheme after another none brought in enough revenue. Since the tax system, like most in those days, relied heavily on tariffs, the generally depressed levels of trade in the late 1830s and early 1840s hurt revenue collection, and U.S. tariffs on goods imported from Texas encouraged smuggling out Texas commodities and smuggling in U.S. goods. Desperate to find some steady stream of revenue, the leaders of the Republic tried one tariff system after another. This constant and ineffective scrambling, combined with costly military ventures pursued during Lamar's presidency, undercut faith in the financial instruments and the financial future of the Republic.[83]

The value of currency and its equivalents in the 1830s and 1840s ultimately rested either on precious metals, credit worthiness, or the public's faith in the stability of the institution that issued the currency. The Republic lacked all three. Behind on its repayment of past debt and existing in a world where major banks and investment companies had grown increasingly skeptical of the soundness of southern and Texas lending, the Republic could not borrow easily or cheaply because not only its current but its future prospects looked bleak. Without sufficient revenue, lacking reserves of precious metals, and facing either non-existent or expensive sources of credit, the value of Texas currency, warrants, and promissory notes plummeted. Texans were caught in a financial vise. The price of perhaps their most significant export, cotton, declined to the point of causing deflation. In the meantime, currency and its equivalent inflated, requiring more and more Texas dollars to buy the same items as before. Cattle, other livestock, and sugar provided some growth, especially as local consumption grew with the population. A basically semi-subsistence economy reliant on barter, the production at home of much of what was needed, and the purchase of relatively few goods shielded smaller-scale landowners and those more distant from market centers. Those who sought larger levels of wealth, however, gazed into the future and saw that annexation offered the best chance of improved prospects.[84]

During and after 1844, conditions brightened. The Atlantic World economy and cotton prices, while still depressed, showed some promise of improvement. Crop yields improved. The chance of either annexation or a long-term financial arrangement with Great Britain promised debt relief, increased confidence in the creditworthiness of Texas and Texans, and heralded the arrival of a more stable government and currency. At the same time, immigration from the South and from Europe grew, adding demand and labor to the local economy. All of these brighter circumstances pushed the value of land and demand for slaves up. New arrivals, however, had little ideological or emotional attachment to the Republic of Texas. Many bet their financial future on annexation, hoping to buy into the Texas economy when the prices of land, slaves, and various other types of property were still low and then see their assets appreciate with the political, military, and financial stability of being part of the United States. As one Texas entrepreneur wrote his son in 1844, "land will go up if you wait, if you could buy any conditionally on time, do so." The dismal financial record of the Republic, repeated difficulties along the southern border with Mexico, recent immigrants' shallow ties to the nation, and the promise of rapid appreciation in the value of what they held made annexation irresistible to most free Texans, especially the elite, by 1845.[85]

By then, from the point of view of Texas slave owners, the government of the Republic had done several essential things. Unlike in the era of Mexican government, slavery enjoyed clear legal protections. It was enshrined in the constitution and regulated by a host of laws. Slave owners filled most significant positions in the government, and they created laws making it possible to buy, sell, trade, rent out, and borrow against slaves. An entire legal code developed that like those in the states of the American South ensured the prosperity and longevity of slavery. Slaveholders feared a closer affiliation with Great Britain in the mid-1840s because Britain led the effort to end slavery in the Atlantic basin. Instead of the Republic possibly continuing to exist in some state of dependency with Britain, slaveholders looked to their government to take one final set of steps ending the life of the Republic and securing annexation to the United States. In that sense, law, culture, and the economy were all moving in the same direction by 1845—toward a Lower South model and full integration into the United States. After the Mexican War and the Compromise of 1850 further stabilized the Texas economy and borders, that Lower South model exploded forward to secession and the disruption of the United States.[86]

Go back to that young stock raiser and his family that Olmsted observed in 1854. Focus on just what seeing Texans as connected to the outside world and both connected and disconnected from each other meant. In terms of the historiography of the South and Southwest, claims that Texas somehow existed as an exceptional or unique place rang hollow. Instead, that stock raiser was part of a growing affiliation of Texas and Texans with the Lower South. Yet his story as well as the stories of all Texans residing outside of the homogenous Lower South cultural islands also qualified that insistence on identification with the Lower South. Certainly, the increasing stream of migrants from states along the Gulf of Mexico, the close connections through New Orleans to the Atlantic World economy, and banking, credit, and law pulled Texas toward the Lower South. It transformed those landowners in Brazoria County into sugar producers. Yet unlike their counterparts in Alabama or Mississippi, they used some Spanish and Mexican herding practices. They never completely duplicated the ways of the Lower South, but Texans also did not totally create a new culture or economy. Insisting on such a complete ethnogenesis obscures reality. Instead, adding a look at the economy tempers the growing emphasis on cultural confrontation and accommodation causing a regeneration or birth of a new culture. Persistence, whether in German labor practices, Comanche raiding and trading patterns, or Upper South affinity for wheat and horses, existed amidst transformation in almost every part of Texas from 1830 to 1850.

Yet two essential Republic-era transformations long influenced Texas. Obviously, Texas grew more like the Lower South, especially in those areas settled largely by blacks and whites from the Lower South and devoted to the cultivation of cotton. Less obviously, a host of cultural islands also emerged and persisted into the 1850s and in many cases beyond to the twentieth century. Acknowledging these twin trend lines places such events as secession in perspective. Secession enjoyed overwhelming support in much of Texas, especially that part that had long been like the Lower South or grew more like the Lower South from 1844 forward. Yet it was often just as stoutly opposed in Upper South, German, or Tejano cultural islands. Contentiousness and close decisions marked the vote on secession in blended communities like San Antonio. Such political outcomes provide clues of the broad and lasting influence of cultural and economic patterns at work by 1850 and suggest a way to make sense of the Texas past.

In conceptualizing Texas, think of tipping points not complete shifts in the dominant paradigm. From 1830 to 1850 and into the 1850s Texas and Texans transformed into a region and a people at home in the Lower South. For much of Texas that transformation long continued as huge swaths of Texas increasingly resembled the Lower South. Yet pockets of different economies and cultures also remained. As soon as they figured out how to do it, Germans in the middle of migrants from the Lower South, returned to growing as many white potatoes as possible. Connections to a broader world between 1830 and 1850 brought persistence as well as transformation. They brought distinctiveness and integration into the Lower South.

Notes

1. Frederick Law Olmsted, *A Journey through Texas: Or a Saddle-Trip on the Southwestern Frontier* (New York: Dix, Edwards & Co., 1857), 101.

2. Olmsted, *Journey through Texas*, 100–102. Also see Francis Richard Lubbock, *Six Decades in Texas or Memoirs of Francis Richard Lubbock*, edited by C. W. Raines (Austin: Ben C. Jones & Co., 1900), 120–140.

3. William Ransom Hogan, *The Texas Republic: A Social and Economic History* (Norman: University of Oklahoma Press, 1946). The book was reprinted with a new preface by Hogan in 1969 and again with a foreword by Gregg Cantrell in 2007. See William Ransom Hogan, *The Texas Republic: A Social and Economic History* (Austin: Texas State Historical Association, 2007), vii–xvii.

4. Hogan, *The Texas Republic*, 298. On the decline of interest in economic history by historians see Eric Foner, "A Brutal Process: 'The Half Has Never Been Told,' by Edward E. Baptist," *New York Times*, October 3, 2014.

5. For elaboration on these points and the evidence to back them up see Walter L. Buenger, "Flight From Modernity: The Economic History of Texas Since 1845," in Buenger and Robert A. Calvert, eds., *Texas Through Time* (1991), 310–341; Buenger, "Three Truths in Texas," in Buenger and Arnoldo De León, eds., *Beyond Texas Through Time: Breaking Away From Past Interpretations* (College Station: Texas A&M University Press, 2011), 1–49; Buenger, "Texas Identity: Alternatives to the Terrible Triplets," in Richard B. McCaslin, Donald E. Chipman, and Andrew J. Torget, eds., *This Corner of Canaan: Essays on Texas in Honor of Randolph B. Campbell* (Denton: University of North Texas Press, 2013), 3–35. On why he ignored other groups see Hogan, preface to the 1946 edition, *The Texas Republic*. On interaction between cultural groups on the local level see Sean M. Kelley, *Los Brazos de Dios: A Plantation Society in the Texas Borderlands, 1821–1865* (Baton Rouge: LSU Press, 2010).

6. For a more full-throated and targeted response to absolutism see Buenger, "Texas Identity."

7. Terry G. Jordan, "The Imprint of the Upper and Lower South on Mid-Nineteenth-Century Texas," *Annals of the Association of American Geographers* 17 (December 1967): 667–690.

8. On distinctiveness within the slave South see Philip D. Morgan, *Slave Counterpoint: Black Culture in the Eighteenth-century Chesapeake and Lowcountry* (Chapel Hill: University of North Carolina Press, 1998); Kelley, *Los Brazos de Dios*, 1–12; Walter Struve, *Germans and Texans: Commerce, Migration, and Culture in the Days of the Lone Star Republic* (Austin: University of Texas Press, 1996). For an introduction to a growing literature on borders see "Margins to Mainstream: The Brave New World of Borderlands History," *Journal of American History* 98 (September 2011): 337–437.

9. *The Texas Almanac, for 1857, with Statistics, Historical and Biographical Sketches, &c., Relating to Texas* (Galveston: Daily News), 100.

10. For population figures from the 1820s to 1850 see Juan N. Almonte, "Statistical Report on Texas, 1835," edited and translated by C. E. Castañeda, *Southwestern Historical Quarterly* (*SHQ*) 28 (January 1925): 177–222; William R. Hogan, "State Census of 1847," *SHQ* 50 (July 1946), 116–118; Abigail Curlee, "A Study of Texas Slave Plantations, 1822–1865" (PhD Dissertation, University of Texas, 1932), 15–16; Marion Day Mullins, *The First Census of Texas, 1829–1836; to which are added, Texas citizenship lists, 1821–1845, and other early records of the Republic of Texas* (Washington: National Genealogical Society, 1959); Randolph B. Campbell, *An Empire for Slavery: The Peculiar Institution in Texas, 1821–1865* (Baton Rouge: Louisiana State University Press, 1989), 54–58; Campbell, *Gone to Texas: a History of the Lone Star State*, 2nd ed. (New York; Oxford University Press, 2012), 157.

11. On the child ladder method used to determine when migrants arrived in Texas, see Barnes F. Lathrop, *Migration into East Texas, 1835–1860* (Austin: Texas State Historical Association, 1949), see especially 60–61, 84–90; William W. White, "Migration into West Texas, 1845–1860" (M.A. thesis, University of Texas, Austin, 1948). The statistical basis for any analysis of the Texas economy and society from 1830 to 1850 remains limited, but for path breaking use of local records see Jesús F. de la Teja and John Wheat, "Bexar: Profile of a Tejano Community, 1820–1832," *SHQ* 89 (July 1985): 7–34; Randolph B. Campbell and Richard G. Lowe, *Wealth and Power in Antebellum Texas* (College Station: Texas

A&M University Press, 1977), especially 138–145. Also see Robert E. Gallman and Ralph V. Anderson, "Slaves as Fixed Capital: Slave Labor and Southern Economic Development," *Journal of American History* 64 (June, 1977); Gavin Wright, *Slavery and American Economic Development* (Baton Rouge: Louisiana State University Press, 2006), 14–128; C. Allen Jones, *Texas Roots: Agriculture and Rural Life before the Civil War* (College Station: Texas A&M University Press, 2005).

12. Travel books and reports offer a useful supplement to the limited statistical records for the Republic Era. Among others see Jean Louis Berlandier, *Journey to Mexico during the years 1826 to 1834,* eds. and trans. Sheila M. Ohlendorf, Josette M. Bigelow, and Mary M. Standifer (Austin: Texas State Historical Association, 1980); Jack Jackson, ed. [translated by John Wheat] *Texas by Terán: The Diary Kept by General Manuel de Mier y Terán on his 1828 Inspection of Texas* (Austin: University of Texas Press, 2000); Jack Jackson, ed., [translated by John Wheat] *Almonte's Texas: Juan N. Almonte's 1834 Inspection, Secret Report, and Role in the 1836 Campaign* (Austin: Texas State Historical Association, 2003); *Texas in 1840 or the Emigrants Guide to the New Republic, Being the Result of Observation, Enquiry and Travel in that Beautiful Country* (New York: W. W. Allen, 1840); William Kennedy, *Texas: the Rise, Progress, and Prospects of the Republic of Texas* (London: R. Hastings, 1841); William Bollaert, *William Bollaert's Texas*, edited by W. Eugene Hollon and Ruth Lapham Butler (Norman: University of Oklahoma Press, 1956); Viktor Bracht, *Texas in 1848,* trans. Charles Frank Schmidt (San Antonio: Naylor Printing, 1931); Ferdinand von Roemer, *Texas: Mit besonder Rücksicht auf deutsche Auswanderung und die physichen Verhältnisse des Landes Nach eigener Beobachtung geshildert* (Bonn: Adolph Marcus, 1849); Olmsted, *A Journey through Texas*.

13. Lubbock, *Six Decades*, 20–178; Terry G. Jordan, *North American Cattle-Ranching Frontiers: Origins, Diffusion, and Differentiation* (Albuquerque: University of New Mexico Press, 1993), 123–240; Terry G. Jordan, *Trails to Texas: Southern Roots of Western Cattle Ranching* (Lincoln: University of Nebraska Press, 1981); Louise S. O'Connor, *Cryin' for Daylight: A Ranching Culture in the Texas Coastal Bend* (Austin: Wexford Publishing, 1989).

14. Berlandier, *Journey to Mexico*, II, 289–300; de la Teja and Wheat, "Bexar," 8–9, 26–34; Almonte, "Statistical Report on Texas, 1835," 192–193; Andrés Reséndez, *Changing National Identities at the Frontier: Texas and New Mexico, 1800–1850* (Cambridge: Cambridge University Press, 2004), 146–170. On Tejano settlements see Andrés

Tijerina, *Tejanos and Texas under the Mexican Flag, 1821–1836* (College Station: Texas A&M University Press, 1994), 5–24; Ana Carolina Castillo Crimm, *De Leon, a Tejano Family History* (Austin: University of Texas Press, 2003); Jack Jackson, *Los Mesteños: Spanish Ranching in Texas, 1721–1821* (College Station: Texas A&M University Press, 1986); F. Todd Smith, *From Dominance to Disappearance: The Indians of Texas and the Near Southwest, 1786–1859* (Lincoln: University of Nebraska Press, 2005); David La Vere, *The Texas Indians* (College Station: Texas A&M University Press, 2004), 103–201. Also see Robert H. Thonhoff, *The Texas Connection with the American Revolution* (Burnet, TX: Eakin Press, 1981), 45–81; Donald E. Chipman and Harriett Denise Joseph, *Spanish Texas, 1919–1821*, rev. ed. (Austin: University of Texas Press, 2010), 174–229.

15. Jordan, *North American Cattle-Ranching Frontiers*, 147–158;

16. Lubbock, *Six Decades*, 138. Also see Jordan, *North American Cattle-Ranching Frontiers*, 147–158.

17. *The Texas Almanac, for 1857, with Statistics, Historical and Biographical Sketches, &c., Relating to Texas* (Galveston: Richardson & Co., 1856), 105.

18. For a description of the importance of cotton and its connection to slavery, see Andrew J. Torget, *Seeds of Empire: Cotton, Slavery, and the Transformation of the Texas Borderlands, 1800–1850* (Chapel Hill: The University of North Carolina Press, 2015). Torget draws his figures on exports from the Republic era from Robert E. L. Crane, Jr., "The Administration of the Customs Service of the Republic of Texas" (M.A. thesis, University of Texas, 1939). For cotton price trends see Stuart Bruchey, *Cotton and the Growth of the American Economy: 1790–1860* (New York: Harcourt, 1967), 14–30. Also, see *Texas Slavery Project* (http://www.TexasSlaveryProject.org).

19. Berlandier, *Journey to Mexico*, 291. Also see Reséndez, *Changing National Identities at the Frontier*, 37–40.

20. S. Deane Wasson, *Fifty Years a Cotton Market: Houston Cotton Exchange and Board of Trade Brochure, 1924* (Houston: Houston Cotton Exchange and Board of Trade, 1924); Avery L. Carlson, *A Monetary and Banking History of Texas* (Fort Worth: Fort Worth National Bank, 1930), 1–18; Walter L. Buenger and Joseph A. Pratt, *But also Good Business: Texas Commerce Banks and the Financing of Houston and Texas, 1886–1986* (College Station: Texas A&M University Press, 1986), 12–39.

21. On the changing demographics of New Orleans see Elizabeth Fussell, "Constructing New Orleans, Constructing Race: A Population

History of New Orleans," *Journal of American History* (*JAH*) 94 (December 2007): 846–855. Also see Jay Gitlin, *The Bourgeois Frontier: French Towns, French Traders, and American Expansion* (New Haven: Yale University Press, 2010); Scott P. Marler, *The Merchants' Capital: New Orleans and the Political Economy of the Nineteenth-Century South* (New York: Cambridge University Press, 2013).

22. *The Seventh Census of the United States: 1850* (Washington: Government Printing Office, 1853) volume I, pp. xxxvi–xxxvii, 505; Terry G. Jordan, "Population Origins in Texas, 1850," *Geographical Review* 59 (January 1969): 83–103; Ralph A. Wooster, "Foreigners in the Principal Towns of Ante-Bellum Texas," *SHQ* 66 (October 1962): 208–220; Terry G. Jordan, "A Century and a Half of Ethnic Change in Texas, 1836–1986," *SHQ* 89 (April 1986): 385–422; David G. McComb, *Galveston: A History* (Austin: University of Texas Press, 1986), 42–120; Lubbock, *Six Decades*, 41–208; Margaret Swett Henson, *Samuel May Williams: Early Texas Entrepreneur* (College Station: Texas A&M University Press, 1976), 45–130.

23. *Galveston Civilian and Gazette,* November 4, 1840; November 2, 1844; *Galveston Zeitung*, August 19, 1855; Robert S. Shelton, "Free and Unfree Workers in Galveston, Texas, 1840–1860," *Journal of Social History* 40 (Spring 2007): 717–730; Robert S. Shelton, "Slavery in a Texas Seaport: The Peculiar Institution in Galveston," *Slavery and Abolition* 28 (August 2007): 155–168.

24. Jordan, "Population Origins in Texas, 1850," 83–103.

25. David B. Edward, *The History of Texas: Or the Emigrant's, Farmer's and Politician's Guide* (Cincinnati: J. A. James, 1836), 278.

26. Kelley, *Los Brazos de Dios*, 48–50. On the international slave trade after it was banned in the United States and its impact on Texas see Ernest Obadele-Starks, *Freebooters and Smugglers: The Foreign Slave Trade in the United States after 1808* (Fayetteville: University of Arkansas Press, 2007), 15–166; Earl Wesley Fornell, *The Galveston Era: The Texas Crescent on the Eve of Secession* (Austin: University of Texas Press, 1961), 241–264; Campbell, *Empire for Slavery*, 50–55. For confirmation of the Africa trade into Brazoria County by one of its chief participants see Monroe Edwards to Mirabeau B. Lamar, May 5, 1840, "Mirabeau Buonaparte Lamar Papers," Texas State Archives, Austin, Texas. Also see Bollaert, *William Bollaert's Texas*, 163–165; "Commerce of Galveston," *The Texas Almanac, 1857*, 120–124, ads for J. S. Sydnor and businesses in New Orleans, inserted between 33–34.

27. Olmsted, *Journey through Texas*, 240. Also see Campbell, *Empire for Slavery*, 50–53; Fornell, *Galveston Era*, 115, 151.

28. Olmsted, *Journey through Texas*, 237–248; Edward, *History of Texas*, 55. Also see Abigail Curlee Holbrook, "Cotton Marketing in Antebellum Texas," *SHQ* 73 (April 1970): 431–455; Henson, *Samuel May Williams*, 45–150.

29. On agricultural practices brought from the South to Texas see Terry G. Jordan, *German Seed in Texas Soil: Immigrant Farmers in Nineteenth-century Texas* (Austin: University of Texas Press, 1966), 8–30; Dewitt Talmage Tarlton, "The History of the Cotton Industry in Texas, 1820–1850," (M.A. Thesis, University of Texas, Austin, 1923), 16–98; Abigail Curlee, "A Study of Texas Slave Plantations, 1822–1865" (PhD dissertation, University of Texas, Austin, 1932). On the use of the mule see R. B. Lamb, *The Mule in Southern Agriculture* (Berkeley: University of California Press, 1963); Jordan, "Imprint of the Upper and Lower South ," 667–690. Also see Kelley, *Los Brazos de Dios*, 130–161; Jones, *Texas Roots*, 93–227; Jack Temple Kirby, *Rural Worlds Lost: The American South, 1920–1960* (Baton Rouge: LSU Press, 1987), 195–204.

30. For descriptions of Texas and its counties by local contributors see *Texas Almanac, 1858*, 53–89. Also see Kelley, *Los Brazos de Dios*, 20–57, 130–161; Gavin Wright, *The Political Economy of the Cotton South: Households, Markets, and Wealth in the Nineteenth Century* (New York: W. W. Norton, 1978); Jordan, *German Seed*, 8–117; William A. Trenckmann, "History of Austin County," typescript and translation of a supplement to the *Bellville Wochenblatt*, June 16, 1899, William A. Trenckmann Papers (Briscoe Center for American History, University of Texas, Austin).

31. Kelley, *Los Brazos de Dios*, 13–161; Torget, *Seeds of Empire*, 57–176; Jordan, *German Seed in Texas Soil*, 31–117; Johann Heinrich Rackuhr and family to Heinrich Kroeger, February 4, 1848; Johann Heinrich Rackurh and family to H. Kroeger, December 10, 1848, Leyendecker Family Papers (Briscoe Center).

32. On the lower Brazos River valley as a distinct plantation region see Kelley, *Los Brazos de Dios*, 13–161. Also see Jordan, *German Seed*, 60–117; Jordan, "Imprint of the Upper and Lower South," 672–675; Fornell, *Galveston Era*, 125–139; "Deed of sale for 45 head of cattle to Johann Leyendecker from Friedriech Zimmerscheid for $200," March 15, 1847; "Receipt from T. W. House and Company," October 9, 1857, Leyendecker Family Papers.

33. Kelley, *Los Brazos de Dios*, 20–129; Thomas Affleck, *Southern Rural Almanac, and Plantation and Garden Calendar for 1854* (Washington, MS: Affleck's Southern Nurseries, 1854), 11–53; Walter D. Kamphoefner, ed., *An Immigrant Miller Picks Texas: The Letters of Carl Hilmar Guenther* (San Antonio: Maverick Publishing Co., 2001); Kamphoefner, "German Texans: In the Mainstream or Backwaters of Lone Star Society?" *Yearbook of German-American Studies* 38 (2003): 119–138.

34. State returns for 42 counties in 1848 were published in the *Texas Almanac, 1857*, 105.

35. Houston *Telegraph and Texas Register*, September 21, 1842; February 1, October 11, 1843; *Texas Almanac, 1857*, 105; I. T. Tinsley, "Letter from I. T. Tinsley, Brazoria Co.," July 28, 1858, *Texas Almanac for 1859*, 76–77; J. D. Waters, "Letter from Col. Waters, of Fort Bend Co.," July 13, 1858, *Texas Almanac for 1859*, 77–80. Also see Kelley, *Los Brazos de Dios,* 102–121; Jones, *Texas Roots*, 115–170; J. Carlyle Sitterson, *Sugar Country: The Cane Sugar Industry in the South, 1753–1950* (Lexington: University of Kentucky Press, 1953); William R. Johnson, *A Short History of the Sugar Industry in Texas* (Houston: Gulf Coast Historical Association, 1961).

36. Jordan, *German Seed in Texas Soil*, 70–73; Torget, *Seeds of Empire*, 228–235.

37. On the changing cultural geography of Texas see Jordan, "A Century and a Half of Ethnic Change."

38. On Texas counties see *Texas Almanac, 1857*, 52–72; *Texas Almanac, 1858*, 53–89. Also see Jordan, "Imprint of the Upper and Lower South"; Jordan, "A Century and a Half of Ethnic Change," 386–389; Jordan, *German Seed*, 8–59; Kelley, *Brazos de Dios*; Armando Alonzo, *Tejano Legacy*; Andrés Tijerina, *Tejano Empire: Life on the South Texas Ranches*;Tijerina, *Tejanos and Texas under the Mexican Flag*; Fornell, *The Galveston Era*, 3–266.

39. On Harrison County and neighboring counties see *Texas Almanac, 1857*, 52–72; *Texas Almanac, 1858*, 53–89; especially B. H. Martin, "Harrison," *Texas Almanac, 1858*, 67–68. Also see Olmsted, *Journey through Texas*, 44–128; James C. Armstrong, "History of Harrison County, Texas, 1839–1880" (M.A. thesis, University of Colorado, 1930); Randolph B. Campbell, *A Southern Community in Crisis: Harrison County, Texas, 1850–1880* (Austin: Texas State Historical Association, 1983); Campbell, *Empire for Slavery*, 115–152; Kelley, *Brazos de Dios*, 92–129; Curlee, "A Study of Texas Slave Plantations";

James David Nichols, "The Line of Liberty: Runaway Slaves and Fugitive Peons in the Texas-Mexico Borderlands," *Western Historical Quarterly* 44 (Winter 2013): 413–433.

40. George P. Rawick, ed., *The American Slave: A Composite Autobiography* (Westport, CT: Greenwood Press, 1979) Supplement Series 2, II 410 (Jacob Branch). On the capitalist motivation of planters see the work of this Washington County, Texas, planter and nurseryman, Thomas Affleck, *Affleck's Southern Rural Almanac and Plantation and Garden Calendar for 1854*; Thomas Affleck, *Affleck's Southern Rural Almanac and Plantation and Garden Calendar for 1860* (New Orleans: H. G. Stetson, 1859). Also see *Texas Almanac, 1857; Texas Almanac, 1858; Texas Almanac, 1859*; "Tait's Plantation Rules," Charles William Tait Papers, Briscoe Center for American History, University of Texas, Austin; "Diary of J. W. Devereux," Julien Sidney Devereux Papers, Briscoe Center; "Blackshear Diary and Memorandum Books," Thomas E. Blackshear Papers, Briscoe Center. On the economics of slavery and variation from plantation to plantation see Campbell, *An Empire for Slavery*, 67–152. On Mississippi and Alabama and their connection to Texas see Edward E. Baptist, *The Half Has Never Been Told: Slavery and the Making of American Capitalism* (New York: Basic Books, 2014). Campbell and Baptist also include many comments from former slaves.

41. Campbell, *Empire for Slavery*, 50–152, 190–208; Curlee, "Texas Slave Plantations"; Ronnie C. Tyler and Lawrence R. Murphy, eds., *The Slave Narratives of Texas* (Austin: Encino Press, 1974).

42. Children often seemed invisible, but sometimes were mentioned in travel books. Bollaert, *William Bollaert's Texas*; Olmsted, *Journey through Texas*. Also see "Devereux Diary;" Crystal Sasse Ragsdale, ed., *The Golden Free Land: The Reminiscences and Letters of Women on an American Frontier* (Austin: Landmark Press, 1976).

43. Olmsted seldom had a good word to say about the diet in Texas, especially eastern Texas. See Olmsted *Journey through Texas*, 44–128. Thomas Affleck, however, who moved from Mississippi to Texas in the 1850s and who long published a widely distributed almanac, indicated that at least the better run plantations produced a variety of food crops, but he too lamented the tendency to not raise your own hogs and garden crops. See Affleck, *Affleck's Southern Rural Almanac and Plantation and Garden Calendar for 1854*, 11–53; Affleck, *Affleck's Southern Rural Almanac and Plantation and Garden Calendar for 1860* (New Orleans: H.G. Stetson, 1859), 95–97, 106–107, 116–127. Also see Bollaert, *William Bollaert's Texas*.

44. On stock raising in plantation districts see Thomas Affleck, "Improved Breeds of Hogs," *Affleck's Almanac, 1860*, 84–85; Olmsted, *Journey through Texas*, 66–91. For livestock statistics see *Texas Almanac, 1857*, 52–72. Also see Jones, *Texas Roots*, 171–194; Jordan, *Trails to Texas*.

45. Mirabeau B. Lamar to David G. Burnet, Albert Sidney Johnston, Thomas J. Rusk, I.W. Burton, and James S. Mayfield; June 27, 1839, *Texas Indian Papers* 1, #36, edited by James M, Day and Dorman Winfrey (Austin: Texas State Library, 1959–1961); Dianna Everett, *The Texas Cherokees: A People between Two Fires, 1819–1840* (Norman: University of Oklahoma Press, 1990); David La Vere, *The Texas Indians* (College Station: Texas A & M University Press, 2004), 153–176; Gary Clayton Anderson, *The Conquest of Texas: Ethnic Cleansing in the Promised Land, 1820–1875* (Norman: University of Oklahoma Press, 2005); Stanley E. Siegel, *The Poet President of Texas: The Life of Mirabeau B. Lamar, President of the Republic of Texas* (Austin: Jenkins, 1977).

46. Daniel Strickland, "Denton," *Texas Almanac, 1858*, 62. For a starting point in understanding this Upper South region see J. T. Allen, *Early Pioneer Days in Texas* (Dallas: Wilkinson Printing, 1918). Allen grew up in antebellum times in Honey Grove, on the border between Lamar and Fannin counties.

47. As late as the mid-1850s cotton remained relatively unimportant in these counties and horses remained more valuable than cattle. See "Statistics for All the Counties," *Texas Almanac, 1857*, 58–72; "Statistics of All the Counties," *Texas Almanac, 1858*, 41–44. For a comparison of these North Texas counties with other areas see *Texas Almanac, 1858*, 53–87; *Texas Almanac, 1859*, 64–85. Also see Jordan, "Imprint of the Upper and Lower South," 667–690; Jordan, "Population Origins in Texas, 1850," 87; A. W. Neville, *The History of Lamar County, Texas* (Paris, TX: North Texas, 1937; rpt. 1986).

48. Allen, *Early Pioneer Days*, 152.

49. Allen, *Early Pioneer Days*, 120. Also see J. W. Latimer, "The Wheat Region and Wheat Culture in Texas," *Texas Almanac, 1859* (Galveston: Richardson, 1858), 64–71; "Statistics for All the Counties," *Texas Almanac, 1857*, 58–72; Jordan, "Imprint of the Upper and Lower South," 677–682. Also see Christopher Long, "Jefferson, TX (Marion County)," Handbook of Texas Online (http://www.tshaonline.org/handbook/online/articles/hgj02), accessed November 10, 2014. Uploaded on June 15, 2010. Published by the Texas State Historical Association.

50. Latimer, "The Wheat Region"; Jordan, "Imprint of the Upper and Lower South."

51. On the game available in the 1830s and 1840s see Allen, *Early Pioneer Days*, 51–56.

52. On this region in the post bellum period see Walter L. Buenger, *The Path to a Modern South: Northeast Texas Between Reconstruction and the Great Depression* (Austin: University of Texas Press, 2001).

53. For an overview of Germans in western Texas see Jordan, *German Seed*, 118–191. Among those who commented on these settlements and especially on cattle raising see Roemer, *Texas*, 147, 277–279; Bracht, *Texas im Jahre 1848*, 88–90; Olmsted, *Journey through Texas*, 278–288.

54. For early accounts of Germans in these counties see Hermann Seele, *A Short Sketch of Comal County, Texas* (New Braunfels: Zeitung, 1885); Robert Penniger, ed., *Fest-Ausgabe zum 50-jährigen Jubiläumder Gründung der stadt Friedrichsburg* (Fredericksburg: A. Hillmann, 1896); John O. Meusebach, *Answer to Interrogatories. …* (Austin: Eugene Von Boeckmann, 1894); Bracht, *Texas im Jahre 1848*; Olmsted, *Journey through Texas*, 182–288; Lorenzo Castro, *Immigration from Alsace and Lorraine: A Brief Sketch of the History of Castro's Colony* (San Antonio: Herald Office, 1871). Also see Rudolph Leopold Biesele, *The History of the German Settlements in Texas, 1831–1861* (Austin: Von Boeckmann-Jones, 1930), 66–138; Moritz Tiling, *History of the German Element in Texas from 1820–1850* (Houston: Rein and Sons, 1913); Julia Nott Waugh, *Castroville and Henry Castro, Empresario* (San Antonio: Standard Printing, 1934); Jordan, *German Seed*, 40–54, 118–191.

55. D. A. Rees, "Kerr," *Texas Almanac, 1858*, 72. Also see Guido E. Ransleben, *A Hundred Years of Comfort in Texas* (San Antonio: Naylor, 1954); Louis Reinhardt, "The Communistic Colony of Bettina," *Texas State Historical Association Quarterly* 3 (1899): 33–40; Ferdinand H. Lohmann, *Comfort: Ein kurzer Überblick über das Leben und Treiben. …* (Comfort: Wilhelm Fellbaum, 1904); A. Siemering, "Die lateinische ansiedlung in Texas," *Der Deutsche Pionier* 10 (1878), 57–62.

56. Olmsted, *Journey through Texas*, 279. On the importance of pecans see Houston *Telegraph and Texas Register*, October 4, 1843. Also see Olmsted, *Journey through Texas*, 157, 231, 277; *Neu-Braunfelser Zeitung*, December 9, 1853; February 10, September 8, 1854; *La Grange Intelligencer*, August 8, 1846; W. M. Von-Maszewski, ed. and trans., *A Sojourn in Texas, 1846–47: Alwin H. Sörgel's Texas Writings* (San Marcos: German-Texan Heritage Society, 1992), 155–157; Bracht, *Texas in Jahre 1848*, 149; Jordan, *German Seed*, 134–142.

57. Brian J. Boeck, "'They Contributed Very Much to the Success of our Colony': A New Source on Early Relations between Germans and Indians at Fredericksburg," *SHQ* 105 (July 2001): 81–91; Karl A. Hoerig, "The Relationship between German Immigrants and Native Peoples in Western Texas," *SHQ* 97 (January 1994): 423–451; Pekka Hämäläinen, *The Comanche Empire* (New Haven: Yale University Press, 2008), 181–320.

58. Terry G. Jordan, "The German Settlement of Texas after 1865," *SHQ* 73 (October 1969): 193–212.

59. José María Sánchez, "A Trip to Texas in 1828," translated by Carlos E. Castañeda, *SHQ* 29 (April 1926): 249–288; Jean Louis Berlandier, *The Indians of Texas in 1830,* edited by John C. Ewers and translated by Patricia Reading Leclerq (Washington: Smithsonian Institution Press, 1969); Manual Mier y Terán, "Noticia de las tribus conocidos que habitan en el Departmento de Tejas, y el número de familias de que consta cada tribu, puntos en que habitan y terrenos en que acampan," *Sociedad de Geografíi y Estadística de la Republica Mexican Boletín* 2 (1870): 264–269; Juan Antonio Padilla, "Texas in 1820," translated by Mattie Austin Hatcher, *SHQ* 23 (July 1919): 47–68; Hämäläinen, *The Comanche Empire*, 141–291.

60. Berlandier, *Indians of Texas*, 35–37; Juliana Barr, *Peace Came in the Form of a Woman: Indians and Spaniards in the Texas Borderland* (Chapel Hill: University of North Carolina Press, 2007), 197–286; James F. Brooks, *Captives and Cousins: Slavery, Kinship, and Community in the Southwest Borderlands* (Chapel Hill: University of North Carolina Press for the Institute of Early American History and Culture, 2002); Hämäläinen, *The Comanche Empire*, 345–361.

61. Robert S. Neighbors, "Na-Ü-Ni, or Comanches of Texas; their Traits and Beliefs, and Divisions and Internal Relations," *Indian Papers of Texas and the Southwest*, 3: 355; Josiah Gregg, *Commerce of the Prairies*, edited by Max L. Moorhead (Norman: University of Oklahoma Press, 1954); Wilson T. Davidson, "A Comanche Prisoner in 1841," *SHQ* 45 (April 1942): 335–342; José María Sánchez, "A Trip to Texas in 1828," translated by Carlos E. Castañeda *SHQ* 29 (April 1926): 249–288; Berlandier, *The Indians of Texas in 1830* ; Manual Mier y Terán, "Noticia de las tribus conocidos que habitan en el Departmento de Tejas, y el número de familias de que consta cada tribu, puntos en que habitan y terrenos en que acampan," *Sociedad de Geografíi y Estadística de la Republica Mexican Boletín* 2 (1870): 264–269; Juan Antonio Padilla, "Texas in 1820" translated by Mattie Austin Hatcher *SHQ* 23 (July 1919): 47–68; Hämäläinen, *The Comanche Empire*, 141–320.

62. Berlandier, *The Indians of Texas in 1830*, 65–134; José Francisco Ruíz, *Report on the Indian Tribes of Texas in 1828*, edited by John C. Ewers and translated by Georgette Dorn (New Haven: Yale University Press, 1972); Padilla, "Texas in 1820," 47–68; Thomas A. Britten, *The Lipan Apaches: People of Wind and Lightning* (Albuquerque: University of New Mexico Press, 2009), 167–201.

63. Brian DeLay, *War of a Thousand Deserts: Indian Raids and the U.S.-Mexican War* (New Haven: Yale University Press, 2008); William D. Carrigan, *The Making of a Lynching Culture: Violence and Vigilantism in Central Texas, 1836–1916* (Urbana: University of Illinois Press, 2004); Samuel Truett, *Fugitive Landscapes: The Forgotten History of the U.S.–Mexico Borderlands* (New Haven: Yale University Press, 2006); Barr, *Peace Came in the Form of a Woman*, 287–291.

64. For a succinct overview of the Tejano areas of Texas see Arnoldo De León and Kenneth L. Stewart, *Tejanos and the Numbers Game: A Socio-Historical Interpretation from the Federal Censuses, 1850–1900* (Albuquerque: University of New Mexico Press, 1989), 8–13. For first hand observations see Berlandier, *Journey to Mexico* II, 412–448; José Antonio Navarro, *Defending Mexican Valor in Texas: José Antonio Navarro's Historical Writings, 1853–1857*, edited by David R. McDonald and Timothy Matovina (Austin: State House Press, 1995); José María Rodríguez, *Rodríguez Memoirs of Early Texas* (San Antonio: Passing Show Printing, 1913); Juan N. Seguín, *A Revolution Remembered: the Memoirs and Selected Correspondence of Juan N. Seguín*, edited by Jesús F. De la Teja (Austin: State House Press, 1991); Antonio Menchaca, *Recollections of a Tejano Life: Antonio Menchaca in Texas History*, edited by Timothy Matovina and Jesús de la Teja (Austin: University of Texas Press, 2013). Also see Arnoldo De León, *The Tejano Community, 1836–1900* (Albuquerque: University of New Mexico Press, 1982); Arnoldo De León, *They Called them Greasers: Anglo Attitudes toward Mexicans in Texas, 1821–1900* (Austin: University of Texas Press, 1983); Tijerina, *Tejanos and Texas under the Mexican Flag*, 137–144; Reséndez, *Changing National Identities at the Frontier*, 146–170.

65. For the argument that economic activity withered below the Nueces between 1830 and 1850 see Leroy P. Graf, "The Economic History of the Lower Rio Grande Valley, 1820–1875," volume 1 (PhD dissertation, Harvard University, 1942); Leroy P. Graf, "Colonizing Projects in Texas South of the Nueces, 1820–1845," *SHQ* 50 (April 1947): 431–448. For a more nuanced view see Armando C. Alonzo,

Tejano Legacy: Rancheros and Settlers in South Texas, 1734–1900 (Albuquerque: University of New Mexico Press, 1998), 67–94; Paul Schuster Taylor, *An American-Mexican Frontier: Nueces County, Texas* (Chapel Hill: University of North Carolina Press, 1934), 14–28; Gilberto Miguel Hinojosa, *A Borderlands Town in Transition: Laredo, 1755–1870* (College Station: Texas A&M University Press, 1983), 25–63; Tijerina, *Tejano Empire*, 3–20. Also see Jordan, *North American Cattle-Ranching Frontiers*, 210–215; Jones *Texas Roots*, 59–76.

66. For an eyewitness account of the area between Laredo and the Nueces see José María Sánchez, "A Trip to Texas in 1828," *SHQ* 29 (April 1926): 249–288. Also see Jordan, *North American Cattle-Ranching Frontiers*, 147–158, 210–221; Alonzo, *Tejano Legacy*, 67–94; Edward Dougherty, *The Rio Grande Valley: A Lecture Delivered before the Lone Star Literary Association of Brownsville, Texas, May 29, 1867* (Brownsville, 1867; reprint, Brownsville, 1955).

67. Alonzo, *Tejano Legacy*, 43–94; Hinojosa, *Borderlands Town*, 25–64; Tijerina, *Tejano Empire*, 21–106; Tijerina, *Tejanos and Texas under the Mexican Flag*, 46–64, 137–144; David Montejano, *Anglos and Mexicans in the Making of Texas, 1836–1986* (Austin: University of Texas Press, 1987), 13–100. For analysis of a similar area see de la Teja and Wheat, "Bexar," 7–34; Raúl A. Ramos, *Beyond the Alamo: Forging Mexican Ethnicity in San Antonio, 1821–1861* (Chapel Hill: University of North Carolina Press, 2008), 15–204.

68. DeLay, *War of a Thousand Deserts*; Hinojosa, *Borderlands Town*, 23–63; Alonzo, *Tejano Legacy*, 85–92; Jordan, "Ethnic Change in Texas," 392–394.

69. On Texas cities see Kenneth W. Wheeler, *To Wear a City's Crown: The Beginning of Urban Growth in Texas, 1836–1865* (Cambridge: Harvard University Press, 1968); Ralph A. Wooster, "Foreigners in the Principal Towns of Ante-Bellum Texas," *SHQ* 66 (October 1962): 208–220.

70. Johnson, *Sugar Industry in Texas*, 10–18; Olmsted, *Journey through Texas*, 244–245; Letter from I. T. Tinley, *Texas Almanac, 1859*, 76–77; letter from Col. Waters, *Texas Almanac, 1859*, 77–80; William J. Jones, "General Hints and Suggestions to the Farmer, Applicable to the Several Months of the Year," *Texas Almanac, 1859*, 80–85.

71. Angela Boswell, *Her Act and Deed: Women's Lives in a Rural Southern County, 1837–1873* (College Station: Texas A&M University Press, 2001); Mark M. Carroll, *Homesteads Ungovernable: Families, Sex, Race, and the Law in Frontier Texas, 1826–1860* (Austin: University

of Texas Press, 2001); Eric Walther, "The Lives of Enslaved Women in Texas: Changing Borders and Challenging Boundaries," in *Texas Women: Their Histories, Their Lives,* eds. Elizabeth Hayes Turner, Stephanie Cole, and Rebecca Sharpless (Athens: University of Georgia Press, 2015), 53–81; Rebecca Sharpless, "Sallie McNeill: A Woman's Higher Education in Antebellum Texas," in *Texas Women*, 82–104.

72. *Debates of the Texas Convention* (Houston: J. W. Cruger, 1846), 37–55; Jean A. Stuntz, *Hers, His, and Theirs: Community Property Law in Spain and Early Texas* (Lubbock: Texas Tech University Press, 2005), 109–174; Woody Holton, "Equality as Unintended Consequence: the Contracts Clause and the Married Women's Property Acts," *JSH* 81 (May 2015): 313–340.

73. Gilbert Jordan, ed. and trans., "William Steinert's View of Texas in 1849," *SHQ* 80 (July 1976): 57–78; 80 (October 1976): 177–200; 80 (January 1977): 283–301; 80 (April 1977: 399–416; 81 (July 1977): 45–72; Kelley, *Los Brazos de Dios*, 58–91; Carroll, *Homesteads Ungovernable*, 76–166; Ann Patton Malone, *Women on the Texas Frontier: A Cross-Cultural Perspective* (El Paso: Texas Western Press, 1983); Jean A. Stuntz, *Hers, His, and Theirs: Community Property Law in Spain and Early Texas* (Lubbock: Texas Tech University Press, 2005).

74. Trenckmann, "Austin County," 31. Also see Kamphoefner, "German Texans," 119–138; Kelley, *Los Brazos de Dios*, 130–161.

75. For eyewitness accounts of the San Antonio area see McDonald and Matovina, *Defending Mexican Valor in Texas: José Antonio Navarro's Historical Writings*; Matovina and de la Teja, *Recollections of a Tejano Life: Antonio Menchaca*; de la Teja, *A Revolution Remembered: The Memoirs and Selected Correspondence of Juan N. Seguín*; John J. Linn, *Reminiscences of Fifty Years in Texas* (New York: Sadlier, 1883), especially 352–354; Olmsted, *Journey through Texas*, 150–167. Also see Ramos, *Beyond the Alamo*, 167–230; De León, *They Called Them Greasers*; De León, *The Tejano Community*, 88–90; David R. McDonald, *José Antonio Navarro: In Search of the American Dream in Nineteenth-Century Texas* (Denton: Texas State Historical Association, 2010).

76. See for example the statistics, information on laws, and various pieces of advice in *Texas Almanac, 1857*.

77. Matovina and de la Teja, *Recollections of a Tejano Life: Antonio Menchaca*, 85. On the various types of money used during the Republic era see James P. Bevill, *The Paper Republic: The Struggle for Money, Credit and Independence in the Republic of Texas* (Houston: Bright Sky Press, 2009).

78. On money, banking, and credit in Texas before 1850 see William M. Gouge, *The Fiscal History of Texas* (Philadelphia: Lippincott, Grambo & Company, 1852); Avery Luvere Carlson, *A Monetary and Banking History of Texas: From the Mexican Regime to the Present Day, 1821–1929* (Fort Worth: The Fort Worth National Bank, 1930), 1–18. Also see Margaret Swett Henson, *Samuel May Williams: Early Texas Entrepreneur* (College Station: Texas A&M University Press, 1976); George D. Green, *Finance and Economic Development in the Old South: Louisiana Banking, 1804–1861* (Palo Alto: Stanford University Press, 1972); Jane Knodell, "Rethinking the Jacksonian Economy: The Impact of the 1832 Bank Veto on Commercial Banking," *Journal of Economic History* 66 (2006): 541–574; Richard H. Kilbourne, *Slave Agriculture and Financial Markets in Antebellum America: The Bank of the United States in Mississippi, 1831–1852* (London: Pickering and Chatto Limited, 2006); Alasdair Roberts, *America's First Great Depression: Economic Crisis and Political Disorder after the Panic of 1837* (Ithaca: Cornell University Press, 2012); Jessica M. Lepler, *The Many Panics of 1837: People, Politics, and the Creation of a Transatlantic Financial Crisis* (New York: Cambridge University Press, 2013); Baptist, *The Half Has Never Been Told*, 215–260.

79. Some local newspapers carried the exchange rate and value of the various types of money available in New Orleans. See Houston *Telegraph and Texas Register*, October 4, 1843. On arbitrage and the general monetary situation of Texas see in particular Thomas F. McKinney to Samuel May Williams, January 7, 1835; Thomas F. McKinney to Sam Houston, March 14, 1837; November 12, 1840, December 31, 1841, all in Thomas F. McKinney papers, Briscoe Center. Also see, Henson, *Samuel May Williams*, 45–150; Carlson, *Monetary and Banking History of Texas*, 1–10; Olmsted, *Journey through Texas* (comments on money throughout); Baptist, *The Half Has Never Been Told*, 254–260.

80. Curlee, "Texas Slave Plantations"; Abner J. Strobel, *The Old Plantations and Their Owners of Brazoria County* (Houston, 1926; rev. ed., Houston: Bowman and Ross, 1930; rpt., Austin: Shelby, 1980); Baptist, *The Half Has Never Been Told*, 261–342; Mark Nackman, "Anglo-American Migrants to the West: Men of Broken Fortunes? The Case of Texas, 1821–1846," *Western Historical Quarterly* 5 (October 1974): 441–455.

81. Woodman, *King Cotton and His Retainers*, 98–138; Henson, *Williams*, 94–113. For sketches of migrants to a Texas plantation region

see Kelley, *Los Brazos de Dios*, 20–57; Baptist, *The Half Has Never Been Told*, 261–307.

82. Henson, *Williams*, 94–113; Carlson, *Monetary and Banking History of Texas*, 1–22.

83. Bevill, *Paper Republic*, 287–290.

84. Gouge, *The Fiscal History of Texas*, 120–160; Edward W. Heusinger, "The Monetary History of the Republic of Texas," *SHQ* 57 (July 1953): 82–90. On the economy and money supply from a merchant's point of view see Linn, *Fifty Years in Texas*; Lubbock, *Six Decades*, 120–189.

85. Nell Mick Pugh, ed., "Contemporary Comments on Texas, 1844–1847," *SHQ* 62 (January 1959): 368. On the lead-up to an annexation see Campbell, *Gone to Texas*, 157–184; Campbell, *Empire for Slavery*, 50–66.

86. On annexation see Pugh, "Contemporary Comments on Texas, 1844–1847," 367–370; Joel H. Silbey, *Storm Over Texas: The Annexation Controversy and the Road to Civil War* (New York: Oxford University Press, 2005); Frederick Merk, *Slavery and the Annexation of Texas* (New York: Knopf, 1972).

PART IV:

Social and Cultural Vistas

Chapter 12
Frontier Bonnets: Women in the Republic of Texas

Mary L. Scheer

In 1827 when Noah Smithwick, a pioneer blacksmith, miller, and memoirist from Kentucky, arrived by schooner into the province of Texas, he described the region as "a dreary place for a lone stranger to land." His first meal consisted of "dried venison sopped in honey," but game was plenty and the soil was rich for future crops. The colonists he encountered consisted of a dozen families, including women and children, who "huddled together for security against the Karankawas." They lived in crude log cabins that were "windowless and floorless," providing meager protection or comfort. The men were hopeful, he observed, and the children delighted in their new environs, but the women, "ah, there was where the situation bore heaviest." Saddened by the family and friends they left behind and the scarcity of basic household items, they endured the hardships, privations, and dangers of a raw frontier. While the men occupied themselves with killing game and cutting trees, there was "little for the women to break the monotony of their lives." As Smithwick famously quoted one old woman, Texas was "a heaven for men and dogs, but a hell for women and oxen."[1]

The conditions that Smithwick and other immigrants described, coupled with social and political instability, characterized life in both Mexican and Anglo Texas. The region was a remote, sparsely populated, northernmost province of Mexico, governed by a regime thousands of miles away with alien customs, religious practices, and a foreign language. Like Smithwick, the Anglo immigrants had arrived beginning in the 1820s from distant American states, lured by cheap lands and the promise of a better future. As newcomers, they too encountered "nothing but wilderness," along with obvious differences between the Mexican people and their own backgrounds. Nevertheless, in about a decade, the Anglo population of Texas outstripped Tejano residents by approximately four to one, declared their independence, fought and won a revolution, and created a newly independent state, the Republic of Texas (1836–1845).[2]

Utilizing the metaphor of "frontier bonnets," women of all colors and stripes resided in the Republic after 1836. Like most groups, they were not homogenous. Many had crossed the Sabine or Red rivers or sailed on schooners to Texas with their husbands and families to build a new life. A few single women and widows came without spouses. Several had participated in the recent revolution, losing husbands and property, while contributing to its ultimate success. Some arrived as chattel property, while others struggled just to hold on to their homes and cultures. Their backgrounds varied as well, from plantation mistresses and farm wives to black slaves and native women. They included Native Americans, Tejanas, Anglos, African-Americans, and foreigners. All claimed a stake in the future of the newly independent nation, whether for land, wealth, status, or freedom.

The birth of the infant Republic was both protracted and difficult. Months of labor pains, marked by political clashes, ethnic differences, and economic conflicts, preceded the final decision to separate and give birth to an independent nation. Two events, the Runaway Scrape and the siege of the Alamo, unfolded while delegates to the constitutional convention met at Washington-on-the-Brazos to declare independence and form a Republic. Both episodes nearly aborted the parturition and significantly touched the lives of women and all Texans.

The first event was the mass exodus of civilian settlers eastward away from the advancing Mexican troops and involved a considerable number of women. Beginning in February 1836 and continuing until the final victory at San Jacinto on April 21, 1836, the chaotic scrape took place "amidst great confusion, disorder, panic, and (in some cases) sheer terror." Many families evacuated without their men and encountered impassable roads due to spring rains. Widow Angelina Peyton recalled the "great commotion—destruction of property—much left on river banks—no wagons scarcely—few horses—many on foot mud up to their knees—women and children." Dilue Rose Harris described over 5,000 people waiting at Lynch's Ferry in southeastern Texas, which became jammed due to waiting refugees. Some also died from the rigors of the journey, such as Dilue's little sister and the infant daughter of Emily Austin Perry, the sister of empresario Stephen F. Austin. As Thomas Jefferson Rusk, a signer of the Texas Declaration of Independence and delegate to the constitutional convention observed: "The women with their little children around them, without means of defense or power to resist, faced danger and death with unflinching courage."[3]

The second event, the siege and then fall of the Alamo on March 6, 1836, was essentially a male affair between two armies, but also affected women, especially those non-combatants who survived the battle. At least seven women and children took refuge behind the Alamo walls, including six *Bexareña* women and one Anglo woman. Mexican soldiers brought those surviving *Bexareña* women and children before General Antonio López de Santa Anna for interrogation. Afterward, Santa Anna forced the captives to pledge allegiance to Mexico, gave them "two silver pesos and a blanket," and permitted them to return to their families. However, their lives were never the same. Many became widows, the children fatherless, and their futures uncertain under the new Republic. For example, Madam Candelaria, who had nursed Jim Bowie at the Alamo, experienced "prolonged periods of loss and deprivation" and did not receive a pension for her services until 1891. Among the most well-known of the Alamo survivors, due in part to the early Anglo-centric narrative of the battle, was Susanna Wilkerson Dickinson and her infant daughter Angelina. They too were brought before General Santa Anna for questioning and then released in exchange for delivering a warning to General Sam Houston. As a widow during the Republic years, Susanna only had her fame and claims to her husband's pension to sustain herself. Only through remarriage was she finally able to regain some semblance of financial support and domestic happiness.[4]

With the sudden victory by General Houston at San Jacinto that secured Texas independence, women and children began returning to their homes following the Runaway Scrape. It was apparent that many families had encountered the effects of the invading army. Homes were looted; towns were burned; and crops were destroyed. One woman, Lydia Ann McHenry, who evacuated to the Trinity River, returned to the Austin colony to find her bed destroyed and "all [her] clothes stolen by plunderers." James and Emily Perry reached their Peach Point plantation near Brazoria only "to find their entire plantation in disarray." Angelina Peyton remembered seeing her home in San Felipe after the war. The "place [was] bare of everything but ruins all my things burnt up. …" And Mrs. George Sutherland, who lost a son at the Alamo, found on her property "nothing in the world worth speaking of." For these Anglo women and their families, as well as the thousands of others who participated in the scrape, their prospects under the new Republic appeared bleak.[5]

As peace and families returned to Texas, women faced challenges under the fragile Republic. How would they rebuild their lives? Could the new Republic restore public order and safety? What roles would women play in the new nation? What rights and benefits, if any, would they realize under an Anglo-controlled government? Answers to these questions were different for each group of Texas women. Clearly, Anglo women were in the best position to benefit from independence and achieve a measure of success. However, according to historian Paul D. Lack, the revolution had failed to overthrow the social fabric, thereby leaving intact the status quo in gender relations and placing greater restrictions on women's legal and economic rights than under Spanish and Mexican laws. Other female groups as well, such as Native American women, Tejanas, and black women were disadvantaged. Some were treated as outcasts, others as enemies, and still others as property. For the foreseeable future, women under the Republic of Texas would continue to be subordinate to men and some even lost ground.[6]

With the inauguration of Sam Houston in 1836 as the first president of the Republic, Texas was still very much Indian territory. The native population at the time totaled about 20,000 and represented a variety of Indian groups from the Comanche and Kiowa to the west, the Caddo and Cherokee in the east, and the Karankawa to the south. Anglo settlements as far north as Austin were frequently subject to Indian raids, which drew reprisals from the new government. Other than Houston, most of the Texan leadership and settlers saw no place for Indians in Texas and sought to remove or exterminate them. Attempts at friendships and alliances were often rejected or later overturned by subsequent administrations. In the end, the force of the Republic's military power, especially under Mirabeau B. Lamar's rule, resulted in curbing Indian resistance and removing many tribes from Texas.[7]

The use of violence and force affected native women, who played essential roles within Indian cultures. Their positions varied according to each tribe's unique history and customs, as well as how the tribe adapted to changing circumstances. According to historian Lindy Eakin, there were three major subsistence groups of Indians living in Texas: village-based groups, hunting/trading groups, and hunter/gathering groups. Each relied on trade with other Indians and Euro-Americans to provide goods, commodities, and horses, as well as alliances, which held many relationships together. Within the various tribes, gendered roles determined the work of native women. A village-based clan such as the Cherokees was organized in a more traditional manner, with women performing the farming, gathering, and caring of the household. Hunting, warfare, and diplomacy were the province of Cherokee men. As Eakin observed: "The differing roles did not imply that one gender's role was more important than the other; instead each complemented each other." Women performed important roles in another village-based tribe: the Caddos of east Texas. According to Hasinai mythology, the human race descended from one woman and Caddo women held matrilineal "ownership" of the household and fields. They cultivated the crops, finished deerskins, and distributed food. Women also played a key role in diplomacy, signaling peaceful intentions with outsiders by their presence. In hunter/trading groups such as the Comanche, men typically had multiple wives, a sign of their wealth and status. Comanche wives were highly esteemed, often symbolizing friendly relations and strong attachments to their husbands. In their villages Comanche women and girls performed necessary tasks such as taking care of the horses and processing buffalo hides. The Karankawa, a hunter/gatherer Indian group, lived along the Texas coast. They came in conflict early with Anglo settlements led by Stephen F. Austin. Restricted to lands west of the Guadalupe River, they were a small fraction of their former numbers during the Republic years and Karankawa women and their families struggled just for survival.[8]

Unlike the Spanish and Mexicans, who adapted to native protocols and reciprocal trade agreements, most Anglo Texans under the Republic adopted President Lamar's injunction against the Indians. He believed that the native population was a major obstacle to Anglo expansion and instituted a policy of removal or extermination. Several tribes therefore found themselves in precarious positions. The Caddos, who lived in the Neches and Angelina valleys, occupied prime land in the area around Nacogdoches. Under pressure from the government and the Texas Rangers, they were forced to relocate several times, adversely affecting women's horticulture and familial roles. Lamar also waged war on the Comanches, which was prolonged and bloody, resulting in hundreds of Comanche men killed, livestock and goods plundered, and women and children left bereft. The treatment of the Cherokees was the harshest. In 1839 Lamar suspected that the Cherokees were involved in a multi-tribe conspiracy and called for their removal from East Texas. Defying Lamar's order to leave peacefully, Chief Bowles (Duwali) and about 100 warriors resisted and were killed at the Battle of Neches. The remaining women and families were then driven north of the Red River into Indian Territory. This removal disrupted their village-based society, brought death and loss, and undermined native women's ability to re-establish households and fields to support their families.[9]

Overall, government policies and Anglo population growth during the Republic years had a devastating effect on native women. Increased pressures and raids on hunting camps destroyed their subsistence systems and displaced many villages. Militia and Ranger attacks made them captives and victims of warfare. While women's roles within those societies did not significantly change, their lives were altered as they struggled just to maintain households, families, and customs. Ultimately, removal or extermination led to life on federal reservations, loss of their way of life, and in some cases, destruction or decline of tribal societies.[10]

Creation of an Anglo Republic also disadvantaged Tejanas and their families. With independence in 1836, the Anglo majority totaling 34,470 outnumbered the minority Mexican population of approximately 3,470. As Anglo leaders claimed more of the land between the Nueces River and the Rio Grande, where most Mexican families lived, Tejanos lost their property, holdings, and cattle. Further, Anglos frequently regarded Hispanics with hostility and viewed them as inferior due their skin color, religion, and culture. While Tejanas enjoyed basic rights of citizenship, their loyalty, and that of their families, was often questioned. Due to the divided allegiance of the Mexican-Texan population during the recent revolution, they were treated as "foreigners in their native land." For example, Anglo Texans often viewed the six *Bexareña* widows who survived the battle of the Alamo as the enemy, while Mexicans saw them as traitors. Their fate under the Republic was one of economic decline and social pariahs. With the 1842 reinvasion by General Santa Anna and his forces, rumors of disloyalty and treason by Tejanos increased. Even Juan N. Sequín, Tejano veteran of San Jacinto and mayor of San Antonio, was suspect. Anti-Mexican sentiment forced Seguín to resign his position and eventually flee to Mexico with his wife María Gertrudis Flores de Abrego, a member of an important ranching family. They did not return for six years. At the same time, Tejano families were often threatened with violence over land disputes with ambitious Anglos. With little knowledge of the law or language, many Mexican families were forced to sell out and leave, such as Patricia de la Garza de León, who helped build the Catholic Church in Victoria. Although she had supported the Texas Revolution, she lost control over her extensive land holdings and was forced to flee Texas and live in poverty in Louisiana. As a result, over a million acres of land changed hands from 1837 to 1842, largely from Mexican landholders, including many Tejanas, to Anglo owners.[11]

As historian Jean Stuntz has pointed out, the immediate daily life of Tejanas during the Republic years changed very little. They continued to live in small villas or towns such as San Antonio. Their lives, as before the revolution, revolved around their families. Women "ground corn to make tortillas, spun thread and wove cloth, took care of their family, and participated in community events." Tejanas also cleaned the house and tended the gardens and livestock. But they also took time for leisure activities, including religious parades, such as the procession of Our Lady of Guadalupe, and street dances known as *fandangos*. On such occasions, Tejanas often encountered Anglo men who would comment on the "sensuous movements of the Mexican women." After 1836, the only difference in their daily lives was that "they now did all this in occupied territory."[12]

As more and more Anglos arrived in the Republic, Tejanas increasingly lost power, land, and status. Many Hispanic women who had survived the revolution were descendants of some of the original families whose ancestors had come as military or civilian settlers. They helped shape the society and culture of Spanish and Mexican Texas, which was characterized by a rigid hierarchy separating elites, small landowners, working class, and peon women. With Anglo occupation, social positions, property, and legal rights eroded. Some wealthier Hispanic families, in an attempt to retain their social standing and gain political influence, married their daughters to promising Anglos. Since Mexican daughters inherited property, often on an equal basis with sons, arranged intermarriages united Mexican landed wealth women with well-positioned Anglo men. For example, Ángela Maria de Jesús Blasa Navarro, the daughter of José Antonio Navarro, a signer of the Texas Declaration of Independence, married the Republic's adjutant general, thereby creating an important base of power between a rich Tejana and an Anglo newcomer.[13]

Nevertheless, intermarriage and accommodation could not prevent Anglo domination. During the Republic years, the ratio of Anglos to the Mexican population was about five to one. With many newcomers bringing their racial prejudices against "people of color," Hispanics became socially and economically marginalized. In cities like San Antonio, which had been mostly Mexican, Anglo customs supplanted Hispanic culture, which "sometimes clashed and sometimes intermingled." Through the control of the government, commercial networks and, in some instances, use of violence and intimidation, the Anglo majority gained hegemonic power. In the process, Tejanas lost the ability to control their own lives or those of their families, with few prospects for political, social, or economic equality.[14]

Whether Mexican or Anglo, women lost significant legal rights under the Republic. During the Spanish and Mexican rule, women held extensive legal rights concerning property, inheritance, and contracts. Their legal identity did not disappear upon marriage, as under Anglo law, and they held the right to own land and conduct business, which "could make them self-sufficient," if necessary. However, with the new Texas Constitution of 1836, Congress stated that as early as practicable, it would "introduce, by statute, the common law of England," which was more familiar to most Texans. This change in law, which the Texas legislature formally enacted on January 20, 1840, meant that women's rights, especially those of married women, could be severely restricted. Utilizing the English doctrine of coverture, a *feme covert*, or married woman, lost her legal existence and became "covered" or controlled by her husband. Yet similar to the Spanish system, Republic women were able to retain certain separate property that she brought to the marriage and share equally in any wealth amassed from the union. This mix of legal traditions created a "hybrid system," which combined Spanish community and separate property laws with the English common law, and protected wives' separate property from their husband's creditors. But women still had certain disabilities under the Republic. For example, without a separate legal identity, she could not sell her separate property without her husband's consent, make contracts, write a will, or sue in court. Legally disadvantaged, Texas women, who were citizens of the Republic, also could not vote or hold office. But as historian Angela Boswell has showed, white women, who were vital economic partners in the household, were active in securing the rights they did have. For example, they independently initiated court cases in their behalf and sought probate of their husband's estates. Still, even with community and separate property laws providing protections to a wife's property, Republic and later statehood women remained worse off than under the earlier Spanish and Mexican systems, which were more equalitarian toward the sexes.[15]

Like Tejanas, Anglo women shouldered much of the burden of daily life under the Republic. Since Anglo women had higher literacy rates and left more of a written record, we know more about their day-to-day lives than other Texas women. Most of their homes consisted of one- or two-room log cabins with dirt or clay floors. Other houses, many in or near the towns, were more substantial with multiple rooms, out buildings, and kitchens. Those residing on small farms such as Sarah Hornsby of Travis County often crossed boundaries between the private and public spheres. She and others like her prepared the food, mended and washed clothes, and took care of the children. They also carded, spun, and wove cotton and wool for clothing. But the women and girls, wearing homespun shirts and dresses with sun bonnets to protect against the hot Texas sun, also worked alongside their husbands and fathers clearing the land, planting the crops, and tending the livestock. Entire families thus shared in the family economy and its solvency. As families became more prosperous and stores more accessible, a few women could obtain ready-to-wear clothes, or at least buy fabric by the yard. Plantation mistresses such as Emily Austin Perry, although expected to maintain a level of refinement, also crossed boundaries to ensure the success of the plantation. Her domestic sphere extended to maintenance of the household by directing necessary tasks, such as tending the gardens, preparing food, and clothing her family and slaves, but she also took an active role in family financial affairs in the public arena. By making independent decisions in the absence of her planter husband or selling off property to provide for the livelihood of the family, she enlarged the scope of women's activities and gender norms to suit the economic realities of a frontier Texas.[16]

The abrupt end of the Texas Revolution and the establishment of the Republic, however, did not necessarily ensure women's safety and comfort. Along with their domestic and economic duties, Anglo women at times took on the public defense of their families when encountering threats from Indian attacks and diseases endemic to a frontier region. Comanches and their allies, the Kiowas, controlled huge expanses of the Republic's lands and regularly raided and plundered frontier settlements. Even the creation of Ranger units by the Congress of the Republic could not eliminate the attacks, leaving women to defend themselves and their property when their husbands were away. For example, Sallie Hornsby, who lived near Bastrop, courageously mustered the women of the settlement against an Indian attack, "commanding them to don male attire, [and] armed them with broom sticks." The Indians, believing that they were outnumbered, retreated. At the same time, epidemics, such as cholera and small pox, spread like prairie fires across Texas communities. Mary Ann Maverick wrote in her *Memoirs*, "Violent influenza with sore throat and measles and scarlenta" felled many San Antonio residents, included several of the Maverick children who became ill and died.[17]

Young Anglo girls and women were also favorite targets of the Indians. Native peoples frequently seized and held them captive as tribal slaves, wives, and concubines, while their children were held for ransom, sold to traders, or adopted into their captors' tribes. In May of 1836, a party of approximately 500 Comanche warriors attacked Fort Parker in current-day

Limestone County, killing several inhabitants and seizing five others. One female captive was nine-year-old Cynthia Ann Parker who subsequently assimilated into Indian society, married a Comanche chief, and gave birth to three children. Over twenty-four years later, on December 19, 1860, she was "recaptured" near the Pease River by the Texas Rangers and returned to the Anglo world. However, she never reconciled to living in white society, yearning to return to her tribal ways and mourning the loss of her Comanche family.[18]

Indians kidnapped and brutalized other Anglo women. Rachel Parker Plummer was a pregnant seventeen-year-old girl with a small child who was abducted by the Comanches who had attacked Fort Parker. Beaten and deprived of her children, she was held captive for thirteen months until ransomed by Mexican traders. In 1838 thirteen-year-old Matilda Lockhart and four other children were taken captive. Two years later on March 19, 1840, sixty-five Comanche warriors entered San Antonio to arrange for Lockhart's ransom. They demanded gunpowder, blankets, and paint in exchange for Lockhart, who had been severely tortured, burned, and mutilated. Mary Ann Maverick described the scene and subsequent battle as a "Day of Horrors." Known as the Council House Fight, 35 Comanches were killed, 27 captured, and 7 Texans died. Lockhart escaped to safety, but her "utterly degraded" condition left the young girl "very sad and brokenhearted" for the rest of her life.[19]

In addition to dangers from Indian raids, rumors often circulated about a re-invasion by Mexican troops and a possible alliance between Mexico and the Comanche tribe. Lydia Ann McHenry reflected such fears in a series of letters to her brother, expressing concern about "another invasion" or a "blockade of our ports" from Mexico. She openly sided with those members of the interim government who favored severe punishment for Santa Anna and his generals who were held captive. Like many others, she feared that if the general was returned to Mexico, then his army, which was "driven out almost to the Rio Grande," would soon return. "The first thing we would know of the enemy," she wrote on August 25, 1836, "he would be at the Colorado."[20]

Her fears proved correct. In March 1842, Santa Anna once again sent an army across the Rio Grande into Texas. The Mexican forces occupied San Antonio, Goliad, and Refugio, but retired a few days later. Despite the short-lived occupation, panic ensued across central Texas, resulting in a second Runaway Scrape. Anglo families, such as the "tribe of Maverick"—Mary Ann, husband Sam, and their three children—made hasty preparations and fled San Antonio on horseback to points beyond the threatened area. Mary Ann recalled that "families ran away from their homes ... and great losses followed." The Maverick house was "robbed of everything" and "all kinds of damage had been done to anything belonging to Americans." Fearful of returning to the city, only 150 miles inland from the Mexican border, they relocated to land across the Colorado River near LaGrange. Unfortunately, Mexican troops returned later that year, capturing Sam Maverick, who was in San Antonio on business, and imprisoning him in Castle Perote in Mexico for seven months.[21]

During the "dark days for the Lone Star republic," the infant government faced numerous dangers and problems, including finding an acceptable location in which to conduct its business. The first Congress had convened at Columbia, a primitive frontier town about 100 miles inland from the Texas coast, but later relocated to Houston, which was nearer to population centers and navigable waterways. New York land speculators John and Augustus Allen had promoted the city as "handsome and beautifully elevated, salubrious and well watered." But not everyone agreed. Millie Gray, who settled in Houston with her husband William in 1837, found the city disagreeable, remarking that she "never saw anything like the mud here." The city's position as the seat of government ended when Congress created a five-member commission to locate the nation's capital "at some point between the rivers Trinity and Colorado and above the old San Antonio road." President Mirabeau B. Lamar favored moving the government away from its east Texas location, which was also his rival Houston's namesake, and further west nearer to Waterloo, later Austin.[22]

In 1842 Texas women joined in the controversy over the location of the nation's capital. Two years prior, the January 1840 census of Austin showed 856 residents and 75 families living there. Like most frontier outposts, men outnumbered women by nine to one. One woman, Julia Lee, had arrived in Austin from Cincinnati, Ohio, with her sister and two brothers. Shortly thereafter, she married George W. Sinks, Lamar's chief postal clerk, and later wrote a series of newspaper articles describing life in Austin. Like most newcomers she was struck by the natural beauty and promise of the town and region. She described the President's House there as a white frame building, which stood "upon the top of one of the pinnacles of green" in Austin. Its stately appearance and location inspired great pride in the young woman, proclaiming it "good enough for a king."[23]

Margaret Moffette Lea Houston, Galveston, circa 1840. Courtesy of Sam Houston Memorial Museum, Huntsville, Texas.

Nevertheless, Austin was a town far from the frontier line of settlements, deep inside Indian Territory, and within striking distance of the Mexican army. During her husband's time in office as president, Margaret Houston worried constantly about his "living in a city that hosted Indian battles in its streets." Further, recent invasions by Mexican troops prompted Secretary of War George Hockley to warn that "if not checked, the next move of the enemy … will be against this place, [Austin] to destroy the archives." These short occupations provided President Sam Houston in his second term with the opportunity to remove the government from Austin. A longstanding opponent of Austin as the capital city, Houston had written Anna Raguet, a young woman of Nacogdoches, that it was "the most unfortunate scite [*sic*] upon earth for the Seat of Government." He therefore decided to do something about it.[24]

One woman, however, stood in the way of Houston's plans. Her name was Angelina Peyton Eberly, a widow and innkeeper who in 1839 had moved to Austin for its economic prospects. She operated a boarding house—the Eberly House—where Houston first encountered her. Angelina soon exhibited her self-reliant, resolute spirit by blocking the removal of the state archives from Austin to Washington-on-the-Brazos where Congress would meet. On December 30, 1842, she observed a group of about twenty armed men ride into town with several wagons, stopping at the General Land Office. She immediately recognized that their mission was to remove the archives to Washington, a distance of about 100 miles. She quickly enlisted the aid of Dr. John Robertson, but he was reluctant to take any action. She was not. Angelina therefore pointed to a six-pound cannon across the street that was kept loaded in the event of Indian attacks. "What is that cannon for?" she cried. She then boldly proceeded to fire the weapon at the men carrying out their orders from Houston. The grapeshot alerted the community and several Austinites gave chase, successfully returning the records to the city. The archives were then unloaded at the Eberly House for safekeeping.[25]

After 1836 Texas women, rather than passive onlookers, had come to believe that they too held a stake in the new nation. The patriarchal model of domesticity and submissiveness, especially in a frontier environment, often gave ground to female autonomy and independent action. They openly expressed opinions about their future in the Republic and initiated actions that ultimately affected the location of the seat of Texas government. Such was the case of Angelina Eberly, who acted out of self-preservation, economic security, and a sense of the nation's rightful seat of government. She knew that with the capital situated in Austin many settlers, "seen on their way to the 'City of Austin,'" would offer a steady supply of boarders for her inn, the Eberly House. The new seat of government would also provide immediate employment for heads of household to plan and build the city, such as carpenter William Stark, and for women to work outside the home, such as his wife, whose "skills lay with needle and thread." Together they provided the "finishing touches to most of Austin's original government buildings." Further, the sale of city lots and farm lands in the area, which would surely increase in value, would attract men, women, and families to Austin as residents and homesteaders. The arrival of the new government also signaled that the future of Texas lay towards the west, at the crossroads of a promising trade network on the banks of the Colorado River. So as Austin's star as the nation's frontier capital rose, fell, and then was secured, so too did the prospects for women and their families to prosper under the Republic of Texas.[26]

Amid the uncertainty about the nation's capital, the Republic claimed two positive achievements that significantly affected women's lives. The first piece of domestic legislation, a Homestead Act (1839), attracted a large number of immigrants to settle in Texas by providing every citizen or head of family with fifty acres of land or one town lot. The second law, an Education Bill (1839), laid the foundations for a public education system in Texas. While these laws contributed to the settlement of Texas and the future education of its citizens, they also uprooted families, necessitated overland or ocean-going travel under perilous conditions, thrust immigrants into a foreign society, created new and unforeseen hardships, and challenged the health, survival, and schooling of frontier children.

Population statistics and newspaper accounts confirm the stunning growth of the Republic, much due to the liberal homestead laws. Shortly after the Texas Revolution, the Anglo population was reported at 34,470, with a slave population estimated at 5,000, Mexicans at 3,470, and Indians at 14,500. By the end of the Republic counts had increased to 102,961 white residents, including those of Mexican and German descent, 38,753 slaves, and 295 free blacks. No accurate estimates of the Indian population exist, but their numbers surely declined due to disease, removal, and war. Overall, the available data indicated that the total population of the Republic had increased over 250 percent, much due to the arrival of Anglo-Americans, Germans, other immigrants, and additional slaves. While the statistics on the numbers of women and children are not easily determined, most followed their husbands to Texas to take advantage of the generous land policy, the promise of a better life, or just "a fair share of curiosity." Whatever their motives, by 1837 the *Telegraph and Texas Register* reported that "crowds of enterprising emigrants are arriving on every vessel," while the next year reports claimed that more than 6,000 immigrants crossed the Sabine River into Texas. Of these, the vast majority lived on homesteads, in remote rural areas, and under primitive conditions.[27]

Many of the new immigrants suffered greatly during their early years in the Republic. Propaganda had circulated widely in Europe exaggerating their prospects, leaving many women ill equipped for the tasks required of them. Most families lacked accurate knowledge of the land, the conditions, or the weather. Women and children were particularly vulnerable due to the difficult journeys, the lack of basic necessities, and the dangers of settling in the fever-ridden river bottoms. Their crude dwellings and bland diets—pork, potatoes, and corn—offered few comforts or variety. Frequent cholera and small pox outbreaks, Indian and Mexican raids, and childbirth all took their toll on immigrant women on the Texas frontier. In addition, many women reacted to the separation from their homelands, leaving reminiscences expressing their feelings of loneliness and terror. Louise Weber Stoehr, one of the earliest German women in Texas, poignantly recalled her frontier isolation: "Like this we lived all alone in the wilderness, it seemed to be lonesome even for the Indians."[28]

The experiences of one German immigrant, Rosa von Roeder Kleberg, was fairly typical. In December 1834 she traveled with her new husband Robert and her parents by ship to New Orleans and then to Texas. Shipwrecked off the coast of Galveston Island, they managed to save all their goods and baggage, "which included everything we thought needful to begin a settlement in a new country." Like others, they were "pulled" to Mexican Texas by its liberal land policies and "pushed" by the political repression in Prussia. They followed family members through a chain migration to the south central part of Texas known as the "German Belt." Arriving in Cat Springs, Rosa and her family moved into a log house with "neither floor nor ceiling." Forced to evacuate her home and family during the Runaway Scrape, she "had to leave behind much that was valuable," which later vanished. In her *Memoirs*, she recalled life after the revolution and under the Republic. Without a home, livestock, money, or crops, she and her husband had to begin life anew, "with less than we had when we started." Rosa and Robert planted their fields, split rails, and built fences while suffering from "chills and fevers." Living near the main road from Houston to Austin, which was clogged with immigrants, Rosa opened a boarding house "since this occupation brought the quickest ready money." But life in frontier Texas was frequently wearisome and lonely. "I came into contact with the outside world very little," she recalled. "I was busy with my household, and had a great deal of work on my hands."[29]

Amusements and entertainments provided occasional escape from the isolation and boredom of everyday living. Women enjoyed visiting with neighbors or travelers, who provided opportunities for gossip and much-needed news. Families participated in house raisings, quilting bees, horse races, dances, concerts, and theatrical performances. Even Rosa Kleberg attended a few social gatherings, such as a grand ball in 1838 at San Felipe to celebrate the battle of San Jacinto. In addition, there were many professional performances centered in Galveston and Houston where one lady commented that the first theatrical company in Texas "not only ran the young people wild, but the old people were not much better." As early as 1838, San Augustine had a thespian troupe, but social standards of the day prohibited women from appearing in amateur theatrical productions. Men therefore played the female parts. The traveling circus also came to Texas, but due to its clientele, no ladies were admitted "unless accompanied by a gentleman." Holidays and special occasions such as weddings were celebrated, marked by drinking, dancing, and merriment. Sunday church services and prayer meetings often took on social, as well as religious significance. Even Indian raids, at least those that were false alarms, according to one young woman, made frontier life less "dull and flat."[30]

Educational opportunities in frontier Texas were also limited. With independence from Mexico, the prevailing sentiment was that the future of the Republic depended on an educated and enlightened citizenry, including women. In his message to the Texas Congress on December 21, 1838, President Lamar therefore urged those assembled to set aside "lands to the purpose of general Education." Congress acted the next month to provide three square leagues of land to each county for primary schools and fifty square leagues of land for the establishment of a university of the "first class." But Lamar's vision to "lay the foundation of a great moral, and intellectual edifice" failed to materialize immediately. Many years were to pass before Texas would have a functional public school system.[31]

In the absence of a "uniform system of free public education," girls were educated at home or in private schools. Teachers often held classes in log cabins "having neither floor or window, or even a door." For Anglo families who could afford the cost, private schools with separate female departments were available. One of the earliest of these schools in 1834 was located at Coles Settlement, founded by Frances Trask. Another was established by Lydia McHenry in Washington County. Curriculums for girls were "both solid and ornamental," ranging from literature to needlework, and aimed at training girls for "refined and cultured womanhood." While Texas had no laws to prevent education of Hispanic or slave girls, opportunities for those Texas women were limited or nonexistent. Since only a few mission or church schools existed in colonial Mexico, Tejanas' schooling was neglected under the Republic and "very few of the Mexican ladies could write. …" For slave women some owners sought to prevent their slaves from reading and writing as "it would lead to running away and other expressions of discontent." Available data reveals, however, that other owners had no objections to their slaves having at least a minimal education.[32]

Higher education in the Republic began at religious-affiliated institutions chartered by the state. Many were co-educational, opening female departments as their student populations grew. Despite their names, most offered little or no college level work. Rutersville College, chartered by the Republic, was established in 1840 by the Methodists near La Grange. It contained the first female department where women could pursue academic studies, as well as music, drawing, and painting. One of the best known was McKenzie College near Clarksville. Opened in 1841, four years later it added a female department and a collegiate department. In 1842, the University of San Augustine opened its doors under the guidance of the Presbyterian Church. It included a grammar school, a female department, and a college, but closed its doors in 1847 due to rising sectarianism, a rival college, and theological intolerance. At the same time, Marshall University was founded as a co-educational school until it organized a separate female department in 1850. One early institution still in existence today is Baylor University, founded in 1845 at Independence by the Baptists. Although it did not open until the next year, it received a charter from the Republic of Texas. Those Texans who desired a more rigorous curriculum and could afford the cost, often sent their children out of state to eastern schools. For example, Emily Austin Bryan enrolled her children in schools in Ohio while Mirabeau B. Lamar sent his daughter to Georgia for her education.[33]

With limited availability of schooling and opportunities during the Republic era, most women were destined for lives of domesticity. Their aspirations were in the private sphere of marriage, family and the home, fulfilling the tenets of "true womanhood." But Texas women were often far from uniform in an unsettled frontier setting such as the Republic of Texas. Whether due to social standing, stressful conditions, or economic necessity, frontier women often contested and transformed entrenched gender roles, functioning in ways traditionally reserved for men. Rather than rigid spheres between the sexes, they were more like "permeable boundaries" where women might share in men's traditional roles through their labor, their property, and their household.[34]

Few women remained single in frontier regions for long. Most married, had children, and contributed to the family economy. Marriage was often an affair of the heart and many wives enjoyed the benefits of a "companionate marriage"—a relationship based on love and mutual affection. But it was not uncommon that "endowments or incomes" were also considerations for couples. As historian Angela Boswell pointed out, "marriage was a financial transaction and a partnership." But according to historian Catherine Kerrison: "It rarely implied an equal partnership. It was clear that men expected to take the initiative and women to follow."[35]

Marital relationships in early Texas reflected the fluid conditions of a frontier region. The unstable social order, economic pressures, and primitive, often dangerous conditions, required men and women to adopt more pragmatic arrangements than they would normally in southern states. Settlers could not always rely on church or secular authorities to officiate their unions, so many were contractual in nature. Known as bond marriages during the Mexican-Texas era, they served to adjust traditional marital practices in isolated areas and promote the orderly distribution of land grants. In theory, these unions would be solemnized later when the clergy arrived to unite the spouses legally. With independence, the new Texas legislature, in an attempt to make legal marriage more accessible, passed a general marriage act of June 5, 1837. This law granted clergy of any faith, as well as government officials, the right to perform marriages, thus bringing a measure of marital order to the often chaotic, social milieu of early Texas.[36]

The marriages of two antagonists during the Republic era—Sam Houston and Mirabeau B. Lamar—are instructive of prevailing practices, at least among the ruling Anglo classes. Both Houston and Lamar had joined the fight to free Texas from Mexico, served as presidents of the Republic, and pursued strongly held visions for the future of Texas. As southerners, they both subscribed to the prevailing code of honor that required high moral standards and ethical behavior, at least in public. If challenged, a man should be willing to defend his personal reputation or that of his wife and family. Further, southern gentlemen measured their manhood in terms of prescribed gender roles. Men, as heads of household, must be strong-willed, rational, and competitive, often placing women on pedestals in need of their protection. Women's sphere was in the home, providing a place of refuge against the harsh forces of politics and the marketplace. There a man could be "soothed, softened, strengthened, cheered, and comforted by domestic tranquility." Both Houston and Lamar defined their manhood in these early nineteenth-century gendered terms, demonstrating their allegiance to southern gentility and a code of honor in their marriages and relationships.[37]

Houston married three times. His first marriage in 1829 was to Eliza Allen of Tennessee. This unhappy union ended after just eleven weeks. Although it is unclear as to the cause for the marriage breakdown, Houston never disparaged the lady's reputation. "It is no part of the conduct of a gallant and generous man" he declared, "to take up arms [accusations] against a woman." Houston never spoke of it again. After resigning his post as governor of Tennessee in disgrace, he married, and then later left his Cherokee wife, Diana Rogers, during his self-imposed exile from Anglo society. Sufficiently recovered, he ended his exile with the Cherokees and re-entered Texas in 1832. There Houston met and courted Anna Raguet, a woman almost half his age, often referring to himself as her "Knighterrant." Then, in 1840, Houston met and married Margaret Moffette Lea, the daughter of Nancy and Temple Lea of Alabama. Margaret was a lively, educated young woman who was twenty-six years Houston's junior. Despite the age difference, she provided Houston with the domestic tranquility that had eluded him in his previous unions. Raised in a strict Baptist environment, Margaret represented the ideal "true woman," observing the social conventions of the day while imposing her moral authority over a husband known as the "Big Drunk." Despite his conversion to abstinence, rumors persisted that he continued to drink out of Margaret's presence. On more than one occasion Houston wrote his wife to assure her of his "newfound ability to abstain from alcohol" and resist "my arch enemy… 'Grog' in any shape or character." Margaret also introduced *Bible* study to her reluctant husband. After her "lovingly merciless barrage," Margaret won him over to religion and Houston accepted baptism by immersion into the Baptist Church in Independence. Clearly, Margaret fulfilled the expectations of true womanhood, exerting a positive effect on Houston by providing a home life that had eluded him and the moral influence to "turn him around."[38]

Lamar, on the other hand, was a widower while president of the Republic. Born in Georgia, he grew to manhood in a plantation environment and received a classical education imbued with moral precepts and a high regard for women. One 1822 description of Lamar stated that he was "a gentleman not more distinguished by the loftiest sentiments of honor, than by mental superiority and devotion to Republican politics." A devoted husband, his first wife Tabitha Jordan died in 1830, a victim of tuberculosis, leaving him devastated and with a young daughter, Rebecca Ann. He found solace in travel and poetry. Two of his poems, "Thou Idol of My Soul" and "At Evening on the Banks of the Chattahoochee" recorded his turmoil and grief. Later, rumors of a courtship with Jane Long, one of the earliest Anglo women in Texas, persisted. Then, in 1843, his daughter died of yellow fever. Again, he plunged into melancholia, turning to travel and poetry to soothe his tormented soul, penning the tribute, "On the Death of My Daughter." Despite his grief, Lamar never forsook his southern code of honor or dreamy-eyed idealism. Unlike Houston, his racial bias toward native tribes would have prevented any possible union with an Indian woman whom he considered inferior. Only in 1851, after his presidency, did Lamar marry again, choosing a traditional patriarchal household that emphasized romantic love, mutual respect, and child rearing. With his second wife Henrietta Moffitt, he had another daughter, and retired to his Richmond plantation.[39]

While marriage and domesticity characterized most Anglo women's gender roles, a few Texas women entered the public sphere of the marketplace. Those who did were usually single or widowed, having certain legal rights as a *feme sole*. But married women also ran businesses, especially operating boarding houses or inns, often times referred to as a hotel. Innkeeping in the Republic era offered one of the few acceptable avenues open to women to live independent lives. While many of these early establishments were run by men, the heavy demand for food and housing in early Texas, especially for travelers, provided women opportunities to take in boarders and provide an income for themselves and their families. These establishments utilized female domestic skills by "providing sleeping quarters, food, and drink." But they also required business entrepreneurship and financial acumen in an occupation where "the problems of hotel proprietorship were formidable" in a frontier region. For example, Jane Long operated several boarding houses at Brazoria and later Richmond, and also owned considerable land, cattle, and slaves. Angelina Peyton Eberly ran the Eberly House in Austin, the Tavern House in Lavaca, and a hotel in Indianola. Pamelia Mann earned a livelihood running an inn at Washington-on-the Brazos and then in Houston when it was the capital. There she earned the reputation as both a businesswoman and "a most notorious character."[40]

Inns not only provided many Anglo women with a source of income, they were also centers for frontier balls and dinner parties. They were one of the few buildings in town large enough to host celebrations and accommodate guests. Many inns contained parlors with pianos, ballrooms for dances, and dining areas decorated with fine china. Boarding houses were often the sites for visiting dignitaries of the Republic. Dilue Rose Harris described one affair at a Houston hotel in which half the men were candidates for office in 1838. The ball formally opened with a grand march or promenade led by Sam Houston and followed by Mirabeau B. Lamar. The Bullock House in Austin was home to all "who came to Austin either for business or curiosity." In 1839 President Lamar arrived in the city and enjoyed a public dinner "of delicacies which graced the festive board" prepared by Mrs. Bullock. In 1841, President-elect Sam Houston returned to Austin and stayed at the Eberly House rather than at the President's House, which, unlike Julia Lee, he described as "in a ruinous and dilapidated condition." Houston later wrote his wife that during his stay he received "the most elegant and hearty greeting that I have ever done. Speeches and a party at night."[41]

Other avenues for women to support themselves were also available. Nancy Tevis, a widow with eight children at Tevis Bluff, now Beaumont, operated a ferry across the Neches River with a headright of land she received after her husband's death in 1836. Another widow with one child, Margaret Hallett, converted her cabin on the Lavaca River into a thriving trading post. Acting as "trader, seller, and clerk," she bartered with local residents and friendly Indians for provisions necessary for survival. With few schools, women also found employment opportunities as school teachers. During the Republic years, Frances Trask operated the first boarding school for "young ladies and misses." She wrote her father in 1835 that her prospects were "improving" and reported, "My school is small, but profitable."[42]

One group of Texas women with little free will, opportunities, or control over their lives, their marriages, or their families were female black slaves. Their fate declined under the "free" Texas government. As long as Texas remained under Mexican rule, there was hope that slavery would be abolished. But with independence and the creation of the Republic, proponents of the revolution took steps to ensure that the "new government will authorize the introduction of slaves into Texas." By March 1836, the delegates to the constitutional convention recognized slavery for life and guaranteed that "Congress shall pass no laws to prohibit emigrants from bringing their slaves into the republic with them." Thus, property rights in slaves were legally upheld, denying women and their families freedom for another thirty years.[43]

Most female slaves arrived in Texas either through the natural increase of the black population or involuntary immigration. Infant mortality among slave babies was high. Pregnant black women at times were worked "so hard, an' didn't give her much care w'en she was sick." Doctors were few and women relied on folk remedies. Those who arrived overland with their masters from the United States experienced many of the same hardships associated with travel by their Anglo counterparts. One slave woman's journey was particularly cruel. Silvia King arrived in Texas through France and then New Orleans. Abducted and held in the hold of a slave ship, she was eventually sold, chained, and marched to her new home near LaGrange. Interviewed at age 100, she recalled: "Dat was a awful time, 'cause us am all chained up and whatever one does us all has to do … and when one get tired or sick, de rest has to drag and carry him." Despite the hardships and powerlessness of black women, the increase in the slave population did have one small advantage. According to historian Angela Boswell, it made their lives less isolated and "easier for black women to form networks within the slave community to help them cope with the system of slavery. And it increased the likelihood of forming families."[44]

The peculiar institution in Texas was particularly harsh on women. Female slaves often did the same work as men. They shucked corn, picked cotton, milked cows, worked as hoe hands, tended gardens, and hauled wood and water, as well as performed routine household tasks. Typically, they worked six days a week "from can see to can't." But if any chores remained undone or they were sick during the week, then they "didn't get no Sunday, either." Sales of slaves, often resulting in the separation of women from their husbands and children, were particularly traumatic. Usually when a slave mother was off working in the fields, the master would collect the children and according to one slave "sold dem jus' like you sell a horse." Such separations were painful and threatened the survival of slave families. One slave recalled, "how Wash Hodges sold off Maw's chillen. I seed her plop down to a settin' and cry about it. But she allowed there weren't nothing could be done, cause it's the slavery law." In addition to the loss of loved ones, female slaves were often victims of sexual abuse or forced breeding to produce children for the master. Matilda (Tildy) Boozie Randon of Washington County recalled how "Young Mawster come up behind her. … [and] He put his hand up under her dress." Rose Williams remembered that she was forced to live with

Rufus, a black plantation slave, against her will. When she resisted, her master demanded, "Woman, I've paid big money for you and I've done that for the cause I want you to raise children." Threatened with a whipping if she continued to resist, Rose yielded.[45]

Treatment of female slaves varied by master. Emily Austin Perry, along with husband James, owned approximately fifty slaves. On their plantation, Emily understood that slaves were property and valuable economic investments. However, according to biographer Light T. Cummins, Emily also manifested "a sincere affection and concern about the slaves living on the plantation." She worried about their clothing, their food, and their health. She was particularly concerned about her house servant Clarissa, cautioning husband James: "If she is sick, she must be taken care of, for she is a good servant and must not be abused." Similarly, Margaret Houston took charge of their slaves during her politician husband's frequent absences. She was particularly fond of house servant Eliza, nursing her when sick and taking her to the governor's mansion to live in 1860. But not all slave owners were paternalistic. The WPA Narratives, a product of the Federal Writers' Project in the 1930s, recorded examples of slave violence and mistreatment. One washday slave woman received a beating every Wednesday for not keeping "de flies from speckin' de clothes overnight." Another female slave received beatings about the head and back because she asked her mistress to let her visit her sick child. Some would succumb to death after the whippings. But the Texas government did provide punishment for the abuse of slaves. In February 1840, Congress imposed fines of $250 to $2,000 for unreasonably cruel treatment. In addition, any person who murdered a slave through intent or mistreatment could be convicted of a felony. Nevertheless, a law in December of 1836, which provided that blacks and mulattos could not be a witness "in any case whatsoever, except for and against each other," meant that slaves could not testify against whites, effectively disadvantaging them legally. Although the legislative protections represented public disapproval of cruelty, courts were generally reluctant to intervene in the "the delicate and responsible relation of master and slave."[46]

Not only was the peculiar institution protected under the Republic, but the opportunity to gain one's freedom was severely restricted. Slaves could only be emancipated by their owner, with the consent of Congress, and on the condition that the slave would be removed from Texas. While manumission of slaves usually occurred through wills as a reward for years of loyal service, in some instances a slave owner would free a favorite slave, concubine, or child. In 1837, James Routh of Galveston freed Sylvia, a black female, at his death and provided her "320 acres of land and money," which later passed to her children. The next year slaveholder Joseph Walling petitioned Congress to emancipate black slave Moriah and her two children because "said woman has long since made to me full and ample satisfaction for her freedom." Although his petition and others were typically refused, many owners disregarded the law when the slave was a long and faithful servant. Many of these freed women and men simply remained in Texas, living in that gray area between bondage and freedom.[47]

Although the number of free blacks in Texas was small, no more than 150, the new Texas government took steps to restrict their presence as well. The Texas Constitution of 1836 stated: "No free person of African descent, either in whole or in part, shall be permitted to reside permanently in the republic, without the consent of congress." In 1837, however, a congressional joint resolution permitted free blacks who resided in Texas on March 1, 1836, to remain "as long as they choose." Three years later another act declared that all free blacks who did not leave by 1842 (later extended to 1845) would be sold into slavery.[48]

Several free black women petitioned Congress to remain in Texas. One such free woman of color was Fanny McFarland of Houston. Seventy-nine Houstonians who recommended her "as a good and useful citizen" signed her 1840 petition. Another free black woman was washer woman Zelia Husk, who in 1841 twice petitioned Congress for permission to remain in Texas. The same year nurse Mary Madison of Galveston, a free black woman, arrived in Texas and was considered to be "a very valuable citizen." She also petitioned for her right to stay in Texas. While Mary's petition was upheld, both Fanny and Zelia were denied. Regardless, like many other free blacks, they stayed anyway.[49]

Female slaves expressed their opposition to slavery in numerous ways. Some women passively resisted their enslavement by becoming "loyal servants," accommodating their masters to ensure that their families could survive. Others feigned illness, worked slowly, stole food, or practiced birth control or abortion. One mulatto slave in Jackson County named Elvira openly showed her rebelliousness in the late 1830s by "her irregularity of conduct and general misbehavior." She was then hired out to another master. Occasionally, slave women, driven to desperation, resorted to violence. In 1841, a $200 reward was posted for "two negro women, Nancy and Isabella" who allegedly murdered their master in Sabine County. But one of the most frequent acts by slaves was running away, either to Mexico where slavery had been abolished, eastward to their prior homes, or simply to live unmolested in the woods. An act of February 1841 gave Texans the right to apprehend runaways and take them before a local justice of the peace for return to their owner. Frequently, rewards for runaways appeared in the local newspapers, such as the one that appeared in the Houston *Weekly Telegraph* of January 8, 1845. The notice offered a $20 reward for the return of a slave girl Eliza, eight or nine years of age with "a light black complexion." Despite displays of agency by resisting enslavement, many women like Mollie Dawson of Navarro County, simply adjusted to their condition and did "the best we could which nearly all of us done."[50]

By 1844 the persistent political, economic, and social uncertainties, as well as the competing visions for Texas by Houston and Lamar, finally caught up to the fragile Republic. Factional politics, quarrelsome personalities, financial instability, Indian raids, Mexican threats, and questions of annexation or independence contributed to a general gloom "over every section of the Republic." Consequently, on October 13, 1845, Texas voters overwhelmingly approved annexation to the United States rather than continued existence as a weak Republic. Although women did not vote on statehood or their new government, they too had a stake in the future of Texas. Julia Lee Sinks reflected the optimistic opinion of many Texas women when she wrote, "the days of gloom and its days of brightness, its rejoicing and it heart-burnings" had all passed away. So at a ceremony in Austin on February 19, 1846, President Anson Jones relinquished his office to the first governor of Texas, J. Pinckney Henderson, and personally lowered the Lone Star flag and raised the American flag. Jones then announced: "This final act in this great drama is now performed; the Republic of Texas is no more."[51]

Visible in the crowd assembled in front of the Texas capitol that day were many "frontier bonnets," worn by Texas women who now looked eastward to the United States. However, not all groups would benefit equally from statehood. Native women would face warfare, destruction of their way of life, and removal from their homes. Tejanas continued to be viewed by the Anglo majority as racially and culturally inferior, losing property, rights, and status. Anglo women, however, had the most to gain by statehood. The first generation of Anglo women had experienced the harsh realities of frontier life, what the anonymous old woman Noah Smithwick quoted eighteen years earlier as "a hell for women and oxen." But by 1845, living conditions had improved somewhat and there were some long-lasting achievements in education, protection of women's property rights, and access to basic necessities. Yet the new Texas state government left in place the status quo in gender relations, exclusion from political life, and continued subordination to men. The most disadvantaged group would still be black females, whose enslavement by the Anglo majority under the short-lived Republic would persist, as Texans ratified a new constitution protecting slavery. Thus, for the foreseeable future, Texas would remain very much a rural, frontier society based on Anglo, male dominance. Texas women, who helped settle the land, raise crops, nurture families, and create communities, would continue to live much as they had under the Republic—as wives, mothers, and helpmates—but also as family business owners, heads of household, land owners, property managers, self-reliant homesteaders, resourceful innkeepers, schoolteachers, and resistors to slavery.[52]

Notes

1. Noah Smithwick, *The Evolution of a State or Recollections of Old Texas Days* (Austin: Steck-Vaughn Co, 1968), 10–15.

2. Estimates of the population of Texas before the revolution and during the Republic period often vary. In 1836 Henry W. Morfit numbered the Anglos at 30,000, Mexicans at 3,470, blacks at 5,000 and Indians at 14,500. Mary Crownover Rabb, *Travels and Adventures in Texas in the 1820's* (Waco, Texas: W. M. Morrison, 1962), 2.

3. Dilue Rose Harris, "The Reminiscences of Mrs. Dilue Harris," *The Quarterly of the Texas State Historical Association* 4 (July 1900-April 1901): 4: 162–167; Paul Lack, *The Texas Revolutionary Experience: A Political and Social History, 1835–1836* (College Station: Texas A&M University Press, 1992), 224. See also Mary L. Scheer, ed., *Women and the Texas Revolution* (Denton: University of North Texas Press, 2012).

4. The surviving *Bexareña* women were Concepción Charlé Gortari Losoya, Andrea Castañon de Villanueva (Madam Candelaria), Juana Navarro Pérez Alsbury, Gertrudis Navarro, Ana Salazar Castro Exparza, and Juana Francisca Losoya Melton. See Dora Guerra, "Two Silver Pesos and a Blanket" in Scheer, ed., *Women and the Texas Revolution*, 123–147.

5. George Nielsen, ed., "Lydia Ann McHenry and Revolutionary Texas," *Southwestern Historical Quarterly*, no. 3 (January 1971): 404; Lack, *The Texas Revolutionary Experience*, 224–237; Mary L. Scheer, "Joys and Sorrow of Those Dear Old Times: Anglo-American Women during the Era of the Texas Revolution" in Scheer, ed., *Women and the Texas Revolution*, 82–83; Light T. Cummins, "'Up Buck! Up Ball! Do

Your Duty!': Women and the Runaway Scrape," in Scheer, ed., *Women and the Texas Revolution, 175.*

6. Lack, *The Texas Revolutionary Experience*, 259.

7. Estimates of the Indian population vary from 14,500 to 40,000. Lindy Eakin, "Continuity, Change, and Removal: Native Women and the Texas Revolution," in Scheer, ed., *Women and the Texas Revolution*, 21.

8. Juliana Barr, *Peace Came in the Form of A Woman: Indians and Spaniards in the Texas Borderlands* (Chapel Hill: University of North Carolina Press, 2007), 277–278, 280–285; Eakin, "Continuity, Change, and Removal," 25–34.

9. See David La Vere, *The Texas Indians* (College Station: Texas A&M University Press, 2004); Randolph B. Campbell, *Gone to Texas*, 2nd ed. (New York: Oxford University Press, 2012), 167–170.

10. Eakin, "Continuity, Change, and Removal," 40.

11. Jean Stuntz, "Tejanas: Hispanic Women on the Losing side of the Texas Revolution," in Scheer, ed., *Women and the Texas Revolution*, 55, 59–60; Jesús F. de la Teja, ed., *A Revolution Remembered: The Memoirs and Selected Correspondence of Juan Seguín* (Austin: State House Press, 1991), 73–74, 92–10; Campbell, *Gone to Texas*, 190; Guerra, "Two Silver Pesos and a Blanket," 129; Ruthe Winegarten and Teresa Palomo Acosta, *Las Tejanas: 300 Years of History* (Austin: University of Texas Press, 2003), 46–47; Cary D. Wintz, "Women in Texas" in Ben Procter and Archie P. McDonald, eds., *The Texas Heritage*, 2nd ed. (Wheeling, IL: Harlan Davidson, Inc., 1992), 265.

12. Stuntz, "Tejanas," 56; Winegarten and Acosta, *Las Tejanas*, 54.

13. Stuntz, "Tejanas," 55, 60; Guerra, "Two Silver Pesos and a Blanket," 127; Winegarten and Acosta, *Las Tejanas*, 52–53.

14. Rupert N. Richardson, et al., *Texas: The Lone Star State*, 10th ed. (Boston: Prentice Hall, 2010), 119; Guerra, "Two Silver Pesos and a Blanket," 129, 146–147.

15. Constitution of the Republic of Texas, 1836, Art. IV, sec. 13; The Texas Constitution of 1845, Art. VII, sec 19. Jean A. Stuntz, "Spanish Law and Women in Colonial Texas, 1719–1821: 'I Wish to Make Use of All the Laws of Texas in My Favor,'" Elizabeth Hayes Turner, Stephanie Cole and Rebecca Sharpless, eds., *Texas Women: Their Histories, Their Lives* (Athens: University of Georgia Press, 2015), 31, 50; See Angela Boswell, *Women's Lives in a Rural Southern County, 1837–1873* (College Station: Texas A&M University Press, 2001), 12–30ff; Jean A. Stuntz,, *Hers, His, and Theirs: Community Property Law in Spain and Early Texas* (Lubbock: Texas Tech University Press, 2005), 168.

16. Annie Doom Pickrell, *Pioneer Women in Texas* (Austin: L. Steck, Co., 1929), 60; William Ransom Hogan, *The Texas Republic: A Social and Economic History* (Austin: University of Texas Press, 1946), 46–48, Light T. Cummins, *Emily Austin of Texas, 1795–1851* (Fort Worth: TCU Press, 2009), 157–165.

17. Smithwick, *The Evolution of a State*, 259; Rena Maverick Green, ed., *Memoirs of Mary A. Maverick: A Journal of Early Texas* (San Antonio: Maverick Publ., Co., 2005), 76–84. See also Paula Mitchell Marks, *Turn Your Eyes Toward Texas: Pioneers Sam and Mary Maverick* (College Station: Texas A&M University Press, 1989).

18. Rachel Plummer, *The Rachel Plummer Narrative* (n.p.: n.p., 1926), 5–12. See also Paul H. Carlson and Tom Crum, *Myth, Memory, and Massacre: The Pease River Capture of Cynthia Ann Parker* (Lubbock: Texas Tech University Press, 2010.

19. Plummer, *The Rachel Plummer Narrative*, 89–118; Green, ed., *Memoirs*, 23–27, 32–33; Scheer, "Joys and Sorrows of Those Dear Old Times," in Scheer, ed. *Women and the Texas Revolution*, 84–87.

20. Nielsen, ed., "Lydia Ann McHenry and Revolutionary Texas," 393, 402; Scheer, "Joys and Sorrows of Those Dear Old Times," 83–84.

21. Jo Ella Powell Exley, *Texas Tears and Texas Sunshine: Voices of Frontier Women* (College Station: Texas A&M University Press, 1985), 89–102; Scheer, "Joys and Sorrows of those Dear Old Times," 84.

22. These two antithetical viewpoints solidified political factions and continued to stir debate long after the commissioners selected the small hamlet of Waterloo on the Colorado River, later Austin, as the permanent site of the capital of Texas. Smithwick, *The Evolution of a State*, 252; Paul Lack, ed., *The Diary of William Fairfax Gray: From Virginia to Texas, 1835–1837* (Dallas: SMU Press, 1997), xxiv; Jeffrey Stuart Kerr, *Seat of Empire: The Embattled Birth of Austin, Texas* (Lubbock: Texas Tech University Press, 2013), 4, 11–25, 59–66.

23. Julia Lee Sinks, vertical file, "Early Days in Texas," 4, Dolph Briscoe Center for American History (DBCAH), University of Texas at Austin. See also Walter P. Freglag, *Chronicles of Fayette; The Reminiscences of Julia Lee Sinks* (n.p: n.p., 1975); Kerr, *Seat of Empire*, 86, 119, 131.

24. Kerr, *Seat of Empire*, 116, 174.

25. Kerr, *Seat of Empire*, 176–188; C. Richard King, "Angelina Belle Peyton Eberly" in Ron Tyler, et al., eds., *The New Handbook of Texas*, 6 vols. (Austin: Texas State Historical Association, 1996), 2: 777; Amelia Williams and Eugene C. Barker, eds., *The Writings of Sam Houston*,

8 vols. (Austin: Pemberton Press, 1970), 5: 322; Martha Anne Turner, *Sam Houston and His Twelve Women* (Austin: The Pemberton Press, 1966), 58–61.

26. Kerr, *Seat of Empire*, 92–127ff; Mark M. Carroll, *Homesteads Ungovernable: Families, Sex, Race and the Law in Frontier Texas, 1823–1860* (Austin: University of Texas Press, 2001), xx.

27. Gifford E. White, *1830 Citizens of Texas*, Appendix A (Austin: Eakin Press, 1983), 239; *Telegraph and Texas Register*, 1837.

28. Ann Patton Malone, "Victorian Womanhood on the Texas Frontier" in Sam W. Haynes and Cary D. Wintz, eds., *Major Problems in Texas History* (Boston: Houghton Mifflin Co., 2002), 200–207; Crystal Sasse Ragsdale, ed., *The Golden Free Land: The Reminiscences and Letters of Women on an American Frontier* (Austin: Landmark Press, 1976), 3.

29. Ragsdale, *The Golden Free Land*, 19–39.

30. Hogan, *The Texas Republic*, 113, 120, 125, 128, 130–131; William Ransom Hogan, "The Theater in the Republic of Texas," *Southwest Review* 19, no. 4 (July 1934): 374–401; Ragsdale, *The Golden Free Land*, 32; Michael L. Collins, "Statehood, 1845–1860," in Procter and McDonald, eds., *The Texas Heritage*, 2nd ed., 81–82; Sinks, Julia Lee, vertical file, 7, DBCAH.

31. "Lamar's Message to Congress, December 21, 1838," in Ernest Wallace, David M. Vigness, and George B. Ward, eds. *Documents of Texas History* (Austin: Texas State Historical Association Press, 2002), 127.

32. Smithwick, *The Evolution of a State*, 231; Campbell, *Gone to Texas*, 175–176; Winegarten and Acosta, *Las Tejanas*, 53; See also "Education" and "Mexican American Education" in Tyler, et al., eds., *The New Handbook of Texas*, 2: 794–796; 4: 671–672.

33. "Education" in Tyler, et al., eds., *The New Handbook of Texas*, 1: 428–429; 2: 788–794; 4: 523; 5: 732; 6: 642; Cummins, *Emily Austin of Texas*, 150–153; Freglag, ed., *Chronicles*, 79–90; "The First College in Texas, 1841–1842," in Wallace, Vigness, and Ward, eds., *Documents of Texas History*, 138–140.

34. Barbara Welter, "The Cult of True Womanhood: 1820–1860," *American Quarterly* 18 (Summer 1966): 151–174; Julie Jeffrey, "Permeable Boundaries: Abolitionist Women and Separate Spheres," *Journal of the Early Republic* 21, no. 1 (Spring 2001): 79–93. See also Sandra L. Myres, *Westering Women and the Frontier Experience 1800–1915* (Albuquerque: University of New Mexico Press, 1982), Adrienne Caughfield, *True Women and Westward Expansion*

(College Station: Texas A&M University Press, 2005) and Harriette Andreadis, "True Womanhood Revisited: Women's Private Writing in Nineteenth-Century Texas," *Journal of the Southwest* 31 (summer 1989): 179–204; Carroll, *Homestead Ungovernable*, 103.

35. Angela Boswell, *Her Act and Deed: Women's Lives in a Southern Rural County, 1837*–1873 (College Station: Texas A&M University Press, 2001), 53.

36. Carroll, *Homesteads Ungovernable*, 112–119.

37. Sylvia D. Hoffert, *A History of Gender in America* (Upper Saddle River, NJ: Prentice Hall, 2003), 167–189; Malone, "Victorian Womanhood on the Texas Frontier," 200.

38. The ideals of true womanhood were purity, piety, domesticity, and submission. See Barbara Welter, Annie Doom Pickrell, *Pioneer Women in Texas* (Austin: E. L. Steck Co., 1929), 5–10; Kerr, *Seat of Empire*, 152, 171; Turner, *Sam Houston and His Twelve Women*, 12–20, 61–78; James Haley, *Sam Houston* (Norman: University of Oklahoma Press, 2006), 49–61, 70, 220, 230, 332–333; *Ever Thine Truly: Love Letters from Sam Houston to Anna Raguet* (Austin: Jenkins Garrett Press, 1975), iii.

39. Philip Graham, *The Life and Poems of Mirabeau B. Lamar* (Chapel Hill: University of North Carolina Press, 1938), 160–165, 236–242; "Mirabeau Buonaparte Lamar," in Tyler, et al., eds., *The New Handbook of Texas*, 4: 37–39. Stanley Siegel, *The Poet President of Texas* (Austin: Pemberton Press, 1977), 130.

40. In 1840 Jane Long owned twelve slaves. William Ransom Hogan, "Pamelia Mann: Texas Frontierswoman," *Southwest Review* 20 (summer 1935): 360–370; Ellen Garwood, "Early Texas Inns: A Study in Social Relationships," *Southwestern Historical Quarterly* 60, no. 2 (October 1956): 219–244; Martha Anne Turner, *The Life and Times of Jane Long* (Waco: Texian Press, 1969), 1–84; Tyler, et al., eds., "Jane Herbert Wilkinson Long, " *The New Handbook of Texas*: 4: 274–275.

41. Garwood, "Early Texas Inns," 232–234, 237–238; Kerr, *Seat of Empire*, 171–173; Ragsdale, ed., *The Golden Free Land*, 32.

42. Evelyn M. Carrington, ed., *Women in Early Texas* (Austin: Texas State Historical Association, 1994), 98, 252; Hogan, *The Texas Republic*, 143.

43. Mexico abolished slavery in 1829, but granted Texas an exemption to continue bringing slaves into the region. The Constitution of the Republic of Texas, 1836, General Provisions, Sec. 9; Angela Boswell, "Traveling the Wrong Way Down Freedom's Trail," in Scheer, ed.,

Women and the Texas Revolution, 113–117; Lack, ed., *The Diary of William Fairfax Gray*, January 10, 1836.

44. Although exact figures are impossible to establish, a report in August 1836 by Henry M. Morfit, a special envoy of Andrew Jackson, revealed that the new Republic had a slave population of about 5,000. By 1840 the tax rolls showed a significant increase in slaves with 12,570 listed. By the end of the Republic in 1845, a total of 27,555 were listed, an increase of more than 450 percent with about half being female. Ruthe Winegarten, *Black Texas Women: A Sourcebook, Documents, Biographies, Timeline* (Austin: University of Texas Press, 1996), 32–33, 255; Wintz, "Women in Texas," 267; Boswell, "Traveling the Wrong Way Down Freedom's Trail," 116–117; Ronnie C. Tyler and Lawrence R. Murphy, eds., *The Slave Narratives in Texas* (Austin: Encino Press, 1974), 3; Norman R. Yetman, ed., *Voices from Slavery* (New York: Holt, Rinehart and Winston, 1970), 198–201; Campbell, *An Empire for Slavery: The Peculiar Institution in Texas, 1821–1865* (Baton Rouge: Louisiana State University Press, 1989), 54–55.

45. The value of slaves depended on their age, sex, and physical condition. A typical female slave in 1848 sold for $200 to $500. Winegarten, *Black Texas Women: A Sourcebook*, 14–16, 18, 21–22; 30–31; Campbell, *An Empire for Slavery*, 154–155, 166–167. See also Eric Walther, "The Lives of Enslaved Women in Texas," in *Texas Women: Their Histories, Their Lives*, Elizabeth Hayes Turner, Stephanie Cole, and Rebecca Sharpless, eds. (Athens; University of Georgia Press, 2015.

46. Campbell, *An Empire for Slavery*, 144–145, 150–152; Cummins, *Emily Austin of Texas*, 161–162; Winegarten, *Black Texas Women: A Sourcebook*, 34; Walther, "The Lives of Enslaved Women in Texas" 63.

47. Boswell, "Traveling the Wrong Way Down Freedom's Trail,"113–115; Winegarten, *Black Texas Women: A Sourcebook*, 2, 4–6, 9; Ruthe Winegarten, *Black Texas Women* (Austin: University of Texas Press, 1995), 6–7.

48. Boswell, "Traveling the Wrong Way Down Freedom's Trail," 113; The Constitution of the Republic of Texas, 1836, General Provisions, Sec. 9.

49. Boswell, "Traveling the Wrong Way Down Freedom's Trail," 114; Winegarten, *Black Women: A Sourcebook*, 1, 9–12; Wingarten, *Black Texas Women*, 2, 4–5.

50. Campbell, *An Empire for Slavery*, 108–109, 177–189; Tyler and Murphy, eds., *The Slave Narratives in Texas*, xxxvii; Winegarten, *Black Texas Women: A Sourcebook*, 33, 35–36; Walther, "The Lives of Enslaved Women in Texas," 72.

51. The vote for annexation was 4,254 to 267 and 4,174 to 312 in favor of ratification of the constitution. Julia Lee Sinks papers, Box 3M11, "Early Days in Texas," 18, DBCAH; Tyler, et al., eds., "Annexation," *The New Handbook of Texas*, 192–193.

52. Fane Downs, "Texas Women: History at the Edges," in Walter L. Buenger and Robert A. Calvert, *Texas Through Time: Evolving Interpretations* (College Station: Texas A&M University Press, 1991), 83; Carroll, *Homesteads Ungovernable*, 99–106.

Chapter 13
American Indians in the Republic of Texas: A Case Study for Moving Beyond Traditional Perspectives

Jody Edward Ginn

The subject of Indians has always figured very prominently in the historiography and popular depictions of the Republic of Texas era. Specifically, the primary focus has been on the numerous battles and other conflicts that took place among the Comanches, Kiowas, Cherokees, and various other tribes during this time, and it has come from vastly different perspectives over time. First, the perspective of the Anglo-American population dominated the earliest study of the history of Indians living in Texas during the Republic period, and that traditionalist literature tended to cast Indians as racially and culturally inferior beings standing in the way of westward expansion and Manifest Destiny. Then, in the mid-twentieth century, the interpretive pendulum began to swing in the other direction, with early revisionists casting Texas Indians as the victims of villainous, land-grabbing Anglos.[1]

This virtually exclusive focus on Texas Indians who were in conflict with the nascent republic led, perhaps unintentionally, to a singular representation of Texas Indians in terms of their mindset, perspectives, and relationships with Anglo Texans, a depiction that even the most rudimentary of historical examinations will not support. Additionally, the ubiquitous practice of collectively referring to the ethnically and culturally diverse peoples who inhabited the Americas prior to Columbus's arrival in 1492 as "Indians" reinforces the idea of them as a singular group, regardless of intent. Pop-culture media of various types have followed that simplistic presentation, which is in keeping with their own crude story-telling formula that pits protagonists ("good guys") against antagonists ("bad guys"), thereby inculcating the minds of a far broader audience with a skewed view of such events. But in fact, the relationships between Indians and the Lone Star Republic's government were more complex and diverse than many scholars have previously acknowledged.

Texas Indians differed widely in their perspectives on many issues, including the subject of how to interact with the fledgling Texas government. During the Republic period, at least sixteen distinct ethno-cultural/linguistic tribal groups resided within the borders claimed by Texas. The total population of Texas Indians following independence was approximately 14,500, as compared to an estimated 30,000 Anglo/Celt-Americans, 5,000 slaves of African descent, and 3,470 Tejanos (Texans of Mexican descent). The Indians of Texas at the time were comprised of diverse peoples from across the continent with distinct languages, cultural practices, and interests, even within individual tribes. Each tribe consisted of varying numbers of sub-tribal bands and familial groups.[2]

Furthermore, leadership was not consolidated in most tribes, as each band was led by its own chief(s) and did not submit to any centralized tribal authority. Contrary to some common scholarly perspectives, there existed as many conflicts between the tribes and bands residing in Texas during the Republic period as there were between American Indians and the Texas government. Finally, many Texas Indians chose, at least at times, to cooperate and collaborate with the Texans—including allying in combat against other tribes whose interests conflicted with their own. For example, men under the leadership of Chief Flacco and Chief Castro of the Lipan Apaches, Chief Placido of the Tonkawas, Chief Bowles of the Cherokees, and Chief Spy Buck of the Shawnees served the Republic at one time or another as scouts, spies, interpreters and even as Texas Rangers. Therefore, the available evidence does not support generalized interpretations that portray the history of Indians in Texas during the Republic period as driven purely by culture conflict. In truth, the Texas Indians were comprised of heterogeneous peoples who sought to protect their own interests by collaborating in various ways with diverse allies (including Anglo Texans) against their enemies.[3]

To demonstrate the necessity for more narrowly tailored studies of the numerous Texas Indians and tribal groups who chose to cooperate and even ally with the Texas Republic in order to pursue a deeper and more nuanced understanding of Texas-Indian relations, this chapter presents a case study of John Conner, whose life reflects the complexities of Indian relations during this era. Conner, a Delaware chief, was the only person known to be of American Indian descent ever to receive a land grant in the Republic or State of Texas. The Texas government awarded Conner the grant because of his unqualified success as a mediator and treaty facilitator between the Anglo-American controlled government and the diverse American Indians tribes residing in the Republic of Texas.

The 1836 and 1845 Constitutions of Texas provided for the distribution of certain public lands to individuals in the form of headright grants, and these constitutions specifically limited the distribution of such grants to those recognized as citizens. Republic and state statutes restricted citizenship to persons of European ancestry and expressly excluded individuals of African or American Indian descent. As a result, neither full nor mixed-blood Africans or American Indians were eligible to receive headright grants under those laws. Out of the countless thousands of men of either African or American Indian heritage living in Texas during that time, only two were ever awarded such grants in contradiction to these discriminatory laws—both by way of special acts passed by the state legislature and signed into law by the sitting governor.

The first was a free mixed-race black man named Samuel McCullough, Jr (sometimes spelled McCullock), who served in the Republic of Texas Army during the revolt of 1836 and was the first man wounded at the Battle of Goliad. Such credentials likely explain his status as a viable exception to the rule forbidding African citizenship.

The second was John Conner, a mixed-race Delaware Indian chief who served as a scout, interpreter, and diplomat for the Texas government from the early 1840s into the mid-1850s. On its face, the nature of his service does not appear to be particularly unique, since many Indians served in such capacities during this and even earlier periods. Among countless others, fellow Delawares Black Beaver, Chief James San (St.) Louis, Jim Ned, Jim Second-Eye, and the even more well-known Jim Shaw (a close associate/subordinate of Conner), many more American Indians all also served in similar capacities at one time or another.[4]

In fact, Shaw has actually received the majority of the attention in the historiography of the period, despite being a subordinate of Conner both within the Delaware Nation and in the eyes of the Texas government. Conner has begun to appear more often, however, in some modern scholarship, although he is usually only briefly noted for having been a scout, interpreter, or guide. Such simplistic references fail to reveal his greater significance as an official diplomatic agent of the Republic, one who was not only able to locate and communicate with the various tribal leaders but also to convince them to attend treaty councils and agree to terms for peace.[5]

In light of these facts, what was it about Conner and his service to Texas that was so exceptional as to have merited a land grant despite the seemingly insurmountable legal obstacle posed by his racial heritage? The answer is that his long-term close relationship with Sam Houston and apparently extensive, unyielding diplomatic efforts were considered by Houston, and later acknowledged by the state legislature and many other public officials, to be vital to Texas's survival. The importance of his role and accomplishments was sufficiently noteworthy to eclipse the otherwise well-appreciated efforts of Conner's Indian colleagues and to merit the expenditure of an incalculable amount of personal and political capital that it took to overcome the racially charged dynamics and core attitudes of the period.

While it is known that Conner thoroughly traversed Texas during his early travels—likely many times—contrary to the assertions of some earlier historians, he was not a member of the "Absentee" Delaware group that had migrated into Texas around 1820. Conner, a chief of the main band of Delawares residing in Kansas by that time, apparently came across the Texas band in his travels and may have resided with them temporarily at various points over time. However, the earliest record of Conner having settled in Texas for any extended period is around 1842, at which time he began working closely with the recently re-elected president of the Republic, Sam Houston. During his second term, President Houston actively sought to repair relations with the various Indian tribes in the wake of Mirabeau Lamar's administration, during which Lamar pursued a policy of attempted expulsion of all Indians, regardless of their disposition towards peaceful coexistence or even the willingness of some to acculturate into white society.[6]

Conner established his legacy in Texas once President Houston chose him to be the lead agent, diplomat, guide, and interpreter for Houston's delegation to all Texas Indians. The president hoped to initiate the process of building a peace with Texas Indians following his re-election to the presidency. However, weather, as well as communications and logistical problems, delayed the delegation from officially embarking until March 1843. Houston's plan was not purely idealistic but was pragmatic and sophisticated. It was designed to achieve three primary goals: (1) appeal to their human nature by plying them with gifts; (2) establish a line of demarcation between the apparently incompatible societies, and; (3) initiate a trading relationship with the tribes so that it would no longer serve their interests to raid Anglo settlements. He fully recognized (and arguably hoped) that the various tribes would raid Mexican settlements instead, which would weaken and distract Santa Anna's forces and introduce more trade goods (especially horses) into the Texas marketplace.[7]

As a result of Lamar's abuses, most tribal leaders at that time were understandably reticent to meet with Anglo leaders, and even the great peacemaker Houston needed inside help to bring the chiefs to the treaty table. Conner was a (if not the) key figure in that effort. He actively, aggressively, and successfully courted leaders from each of the tribes living in Texas at that time, including the Comanches. A trader like his father, he used his business relationships and resources to lavish gifts upon the chiefs (even those whose people had suffered directly at the hands of the Lamar administration) to entice them to negotiate with Houston.[8]

Lamar lacked both experience with, and sympathy for, the Indians of Texas, regardless of their willingness to cooperate or acculturate. He completely disavowed their claims to the lands on which they lived, and aggressively pursued the expulsion of even those tribes that had allied themselves with the Texas government against Mexico, as well as the generally more unpredictable and combative tribes, such as the Comanche. Of particular note was his stance against the Cherokee, whom he drove out of the country in a bloody war, along with most of the Absentee Delaware and other peaceful tribes. With those expulsions and his unrelenting war against the Comanche, Lamar succeeded in making Texas larger and arguably safer (in the short-term), but poorer both monetarily and diplomatically, as he ran up the public debt and obliterated the fragile bonds between Anglos and many of the Indian tribes that had been carefully cultivated by Houston and others in the years before Lamar took office.[9]

Lamar's indiscriminate policies and abuses had made even the (previously) most affable and cooperative chiefs wary of the Texans. Houston's plan was merely a fantasy if he could not convince the chiefs to even talk to him. By this time, most Indians, especially Comanches and Kiowas, had moved well beyond the reach of even the most aggressive ranging companies and into territory where no white men had ever gone before or would dare venture into on their own. This was exactly where Conner, a ranking member of a nation with a tradition as intertribal mediators, and his associates came into play: Conner began by making trips to negotiate with the various tribes on Houston's behalf, traveling either by himself or in the company of two Indian companions. On few, if any, occasions did Anglo agents travel with him on his initial foray into the frontier. Next, once Conner convinced the various chiefs to meet with Houston's Anglo agents, he led those delegations to the various villages and camps, initiated communications and translated for all parties, negotiated terms, and perhaps most important, kept the members of the delegations alive throughout the process.[10]

Sometime in 1842, after returning to the office of president of the Republic, Houston specifically solicited Conner's help in carrying out the objectives of his peace policy. Texas's Constitution prevented anyone from serving consecutive terms. That provision kept Houston off the ballot in 1838 and led to Lamar's victory over a relatively unknown candidate who had replaced two earlier candidates (both of whom had died during their campaigns) a mere few weeks prior to the election. Once elected, Lamar immediately implemented his aggressive and unyielding Indian removal policies, which Houston openly and persistently criticized throughout Lamar's term. However, some modern scholars have erroneously asserted that Lamar "defeated" Houston and thereby construed Lamar's election as an indicator of proof of widespread public support for Lamar's Indian policy over that of Houston's. However, that presumption does not appear to have been tested through a published scholarly inquiry.[11]

Houston's popularity never ebbed and he won reelection to the presidency in a landslide in 1841, after which he returned determined to rectify the situation and build a lasting peace between white Texans and Indians. Houston recognized that he needed a man with Conner's unique combination of knowledge, reputation, and skills to reach out to the chiefs whom Lamar had so thoroughly alienated and antagonized, especially considering that Houston's agents had previously failed to make contact with many of those tribes during his first term. Therefore, Conner was "employed by Gen. Houston as an Interpreter, guide, and agent" and was specifically tasked with "opening negotiations, effecting treaties, and conducting conciliatory measures with the various Indian tribes then hostile to Texas." If Conner were successful in convincing the various chiefs to agree to a treaty, then he would receive a league of land in return for what must have been regarded at the time as a virtually impossible mission. Exactly how Houston came to know Conner and that he was so uniquely "fitted … for this difficult employment" remains a mystery, but the outcome became apparent in short order.[12]

Considering the hostility level towards Anglos resulting from Lamar's Indian policies, it was clear that no white man would even survive the journey to seek out the tribal leaders, much less find them or convince them to attend a parley. Furthermore, a league of land in the fledgling nation, which was land-rich but cash-poor, would be a tiny price to pay for such services. It was certainly far cheaper than continuing Lamar's war, the costs of which had greatly diminished his rival's popularity (any racial hostilities notwithstanding).[13]

Houston needed Conner's skills and expertise not only to make peace between Anglos and Indians, but also between the various tribes, who continued to raid each others' camps and villages as frequently as they did those of non-Indians. Again, establishing trade relationships was key to that effort, and Conner's store, which was located near the proposed boundary between Indian lands and Anglo settlements, was ideally situated as the point of exchange for both trade and the return of stolen merchandise. The fact that certain tribes were willing to seek Houston's aid in mediating inter-tribal conflicts in hopes of regaining their property indicates great confidence in Houston's ability to produce results. Many chiefs even abided by Houston's admonitions not to retaliate when wronged, demonstrating a willingness to settle such matters through negotiations rather than armed conflict. It was due to Conner's efforts as his agent that the president was able to accomplish such goals.[14]

Conner made the first major step towards building a lasting peace according to Houston's plan by bringing together the chiefs of almost every known tribe in or around Texas at that time, beginning with the more sedentary agricultural tribes. Leaders of tribes generally more disposed to cooperate with the Texas government (despite Lamar's abuses), such as the Delaware, Shawnee, and certain Caddo bands including the Hainais participated, as well as leaders of typically more combative tribes such as the Nadacos, Wacos, Tawakonis, Kichais, and Wichitas. Representatives from the United States government were also notably in attendance at each of these councils, which were held at the Torrey Trading House on Tawakoni Creek near present Waco. Leaders from each tribe, the government of Texas, and those for the United States each spoke, all in favor of solidifying a permanent peace accord, and signed an "article of agreement" committing to do just that. The fact that such a gathering occurred in the wake of the Lamar years was in and of itself an outstanding achievement, regardless of the final outcome.[15]

Houston certainly recognized that Texans had more to gain from peace than war with the Indians, as did many of the Indian leaders. A cease-fire was arranged to suspend hostilities as they prepared for a "Grand Council" to sort out the details of a more lasting peace agreement. Many chiefs also agreed to encourage other tribal leaders not present at that first gathering to join in the process. Having laid the diplomatic groundwork with the Comanches and other more reticent tribes the previous year, in May 1843, Conner and Shaw escorted Indian agents, Colonel Joseph Eldredge and

Thomas Torrey, into Comanche country, carrying gifts and two Comanche prisoners, who had remained in the custody of the Texas government since the infamous Council House Fight in 1840. Their mission was to convince the Comanche chiefs to attend the Grand Council meeting. Conner and Shaw were not merely guides and interpreters; they were also there to vouch for Houston's integrity and try to convince the chiefs to come to the council. Only the word of a fellow Indian could possibly persuade the Comanche chiefs, who were understandably suspicious of Anglo promises, to reevaluate their stance regarding the Texans. Again, pragmatism guided Houston's plan: he sent gifts, but only enough to entice the Comanche chiefs to attend the Grand Council, and promised to give them much more once a treaty was concluded.[16]

While the Comanches did not attend either the initial Tehuacana Creek Council or sign the Fort Bird Treaty in 1843, Chief Pahayuco did enter into separate negotiations with Houston, agreeing to a cease-fire. This agreement was reached primarily as a result of the efforts of Conner, Shaw, Eldredge, Torrey, and others. Under the direction and authority of the president of the Republic of Texas, Conner and other negotiators continued to meet with Pahayuco throughout Houston's final term of office. The president himself provided Conner with a paper proving his authority to act on behalf of the Republic. In this document, Houston expressed "great confidence in John Conner," and directed him to "promot[e] the object of peace," among the Indians of Texas. President Houston's confidence was not offered blindly: he inquired through his private secretary, Washington D. Miller, as to "the fidelity with which [Conner and his Delaware colleagues] have kept their engagements with the government." Clearly, these reports came back positive, as Miller was eventually named by Attorney General Ebenezer Allen to be the primary witness to the Texas Legislature regarding Conner's land petition.[17]

Although it took nearly three years and half dozen councils and preliminary treaties, Houston's peace policy eventually bore full fruit. Conner and Houston periodically met and maintained correspondence regarding the progress being made, in which Conner went so far as to commit to taking his tribe to war on behalf of Texas against the Comanche. Because Conner was illiterate, this correspondence was written and witnessed by Anglo Texan agents, including E. L. Wheelock, who attested to the authenticity of the letters. By November 1845, every known tribe in and around Texas had signed agreements and exchanged gifts and prisoners with the Texas government. This accomplishment is testament to Conner's influence within the hostile tribes, as well as to his tenacity and courage in seeing the process through to fruition.[18]

These treaties were ratified by the Texas Senate and honored by Houston's successor, Anson Jones, who was the last president of the Republic of Texas. After Texas was annexed by the United States in February of 1846, responsibility for Indian affairs fell to the federal government. Conner had thus fulfilled his obligation to "open … negotiations, effect … treaties, and conduct … conciliatory measures with the various Indian tribes then hostile to [the Republic of] Texas."[19]

Under the terms of his agreement with Houston, Conner earned what no other person known to be of American Indian descent would ever receive in Texas: a headright grant of land. But, it would take another decade before the Indian agent could gain legal title to his land and, in the meantime, Conner continued to serve the Texas government until he was promoted to the position of principal chief of the Delaware Nation in 1857. After earning the title of principle chief, Conner sold his land and moved out of Texas, permanently. [20]

Although John Conner had fulfilled his commitment to the Republic of Texas by the time that annexation to the United States was complete, he continued to serve the new state. In 1847, Conner successfully helped to negotiate the famous Meusebach-Comanche Treaty, which opened up more than three million acres of West Texas land to German settlers. Conner's commitment to establishing and maintaining peace between Anglos and Indians was an unwavering and unending personal endeavor, and he continued to serve the State of Texas and the United States with the same dedication and vigor that had earned him both the right to own land in Texas and an unquestioned reputation as a loyal and effective diplomat.

By the early 1850s, Conner was living with a band of Delaware near Fort Martin Scott, near modern-day Fredericksburg, where he became "great friends" with the then-young United States Army officer, Colonel Richard Irving Dodge (aide-de-camp to General William Tecumseh Sherman). Dodge noted in his treatise on his life and experiences among the American Indians, *Our Wild Indians: Thirty-Three Years' Personal Experience among the Red Men of the Great West*, that Conner was around fifty years old by this time. Conner shared with Dodge many stories of traversing the continent in his earlier days, impressing the young officer with his geographical knowledge and thrilling him with his tales of adventure. It was around this time that Conner first attempted to legally assert his right to the land promised him by Sam Houston nearly a decade before.[21]

There are numerous myths perpetuated throughout most of the modern scholarship and publications referencing Conner and his land grant. These include assertions that Conner received full citizenship and even voting rights in Texas along with the grant; that the grant was intended for the tribe rather than for Conner personally; and misrepresentation of the reasons that he was given the grant in the first place. Although the existing historical record has repeatedly reported that Conner was awarded a league of land for his services to the Chihuahua-El Paso expedition, this was not the case. Conner's petitions and a supporting affidavit by then-State Attorney General Ebenezer Allen (previously Attorney General of the Republic) document that the land was compensation for his services as "lincaster [interpreter] and agent" to then-president of the Republic of Texas, Sam Houston, during his second term from 1842-45. Conner submitted his first petition to the 3rd Legislature of Texas in 1850, requesting legal title to a league of land and noting that he had "for many years been engaged in behalf of the Government … in endeavoring to conciliate the various hostile tribes."[22]

The success achieved by the second petition was bolstered by the supporting affidavit filed by Allen, who named Houston's private secretary, Washington D. Miller, as the primary witness to Houston's agreement with Conner and Conner's successful compliance with the terms of that agreement. No record as to whether Miller was ever called to testify on Conner's behalf before either house of the Texas Legislature has survived, although the fact that the special act was passed (and signed into law by Governor Peter H. Bell, a former Texas Rangers commander) is, alone, proof that the Legislature was convinced of the legitimacy of Conner's claim. The act, ordering the Land Commissioner of Texas to issue a certificate for a league of land to "John Conner, Delaware Chief" (and exempting him from any fees or dues for such certificate) passed and was signed into law on February 7, 1853.[23]

This account of Conner as the lead agent on behalf of Sam Houston and the Republic of Texas necessarily raises the question of just who he was, how he came to be selected for such a unique and important role, and why he was willing to accept it. John Conner, Delaware Chief, was an illiterate hyperpolyglot who helped forge peace in the borderlands on the nineteenth-century frontier of what is now commonly referred to as the American West, including Texas. Conner worked alongside some of the most famous Anglo and Indian political and military leaders of the period, and he was highly respected by them all.

John Conner—whose Lenape name has been lost to history—was in every way a product of the matrilineal culture of the Delaware Indians who taught their own to pursue peace when possible, yet not be afraid to fight, and to fight to the finish when the time was at hand. His Delaware mother, Mekinges—a direct descendant of the Lenape principal chiefs dating back to the seventeenth century—raised Conner in a Delaware household, in a Delaware village, to be a Delaware man who lived his entire life consistent with Delaware values and customs, and who eventually ascended to the highest position within the tribe in strict accordance with those customs.[24]

A deeper look at Conner reveals that his Anglo-American contemporaries recognized, utilized, and greatly appreciated his unique skill set and his unwavering commitment to establishing peace between the Anglo-European dominated governments and the Indian tribes of the American West. Some of the most famous Anglo-American pioneers and leaders of the period, such as Sam Houston, Richard Dodge, Randolph B. Marcy, Ferdinand Roemer, Robert Neighbors, William Highsmith, John Holland Jenkins, James Pike, and even the noted Indian provocateur, John Robert Baylor, lauded him as a trustworthy and effective diplomat, interpreter, guide, and fierce warrior.

In addition to his vast knowledge of North American geography and his ability to speak at least six different Indian languages plus English and Spanish, Conner had a high level of credibility among even the most combative Indian tribes. This credibility allowed him to move in and out of Indian Territory and to safely escort Anglo Texans through the heart of Comancheria and bring even the most intractable war chiefs to treat for peace. Scholars should note that Conner was as respected within his own tribe as he was among Anglo-Americans and other American Indian nations. He spent the last fifteen years of his life as the principal chief of the Delaware and, in that capacity, led them in the final stage of their westward migration, from Kansas to the Indian Territory in Oklahoma.

Eventually John Conner came to command the respect of some of the most famous (and in some cases, notorious) trailblazers and military commanders of the Western frontier. Many of these were men who spent the better part of their lives in mortal combat against most Indians, yet they extended a level of praise and deference to Conner at times that exceeded any they ever attributed to any other white men (much less an Indian). And although some might think that it was simply because technically speaking, Conner was half white, and therefore they regarded

Delaware Indian Council in Washington D.C., 1867: Principal Chief John Conner, seated center (arms crossed). Courtesy Bartlesville Area History Museum.

him as white, his white admirers' descriptions of him, as well as his thoroughly Indian upbringing, defy such a theory.

The only documented physical descriptions of Conner are from his time of middle age, in the mid to late 1840s. He was described as a "fine, portly man, about forty-five years old, and of very light complexion, with long, black hair and moustache." Another even refers to Conner as looking "Arab." At least one photo of him from approximately twenty years later confirms those descriptions, although his hair was cut short, most likely because he was in Washington D.C. at the time, engaged in treaty negotiations with the Cherokee Nation.[25]

In addition to his distinctively non-white physical appearance, Conner's accent, behaviors, and mannerisms, and even some of the very skills he was lauded for clearly demonstrated to anyone who met him that he was an Indian. Conner was raised by an Indian mother, in an Indian household, speaking an Indian dialect as his first language. Even his white father had also been acculturated to an extent by a mother who had been captured and raised by Shawnees. John Conner's "Indianness" was readily apparent to all, and perhaps most importantly, Conner self-identified as such. He eschewed white societal norms in favor of an observably Lenape Indian lifestyle.[26]

Conner's Anglo-American contemporaries respected and appreciated him, but they clearly did not consider him to have been "white." Their admiration notwithstanding, the praise they lavished upon him was often tainted with the various racial stereotypes that were prevalent at the time among those Americans of European ancestry. Many such descriptions had such racially charged qualifiers, whether expressed or implied, like "for an Indian," attached, and some were even less subtle. Dr. Ferdinand Roemer, author of the widely disseminated and highly regarded travelogue, *Roemer's Texas* …, went so far as to write that [Conner] was, "a six-foot-tall, strong Delaware chief [who] … looked quite civilized … [when] viewed from the rear." This overtly racist depiction went on to pronounce that "viewed from in front, his brown features, however, betrayed his Indian origin immediately." Considering Roemer's numerous other remarks about American Indians and their respective cultures throughout his book, it is fair to say that he generally regarded them as inferior.[27]

But not all of Conner's colleagues were as racially biased in their descriptions of, and references to, Conner as Roemer was. In fact, even some who were known for their anti-Indian sentiments generally nevertheless held Conner in the highest regard. Perhaps the most unexpected Conner enthusiast was John Robert Baylor, the former

Texas Indian agent who went on an infamous statewide anti-Indian campaign.[28]

On January 1, 1857, Baylor penned what can best be described as a letter of reference for Conner, attesting to his "truth, honesty, and integrity," and commending him for the many "important services … rendered to the … State [and] people of Texas." Baylor notes that such services were so significant that Conner was granted "a league of land and made … a citizen of the State." Baylor further explains that Conner had "devoted the best of his life to make peace with the wild and warlike tribes … [and] often risked his life and lost his property," in the process. Baylor closed by requesting that "all good citizens … meet [Conner] with the kindness he so well deserves." Those familiar with Baylor's anti-Indian efforts will likely find such adulation by him for an Indian to be counterintuitive.[29]

While it is certainly notable that someone best known historically for their perceived animosity towards Indians to have given such praise to Conner, Baylor was far from the most famous or respected person to do so. In 1844, President Sam Houston of the Republic of Texas expressed in writing his "great confidence" in Conner, and later promised him a headright land grant as compensation for his successful efforts to bring the Comanches and other hostile tribes to treat for peace. Considering that under the constitution and laws of the Republic (and subsequent State) of Texas, it was illegal to issue a headright land grant to anyone of Native American descent, it was no small promise when made, and it took nearly a decade and a literal act of the state congress to honor it.[30]

While Sam Houston provided Conner with the highest accolades and most tangible reward that he would receive, there were many other men of note who were never short of praise for the Delaware chief. The renowned Texas Indian agent, Major Robert Neighbors, regarded Conner as "faithful," employed him as his guide, interpreter, and agent for over a decade, and supported Conner's application for the land grant he was eventually awarded in 1853. Noted Texas Ranger James Pike called Conner (along with Jim Shaw), "the great Delaware scout … who [was] to the Texas frontier what Black Beaver was to the territory farther north."[31]

Ebenezer Allen, who held the office of Attorney General for both the Republic and State of Texas, wrote a letter supporting Conner's application for the land grant originally promised to him by Houston. In that letter, Allen affirmed that Conner's "fidelity never was questioned and the importance and value of his services, which were often hazardous and arduous." Allen also noted that there were then "many living in the

Capitol who [could] bear honorable testimony to the merits and great utility of his services." In particular, Allen named Washington D. Miller, Houston's former private secretary from his terms as president of the Republic, as the primary witness who would corroborate Allen's attestations of Conner's merit and character. Allen wrote that Miller would also affirm Houston's promise to obtain the land grant for Conner in exchange for his services to the Republic and State in securing a peace treaty with the Comanche and other previously hostile—due mainly to persecution by Mirabeau Lamar—tribes.[32]

Furthermore, many naïve but courageous visionaries such as John O. Meusebach and John Coffee "Jack" Hays might have disappeared without a trace during their various excursions into Comancheria out on the Texas frontier without the guidance and protection of Conner and his fellow Delaware scouts, guides, interpreters, ambassadors, and frontiersmen. John Holland Jenkins (the youngest soldier of the Texas Revolt, a Texas Ranger, and Confederate veteran) described how the "celebrated chief of the Delawares, John Connor [*sic*]," saved the lives of Texas Ranger Captain Samuel Highsmith and his company (of which, Jack Hays was a member) on one occasion, and scoured Comancheria to find the kidnapped Thomas Coleman for his aggrieved family on another. Colonel Richard Irving Dodge extolled Conner as "having … more minute and personal knowledge of the North American Continent than any other man ever had," including that of the famous U.S. Army scout, Black Beaver. Dodge insisted that Conner had memorized every aspect of the geography of North America, and that he was able to navigate up, down, and across the continent with ease. Dodge said that Conner was equally able to provide detailed instructions to those wishing to travel "in any direction, or for any distance."[33]

Many generally forgotten yet important men of the time also held Conner in high esteem. Indian commissioners J.C. Neill and E. Morehouse wrote to President Houston on October 20, 1844, that, in their opinions, Conner was more deserving of the credit for "bringing in" the previously hostile Comanche and other tribes that signed the Treaty of Tehuacana Creek just eleven days earlier. Thomas G. Western, Superintendant of Indian affairs for Texas, referred to Conner as an "excellent and competent [man]" when authorizing a subordinate to procure his services if possible under "any arrangement [he] might make" in order to do so. L.H. Williams described Conner as a "source that I cannot doubt." These more obscure affirmations of Conner's status as an effective and trustworthy intermediary would indicate that he was not merely being praised out of any sort of disingenuous political agenda but was being honestly assessed by those who knew him best and relied on him in the course of their daily responsibilities.[34]

Although many of Conner's contemporaries were willing to express the high levels of esteem in which they held him in both private and public correspondence, some even going so far as to press for legislation at a time and from a body that was generally predisposed to disregard the rights of Indians (at best), later historians have consistently failed to accurately and fairly document Conner's place in the history of the American West. That failure can be explained in part by general prejudice, manifested in a tendency to minimize his role by misrepresenting his actual level of responsibility and authority and therefore the corresponding recognition due to him. The most common tactic was to simply refer to him as an "interpreter," "guide," or "scout," and leave it at that, ignoring his role as an agent of the government who was often responsible for "opening negotiations, affecting treaties, and conducting conciliatory measures." Not to mention the fact that, at times, no white man could have found their way to, or lived through, a meeting in some of the tribal territories without Conner at their side.[35]

Preliminary theories of potential misidentification notwithstanding, it is clear that Conner's legacy on the Texas and Western Frontiers has long been obscured by a Euro-centric dominated historiography bent on emphasizing and romanticizing white "accomplishments" in the "taming of the Wild West." Any admission of the substantial roles played by Conner and countless other Native Americans would have undermined notions of Anglo-European exceptionalism and Manifest Destiny. In addition to the longstanding tribal traditions of frequent and extensive travels, Conner and his Delaware contemporaries—like Black Beaver and many other notable Delaware scouts, interpreters, and diplomats—frequently took work with various regional governments when available. They regularly worked for the armies and Indian agencies of Texas, the United States, and Mexico, on assignments that took them away from home for extended periods, excursions from which they always returned.

In the final analysis, John Conner, Delaware chief, was one of the most erudite frontiersmen and effective conciliators in the borderlands of the nineteenth century American West. As such, his role was pivotal, yet has been largely overlooked within the existing historiography. Despite Conner's undeniably positive reputation among his contemporary Anglo military and government leaders and apparently equivalent prestige among American Indian tribal leaders, his place in the history of the borderlands of the American West has been given short shrift up until now. The very fact that Conner's role has been obscured by error and omission, whether deliberate or inadvertent, provides the most striking reason for an intensive and introspective scholarly examination of not only his life and times, but of the many other American Indians of the period who collaborated and allied with the Republic of Texas.

As with Conner, the thousands of individuals of the many tribes of American Indians who lived in Texas during the period of the Republic were often as different culturally and politically from each other as they were from their Anglo and Latino Texan neighbors. Therefore, any attempt to interpret the perspectives of such diverse peoples will require an in-depth examination of the actions and documented statements of specific individuals, bands, and tribes as a starting point. The numerous and certainly significant conflicts between various tribal groups or bands and the fledgling Texas Republic have been, for the most part, thoroughly documented and analyzed, and from multiple perspectives, in the existing historiography of the period. What is currently lacking is a thorough examination and nuanced analysis of the actions, motives, and perspectives of the many Texas Indians during the Republic period who, for their own reasons, chose to collaborate and ally with the fledgling Texas government. Giving due attention to this aspect of the history of Texas Indians will not only recognize their agency in regard to their own affairs, but also finally acknowledge their contributions to the development of modern Texas.

Notes

1. Two leading examples of the Anglo-traditionalist and "early revisionist" (author's term) approaches, respectively: T. R. Fehrenbach, *Lone Star: A History of Texas and the Texans* (New York: Macmillan, 1968); Gary C. Anderson, *The Conquest of Texas: Ethnic Cleansing in the Promised Land, 1820–1875* (Norman: University of Oklahoma Press, 2005).

2. Randolph B. Campbell, *Gone to Texas: A History of the Lone Star State* (New York: Oxford University Press, 2003), 157.

3. David La Vere, *The Texas Indians* (College Station: Texas A&M University Press, 2004), 169–71; Stephen L. Moore, *Savage Frontier, Volume I–IV: Rangers, Riflemen, and Indian Wars in Texas.* (Denton: University of North Texas Press 2006–2010); Carol A. Lipscomb, "DELAWARE INDIANS," *Handbook of Texas Online* http://www.tshaonline.org/handbook/ online/articles/bmd08, (accessed November 25, 2010).

4. H. P. N. Gammel, ed. and comp., *Laws of Texas, 1822–1897.* 10 vols. (Austin: Gammel Book Company, 1898), 1: 1069; Stephen L. Moore. *Savage Frontier, Volume I, 1835–1837: Rangers, Riflemen, and Indian Wars in Texas* (Plano: Republic of Texas Press, 2002); Carol A. Lipscomb, "DELAWARE INDIANS," *Handbook of Texas Online* http://www. tshaonline.org/handbook/online/articles/bmd08, (accessed November 25, 2010).

5. Ferdinand Roemer, *Roemer's Texas,* Oswald Mueller, ed. (San Antonio: Standard Printing Company, 1935), 235. A possible explanation for Shaw's prominence over Conner in Texas historiography may be the fact that Ferdinand Roemer appears to have mistakenly identified Conner as Shaw—a palpable error—in his landmark survey of Texas geography, translated into English by Oswald Mueller as *Roemer's Texas*. The error of fact is easily ascertained in that Roemer noted two Delaware having accompanied Robert Neighbors when he met them, one a chief and the other clearly a subordinate. From there Roemer consistently referred to Shaw as the Delaware chief and never named the subordinate. It is well documented that Shaw never held the position of chief of any level in his tribe, not to mention that he was many years, possibly two decades or more, Conner's junior. The question of whether Roemer misidentified Shaw as Conner is by no means a settled matter, as one scholar also researching these events has raised a challenge to the theory, although his query has yet to be fleshed out. Dr. James Kearney of Weimar, Texas, is a German language specialist who studies German immigrants in early Texas, researching their activities in heretofore un-translated or referenced German documents of that period. Dr. Kearney does not currently believe that Conner was on the Meusebach-Comanche expedition at the time that the key negotiations took place, an opinion primarily based on a secondary account which this researcher has found to be in error on several related matters, including the misdating and identification of a well-documented photo of Conner. Information included in an email series from Dr. James Kearney, February 23, 2012. In any event, Conner and Shaw were on both on that expedition together with Roemer, a fact confirmed by the presence of their names and marks on the famous Muesebach-Comanche Treaty. Roemer also fails to describe the full extent of Conner and Shaw's participation in that matter: this further calls his account of events into question. Despite the fact that Roemer was a scientist interested in geology rather than history, his expansive influence over the last 160+ years has resulted in his errors and omissions having been repeated by multiple generations of historians without

scrutiny, contributing directly to Conner's severely diminished presence in the canon of Texas historical literature.

6. Timothy Crumrin, "An American Life: Captain John Conner of Indiana and the West," http://www.connerprairie.org/Learn-And-Do/Indiana-History/Conners-And-The-Lenape/Captain-John-Conner.aspx, (accessed December 2, 2010).

7. H. Allen Anderson, "The Delaware and Shawnee Indians and the Republic of Texas, 1820–1845," *Southwestern Historical Quarterly* 94 (October 1990): 246–248; Gary C. Anderson, *The Conquest of Texas: Ethnic Cleansing in the Promised Land, 1820–1875* (Norman: University of Oklahoma Press, 2005), 209; Sam Houston, *The Writings of Sam Houston, 1813–1863*, edited by Amelia W. Williams and Eugene C. Barker, 8 vols. (Austin: University of Texas Press, 1938–1943), 3: 344, 363–64 (hereafter cited as *Writings of SH*); W. E. S. Dickerson, "Indian Relations" http://www.tshaonline.org/handbook/online/articles/bzi01 (accessed November 5, 2010).

8. Thomas W. Kavanagh, *Comanche Political History: An Ethnohistorical Perspective, 1706–1875* (Lincoln: University of Nebraska Press, 1996), 265, 290.

9. Dickerson, "Indian Relations."

10. Ibid.; Weslager, *The Delaware Indians*, 288–99; Amy C. Schutt, *Peoples of the River Valleys* (Philadelphia: University of Pennsylvania Press, 2007), 4–5, 124–125, 141–149; Gunlög Fur, *A Nation of Women: Gender and Colonial Encounters Among the Delaware Indians* (Philadelphia: University of Pennsylvania Press, 2009), 61–63.

11. David La Vere, *Contrary Neighbors: Southern Plains and Removed Indians in Indian Territory* (Norman: University of Oklahoma Press, 2000), 84–85; Pekka Hamalainen, *The Comanche Empire* (New Haven: Yale University Press, 2008), 215. In *The Comanche Empire*, Pekka Hamalainen claimed that Lamar defeated Houston in the 1838 election, and then asserted that the erroneous electoral outcome was proof of widespread support in Texas of Lamar's Indian policy over that of Houston. In fact, Houston did not run in the 1838 election, and indeed could not have, due to the Constitutional bar on holding that office for consecutive terms. David La Vere originally made the same claim in *Contrary Neighbors*, although he later corrected the factual error without comment while leaving in the original assertion regarding public opinion, in *The Texas Indians*. In any event, interpreting the outcome of the 1838 election as a definitive statement on the majority of Anglo voters' position on Indian policies constitutes an oversimplification of a complex state

of affairs. The cited works in *Contrary Neighbors, The Texas Indians,* and *The Comanche Empire* do not provide detailed information on that issue, indicating that it may be ripe for a focused study. First, Indian policy was not the only important political question of the day: the Republic was also facing significant issues regarding foreign policy, the question of annexation to the United States, relations with Mexico, land policy, and financial policy. Additionally, any assessment of the efficacy of Houston's first-term Indian policy is constrained by the fact that it was never fully implemented, as the Congress refused to ratify the treaty that Houston had made with the Cherokee, and his agents had been unable to establish contact with the Comanches and many of the other plains tribes. Perhaps more importantly, however, the 1838 election was considered to have been essentially uncontested. The candidates originally opposing Lamar, Attorney General Peter Grayson and later, Chief Justice James Collinsworth, both committed suicide. Shortly before the election, a little-known senator "who had no chance of winning" named Robert Wilson became the candidate, and Lamar easily defeated him. During Lamar's term, Houston remained a vocal critic of Lamar's Indian policies, accusing the administration of "duplicity and fraud in unjustifiably driving the Indians from their homes and lands." Houston was eligible to run again in 1841, and he defeated Lamar's vice president and fellow "Houston-hater," David G. Burnet, in a landslide. Also see Campbell, *Gone to Texas*, 163–73.

12. Legislative history, letter to pres of senate from committee on Indian affairs chair recommending passage of bill on to senate for a full vote TSLA; letter from Ebenezer Allen (Attorney General of Texas—and formerly of the Republic) to the Senate committee on Indian affairs, January 12, 1852; Campbell, *Gone to Texas,* 164–73.

13. Conner petition dated January 11, 1850. No. 41, Box 14. Legislative Records, Texas State Library and Archives, Austin (hereafter cited as TSLA); *Writings of SH* 3: 195, 32–33, 344–45, 359–60; Campbell, *Gone to Texas,* 167–73.

14. *Writings of SH* 3: 344, 363–64. Houston makes reference to the "Delaware Trading House" in a letter to Waco Chief Acaquash, with no indication as to its specific location.

15. Minutes of council and article of agreement, Tawackanoo Creek Council, March 28–31, 1843, Winfrey, Dorman H. and Day, James M., eds. *The Indian Papers of Texas and the Southwest, 1825–1916.* 5 vols. (1966. reprint, Austin: Texas State Historical Association, 1995) (hereafter cited as *Indian Papers*).

16. Ibid.; *Writings of SH* 3: 370–74.

17. *Indian Papers,* 2: 129, 231–32, 397; Presidents agreement with D.G. Watson and John Conner, February 5, 1844. *Writings of SH* 4: 330, 369–70; Conner Land Petition, Affidavit by Ebenezer Allen, dated January 12, 1852. No. 73, Box 15. Legislative Records, TSLA.

18. Dickerson, "Indian Relations."

19. Ibid.

20. *Writings of SH* 4: 330; Garrison, ed., *Diplomatic Correspondence of the Republic of Texas*, 2: 212–17; THOTO Indian Affairs; Ibid.; Ebenezer Allen Affidavit; Birds Fort Treaty, letter from John Conner to Sam Houston, July 9, 1844, Indian Papers; Gary Clayton Anderson, *The Conquest of Texas: Ethnic Cleansing in the Promised Land 1820–1875* (Norman: University of Oklahoma Press, 2005), 202–203, 205, 208–209. Some modern historians have attempted to diminish Indian participation in the Tehuacana Creek Councils, and thus the overall significance of those events, but this approach runs counter to the primary documents from the period. A prime example is the claim by Gary Anderson, in his controversial work, *The Conquest of Texas. ...* , that only the "Delaware and Shawnee interpreters and their relatives" participated in the council of March 28, 1843, and signed the articles of agreement. Anderson also mistakenly refers to it as a "treaty," even though the supporting documents make clear that the council was merely the first step in a process of developing a permanent and wide-ranging treaty. Despite Anderson's citation to the original document, which is located in the Indian Papers at the Texas State Library and Archives, the document contradicts these claims: it was also signed by Chiefs for the Caddos, "Ironises," "Anadarkos," "Tiwacones," Wacos, Witchitas, and "Ketchies." The author makes similar erroneous claims regarding the Fort Bird Treaty, also available at TSLA. Additionally, Anderson provides no source for his claim regarding the state of mind of Conner and Shaw during a particular visit to Payuco's village in July 1843, so the basis for that claim is unclear.

21. R.I. Dodge. *Our Wild Indians: Thirty-Three Years' Personal Experience among the Red Men of the Great West* (1882; repr., Lavergne, TN: Kessinger Publishing, 2010), 554–555.

22. Crumrin, "An American Life ..."; H. Allen Anderson, 259; Carol A. Lipscomb, "Delaware Indians"; Clinton A. Weslager. *The Delaware Indians: A History* (New Brunswick: Rutgers University Press, 1972), 389; Conner petition dated February 11, 1850. TSLAC legislative records.

23. Special Act for the Relief of John Conner, Delaware Chief, Gammel's *Laws*, 3: 1402.

24. Regula Trenkwalder Schoenberger, *Lenape Women, Matriliny, and the Colonial Encounter< Resistance and Erosion of Power (c. 1600–1876): An Excursus in Feminist Anthropology* (New York: Peter Lang, 1991), 238–249; Ruby Cranor, *Kik Tha We Nund: The Delaware Chief William Anderson and His Descendants* (Bartlesville: Delaware Tribe of Indians, 2004), 1–2, 144; Henry Lewis Morgan, *Ancient Society, or, Researches in the Lines of Human Progress from Savagery through Barbarism to Civilization* (London: Macmillan & Company, 1877), 117; Weslager, *Delaware Indians*, 63–65. While Conner's Lenape name appears to have been lost to history, it should be noted that Lenape linguists have long-ago confirmed that the alleged Lenape name given to L. H. Morgan by Sally Williams-Journeycake for Conner is a nonsensical and arguably offensive phrase without connection to any traditional Lenape names. Modern tribal elders and historians therefore consider it likely to have been an intentional slight against Conner. Their suspicions arise from the combined fact that the only source for this "name" was Sally Williams-Journeycake, the mother of Charles Journeycake, Conner's intra-tribal political rival. It is of related note that Williams-Journeycake fraudulently claimed Lenape Wolf clan heritage for herself—and by extension, for her son—in order for him to assert a claim to a tribal leadership position. That fact was documented within a favorable biography of Charles Journeycake (endorsed by his own descendants) that was published in 1970—two years prior to Weslager's *Delaware Indians: A History*, and eight years prior to his *The Delaware Indian Westward Migration*. That biography unequivocally states that Williams-Journeycake was not a Delaware at all. Instead it says that, at best, she was a half-white/half-Wyandot who had married into the Delaware tribe. That fact establishes that Charles's eventual ascension to principal chief following Conner's death constituted a usurpation of the post according to the Lenape tradition of matrilineal succession; Also see, Harry M. Roark, *Charles Journeycake, Indian Statesman and Christian Leader* (Dallas: Taylor Publishing Co., 1948), 20. Jim Rementer, Lenape Linguist, Bartlesville, Oklahoma, email(s) to author regarding Weslager's correspondence with the late Lenape linguist and elder, Nora Dean, February 2 and 10, 2012.

25. Crumrin, "An American Life …"; Weslager, 425; W. B. Parker, *Through Unexplored Texas in the Summer and Fall of 1854* (Austin: Texas Historical Commission, 1990), 117.

26. Some Anglo-American observers even quoted Conner using the stereotypical broken English speech patterns associated with Indians of

that era. Parker, 116–117, 124, 144–47, 163, 166–168, 221–222; Ferdinand Roemer, *Roemer's Texas,* 235–281.

27. *Roemer's Texas,* 235, 250–281. It should be mentioned to Roemer's credit that, at least, he specifically acknowledged Shaw and Conner's participation at all, which is more than can be said for the venerated German leader of that expedition, John O. Meusebach. Otto W. Tetzlaff, "Meusebach-Comanche Treaty," http://www.tshaonline.org/handbook/online/articles/mgm01, (accessed November 5, 2010). Meusebach's "*Answers to Interrogatories.*"

28. Jerry Thompson, "BAYLOR, JOHN ROBERT," *Handbook of Texas Online* (http://www.tshaonline.org/handbook/online/articles/fbaat), (accessed January 27, 2012). Published by the Texas State Historical Association.

29. Richard C. Adams, "A Brief History of the Delaware Indians," *U.S. 59th Cong. 1st Session. Vol. 8, no. 501.* (Serial Document 4916 no. 501), 42. The notion that Conner was "made a citizen" of Texas is as yet unproven. The claim is founded on the logic that, technically, one had to be a citizen in order to obtain a land grant. The only contemporary source to make that claim is the "letter of recommendation" by John Robert Baylor. However, Baylor had no official role in that process and therefore appears to have also been making an assumption. Some historians have even made the leap to claiming that Conner was eligible to vote. However, Conner's grant was made possible via a special act of the legislature that never mentions citizenship or voting rights, only the land as compensation for his services to the Republic. There is no contemporary official record to indicate that actual citizenship or the right to vote was ever conferred on Conner.

30. *Writings of SH* 4: 330; Conner petition 1853, Allen affidavit 1852, No. 73, Box 15. Legislative Records, TSLA; Gammels, *Laws*, "Special Act for the Relief of John Conner, Delaware Chief." Texas's history of the marginalization of Indians and other minorities is so engrained in the modern consciousness—at least for those even somewhat educated in the matter—that when this author first contacted the Texas General Land Office (GLO) Archives Division to request copies of Conner's grant and related documents, several archival staffers argued, politely but persistently, that I must be mistaken. Needless to say they were more than a bit surprised when I provided them the patent and volume numbers from their own online digitized index. Both the act and the patents were issued in the name and title of "John Conner, Delaware Chief."

31. Kenneth Franklin Neighbors, *Robert Simpson Neighbors and the Texas Frontier, 1836–1859* (Waco: Texian Press, 1975), 38, 107, 133; James Pike, *Scout and Ranger: Being the Personal Adventures of James Pike of the Texas Rangers in 1859–1860* (Cincinnati, OH: Princeton University Press, 1865), 63.

32. Allen affidavit 1852. No. 73, Box 15. Legislative Records, TSLA.

33. Dodge, 554–555; John H. Jenkins, *Recollections of Early Texas: The Memoirs of John Holland Jenkins*, John Holmes Jenkins, ed. (Austin: University of Texas Press, 1958), 151, n6.

34. *Indian Papers* 2: 129, 231–32, 397.

35. Allen affidavit 1852. No. 73, Box 15. Legislative Records, TSLA.

Chapter 14
Freedom and Slavery in the Republic: African American Experiences in the Republic of Texas

Alwyn Barr

African Americans in Texas during the Texas Revolution and Republic faced abrupt changes and challenging choices that could lead to freedom or increased limitations on their lives. Slaves far outnumbered free blacks in Texas throughout the period from 1835 to 1846. There had been scattered numbers of slaves and free African Americans among the region's settlers in the period of Spanish rule up to 1821. The number of slaves increased after Stephen F. Austin and other empresarios received approval in the 1820s from the new Mexican government to bring Anglo settlers from the United States, including southern slaveholders. The slaves who accompanied their owners often suffered an arduous journey walking behind their masters' wagons or traveled aboard ships, usually below deck, from New Orleans.

The slave population in Texas grew slowly in the late 1820s and early 1830s because leaders in the Mexican government expressed ambivalence about slavery, which had declined in the more heavily populated areas of Mexico. Moves to abolish the institution alternated with decisions to exempt Texas where slave labor apparently contributed to economic development. Additionally, Anglo slaveholders in Texas often circumvented anti-slavery laws by using legal documents to define their laborers as indentured servants.

Most Texas slave owners claimed fewer than ten slaves; yet some could be described as members of the planter class, owning twenty or more slaves. The earliest example, Jared Groce, came with ninety slaves to create his Brazos Valley plantation in 1822. By 1834, at least 2,000 slaves labored in the Anglo settlements, probably more.[1] The background and process of arrival of Texas slaves differed. Before the Texas Revolution, slave traders, including noted Alamo defender James Bowie, smuggled slaves through Texas and into the United States, which had made the importation of slaves illegal in 1808. Seven ships brought slaves, originally captured in West Africa, from the Spanish colony of Cuba to labor in Texas between 1833 and 1835. Five more ships landed African slaves in 1836–1837. Four ships carried a total of 705 bondsmen, three landed perhaps another hundred Africans, and the number of people on the remaining five ships is unknown. It seems likely that a thousand Africans entered Texas through a slave trade viewed officially as forbidden by the laws of Mexico and the United States. Among those involved in the smuggling, Sterling McNeel became a prominent planter, while James Fannin died as a military leader in the Texas Revolution. Sean M. Kelley, in his study of slaveholding "in the Texas borderlands," explains that the thousand smuggled African slaves represented roughly 20 percent of the entire slave population of about 5,000 by 1836, with an even higher percentage of up to 50 percent in Brazoria County by 1837. Because many of the Africans worked on large plantations near the coast, they could often establish families with African spouses and keep alive some memories of African culture during the Republic period.[2]

Free African Americans in much smaller numbers, perhaps 150, came to Mexican Texas in the late 1820s and early 1830s. They arrived for social, economic, and legal-political reasons. Interracial couples found greater acceptance in Mexico than in the United States. William Goyens with his Anglo wife lived in Nacogdoches. There Goyens at various times successfully operated an inn, worked as a blacksmith, engaged in transporting goods, and speculated in property. David Town, an Anglo, migrated from Louisiana to Texas so he could free his slave wife and their children. Another white settler near Bastrop, John F. Webber, married a former slave named Silvia. They later moved to South Texas to avoid growing discrimination in Central Texas. A number of families named Ashworth, who arrived in Texas from Louisiana, reflected multi-racial relationships.[3]

Other free African Americans joined white frontiersmen in the hope of improving their economic status. Robert Thompson acquired property to raise cattle, hogs, and horses in Montgomery County. In Brazoria County, Emanuel J. Hardin established himself as a farmer on his own land. Greenbury Logan came from Missouri to support himself as a blacksmith. Free African American women also arrived in Texas. Zelia Husk and Diana Leonard worked as washerwomen. In addition to his economic success, Goyens cast a ballot in Nacogdoches elections and appeared in court during legal transactions.[4]

In the early 1830s, a variety of issues and conflicts arose between Anglo settlers in Texas and some Mexican government administrations.

Slavery played a role in these disputes, with historians offering varied views on its importance. Randolph Campbell described it as "an underlying cause of the struggle" but not "the immediate cause." Ernest Obadele-Starks focused on the active roles of several slave smugglers and traders in the developing opposition to the Mexican government. Paul Lack discusses Anglo Texan fears of Mexican anti-slavery action as events moved toward conflict in 1835. Jodella Kite (Dyerson) studied the "war" and "peace" parties among Anglo settlers that favored challenging or conciliatory approaches toward the government. She found the groups included similar percentages of slaveholders, with more planters in the aggressive faction. Andrew Torget concludes that the growing production of cotton with slave labor in Texas conflicted with Mexican opposition to slavery and became a major stimulant to revolution. Campbell and Lack also recognize the irony of Anglo Texans describing their decision to declare independence as a "contest for liberty or slavery."[5]

As the possibility of war loomed in 1835, it brought with it the threat of political, social, and economic disruption, including impacts on slaves and free African Americans. For slaves, chaos could create opportunities to escape or revolt in search of freedom. An awareness of Mexican ambivalence towards slavery had led to some runaways before the conflict. Yet other bondsmen might enhance their status in the eyes of owners or perhaps earn individual emancipation by contributing to the revolutionary cause. Anglo Texans recognized both of these possibilities, fearing and seeking to control actions aimed at freedom, while encouraging or requiring labor that supported opposition to Mexican authority.

The first effort to achieve freedom came in October 1835 when up to a hundred slaves in the lower Brazos River valley sought to break away from their owners' control. Better armed slaveholders defeated the revolt, hanged suspected leaders, and whipped many others.

With the spring of 1836, Mexican armies under Generals Antonio Lopez de Santa Anna and Jose Urrea advanced into Texas and defeated Texan troops at the Alamo in San Antonio and at Coleto Creek near Goliad. Many Texas families began to flee the Mexican advance in what became known as the "Runaway Scrape," trying to take their slaves with them. During that time, some slaves seized the opportunity to escape, either seeking protection from the Mexican armies or making their own way south toward Matamoros below the Rio Grande. Arch, a determined runaway, was captured several times, but broke his chains on two occasions and successfully fled again after the last recapture. In East Texas along the Trinity River slaves seemed on the verge of open resistance in March. That led Anglos to put down the potential uprising, killing one leader and whipping a second, although a third one escaped.

The loss of slaves appeared significant to Anglo Texans. After Sam Houston's army defeated Santa Anna's troops at San Jacinto in April, the Texans included the surrender of escaped slaves and other property as a clause in the independence treaty signed by the captured Santa Anna. General Vicente Filisola made some attempt to comply, but Urrea rejected the surrender of any slaves who were then traveling with his troops. Earlier, after the Mexican army captured the Alamo and killed its defenders, Santa Anna allowed Joe and Sam, the slaves of Travis and Bowie, to depart with word of the battle. Despite his service with the Texan army, Joe continued to be a bondsman of the Travis estate after the war. To remedy that result, Joe escaped in April 1837, thus creating "his own method of celebrating the first anniversary of the battle of San Jacinto," in the words of historian Paul Lack.[6]

Most slaves in Texas remained under the control of slaveholders. Sam Houston sent a young male slave away from the contested areas to work for a friend. Other owners took slaves with them during the "Runaway Scrape" toward East Texas. Texan government officials hired or temporarily requisitioned slaves from their owners to build defenses for Galveston where the government retreated, while other slaves were used on riverboats carrying people and supplies to the island.

Josiah H. Bell employed slaves Sam and Peter to protect families amid the disruptions. Thomas F. McKinney directed his bondsman Cary to take information to military officers. Wyly Martin, who frequently hired out his slave Peter to move freight, allowed him to deliver supplies for the Texas army. Like Joe and Sam at the Alamo, other slaves participated in military campaigns. In December 1835, Thomas Stephens fought along with the Texans who seized San Antonio from the Mexican army. In the San Jacinto campaign, Houston apparently received word from some slaves concerning Mexican troop movements. Slave James Robinson guarded supplies for the Texas troops, while another bondsman, Mark Smith, joined the attack at San Jacinto. Yet it appears that only Cary McKinney and Peter Martin won their freedom as a result of their service in support of the revolution.[7]

Free African Americans generally had faced less prejudice in Mexican Texas than in the United States. They usually had settled near white Texans, however, and sought to protect their status of freedom in those communities. Samuel McCullough, a free black from Matagorda, probably suffered the first wound of the war when the Texans captured a small Mexican garrison at Goliad in October 1835. McCullough's injuries left him with a serious disability for the remainder of his life. Later that month other Texas troops, including Greenbury Logan, advanced on San Antonio. At Concepcion mission, Logan as a member of Fannin's company, helped hold off Mexican attacks. During the assault on San Antonio in December 1835, Logan was among the Texans wounded in battle. Like McCullough, Logan suffered permanent injury.

United States volunteers joined the Texans under James Fannin during the winter at Goliad. They included Peter Allen, a free black from Pennsylvanian, who faced capture and death before a firing squad with the other prisoners in March 1836. In another incident, when Houston sent his men forward in their surprise attack at San Jacinto in April 1836, their marching music came in part from Dick the Drummer, another free African American. After Texas was annexed to the United States, Dick again joined the army, serving in the conflict between the United States and Mexico in 1845.

Beyond the battlefields, African Americans contributed to the Texas war for independence in varied ways. William Goyens of Nacogdoches used his ability to communicate with the Cherokee in East Texas to interpret for Sam Houston's successful effort to maintain peaceful relations and avoid fighting on another front. Supplies and cattle for the Texas armies came from the Ashworths, a free black family who had gained prominence in East Texas. Another free black rancher, Robert Thompson, sent a rifle and a horse for military use.[8]

The complicated story of Emily West may be added to the list of possible involvements by an African American. Although early accounts described her as a slave, she served as a free woman who worked for James Morgan, a supporter of Texas independence. Some of Santa Anna's troops captured Emily at New Washington on Buffalo Bayou before she and other workers could leave for Galveston. One account suggests that Santa Anna found her attractive, which may have distracted him at the moment the Texans attacked at San Jacinto. She found her way to the Texas lines after Houston's army won its victory.[9]

The success of the Texas Revolution brought with it a constitution for the new Republic of Texas. The authors of that document confirmed the legality of slavery, removing the previous concern that Mexico might emancipate Texas bondsmen. The Texas constitution added further protection for slavery by declaring that no slaveholder could free a slave without the approval of the Texas Congress. Assured by the clear protection of slavery, the immigration of slaveholders to Texas with their slaves increased. An expanded slave trade overland and by ship from New Orleans and other ports brought additional slaves to the new Republic for sale. From the estimated 5,000 slaves in 1836, roughly 13 percent of the Texas population, the number counted by Texas assessors in 1840 rose to 12,570, a growth of over 100 percent. By 1845 at the end of the Republic period, tax assessors found 27,555 slaves. An early state census in 1847 set the slave figure at 38,753, or 27 percent of the population. Thus, the slave population grew faster than the free white population during the Republic era.[10]

During the days of the Republic, Texans recognized the Rio Grande as the border with Mexico although Anglo settlement below the Nueces River remained limited and accompanied by few slaves. As before and during the war for independence, some slaves continued to seek freedom in Mexico, usually in small groups ranging from two or three up to twenty-five in one instance. While slaveholders and slave hunters recaptured some, others proved successful. In 1851, Texas slave owners believed 3,000 escaped bondsmen lived at Matamoros or in other communities below the Rio Grande. Early in the Republic years, African born slaves appeared most likely to run away. That began to change with the growing number of slaves from the South. While runaways who reached Mexico achieved a practical freedom, Mexican law contained complications in gaining legal citizenship for the newly arrived African Americans. Still, in the borderlands of northern Mexico that may not have been a major issue for working class people if they found a role in local communities.[11]

While the number of slaveholders grew rapidly during the years of the Republic, they did not form a majority of the white population. Most non-slaveholding Anglos supported the institution, however, because they hoped to acquire bondsmen in the future. Regardless of economic factors, most whites had matured in a society that believed in their racial superiority, which allowed them a status above that of all African Americans. A few individuals did hold alternate views. Stephen Pearl Andrews, a northern attorney who settled in Texas prior to 1839, suggested the Republic could eliminate its debt by ending slavery in return for British financial aid and reimbursements to slaveholders. After some early interest in Andrew's ideas, strong opposition arose, eventually forcing the strategizing abolitionist to leave Texas.[12]

Two groups did not become as involved in slaveholding as did Anglos from the United States. Few Mexican Texans, who lived primarily in

South Texas, owned slaves. Some Tejanos shared Mexican doubts about slavery and on occasion assisted bondsmen fleeing toward Mexico. As a result, Tejanos faced suspicion from Anglos. German immigrants, who began to settle in south central Texas in the 1830s, also owned fewer slaves than Anglos from the South. Since most became owners of small farms, they often could not afford the cost of slaves. They also reflected a culture in which members of the working class usually were not of a different race, although slavery did appear similar to European serfdom. For example, the German group promoting immigration to Texas in the 1840s, commonly called the Adelsverein, directed Count Joseph of Boos-Weldeck to acquire land and slaves, initially seventeen, to create the Nassau plantation in Fayette County. Three of the slaves ran away and hid in the Brazos River bottom, perhaps because of a hard driving Anglo overseer. When caught, one surrendered, but the other two escaped again and may have reached Mexico. The success of the plantation fluctuated with changes in overseers that included an experienced slave blacksmith called Negro Jim in 1847.

German immigrants in the region from Galveston to San Antonio settled among Anglos who came mainly from the South. Thus, the Germans generally sought the acceptance of their neighbors. German immigrants who became a majority in the Hill Country beyond San Antonio on small farms or ranches probably felt less need to conform to southern views. Thus, escaping slaves may have found occasional aid in that region. The sense of cultural differences led some Anglos to take a wary view of their German neighbors.[13]

As slavery in Texas grew during the Republic years, it had changing impacts on the lives of bondsmen. When slaveholders and slave traders moved large numbers of people from the South into the new republic, many found themselves separated from family members—parents, children, and other kinfolk.[14] Yet they had little time to mourn such changes because of the hard labor clearing land for farming on the still developing Texas frontier. More slaves meant expanded agriculture, especially the dominant commercial crop cotton, which witnessed production increases from 4,000 bales in 1833–1834 to 58,000 bales by 1850.[15]

While most bondsmen labored in the fields on farms and plantations, the increase in slave population led to more diversity of occupations and skills. Even field hands raised food crops, as well as cotton, with the hardest work faced by those on sugar plantations employed in cutting and transporting cane. Others herded and cared for cattle and horses on ranches. On plantations and in the developing small towns, slavery also included house servants who cooked, sewed clothes and quilts, and cared for children. A variety of tasks required smaller numbers of skilled craftsmen such as blacksmiths, carpenters, leather tanners, brick masons, and dock workers in ports. Most constructed their own cabins and furniture and in some cases the larger homes and more polished furniture of their owners.[16]

The concentration of more slaves on plantations did allow the growth of a separate sense of community. Those slaves could expect to create new families and maintain some aspects of African and African American culture. Spiritual ideas might be reflected in charms and in religious gatherings at night to express hope more openly. Folklore that contained humor could be shared. Most popular in Texas, the Old John stories appear. These stories were similar to the Brer Rabbit tales that involved subtle criticism of slaveholders through analogies and double meanings.[17]

Slaves also provided music for themselves and for owners, in some cases with banjos they constructed. Bondsmen might join in a chant to create a reasonable speed for various group work. More lively tunes accompanied opportunities to enjoy time for themselves on Saturday evening or to celebrate the end of harvest in the fields. The words of some tunes might express more than one idea or send a warning to other slaves.[18]

One might expect free African Americans to fare better than slaves in the new republic since several had aided in its creation. Yet slaveholders feared the influence of free blacks on slaves as examples of a status slaves could not share. Thus, the 1836 Constitution of the Republic of Texas stated that free African Americans could not remain in Texas unless approved by congress.[19]

The new Texas Constitution also prohibited slaveholders from freeing any of their bondsmen without the approval of the Texas Congress, which seem to imply that such approval would be hard to achieve. As a result of petitions by and for two slaves who had served the cause of independence, they did receive their freedom in 1839–1840. Wyly Martin freed Peter, while Thomas F. McKinney allowed Cary to buy his freedom. In each case, however, Congress required a $1,000 security bond that these men would not become dependent on the republic. The declining value of Texas paper money probably made that more manageable. Other petitions to emancipate slaves met rejection. By an 1840 ruling of the Texas Supreme Court, African American women who lived as free persons with Anglo men also were considered legally free.[20]

Free African Americans already in Texas by 1836 petitioned to remain in the Republic. Congress debated that question and agreed in 1837 to let them stay. Yet free blacks could no longer vote or testify in court against Anglos. To retain ownership of property, free African Americans sent petitions to Congress, often with the supporting signatures of neighbors, but Congress neither approved nor rejected them. Even those who served in the military could only receive cash payments rather than land. Surprisingly, it seems that no free African Americans lost land they already owned in 1836.[21]

New debate arose in Congress during 1839 reflecting fears of free black influences. Action by the Houston city government probably contributed to discussions in Congress. Houston government leaders sought to expel free blacks through a local law, describing them as "useless" and a threat to slavery. Yet that effort failed to receive support in a local court. Congress in February 1840 then adopted a new law against immigration into Texas with sale as slaves to punish any new arrivals who did not depart. Ironically, the law appears similar to but harsher than the Mexican law that attempted to end Anglo entry into Texas in 1830. A more sweeping section of the 1840 law declared all free African Americans must remove themselves from the Republic by the beginning of 1842.[22]

Opposition to that requirement developed quickly. Free blacks successfully gained defenders including friends, neighbors, and white relatives. Anglo men who had served with African Americans in the military also offered their support, as did other whites who saw the value of skilled blacks who included barbers and nurses. Petitions to the next Congress in late 1840 in favor of several free blacks stimulated a review of the previous law. In December 1840 Congress adopted a new act allowing all free African Americans in Texas before the declaration of independence in 1836 to continue their residence in the republic. In 1843, Congress confirmed property ownership for a few who had served in the war of independence, but rejected other requests regarding land.[23]

The earlier law against free black immigration into Texas after the declaration of independence remained in force. Several individuals petitioned for exemptions with the support of white Texans in varying numbers. Although Congress did not act upon those appeals, President Sam Houston in 1842 put off the deadline requiring their departure for a year. In 1843, he extended the deadline until 1845. No further action occurred during the final days of the Republic.

Other limitations continued, such as the inability of African Americans to testify in court, or vote, or legally marry anyone white. There also existed the possibility of a free black being claimed as a runaway slave by a white man. William Goyens had to ransom himself from such a claim at one time.[24]

Despite the fluctuations in congressional legislation and the continuation of legal limitations, the lives of free African Americans at the local level appear to have included more flexibility and opportunity than might have been expected. Although a law existed against emancipation of slaves, James Routh in his 1837 Harris County will freed Sylvia and the six children he probably had fathered with her. The executor of the will tried to deny her freedom, but she and her children clearly became free and also inherited 320 acres of land from Routh. In a Bexar County case that also involved interference by an executor, Harriet Arnold won her freedom in local court based on the 1846 will of Hendrick Arnold, her father, despite her mother being a slave named Dolly. Other similar cases also occurred, suggesting that the free status of a white father carried more weight than the slavery of a black mother in local Texas courts.[25]

Despite the mixed results for petitions to confirm free black property ownership, William Goyens owned property including 5,000 acres of land in 1840. Ann Tucker bought a lot in Houston during 1840. Fannie McFarland, who had been freed in 1835, acquired land and profited from its sale. After his emancipation, Peter Martin owned land in Fort Bend County for raising cattle and horses during the 1840s, under a trust agreement with a white landowner. Other land-owning ranchers who retained their property included the Ashworths and Robert Thompson.[26]

Many free African Americans supported themselves by their skilled occupations. Cary McKinney operated a livery stable. Goyens and James Richardson served as innkeepers in Nacogdoches and on the coast respectively. Nelson Kavanaugh, Henry Tucker, and Henry Lloyd acted as barbers for white men. Charity Bird sold baked goods. Zelia Husk and Diana Leonard washed clothes to earn a living. Several men enlisted in military companies during the Republic period: Pleasant Bious, Henry Bird, Thomas Cevallos, Gibson Perkins, Joseph Tate, and Joseph Taylor. Historian John Garrison Marks argues that most free African Americans in Texas achieved various forms of positive status at the community level. They earned the respect of white Texans who in numerous petitions described their black neighbors and employees as "good," "industrious," and "useful."[27]

The increasing numbers of slave laborers brought from the United States and Africa to Texas in the 1820s and 1830s, as well as fears that Mexico might abolish slavery, created one of the important causes of the Texas revolution. Texas independence confirmed the continuation of slavery, which foreshadowed rapid expansion during the years of the Republic. Yet some slaves escaped to Mexico during the conflict and increasing numbers followed in the next ten years. Other bondsmen aided the revolution in the hope of freedom or greater opportunities, while others served when required. For the slaves in Texas, work roles and slave culture became more diverse during the Republic years.

A much smaller group of free African Americans had come from the United States to Mexican Texas seeking economic opportunity or greater freedom from discrimination. Yet they generally aided the Texas Revolution as soldiers or contributors of supplies or other skills to protect their status in the Anglo settlements. White fears that the presence of free blacks might cause unrest among slaves led to new limitations on the roles of free African Americans in society and even threats of expulsion. Their contributions to local communities through various occupations created positive images of them among their white neighbors that allowed them to remain and in some cases acquire property in the Republic.

The roles of African Americans in the Texas Revolution and their status during the Republic years in some ways paralleled those of slaves and free blacks in the South during and after the longer American Revolution. Some slaves had escaped to freedom on the British side, while some free blacks had fought on the American side. Paul Lack also suggests some comparisons, as well as differences, between the Texas Revolution and the longer American Civil War. Some slaves and free blacks joined the Union army, while others were used or pressed to aid the Confederacy. Recognizing emancipation in 1865 as a major difference, Lack concludes: "For Texas Confederates, the Civil War represented a failed attempt to replicate their past."[28]

Notes

1. Randolph B. Campbell, *An Empire for Slavery: The Peculiar Institution in Texas, 1821–1865* (Baton Rouge: Louisiana State University Press, 1989), 10–34.

2. Ernest Obadele-Starks, *Freebooters and Smugglers: The Foreign Slave Trade in the United States After 1808* (Fayetteville: University of Arkansas Press, 2007), 60–62, 75–87; Sean M. Kelley, *Los Brazos de Dios: A Plantation Society in the Texas Borderlands 1821–1865* (Baton Rouge: Louisiana State University Press, 2010), 48–56, 72–82, 121–128, 203.

3. Harold Schoen, "The Free Negro in the Republic of Texas, I," *Southwestern Historical Quarterly* 39 (April 1936): 294–300; Victor H. Treat, "William Goyens: Free Negro Entrepeneur," in *Black Leaders: Texans for Their Times*, ed. Alwyn Barr and Robert A. Calvert (Austin: Texas State Historical Association, 1981), 19–47.

4. Schoen, "Free Negro in the Republic of Texas, I," 299–302; Treat, "Goyens," 22, 28. See also Ruthe Winegarten, *Black Texas Women: 150 Years of Trial and Triumph* (Austin: University of Texas Press, 1995), 3–4.

5. Campbell, *Empire for Slavery*, 40–41, 48; Obadele-Starks, *Freebooters and Smugglers*, 75–87; Paul Lack, *The Texas Revolutionary Experience: A Political and Social History, 1835–1836* (College Station: Texas A&M University Press, 1992), 238–244; Jodella Dorothea Kite, "The War and Peace Parties of Pre-Revolutionary Texas, 1832–1835" (M.A. thesis: Texas Tech University, 1986): 86; Andrew J. Torget, *Seeds of Empire: Cotton, Slavery, and the Transformation of the Texas Borderlands, 1800–1850* (Chapel Hill: University of North Carolina Press, 2015).

6. Lack, *Texas Revolutionary Experience*, 242–248. See also James W. Russell, *Escape from Texas:A Novel of Slavery and the Texas War of Independence* (Cornwall-on-Hudson, NY: Sloan Publishing, 2012).

7. Lack, *Texas Revolutionary Experience*, 247–249; Schoen, "Free Negro in the Republic of Texas, II," *Southwestern Historical Quarterly* 40 (July 1936): 32–33.

8. Lack, *Texas Revolutionary Experience*, 248; Schoen, "Free Negro in the Republic of Texas, II," 26–34.

9. Margaret Swett Henson, "West, Emily D." *Handbook of Texas Online*. Accessed December 12, 2014. Uploaded June 15, 2010. Published by the Texas State Historical Association. Jeffrey D. Dunn and James Lutzweiler, "Yellow Rose of Texas," ibid. Accessed December 12, 2014. Uploaded June 15, 2010. Modified April 24, 2014. Dunn and Lutzweiler find no connection between Emily West and the song "The Yellow Rose of Texas," which had been suggested by some writers. For a fictional account see: Anita Bunkley, *Emily: The Yellow Rose* (Houston: Rinard Publishing, 1989).

10. Lack, *Texas Revolutionary Experience*, 250–252; Campbell, *Empire for Slavery*, 54–55; Michael Tadman, *Speculators and Slaves: Masters, Traders, and Slaves in the Old South* (Madison: University of Wisconsin Press, 1989), 28.

11. Campbell, *Empire for Slavery*, 62–63, 180; Kelley, *Los Brazos de Dios*, 100–101; Ronnie C. Tyler, "Fugitive Slaves in Mexico," *Journal*

of Negro History 57 (January 1972): 1–12; Rosalie Schwartz, *Across the Rio Grande to Freedom: United States Negroes in Mexico* (El Paso: Texas Western Press, Southwestern Studies, No. 44, 1975); Sarah E. Cornell, "Citizens of Nowhere: Fugitive Slaves and Free African Americans in Mexico, 1833–1857," *Journal of American History* 100 (September 2013): 351–374.

12. Campbell, *Empire for Slavery*, 68, 209–215, 221–222.

13. Ibid., 215–219; Kelley, *Los Brazos de Dios*, 130–134, 148–152; James C. Kearney, *Nassau Plantation: The Evolution of a Texas-German Slave Plantation* (Denton: University of North Texas Press, 2010), 63–74, 89, 131.

14. Campbell, *Empire for Slavery*, 50, 163; Kelley, *Los Brazos de Dios,* 35.

15. Campbell, *Empire for Slavery*, 34; Karen Gerhardt Britton, Fred C. Elliott, and E. A. Miller, "Cotton Culture," *The New Handbook of Texas* (Austin: Texas State Historical Association, 1996), II, 354.

16. Alwyn Barr, *The African Texans* (College Station: Texas A&M University Press, 2004), 15–21; Campbell, *Empire for Slavery*, 119–128.

17. Kelley, *Los Brazos de Dios*, 74–76, 122–127; Barr, *African Texans,* 25–26.

18. Campbell, *Empire for Slavery*, 174–175; Kelley, *Los Brazos de Dios*, 122.

19. Schoen, "Free Negro in the Republic of Texas, III," *Southwestern Historical Quarterly* 40 (October 1936): 93.

20. Ibid., 98–113.

21. Schoen, "Free Negro in the Republic of Texas, IV," *Southwestern Historical Quarterly* 40 (January 1937): 174–178.

22. Ibid., 183–197.

23. Ibid., 197–199; Schoen, "Free Negro in the Republic of Texas, V," *Southwestern Historical Quarterly* 40 (April 1937): 267–274, 285–289.

24. Schoen, "Free Negro in the Republic of Texas, VI," *Southwestern Historical Quarterly* 41 (July 1837): 104; Treat, "Goyens," 30.

25. Andrew Forest Muir, "The Free Negro in Harris County, Texas," *Southwestern Historical Quarterly* 46 (January 1943): 225–228; Schoen, "Free Negro in the Republic of Texas, III," 94–98.

26. Treat, "Goyens," 28–29; Michael Rugeley Moore, "Peter Martin: A Stockraiser of the Republic Period," in *Black Cowboys of Texas*, ed. Sara R. Massey (College Station: Texas A&M University Press, 2000), 39–47; Schoen, "Free Negro in the Republic of Texas, V," 275–287.

27. Ibid., 281, 286; Schoen, "Free Negro in the Republic of Texas, VI," 97–102; John Garrison Marks, "Community Bonds in the Bayou City: Free Blacks and Local Reputation in Early Houston," *Southwestern Historical Quarterly* 117 (January 2014): 267–282.

28. Paul Lack, "Slavery and the Texas Revolution: A Comparison with the American Civil War," in *Invisible Texans: Women and Minorities in Texas History*, ed. Donald Willett and Stephen Curley (New York: McGraw- Hill, 2005), 72.

Chapter 15

A Tainted Friendship: The Betrayal of Tejanos in the Republic of Texas

Francis X. Galán

Two weeks after leading a company of regulars in victory over Santa Anna at the Battle of San Jacinto, Col. Edward Burleson wrote Gen. Thomas Rusk noting the bravery of Tejanos under the command of Capt. Juan Seguín from San Antonio. Burleson expressed his desire "to see them enjoy liberty to the full extent" for having been "honestly engaged in the noble cause of freedom."[1] General Rusk, focused upon the withdrawal of Mexican troops from Texas, had proclaimed neutrality no longer remained an option for Tejanos who helped Mexico.[2] Anxiety over possible military reoccupation reverberated into the fall of 1836 when the *Columbia Telegraph and Texas Register* reported that Tejanos at San Antonio were the "pretended friends" of Texas.[3] In essence, Tejanos weighed the prevalent dangers of becoming a stateless people while their responses reflected local interests in defense of their land, families, and traditions. Tejano contributions to the Texas Revolution mattered less than perceptions of patriotism and whether or not Tejanos were on board with securing the borders of the new nation.

This essay examines the major Mexican-populated communities in the Republic of Texas, 1836–1845, including Nacogdoches, San Antonio, Goliad, and Victoria, collectively "Tejano."[4] Born into an Old World under Spanish imperialism and bred to defend the Texas frontier against foreign penetration of Mexico's silver trade, Tejanos fought for survival based upon a mixed economy of ranching, farming, and smuggling far from Mexico City and closer to Comanche and U.S. expansionism. Tejanos endured brutal retaliation from Spanish royalists for aligning with Indians and Anglo Americans in the Battle of Medina (1813) during Mexico's war of independence against Spain, 1810–1821. Tejanos soon thereafter ushered Stephen F. Austin into Mexican Texas from Natchitoches, Louisiana, along the Camino Real and together experienced greater troubles during the First Republic of Mexico, 1824–1835, following brief monarchical rule. Domestic and foreign issues that confronted Tejanos before 1836 included Centralist and Federalist political factions of Mexico concerned about the devastated economy, European reconquest, Indian raids, and greater numbers of American immigrants arriving in Texas.[5] Meanwhile, Anglo and African Americans quickly outnumbered the 3,500 Tejanos by more than ten to one, not including another 12,000 Comanches on the Southern Plains. It appeared as though the world rushed into Texas where Tejanos remained a distinct minority as the smoke cleared following the Texian victory over Santa Anna at San Jacinto.[6]

By late June 1836, after General Rusk established his headquarters in Victoria, located about 115 miles southeast from San Antonio, Anglo Texans ("Texians") arrested *don* Fernando de León, the son of a Mexican *empresario* who founded the colony of Victoria in 1824, as a traitor for turning over supplies to Gen. José Urrea during the Texas Revolution. It did not matter to Rusk that General Urrea held De León prisoner for aiding the Texian revolt. Ironically, Carlos de la Garza, from nearby Goliad, raised a company of Tejanos in opposition to Texas independence but avoided prison and stayed on his ranch unlike De León, who was exiled and his property confiscated. Juan Seguín of San Antonio also raised a company of Tejanos, but sided with Anglo Texans in their bid for independence. However, just as De León suffered from his involvement in the war, Seguín's loyalty resulted in Mexican troops pillaging his ranch, which Texians later burned.[7] In East Texas, on the other hand, Gen. Sam Houston, residing at Nacogdoches, urged fellow Texians to display benevolence toward Tejanos who had professed neutrality and "*by no means* treat them with *violence*." It made little difference to Texians in Nacogdoches who eventually ran Tejanos out of town.[8] Events such as these became all too common during the era of the Republic, leaving many Tejanos wondering why their allies during the revolution had now decided to betray them. Tejano responses to their predicament ranged broadly from accommodation to resistance and reveals, in the words of historian Andrés Tijerina, why "defense had become a part of their unique culture."[9] If anything, Tejanos learned through lengthy experience on the Texas frontier to stick close to their guns and never surrender.

Scholars generally agree that Tejanos experienced declension during the Republic of Texas. Arnoldo De León refers to this era as one of "cataclysmic changes" in a "cycle of land displacement, dilution of political power, occupational degradation, and racial subordination."[10] Timothy Matovina explains Tejano representation in the National Congress of Texas "declined in political clout." Meanwhile, San Antonio Tejanos no longer held a "monopoly" in the mayor's office and witnessed Catholic Church leadership change from native to European clergy after Texas independence from Mexico.[11] Fighting alongside Bowie, Crockett, and Travis at the Alamo and maintaining a rear guard in the Battle of San Jacinto proved insufficient for Tejano loyalties to the new nation. Military, political, economic, and social bonds that Tejanos had forged on native ground during the previous Spanish and Mexican eras no longer mattered as they had to renegotiate terms favorable to Anglos. Even those Tejanos who sought refuge on South Texas ranches between the Nueces River and Rio Grande, a vast region that remained predominantly ethnic Mexican, found their "world much contracted" by Comanches who expanded southward into northeastern Mexico.[12] By comparison, however, Mexicans in the Rio Grande borderlands continued to use the river to subvert national control and took advantage of opportunities well into the late nineteenth century, which Tejanos in San Antonio, Goliad, and East Texas found increasingly difficult under the Republic of Texas as the border moved further west.[13] According to Raúl Ramos, Tejanos sought to consolidate their own political identity based upon regional autonomy and stability, yet learned "to live with a degree of tension and danger tempering" their goals.[14] Tejanos found themselves fighting the same struggles as Native Americans but with a hand still in play having served in the Texas Revolution.

Even so Tejanos held no guarantees about equality, justice, or citizenship in the new nation and fought against subjection of their status to that of free blacks and Indians. Historian Jesús (Frank) De la Teja notes that the Republic of Texas Constitution denied citizenship to African Americans and Native Americans while that of Tejanos remained in the balance.[15] Ironically, Tejanos were also uncertain about rights and freedom under Centralist Party rule in Mexico, especially after Santa Anna returned to power amidst continued foreign threats and rebellions. Matovina explains that San Antonio Tejanos "demonstrated loyalty to their Mexican heritage, not the Mexican government," which Anglo Texans misunderstood or could not fully accept.[16] Historian Andrés Reséndez adds that Tejanos held "pecuniary interests that were also central in determining peoples' loyalties and ultimately their national identity" much like the Texas Cherokees.[17] Tejanos became a class apart during the Republic of Texas through persistence of their language, traditions, and a traditional ranching economy in stark contrast to a new country transforming itself into a plantation society with an identity and character more American if not Southern.[18] During the Republic of Texas era, Tejanos naturally refused to become "foreigners in their native land."[19]

The Tejano community at Nacogdoches perhaps fell under greatest suspicion because they did not take up arms against their own countrymen throughout the Texas Revolution. Although individual Anglos had resided at Nacogdoches since the 1790s and established enduring relationships beyond Mexican independence from Spain, many large Anglo family settlements quickly became the majority in East Texas with less inclination toward accommodation.[20] The newly created municipalities at Liberty (1831), San Augustine (1834), Shelby/Teneha (1835), Red River (1835), Bevil/Jasper (1835), and Sabine (1835) were all carved from the vast Nacogdoches District while other Anglos still resided at Nacogdoches.[21] The total population alone from the Nacogdoches Census of 1835 counted 1,490 residents with 265 households (163 Tejano and 102 Anglo) and 128 black servants/slaves, the latter who comprised 9 percent of the total. The increasing presence of Anglo-Americans at Nacogdoches and elsewhere in East Texas together with African Americans and Native American arrivals from the East made the Tejano community at Nacogdoches aware of their own vulnerability to disfranchisement after barely avoiding such a measure by "American citizens" to remove this right in September 1836.[22]

Although Tejanos at Nacogdoches became accustomed to *de facto* slavery prior to the Texas Revolution through their civic duties as *alcalde* (municipal official), presiding judge, or *testigos* (witnesses) to contracts for sale, they were not assured of such roles afterward under Texian rule.[23] For example, on September 27, 1830, John Durst, local resident, acted as a witness along with Luís Procela under Vicente Cordova, alcalde at Nacogdoches, who presided over the sale of a slave named Sarah (age twenty-four) from Daniel Clark to Frost Thorn for 600 pesos. Two months later, Cordova also presided over a case whereby a black servant named Silvia (age unknown) appeared before him to purchase her freedom. Cordova permitted the transfer of her personal services from the "foreigner" Thomas Ruel, whom Silvia owed 600 pesos, to Adolphus Sterne, a resident of Nacogdoches. Silvia in turn had to pay Sterne fifteen pesos a year until the debt from her previous master was paid off and only then could she attain her freedom. In October of 1831, another alcalde, Manuel de los Santos Coy, presided over the sale of a black slave named Harry, age twenty-five, from Harrison E. Watson, a resident from the Ais District east of Nacogdoches along the Sabine River, to Frost Thorn for 550 pesos. More such examples followed as the importance of servitude or slavery grew in significance together with land sales.[24] However, John Durst, whom the Nacogdoches Census of 1835 lists as thirty-seven years old and married to Harriet M. Jameson, age twenty-seven, with four children and twenty-two black servants, is indicative of power shifts away from Tejanos. On May 27, 1836, barely one month after Santa Anna surrendered at San Jacinto, Durst sold his Angelina plantation, which totaled 40,000 acres west of Nacogdoches and included "his farm with seventeen negroes and mulatoes." to a small group of investors from Natchitoches, Louisiana, in the amount of $10,000 and made payable to John Bernardo Davenport of Natchitoches.[25] Tejanos increasingly lost power presiding over such transfers and slave sales as their own professional roles were challenged under Anglo rule.

The sale of Durst's plantation, if anything, foreshadowed the transfer of more land titles under the Republic of Texas as new settlers received first-class headrights and citizenship that fed growing resentment among Tejanos. Historians particularly note that only 18 percent of Tejanos in East Texas were able to patent their claims while just 25 percent of San Antonio-Goliad claimants patented theirs.[26] By the fall of 1836, despite General Houston's caution against Texians from doing any harm, individual Tejanos were harassed under the law, detained illegally by private citizens, whipped, and forced into labor for minor offenses. In addition, a group of eighty-two "American citizens" petitioned the National Congress of Texas and urged disenfranchisement of "the Mexican Population residing in the Municipality of Nacogdoches." According to historian Paul Lack, the majority of Anglo-Texan sentiment evidently prevailed as no records indicate any Mexican voting controversies in 1837 and 1838.[27]

Lack also notes the infamous Cordova Revolt followed the ambitious plans of another Nacogdoches resident named Richard Sparks for settlement of the Texas frontier. In March of 1837, Sparks lost fourteen horses to a band of Nadaco (Caddo) Indians allegedly led by Telesforo Cordova, whose surname alone raised suspicion about his ties with Vicente Cordova. The Cordova family had roots in East Texas dating back a hundred years to the old Spanish fort at Los Adaes in northwestern Louisiana and the establishment of Nacogdoches in 1779. East Texas Tejanos became familiar with the Caddoan language and traded with everyone, including slaves from Louisiana. In turn, as Lack explains, runaway slaves sought "refuge among Indians who often held longstanding friendships with Tejanos" while a Texas Senate committee reported how Caddos "all understand and speak the Castilian language." The presumption on the part of Anglo Texans was that East Texas Tejanos, like the Indians, were horse thieves and could not be trusted. Undeterred, Sparks attempted to settle on a disputed tract of land and continued surveying near the headwaters of the Trinity River until he and Indian Agent Jess Watkins were killed by an unidentified party in the spring of 1838. After his death, 115 men gathered at Nacogdoches in fear that all Anglos would be driven out of town by a combined Indian-Tejano alliance, so they asked Congress to respond with a preemptive strike. After inaction from Congress, the men responded with the formation of a volunteer guard unit ready to defend Nacogdoches and their families from any potential attacks while President Sam Houston only wished to avoid indiscriminate killing on both sides.[28]

Meanwhile, Vicente Cordova, Antonio Menchaca, and several other Tejanos from Nacogdoches articulated their community's concerns about "tranquility," including "more security of their property" and an end to Anglo-Texan attitudes "that they should be considered as Enemies." Periodic outbreaks of violence and military mobilization, however, continued with no reassurances from Congress.[29] East Texas Tejanos, particularly those like Cordova and Menchaca who fought and worked alongside many Anglo Americans before the Texas Revolution, found working with greater numbers of recent immigrants from the United States more difficult afterwards. "Older" Anglo-American residents themselves came under greater scrutiny and had to decide for themselves whether to back their Tejano friends in a rapidly transforming region. After all, many Texians were already anxious about the viability of their new republic. Historian Andrew Torget notes that Anglo Texans were unable to secure foreign recognition of their republic as well as trade agreements, military assistance, and loans.[30] Such failure in foreign policy only exacerbated anxieties internally about any rebellion, which in turn affected Anglo-Tejano relations.

By the summer of 1838, tensions in East Texas reached a boiling point when Gen. Vicente Filisola's memorandum circulated among Tejanos from a small, ill-supplied party of Mexicans under Pedro Julían Miracle who had arrived in Choctaw Indian country east of the Trinity River. General Filisola, Commandant-in-Chief of Mexico's northern defenses, had promised military support from Mexico should Tejanos join with Indians in armed revolt. In early July, Vicente Cordova and other Nacogdoches leaders met with these Mexican emissaries and together visited Texas Cherokee Chief Bowl's village seeking his support. Meanwhile, President Houston learned from an army officer in Bastrop, Texas, that the Comanches had rejected an invitation the previous month to join a Mexican-Cherokee-Tejano "confederation." Houston informed a Cherokee agent that trouble was on the horizon, while General Rusk and

Joseph Durst (John Durst's older brother), who monitored Tejano movements, were the only ones the president wanted to be informed of recent developments. Without firm commitments from any Indian nations, the most Cordova could expect was a force of 540 men. Cordova wrote Manuel Flores, another Tejano from Nacogdoches with a commission from General Filisola, and requested reinforcements. He left the meeting on July 20 under the belief that Indian chiefs promised to unite and assist Tejanos even if their plans were discovered. Cordova also believed rumors that a Mexican invasion had already begun at Goliad.[31]

Fighting apparently commenced August 4, 1838, as mounted Tejanos fired upon a party of eight to ten Anglo Texans, killing one, after they had left Nacogdoches in search of stolen horses secretly kept at a neighboring Mexican settlement. Several days later, John Durst alleged that he had personal contact with a Tejano rebel patrol and provided details about a general revolt, which was reported to General Rusk who was in the vicinity of Nacogdoches. The next day, August 8, President Houston dispatched a letter offering Cordova an armistice, stating that the Tejano rebels could return to their homes "as good citizens," but those who did not lay down their arms would be subject to the "crime of treason," punishable by a loss of property and life. While he attempted diplomacy, President Houston simultaneously prepared for war and warned the Cherokees not to join with Tejano rebels as General Rusk marched the Nacogdoches guard toward Cordova's camp thirty-two miles west along the Angelina River. They also called upon other militias elsewhere in East Texas as President Houston requested arms from the U.S. Army. Among the public's concern was the Tejano reputation as fighters, numbering over 100 men about whom one reporter stated on August 9, "I have fought side by side with these Mexicans" and "they are brave men and sharpshooters."[32]

Vicente Cordova evidently made an official proclamation of rebellion on August 10, 1838, which he and eighteen other co-conspirators signed, including three Anglos and one African American. It declared that "the citizens of Nacogdoches, tired of suffering injustices and the usurpation of their rights" held firm to their guns and were "determined to shed their last drop of blood in order to protect their individual rights and those of the Nation to which they belong." They asked only that their families not be harmed and in return promised kind treatment to Tejano families.[33] One of the Tejano rebels, named Guillermo Cruz, years later recounted how he explained to his former employer, Joseph Durst, that Tejanos had been treated like "dogs long enough" and thus fought for their civil rights.[34] Interestingly, both these names appear on the same Census for

Nacogdoches in 1835, west of town to the Angelina River, precisely in the area of Cordova's rebel base.[35] That Cruz worked for Joseph Durst suggests Tejanos knew firsthand the plight of African Americans on plantations and did not want to be treated like slaves. Regardless, General Rusk believed the Tejano rebels were "reckless desperados." President Houston just thought their rebellion came in response to alleged horse stealing, though he penned a letter to Andrew Jackson in the United States and stated, "the violence of the American character was one cause, and measures were taken without my knowledge or consent." For Tejanos, their revolt symbolized self-preservation.[36]

Cordova managed to recruit individual Indians and with a force of around 200 men defeated a company of fifty mounted Texians in late September 1838, but time worked against him. The lack of provisions led him to raiding farms, stealing livestock, and deaths of more Anglo settlers. He held off General Rusk's slightly larger Texas militia in the fall and winter, but by March 1839, he received word from Matamoros, located across the present U.S.-Mexico border from Brownsville, Texas, that the assistance promised would not come due to renewed civil war in the Mexican states of Tamaulipas and Sonora. Instead, Mexico's authorities recommended that Cordova engage in guerrilla warfare against the Anglos and move his operations northwest of San Antonio to avoid East Texas and its dangerous border with Louisiana. Following this advice, Cordova suffered new problems. When he moved his operation, only seventy-five men joined him, mostly Tejanos and blacks, most of whom refused to enter unfamiliar territory under Comanche dominance. By late March, Cordova emerged near Anglo settlements on the upper Colorado River. The residents in this area quickly alerted Texas Ranger companies. As a result, Cordova's force suffered about fifty-three casualties after a Ranger company attacked their camp near the Guadalupe River. One of the rebels taken captive, a wounded African American named Raphael, stated that Cordova and many of his men had been wounded during the attack. Chased by two other ranger companies numbering 130 Texans, Cordova split his remaining rebels and reached Matamoros, where he regrouped with anywhere from 50 to 100 men—Mexicans, blacks, and Indians—and launched retaliatory strikes across the border in South Texas during the winter of 1839 and spring of 1840. As historian Lack relates, the Cordova revolt in East Texas "failed, but not because of its leader's want of courage."[37] In part, because of Cordova's activities, Anglos forced more than 100 Tejano families to abandon their homes in Nacogdoches, many of whom sought refuge by crossing the border into northwestern Louisiana.[38]

The Tejano community at San Antonio also experienced conflict in defense of their own lands, but held onto power longer than their counterparts at Nacogdoches. Potential threats to the sustainability of Texas independence from a combination of Santa Anna's army returning to Texas, Comanche expansion into northern Mexico, and fugitive slaves placed a heavy burden upon Anglo-Tejano relationships. The civic and military service of San Antonio Tejanos to the Republic of Texas and the mitigating effects of social ties among local elites were not enough to stem the tide of raised anxieties in the new nation. While tensions simmered over land transfers with Texas headright claims, Anglo Texans at San Antonio needed Tejano allies more than their compatriots did at Nacogdoches, especially given that they were still outnumbered and possibly outgunned amidst the smoldering remains of the Alamo. The Texas Rangers employed Tejano "volunteer" companies against Comanches on the Southern Plains and Mexican desert, where the threat of incursions from Indians and bandits across the border were just as problematic as the potential return of Santa Anna's troops.[39]

General Sam Houston placed his trust in Capt. Juan Seguín after his service at the Battle of San Jacinto. Seguín's first duty involved observing the withdrawal of Mexican troops from Texas and making sure they did not take slaves or any other property with them. But Seguín also tended to wounded Mexican soldiers left behind during the retreat of Santa Anna's forces. By late May 1836, he received orders from General Rusk, who took command of the Texas Army, to take possession of San Antonio and raise a battalion to defend the Texas frontier. Captain Seguín and his company of twenty-two men reached San Antonio on June 4, 1836, where the few Mexican soldiers on duty departed just two days later. Historian Frank de la Teja explains that Seguín's command found recruitment of men difficult because "the majority of citizens do not want to take up arms against Mexican soldiers" and instead "wish to remain neutral." Since Seguín's company remained relatively small, General Rusk sent a detachment of 180 men to stay temporarily at San Antonio and help establish order. By June 21, however, Seguín grew uncomfortable with the situation emerging in San Antonio and informed his fellow *Bexareños* (Tejano citizens from San Antonio de Béxar) of his plans to evacuate the town and requested their help to drive cattle away from retreating Mexican troops. Captain Seguín was concerned they would be treated unfairly as real enemies by angry, war-weary Mexican troops and by Anglo Texans bent upon revenge for the Alamo and Goliad massacres. Tejanos did not abandon their town and indeed suffered the consequences. By October 1836, Mexican cavalry rode into an unprotected San Antonio in search of cattle.[40]

Meanwhile, President David Burnet promoted Seguín to lieutenant colonel and ordered him to raise a battalion for the purpose of defending San Antonio. Seguín, who had been away tending to his family and ranch near San Antonio, quickly raised another forty-two men and, by the time he entered San Antonio in November, had eighty men under his charge. However, despite solving his earlier recruitment problems, Seguín and his men faced new hardships with carrying out their orders: Gen. Felix Huston, the new commander of the Texas Army. General Huston wrote President Houston in November 1836 that Seguín was unfit for command because "he cannot speak our language." In the same letter, Huston also recommended the abandonment of San Antonio. Colonel Seguín blocked Huston's attempt to evacuate San Antonio, having dispatched Blas Herrera, a former scout for Colonel Travis, to relay his appeal to President Houston. According to De la Teja, Seguín found himself increasingly alienated from his fellow Bexareños primarily because he had ordered the confiscation of horses and mules as well as city funds in order to provision his men, a force that had grown to include 118 men by the end of 1836. Still, he succeeded with providing intelligence to the Texas government about Mexican military movements and he oversaw the ceremonial burial of the Alamo defenders. On February 25, 1837, before he left San Antonio, Seguín ordered the ashes of the defenders to be collected and properly interred with full military honors. He addressed the audience in Spanish and Major Thomas Western, Seguín's second-in-command, delivered his speech in English. Seguín addressed those who gathered as "Companions in Arms!" and referred to the defenders as "valiant heroes" who "preferred to die a thousand times rather than submit themselves to the tyrant's yoke." He closed with "Texas shall be free and independent, or we shall perish in glorious combat."[41] This symbolic act of burying the dead, most of whom were Anglos from the United States, along with nine Tejanos, and other defenders who were immigrants from Europe, proved significant because it appeared patriotic and enabled some Anglo-Tejano cooperation in San Antonio.

A process of Tejano political and economic loss in San Antonio on the other hand also underlies paying homage to the Alamo defenders. According to De la Teja, Gen. Felix Huston and some of his associates might have schemed to clear out San Antonio so that they could buy up its lands more cheaply.[42] Tejano elites of San Antonio likely became aware of what happened to don Ramón Múzquíz and don Fernando de León.

Historian Andrés Reséndez explains that Múzquiz was the "ultimate insider" at San Antonio, a businessman originally from Monclova (Coahuila) whose father was a lieutenant in the military under Spain and commandant at Nacogdoches in 1800 when Ramón was just a few years old.[43] Ramón Múzquiz entered politics when the governor of Coahuila tabbed him as *jefe político* (political boss) of Texas in 1828 and well understood the importance of slave labor to the Texas economy as evident in Stephen F. Austin's colony. As political boss, Múzquiz had urged President Vicente Guerrero of Mexico, who had abolished slavery in September 1829, to grant an exemption for Texas, which the chief executive did later that same year. In the words of historian Reséndez, "Múzquiz put his career on the line to protect the livelihood of the Anglo-American colonies of Texas." Ramón Múzquiz and prominent San Antonio Tejanos, such as Erasmo Seguín (and his son Juan), José Antonio Navarro, Juan Martín de Varamendi, whose daughter (Ursula) married Jim Bowie, and other local elites, represented the new generation of Mexican business leaders under the Federalist banner who favored commercial ties with the United States. However, as Reséndez accurately claims, Múzquiz was also a Mexican nationalist whose goal remained "to develop Texas *as part of the Mexican nation*."[44] This placed the San Antonio politician in a precarious position as Ramón Múzquiz distrusted Santa Anna's government, which he considered a "military and ecclesiastical theocracy."[45]

The ability of Ramón Múzquiz to play off both Mexican and Anglo sides in the Texas Revolution quickly disappeared afterward. Having witnessed the fall of the Alamo and helped to identify the bodies of Travis, Crockett, and Bowie, Múzquiz left San Antonio for good in May 1836, perhaps sensing his own loyalty suspect after Santa Anna's defeat at the Battle of San Jacinto. It did not matter which side he supported in the Texas Revolution because he lost much of his wealth at the hands of both the Mexican and Republic of Texas governments. The Mexican warship, *Moctezuma,* seized his goods valued at more than 30,000 pesos that he had purchased on his last trip to New Orleans the year before. He also lost his home in San Antonio to Texas Ranger Erastus "Deaf" Smith sometime after President Sam Houston enacted legislation in November 1836, enabling Smith to select any property of his choosing. By the late 1830s, Múzquiz managed to hold onto several pieces of scattered land, but only returned to politics in Mexico and not Texas.[46]

Meanwhile, the question became who would assume Tejano leadership at San Antonio and become the ultimate insiders in the new Republic of Texas. How would they respond to Anglo Texan expansion into the Alamo city? At this point, Juan Seguín and José Antonio Navarro ushered what historian Raúl Ramos refers to as a "new style of asserting political power" to advocate for their Tejanos. Although Seguin almost single-handedly saved San Antonio by sticking close to President Sam Houston's support, he needed time to think about his own future and, like Múzquiz, left San Antonio by the fall of 1837 after reaching the conclusion that Mexican troops would not return to the city and saw that Tejanos became more involved in local politics. San Antonio had just incorporated its city council under the laws of the Republic of Texas with John W. Smith elected its first "official" mayor on September 18, 1837, over Navarro. Tejanos made up the entire city council while Smith, who held the position as the council's president, proved a different leader from other commanders who had governed locally. Smith actually lived in San Antonio several years before the Texas Revolution and became well integrated, if not totally assimilated, by learning Spanish and earned the nickname *El Colorado* (the Red). He married María de Jesús Delgado Curbelo, a local Tejana with roots from one of the Canary Islander families who founded the civilian settlement of San Antonio. Their union represented one of a growing number of intermarriages in San Antonio despite suspicion of Tejano loyalties.[47]

José Antonio Navarro, despite his defeat for mayor by John Smith, served in the first Bexar County government as an associate justice while his family's interests were well represented in the new San Antonio city council. Navarro advanced funds for the defense of Bexar in case Santa Anna's troops returned, especially after the National Congress authorized counties in June 1837 to levy a property tax to help pay for costs of governing. Historian David McDonald explains that Navarro's other various duties as county commissioner included overseeing the admission of wills, serving as probate judge, and certifying sales of land claims known as headright grants that were promised under the Texas Constitution to heads of households and single men living in Texas as of March 4, 1836 (effective date of the Texas Declaration of Independence).[48] Headright claims each measured a league (4,428 acres) and one labor (177 acres) of land and recorded as a contract or sale in the county deed records. Navarro also recorded loyalty statements from Tejanos, one of the conditions required under the constitution for anyone wanting a headright claim. As historian Tijerina explains, the swearing of loyalty meant not having helped the Mexican army in the revolution and agreeing to defend Texas against Indian incursions. The headright claims were also divided into 1st Class (residency to 1836), 2nd Class (to 1837), and 3rd class (to 1840) as bounty for service in the Texas Revolution and donation grant.[49] These headright claims became controversial and subjected to speculation, but business apparently went well for Navarro.

Navarro had ensured his own progress at least through 1837 after having signed the Texas Declaration of Independence, supplying the Texian cause against Santa Anna, and remaining loyal to the new republic. The Bexar County tax assessment for that year shows his rural landholdings totaled 30,996 acres, most of which was located along the Atascosa River southeast of San Antonio with nearly 9,000 acres acquired after 1834. He listed other property valued at $15,700 that included 5 lots in town and 234 head of cattle (valued at $1,200), a herd larger than any other Bexareño, along with several horses and four mules, though most of his livestock had been lost during the Texas Revolution. Other family members collectively held thousands of acreage, lots and livestock in Bexar and Victoria. His uncle, Francisco Ruiz, the only other Tejano who signed the Texas Declaration of Independence, also became a large landowner with nearly 40,000 acres.[50] Navarro's status and wealth evidently continued into the Republic of Texas era, a testament perhaps to a Tejano dream neither wholly Mexican nor American.

In the intervening time, Sequín needed a break once again from San Antonio for both personal and material reasons. He tended to business in New Orleans until early 1838 and, upon his return to San Antonio, learned that voters had elected him to the Texas Senate. Seguín traveled to Houston, first site for the capital of the new Republic, then abruptly resigned his senate seat on May 14, 1838, and obtained his pay in 1,280 acres of land as bounty, as well as another 640 acres of land as a donation grant for his services at the Battle of San Jacinto.[51] Seguín ventured away from businessman, judge, rebel, and politician just a few short years.

Seguín as well as Navarro perhaps felt most heavily the burdens about safety and civil rights of the Tejano community at San Antonio as well as concern for their own wellbeing. Seguín made quick, significant decisions during the nine days he served as a Texas senator. De la Teja notes he worked tirelessly "at making the coexistence of Tejano and Texan a reality." Seguín introduced a bill with the help of a translator that provided relief for the widows and orphans of those who perished at the Alamo.[52] Seven female survivors—Concepción Charlé Gortari Losoya, Gertrudis Navarro, Juana Navarro Pérez Alsbury, Andrea Castañon de Villanueva (aka Madam Candelaria), Ana Salazar de Esparza, Juana Francisca Losoya Melton, and Susanna Wilkerson Dickinson—were actually inside the Alamo when it fell to Santa Anna. According to historian Dora Guerra, "each had a husband, son, brother, or brother-in-law fighting on the Texas side of the revolution."[53] The stories of these forgotten women and children of the Alamo, indeed the civilian casualties of the Texas Revolution, likely fueled Seguín's passion to serve his Tejano community more than ever, as well as sympathetic Anglo-Texans who proved to be important allies at the local and national level.

Public service and cooperation also became one of the principal strategies promoting Tejano life with regards to education and religion.[54] Seguín and Navarro, the latter elected in September 1838 as the only Tejano in the House of Representatives, were the only native Texans overall in the legislative session of the Third National Congress from November 1838 through January 1839. Both attempted to establish a religious-based academic institution in San Antonio through the assistance of Father John Timon, whom the bishop of New Orleans appointed to access church affairs in Texas, and planned to endow a Catholic college with four leagues (17,714 acres) of land from the Republic. Other crises temporarily put a hold on education, as funds were just not there since priorities of the Third Congress remained the defense of Texas from the Mexican army and Indian attacks. Apparently, Catholic leadership underwent somewhat of a transformation in order to support and sustain higher education. Seguín in particular helped Father Timon remove a local priest from San Antonio, named Fr. Refugio de la Garza, whose political leanings under Mexico tilted toward centralism over federalism and likely hurt his status in San Antonio, if not his administration and poor management of his parish.[55] Historian Father Robert Wright adds that the emergence of "an increasingly public and anti-Catholic Protestantism" might have fed Father De la Garza's nationalism absent the economic interests expressed by pro-settler Tejano elites.[56] Anglos were willing to accept Tejano education and Catholicism in San Antonio so long as each reflected the interests of the Republic of Texas.

The majority of Anglos, however, were unwilling to compromise on the issue of slavery, making it one of the more troubling dilemmas Tejano politicians faced. As De la Teja explains, Seguín displayed "sensitivity" in at least one case regarding African-American freedom. Despite the exclusion of free blacks from citizenship under the Constitution of 1836, Seguín sided with Wily Martin's efforts to petition the Texas Congress and allow his emancipated slave, Peter, to remain in the Republic. There were about 5,000 African American slaves in Texas by 1835 whose numbers alone surpassed the Tejano population. Peter fought behind the lines during the Texas Revolution as Martin's slave, having delivered messages and supplies for the Texas Army as did another slave named Cary, who belonged to Thomas F. McKinney. Seguín also might have learned that the slaves Joe and Sam, who belonged to Colonel Travis and Jim Bowie, respectively, fought Mexican troops from inside the Alamo. Joe and Sam survived its fall by persuading Santa Anna's troops that they were mere slaves and could inform other Texans about the outcome of this battle. Two slaves also happened to serve at the Battle of San Jacinto, one named Mark Smith, who joined in the fighting, while another named James Robinson performed guard duty in the Texas camp. As historian Alwyn Barr explains, they likely aided the Texas cause either because they hoped to earn their freedom or because they had no other choice.[57] Although most did not own slaves, Tejano elites did not oppose slavery outright and knew very well that Anglos might interpret abolition as disloyalty to the Republic of Texas much less than sympathy for individual cases of manumission.

Regardless of how Tejanos felt personally about Mexico's abolition of slavery, the tradition of indentured servitude at San Antonio went unchanged under the Texas Constitution of 1836 or laws under the Republic. In early 1838, Cornelius P. Van Ness, a Vermont native and lawyer, who arrived in San Antonio the year before and was apparently an abolitionist, argued with Navarro about the services of a female servant. In his own defense, Navarro responded, "she is a woman in whose presence I paid a quantity of gold and silver and she was obliged by the previous laws, still in effect, to serve me as a cook or to repay me the money if she no longer wishes to serve." Navarro emphasized that indenture was legal under the laws and customs in Texas and that Van Ness well knew there were "numerous servants" in Bexar County in the same condition as his female servant. Evidently, Navarro had a dispute previously over a servant named Rocque Charles whose services Navarro sold to Josefa de la Garza, but the servant ran away before completing his term. To be sure, the 1837 Bexar County tax assessment listed no slaves for Navarro and he admitted "I will be the first to procure the individual liberty of these poor servants on the day the Congress provides a general [legislative] measure for it."[58] Even if Navarro genuinely sympathized with the status of black slaves, as did Seguín, they had to be cautious about objecting to the institution of slavery, especially as they understood the importance of slave labor to the production of cash crops in the Atlantic world.[59]

Another area of great concern to Navarro was the presence of ruffians and vagabonds in San Antonio, some of them Anglos and others former soldiers in Santa Anna's army. Before voters elected him to the

Texas House of Representatives, Navarro's younger brother Eugenio was murdered in cold blood. Eugenio Navarro had become wealthy like his brother and helped operate one of their general stores in San Antonio known as "the Navarro Corner," near the northeast corner of Plaza de Armas on Flores Street. After José Antonio Navarro evidently exitted the store to take a morning stroll, a man named Tinsley, described as a thug and gambler, entered and reached across the store counter, pistol-whipped Eugenio in the face with his pistol, and then shot him in the chest. Eugenio managed to plunge a knife into Tinsley's chest, striking a mortal wound before his own death. The cause of the incident was something of a mystery. Tinsley allegedly took out his anger against Eugenio after a heated confrontation with a female neighbor, but robbery might have been the primary motive. José Antonio Navarro found some comfort in that his brother's burial was inside San Fernando Church, an honor that church officials normally prohibited during this time. Historian McDonald notes that José Antonio Navarro acquired the "Navarro House" from his brother's estate.[60]

By 1838, Navarro and Seguín also became very concerned about Tejanos' land loss. In October, the heirs of Joaquín Leal, led by José de la Garza and his wife, Consolación Leal, filed a lawsuit against John W. Smith, Ephraim Bollinger, William McCraven, John Neill, William Richardson, John S. Simpson, and Robert C. Trimble to prevent the loss of their family's land along the San Antonio River that had been part of a Spanish grant to the Leals in 1778. However, Spanish records and confirmations of land grants were lost after the Battle of Medina in 1813 when royalists occupied San Antonio and threatened to kill any Tejano who rebelled against Spain. The turmoil of the Texas Revolution similarly muddied the management of land records. Smith, at the time Bexar County Clerk after his previous service as mayor, along with the other defendants, had examined Tejano land records searching for questionable titles. As a result, they initiated proceedings to have the Leal property declared as public domain because the family did not have valid proof of title to the land. Trimble was the county surveyor while Neill had physically squatted on part of the Leal property, began plowing it, moved cattle onto it, and chopped down trees evidently to build his home. The Leals hired former mayor Henry Daingerfield as their attorney and requested the following: 1) the immediate eviction of Neill; 2) a prohibition on further surveys or issuance of titles; and 3) reasonable time to obtain their titles, which they believed were in the archives of Mexico. Judge James Robinson acted swiftly in favor of the Leals and ordered John Borden, commissioner of the General Land Office, not to issue any patent or title from the Leal land to any of the defendants.[61]

Although Anglo-Texan allies helped the Leal family ward off land loss in San Antonio, Seguín and Navarro were aware of the Cordova Revolt in East Texas and prepared a bill in the Third National Congress authorizing the Texas General Land Office to issue titles to all Tejanos. Navarro and his fellow House member from San Antonio, Van Ness, defended the bill against an objection from a representative of Nacogdoches. Navarro used arguments from the Leal-De la Garza petition to benefit other Tejanos facing similar challenges to their land titles, but tried to placate their fellow legislators by stating that only a limited number of Spanish land grants existed. As David McDonald explains, Navarro cited law and common practice that secured Tejano rights to their land, but also expanded upon the issue of legality by describing two classes of landowners whose property was threatened: 1) those who at one time possessed written titles lost, stolen, or disappeared from damage and destruction of public records in the Bexar archives; and 2) those who had been unable to obtain title due to war. Navarro added that Spanish laws, subsequently adopted under Mexico, provided that an individual in peaceable possession of any portion of public land not appropriated to municipal or national purposes for ten years thereby acquired a right to obtain a title in good faith upon payment of proper fees. However, despite the validity of their arguments, Navarro and Van Ness's bill was defeated. Navarro delivered his speech in favor of the bill without the services of a translator and only later did his words appear in English after the Third Congress had adjourned. Even so, it is likely that the bill was doomed from the beginning given Navarro's public criticism of President Mirabeau Lamar's administration and his political appointments.[62]

Meanwhile, Tejanos at Goliad and Victoria also experienced land loss while relationships with Anglo-Texans grew tense. Family historian Alonzo Salazar notes that the situation rapidly deteriorated after the Battle of San Jacinto as Anglo-American veterans and newcomers quickly settled and claimed the most desirable tracts of land. It appeared that General Thomas Rusk naturally had a difficult time controlling the anger of his own men after having returned to his headquarters in Victoria following the burial of Col. James Fannin's men at Goliad. According to the memoirs of John Linn, alcalde of Victoria, "their creed was the total extermination of the Mexican race and the appropriation of their property to the individual use of the exterminators." Apparently, Isaac Watts Burton and his company of rangers from East Texas traveled among General Rusk's infantry companies to Victoria and then Goliad. Before the Texas Revolution, Burton became the captain of a new company in the Corps of Rangers, which consisted of fresh recruits from regions near the Sabine River. Given the likelihood that many of Burton's recruits were among the 5,000 or so volunteers who arrived in Texas after October 1835 and were hell-bent upon revenge for the Alamo and Goliad massacres, General Rusk's task of maintaining order was darn near impossible. Widespread banditry affected the Carlos de la Garza Ranch in Goliad just as it did the rest of the Tejano population. There were many Texas outlaws and, as Lt. John Browne of the Texian army wrote, "a group of twenty of these men met in a Goliad public house and planned to burn down Carlos Rancho and take all the cattle."[63] Linn reported in 1839 that the men who called themselves "a band of brothers" were in the "cow stealing business, and are scattered all over this frontier." Evidently, they stole cattle from the Carlos Ranch, ran off with other cattle belonging to Juan Seguín, and killed eight men from a party of Mexican traders on the Nueces River.[64]

The only reason Carlos de la Garza held onto his ranch despite aiding the Mexican side of the Texas Revolution was that he had established close friendships with influential Anglos whom he saved from the Goliad Massacre, including John and Nicholas Fagan, James Byrne, Edward Perry, and John and Anthony Sydick. Shortly after his arrival at Victoria in June 1836, General Rusk dispatched his soldiers to Carlos Rancho with orders to force Carlos de la Garza off his land and to leave Texas. De la Garza listened, but did not obey the soldiers. Coming to his defense, De la Garza's friends stepped in front of the troops and allegedly stated, "You can read it to him, but you don't touch him," and "none durst molest him."[65] What is perhaps least understood about Anglo-Tejano relationships was that another empresario colony, consisting of largely Irish-Catholic settlers, existed nearby, virtually in the shadows of Austin's colony. The mostly Irish and Tejano settlers at Refugio, Goliad, and Victoria, became the last line of counties to be included in the Republic of Texas. Because these counties were located closer to the border with Mexico, fewer Anglos lived there, leaving the residents there to develop their own loyalties to each other based upon trade, kinship, and religious bonds. Historian Stephen Hardin notes that General Rusk could easily be described as a "racist thug" who began a Tejano "Trail of Tears." Yet Rusk truly believed Mexicans were about to launch another offensive in

Texas while blinded by his own cultural bias, which did not help matters. General Rusk's 350 troops were the new republic's first line of defense while local Tejanos such as don Carlos, who did not support the goals of the Texas Revolution, were viewed with great suspicion.[66]

Interestingly, Manuel Sabriego of Goliad, who fought for Mexico during the Texas Revolution and left with the retreating Mexican army, eventually lost his land in a legal proceeding. He was compensated ninety-six dollars for his 11,000-acre ranch. Sabriego subsequently joined Mexico's army and evidently returned to Texas in 1838 as leader of several Mexican raids against Anglo-Texan ranching interests just as tensions flared in East Texas with the Cordova Revolt. As historian Jimmy Bryan notes, Anglo Texans had acquired dubious titles to forty of the forty-nine-total Tejano ranches in the Goliad area north of the Nueces River. While Texians felt justified taking lands in the revolution's aftermath, greed proved another motivating factor in the displacement of settlers besides Anglo notions about whiteness and patriotism.[67] Tejanos fully understood the importance of Anglos with whom they cooperated and established intimate bonds, but Tejanos also realized that in order to defend their land in Texas they had to stay and utilize any means necessary.

The case of don Fernando De León from Victoria is illustrative of lost land and those Tejanos forced from town on suspicion of helping Mexico or outright hatred for any Mexicans over what happened at the Alamo and Goliad. Though imprisoned by General Rusk for disclosing to Mexican forces the location of supplies during the Texas Revolution, his captors allowed De León to cleanse himself daily in the river. During one such occasion, a Texian volunteer named Brantley and his friends shot and wounded him. Rusk displayed sympathy for don Fernando and set him free to return to his ranch. Due to lack of provisions from a fledgling new republic, Texian volunteers/rangers pillaged homes and ranches throughout Texas. General Rusk was powerless to do anything about complaints received from De León and his wife, *doña* Patricia. After General Rusk ordered all Tejanos to move east and avoid helping retreating Mexican troops, and with don Fernando convalescing, doña Patricia planned to move the entire De León family to New Orleans in the summer of 1836. As the family loaded up what belongings and goods they could on mules rented from Philip Dimmitt, other Texians jeered and stole what remained of their possessions, including horses.[68] Fortunately, the De León family had good credit among the mercantile and banking elite at New Orleans who helped them avoid abject poverty upon their arrival in the Crescent City.

Historian Ana Carolina Castillo Crimm explains that land fraud grew more rampant in the absence of don Fernando De León, who had worked as a local land commissioner for Victoria, where Anglo and Tejano allies defended their lands. Volunteers continued to arrive in Texas even after the revolution had ended, yet still expected large land grants. The Republic of Texas created the General Land Office to regulate land sales. San Jacinto veterans could claim payment in land, but the acreage awarded declined from the Mexican league of over 4,428 acres to the American standard of 640 acres. Volunteers actually targeted settlers regardless of background, taking the best lands for themselves. Newcomers felt free to settle on the wide-open spaces perhaps unknowingly squatting on someone's land, often leaving landowners, who were often unaware of the squatters' presence on their lands, to prove their boundary claims in court. Don Fernando's friend, Edward Linn, who served as local surveyor in Victoria, tried unsuccessfully to protect his ranching empire. Linn, along with relatives of De León, paid the taxes on the land and ran off squatters for as long as possible. The De León family did not return from their Louisiana exile until after statehood in 1845 and managed to recover half of their 100,000-acre ranch.[69] Tejano justice at Goliad and Victoria apparently came with a price and no guarantee of life or property.

As Tejanos struggled to retain their livelihood, military service became another means to display the highest level of patriotism to their new nation and defend their family honor. Violence at both ends of the Republic only reaffirmed the need for deployment of Texas Ranger companies to hold off Comanches from making San Antonio part of their own empire or outright destruction like Mission San Sabá previously under Spain. A confluence of events occurred from the Cordova Revolt in late 1838-early 1839 through the infamous Council House Fight in 1840 that tainted all relationships with Anglos in Texas. Mirabeau Lamar, who succeeded Sam Houston as president of Texas and served from early December 1838 through early December 1841, discontinued Houston's moderate Indian policies and went on the offensive against Cherokees in 1839 until their complete removal from Texas, followed by all-out war against Comanches. In Mexico, Santa Anna returned to the presidency temporarily from March to July 1839 as Conservatives ruled the new Centralist Republic of Mexico between 1835 and 1846, and appointed him interim president when President Anastacio Bustamante stepped away from the office to quell other Federalist rebellions. For example, General José de Urrea, who ironically fought under Santa Anna in the

Texas Revolution and won at Goliad, became upset at him following the Battle of San Jacinto for ordering the withdrawal of Mexican troops from Texas despite outnumbering Texian soldiers more than two-to-one (roughly 2,500 to 900). By 1837, General Urrea turned against Santa Anna and fought against him in the Battle of Mazatlán (1838). Another rebellion occurred in the southern state of Chiapas after an invasion from a general based across the border in Guatemala. The Republic of Texas and Republic of Mexico were in no mood for tolerance of any border rebellions, including Indians intent upon exposing the weaknesses of their respective nations. Tejanos leveraged military service on both sides of the border to their own political advantage as much as possible.

By the summer 1839, the growing threat from Comanches and Santa Anna's reemergence as president of Mexico once again pulled Juan Seguín into military service to the Republic of Texas that reflected closer ties between elite Tejanos and Anglos at San Antonio.[70] Under orders from President Lamar, two companies of fifty-four volunteers each were recruited in San Antonio to fight Comanches, one composed of Tejanos and another of Anglo-Texans for which Seguín and L. B. Franks were made captains and took command, respectively, while Henry Karnes was elected commander of both companies. Among those who served under Captain Seguín were Nepomuceno Flores, who had also served in Seguín's company at San Jacinto, and another eleven Tejano volunteers who had served earlier in the Texas Revolution, including Trinidad Coy and Ambrosio Rodriguez. Other volunteers came from pioneering Tejano families dating back to the original founders of San Antonio. Among this group were Marcos Veramendi, Luciano Navarro, José Luis Carvajal, Miguel Arciniega, Jr., and Manuel Leal.[71] Both companies ventured into the Texas Hill Country, northwest of San Antonio, in pursuit of Indians on the headwaters of the Medina River, near Hondo Seco, and Cañon de Uvalde. One of the Texas Revolution veterans, Pedro Flores Morales, was killed in action.[72]

There were other veterans of the Texas Revolution whose names subsequently appeared on the muster rolls for the Texas Army of the Republic under the Command of Major James W. Tinsley, Company B, 1st Regiment and Cavalry. Four of these were Tejano veterans at the Battle of San Jacinto under Seguín, including Manuel Flores, Jacinto Peña, Eduardo Ramirez, and Pedro Herrera, plus Antonio Cruz, who had arrived elsewhere from Mexico on the eve of the Texas Revolution. Flores and Peña were furloughed June 10, 1836, while the other three were furloughed November 5, 1836. Two other Tejanos, Manuel Bueno and Miguel Mata, had served with Flores, Herrera, Peña, and Ramirez in the Siege at Bexar, October–December 1835. A total of nineteen Tejanos and Mexicans were furloughed at various times through early 1837.[73] Other records indicate that some Tejanos reenlisted for Texas military service on the furlough date. For example, on November 5, 1836, Cruz enlisted as 1st Sergeant and Herrera as 4th Sergeant with Lt. Manuel Flores's company.[74] Their duties entailed patrolling the countryside along with Seguín and Flores to look for any signs of Santa Anna's troops returning to the region, check banditry, or apprehend fugitive slaves.[75]

Tejanos grew accustomed to serving alongside Anglo Texans and vice-versa in rare circumstances that kept racism in check during the Republic of Texas. A list for Company B of Seguín's regiment, signed by him and Manuel Flores on December 31, 1836, at their headquarters in San Antonio, reveals such names as Englebert Bader, Michael Dugan, Michael Fox, Thomas Hays, John Huffman, Walter Lambert, Lewis Mallet, Thomas O'Connor, John Rockwell, Joseph Walker, and John Williams.[76] Antonio Menchaca, from San Antonio (not to be confused with his namesake in Nacogdoches), served as first lieutenant under Seguín from October 1836 to March 1837 and then as captain until Seguín's command was disbanded in October 1837. Apparently, Menchaca subsequently provided additional military service as a cavalry captain from February to April 1838 under General Albert Sidney Johnston, whom Rusk appointed adjutant general in August 1836 and then replaced Gen. Felix Huston as a brigadier general in early 1837.[77] Military service for the Republic of Texas perhaps proved an exception than the norm, but significant nevertheless for many Tejano families accustomed to military duty on the frontier.

In reality, however, not even Juan Seguín entirely escaped suspicion for being Mexican despite his own connections with Sam Houston through the Battle of San Jacinto and other Anglo military officers in the Republic of Texas. For example, Mary Maverick of San Antonio tainted Seguín's character when she suggested he was less than courageous because after only ten days out on the Comanche campaign, he returned only to report "the woods full of Indians and predicting that our men would surely be killed." It also did not help Seguín that he participated in land speculation, headright claims and donation, including the purchase of lands from other Tejanos.[78] Speaking up for Tejano civil rights or other minorities only raised more doubts about him. While serving in the Fourth Congress of the Texas Republic at Houston, Seguín sensed a growing disregard for Tejano interests with much of Texas overwhelmingly

Anglo Texan compared to San Antonio. His address to the Texas Senate in February 1840 raised concerns from Tejano constituents who had not seen laws translated or printed in Spanish and believed that they had been denied "rights guaranteed to them" by the Constitution and laws of the new republic. He reminded his fellow senators that "the Mexico-Texians were among the first who sacrificed their all in our glorious Revolution, and the disasters of war weighed heavy upon them." Seguín added, "as a representative from Bexar, I never shall cease to raise my voice in effecting this object."[79]

By 1840, Seguín was swept into Mexico's political affairs by favoring the "Republic of the Rio Grande," yet another Federalist attempt to break away from the Centralist Republic and establish a confederation that encompassed the northeastern Mexican states of Coahuila, Nuevo León, and Tamaulipas with Laredo as capital. After the short-lived republic's army commander, General Antonio Canales Rosillo, defected to the Centralist government, Seguín was left exposed for having raised a company of men and invested $3,000 in supplies. As historian De la Teja notes, Seguín soon engaged in a smuggling operation to pay off his debts, which only brought him into further contact with Mexican military officers still intent upon recovering Texas for Mexico. All of his previous service in the military for the Republic of Texas and warning to Sam Houston about the possibility of Mexican troops invading from Laredo or Matamoros only fueled Anglo anxieties about Indian raids and Tejano duplicity.[80] In addition, "Reconquest" rhetoric appeared frequently in the press of Mexico City a year after the Battle of San Jacinto and spread to northern Mexico, which only fueled Texian concerns about the border, or that Tejanos kept ties south of the Rio Grande and acted as double spies by informing Mexican authorities about hostile Comanche movements.[81] Mexican politics and Indian movements kept the Republic of Texas on the defensive whether or not Tejanos actually played a role.

The gravest threat to the Republic of Texas came directly from Comanches on the Southern Plains expanding their own trade markets across the northern frontier of Mexico and Texas. As historian Brian De Lay explains, President Houston's policy of coexistence and diplomacy with Indians had been discredited by the fall of 1838 after a Texas Rangers attack on a Comanche party led to a cycle of retaliatory raids just as troubles with Tejanos and Cherokees flared in East Texas. After Lamar became president of Texas in December 1838, he repudiated agreements Houston made with the Cherokees and other Indians in East

Texas and drove them from the republic. President Lamar also employed plunder-hungry rangers in a program of aggressive campaigns designed to terrorize Comanche families and drive them away from Texas settlements. Perhaps unbeknownst to Lamar, some Tejanos from San Antonio actually rode with Comanches in the border state of Coahuila and in one documented instance at least sacked a small, isolated Mexican community. For good measure, Lamar turned to the Lipan Apaches, an old foe of the Comanches, and entered into a treaty of peace, commerce, and friendship with their leader, Cuelgas de Castro. By early 1839, Lipan scouts were back on the Southern Plains spying on Comanches and hunting bison. The Southern Plains economy of hides and robes attracted traders from all backgrounds and threatened to unhinge a slave-based plantation model still rising in the Texas Republic.[82]

Tejanos found it increasingly difficult to resume their roles as cultural brokers that they played before the Texas Revolution in re-establishing trade and treaty with Comanches.[83] The Comanches moved from a largely neutral stance during the Texas Revolution toward greater assertiveness of their own sovereignty, as former president Houston's containment approach proved insufficient. President Lamar hoped to remove Comanches as with East Texas Indians to ensure space and safety. He needed soldiers to punish Indians, not cultural intermediaries. What President Lamar got was a bloodbath in the so-called Council House Fight at San Antonio in March 1840 between Comanche chiefs and Anglo Texans that resulted in the collapse of diplomacy and all-out war. Thirty-five Comanches died during the melee with another thirty-seven taken prisoner, while seven Texans perished. Neither neutrality nor accommodation became possible between Comanches and Anglo Texans, which also colored Tejano-Anglo friendships.[84] Around this time, some members of José Antonio Navarro's family lived in a newly constructed house on his San Geronimo Ranch along the Guadalupe River where a desperate young man, named Joseph Powell, arrived at the door after he escaped from captivity among the Comanches. The Navarros took care of him and saw that he returned to his family while Navarro negotiated to sell cattle to Texas Army Colonel William Cazneau.[85] Tejanos preferred peace between both nations, but got none. Cooperation with Anglo Texans through politics and military service remained vital for self-preservation in the face of Comanche warfare and the continued threat of reconquest from Mexico.

Tejanos subsequently faced the dilemma of whether to support an Anglo-Texan offensive into New Mexico and capture of the Santa Fé trade as part of expansion toward the Pacific. Mexico appeared vulnerable from Indian raids, yet was still a formidable opponent on the battlefield. Although Anastacio Bustamante returned to Mexico's presidency in mid-July 1839 and remained in power through September 1841, Santa Anna reassumed the presidency several more times in late 1841, early 1843, and mid-1844, so the fear of another invasion in Texas remained as long as he stayed involved in Mexico's political affairs. Santa Fé, located on the western edge of Comanchería along the Upper Rio Grande, served as the capital of New Mexico long after its establishment by Spain in the early 1600s and stood atop the central corridor of the Camino Real from Mexico City. Hispanos of Santa Fé had long been engaged in the silver trade with the city of Chihuahua, located about 300 miles due south from El Paso, in exchange for hides and woolen clothes. After 1821, Santa Fé increasingly became the nexus of trade between Chihuahua and emerging American markets in Missouri.[86] Virtually no Tejanos answered this call for Anglo-American expansion.

The only Tejano who did and joined the "Santa Fé Expedition of 1841" was José Antonio Navarro. Historian David McDonald refers to Navarro's commitment to Lamar and the expedition as his grandest blunder. Perhaps Navarro tried soothing over his prior public challenge to Lamar over new political appointees after the latter became president. Navarro played off Anglo-Texan animosity, anger, and resentment against Tejanos after the Cordova Revolt, having warned President Lamar of an imminent threat from Mexican troops in early 1840. Navarro also had predicted misfortune for Lamar's administration before the Council House Fight. After Anglo-Comanche relations reached its nadir and Santa Anna kept meddling with Mexico's presidency, Navarro needed to reassure Anglo Texans of his credentials as a true patriot rather than rely upon his elevated status as a signer of the Texas Declaration of Independence.[87]

President Lamar, in turn, needed José Antonio Navarro in 1841 for expansion into New Mexico as much as former president Houston needed Juan Seguín at San Antonio after the Texas Revolution. Historian Andrés Reséndez highlights several themes that came out of American and Texas newspapers about the Santa Fé Expedition: 1) the profits from capturing the wealth of the Santa Fe-Chihuahua Trail, noting a market valued anywhere from $75,000 to one million dollars; 2) its Anglo-Saxon character that appealed to its readers, filled with a sense of repulsion at Mexico's mixed racial heritage; and 3) the unchartered, savage, and exotic nature of the country, filled with the "roaming" Indian in a pristine environment.[88] Meanwhile, Mexican newspapers quipped that the rapaciousness of the *norteamericanos* (North Americans) had to be stopped in Texas, or they would impose an alien religion, language, and culture on Mexico. The newspaper of Chihuahua, *La Luna*, inflamed passions on June 29, 1841, when it claimed that if Anglo Americans and, by implication, their system of racial slavery, were not stopped that Mexicans would be "sold as beasts" because "their color was not as white as that of the conquerors."[89]

Tejanos became a political pawn amidst this racial rhetoric and likely found it odd that Anglo Texans did not invite Indians to serve as scouts on the expedition. President Lamar at least felt having Tejanos on the expedition could help convince New Mexicans of the joys and advantages conferred with sovereignty under the Republic of Texas. Lamar even traveled to San Antonio to make his case, having attended a ball thrown in his honor with Juan Seguín, who at the time was the mayor of San Antonio, his wife, as well as other elite Tejanos in attendance. Still, mistrust prevailed as rumors circulated that Mayor Seguín kept close contact with Mexican officials and informed them about an invasion from Texas.[90] Republic of Texas Army General Hugh McLeod encountered opposition from the Seguíns to the expedition and noted, "Seguin is my enemy … but the Navarro family can neutralize him, and I may count on the Veramendis." General McLeod happened to be the commanding officer at the Council House Fight and was not taken for a fool.[91]

McDonald offers a number of reasons why Navarro agreed to participate as a commissioner on the Santa Fé expedition. These factors included: 1) unwise to continue opposing the president, which reflected badly upon his loyalty, especially with raised racial animosities; 2) the president played upon Navarro's humanitarian sentiments, suggesting that violence could be avoided if Navarro spoke directly to the citizens of Santa Fé; and 3) material reward, as the job of commissioner paid well. By June 1, 1841, Navarro finally accepted Lamar's offer and then walked into a store owned by Duncan C. Ogden and George T. Howard in San Antonio to collect an advance payment of $1,000 for goods. Upon his return from New Mexico, Navarro would receive the remaining balance of $2,000. Aside from personal aggrandizement and business interests, perhaps Navarro reluctantly agreed because he recognized troubling warning signs the previous year when the Texas Congress adopted the English common law for all legal proceedings and expunged most Mexican legislation from the legal code, not to mention the recent bloodshed between Anglos and Tejanos in East Texas.[92] Moreover, incorporating New Mexico under the Texas flag would also vastly increase the Hispanic population and could potentially increase economic and political power for Tejanos. Navarro primarily served as translator for the expedition in addition to cultural broker.[93]

The Santa Fé Expedition proved a disaster from the start while Navarro's capture, trial, and imprisonment in Mexico City fueled Santa Anna's determination to exact revenge on Texas in 1842. On March 5, General Rafael Vasquez occupied San Antonio and, while the Anglo families fled town, many Bexareños stayed and cooperated. Some of the Bexareños held a public meeting and agreed to an unsigned petition for armed opposition to the Republic of Texas. Vasquez stayed for only a few days, satisfied with his efforts, and returned to Mexico along with several Bexareño families. Juan Seguín, as mayor of San Antonio, still had the support of Gen. Edward Burleson, who refused to hear charges against Seguín and ordered him to ride out with Captain Jack Hays onto the ranches along the San Antonio River in pursuit of General Vasquez. Upon Seguín's return, however, Anglos branded him a traitor under suspicion of being involved with the recent Mexican invasion. On April 18, 1842, he resigned as mayor of San Antonio and fled with his family to Mexico. The following month, Adolphus Sterne of Nacogdoches remarked in his diary, "Col. Seguin has joined them, and as is usually the case, when our warm Friends turn against us, they become the most inveterate foes." Sam Houston, who had returned to the presidency after voters elected him to a second term in December 1841, was not so quick to judge and instead wrote Juan's father, Erasmo Seguín, saying he could not "denounce Colonel John N. Seguin, without a most perfect understanding of the circumstances of his absence." Not even Houston's successor, Anson Jones, the last president of Texas before annexation, believed that Seguín, who "fought as well at San Jacinto as any man there … has turned traitor." As De la Teja describes, Juan Seguín could find neither rest nor peace.[94]

Santa Anna wanted to punish Texas again after General Vasquez's quick withdrawal so another force from Mexico reoccupied San Antonio when General Adrian Woll entered on September 11, 1842, with 1,000 regular infantry, 500 cavalry, and two cannons. The French-born Woll had served in the Napoleonic armies before his immigration to Mexico where he fought for its independence movement from Spain before he became an officer under Santa Anna. During the Texas Revolution, he served as quartermaster in the Mexican army and remained a Centralist afterwards. Ironically, Juan Seguín served in Woll's army after his first exile from San Antonio to Mexico in much the same way he served the Texas Republic as a vanguard, scout, and forager. Seguín later claimed he had to serve either in the Mexican military or face imprisonment. Seguín commanded a unit called the "Defenders of Bexar," which included none other than Vicente Cordova and Antonio Perez, who had served previously as Jack Hays's former co-captain. Cordova had received a pardon from President Lamar for his involvement in the earlier failed revolt at Nacogdoches and fled Texas shortly afterwards. From Mexico, Cordova launched raids into South Texas during the winters of 1839 and spring 1840 with a combined force of 50 to 100 men, composed of Indians, Mexicans, African Americans, and Anglo Americans.[95]

Other Tejanos hedged their bets and defended of San Antonio as the Republic of Texas organized two companies under Jack Hays with one composed of 100 Tejanos led by Salvador Flores. Woll's forces held the upper hand with Seguín and Cordova on his side and captured several Tejanos, including Antonio Menchaca, before taking the city. Woll also restored Father Refugio de la Garza as the town priest then freed Menchaca after he promised never to take up arms against Mexico again. Perhaps sensing retribution against all Tejanos of San Antonio after his planned departure, General Woll made the fifty-one Anglo-Texan prisoners sign a statement on September 14, 1842, with language that recommended the local Mexican population be treated "with lenience and kindness" nor should they be "disturbed or injured either in person or property" in the event that San Antonio fell again under Texan control. Seguín might have influenced the wording and rationalized his own actions as an extreme form of fighting for civil rights.[96]

Tejanos once again were caught in the middle of violent conflict between Texians and Mexico. Just four days later, the Texas Republic confronted General Woll's forces in the "Battle of Salado Creek," seven miles north of San Antonio. After initial skirmishes, General Woll retreated to the Rio Grande certain his movements would draw out more Texas volunteers. During the fall of 1842, storms had dumped large amounts of rain in the region south of San Antonio, making the Medina River, as well as other streams and creeks, nearly impassable. Such conditions served to slow the Texian pursuit of Woll's retreating forces. The casualties at the "Battle of Salado Creek" reportedly included sixty Mexican troops who died and many more wounded. Vicente Cordova was among those Mexican soldiers killed in action. On the other side, one Anglo Texan was killed and approximately twelve wounded.[97]

Aside from its failure, the Vasquez and Woll occupations of San Antonio in 1842 represented the nadir of Tejano and Anglo-Texan animosity toward each other similar to that between Comanches and Anglo Texans after the Council House Fight of 1840 in San Antonio. Tejanos began to question their own fate in the Texas borderlands and many had begun an exodus either to Louisiana or Mexico. About 200 Bexareño families actually left San Antonio with General Woll and lived with Seguín south of the Rio Grande. They abandoned their beloved city because they feared Anglo-Texan reprisal against all Mexicans in the Republic of Texas as tensions only increased with rhetoric from both Mexico and the United States. Historian Raúl Ramos argues that reconquest politics in Mexico and the increased involvement of the United States in Texas affairs "accelerated the transformation of the ethnic Mexican populations in San Antonio to that of minority status."[98] Racial attitudes hardened and did not help matters any.[99] The responses of Tejanos at San Antonio to the Mexican occupations in 1842 ranged from neutrality to ambivalence to participation, which reflected an "instinct to survive" in the words of historian Timothy Matovina. Tejanos found it increasingly difficult to live quietly inside the Republic of Texas as their ancestors had sought to do during the Spanish era, as warfare kept raising its ugly head. Most Tejanos believed their status under Anglo Texan rule had been reduced to barely above that of Indians and African Americans, but enough to be considered a separate class if not yet invisible Texans.[100]

Ironically, Navarro weighed his own fate inside the national jail of Mexico City as Anglo friends stuck by him. In late 1843, General McLeod sought help from Charles Elliot, British chargé d'affaires to the Republic of Texas. Elliot, in turn, contacted Foreign Secretary George Hamilton-Gordon, Earl of Aberdeen, to instruct Britain's ambassador in Mexico to negotiate the release of Navarro. By February 1844, George Van Ness managed to visit Navarro in prison and noted that Navarro lived in constant fear of personal attacks and had a badly infected leg that left him in pain. By the end of 1844, however, Santa Anna was no longer president of Mexico when General Mariano Paredes, once an ally, charged Santa Anna with military and fiscal mismanagement and joined forces with other generals to remove him from power. Some of his "friends" helped free Navarro even before the new president granted him a pardon and boarded a ship from Veracruz, Mexico, to Havana, Cuba, where he booked passage on another ship headed for New Orleans. On January 29, 1845, Navarro arrived in Galveston and by early February, Mayor Edward Dwyer of San Antonio met him on the outskirts the city and provided him an escort into town.[101]

Mayor Dwyer made certain that Anglo Texans treated Navarro as a patriot, which could not be said for San Antonio's other native son and former mayor, Juan Seguín, who fought for Texas independence from

Mexico only to be considered a traitor among many Anglos by the end of the Republic. In greater irony, Navarro arrived just in time to witness the admission of Texas into the Union as a slave state and joined the Constitutional Convention in Austin. Navarro and Volney Howard, a lawyer and newspaper editor from Maine, who had just arrived at San Antonio, were chosen to represent Bexar County. At Navarro's request, Howard introduced a resolution calling for Spanish translations of the recent annexation and military protection of Texas. As historian McDonald notes, two of Navarro's closet allies at the convention were George Fisher and Henry L. Kinney, both of whom spoke fluent Spanish and were considered friends of the Tejano community. Navarro selected Fisher as his official translator against a resolution that potentially threatened Tejano land titles through forfeiture. Through his efforts, the resolution was tabled temporarily. Kinney was a delegate from San Patricio County in South Texas and represented many Tejanos. Since U.S. law defined citizenship, the convention's main issue concerned voting rights. Among the wording in the requirements they debated were "free white male person" with United States or Republic of Texas citizenship and satisfying a residency requirement. Both Kinney and Navarro made speeches against the inclusion of the word "white" in the state constitution. Kinney remarked that he knew of instances where individuals known to be citizens, who had served in the military and took an oath of allegiance, were denied the right to vote under the pretext "that they could not be considered white persons; they were Mexicans." The convention voted forty-two to fourteen in favor of deleting the word "white," which historian David McDonald explains was Navarro's greatest achievement and, with some Anglo allies, prevented the total disenfranchisement of Mexican Americans in Texas after 1845 under the state constitution.[102]

Unfortunately, Tejanos experienced considerable declension during the Republic of Texas era as friendships with Anglos became tainted amidst incessant warfare, conflict, and mistrust with Indians and Mexico. The erosion of their land base ensued with the Texas Revolution through the confiscation of property by Mexican and Texian forces, who were anxious about Tejano contributions to either side. Within the first couple years under Texian rule, Anglo and Tejano speculators bought over 200 headright certificates from San Antonio citizens that included outlying ranches. From 1837 to 1842, thirteen of the most prominent "American buyers" purchased 1,368,574 acres from 358 Mexicans, while fourteen of the most prominent Tejano buyers purchased 278,769 acres from 67 of their fellow Tejanos. Among the latter were Juan Seguín, who purchased ten of these headright grants, and fellow Bexareño, José Antonio de la Garza, who bought between eight and thirteen such grants.[103]

Tejanos held onto to a majority of the town lots in San Antonio, but the downward trend continued as Anglo Texans and other European immigrants became more entrenched within the Alamo City. Although Tejanos still controlled a majority of city-council seats, Anglo Texans held the mayor's office for most of the period while the presence of French, Irish, and German immigrants added to the cultural milieu by the end of the Republic. Intermarriage continued in San Antonio on a small scale and facilitated accommodation. Around 8 percent of all intermarriages were Anglo and Mexican (23 of 294), mostly between Anglo men and Hispanic women. Half of these Anglo-Tejano unions were among elite families, including Mayor John W. Smith, who moved to San Antonio in 1827 after leaving Green DeWitt's colony. Smith became Catholic before his marriage in 1830 to María de Jesús Delgado Curbelo, maiden from a prominent Canary Island family, and together they had six children. Smith got reelected several times during the Republic of Texas. Mayor Edward Dwyer himself married a Tejana, named Marianna Leal Ramón, who also hailed from distinguished founding families. Historian David Montejano explains how intermarriage formed part of an important peace structure among Anglos and elite Mexican families in South Texas, which led to land loss by other means.[104]

Tejanos in East Texas could not expect the same kind of accommodation with Anglo Texans, as they were greatly outnumbered demographically and intermarriage was less likely to occur. Their neutrality during the Texas Revolution and the Cordova Revolt especially made all Tejanos suspect in Anglo-Texan eyes as traitors more likely to rejoin Mexico, if not Indians. Consequently, they could not expect to participate in the mercantile trade or share power in city government like their counterparts at San Antonio. A hardened Indian policy and deeper entrenchment of black slavery did not help racial attitudes towards Tejanos in East Texas as Anglos acquired more land for plantations and patrolled the countryside for rebels and fugitive slaves. East Texas Tejanos essentially became a stateless people, kicked out of Nacogdoches with refuge closer on the other side of the border in Louisiana than Mexico. Others persisted into statehood within smaller, outlying communities like Cherino and Moral, as historian Paul Lack refers, "in a kind of defensive segregation."[105] Vicente Cordova and his fellow Tejanos refused to give up their guns, like Seguín and his most ardent followers, yet paid dearly with their lives to protect regional interests.

For Tejanos in the Goliad and Victoria region, the experiences of Carlos de la Garza and Fernando De León fell somewhere between the actions of their counterparts in San Antonio and East Texas. Carlos de la Garza made up for the havoc he created during the Texas Revolution by saving the lives of his Anglo-Irish friends from the Goliad massacre. His ranch became like a fortress and he offered it as a place of refuge to settlers after a Comanche raid on Victoria in 1840 and the Mexican invasion two years later. He also provisioned the Republic of Texas Army in pursuit of retreating Mexican troops from San Antonio.[106] Meanwhile, Fernando De León helplessly watched his lands be confiscated for helping both sides during the Texas Revolution. He re-established business contacts with Anglos from exile in New Orleans and, upon his return to Texas, reentered the land and cattle trade and eventually the promotion of railroads. Don Fernando's leadership was lost during the Texas Republic then found after statehood.[107] Both Carlos de la Garza and eventually Fernando De León learned that what mattered most during the Republic of Texas era was how they had recently handled Anglos.

The individual paths of Juan Seguín and José Antonio Navarro were at a crossroads after 1842 and dictated their controversial legacies for siding with Mexico or Texas. Seguín's participation at the Battle of San Jacinto and close working relationship with Sam Houston were not enough against insurmountable distrust following his own business dealings at San Antonio, exile to Mexico following General Vasquez's invasion, and subsequent military service to Mexico against Anglo-Americans. While incredibly difficult Anglo-Comanche relations appeared to pull Seguín on the side of the Texas Republic, heightened anxieties Anglos felt toward Santa Anna and his return to Texas left Seguín wishing perhaps he and his fellow Bexareños could be left alone to enjoy the freedom and opportunity that the frontier offered those who had sacrificed themselves for family, land, and traditions. Perhaps he too might have joined Navarro in the Santa Fé expedition, but he likely surmised Texian expansion westward would not be well received among Hispanos who themselves had troubled times with Comanches and preferred trade agreements with Anglo-Americans from Missouri rather than conquest from Texas. Greed played a part on all sides, but so too did self-preservation. Once Seguín and his fellow Tejano loyalists felt the Republic of Texas was no longer sustainable, they took their chances in Mexico. Seguín did return eventually to Texas as the land of his birth when it appeared safer to do so. Seguín, as it turned out, was a rebel and Federalist at heart who sought defense of home and family all the while he was made to feel a "foreigner in my native land."[108]

Navarro perhaps remains the most enigmatic of Tejano non-combatant leaders in the Republic of Texas era and beyond. Arnoldo De León argues that Navarro was not the monolithic "all-American" or "Uncle Tom" that traditionalist and revisionist historians have painted. Navarro represented an elitist, local perspective of the various roles and personal motives that called for certain behaviors. De León adds that "even poorer Tejanos did not all fit into a convenient stereotype" as represented in the rank-and-file Tejano forces and volunteers or communities-at-large whose encounters with Anglo Texans ranged from friendly and cooperative to openly hostile.[109] Scholars have described Navarro as an "Americanized Texian" or "Anglicized Mexican," especially since Anglo Texans emphasized his European roots even though he remained culturally Mexican.[110] Above all, Navarro became the ultimate Tejano insider during the Republic of Texas. As the fortunes of Navarro and other Tejanos ebbed and flowed, so too did the Republic which could not have survived independently from other nations for as long as it did without support from Tejanos who held the joker's wild card.

Tejanos paradoxically never knew for certain which nations might prevail, whether the Republic of Texas, Mexico, or Comanche, but could ill afford to become stateless like Texas Indians who faced removal or extinction. Tejanos emerged from the Texas Revolution in cooperation with whomever best served their own interests at the moment only to see their world pulled apart. They could no longer play off opposing forces or remain neutral as revealed with the Cordova Revolt (1838), Council House Fight (1840), Santa Fé Expedition (1841), or Mexican military occupations of San Antonio (1842), which tainted relationships with Anglos and left feelings of betrayal throughout the Republic. The varied responses of Tejanos to Anglo-Texan rule foreshadowed the history of Mexican-American struggle for equality, justice, and freedom into statehood and the following century. As the late historian David Weber remarked, the Tejano communities "were caught in the middle, just as they have been ever since."[111]

Notes

1. Letter, Edward Burleson to Thomas Rusk, May 5, 1836, as quoted in Jesús F. de la Teja, ed., *A Revolution Remembered: The Memoirs and Selected Correspondence of Juan N. Seguín* (Austin: Texas State Historical Association, 2002), 27.

2. Stephen L. Hardin, "Plácido Benavides: Fighting Tejano Federalist," in *Tejano Leadership in Mexican and Revolutionary*

Texas, ed. Jesús F. de la Teja(College Station: Texas A&M University Press, 2010), 69.

3. *Columbia* (later Houston) *Telegraph and Texas Register*, November 9, 1836, as quoted in Timothy M. Matovina, "Between Two Worlds," in *Tejano Journey, 1770–1850*, ed. Gerald E. Poyo (Austin: University of Texas Press, 1996), 74.

4. Poyo, *Tejano Journey*, xiv, explains that the "Tejano identity" of the nineteenth century emerged from the Spanish colonial communities of San Antonio de Béxar, La Bahía (Goliad), and Los Adaes (Nacogdoches) established between 1716 and 1718. Only Victoria was established more recently under the Republic of Mexico following independence from Spain. See also, Andrés Tijerina, "Constructing Tejano Memory," in Gregg Cantrell and Elizabeth Hayes Turner, eds., *Lone Star Pasts: Memory and History in Texas* (College Station: Texas A&M University Press, 2007), 179. Tijerina defines *Tejano* as "the native Mexican of Texas" who arrived before Anglo-American immigrants and "includes any Spanish-surnamed Texans whose historical or cultural roots are in Texas."

5. For background on Spanish and Mexican Texas, see Donald E. Chipman and Harriet Denise Joseph, *Spanish Texas, 1519–1821* (Austin: University of Texas Press, 2010); Pekka Hämäläinen, *Comanche Empire* (New Haven: Yale University Press, 2008); Juliana Barr, *Peace Came in the Form of a Woman: Indians and Spaniards in the Texas Borderlands* (Chapel Hill: University of North Carolina Press, 2007); Raúl Ramos, "Finding the Balance: Béxar in Mexican/Indian Relations," in *Continental Crossroads: Remapping U.S.-Mexico Borderlands History* (Durham: Duke University Press, 2004), 35–65; Jesús F. de la Teja, *San Antonio de Béxar: A Community on New Spain's Northern Frontier* (Albuquerque: University of New Mexico Press, 1995); Andrés Tijerina, *Tejanos and Texas Under the Mexican Flag, 1821–1836* (College Station: Texas A&M University Press, 1994); David J. Weber, *The Spanish Frontier in North America* (New Haven: Yale University Press, 1992); and Weber, *The Mexican Frontier, 1821–1846* (Albuquerque: University of New Mexico Press, 1982).

6. Weber, *The Mexican Frontier*, 177; Brian De Lay, *War of a Thousand Deserts: Indian Raids and the U.S.-Mexican War* (New Haven: Yale University Press, 2008), 27, 38. De Lay notes the Tejano population in 1830 numbered around 3,000 compared to more than 7,000 Anglo colonists and African slaves; J.S. Holliday, *The World Rushed In: The California Gold Rush Experience* (Norman: University of Oklahoma Press, 2002); see also, Andrew J. Torget, *Seeds of Empire:*

Cotton, Slavery, and the Transformation of the Texas Borderlands, 1800–1850 (Chapel Hill: University of North Carolina Press, 2015), 13. Torget notes that more than 30,000 Americans left the United States for Texas during the 1820s and 1830s.

7. Ana Carolina Castillo Crimm, "Finding Their Way," in Gerald E. Poyo, ed., *Tejano Journey*, 120–121; Alonzo Salazar, "Carlos de la Garza: Loyalist Leader," in De la Teja, *Tejano Leadership*, 202–203; and Tijerina, *Tejanos and Texas Under the Mexican Flag*, 137. This essay follows Torget's use of the term "Anglo-Texans" for the 1830s and 1840s. Torget says Anglo Americans "began developing a national identity distinct from both Mexico and the United States." Anglo-Texans are also referred to as *Texians*. Torget uses the terms "Anglo-Americans" and "Anglos" to refer to citizens of the United States who immigrated to Texas during the early 1810s through the early 1830s; Torget, *Seeds of Empire*, xi.

8. Paul D. Lack, "The Córdova Revolt," in Poyo, *Tejano Journey*, (Quotation) 94, 96–97.

9. Tijerina, *Tejanos and Texas Under the Mexican Flag*, 144; see also, Jimmy L. Bryan. Jr., "The Enduring People: Tejano Exclusion and Perserverance in the Republic of Texas, 1836–1845," *Journal of the West* (Summer 2008), 43–44. Bryan explains Tejanos applied "strategies of perseverance" that ranged from active resistance, self-exclusion or mass removal, neutrality, and cooperation either through political and judicial participation or military service in Ranger companies in defense of the Republic of Texas.

10. Arnoldo De León, *Mexican Americans in Texas: A Brief History* (Wheeling, IL: Harland Davidson, Inc., 1999), 35–36; see also, De León, *They Called Them Greasers: Anglo Attitudes toward Mexicans in Texas, 1821–1900* (Austin: Univrsity of Texas Press, 1983), which includes racial attitudes towards Indians and Native Americans. See also, Teresa Palomo Acosta and Ruthe Winegarten, who also note the lack of freedom and safety of Tejanos like slaves and land dispossession like Native Americans in *Las Tejanas: 300 Years of History* (Austin: University of Texas Press, 2003), 46.

11. Timothy M. Matovina, *Tejano Religion and Ethnicity: San Antonio, 1821–1860* (Austin: University of Texas Press, 1995), 25.

12. De Lay, *War of a Thousand Deserts*, 74; Tijerina, *Tejanos and Texas Under the Mexican Flag*, 138.

13. Omar S. Valerio-Jiménez, *River of Hope: Forging Identity and Nation in the Rio Grande Borderlands* (Durham, NC: Duke University Press, 2013),10–11.

14. Ramos, "Finding the Balance: Béxar in Mexican/Indian Relations," 59.

15. De la Teja, "Juan N. Seguín: Federalist, Rebel, Exile," in De la Teja, *Tejano Leadership*, 225.

16. Matovina, *Tejano Religion and Ethnicity*, (Quotation) 48; see also, Andrés Reséndez, *Changing Identities at the Frontier: Texas and New Mexico, 1800–1850* (Cambridge, UK: Cambridge University Press, 2005), 170. Reséndez states there were competing appeals on the part of Mexican centralists who "emphasized collective identities based on religion, or linguistic and ethnic solidarity" besides historic ties between Texas and its Spanish-Mexican roots.

17. Reséndez, *Changing Identities at the Frontier*, 163–164, 170 (Quotation), who adds that Cherokees initially sought permission from Spain to settle in Texas and then a Mexican land grant, also felt uncertain about their future and steered a neutral course between Mexico and the United States during the Texas Revolution; see also, Dianna Everett, *The Texas Cherokees: A People Between Two Fires, 1819–1840* (Norman: University of Oklahoma Press, 1990).

18. Ramos, *Beyond the Alamo*, 167; De León, *The Tejano Community*, xviii. On the expansion of cotton production in Texas, see Torget, *Seeds of Empire*, 181, who refers to Texas as "cotton country;" see also, Randolph B. Campbell, *An Empire for Slavery: The Peculiar Institution in Texas, 1821–1865* (Baton Rouge: Louisiana State University Press, 1989).

19. David J. Weber, *Foreigners in Their Native Land: Historical Roots of the Mexican Americans* (Albuquerque: University of New Mexico Press, 1973).

20. Census Report of Nacogdoches, May 31, 1809, in "Blacks of Texas," Microfilm 79.52, Roll 2, Frame Nos. 0052–0065, Special Collections, DeGolyer Library, Southern Methodist University, Dallas, Texas; English Transcription. East Texas had witnessed an immediate influx of Anglo Americans in the early 1830s despite Mexico's attempts to bar illegal immigration into Texas across the Sabine River border with Louisiana. Fear of further Anglo-American conquest over northern Mexico lay behind the Republic of Mexico's continued refusal to recognize Texas Independence; Weber, *The Mexican Frontier*, 267.

21. Joe E. Ericson, comp., and Carolyn R. Ericson, ed., *They Came to East Texas, 500–1850: Immigrants and Immigration Patterns* (Westminster, MD: Heritage Books, 2005), 99–121. For discussion of Spanish ranching settlement patterns around Nacogdoches, see Jack Jackson, *Los Mesteños:*

Spanish Ranching in Texas, 1721–1821 (College Station: Texas A&M University Press, 1986), 491–493.

22. Census Report of Nacogdoches, April 30, 1835 (668 residents); Census Report of Nacogdoches, [?] 1835 (293 residents); Census Report of Nacogdoches, East of Town to Attoyac, [?] 1835 (118 residents); Census Report of Nacogdoches, Southwest of Nacogdoches, April 25, 1835 (33 residents); Census Report of Nacogdoches, Northwest of Nacogdoches, [?] 1835 (71 residents); Census Report of Nacogdoches, (Radford) Berry Settlement, [?] 1835 (12 residents]; Census Report of Nacogdoches, from West to Angelina, [?] 1835 (177 residents); Census Report of Williams Settlement [near Nacogdoches], April 21, 1835 (118 residents), in "Blacks of Texas," Microfilm 79.52, Roll 3 [multiple frames], Special Collections, DeGolyer Library, Southern Methodist University, Dallas, Texas; English transcription. The population total from censuses for the other municipalities in East Texas numbered around 3,337 mostly Anglo residents, except for 329 servants (of whom 103 are described as black) or approximately 10 percent of the total. The majority of the servants were found in Sabine (138), followed by Jasper (103) and San Augustine (83). The Tenaha Census, which contained very few families with servants, separately listed an additional 154 Choctaws and 53 Houma/Caddos. See also, Census Report of San Augustine, latter part of 1835 (404 residents); Census Report of Teneha, [1835] (741 residents); Census Report of Sabine, [?] 1835 (1,479 residents); Census Report of Bevil (Jasper), [?] 1835 (713 residents); in "Blacks of Texas," Microfilm 79.52, Roll 3 [multiple frames]; English transcription; Torget, *Seeds of Empire*, (Quotation) 204.

23. Bill of Sale, William R. Bracken to Pormile Parchman, for three slaves, Nacogdoches, September 2, 1826, *Nacogdoches Archives* (hereafter *NA*), 215–216, compiled by R.B. Blake, Special Collections, DeGolyer Library, Southern Methodist University, Dallas, Texas; Spanish transcription.

24. Bill of Sale, Daniel Clark to Frost Thorn, for one slave, Nacogdoches, September 27, 1830, *NA*, 270–271; Spanish transcription; Contract of Transfer of Services, Thomas Ruel to Adolphus Sterne, for Silvia, Nacogdoches, November 3, 1830, *NA*, 277–278; Spanish transcription; Bill of Sale, Harrison E. Watson to Frost Thorn, for one slave, October 8, 1831, *NA*, 288–289; Spanish transcription. See also, Bill of Sale, John Durst to William Goyens, for one slave, Nacogdoches, January 3, 1829, *NA*, 239; Bill of Sale, Retson Morris to Elisha Roberts, for one slave, Nacogdoches,

May 25, 1829, *NA*, 251; Spanish transcription. Pedro Garza and Juan Garza served as witnesses to the latter contract. On January 3, 1829, Jesús de los Santos Coy and José Piñeda acted as witnesses under José Ignacio Ybarbo, alcalde of Nacogdoches, who presided over the sale of a black slave named Jerry (age 26) "for life" from *don* John Durst to William Goyens at the price of 700 pesos. On May 25, 1829, the alcalde Ybarbo also presided over the sale of a mulatto slave named Juan (age 21) from "the foreigners" Retson Morris to Elisha Roberts in the amount of 575 pesos.

25. Sale of land and slaves, John Durst to Samuel Price, Russell, Theophilus and Marcelina Tausin, Cable, and Bullard, Nacogdoches, May 27, 1836, *NA*, 131–133; English transcription. Among the servants were Nelly and her four children (Manuel, Victoria, Zical, and Jefferson); a "negro boy named Andres; a negro man named Moses and his wife Rosa; a negro woman named Phyllis; a negro man named Isaac and his wife Mary; Peter, Julia, and George; a mulatoe girl named Mariana; a mulatoe boy named Antonio; and girl named Lydia." Durst, described as the "Paul Revere" of the Texas Revolution for warning Texans about the approach of Santa Anna, afterwards served as captain of a company together with General Rusk against Cherokee and Kickapoo Indians; see Joe E. and Carolyn Reeves Ericson, "DURST, JOHN MARIE," *Handbook of Texas Online* (http://www.tshaonline.org/handbook/online/articles/fdu27), accessed May 20, 2015. Uploaded on June 12, 2010. Published by the Texas State Historical Association. On the decline of Indians in Texas, see F. Todd Smith, *From Dominance to Disappearance: The Indians of Texas and the Near Southwest, 1786–1859* (Lincoln: University of Nebraska Press, 2005).

26. Tijerina, *Tejanos and Texas Under Mexico*, 139; Lack, "The Córdova Revolt," 95. Curiously, 65 percent of Rio Grande claimants succeeded with their patents, after the area had become "Neutral Ground" after the Texas Revolution.

27. Lack, "The Córdova Revolt," 94–95.

28. Lack, "The Córdova Revolt," 95–96. See also, David La Vere, *The Texas Indians* (College Station: Texas A&M University Press, 2004), 170. La Vere notes that the Caddos were even more anti-Texas in March 1836 than the Cherokees and more amenable to Mexican agents. The Cherokees, who were refused discussion of a peace treaty by Mexico, were divided into pro-Mexican and pro-Texan factions and opted to remain neutral through the Texas Revolution like East Texas Tejanos. After Texas independence, the Caddos and Cherokees of East Texas became caught in the middle as did Tejanos. Richard Sparks appears on the Nacogdoches

Census of 1835, northwest of town, as a 42-year-old married father with six children and six blacks (3 male, 3 female) without mention of his occupation or place of origin. He lived in a small community of 71 total residents containing 11 Anglo families, 18 blacks (9 male, 9 female) without any occupations listed; Census of Nacogdoches, [?] 1835, Northwest of Nacogdoches, in "Blacks of Texas," Mf 79.52, Roll 2.

29. Lack, "The Córdova Revolt," 96.

30. Torget, *Seeds of Empire*, 261.

31. Lack, "The Córdova Revolt," 98. At the same time, the leader of the Mexican party, Pedro Miracle, tried to recruit Kickapoo and Chickasaw villages where he waited without success for assistance from the Kichais, Wacos, or Tahuacanos. The following month, Miracle headed toward Caddo villages and was killed during a skirmish along the Red River on August 20. Miracle's journal and the Filisola memorandum had fallen into the hands of Texas government officials, but hostilities apparently had already begun.

32. Ibid., 99–100. Most interesting is Lack's discussion that General Rusk's emissary, Antonio Menchaca, allegedly agreed that "the Mexicans were doing wrong and that he would get as many of them to leave Cordova as he could and return to their homes." Menchaca returned to Nacogdoches on August 7, 1838, supposedly having convinced some to do so, when he learned of John Durst's news that Tejanos planned a rebellion. Although Lack does not mention why Menchaca would have seemingly turned against Vicente Cordova, he must have rejoined him because Menchaca was the only one found guilty in the revolt during the trial afterwards and was then pardoned by President Lamar. See also, Roderick B. Patten, "MENCHACA, JOSE ANTONIO [1795-?]," *Handbook of Texas Online* (http://www.tshaonline.org/handbook/online/articles/fme13), accessed May 21, 2015, which states he is "not to be confused with the pro-Texas revolutionary of the same name" from San Antonio.

33. Lack, "The Córdova Revolt," 97.

34. Ibid.

35. Census Report of Nacogdoches, from West to Angelina, [?] 1835, *NA*, Roll 3.

36. Lack, "The Córdova Revolt," 97.

37. Ibid., 99, 102–104, 108–109. Ironically, Chief Bowl and the Cherokees were also betrayed by the Texas government despite their official neutrality during Cordova's revolt and chose to stand against eviction in the summer of 1839 when Chief Bowl died during the fighting

and the remaining Cherokees, along with other surviving Delaware, Shawnee, and still other Indians, were removed from Texas.

38. Montejano, *Anglos and Mexican in the Making of Texas*, 27.

39. For additional background on the difficulty of establishing colonization and relations with Native Americans in broader perspectives, see the classic works of Edward H. Spicer, *Cycles of Conquest: The Impact of Spain, Mexico, and the United States on the Indians of the Southwest, 1533–1960* (Tucson: University of Arizona Press, 1962); and Elizabeth A.H. John, *Storms Brewed in Other Men's Worlds: The Confrontations of Indians, Spanish, and French in the Southwest, 1540–1795* (Lincoln: University of Nebraska Press, 1975). For such recent works more specific to the Republic of Texas era and Native Americans, see Smith, *From Dominance to Disappearance*; Hämäläinen, *Comanche Empire*; and De Lay, *War of a Thousand Deserts*.

40. De la Teja, *A Revolution Remembered*, 28–29.

41. Ibid., 29–32; De la Teja, *Seguín: Federalist, Rebel, Exile*, 224–225.

42. Ibid., 31.

43. Andrés Reséndez, "Múzquiz: The Ultimate Insider," in De la Teja, *Tejano Leadership*,129–131. Ramón Múzquíz's father was among the Spanish troops that killed the infamous horse trader Philip Nolan the following year, regularly visited Indian camps and was even himself accused of smuggling later at La Bahía (Goliad). Ramón Múzquiz did not go the military route and instead became postmaster at Monclova and oversaw regular mail deliveries to San Antonio. Mexican independence from Spain eased trade restrictions with the United States where Mexican traders were legally able to open lines of credit. Múzquiz jumped at these commercial opportunities, first by transporting goods from Coahuila, including one instance of 58 mule loads in 1823 carrying goods that included wine and *aguardiente* (strong Mexican liquor), followed by regular business trips to New Orleans and quickly became a very successful Mexican merchant in Texas.

44. Ibid., 129, 132–136, 138. Ramón Múzquiz's family was so integrated into elite Mexican society that one relative, Melchor Múzquiz, even briefly served as president of Mexico in 1832. Interestingly, Melchor Múzquiz represented the Popular York Rite interests within the Liberal (federalist) Party and was only appointed interim president when Antonio Bustamante of the Conservative (centralist) Party left the presidency to fight against Santa Anna, who had launched a rebellion under his Plan of Veracruz against centralist rule. For discussion of the struggle between

Scottish and York Rite Freemasonry in Mexico at this time, as well as Tejanos, see Reséndez, *Changing National Identities at the Frontier*, 68–70.

45. Reséndez, "Múzquiz: The Ultimate Insider," 138–140, which includes discussion of Ramón Múzquiz's role as intermediary between Anglos and Mexicans during the Texas Revolution having been reelected by Tejanos as political boss of San Antonio.

46. Reséndez, "Múzquiz: The Ultimate Insider," 140.

47. Ramos, *Beyond the Alamo*, 170–171; De la Teja, *A Revolution Remembered*, 33.

48. McDonald, *José Antonio Navarro*, 139–141.

49. Tijerina, *Tejanos and Texas Under the Mexican Flag*, 140.

50. McDonald, *José Antonio Navarro*, 144–145.

51. De la Teja, *A Revolution Remembered*, 33; Matovina, *Tejano Religion and Ethnicity*, 79. For discussion about the politics of bilingualism in the Republic of Texas era, see Carlos Kevin Blanton, *The Strange Career of Bilingual Education in Texas, 1836–1981* (College Station: Texas A&M University Press, 2004), 16–17, who states that bilingual instruction in schools was not legally prohibited.

52. De la Teja, *A Revolution Remembered*, 33.

53. Dora Elizondo Guerra, "Two Silver Pesos and a Blanket: The Texas Revolution and the Non-Combatant Women Who Survived the Battle of the Alamo," in *Women and the Texas Revolution,* ed. Mary L. Scheer (Denton: University of North Texas Press, 2012), 123.

54. Matovina, *Tejano Religion and Ethnicity*, 79.

55. De la Teja, *A Revolution Remembered*, 34; McDonald, *Jose Antonio Navarro*, 148, 150–151; Robert E. Wright, O.M.I, "Father Refugio de la Garza: Controversial Religious Leader," in De la Teja, *Tejano Leadership*, 84, 86. Seguín's allegations about Father De la Garza's neglect of the community's religious needs and his scandalous behavior, living with "different lovers, from whom he has had illegitimate children," triggered the priest's downfall.

56. Wright, "Father Refugio de la Garza," 86. On this point about perceived anti-Catholicism and economic interests, timing meant everything as the Catholic Church became concerned about losing its *fueros* (or special rights of immunity from prosecution) and its property. Both the church and the military favored the centralists and this might explain, at least in part, why Santa Anna returned to Mexico City from his country estate in Veracruz and suddenly became a Centralist after he rebelled against centralism in the first place; see Buchenau, *Mexican Mosaic*.

57. De la Teja, *Seguín: Federalist, Rebel, Exile*, 225; Alywn Barr, "The Influence of War and Military Service on African Texans," in Alexander Mendoza and Charles David Grear, eds., *Texans and War: New Interpretations of the State's Military History* (College Station: Texas A&M University Press, 2012), 99–100.

58. McDonald, *José Antonio Navarro*, 145–146.

59. See Amy M. Porter, *Their Lives, Their Wills: Women in the Borderlands, 1750–1846* (Lubbock: Texas Tech University Press, 2015), 61. Porter states that "slavery in San Antonio" during the Spanish and Mexican eras "was not as permanent an institution as in Saltillo [Coahuila], where there were more slaves and more wealth." This stands in sharp contrast to slavery in Texas after 1836; see Campbell, *An Empire for Slavery* and Torget, *Seeds of Empire*.

60. McDonald, *José Antonio Navarro*, 147–148.

61. Ibid., 152.

62. Ibid., 153–154.

63. Salazar, "Don Carlos de la Garza: Loyalist Leader," in De la Teja, *Tejano Leadership*, 202–203 (Quotations); John W. Crain, "Isaac Watts Burton: The Glorious Years, 1832–1843," *Southwestern Historical Quarterly* (October 2005); 176–177; Bryan, "The Enduring People," 42.

64. Ibid., 203.

65. Ibid., 201–202 (Quotation); Stephen L. Hardin, "Plácido Benavides: Fighting Tejano Federalist," in *De la Teja, Tejano Leadership*, 69.

66. Hardin, "Benavides: Fighting Tejano Federalist," 70.

67. Bryan, "The Enduring People," 42, see also Note #11, p. 46; Salazar, "Don Carlos de la Garza: Loyalist Leader," 202; McDonald, *José Antonio Navarro*, 151.

68. Carolina Castillo Castillo Crimm, De León: Leadership Lost," in De la Teja, *Tejano Leadership*, 115–117.

69. Ibid., 117–118.

70. McDonald, *José Antonio Navarro*, 156.

71. Affidavit, Seguín's Company for the 1839 Indian Campaign, P.L. Buquet, San Antonio, September 28, 1860, Bexar County, Texas, in De la Teja, *Revolution Remembered*, 184–186; L. Lloyd MacDonald, *Tejanos in the 1835 Texas Revolution* (Gretna, LA: Pelican Publishing Co., 2009), 72–75; see also, Robert Garcia and Sylvia Jean de Jesús Garcia, *Tejano Participants in the Texas Revolution, 1835–1836* (San Antonio, TX: Paso de la Conquista, 2006); John C. Barron, et al., *Republic of Texas*

Pension Application Abstracts (Austin: Morgan Printing & Publishing Inc., 1987).

72. De la Teja, *Revolution Remembered*, 185.

73. Karen R. Thompson, ed., *Defenders of the Republic of Texas, Volume I, Texas Army: Muster Rolls, Receipt Rolls and Other Rolls, 1836–1841* (Austin: Laurel House Press, 1989), 293, 295–296; List, Seguín's Company at the Siege of Béxar, in De la Teja, *A Revolution Remembered*, 182–183.

74. *Veteran Biographies*, The Albert and Ethel Herzstein Library, San Jacinto Museum of History, La Porte (Houston), Texas.

75. Ironically, Major Tinsley was defeated in a fight against Indians near Victoria in March 1837, but died over a year later at San Antonio in a duel with Major Stiles Leroy around the same time that Navarro's brother was murdered; see Thomas W. Cutrer, "TINSLEY, JAMES W.," *Handbook of Texas Online* (http://www.tshaonline.org/handbook/online/articles/fti03), accessed May 27, 2015.

76. Muster Roll, Company B, Seguín's Regiment, Bexar, December 31, 1836, in De la Teja, *A Revolution Remembered*, 149–150.

77. Matovina and De la Teja, eds., *Recollections of a Tejano Life*, 96 note 52; Jeanette H. Flachmeier, "JOHNSTON, ALBERT SIDNEY," *Handbook of Texas Online* (http://www.tshaonline.org/handbook/online/articles/fjo32), accessed May 27, 2015.

78. De la Teja, *A Revolution Remembered*, 35.

79. Juan Seguin's Address in the Senate, February 1840, Houston, Texas, in De la Teja, *A Revolution Remembered*, 174.

80. David M. Vigness, "REPUBLIC OF THE RIO GRANDE," *Handbook of Texas Online* (http://www.tshaonline.org/handbook/online/articles/ngr01), accessed May 27, 2015; De la Teja, "Seguín: Federalist, Rebel, Exile," 226; Letter, Juan Seguín to Secretary of War, Béxar, January 26, 1837, in De la Teja, *A Revolution Remembered*, 153–154; Letter, Juan Seguín to President Lamar, December 26, 1840, Austin, in De la Teja, *A Revolution Remembered*, 176–178. By this time, the capital of the Texas Republic had moved to newly created Austin, Texas.

81. Ramos, *Beyond the Alamo*, 180; De Lay, *War of a Thousand Deserts*, 74.

82. De Lay, *War of a Thousand Deserts*, 74, 76, 92–93, and 112.

83. Ramos, *Beyond the Alamo*, 53, 55, 60–62, which mentions that Tejano Francisco Ruiz became a cultural broker with Comanches, having lived among them for eight years, and that Comanches were often at war

with the Apaches. For a much broader perspective on new Indian history, see Hämäläainen, *Comanche Empire*.

84. De Lay, *War of a Thousand Deserts*, 77–78.

85. McDonald, *José Antonio Navarro*, 158.

86. Cheryl English Marin, *Governance and Society in Colonial Mexico: Chihuahua in the Eighteenth Century* (Stanford: Stanford University Press, 1996); Weber, *The Spanish Frontier in North America*; Weber, *The Mexican Frontier*; De Lay, *War of a Thousand Deserts*; Buchenau, *Mexican Mosaic*.

87. McDonald, *José Antonio Navarro*, 154–155, 166.

88. Reséndez, *Changing National Identities at the Frontier*, 206–210.

89. Weber, *The Mexican Frontier*, 267.

90. Reséndez, *Changing National Identities at the Frontier*, 205–206, 208.

91. McDonald, *José Antonio Navarro*, 164; De Lay, *War of a Thousand Deserts*, 77.

92. Ibid., 166; Reséndez, *Changing National Identities at the Frontier*, 208.

93. McDonald, *José Antonio Navarro*, 166–167.

94. Ramos, *Beyond the Alamo*, 185–186; De la Teja, "Seguín: Federalist, Rebel, Exile," 226–227; Matovina and De la Teja, *Recollections of a Tejano Life*, 99; De la Teja, *A Revolution Remembered*, 44.

95. Ramos, *Beyond the Alamo*, 188, 189 (Quotations), 190; Matovina and De la Teja, *Recollections of a Tejano Life*, 89 Note 32, 101; De la Teja, "Seguín: Federalist, Rebel, Exile," 226; De la Teja, *A Revolution Remembered*, 45–46; Lack, "The Cordova Revolt," in Poyo, *Tejano Journey*, 109.

96. Thomas W. Cutrer, "SALADO CREEK, BATTLE OF," *Handbook of Texas Online* (http://www.tshaonline.org/handbook/online/articles/qfs01), accessed May 30, 2015.

97. Ibid.; Lack, "The Cordova Revolt," in Poyo, *Tejano Journey*, 109. Approximately two hundred Texian volunteers under Capt. Matthew Caldwell joined with Capt. Hays and his Texas Rangers, including Henry E. McCulloch, William A. A. "Bigfoot" Wallace, Robert A. Gillespie and 34 other Texans, who boldly lured General Woll and his troops out of San Antonio to the Salado Creek. Back near San Antonio, Caldwell's and Hays' command met up with the vanguard of General Edward Burleson's forces. In other fighting, the 53 men under Capt. Nicholas Dawson had surrendered to a separate column of 300 Mexican cavalry. Most of them were shot after laying down their arms while the rest were taken

to the Perote Prison in Mexico from where the members of the Santa Fe expedition had just been released by Santa Anna before Woll's invasion of San Antonio.

98. Ramos, *Beyond the Alamo*, 178, 190, 191 (Quotation).

99. De León, *They Called Them Greasers*, 16–17. For example, De León relates that in May 1842, after the Vasquez invasion and Anglo-Texans were still imprisoned in Mexico, Adolphus Sterne, Justice of the Peace in East Texas, remarked at the marriage between a Tejano and a white woman that "if their [groom's compatriots] hair would be a little curly" that "they would be taken anywhere for Negroes." Francis S. Latham, traveling in Texas that same year said that Mexicans were nothing else than "the mongrel and illicit descendants of an Indian, Mexican, and Spanish penciled with a growing feintline of the Anglo Saxon ancestry." American attitudes about miscegenation between whites and blacks transferred similarly to Mexicans, but the latter in turn fed off a lengthier Black Legend against Spanish conquest in the New World.

100. Matovina, "Between Two Worlds," in Poyo, ed., *Tejano Journey*, 75–76; Ruthe Winegarten (with Cary Schechter), *Invisible Texans: Women and Minorities in Texas History* (New York: McGraw-Hill, 2005).

101. McDonald, *José Antonio Navarro*, 195, 199–202. The interim president of Mexico, José Joaquín de Herrera, received a petition from Navarro's attorney while Navarro himself wrote President Herrera in mid-January 1845 about the many grievances he had suffered under Santa Anna. President Herrera ordered Navarro to be set free, but the local commander at Veracruz, Ignacio de Mora, reported back that Navarro was already gone, apparently after an officer allowed him to wander about town. One of the first persons Navarro wrote in the United States was William C. Cooke, a friend and fellow Santa Fe expedition member, whom he asked to deliver another letter he wrote to his wife, Margarita. While in New Orleans, another friend, George Kendall, provided him with lodging.

102. McDonald, *José Antonio Navarro*, 205–207, 208 (First Quotation), 211 (Second and Third Quotation), 213. Navarro was also concerned about the addition of the words "Indians not taxed, Africans and descendants of Africans" after free white men, which could potentially disenfranchise Tejanos based upon Anglo-American anti-miscegenation attitudes.

103. Ramos, *Beyond the Alamo*, 197–199; Montejano, *Anglos and Mexicans in the Making of Texas*, 28.

104. Matovina, "Menchaca: Narrating a Tejano Life," in De la Teja, ed., *Tejano Leadership*, 177–179; Ramos, *Beyond the Alamo*, 193, 195; Matovina and De la Teja, eds., *Recollections of a Tejano Life*, 15–17;

Matovina, *Tejano Religion and Ethnicity*, 38; Matovina, "Between Two Worlds," in Poyo, ed., *Tejano Journey*, 80; *Handbook of Texas Online*, Cecil Collins Scanlan, "Smith, John William," accessed August 20, 2016, http://www.tshaonline.org/handbook/online/articles/fsm30; *Handbook of Texas Online*, "Dwyer, Edward," accessed August 20, 2016, http://www.tshaonline.org/handbook/online/articles/fdw01. See also, Montejano, *Anglos and Mexicans in the Making of Texas*, 34, for discussion of the peace structure among elites.

105. Lack, "The Cordova Revolt," in Poyo, ed., *Tejano Journey*, 108–109.

106. Salazar, "Dn Carlos de la Garza: Loyalist Leader," in De la Teja, ed., *Tejano Leadership*, 204. In 1842, don Carlos, Nicholas Fagan, and Tom O'Connor rescued the Gilleland children, Rebecca and William, after they were left for dead along the San Antonio River following the death of their parents at the hands of Comanches who took the children captive. General Albert Sydney Johnston utilized the don Carlos Ranch as his headquarters during the Gilleland murders and chased after the Comanches. The ranch even served as headquarters for Vincentian priests suggesting cooperation with greater European control over the previous native Father Valdez.

107. Castillo Crimm, "De León: Leadership Lost," in De la Teja, ed., *Tejano Leadership*, 122.

108. David J. Weber, *Foreigners in Their Native Land: Historical Roots of the Mexican Americans* (Albuquerque: University of New Mexico Press, 1973), 177.

109. De León, *The Tejano Community*, xxii (First Quotation)-xxiii (Second Quotation).

110. McDonald and Matovina, in *Defending Mexican Valor in Texas*, (pages 16 [Quotation], 19–20, 22), note that in San Antonio, five of the eight city council members were still Tejanos in 1845, but there were none on city council on the eve of another civil war in 1860.

111. Weber, *Foreigners in Their Native Land*, 93.

Chapter 16
God Bless Texas: Religion in the Lone Star Republic

John Storey

Aside from having been a province of Spain and then Mexico, both nations in which Roman Catholicism was the exclusive and required faith of all citizens, there was nothing particularly exceptional about the religious development of the Texas Republic. With a population estimated at 34,470 in 1836, the vast majority of Texans consisted of Anglos primarily of Protestant heritage from the United States, especially Louisiana, Alabama, Arkansas, Tennessee, and Missouri. Thus, by the 1830s and 1840s, Anglo Texans reflected essentially the attitudes and impulses typical of Protestantism in the United States in general and the South in particular: an intense hostility toward Catholicism, a belief that education should buttress the churches' view of public morality, a desire for a Christian Sabbath, prohibition of John Barleycorn, and an evangelical zeal to redeem individual sinners, thereby creating a more wholesome society, something the godly all agreed was sorely lacking west of the Sabine River. As a Presbyterian traveler lamented in 1836, the morality of "Texasians" was "Bad-bad! Superlatively bad!!"[1] Clearly, thought the righteous, Texas desperately needed God's blessing, and so they set out to tame the wicked land and to bring the new Republic into God's fold.

That the fledging Republic of Texas tested the fervor of the saints is undeniable, for by the 1830s, the prevailing mood of most Texans was decidedly secular, and skepticism, if not outright hostility, toward organized religion of any sort was widespread. It pleased one early settler, for example, that Texas was free of the "strifes and animosities," the "ravings and … rompings, or indecorous and indecent exhibitions" that usually accompanied "the cause of true religion."[2] Notably, Texas politicians saw to it that preachers would not blemish their ranks with such indecent behavior. The Texas Constitution of 1836 prohibited ministers of the gospel from holding public office in the new nation. The rationale for this provision, that ministers should not be diverted from their lofty calling to serve God and to rescue wayward souls by occupying political positions, smacks of disingenuousness.[3] Such an attitude toward religion was perhaps to be expected, for prior to independence places of worship, whether Catholic or Protestant, were few and far between, church membership was negligible, and Sunday, which Texans certainly recognized as a "day off," was more an occasion for fun and frolic than a time for spiritual nourishment. Wrote one female emigrant from Virginia, "Sunday is spent by most Texans in hunting and fishing and breaking wild horses."[4] Or, as an early Baptist missionary put it, even those who claimed to be fellow Baptists demonstrated by their behavior that "they love the ballroom better than they love the church of Christ."[5]

Although Catholicism had been the established faith of Texas, it had never been as strong in practice as it was on paper. The very few priests in the province never numbered enough to carry out the functions expected of a religious institution. This had created a serious dilemma for Stephen F. Austin, who was more of a Jeffersonian Deist than anything else and who apparently never affiliated formally with any religious body. Motivated it seems more by a desire for political harmony than religious conviction, he had earnestly encouraged settlers in his colony to comply with Mexican law. His problem was twofold. In the first place, those Anglo Americans coming to Texas for cheap land and economic opportunity were not much inclined toward religion of any sort, much less Catholicism, and, in the second place, the failure of the Catholic Church to provide enough priests to christen children, perform baptisms, legalize marriages, conduct funerals, and offer other services gave Anglos an easy excuse to ignore the established faith. The good-natured Padre Miguel Muldoon had arrived in San Felipe in 1831 and stayed little over a year, but his assembly-line conduct of the sacraments, hefty fees, and fondness of booze at weddings served mainly to reinforce the existing anticatholicism of many Anglos.[6] Actually, for some settlers the religious requirement had posed no problem. As one had explained to Austin, he could be as good a Christian in Texas as anywhere else, for it was "only a name anyhow."[7] Most Anglos had simply ignored the requirement. By 1836, no more than 25 percent had acknowledged Catholicism.[8]

This low percentage is even more striking considering that Mexico had made it relatively easy to comply with the law. Since Mexican authorities used the terms "Christian" and "Catholic" synonymously, one could satisfy the law with an affirmation to the Christian faith rather that a declaration of Catholicism. This was an easy remedy for Anglo Texans who had qualms about proclaiming themselves Catholics. Easier still, the law could be met with an admission of the "errors" of Protestantism. To be sure, Mexican officials took the religious requirement seriously and never wavered on the matter. Regardless, though the noncompliance of Texans had concerned them, Mexico never vigorously enforced the law. Admittedly, violators could be banished and some arrests were made, as in the cases of the Baptist preacher Joseph Bays and the Cumberland Presbyterian Sumner Bacon. However, by the 1830s the more relaxed attitude of the commandant at Nacogdoches, Col. José de las Piedras, had become typical. When informed of a nearby Methodist-Presbyterian camp meeting in 1832, he instructed that unless the worshippers were stealing horses or killing people they were to be left alone. A state law of 1834, which had provided for a measure of religious tolerance, albeit in violation of the Constitution of 1824, reflected Piedras's sentiment. So long as Protestants did not disturb the peace, they were not to be molested for practicing their faith—quietly.[9]

Prior to independence, and in defiance of Mexico, preachers from all the major Protestant denominations had slipped into Texas to challenge "the tyranny of priestcraft." Indeed, the more lurid the reports about the lawlessness and godlessness of the Texas frontier, the more determined were the righteous to confront Satan on his own turf. In 1815 a Methodist had preached the first Protestant sermon in Northeast Texas. A Baptist preacher had crossed the Sabine River into East Texas in 1820, and four years later a Cumberland Presbyterian had arrived. An Episcopal minister had located at Brazoria in 1831. Primitive Baptists, an antimissionary group, had a congregation near LaGrange by January 1834, followed two years later by a restoration group at Clarksville, the Disciples of Christ, seeking to "restore" Christianity to its presumed biblical purity and New Testament simplicity. By 1836, Protestant activity had already become rather common around Nacogdoches-San Augustine, San Felipe, and Houston-Galveston, with Methodists leading the way in total numbers. There were at least thirty-three ministers in the field on the eve of the Texas Revolution: thirteen Baptists, twelve Methodists, three Cumberland Presbyterians, three regular Presbyterians, one Episcopal, and one Disciple. Yet, there were no formal denominational structures. That came after independence.[10]

Religion was not a factor contributing to the Texas Revolution, but it was prominently cited in the Declaration of Independence and elsewhere once the decision to break from Mexico had been made. Specifically, the declaration of March 2, 1836, accused Mexico of denying Texans "the right of worshipping the Almighty according to the dictates of our own consciences, by the support of a national religion calculated to promote the temporal interests of its human functionaries rather than the glory of the true and living God."[11] The Constitution of 1836 likewise declared, "every person shall be permitted to worship God according to the dictates of his conscience." Moreover, Stephen Austin, writing to Sam Houston in late 1835, now proclaimed his wish "to see Texas free from the trammels of religious intolerance, and other antirepublican restrictions." Some weeks later, he asserted that Texans were fighting "for the right of self-government, and of worshipping God according to the dictates of our consciences."[12]

This sudden religiosity on the part of people who had heretofore given little heed to matters spiritual tempts one to accuse them of cynical exploitation. Although some Texans had obviously found it offensive, they had not protested against the religious requirement in the years prior to 1835–1836. In fact, those Americans migrating to Texas in the 1820s and 1830s knew perfectly well what they were doing. They were leaving a land in which religious freedom had been largely achieved for one in which Catholicism was the established and exclusive faith. Stephen Austin had raised no objection, but instead had willingly complied and time-and-again had urged Mexico to send priests to his colony. Temptation notwithstanding, however, it would be a mistake to dismiss this outbreak of religious rhetoric as nothing more than a cynical ploy. Austin obviously had long held Catholicism in contempt, as shown in private letters from the early 1820s in which he had labeled priests "enemies of liberty, of human happiness and of the human race." Because of them, he added, Mexico was "enslaved by superstition and fanaticism."[13]

Such sentiments were common among those Americans who had migrated to Texas. Yet, like Austin, they had suppressed their feelings in return for cheap land. Catholicism was the established faith in Mexico; the settlers understood that; and they had lived with it not only because there was no alternative, but also because religion was of little importance to most of them. That all changed with the events of 1835–1836. Austin and others were now free to voice publicly what they had thought privately for a long time. It was Branch T. Archer, however, president-elect of the revolutionary government, the Consultation, who first employed biblical imagery and cast the struggle in terms of freedom and religious bigotry. This elevated the Texas Revolution from merely a political contest into a noble cause for freedom of conscience, a theme that resonated well with Americans back in the United States whose support would be critical to Texas in the years ahead.[14] Also seen here is the beginning of a Texas civil religion in which the new nation's struggle for independence was cast as a divinely sanctioned battle for religious freedom over Mexican tyranny, and the Alamo and San Jacinto provided a pantheon of martyrs and heroes. Just as the hand of providence had presumably guided George Washington, so now it directed Sam Houston.[15]

These subsequent pious renditions notwithstanding, religion was not a causal force in the Texas Revolution; however, independence definitely contributed to the swift advancement of Protestantism. Now freed of all legal restrictions, Protestants were poised to take the battle to Satan and to rescue the souls of wayward Texans. Methodists, Baptists, Presbyterians, and others moved rapidly across the landscape busily forging organizational structures and aggressively promoting the gospel. By the late 1840s Methodist circuits and conferences, Baptist associations and conventions, Presbyterian presbyteries and synods, and Episcopal parishes covered the Lone Star Republic. This had been no easy task. Travelling horseback through isolated terrain, preachers confronted daunting challenges from the weather, swollen rivers, a lack of ferries and bridges, occasional Mexican forces, physical assaults, and hostile Indians. Comanche attacks were fairly frequent, as related by the Baptist preacher Z. N. Morrell. "Just about the time we closed the services on Sunday," wrote he in 1837, "the Indians dashed upon us and killed two men, in sight of the congregation." In response, many of the faithful obviously preferred Old Testament "eye for an eye" justice to New Testament "turn the other cheek" love. Again Morrell: "From north, east and west, rumors reached us of Indian outrages, that make our blood chill sometimes fear, and then by turns boil with feelings of furious revenge."[16] Circumstances such as these obliged many ministers, Methodists, Baptists, and Presbyterians, to set aside theological differences and travel together, a kind of coerced frontier ecumenism.

Less deadly but no less a concern were the rowdies who regularly showed up at religious services more intent on raising hell and mocking the faithful than contemplating eternal verities. Typical of such behavior was an incident Morrell witnessed at Washington-on-the-Brazos in 1838. "Loafers and gamblers" had assembled outside the meeting place, "a vacated billiard-room on Main Street," where a joint Methodist-Presbyterian service was in progress. "Without the fear of God or man before their eyes," the sinners entertained themselves at the expense of the saints. One man stood just outside the building, behind the pulpit area, holding a chicken by the neck that was made to squall every time the congregation began to sing. And positioned near an open window was a "partly intoxicated" black man who on cue from "some twenty or more … lewd fellows around him," stuck his head through the window and loudly shouted, "Glory to God!" whereupon the sinners all responded, "Amen and amen!" On other occasions, the saloon became the site for a mock communion, as "these mockers of God's religion" administered "the bread and wine, emblems of a Saviour's love." If the troublemakers expected their antics to quench the zeal of the godly, they had badly misjudged the toughness of preachers like Morrell. "We are determined, as ministers of the gospel," he asserted, "that we will not be run out of Texas, nor out of this town [Washington]." Even so, because of the presence of such characters, coupled to the danger of an Indian attack, preachers usually carried weapons—even in the pulpit. According to Morrell, "preacher and people carried carnal weapons with them in the House of God in those days, and did not for a moment suppose they were violating the Scriptures."[17]

While most preachers on the Texas frontier were genuinely devoted to their calling, the profession's standing with the general populace was diminished by the presence of a good many bogus men of the cloth. These charlatans in clerical garb were better acquainted with the rules of Hoyle than the Holy Writ and fonder of hard liquor than ministerial routine. A case in point was an alleged Hardshell Baptist called "Daddy Spraggins" at Velasco, near the mouth of the Brazos River. The saloon was his source of inspiration before preaching and his place of relaxation afterwards. According to the Baptist missionary James Huckins, "when this man preaches drunkards, blacklegs and the vile of every description are sure to attend," and during the preaching they "applaud by clapping their hands and stomping … their feet." At the end of the service, said Huckins, preacher and congregation "proceed to the grogshop," where they all ate, drank, and got drunk together. "O Lord!" cried Huckins, "how long shall thy precious cause bleed by our being allied in name to such men."[18] No denomination was immune to such scoundrels, and the situation became so acute that a group of Methodists, Baptists, and Presbyterians in Houston formed the Ecclesiastical Committee of Vigilance for Texas in May 1837. Its purpose, explained Z. N. Morrell, a founding member of the committee, "was to prevent impostors from securing the confidence of the people, in the exercise of ministerial functions." Hereafter no minister would be recognized "until he exhibited unmistakable credentials of authority from his denomination." A noble objective, to be sure, but its enforcement was almost impossible. Closer ministerial scrutiny awaited the development of stronger denominational organizations.[19]

Relied on heavily by Methodists, Baptists, and Cumberland Presbyterians, the protracted camp meeting, often lasting two weeks or more, was an effective means of kindling spiritual fires and extending denominational outreach. Emotional fervor ran high at these tempestuous gatherings, as enthusiastic evangelists aroused penitents by graphically contrasting the horrors of spending eternity in hell to the joys of a heavenly paradise. Raising the level of intensity, overly exuberant preachers were described by one observer as running from one side of the pulpit to the other, "talking loudly" and using "gestures of the most violent character." Under such pressure, many seekers, at least in the opinion of critics, abandoned all restraint, apparently overcome by the Holy Ghost. An "old woman" was said to have had "fits" at an 1841 meeting near Independence, while a skeptical observer of an 1845 Methodist gathering in Houston concluded, "no pen or tongue could give … an adequate description of those riotous scenes—a person must see and hear in order to be convinced of their mad extravagances. … [And] they call it revival." While such criticism is understandable, the camp meetings were nonetheless significant not only for religious but also social reasons. They offered rural and small-town Texans an opportunity to socialize with neighbors, to escape for a moment the loneliness and tedium of their daily routine. For women in particular, whose daily life on the Texas frontier was toilsome and rather solitary, the camp meeting was something to look forward to, a breath of fresh air.[20]

Once the excitement of a camp meeting had faded, the challenge for the churches was how to continue the spiritual fires and to cultivate a habit of regular attendance among people who, given years of Catholic neglect and restricted Protestant activity, had grown apathetic. To maintain contact with and to ensure the regularity of services for scattered congregations, many numbering no more than five to twenty members, Methodists and Presbyterians relied heavily on itinerant preachers, or circuit riders. The advantage of this practice was that it allowed a small group of trained ministers to shepherd several isolated churches. The disadvantage was that it permitted those congregations to avoid making the financial arrangements necessary to support resident pastors. Baptists, too, used itinerants, but they preferred resident pastors, an objective too frequently achieved with men of scant education or training. Struggling to survive, churches of different denominations sometimes shared the same building on alternate Sundays, a practice Z. N. Morrell strongly discouraged among Baptists. "To develop strong churches, maintain Sunday-schools and prayer meetings, and properly impress our doctrines upon the people," declared he, "we must have houses of our own."[21]

For the supporting denominations back in the United States, the freedom now to establish churches in the Texas Republic posed a dilemma. Was Texas, now an independent nation, but one populated primarily by Anglo Americans, a "domestic" or "foreign" mission field? This simple question vexed both American and Texas Protestants. Presbyterians never figured it out and Episcopalians dithered until 1844. The American Baptist Home Mission Society, after some initial confusion among both Texans and Americans, came to a novel solution. Georgia Baptists were permitted to "adopt" Texas, subsequently forging a longstanding tie between Georgia and Texas Baptists. Methodists followed the same pattern, turning Texas over to Mississippi Methodists, who in turn never quite decided whether Texas was domestic or foreign.[22]

Whatever their status, Texas Protestants made impressive strides from 1836 to 1845. With their system of circuit riders and utilization of camp meetings, the Methodists easily outpaced all others. They aggressively pursued ornery Texans, as noted by one of their ministers in 1843: "The backwoodsman has gone into the forest, and the panther is scarcely more keen scented for his blood than the Methodist preacher is for his soul."[23] Determined to take Methodism to every hamlet in the Republic, three missionaries, with the blessing of their Mississippi brethren, arrived in 1837. Of the trio, the Rev. Martin Ruter was named superintendent of the Texas Mission. By 1840, some 1,900 Methodists resided in Texas, enough to sustain the creation of the Texas Conference in December 1840. Rapid growth followed, and by 1844 Methodists claimed over 6,000 members, enough to divide the Texas Conference into the Eastern and Western Conferences.[24]

If not in number, Baptists matched the Methodists in enthusiasm. Their efforts were divided, however, by sharp differences between antimissionary and missionary factions, exemplified by Daniel Parker and Z. N. Morrell, respectively. Organized in Illinois in July 1833 and relocated in Texas in January 1834, Parker brought the first Baptist church to Texas, called the Pilgrim Church of Predestinarian Regular Baptists. Intensely Calvinistic and fiercely committed to local congregational autonomy, this group objected to organized mission societies, Bible societies, Sunday schools, and seminaries, considering them unscriptural and a threat to congregational purity. On the other hand, Morrell and the missionary Baptists believed cooperation by locally independent congregations was the best way to advance the cause of Jesus. The influence of the Parker group was considerable, primarily in East Texas, but it steadily lost ground to Baptists of Morrell's persuasion, such as James Huckins and William M. Tryon, both important to the cause of Baptist education. In October 1840, missionary Baptists, with three ministers, three churches, and forty-five members, founded the Union Baptist Association. Coincidentally, just a few days later Parker's followers formed the Union Association of Regular Predestinarian Baptists. By the end of the Republic, total membership of all Baptist groups was less than 2,000.[25]

The Cumberland Presbyterians were the first of that denomination to arrive in Texas, and the man who led them was Sumner Bacon. His education was meager, a worrisome matter to scholarly Presbyterians, but his passion to proclaim the Word was boundless. Emerging from the raucous revivalism of the early 1800s in Tennessee, the Cumberland Presbyterians readily adapted to the frontier conditions of Texas. They diluted Calvinistic predestination with a dose of free will, embraced the camp meeting as enthusiastically as the Methodists, and ordained for the ministry men whose lack of schooling would have rendered them unacceptable to "Old School" Presbyterians. Bacon and the Cumberlands were made for one another, albeit even the Cumberlands had some qualms about his literary deficiencies. In 1836, Bacon organized the first Presbyterian church in the Republic, and when the Texas Presbytery was established at San Augustine in November 1837, he was its first moderator. Likewise, when the Texas Synod was created in 1843, he became its first moderator. By the time Texas entered the Union, this body had over 1,000 communicants, almost thirty ordained ministers, and thirty-seven congregations.[26]

As with the Baptists, the Presbyterian fellowship was divided. Adhering closely to Calvinism, frowning upon the excesses of the camp meetings, and insisting upon a learned ministry, Old School Presbyterians seemed poorly suited for the frontier. Yet, in 1834 an Old School minister arrived in Austin's colony, and in 1837, under the direction of the Mississippi Synod, the Board of Domestic Missions assumed responsibility for Texas. In 1838, the Rev. Hugh Wilson formed the Republic's first Old School church near San Augustine. Two years later Wilson, joined by ministers William Y. Allen, John McCullough, and Elder John McFarland, organized the Texas Presbytery, later rechristened the Presbytery of Brazos. But whether Texas was a domestic or foreign mission field had always troubled some Old Schoolers, and so in 1843 the Board of Foreign Missions took control. Whether domestic or foreign, the Old School branch of the faith could never keep pace with the more evangelistic, frontier oriented Cumberlands. In 1846, Old School Presbyterians claimed only about 200 members. Even so, with their emphasis upon schooling, they offered the gospel to Texans of a more literate sort, as did the Protestant Episcopal Church.[27]

Numerically speaking, Episcopalians never amounted to very much in the Republic of Texas. Few clerics cared to venture to that untamed wilderness, and China, or Africa, or Greece were far more likely than Texas to receive foreign mission gifts from the membership. The evangelistic zeal that drove Methodists, Baptists, and Cumberland Presbyterians to aggressively pursue lost souls and welcome them with open arms into the fellowship of saints was simply alien to Episcopalians, as evidenced by an 1843 resolution. That year Episcopal missionaries in Texas agreed not to accept emigrants into the church without satisfactory testimonials of Christian character from their previous rectors. At Christmas 1838, the Rev. Caleb S. Ives conducted the first service in Matagorda, and in January 1839, he organized Christ Church in that community, the first Episcopal church in Texas, the mother church of Texas Episcopalians. Christ Church of Houston was established in 1839, and Trinity Church of Galveston, 1841.[28]

Smaller groups scattered across Texas by 1845 included the Disciples of Christ, known as "Campbellites" to their detractors. Restoring Christianity to the presumed unity and purity of the apostolic era was this group's mission, but a wariness of external control over locally independent congregations prevented it from forging a denominational structure until the late nineteenth century. In the fashion of Daniel Parker, a Disciples church, dubbed "the church on wheels," was organized outside Texas and moved to Clarksville under the leadership of Lynn D'Spain and Mansil Matthews in 1836. D'Spain subsequently started a church in Nacogdoches, while Matthews sought converts across northern Texas. By 1845, the Disciples had several congregations in the Republic, including one at San Patricio, which reportedly had 100 members. There were a few small independent Evangelical congregations among the growing number of German settlers entering the Republic, as well as a tiny band of Millerites expectantly awaiting the millennium. A small group of Mormons resided near Austin, and Jews, though negligible, were also present. In 1836, about 200 Hebrews dwelled in the Republic, and at least a dozen of them were veterans of the Texas Revolution. When Texas joined the Union, the only Jewish institution was a Houston cemetery consecrated by a visiting rabbi. At the same time, at least one Universalist, the Rev. Levi Chase, roiled the baptismal waters at Washington-on-the-Brazos with the announcement of Satan's death. Bemused residents promptly voiced their sympathy over the passing of Chase's father.[29]

The status of Catholicism was paradoxical. Although the established faith during the colonial era, it had always been a negligible force, and Anglo Texans who now dominated the Republic saw no reason for that condition to change, presuming as they did that only Protestantism could ensure a future nation of virtuous citizens committed to the highest moral standards. If Catholics had been guilty of equating Christianity to Catholicism, Protestants were equally prone to reducing it to Protestantism. Accordingly, "priest-ridden" and "superstition-bound" Catholics, whether Mexicans or Germans, could become "true" Texans only by embracing the Protestant faith of the dominant Anglos. Implicit here was an assumption of superiority, proof of which was seen in the language so easily and readily employed by Protestants: "the tyranny of priestcraft," "the man [Catholicism] of sin," "the blindest superstition," and "a semi-savage people [Mexican Catholics]." Put succinctly by Z. N. Morrell, because of Catholicism the Mexican "multitudes [were] oppressed by superstitions and moral degradation," and "our German population is in a condition scarcely less deplorable."[30]

Such blatant anticatholicism was not the only challenge confronting the Catholic Church in the decade following independence. As one observer recalled, this was a period when "troubles followed troubles." Churches lay in ruins, and the few parishioners who remained faithful lacked "the instruction necessary to render" Catholicism's "teaching intelligible to themselves or to enable them to transmit" those teachings "to their children in … purity."[31] There was also a delicate diplomatic issue for the Church. Should the Vatican recognize Texas independence, thereby surely alienating a devoutly Catholic Mexico, or withhold recognition and risk losing any influence in the new Republic? Rome never officially recognized the Texas Republic, but it nonetheless refocused Texas Catholicism, turning it more toward Galveston and New Orleans than San Antonio. To begin the process of rebuilding, for instances, the bishop of New Orleans selected Vincentian Father John Timon to inspect conditions in Texas, an assignment he carried out from late December 1838 to early January 1839, along the way conducting the first masses in Galveston and Houston. Perhaps Timon's most significant contribution was the delegation of responsibility for the Republic to Father Jean Marie Odin, a French Vincentian who would come to be regarded as the father of modern Catholicism in the Lone Star State.

Along with three fellow Vincentians, Odin arrived in Texas in July 1840 and quickly assembled a cadre of able priests who worked productively among the expanding numbers of German, French, and Irish migrants. In July 1841, the papacy made Texas a vicariate with Odin the first vicar. Largely due to his tireless efforts, and the assistance of his fellow priests, Texas, showing healthy signs of growth, became a diocese in 1847. Odin was the first bishop. Notably, he was seated not in San Antonio, the heart of Spanish Catholicism, but in Galveston, geographically situated and culturally tied more closely to the United States. Galveston's St. Mary's Cathedral, the "mother church" of Texas Catholicism, was dedicated in November 1848. When Odin left Texas in 1861 to become archbishop of New Orleans, Catholicism was on a solid foundation.[32] And lest anyone doubt, Catholics were quite adept at returning Protestant invective. According to a priest in Brownsville in the late 1840s, for example, thc area swarmed with Methodists and ants, neither of which did much to improve the community. Said he: "The greater part of the Methodist, Presbyterian, Baptist, and other ministers of Texas are as ignorant as their disciples."[33]

The work of the churches on the Texas frontier did not stop with the redemption of lost souls and spiritual nurture, though certainly that was uppermost. More broadly, the churches were civilizing institutions, creating social bonds, encouraging sobriety, fostering education, and striving for order. With its reputation for disorderliness and violence, the Lone Star Republic definitely stood in need of refinement, beginning with the primary undertaking of curtailing alcoholic consumption. It was instantly obvious to Martin Ruter upon his arrival in 1837 that the Texas Republic was in dire need of temperance. He was convinced that the unruliness so often brought about by public drunkenness might be eradicated by the outlawing of "demon rum." "Profaneness, gaming, and intemperance," he declared in 1838, were the "prevailing vices against which" Texans had "to contend." Baptist Z. N. Morrell heartily concurred. Saloons, "these sinks of sin" he called them, were "the enemy to peace and good society, to say nothing of Christianity." Methodists, Baptists, and Presbyterians led the fight against John Barleycorn. William Y. Allen, an Old School Presbyterian, joined others in starting the Texas Temperance Society at Houston in February 1839. Sam Houston, well-known for his bouts with the bottle, spoke at length on this occasion, cautioning listeners "to do as he advised, ... not as he had done." Sam Corley, a Cumberland Presbyterian, soon joined the effort. When Baptists founded the Union Association in October 1840, "the eternally troublesome liquor question" was high on the agenda. The association urged the creation of temperance societies in every community to battle this "stream of liquid fire which has desolated other countries" and threatens "the rising prospects of this young and interesting [Texas] republic." Although this movement gained some momentum, especially after the Sons of Temperance, a national organization, entered the state in 1848, most Texans of the republican era continued doing as Houston had done.[34]

More satisfying success came in the area of education, inasmuch as all the churches valued schooling. As early as 1829, Thomas J. Pilgrim, a Baptist layman from New York, established an interdenominational Sunday school at San Felipe. Although "free from any denominational leanings," this bold affront to Mexican law lasted less than a year. Pilgrim continued his work elsewhere, however, and soon Old School Presbyterian William Y. Allen gave his support. By 1838, Sunday schools operated in Houston, San Antonio, Nacogdoches, and Washington-on-the Brazos, affording teaching opportunities for many women. Noting that Baptists had initiated this movement, Z. N. Morrell could not resist scoring a few denominational points. For their refusal to "sprinkle" children, he wrote, "Baptists have often been charged with indifference about the spiritual welfare of children," a claim the Sunday school movement supposedly disproved.[35] Since literature peculiar to specific denominations was in short supply on the frontier, Sunday schools were often nondenominational, or "union" schools. Religion, of course, was their primary purpose, but they contributed more broadly to the educational advancement of those communities in which they existed. Libraries were sometimes spawned by Sunday schools, as well as temperance societies and a curiosity about other academic institutions and intellectual pursuits.[36]

Meeting the educational needs of elementary, secondary, and college students definitely weighed heavily on many of the faithful. In 1839 Z. N. Morrell lamented that "no schools yet, worthy of the name," existed in the Lone Star Republic, and his "hopes of educating" his three young children in Texas "had all vanished." This condition could not be attributed to a lack of interest. Pilgrim, for instance, attempted to fill the need by exposing students who attended his Sunday school at Gulph Prairie in Brazoria County to English grammar, geography, rhetoric, history, composition, arithmetic, natural philosophy, moral philosophy, languages, and mathematics. One of the first acts of the Union Baptist Association was the creation of the Texas Baptist Education Society in October 1841. With preachers doubling as teachers, a multitude of church-sponsored academies, institutes, and colleges soon sprinkled the landscape. That most of these efforts were short-lived seems not to have dampened the resolve of the churches.[37]

With older students in mind, the Republic of Texas chartered nineteen educational institutions between 1836 and 1845, and the state chartered 117 more from 1845 to 1861. Credit for the vast majority goes to Methodists, Baptists, Presbyterians, Catholics, Lutherans, and Episcopalians. Of varied academic respectability, most of these failed sooner or later; many were relocated or consolidated; and all bore the stamp of their respective denominations. Methodists led the way, and the inspiration was Martin Ruter. This indefatigable missionary's stay in Texas was brief, lasting only from his arrival in November 1837 until his death in May 1838. He was a whirlwind of activity. Within weeks, he had formed circuits at San Augustine and Washington-on-the-Brazos and had plans for a third at Houston, all the while promoting a college. With his untimely death in his early 50s, the actual task of creating a college devolved largely upon Robert Alexander. Under his supervision, the appropriately named Rutersville College, located near LaGrange, commenced in February 1840. It peaked with 194 students in 1844–1845, and until about 1850 was Texas's premier educational institution.[38]

Begun as a high school in 1841, McKenzie College, near Clarksville, was founded by the Methodist minister John W. P. McKenzie. In 1845, the school added female and college departments. Although a state school, the University of San Augustine, which opened in 1842, had close ties to the Presbyterian Church, a situation that irritated the sizeable Methodist population of that area. William M. Tryon, a native New Yorker, was a major force for education among Baptists, and in February 1845, he and R. E. B. Baylor, formerly an Alabama congressman, secured a charter for a college at Independence. Tyron's name probably should have graced the school, but the New Yorker deferred to the Alabamian. By the late 1850s, Baylor University was awarding more degrees than all other Texas colleges combined. Regarding schools of a secular nature, so long as they were "under proper influences" the churches generally supported them. And why not? Most of the teachers usually were preachers. Of the fourteen Presbyterian ministers who entered Texas as missionaries during the Republic, for instance, nine taught school. As late as 1866, eighteen of the thirty-five teachers who attended the Texas teachers' state convention were preachers. So whether Christian or secular, religion exercised vast influence over Texas education. To be sure, the education of ministers was a major function of Christian schooling, but the schools did far more than that. They afforded women academic opportunities often in a coeducational setting; within the limits allowed by their respective denominations, they nurtured a spirit of critical inquiry; and they improved the literacy of frontier Texans. Among whites, by 1860 illiteracy was under 4 percent for men and just over 5 percent for women.[39] Religiously inspired schools surely deserve much of the credit.

On the increasingly troublesome matter of slavery, the Texas churches reflected the culture of the Old South, particularly those dominant Protestant ones whose members hailed largely from the southern states. Quite a few ministers owned one or more slaves. William Tryon had acquired several slaves by way of his marriage in Alabama, and the couple brought them to Texas. James Huckins acquired a household servant to assist his wife, which created problems with the American Baptist Home Mission Society but seems not to have hindered his work among slaves in the Galveston area. When the Methodist Church split over slavery in 1844, Texas Methodists followed their southern brethren, as did Texas Baptists in 1845. Although Presbyterians and the Disciples of Christ avoided a schism, neither group opposed the "peculiar institution." Basically, the Texas churches were at ease with slavery, and evangelization rather than emancipation was their remedy to the issue of race.[40]

There was little need for the churches to send missionaries to Africa, for it seemed that Africa had come to Texas. Throughout the republican era slaves constituted a significant portion of the population, numbering about 5,000 in 1836 and increasing rapidly to 38,753 in 1847, or about 27 percent of the total population. Here was an opportunity for the churches not only to redeem lost souls but also to inculcate habits pleasing to the owners. A Texas Methodist gave expression to a view echoed across the American South. Religion, he asserted, would make slaves "honest, industrious and more obedient to those who controlled them, greatly to the advantage of both servants and the masters."[41] In other words, the church was both a source of spiritual nurture and a means of control. Although Methodists and Baptists took the lead in evangelizing the African population, the pattern was the same for all denominations. Slaves were admitted to membership and either attended services with whites, sitting in designated areas, or had separate services of their own, closely scrutinized by whites. In the early 1840s slaves made up 60 percent of a Baptist congregation in Galveston, and of the sixty-eight members of the newly formed Methodist congregation in Houston, almost half were free blacks and slaves. In 1845, African Americans made up 20 percent of Methodism's total membership in Texas.[42]

Blacks occasionally were allowed to organize their own churches, generally with a white pastor. Black preachers were rare, but one who rose to prominence among Methodists was "Uncle Mark," or the Rev. John Mark. This exceptional Washington County slave preached to both whites and blacks, and with contributions from whites, he eventually purchased his freedom. Z. N. Morrell related the story of another slave preacher named "Jerry." In 1846, this "very remarkable negro boy" sought Morrell's permission to join the church. Satisfying Morrell of his "deep convictions and joyful deliverance," Jerry was instructed "to confer with his owner," who raised no objections. Jerry subsequently convinced the Baptist congregation "that he not only had a soul," but also that "his spirit had been moved by the power of God." And so, said Morrell, "I baptized him with some others." Thereafter Jerry learned to read and was "encouraged by the church to preach to his people."[43]

By the end of 1845, religion had become well established in Texas. By far, Methodists had the strongest voice, with over 6,000 members and sixty-four local ministers. Baptists were a distant second with a membership of approximately 2,000, followed in order of numerical strength by Presbyterians, Cumberlands and Old Schoolers combined claiming about 1,500 communicants; the Disciples of Christ, only a few hundred at best; Catholics, now reestablished on a firm footing with ten churches, most in or around San Antonio; and Episcopalians, with congregations in Matagorda, Houston, and Galveston. The extent and diversity of the Republic's religious presence by 1845 impressed a visitor to Houston, who recorded being awakened one Sunday morning by the bells of a Catholic mass. During the course of that day, he subsequently attended a Methodist Sunday school, heard a Baptist sermon, went to a Presbyterian Bible class, and ended the day back at the Methodist church. How different that was from Z. N. Morrell's experience just eight years earlier, who upon arrival in Houston in 1837 "was informed that there never had been a sermon preached in the place." Clearly, substantial progress had been achieved since 1836. Yet, from the viewpoint of the righteous, the work of the Lord is never finished. And that certainly was true of Texas as it entered statehood. The frontier was still untamed, and in 1847, at least 85 percent of Texans claimed no religious affiliation. Even so, the saints saw cause for optimism as they surveyed the religious horizon. "No year … dawned upon us with brighter prospects than 1847," exclaimed Morrell, who now "rejoiced that the wilderness was blooming as the rose."[44] Even more euphoric about the future of Texas was fellow Baptist J. H. Stribling, who proclaimed that "Already has the desert waste begun to blossom as the rose, some fruit has been manifest, precious souls have been redeemed, light is spreading, darkness is receding, and the leaven of truth is spreading through the minds of our population."[45] Surely, God had blessed Texas!

Notes

1. Rupert N. Richardson, Adrian Anderson, and Ernest Wallace, *Texas, The Lone Star State*, 7th ed. (Upper Saddle River, NJ: Prentice Hall, 1997), 71, 138; John W. Storey, "Religion," in *New Handbook of Texas*, 6 vols., ed. Ron Tyler et al. (Austin: Texas State Historical Association, 1996), 5: 523; John W. Storey, "Battling Evil: The Growth of Religion in Texas," in *Texas, A Sesquicentennial Celebration*, ed. Donald W. Whisenhunt (Austin: Eakin Press, 1984), 371.

2. Storey, "Battling Evil," 371.

3. William Stuart Red, *The Texas Colonists and Religion, 1821–1836*, (Austin: E. L. Shettles, 1924), 93; Richardson, *Texas*, 108.

4. Storey, "Battling Evil," 372.

5. Z. N. Morrell, *Flowers and Fruits in the Wilderness*, 3rd ed., rev. (St. Louis: Commercial Printing Co, 1872), 109.

6. James Vanderholt, "Padre Miguel Muldoon: The Forgotten Man of Texas History," *Catholic Heritage* (Nov.– Dec. 1993): 27–28; Richardson, *Texas*, 75–76; Storey, "Religion," 523; Storey, "Battling Evil," 371–72; Howard Miller, "Stephen F. Austin and the Anglo-Texan Response to the Religious Establishment in Mexico, 1821–1836," *Southwestern Historical Quarterly* 91, no. 3 (Jan. 1988): 284–88, 292–94; W. E. Estep, "Religion in the Lone Star State: An Historical Perspective," *International Review of Mission* 78, no. 31 (Apr. 1989): 180–81.

7. Red, *The Texas Colonists*, 8.

8. Ibid., 18. See also Estep, "Religion," 182; "A Brief Sketch of Texas History," in *Texas Almanac, 2008–2009*, ed. Elizabeth Cruce Alvarez (Dallas: Dallas Morning News, Inc., 2008), 54.

9. Richardson, *Texas*, 76; Miller, "Stephen F. Austin," 290, 296, 300–02; Red, *The Texas Colonists*, 74–75, 136–38; Morrell, *Flowers*, 33.

10. Morrell, *Flowers*, 6; Storey, "Religion," 524; Red, *The Texas Colonists*, 70–84, 135–41.

11. "A Brief Sketch," 463.

12. Estep, "Religion," 183; Miller, "Stephen F. Austin," 313.

13. Miller, "Stephen F. Austin," 304.

14. Ibid., 293, 301–04, 311–14. See also Estep, "Religion," 183; Richardson, *Texas*, 100.

15. Robert Wuthnow, *Rough Country, How Texas Became America's Most Powerful Bible-Belt State* (Princeton and Oxford: Princeton University Press, 2014), 91–94.

16. Morrell, *Flowers*, 30, 42, 49, 106, 125, 128, 225.

17. Ibid., 30, 38–39, 40; Wuthnow, *Rough Country*, 36.

18. J. M. Carroll, *A History of Texas Baptists* (Dallas: Baptist Standard Publishing Co., 1923), 154–55; and Howard Miller, "Texas," in *Religion in the American South, A Historical Study*, ed. Samuel S. Hill (Macon, GA: Mercer University Press, 1983), 319.

19. William Ransom Hogan, *The Texas Republic, A Social and Economic History* (Austin: Texas State Historical Association, 1946), 209–10; Storey, "Battling Evil," 372; Morrell, *Flowers*, 33; Estep, "Religion State," 185.

20. Quotation in Hogan, *The Texas Republic*, 212, 216; Storey, "Religion," 525; Morrell, *Flowers*, 42–43; Richardson, *Texas*, 71, 177.

21. Storey, "Religion," 525; Morrell, *Flowers*, 130, 146, 224.

22. Miller, "Texas," 318–19; Carroll, *A History*, 158–61.

23. Quotation in Hogan, *The Texas Republic*, 194.

24. Ibid., 194–95. See also Walter N. Vernon, *The Methodist Excitement in Texas, A History* (Dallas: Texas United Methodist Historical Society, 1984), 40–50.

25. Carroll, *A History*, 46–50, 71, 77–86, 150–58; Hogan, *The Texas Republic*, 198–99; Morrell, *Flowers*, 32, 67–69, 80–81, 101–04.

26. Hogan, *The Texas Republic*, 199; Storey, "Battling Evil," 373; Red, *The Texas Colonists*, 135–41; R. Douglas Brackenridge, *Voice in the Wilderness: A History of the Cumberland Presbyterian Church in Texas* (San Antonio: Trinity University Press, 1968), 16–19, 40–42.

27. John R. Hendrick, "Presbyterian Church," in *New Handbook of Texas*, 5: 327; Hogan, *The Texas Republic*, 200–01.

28. Dubose Murphy, *A Short History of the Protestant Episcopal Church in Texas* (Dallas: Turner Co., 1935), 10–14; Lawrence L. Brown, "Protestant Episcopal Church," in *New Handbook of Texas*, 5: 359.

29. Colby D. Hall and Kenneth L. Teegarden, "Christian Church (Disciples of Christ)," in *New Handbook of Texas*, 2: 98; Carter E. Boren, *Religion on the Texas Frontier* (San Antonio: The Naylor Co., 1968), 6–7, 9–15; Hogan, *The Texas Republic*, 202; Hollace Ava Weiner, *Jewish Stars in Texas: Rabbis and Their Work* (College Station: Texas A&M University Press, 1999), xv.

30. Timothy M. Matovina, "Religion and Ethnicity in San Antonio: Germans and Tejanos in the Wake of United States Annexation," *Catholic Southwest, A Journal of History and Culture*, 10 (1999), 31–32; Morrell, *Flowers*, 2, 6, 59, 98, 144.

31. A. A. Lambing, "Scenes from the Texas Mission of Half a Century Ago," *American Catholic Historical Researches* 3 (1887), 2.

32. Storey, "Battling Evil," 373–74; Miller, "Texas," 320–21; Patrick Foley, "Timon, John," in *New Handbook of Texas*, 6: 500; Patrick Foley, "Odin, Jean Marie," in *New Handbook of Texas*, 4: 1111–12.

33. Quotation in Wuthnow, *Rough Country*, 35.

34. Hogan, *The Texas Republic*, 219–21; Morrell, *Flowers*, 133; Richardson, *Texas*, 184–85; Storey, "Religion," 525; *The Union Baptist Association, Centennial History, 1840–1940* (Brenham, TX: Banner-Press, Inc., n.d.), 9.

35. Morrell, *Flowers*, 33.

36. Ronald C. Ellison, *Texas Baptist Sunday Schools, 1829–1996* (Dallas: Baptist General Convention of Texas, 1997), 10–16, 19; Storey, "Religion," 525.

37. Morrell, *Flowers*, 60, 67–68; Ellison, *Texas Baptist*, 13; Storey, "Religion," 525.

38. Storey, "Religion," 525; Vernon, *The Methodist Excitement*, 29ff; Richardson, *Texas*, 185–86.

39. Norman W. Spellmann, "McKenzie, John Witherspoon Pettigrew," in *New Handbook of Texas*, 4: 415; B. E. Masters, "McKenzie College," in *New Handbook of Texas*, 4: 416; Nancy Beck Young, "University of San Augustine," in *New Handbook of Texas*, 6: 642; Morrell, *Flowers*, 66–70, 118, 232; Carroll, *A History*, 229–30; Richardson, *Texas*, 185–86.

40. Eugene W. Baker, "James Huckins: First Baptist Missionary to Texas," *Texas Baptist History, The Journal of the Texas Baptist Historical Society* 4 (1984): 7; Brackenridge, *Voice Wilderness*, 72–75; Boren, *Religion Frontier*, 32–34.

41. Quoted in Vernon, *The Methodist Excitement*, 70.

42. Richardson, *Texas*, 72,161; Baker, "James Huckins," 7; Vernon, *The Methodist Excitement*, 75–76.

43. Hogan, *The Texas Republic, 197*; Morrell, *Flowers*, 128–29.

44. Vernon, *The Methodist Excitement*, 75ff; Hogan, *The Texas Republic*, 195, 199, 201, 202, 203; Boren *Religion Frontier*, 46–47; Miller, *Texas*, 320–21; Morrell, *Flowers*, 29, 141–44.

45. Morrell, *Flowers*, 144.

Selected Bibliography

Adams, Ephraim D. *British Interests and Activities in Texas, 1838–1846*. Baltimore: Johns Hopkins University Press, 1910.

Adams, John A., Jr. *Conflict and Commerce on the Rio Grande: Laredo, 1755–1955*. College Station: Texas A&M University Press, 2008.

Alonzo, Armando C. *Tejano Legacy: Rancheros and Settlers in South Texas, 1734–1900*. Albuquerque: University of New Mexico Press, 1998.

Anderson, Gary Clayton. *The Conquest of Texas: Ethnic Cleansing in the Promised Land*. Norman: University of Oklahoma Press, 2005.

Barker, Eugene C. *The Life of Stephen F. Austin, Founder of Texas, 1793–1836*. Austin: University of Texas Press, 1990.

Barker, Nancy N., ed. and trans. *The French Legation in Texas*. 2 vols. Austin: University of Texas Press, 1964.

Barr, Alwyn, and Robert A. Calvert, eds. *Black Leaders: Texans for Their Times*. Austin: Texas State Historical Association, 1981.

Barr, Alwyn. *Black Texans: A History of African Americans in Texas, 1528–1995*. 2nd ed. Norman: University of Oklahoma Press, 1996.

Barr, Juliana. *Peace Came in the Form of a Woman: Indians and Spaniards in the Texas Borderlands*. Chapel Hill: University of North Carolina Press, 2007.

Bass, Feris A., Jr., and B.R. Brunson. *Fragile Empires: The Texas Correspondence of Samuel Swartout and James Morgan, 1836–1856*. Austin: Shoal Creek Publisher, 1978.

Bate, W. N. *General Sidney Sherman: Texas Soldier, Statesman, and Builder*. Waco: Texian Press, 1974.

Bevill, James P. *The Paper Republic: The Struggle for Money, Credit, and Independence in the Republic of Texas*. Houston: Bright Sky Press, 2009.

Biesele, Rudolph Leopold. *The History of German Settlements in Texas, 1831–1861*. Austin: Von Boeckmann-Jones, 1930.

Boren, Carter E. *Religion on the Texas Frontier*. San Antonio: The Naylor Co., 1968.

Boswell, Angela. *Women's Lives in a Rural Southern County, 1837–1873*. College Station: Texas A&M University Press, 2001.

Brackenridge, R. Douglas. *Voice in the Wilderness: A History of the Cumberland Presbyterian Church in Texas*. San Antonio: Trinity University Press, 1968.

Braider, Donald. *Solitary Star: A Biography of Sam Houston*. New York: G.P. Putnam's Sons, 1974.

Brazos. *Life of Robert Hall: Indian Fighter and Veteran of Three Great Wars*. Austin: State House Press, 1992.

Brice, Donaly E. *The Great Comanche Raid: The Boldest Indian Attack of the Texas Republic*. Austin: Eakin Press, 1987.

Britten, Thomas A. *The Lipan Apaches: People of Wind and Lightning*. Albuquerque: University of New Mexico Press, 2009.

Brown, Lawrence L. *The Episcopal Church in Texas*. Austin: The Church Historical Society, 1963.

Buenger, Walter L., and Arnoldo de Leon, eds. *Beyond Texas through Time*. College Station: Texas A&M University Press, 2011.

Buenger, Walter L., and Robert A. Calvert. *Texas through Time*. College Station: Texas A&M University Press, 1991.

Campbell, Randolph B., and Richard G. Lowe. *Wealth and Power in Antebellum Texas*. College Station: Texas A&M University Press, 1977.

Campbell, Randolph B. *An Empire for Slavery: The Peculiar Institution in Texas, 1821–1865*. Baton Rouge: Louisiana State University Press, 1989.

———. *Gone to Texas: A History of the Lone Star State*. New York: Oxford University Press; 2003.

———. *Sam Houston and the American Southwest*. 2nd ed. New York: Pearson-Longman, 2002.

Cantrell, Gregg. *Stephen F. Austin: Empresario of Texas*. New Haven: Yale University Press, 1999.

Carlson, Paul H., and Tom Crum. *Myth, Memory and Massacre: The Pease River Capture of Cynthia Ann Parker*. Lubbock: Texas Tech University Press, 2010.

Carrigan, William D. *The Making of a Lynching Culture: Violence and Vigilantism in Central Texas, 1836–1916*. Urbana: University of Illinois Press, 2004.

Carroll, J. M. *A History of Texas Baptists*. Dallas: Baptist Standard Publ. Co., 1923.

Carroll, Mark M. *Homesteads Ungovernable: Families, Sex, Race, and the Law in Frontier Texas, 1826–1860*. Austin: University of Texas Press, 2001.

Cartwright, Gary. *Galveston: A History of the Island*. Fort Worth: Texas Christian University Press, 1991.

Casteneda, Carlos E. *Our Catholic Heritage in Texas*, 6 vols. Austin: Von Boeckmann-Jones Co., 1936–1958.

Caughfield, Adrienne. *True Women and Westward Expansion*. College Station: Texas A&M University Press, 2005.

Clarke, Mary W. *Chief Bowles and the Texas Cherokees*. Norman: University of Oklahoma Press, 1971.

———. *Thomas J. Rusk: Soldier, Statesman, Jurist*. Austin: Jenkins Publishing Company, 1971.

Conner, Seymour V. *Adventure in Glory: The Saga of Texas, 1836–1849*. Austin: Steck-Vaughn Co., 1965.

Costeloe, Michael P. *The Central Republic of Mexico, 1835–1846*. London: Cambridge University Press, 1993.

Cox, Michael. *The Texas Rangers: Wearing the Cinco Peso, 1821–1900*. New York: Forge, 2008.

Crane, William C. *Life and Select Literary Remains of Sam Houston of Texas*. Dallas: William G. Scharff, 1884.

Crawford, Anna Fears. *The Eagle: The Autobiography of Santa Anna*. Austin: State House Press, 1988.

Crimm, Ana Carolina Castillo. *De Leon: A Tejano Family History*. Austin: University of Texas Press, 2003.

Crisp, James E. *Sleuthing the Alamo: Davy Crockett's Last Stand and Other Mysteries of the Texas Revolution*. New York: Oxford University Press, 2005.

Cummins, Light T. *Emily Austin of Texas, 1795–1851*. Fort Worth: Texas Christian University Press, 2009.

Cutrer, Thomas W. *Ben McCullough and the Frontier Military Tradition*. Chapel Hill: University of North Carolina Press, 1993.

———. *The English Texans*. San Antonio: UT Institute of Texan Cultures, 1985.

Davis, William C. *Lone Star Rising: The Revolutionary Birth of the Texas Republic*. College Station: Texas A&M University Press, 2004.

Dawson, Joseph G., III. *The Texas Military Tradition: From the Texas Revolution to World War II*. College Station: Texas A&M University Press, 1995.

Day, James M., and J. Dorman Winfrey, eds. *Texas Indian Papers*, 5 Vols. Austin: Texas State Library, 1959–1961.

De Bruhl, Marshall. *Sword of San Jacinto: A Life of Sam Houston*. New York: Random House, 1993.

De la Teja, Jesús F. *San Antonio de Bexar: A Community on Spain's Northern Frontier*. Albuquerque: University of New Mexico Press, 1995.

De Leon, Arnoldo. *Mexican Americans in Texas: A Brief History*. Wheeling, IL: Harland Davidson, Inc., 1999.

De Leon, Arnoldo. *The Tejano Community, 1836–1900*. Albuquerque: University of New Mexico Press, 1982.

———. *They Called Them Greasers: Anglo Attitudes toward Mexicans in Texas, 1821–1900*. Austin: University of Texas Press, 1983.

DeLay, Brian. *War of a Thousand Deserts: Indian Raids and the U.S.-Mexican War*. New Haven: Yale University Press, 2008.

Eckstein, Stephen D. *History of the Churches of Christ in Texas, 1824–1950*. Austin: Firm Foundation Publ., 1963.

Edward, David B. *The History of Texas: Or the Emigrant's, Farmer's, and Politicians Guide*. Cincinnati: J. A. James, 1836.

Eller, E. M., et al. *The Texas Navy*. Washington, D.C.: Naval History Division, Navy Department, 1968.

Ericson, Joe E., comp., and Carolyn R. Ericson, ed. *They Came to East Texas, 1500–1850: Immigrants and Immigration Patterns*. Westminster, MD: Heritage Books, 2005.

Everett, Dianna. *The Texas Cherokees: A People Between Two Fires, 1819–1840*. Norman: University of Oklahoma Press, 1990.

Exley, Jo Ella Powell. *Frontier Blood: The Story of the Parker Family*. College Station: Texas A&M University Press, 2001.

———. *Texas Tears and Texas Sunshine: Voices of Frontier Women*. College Station: Texas A&M University Press, 1985.

Fehrenbach, T. R. *Lone Star: A History of Texas and the Texans*. New York: American Legacy Press, 1983.

Fischer, Ernest C. *Robert Potter: Founder of the Texas Navy*. Gretna, LA: Pelican Publishing, 1976.

Flannery, John Brendan. *The Irish Texans*. San Antonio: The University of Texas Institute of Texan Cultures, 1980.

Fornell, Earl Wesley. *The Galveston Era: The Texas Crescent on the Eve of Secession*. Austin: University of Texas Press, 1961.

Fowler, Will. *Santa Anna of Mexico*. Lincoln: University of Nebraska Press, 2002.

Francaviglia, Richard V. *From Sail to Steam: Four Centuries of Texas Maritime History, 1500–1900*. Austin: University of Texas Press, 1998.

Friend, Llerena. *Sam Houston: The Great Designer*. Austin: University of Texas Press, 1954.

Fur, Gunlog. *A Nation of Women: Gender and Colonial Encounters among the Delaware Indians*. Philadelphia: University of Pennsylvania Press, 2009.

Gambrell, Herbert Pickens. *Anson Jones: The Last President of Texas*, 2nd ed. Austin: University of Texas Press, 1964.

———. *Mirabeau Buonaparte Lamar: Troubador and Crusader*. Dallas: Southwest Press, 1934.

Gammel, H. P. N., comp. *Laws of Texas, 1822–1897*. Austin: Gammel Book Co., 1898.

Garrison, George P., ed. *Diplomatic History of the Republic of Texas*. Washington, D.C.: Government Printing Office, 1908–1911.

Glasrud, Bruce, Light Townsend Cummins, and Cary D. Wintz, eds. *Discovering Texas History*. Norman: University of Oklahoma Press, 2014.

Gouge, William M. *The Fiscal History of Texas*. Philadelphia: Lippincott, Grambo and Company, 1852.

Graham, Philip. *The Life and Poems of Mirabeau B. Lamar*. Chapel Hill: University of North Carolina Press, 1938.

Green, Rena Maverick, ed. *Memoirs of Mary Maverick: A Journal of Early Texas*. San Antonio: Maverick Publ. Co., 2005.

Gulick, Charles A., ed. *The Papers of Mirabeau Buonaparte Lamar*, 6 vols. Austin: Texas State Library, 1920–1927.

Haley, James L. *Most Excellent Sir: Letters Received by Sam Houston, President of the Republic of Texas, Columbia, 1836–1837*. Austin: Duncan and Gladstone, 1987.

———. *Passionate Nation: The Epic History of Texas*. New York: Free Press, 2006.

———. *Sam Houston*. Norman: University of Oklahoma Press, 2002.

Hamaleinen, Pekka. *The Comanche Empire*. New Haven: Yale University Press, 2008.

Hammett, A. B. J. *The Empresario: Don Martin De Leon*. Waco: Texian Press, 1973.

Hardin, Stephen L. *Lone Star: The Republic of Texas, 1836–1846*. Carlisle, MA: Discovery Enterprises, 1998.

———. *Texian Iliad: A Military History of the Texas Revolution, 1835–1836*. Austin: University of Texas Press, 1994.

———. *Texian Macabre: The Melancholy Tale of a Hanging in Houston*. Abilene: State House Press, 2007.

Haynes, Sam W. *Soldiers of Misfortune: The Somervell and Mier Expeditions*. Austin: University of Texas Press, 1990.

Hendrickson, Jr., Kenneth E. *The Chief Executives of Texas: From Stephen F. Austin to John B. Connally, Jr.* College Station: Texas A&M University Press, 1995.

Henson, Margaret Swett, comp. and Donald E. Willett, ed. *The Texas That Might Have Been: Sam Houston's Foes Write to Albert Sidney Johnston*. College Station: Texas A&M University Press, 2009.

Henson, Margaret Swett. *Samuel May Williams: Early Texas Entrepreneur*. College Station: Texas A&M University Press, 1976.

Hietala, Thomas R. *Manifest Design: American Exceptionalism and Empire*. 1985; rev. ed., Ithaca, NY: Cornell University Press, 2003.

Hinojosa, Gilberto Miguel. *A Borderlands Town in Transition: Laredo, 1755–1870*. College Station: Texas A&M University Press, 1983.

Hogan, William Ransom. *The Texas Republic: A Social and Economic History*. 1946; reprint: Austin: Texas State Historical Association, 2007.

Howe, Daniel Walker. *What Hath God Wrought: The Transformation of America, 1815–1848*. New York: Oxford University Press, 2007.

Humphrey, David G. *Peg Leg: The Improbable Life of a Texas Hero, Thomas William Ward, 1807–1872*. Denton: Texas State Historical Association, 2009.

James, Marquis. *The Raven: A Biography of Sam Houston*. Austin: University of Texas Press, 1929.

Jenkins, John H., ed. *The Papers of the Texas Revolution*. 10 Vols. Austin: Presidential Press, 1973.

Jenkins, John H., and Kenneth Kesselus. *Edward Burleson: Texas Frontier Leader*. Austin: Jenkins Publishing Company, 1990.

Johnson, Frank W. and Eugene C. Barker, ed. *Texas and Texians* Vol. 1. Chicago: American Historical Society, 1916.

Johnson, Melvin C. *Polygamy on the Pedernales: Lyman Wight's Morman Villages in Antebellum Texas, 1845–1858*. Logan: Utah State University Press, 2006.

Johnson, William R. *A Short History of the Sugar Industry in Texas*. Houston: Gulf Coast Historical Association, 1961.

Jones, Anson. *Memoranda and Official Correspondence Relating to the Republic of Texas, Its History and Annexation*. El Paso: Forgotten Books, 2012.

Jones, C. Allen. *Texas Roots: Agriculture and Rural Life before the Civil War*. College Station: Texas A&M University Press, 2005.

Jordan, Jonathan W. *Lone Star Navy: Texas, the Fight for the Gulf of Mexico, and the Shaping of the American West*. Washington, D.C.: Potomac Books, 2006.

Jordan, Terry G. *German Seed in Texas Soil: Immigrant Farmers in Nineteenth-century Texas*. Austin: University of Texas Press, 1966.

Jordan, Terry G. *North American Cattle Ranching Frontiers: Origins, Diffusion, and Differentiation*. Albuquerque: University of New Mexico Press, 1993.

Jordan, Terry G. *Trails to Texas: Southern Roots of Western Cattle Ranching*. Lincoln: University of Nebraska Press, 1981.

Kamphoefner, Walter D., ed. *An Immigrant Miller Picks Texas: The Letters of Carl Hilmar Guenther*. San Antonio: Maverick Publishing Co., 2001.

Kavanagh, Thomas W. *Comanche Political History: An Ethnohistorical Perspective, 1706–1875*. Lincoln: University of Nebraska Press, 1996.

Kearney, James C. *Nassau Plantation: The Evolution of a Texas-German Slave Plantation*. Denton: University of North Texas Press, 2010.

Kelley, Sean M. *Los Brazos de Dios: A Plantation Society in the Texas Borderlands, 1821–1865*. Baton Rouge: Louisiana State University Press, 2010.

Kemp, L. W. *The Signers of the Texas Declaration of Independence*. Houston: Anson Jones Press, 1944.

Kendall, George Wilkins. *Narrative of the Texan Santa Fe Expedition*. Gerald D. Saxon and William Taylor, eds. 2 vols. Dallas, TX: DeGolyer Library and William P. Clements Center for Southwest Studies, 2004.

Kennedy, William. *Texas: The Rise, Progress, and Prospects of the Republic of Texas*. 2 Vols. London: R. Hastings, 1841.

Kerr, Jeffrey Stuart. *Seat of Empire: The Embattled Birth of Austin*. Lubbock: Texas Tech University Press, 2013.

King, Irene Marshall. *John O. Meusbach: German Colonizer in Texas*. Austin: University of Texas Press, 1967.

King, Richard C. *James Clinton Neill: Shadow Commander of the Alamo*. Austin: Eakin Press, 2002.

Lack, Paul D. *The Texas Revolutionary Experience: A Political and Social History*. College Station: Texas A&M University Press, 1992.

Lankevich, George. *The Presidents of the Republic of Texas*. Dobbs Ferry, NY: Oceana Publishing, 1979.

Lathrop, Barnes F. *Migration into East Texas, 1835–1860*. Austin: Texas State Historical Association, 1949.

LaVere, David. *The Texas Indians*. College Station: Texas A&M University Press, 2004.

Lindley, Thomas Ricks. *Alamo Traces: New Evidence and New Conclusions*. Lanham, MD: Republic of Texas Press, 2003.

Linn, John J. *Reminiscences of Fifty Years in Texas*. 1883; reprint: Austin: State House Press, 1986.

Loomis, Neal. *The Texan-Santa Fe Pioneers*. Norman: University of Oklahoma Press, 1958.

Lubbock, Richard Francis. *Six Decades in Texas, or Memoirs of Francis Richard Lubbock*. Edited by C.W. Raines. Austin: Ben C. Jones & Co., 1900.

Malone, Ann Patton. *Women on the Texas Frontier: A Cross-Cultural Perspective*. El Paso: Texas Western Press, 1983.

Malsch, Brownson. *Indianola: The Mother of Western Texas*. Austin: State House Press, 1988.

Marks, Paula Mitchell. *Turn Your Eyes toward Texas: Pioneers Sam and Mary Maverick*. College Station: Texas A&M University Press, 1989.

Matovina, Timothy M. *Tejano Religion and Ethnicity: San Antonio, 1821–1860*. Austin: University of Texas Press, 1995.

McBeth, Harry Leon. *Texas Baptists: A Sesquicentennial History*. Austin: Eakin Press, 1998.

McCaslin, Richard B., Donald Chipman, and Andrew Torget, eds. *This Corner of Canaan: Essays on Texas in Honor of Randolph B. Campbell*. Denton: University of North Texas Press, 2013.

McCaslin, Richard B. *Fighting Stock: John S. "Rip" Ford of Texas*. Fort Worth: Texas Christian University Press, 2011.

McComb, David G. *Galveston: A History*. Austin: University of Texas Press, 1986.

McCutcheon, Joseph D., and John Milton Nance, ed. *Mier Expedition: A Texas Prisoner's Account*. Austin: University of Texas Press, 1978.

McDonald, Archie P. *Texas: All Hail the Mighty State*. Austin: Eakin Press, 1983.

———. *The Texas Experience*. College Station: Texas A&M University Press, 1986.

McDonald, David. *Jose Antonio Navarro: In Search of the American Dream in Nineteenth Century Texas*. Denton: Texas State Historical Association, 2010.

Meed, Douglas V. *The Fighting Texas Navy, 1832–1843*. Plano, TX: Republic of Texas Press, 2001.

Menchaca, Antonio. *Recollections of a Tejano Life: Antonio Menchaca in Texas History*. Edited by Timothy Matovina and Jesús F. De la Teja. Austin: University of Texas Press, 2013.

Mendoza, Alexander, and Charles D. Grear, eds. *Texans and War: New Interpretations of the State's Military History*. College Station: Texas A&M University Press, 2012.

Merk, Frederick. *Slavery and the Annexation of Texas*. New York: Knopf, 1972.

Merry, Robert W. *A Country of Vast Designs: James K. Polk, the Mexican War, and the Conquest of the American Continent*. New York: Simon and Schuster, 2009.

Miller, Hunter. *Treaties and Other International Acts of the United States*, 8 vols. Washington, D.C.: Government Printing Office, 1931–1948.

Montjano, David. *Anglos and Mexicans in the Making of Texas, 1836–1986*. Austin: University of Texas Press, 1987.

Moore, Stephen L. *Eighteen Minutes: The Battle of San Jacinto and the Texas Independence Campaign*. Lanham: MD: Republic of Texas Press, 2004.

———. *Savage Frontier: Rangers, Riflemen, and Indian Wars in Texas*, 4 vols. Denton: University of North Texas Press, 2002–2010.

Moretta, John Anthony. *William Pitt Ballinger: Texas Lawyer, Southern Stateman, 1825–1888*. Austin: Texas State Historical Association, 2000.

Morgenthaler, Jefferson. *Promised Land: Solms, Castro, and Sam Houston's Colonization Contracts*. College Station: Texas A&M University Press, 2009.

Morrell, Z. N. *Flowers and Fruits in the Wilderness or Thirty-Six Years in Texas and Two Winters in Honduras*. Boston: Gould & Lincoln 1872.

Muir, Andrew Forest. *Texas in 1837: An Anonymous, Contemporary Narrative*. Austin: University of Texas Press, 1958.

Mullins, Marion Day. *The First Census of Texas, 1829–1836; to which are added, Texas citizenship lists, 1821–1845, and other early records of the Republic of Texas*. Washington, D.C.: National Genealogical Society, 1959.

Mulroy, Kevin. *Freedom on the Border: The Seminole Maroons in Florida, the Indian Territory, Coahuila, and Texas*. Lubbock: Texas Tech University Press, 1993.

Murray, Ellen M. *Notes on the Republic*. Washington-on-the-Brazos: Star of the Republic Museum, 1991.

Myres, Sandra L. *Westering Women and the Frontier Experience, 1800–1915*. Albuquerque: University of New Mexico Press, 1982.

Nackman, Mark E. *A Nation within a Nation: The Rise of Texas Nationalism*. Port Washington, NY: Kennikat Press, 1975.

Nance, Joseph Milton. *After San Jacinto: The Texas-Mexican Frontier, 1836–1841*. Austin: University of Texas Press, 1959.

Nance, Joseph Milton. *Attack and Counterattack: The Texas-Mexican Frontier, 1842*. 1964; Digital edition, TSHA Online: A Digital Gateway to Texas History.

Newsome, Roy S. Jr and James B. Collingsworth, Jr. *Too Good to be True: James Collingsworth and the Birth of Texas*. Kingston Springs, TN: Westview, 2012.

Oates, Stephen B., ed. *The Republic of Texas*. Tracy, CA: American West Publ. Co., 1968.

Obermeyer, Brice. *Delaware Tribe in a Cherokee Nation*. Lincoln: University of Nebraska Press, 2009.

Olmsted, Frederick Law. *A Journey Through Texas: Or, a Saddle Trip on the Southwestern Frontier*. New York: Dix, Edwards & Co., 1837.

O'Neal, Bill. *War in East Texas: Regulators vs. Moderators*. Lufkin: Best of East Texas Publ., 2006.

Pickrell, Annie Doom. *Pioneer Women in Texas*. Austin: E.L. Steck Co., 1929.

Pierce, Gerald S. *Texas Under Arms: The Camps, Forts, and Military Towns of the Republic of Texas*. Austin: Encino Press, 1969.

Poage, W. R. *Politics—Texas Style*. Waco: Texian Press, 1974.

Ragsdale, Crystal Sasse, ed. *The Golden Free Land: The Reminiscences and Letters on an American Frontier*. Austin: Landmark Press, 1976.

Ramos, Raul A., and Monica Perales, eds. *Recovering the Hispanic Heritage of Texas*. Houston: Arte Publico Press, 2010.

Ramsay, Jr., Jack C. *Thunder on the Brazos: A Biography of Mirabeau B. Lamar*. Austin: Eakin Press, 1985.

Red, William Stuart. *A History of the Presbyterian Church in Texas*. Austin: Steck Co., 1936.

———. *The Texas Colonists and Religion, 1821–1836* Austin: E.L. Shettles Publ., 1924.

Reichstein, Andreas V. *Rise of the Lone Star: The Making of Texas*. College Station: Texas A&M University Press, 1989.

Reid, Stuart. *The Secret War For Texas*. College Station: Texas A&M University Press, 2007.

———. *The Texan Army, 1835–1846*. Oxford: UK: Osprey Publishing, 2003.

Resendez, Andres. *Changing Identities at the Frontier: Texas and New Mexico, 1800–1850*. Cambridge, UK: Cambridge University Press, 2005.

———. *Texas Patriot on Trial in Mexico: Jose Antonio Navarro and the Texan-Santa Fe Expedition*. Dallas, TX: DeGolyer Library, 2005.

Robenalt, Jeffrey. *Tales from the Texas Republic: A Glimpse of Texas's Past*. Charleston, SC: History Press, 2013.

Roberts, Madge Thornall. *The Personal Correspondence of Sam Houston*, 4 Vols. Denton: University of North Texas Press, 1996–2001.

Rodriguez, Jose. *Maria Rodriguez Memoirs of Early Texas*. San Antonio: Passing Show Printing, 1913.

Roemer, Ferdinand, and Oswald Mueller, ed. *Roemer's Texas*. San Antonio: Standard Printing Company, 1935.

Scheer, Mary L., ed. *Women and the Texas Revolution*. Denton: University of North Texas Press, 2012.

Schoenberger, Regula Trenkwalder. *Lenape Women, Matriliny, and the Colonial Encounter, Resistance and Erosion of Power (1600–1876): An Excursus in Feminist Anthropology*. New York: Peter Lang, 1991.

Schutt, Amy C. *Peoples of the River Valleys*. (Philadelphia: University of Pennsylvania Press, 2007).

Schwartz, Rosalie. *Across the Rio Grande to Freedom: United States Negroes in Mexico*. El Paso: Texas Western Press, Southwestern Studies, no. 44, 1975.

Scmitz, Joseph W. *Texan Statecraft, 1836–1845*. San Antonio: Naylor Co., 1941.

Seguin, Juan N. *A Revolution Remembered: The Memoirs and Selected Correspondence of Juan N. Seguin*. Edited by Jesús F. De la Teja. Austin: State House Press, 1991.

Siegal, Stanley E. *A Political History of the Texas Republic, 1836–1845*. Austin: University of Texas Press, 1959.

Siegal, Stanley E. *The Poet President of Texas: The Life of Mirabeau B. Lamar, President of the Republic of Texas*. Austin: Jenkins, 1977.

Silbey, Joel H. *Storm over Texas: The Annexation Controversy and the Road to the Civil War*. New York: Oxford University Press, 2005.

Silver, James W. *Edmund Pendleton Gaines, Frontier General*. Baton Rouge: Louisiana State University Press, 1949.

Silverthorne, Elizabeth. *Ashbel Smith of Texas: Pioneer, Patriot, Statesman, 1805–1886*. College Station: Texas A&M University Press, 1982.

Sitterson, J. Carlyle. *Sugar Country: The Cane Sugar Industry in the South, 1753–1950*. Lexington: University of Kentucky Press, 1953.

Sitton, Thad, and Dan K. Utley. *From Can See to Can't: Texas Cotton Farmers on the Southern Prairies*. Austin: University of Texas Press, 1997.

Smith, F. Todd. *From Dominance to Disappearance: The Indians of Texas and the Near Southwest, 1789–1859*. Lincoln: University of Nebraska Press, 2005.

Smith, Justin. *The Annexation of Texas*. New York: Barnes and Noble, 1941.

Smithwick, Noah. *The Evolution of a State, or Recollections of Old Texas Days*. 1900; reprint: Austin: University of Texas Press, 1983.

Spellman, Paul. *Forgotten Texas Leader: Hugh McLeod and the Texan Santa Fe Expedition*. College Station: Texas A&M University Press, 1999.

Stevens, Kenneth R. *The Texas Legation Papers, 1836–1845*. Fort Worth: Texas Christian University Press, 2012.

Struve, Walter. *Germans and Texans: Commerce, Migration, and Culture in the Days of the Lone Star Republic*. Austin: University of Texas Press, 1996.

Stuntz, Jean A. *Hers, His, and Theirs: Community Property Law in Spain and Early Texas*. Lubbock: Texas Tech University Press, 2005.

Sullivan, Roy F. *The Texas Navies*. Bloomington, IN: Authorhouse, 2010.

Thompson, Charles N. *Sons of the Wilderness: John and William Conner*. Nobleville: Indiana Historical Society, 1937.

Thompson, Karen R., ed. *Defenders of the Republic of Texas, Volume I, Texas Army: Muster Rolls, Receipt Rolls, and Other Rolls, 1836–1841*. Austin: Laurel House Press, 1989.

Tijerina, Andres. *Tejanos and Texas under the Mexican Flag, 1821–1836*. College Station: Texas A&M University Press, 1994.

Tiling, Moritz. *History of the German Element in Texas from 1820–1850*. Houston: Rein and Sons, 1913.

Tinkler, Robert. *James Hamilton of South Carolina*. Baton Rouge: Louisiana State University Press, 2004.

Torget, Andrew. *Seeds of Empire: Cotton, Slavery, and the Transformation of the Texas Borderlands, 1800–1850*. Chapel Hill: University of North Carolina Press, 2015.

Truett, Samuel. *Fugitive Landscapes: The Forgotten History of the U.S. - Mexico Borderlands*. New Haven: Yale University Press, 2006.

Turner, Elizabeth Hayes, Stephanie Cole, and Rebecca Sharpless, eds. *Texas Women: Their Histories, Their Lives*. Athens: University of Georgia Press, 2015.

Turner, Martha Anne. *Sam Houston and His Twelve Women*. Austin: The Pemberton Press, 1966.

———. *The Life and Times of Jane Long*. Waco: Texian Press, 1969.

Tyler, Ronnie C., and Lawrence W. Murphy, eds. *The Slave Narratives in Texas*. Austin: Encino Press, 1974.

Utley, Robert M. *Lone Star Justice: The First Century of the Texas Rangers*. New York: Oxford University Press, 2002.

Valerio-Jimenez, Omar S. *River of Hope: Forging Identity and Nation in the Rio Grande Borderlands*. Durham, NC: Duke University Press, 2013.

Vernon, Walter N. *The Methodist Excitement in Texas, A History*. Dallas: Texas United Methodist Historical Society, 1984.

Vernon, Walter N. *William Stevenson, Riding Preacher*. Dallas: Southern Methodist University Press, 1964.

Vigness, David. *The Revolutionary Decades: The Saga of Texas, 1810–1836*. Austin: Steck-Vaughn Co.,1965.

Wallace, Ernest, David M. Vigness, and George B. Ward, eds. *Documents of Texas History* Austin: Texas State Historical Association, 2002.

Waugh, Julia Nott. *Castroville and Henry Castro, Empresario*. San Antonio: Standard Printing, 1834.

Webb, Walter Prescott. *The Texas Rangers: A Century of Frontier Defense*. Austin: University of Texas Press, 1935.

Weber, David J. *Foreigners in Their Native Land: Historical Roots of the Mexican Americans*. Albuquerque: University of New Mexico Press, 1973.

———. *The Mexican Frontier, 1821–1846*. Albuquerque: University of New Mexico Press, 1982.

———. *The Spanish Frontier in North America*. New Haven: Yale University Press, 1992.

Weems, John Edward. *Dreams of Empire: A Human History of the Republic of Texas, 1836–1846*. New York: Barnes and Noble, 1995.

Wells, Tom Henderson. *Commodore Moore and the Texas Navy*. Austin: University of Texas Press, 1960.

Whisenhunt, Donald W., ed. *Texas: A Sesquicentennial Celebration*. Austin: Eakin Press, 1984.

Willett, Don, and Stephen Curley, eds. *Invisible Texans: Women and Minorities in Texas History*. New York: McGraw-Hill, 2005.

Williams, Amelia W., and Eugene C. Barker, eds. *The Writings of Sam Houston, 1813–1863*, 8 vols. Austin: University of Texas Press, 1938–1943.

Williams, John Hoyt. *Sam Houston: A Biography of the Father of Texas*. New York: Simon and Schuster, 1993.

Winchester, Robert Glenn. *James Pinckney Henderson: Texas's First Governor, U.S. Senator, Statesman, Diplomat, General*. San Antonio: Naylor, 1971.

Winders, Richard Bruce. *Sacrificed at the Alamo: Tragedy and Triumph in the Texas Revolution*. Abilene: State House Press, 2004.

Winegarten, Ruthe, and Teresa Palamino Acosta. *Las Tejanas: 300 Years of History*. Austin: University of Texas Press, 2003.

Winegarten, Ruthe. *Black Texas Women: 150 Years of Trial and Triumph*. Austin: University of Texas Press, 1995.

———. *Black Texas Women: A Sourcebook, Documents, Biographies, Timeline*. Austin: University of Texas Press, 1996.

Wright, Gavin. *The Political Economy of the Cotton South: Households, Markets, and Wealth in the Nineteenth Century*. New York: W.W. Norton, 1978.

Wuthnow, Robert. *Rough Country: How Texas Became America's Most Powerful Bible Belt State*. Princeton, NJ: Princeton University Press, 2014.

List of Contributors

Alwyn Barr is an American historian who specializes in African American studies, the American South, the American Civil War, and Reconstruction. He is a professor emeritus and former chairman of the history department at Texas Tech University in Lubbock, Texas. His five authored books include: *Black Texans: A History of African Americans in Texas, 1528–1995* (2nd ed. 1996) and *African Texans* (2004). He is a Fellow and former president of the Texas State Historical Association.

Walter L. Buenger, a native of West Texas, received his Ph.D. from Rice University in 1979 and began teaching at Texas A&M University that same year. He teaches courses in U.S. History, The History of the South, and Texas History. Five students have received a Ph.D. under his direction and ten students have received an M.A. His own research focuses on comparative border studies, the South, and Texas since 1820, and he has written or edited numerous books and articles. His book *The Path to a Modern South: Northeast Texas between Reconstruction and the Great Depression* won the Coral H. Tullis Award for the best book on Texas published in 2001. He is a Fellow of the Texas State Historical Association. His current research project examines the interaction between history and memory in Texas after 1820.

James E. Crisp was born in Wichita Falls, Texas, in 1946 and was raised and educated in Henrietta, in Clay County. He graduated from Rice University with Honors in History in 1968, and received his M. Phil. and Ph.D. degrees from Yale University in the 1970s. Since 1972 he has taught at North Carolina State University, where as Professor of History he recently entered the phased retirement program. Crisp plans an active retirement. His next project is the biography and annotated memoir of the Prussian-born Texas Revolutionary soldier Hermann Ehrenberg, one of the very few citizens of the Texas Republic to publish a book during that nation's existence. Crisp's *Sleuthing the Alamo: Davy Crockett's Last Stand and Other Mysteries of the Texas Revolution* (Oxford Univ. Press, 2004) received the Fehrenbach Award from the Texas Historical Commission. His presentations and articles have won both national and international prizes, including the H. Bailey Carroll prize for "Sam Houston's Speechwriters: The Grad Student, the Teenager, the Editors, and the Historians," published in the October 1993 issue of the *Southwestern*

Historical Quarterly. He is a Fellow of the Texas State Historical Association and a member of the Philosophical Society of Texas. Crisp has contributed chapters or other essays in each of the following works: *With Santa Anna in Texas: A Personal Narrative of the Revolution*, by José Enrique de la Peña, Carmen Perry, ed.; *The Texas Military Experience: From the Texas Revolution through World War II*, Joseph G. Dawson III, ed.; *Lone Star Pasts: Memory and History in Texas*, Gregg Cantrell and Elizabeth Hayes Turner, eds.; *Tejano Leadership in Mexican and Revolutionary Texas*, Jesús F. de la Teja, ed.; *Recovering the Hispanic History of Texas*, Monica Perales and Raúl A. Ramos, eds.; and *How Did Davy Die: And Why Do We Care So Much?*, by Dan Kilgore and James E. Crisp.

Joseph G. Dawson III was born in Ohio, but has lived most of his life in the South, including the states of Georgia, Florida, North Carolina, Louisiana, and Texas. Dawson's research focuses on the American military in the 19th century, including aspects of the regular army, volunteer army, the navy, the Marine Corps, the military's interaction with society, and military government. He served as Director of A&M's Military Studies Institute from 1986 to 2000. His publications include *Doniphan's Epic March: The 1st Missouri Volunteers in the Mexican War* (Lawrence: University Press of Kansas, 1999); *The Late 19th Century U.S. Army, 1865–1898: A Research Guide* (Westport, CT: Greenwood Press, 1990); *Army Generals and Reconstruction: Louisiana, 1862–1877* (Baton Rouge: Louisiana State University Press, 1982; paperback, 1994). He is also the editor of *The Texas Military Experience: From the Texas Revolution through World War II* (College Station: Texas A&M University Press, 1995); *Commanders in Chief: Presidential Leadership in Modern Wars* (Lawrence: University Press of Kansas, 1993); *The Louisiana Governors: From Iberville to Edwards* (Baton Rouge: Louisiana State University Press, 1990). He is also the associate editor of *American Military Leaders* (Westport, CT: Praeger, paperback, 1989); and *The Dictionary of American Military Biography*, 3 vols. (Westport, CT: Greenwood Press, 1984).

Francis X. Galán is now a Visiting Professor of History at Texas A&M University, San Antonio where he teaches Texas, Mexico, and Latin American history. He earned a Ph.D. in history from Southern Methodist University in 2006, an M.A. in history from the University of Texas at San Antonio, and B.A. in Latin American Studies from the University of Texas at Austin. Among his publications are

"Between Imperial Warfare: Crossing of the Smuggling Frontier and Transatlantic Commerce on the Louisiana-Texas Borderlands, 1754–1785," in *Texans and War: New Interpretations of the State's Military History*, pp. 157–177, edited by Alexander Mendoza and Charles David Grear (College Station: Texas A&M University Press, 2012) and "Lost in Translation: Tejano Roots on the Louisiana-Texas Borderlands, 1716–1821," in *Recovering the Hispanic History of Texas*, pp. 3–18, edited by Raúl A. Ramos and Monica Perales (Houston: Arte Público Press, 2010). He has revised his dissertation about the Spanish fort of Los Adaes, Texas, into a book manuscript titled, *Broken Border: Los Adaes, Smuggling, and Early American Westward Movement to Mexico*.

Jody Edward Ginn received a B.S.C.J. and an M.A. in Public History from Texas State University, and a Ph.D. in History from the University of North Texas. Dr. Ginn has published articles and contributed book reviews on a variety of topics, including the chapter, "Texas Rangers in Myth and Memory" in *Texan Identities* (University of North Texas Press, 2015). Dr. Ginn has also presented academic papers at numerous academic conferences, including the Texas State Historical Association Annual Conference (TSHA) 2005, 2011, and 2015 and at the Windy City History Conference at the University of Illinois-Chicago, 2011. Dr. Ginn has twice won the Fred White Jr. Research Fellowship in Texas History from the TSHA, and was formerly chief investigator for the Hays County Criminal District Attorney's Office in San Marcos, Texas.

Bruce A. Glasrud is Professor Emeritus of History, California State University, East Bay; Retired Dean, School of Arts and Sciences, Sul Ross State University; and a resident of San Antonio, Texas. Born and raised in Minnesota, Glasrud earned his master's degree at Eastern New Mexico University and received his Ph.D. in history from Texas Tech University—one of the early products of the "Texas Tech School of Black History." Glasrud is a Fellow of the Texas State Historical Association as well as two Texas regional associations, East and West. Among his twenty-five books, he is co-editor of *The African American West: A Century of Short Stories, The Harlem Renaissance in the West, Texas Labor History*, and with Harold J. Weiss, two volumes on *Tracking the Texas Rangers* (University of North Texas Press, 2012, 2013).

James L. Haley is an independent scholar living in Austin. His biography *Sam Houston* (University of Oklahoma Press, 2002) won the Spur Award from the Western Writers of America, the Coral Horton Tullis Award as the best book on Texas history from the Texas State Historical Association, the T. R. Fehrenbach Book Award from the Texas Historical Commission, the Deolece Parmelee Award from the Texas Historical Foundation, and the Award of Merit from the Philosophical Society of Texas.

Kenneth W. Howell received his B.S. degree in history from the University of Texas— Tyler, his M. A. degree in history from Texas A&M University—Commerce and his Ph. D. in history from Texas A&M University in College Station. He taught for twelve years in the Texas public school system before becoming an Assistant Professor of History at Prairie View A&M University in the fall of 2004. In 2014, Howell accepted a new position at Blinn College, where he serves as a Professor of History and the Executive Director of the Central Texas Historical Association. He has also taught at Texas A&M University (College Station), North Harris Montgomery Community College, and Trinity Valley Community College. Howell has several publications that focus on the history of Texas and the Old South, including *Henderson County, Texas, 1846–1861: An Antebellum History* (Eakin Press, 1999), *The Devil's Triangle: Ben Bickerstaff, Northeast Texans, and the War of Reconstruction* (Best of East Texas Publisher, 2007), *Texas Confederate, Reconstruction Governor: James Webb Throckmorton* (Texas A&M University Press, 2008), *Beyond Myth and Legend: A Narrative History of Texas* (Abigail Press, 2008), *Seventh Star of the Confederacy: Texas During the Civil War*, ed. (University of North Texas Press, 2009), *Still the Arena of Civil War: Violence and Turmoil in Reconstruction Texas, 1865–1874* (University of North Texas Press, 2012); "George Adams: A Cowboy All His Life," in *Black Cowboy of Texas*, ed. Sarah Massey (Texas A&M University Press, 2000); "Black Women in the Modern Era, 1974–2000" in *African American Women in Texas: A Collaborative History*, eds. Bruce Glasrud and Merline Pitre (Texas A&M University Press, 2008), "'When the Rabble Hiss, Well May Patriots Tremble': James Webb Throckmorton and the Secession Movement in Texas, 1845–1861," *Southwestern Historical Quarterly* (April 2006). Additionally, Howell has published numerous articles and book reviews in the *Southwestern Historical Quarterly*, *East Texas State Historical Journal*, *Southern Studies: An Interdisciplinary Journal of the South*, *The Southern Historian*, *West Texas Historical Association Yearbook*, the *Journal of South Texas*, and *Diálogos Latinamericanos*.

Gary D. Joiner is a cartographer, an associate professor of history professor at LSU-Shreveport, and the director of the Red River Regional Studies Center. Joiner has written and edited numerous books, including *Shiloh and the Western Campaign of 1862*; *One Damn Blunder From Beginning to End: The Red River Campaign in 1864*; *Through the Howling Wilderness: The Red River Campaign and Union Failure in 1864*; *Red River Steamboats*; and *Mr. Lincoln's Brown Water Navy: Mississippi Squadron*. Since 2006, he has aired a weekly radio program called *History Matters* for Red River Radio and is an experienced and popular lecturer on history, geography and archaeology. His myriad affiliations include the Civil War Preservation Trust, U.S.; the North Louisiana Historical Association (former board of directors, former editor of *North Louisiana History*); the DeSoto Parish Historical Society (former president); the Southern Historical Association; the Louisiana Historical Association; the Oakland Cemetery Preservation Society; the Spring Street Historical Museum; Red River Radio; the Red River Heritage Association; the Sons and Daughters of Pioneer River Men; and the Historic Shreveport Preservation Society.

Mary L. Scheer is an associate professor and chair of the Lamar University history department. In 2004 she was a Fulbright Scholar to Germany. Dr. Scheer has authored or edited several books, including *Foundations of Texan Philanthropy* (2004), *Twentieth-Century Texas: A Social and Cultural History* (2008) with co-editor John W. Storey, and *Women and the Texas Revolution* (2012), which was a co-winner of the Liz Carpenter Award for women's history. She has also written several scholarly articles and book chapters. She is a past board member of the Texas State Historical Association and in 2009 received the Ottis Lock Award as Educator of the Year from the East Texas Historical Association.

Paul N. Spellman received his Ph.D. in History from the University of Houston. Spellman currently teaches Texas and American history at Wharton Junior College. He is a native Texan and descendant of the Old Three Hundred family of Zadock and Minerva Cottle Woods. Spellman has authored six books on Texas history, including *Old 300, Gone to Texas* (CreateSpace, 2014), *Race to Velasco* (Hendrick Long Publishers, Dallas, 1995); *Forgotten Texas Leader: Hugh McLeod and the Texan Santa Fe Expedition* (Texas A&M Press, College Station, 1999); *Spindletop Boom Days* (Texas A&M Press, College Station, 2001); *Captain John H. Rogers, Texas Ranger* (University of North Texas Press, Denton, 2003); *Captain J. A. Brooks, Texas Ranger* (University of North Texas Press, Denton, 2007). Spellman has also published professional articles in refereed journals, including the *Southwestern Historical Quarterly*, the *South Texas Journal of History*, the *Oil Industry History*, and *The Texas Ranger Dispatch*. Furthermore, he has presented papers at the Texas State Historical Association, the East Texas Historical Association, 2007, and the Stormont Lectures in Victoria, Texas.

Kenneth R. Stevens. After serving four years in the Navy, Ken Stevens returned to academia to pursue his Ph.D. at Indiana University, where he also worked as an editorial assistant at the *American Historical Review*. He has published five books, including the *Texas Legation Papers, 1836–1845*; *Border Diplomacy* (a study of 19th century Anglo-American-Canadian relations), two volumes of the Diplomatic Papers of Daniel Webster; and an annotated bibliography of President William Henry Harrison. In addition to the U.S. history survey, he teaches courses in U.S. Constitutional History, the American Presidency, and the Age of Jackson.

John Storey is a Distinguished Regents Professor Emeritus at Lamar University. Storey received his Ph. D. degree from the University of Kentucky. He has written several books on the history of religion, including *Texas Baptist Leadership and Social Christianity, 1900–1980* (1986); *Southern Baptists of Southeast Texas, A Centennial History, 1888–1988* (1988); *The Religious Right, A Reference Handbook* (3rd edition, 2007); and "Pagodas amid the Steeples: The Changing Religious Landscape," in *Twentieth-Century Texas, A Social and Cultural History* (2008).

Charles Swanlund has been a Professor of History at Blinn College in Bryan, Texas, for the past ten years, where he teaches primarily Texas History, but also United States History. He is co-editor of *A Lone Star Reader*, and has published several book reviews for the East Texas Historical Association, West Texas Historical Association, and Central Texas Historical Association. Prior to entering the world of academia, he spent fourteen years working in the sports and entertainment industries.

Harold J. Weiss, Jr. is Emeritus Professor of History, Government, and Criminal Justice at Jamestown Community College, Jamestown, New York. He holds degrees from the following institutions: BS in history from the University of Scranton (Pa.), magna cum laude; MA in history from Pennsylvania State University; and a Ph.D. in history from Indiana University at Bloomington. He has presented papers on western law and order at meetings of the Western History Association, Texas State Historical Association, East Texas Historical Association, and other historical bodies. His articles on the Texas Rangers and Captain Bill McDonald have appeared in numerous journals, such as the *Southwestern Historical Quarterly* and the *Journal of the West*. He has published a highly acclaimed biography of Ranger Captain Bill McDonald—the first one to appear in a hundred years. He is also co-editor of a two-volume anthology on the Texas Rangers in the nineteenth and twentieth centuries. In all these endeavors, Weiss found out that Texas is not just a place, but a state of mind in the American psyche.

Richard Bruce Winders earned his doctorate from Texas Christian University in 1994. A specialist in the areas of the early American military and the Southwest, Winders is widely published on the topic of the Texas Revolution and Mexican War. His book entitled *Mr. Polk's Army: The American Military Experience in the Mexican War* won the Jerry Coffey Memorial Book Prize for the best work in the field of military history for 1997. He served as assistant editor on *The United States and Mexico at War*, an encyclopedia project for Macmillan released in 1998. His second book, *Crisis in the Southwest: The United States, Mexico and the Struggle over Texas* was named an "Outstanding Academic Title for 2002" by *Choice*, the journal of academic and research libraries; it also won the Sons of the Republic of Texas's 2003 Summerfield G. Roberts Award for the best work on the Republic of Texas as well as was runner up for the TSHA Bates Award for best research in the field of early Texas history. A third book, *Sacrificed at the Alamo: Tragedy and Triumph in the Texas Revolution*, was released in spring 2003. He has provided several chapters to collaborative efforts, including "Colonization, 1821–1836" in *Going to Texas: Five Centuries of Texas Maps* published in 2007. Winders's work was profiled in *How Historians Work*, published in 2010. He also writes for local visitor publications. Winders has appeared in several documentaries that have aired on the Discovery Channel, the History Channel, and on PBS. He recently completed a manuscript entitled *Panting for Glory: The Mississippi Rifles in the Mexican War, 1846–1848*, which is under review by Texas A&M University Press. Winders has served as Alamo Historian & Curator since 1996.

Index

B

C

I

M

S

T

Y

Z